The Yugoslav Search for Man:

Marxist Humanism
In Contemporary Yugoslavia

OSKAR GRUENWALD

J.F. BERGIN PUBLISHERS, INC.

Library of Congress Cataloging in Publication Data

Gruenwald, Oskar.
  The Yugoslav search for man.

  Bibliography: p.
  Includes indexes.
  1. Communism—Yugoslavia. 2. Communism and Philosophy. 3. Humanism. I. Title.
HX365.5.A6G78   335.43@44   82-4290
ISBN 0-89789-005-1   AACR2

All rights reserved
J.F. Bergin Publishers, Inc.
670 Amherst Road
South Hadley, Mass. 01075

0123456789   056   987654321

Printed in the United States of America

Contents

PART ONE: THE GENERAL FRAMEWORK

Chapter I What is Marxist Humanism? *1*

Chapter II East-West Dialogue and Marxist Humanism *16*

Chapter III Titoism: Alternative To Stalinism? *34*

List of Tables

List of Illustrations

A Map of Yugoslavia appears on page 320

Preface

This is a study of a modern odyssey: the Yugoslav search for man. However farfetched the statement might appear, the study follows the peregrinations of two essential threads that help define the phenomenon of man. One of them is the esoteric concept of alienation, the radical disjunction between man's essence and his everyday existence, which weaves like Ariadne's thread through the entire Western cultural heritage. The other is the equally inscrutable thread of Marxist-Leninist ideology, whose historicism, dialectic, and utopianism form an enchanted universe fading into distopia. Where the two threads cross, there is the moment of man.

Though mortal, limited, and imperfect, man was not born to die but to begin, as Hannah Arendt put it. It is ambiguity, imperfection, incomplete knowledge, trying, failing, and beginning anew that seem to characterize the human condition. Avant-garde Yugoslav Marxist humanists call the essential capacity and modality of man's authentic existence *praxis,* that is, free, creative, and self-creative (self-actualizing) activity. This emphasis on individual human self-realization and freedom constitutes a Copernican revolution in Marxism. Man as a free, creative being of *praxis* signifies a new Archimedean point for judging both individual and societal action, whether in capitalism, state capitalism (Stalinism), or socialism (communism). What follows is an attempt to delve deeper into the forbidding territories delimited by alienation and ideology. Our aim is to excavate, analyze, and separate, as far as possible, the humanist, democratic, and liberal elements in the Marxist-Leninist world view from its anti-humanist, totalitarian, and dogmatic aspects.

In the final analysis, the crucial question is not one of mere ideology, philosophy, politics, sociology, law, economics, or the sciences, but of human self-understanding and the relationship between theory and practice. That socialist practice has become widely separated from Marxist theory hardly needs elaborating. But that Marxist theory as well as socialist practice might harbor conflicting seeds of humanism and terror, liberation and enslavement, self-government and dictatorship, ecstasy and agony, is less well understood. We may not be able to liberate completely either societies or men from the iron grip of ideologies and the straitjacket of dogma. But it should be possible, at least, to humanize both ideologies and men. That is the quintessential challenge of the twentieth century. But it is not the challenge of history. It is the challenge of man.

In the lengthening shadows of late twentieth century, man has arrived at a fateful crossroads. Either he will affirm the humanity of man and assure the survival and growth of the species commonly known as *homo sapiens,* or he will fritter away his evolutionary chances in a tragic struggle against himself, his fellow men, and nature. We cannot turn the clock back to man's infancy. We live in the present. But do we dare to look into the future? We see the solution to the riddle of history in the rebirth of the man-child, as in Stanley Kubrick's adaptation of Arthur C. Clarke's *2001: A Space Odyssey.* But that means only that we have met our challenge. That challenge is—us.

This is an interdisciplinary study that explores theory and policy in one of the most fascinating socio-economic-political experiments in the world—Yugoslavia. Its threefold aim is a critical assessment of (1) the *Praxis* school of thought—a phenomenal reconstruction of the Marxist-Leninist intellectual heritage and critique of socialist practice in contemporary Yugoslavia by avant-garde Marxist humanist philosophers and sociologists (banned in 1975); (2) Yugoslav theory and practice in light of the avant-garde critique; and (3) a positive transcendence *(Aufhebung)* of the Marxist *Weltanschauung,* culminating in a definitive refutation of Marxism-Leninism. The major question and *leitmotif* of the study is: how and why do utopian assumptions in theory lead to their opposites—distopia, totalitarianism, and dictatorship—in everyday practice? The study thus has far-reaching theoretical as well as policy implications for both East and West.

Yugoslav neo-Marxist or Marxist humanist theorists are "avant-garde" in at least four related senses: (1) *historically,* since they are contemporary interpreters of Marxist-Leninist teachings; (2) *culturally,* since they have transformed the social sciences and humanities, and contributed to a unique socialist humanist culture; (3) *philosophically,* and most important, since they have elaborated the most radical, comprehensive, and far-reaching reconstruction of Marxist-Leninist theory, and the most incisive Marxist critique of socialist practice in the communist world; and (4) *politically,* since their critique of Stalinism, monolithism, and one-party dictatorship have led to the most severe *Marxist* theoretical challenge to communist one-party rule thus far.

The Delphic title, *The Yugoslav Search for Man,* was chosen because the scope of this work far surpasses the narrow framework of a single country study by its emphasis on discovering what makes all of us essentially *human*—in ideology, philosophy, politics, economics, culture—as individuals and as a society. Just as Homer three millennia ago summed up the prevailing civilization and culture of an entire epoch in his *Iliad* and *Odyssey* in the language of *myth,* so our study attempts to sum up contemporary civilization and culture at the crossroads between East and West, embodied in the Yugoslav experiment, in the language of *science.*

Although the text was completed by 1981, this book looks forward to 2001. It addresses itself to those who desire real intellectual challenges and are seeking their own identity. The spirit of our exploration is even more important than the scholarship, since for genuine understanding it is important that, whenever we refute Marx, we are also with Marx, and not simply against him. Thus, when Marx talks about alienation, we dialogue with him; when he agonizes over human degradation and dehumanization, we empathize with him. But this means also that the real *dramatis personae* are the readers who are called upon to confront their own White Whale of myths/symbols/ideology/prejudice and to tame it by conquering themselves. That is the quintessential challenge of a modern odyssey.

Acknowledgments

The present study grew out of my doctoral dissertation, "Humanism and Marxism: The Yugoslav Perspective," at Claremont Graduate School (1971). Post-doctoral research was conducted in Yugoslavia, the Federal Republic of Germany, and the United States. Preliminary research findings were presented at a number of conferences here and abroad, and published in scholarly journals. The first major summary of research in *Orbis*, Fall 1974 (revised as Chapter I), led to nomination to Delta Tau Kappa, the International Social Science Honor Society, for outstanding scholastic achievement. The Ludwig Vogelstein Foundation extended a grant for research and writing, 1976–1977. And the Russian and East European Center at the University of Illinois at Urbana-Champaign graciously hosted me during its 1976 and 1979 Summer Research Laboratories, providing access not only to its extensive Slavic collections, but also to an expert staff. A measure of the vast intellectual debt owed to colleagues worldwide is reflected in the References and the Selected Bibliography.

A book can be a work of art. If this volume approaches that ideal, it is thanks to the knowledge, patience, and editorial acumen of James K. Fleming, as well as the personal attention of J.F. Bergin and his staff.

O. Gruenwald
Santa Monica

The White Whale swam before him as the monomaniac incarnation of all those malicious agencies which some deep men feel eating in them, till they are left living on with half a heart and half a lung. That intangible malignity which has been from the beginning; to whose dominion even the modern Christians ascribe one-half of the worlds; which the ancient Ophites of the east reverenced in their statue devil;—Ahab did not fall down and worship it like them; but deliriously transferring its idea to the abhorred white whale, he pitted himself, all mutilated, against it. All that most maddens and torments; all that stirs up the lees of things; all truth with malice in it; all that cracks the sinews and cakes the brain; all the subtle demonisms of life and thought; all evil, to crazy Ahab, were visibly personified, and made practically assailable in Moby Dick. He piled upon the whale's white hump the sum of all the general rage and hate felt by his whole race from Adam down; and then, as if his chest had been a mortar, he burst his hot heart's shell upon it.

*   *   *

Not reasoning; not remonstrance; not entreaty wilt thou hearken to; all this though scornest. Flat obedience to thy own flat commands; this is all thou breathest. Aye, and say'st the men have vow'd thy vow; say'st all of us are Ahabs. Great God forbid!—But is there no other way?

Herman Melville, *Moby Dick* (1851)

Chapter I · What is Marxist Humanism?

> ... the ideas of economists and political philosophers, both when they are right and when they are wrong, are more powerful than is commonly understood. Indeed the world is ruled by little else. Practical men, who believe themselves to be quite exempt from any intellectual influences, are usually the slaves of some defunct economist. Madmen in authority, who hear voices in the air, are distilling their frenzy from some academic scribbler of a few years back. I am sure that the power of vested interests is vastly exaggerated compared with the gradual encroachment of ideas... But, soon or late, it is ideas, not vested interests, which are dangerous for good or evil.
>
> John Maynard Keynes, *The General Theory of Employment, Interest and Money* (1936)

1.   Prometheus Unbound

One of the most striking developments in recent intellectual history is the reinterpretation of Marx by Marxist philosophers in such a way that he is barely recognizable to those who hold a dogmatic conception of Marxism-Leninism, or—as the Yugoslavs put it—a "Stalinist" conception. Marxist humanist thought, a relatively recent phenomenon, came into its own in the 1960s. Its most radical exponents are the avant-garde Yugoslav Marxist philosophers and sociologists. Gajo Petrović, Mihailo Marković, and Svetozar Stojanović are among the most significant interpreters; but the majority of Yugoslavia's Marxist philosophers have contributed to this school of thought. Theirs is a new perspective, trend or *Weltanschauung* which—if not expressly stated in the country's social sciences—at least constitutes their philosophical inspiration.

Marxist humanism is part of a larger context of contemporary humanist renaissance in which Christians and Marxists, democrats and communists, scientists, philosophers, theologians and laymen, passionately concerned with the future of man, are engaged in the most promising dialogue of our age—a dialogue seeking to bridge ideological gaps and improve understanding among peoples and nations in a common effort to build a safer and more humane world.[1] Thus, we have the Christian-Marxist dialogue, initiated by the German Paulus Society and the prominent French Marxist philosopher, Roger Garaudy. In Eastern Europe, leading Marxists like Adam Schaff and Leszek Kolakowski in Poland, Karel Kosik and Ivan Svitak in Czechoslovakia, György Lukacs and his followers in Hungary, and others have engaged in the promising enterprise of opening up Marxism-Leninism to the dilemmas and needs of man in the latter part of the twentieth century. Even in the USSR, prominent scientists like Andrei Sakharov have joined in the humanist renaissance by pointing out the need to humanize existing societies and engage in a constructive dialogue in order to escape the Armageddon of nuclear war and famine. The Nobel-Prize-winning author and humanist Aleksandr I. Solzhenitsyn constantly reminds us of the tragic results of a radical disjuncture between means and ends and of insensitivity to man causing human suffering on an enormous scale—the color of the flag or the proclaimed state and party ideals notwithstanding.

Although Marxist humanists have been active elsewhere in Eastern Europe, especially before the invasion of Czechoslovakia in 1968, it is only in Yugoslavia that they have been allowed to reach maturity and become the predominant cultural orientation in the social sciences. The Yugoslav avant-garde Marxists have exerted considerable influence both within and outside the country's boundaries, paralleling the impact of the Yugoslav model of self-managing socialism on countries in the Soviet bloc and the Third World.

It is well known that the Yugoslavs, following their break with Stalin in 1948, pioneered new social, political, and economic institutions, for example, establishing workers' councils and communes, decentralizing the economy and the administration, abandoning collectivization of agriculture, and reorganizing the Communist Party (known, since 1952, as the League of Communists of Yugoslavia). These developments found their way also into new theoretical systems elaborated to justify Yugoslavia's "independent road to socialism." The Yugoslav innovations in Marxist-Leninist theory have not yet been fully understood in either East or West. Even less well understood is the transformation of Marxist-Leninist ideology by avant-garde Marxist theoreticians into a distinct critical philosophy and a more humane faith.[2]

Contrary to the prediction by some Western experts that the trend in Marxist movements is toward deradicalization, in Yugoslavia the avant-garde Marxists have been radicalizing Marxist theory, if not socialist practice.[3] They are contributing to a genuine renaissance of both Marxist and humanist thought, seeking to raise Marxist philosophy out of its protracted and deadly slumber as an ossified, dogmatized system of absolute and unchanging truths or ideology, onto the level of critical philosophy in the classic sense.

This revolutionary reinterpretation of Marxist-Leninist theory is one of the major issues in Yugoslavia today and an important point of controversy between the official guardians and the unofficial interpreters of the faith. It is possible that the only future for the Marxist humanists may, ironically, be their past, since their devastating critique of all existing societies, institutions and practices, including those of socialist Yugoslavia, may bring down upon them at any moment the full wrath of the communist leadership, already frustrated by unprecedented problems of ethnic divisions, difficulties in economic planning, inflation, unemployment, student unrest, labor demands, corruption, and rising discontent within and outside the party's ranks. The Yugoslav avant-garde—which gathered around the radical Marxist journals *Praxis* and *Filosofija* and which in 1963 instituted an annual International Summer School on the island of Korčula, supplemented since 1971 by Winter Philosophical Meetings in Serbia—has been attacked by regime spokesmen for a wide variety of wrongs, ranging from alleged opposition to economic decentralization of Yugoslavia's emerging market economy, opposition to workers' self-management, advocacy of political centralism, "etatism" (statism), unitarianism and the multi-party system, to an "inexact" interpretation of Marx and "anticommunism" in its contemporary form.[4] Another accusation against the members of this group—that they have "opened the door to nationalism" and thus by implication added fuel to the rising ethnic divisions, particularisms and strife undermining the "brotherhood and unity of the Yugoslav peoples"—may have been the final "kiss of death."[5] In a 1972 article, entitled "For Freedom of Academic Discussion," the editorial board of *Praxis* asserted that the regime's accusations against one of its members—of making nationalist statements, together with administrative measures such as the withholding of travel documents from members of the University of Belgrade's Faculty of Philosophy (i.e., Social Sciences)—were in reality aimed at the exponents of creative Marxism who oppose all dogmatism and etatist models of socialism.[6]

We may, at present, be witnessing the final act in a drama with overtones of a classic Greek tragedy whose protagonists, like Socrates, are accused of misleading and corrupting the youth, attempting to transform a student rebellion and dissatisfaction into a "broad confrontation between the young people and the foundation of the socio-political system," forming "tactical alliances with currents of opposition," undermining the leading role of the League of Communists, and thus allegedly abrogating the achievements of Yugoslav socialism.[7] The party, acting via the Belgrade University Council, instituted formal (legal) proceedings to remove the "Belgrade Eight"—seven men and one woman—from their teaching posts and ordered the party members of *Praxis'* editorial board and on the Faculties of Philosophy at Zagreb and Belgrade Universities to "differentiate" themselves from and "settle accounts with the carriers of viewpoints unacceptable to the League of Communists."[8] The late President Tito himself, at the Tenth Party Congress of May 27-30, 1974 (dubbed the "Congress of Unity and Revolutionary Decisiveness"), called for a continued ideological-political offensive, and resolutions were passed at the Congress urging a struggle without compromise against all "alien" ideologies, their carriers, and political practices based on them.[9] In the face of this massive campaign by the regime, the support by faculty colleagues and students must certainly have been gratifying to the avant-garde, though it turned out to be a rather thin reed to hang on to for professional and personal survival in a social system which once more insists rigidly on "partyness," "classness," and the ideological "correctness" and "truthfulness" even of academic discourse (see Chapter X).[10]

With the passage in 1968 of a new law in Yugoslavia, which Mihailo Marković, among others, considers "undemocratic," all publications that "upset the citizenry" can be banned.[11] Thus, in August 1971 a number of periodicals— *Praxis, Student, Kultura, Književne novine, Prosvjeta, Hrvatski tjednik* and *Široki brijeg*—received staying injunctions, most of which, however, were later removed, wholly or partially.[12] Yet, if the past is any guide to the future, it seems likely that Yugoslav avant-garde Marxist humanist thought—like "Djilasism"—cannot be abolished via administrative measures. An idea cannot be vanquished by guns, police or bureaucracies; it can be fought successfully only with a better idea.

2. A Modern Odyssey: The Yugoslav Search for Man

There are two integral aspects to Marxist humanist thought: (1) Marx's philosophy of man, and (2) Marx's conception of the dialectic, and of science and technology that go with it. It is significant that the Yugoslav avant-garde philosophers have gone back to the early or young Marx who wrote the *Economic and Philosophical Manuscripts* (known as the "Paris Manuscripts") of 1844, in order to discover an "authentic Marxism" whose major concern is human alienation and which the Yugoslavs claim is, ipso facto, a humanist view. According to them, authentic Marxism—authentic socialism —is humanist in content.

Gajo Petrović, in his *Marx in the Mid-Twentieth Century*, contrasts the "Stalinist" version of Marxism-Leninism with the humanist.[13] One of the major elements in the "dogmatic" view is the conception of the state as the instrument of change in society from capitalism to socialism. This conception of the state degenerated in the Stalinist framework into a totalitarian system, a police dictatorship. Stalinism was a system designed to utilize the state as a "dictatorship of the proletariat" in order to do away with private property, collectivize agriculture, and eradicate the remnants of "bourgeois" mentality, class relationships, exploitation and conflict in society. In practice, the Yugoslavs point out, the Stalinist version of Marxism resulted in "state capitalism," that is, in the domination of totalitarian forms of the state machinery and bureaucratic apparatus over the proletariat. While private property was abolished as the primary exploitative agency in society, its role was assumed by state ownership and control of nationalized property. This, in effect, meant control by a huge governmental, party and state bureaucracy.

The Yugoslav system, on the other hand, evolved from a Stalinist prototype police state (1945-1950) in search of an "independent road to socialism," following the break with Stalin in 1948.   This search, outside Russian hegemony, was influenced by the West, especially through U.S. economic and military aid. Western—notably French humanist and individualist—cultural influence has traditionally been strong in Yugoslavia, since many Yugoslav intellectuals have studied in the West.   These factors, by giving Yugoslavia a breathing spell from Russian pressure, made it possible for her to bring about a more liberalized, less totalitarian version of socialism or communism.   The 1960s marked a radical, though still poorly understood, development in the Yugoslav system with the inauguration of the New Economic Policy in 1965, leading to a "market-planned" economy in which the Yugoslavs have experimented with new methods of decentralizing the economy as well as the governmental machinery, the administration, and even the party.[14]   This framework of liberalized institutions and practices provided greater opportunity for free expression and creative thinking.

The focal point and the essential distinguishing aspect of Marxist humanism is that it turns away from contemplating abstract entities such as the state, collectivities, socialism and communism, and focuses instead on man, the individual human being. It reinterprets man as essentially a free, creative, and self-creative being, or a being of *praxis*.[15]   The idea of *praxis* implies human potentiality and capability to transform the world, that is, to change both one's self and one's environment. This radicalization of Marxist thought shifts the balance of Marx's economic and historical determinism from the determinist toward the voluntarist or action-oriented end of the scale.   The avant-garde Marxist philosophers emphasize that—while consciousness is determined by life and men are prisoners of their circumstances—men can also change these circumstances.[16]

This action-oriented outlook restores to the Marxist view and analysis of history, society and man the critical perspective, which was an essential element in the *Weltanschauung* of the young Marx. The major concept for the young Marx was the *alienation* of man due to the exploitation and alienation of his labor in capitalist (class) society.   In the Yugoslav conception, Marxist theory undergoes a searching re-evaluation and becomes once more a *method of critique*, but this time a critique of all existing societies, whether capitalist, state capitalist (Stalinist), or socialist (communist).[17]   This is the essence of the Yugoslav avant-garde's radical reconstruction of Marxist philosophy.   In their view, the dogmatized Stalinist version of Marxism-Leninism was used as an excuse, an apologetic, for current malpractices rationalized in terms of the alleged need for the "dictatorship of the proletariat" to effect economic development, industrialization, urbanization, and capital accumulation.[18] They maintain that Marxist philosophy ought to retrieve its erstwhile Promethean function of radical critique of all existing societies, institutions, and practices that hinder the freedom, creativity, and all-round development of man, instead of being a servant of politics. This is a fundamental shift in emphasis away from the generally accepted Marxist viewpoint and socialist practice of looking only at the necessity of reaching a classless society, the "dictatorship of the proletariat," and the like, with no compunction as to the means utilized to attain the end. As Marković puts it: " . . . some Marxists (although by no means only Marxists) have been behaving as though they accepted 'the end-justifies-the-means' principle."   Marxist humanism, he says, "rejects both this principle and the practice of permanent subordination of morals (and science, and law, and art) to politics."[19]

The Yugoslav philosophers point out that the ultimate goals have a tendency to recede into the future and that we are left with the means, humane or otherwise. Danko Grlić maintains that "the end must always be present in the means . . . ."[20] The Yugoslav avant-garde thus contradicts Marx's and especially Lenin's moral/ethical relativism which assumes that the ends justify the means. Its members see a pressing need to *integrate* means and ends, that is, to pursue socialist ends via humane ("socialist") means. There can no longer remain the radical disjuncture, as has so often been the case in the past, of pursuing lofty ideals of a classless, conflictless, non-exploitative society through the abuse of real human beings. This is undoubtedly one of the major revolutionary and humanist contributions of Yugoslav Marxist humanism.

The Yugoslav avant-garde remains "Marxist," although of a quite different hue. It still maintains that capitalist society is characterized by exploitation of labor, division into antagonistic classes, class conflict, and the creation of *homo duplex*—the alienation of man, his fragmentation into various conflicting roles or spheres, and consequent division into a moral citizen and an immoral private person. The Yugoslavs thus continue to subscribe to Marx's and Engels' view of the nature of man, expressed in *The German Ideology* and elsewhere, as well as to their description of how man undergoes alienation in a class society, ceases to be a whole man, an integral human being through the exploitation of his labor, and becomes an appendage to the machine. According to Marx and Engels, human nature is transformed in capitalist society in such a way that man is reduced to the role of worker instead of being the whole man who creates himself and his world—a metaphysical idea in a sense, but an impressive notion that lies at the basis of the whole concept of alienation. It is significant that the concept of alienation pertains to man and refers to the disjunction between what man is, his *existence*, and what he could or should be, his *essence*.

At this point the Yugoslav Marxist philosophers get into some trouble, because they imply that there is an "ought" or an "essence" of man. Is this essence independent of space and time and various social formations? Actually, Marković states that there are "certain elements (truths, values)" of "lasting human significance" that are not relative to place and time.[21] But this implies that these truths and values are independent of history, the dialectic, and the economic "substructure." This is obviously "un-Marxist" in the usual sense of the term, since according to Marx all moral/ethical standards of truth, values, systems of justice, politics, the state, the arts, and culture in general are but "superstructures" derived from and based on specific economic "substructures" or the systems of the organization of production at different historical stages in society's development.

In the generally accepted Marxist view, law, state, and politics are all alienated social forms characterizing capitalist society in which the government apparatus is but the "executive committee" of the ruling class—the "bourgeoisie." The avant-garde Marxists maintain, surprisingly, that the state machinery, bureaucracies, hierarchies, division of labor, specialization, economic development, market and money— resulting in a "fetishism" of commodities and the reification of man (man relating himself to other men via commodities)—are all sources of alienation not only in the class society of capitalism and in state capitalism *but also in socialism.*[22] This is a major innovation in Marxist theory. In Marxist-Leninist thought alienation was the hallmark exclusively of class society. The classic Marxist view was that of exploitation, of the capitalists opposing the wage-earning proletariat in a life-and-death class struggle, a zero-sum game in which the winner takes all and the loser loses all. The aim of the proletarian revolution was, first of all, the abolition of private property, the nationalization of the means of production; second, the bourgeois state machinery was to be uprooted and discarded to make way for a revolutionary "dictatorship of the proletariat" whose aim was, originally, to bring about, in Engels' much vaunted words, the "withering away" of the state in socialism and communism.

This concept of the withering away of the state was relegated farther and farther into the background by orthodox Marxists, whereas to the Yugoslavs it is precisely the need to do away with the remnants of the institutions of the state, bureaucracy, and politics—for the avant-garde not excluding *the party itself*—that should be the primary goal for Marxist theory and socialist practice.[23] The League of Communists thus adopted at its Ninth Congress in 1969 a resounding "Resolution on the Ideological-Political Foundations for the Further Development of the League of Communists of Yugoslavia," urging that the communist vanguard

> must be a party of the revolution, of the ceaseless revolutionizing
> of social relationships, of *the abolition of all monopoly, including*

> *its own*; it must be a party that keeps moving forward and not one
> that conserves relationships dating from the early phase of social-
> ism, and fossilizes them.[24]

By the Tenth Party Congress of May 1974, however, the League had changed
its mind, reasserting its total and unconditional ideological-political monopoly as
the vanguard of the working class in the building of socialism. Tito's address on
May 27 heralded the entrance into a "new phase" in the struggle for Yugoslav
socialism, coupled with an equally controversial promise (given Marxism's generic
paradoxes) regarding the role of workers:

> The essence and the basic goal of this struggle is that *political
> power in the name of the working class be transformed into
> political power of the class itself* and of all the working people,
> that workers in associated work may decide directly on the means,
> conditions and fruits of their labor and on social life generally.[25]

In Marx's conception, the state machinery, bureaucracy, and politics are
alienating forces standing above man. Hence, according to Marx and Engels, the
end goal of the classless communist society will be achieved when *political* power
loses its suppressive nature and becomes *social* power. Political power would lose
its dominance over man and yield in the classless society to the "administration of
things."[26] The Yugoslav innovation is the insistence that statism, bureaucracy,
hierarchy, division of labor, law, politics, and— until recently—the party, must all
begin to wither away now, to be supplanted by direct participatory democracy or
workers' self-management. The Yugoslavs see their institution of workers' councils
and communes as the germ of direct or participatory democracy, developing in the
direction of Engels' notion of the "administration of things." Their vision of
communism is that of a classless society in which power has lost its political
character, in which there is no longer the need to suppress class conflict and
exploiting classes, and in which the associated producers (workers) control and
manage production and distribution.

One of the fundamental new concepts of the Yugoslav avant-garde is its
emphasis on the need to revive Marx's philosophy of man, focusing on the
conception of man as a free creative being who can realize his potentialities and
change the world through *praxis*—creative activity, immediate production, work.
This focus on labor as the key to the de-alienation of man is a central element in
Marx.   The avant-garde has significantly connected Marx's emphasis on man's
creative activity and labor to the possibility of *freedom* and thus enhanced the
definition of man as a free, creative, and self-creative being who alone is capable
of fulfilling Marx's injunction to philosophers to change the world.   But the
definition of man as an active agent in history rather than its captive clearly
implies abandonment of Marx's economic and historical determinism in which the
outcome of the historic struggle is known in advance. The Yugoslav Marxists try to
deal with this problem by stating that the "ought," which implies that man should
develop his creative potentialities, rests in the final analysis in the economic
substructure. They point out, however, that the substructure is not isolated from
the superstructure and that there are forces which have dynamics of their own
within the different spheres of the superstructure. The Yugoslavs thus see the two,
the economic sphere and the political, legal, cultural, philosophical sphere, as
interacting—approaching the Weberian concept of interaction between the material and spiritual-religious realms.   They continue to insist that ultimately the
economic aspect still determines all the rest, but they have given a lot of leeway
by acknowledging the fact of interaction between the different spheres in
society.[27]

Significantly, the Marxist humanists claim that within the constraints imposed
on human freedom by economic and historical factors, man retains degrees of
freedom. This is crucial if their central conception of man as a being of *praxis* is
to be meaningful at all. The truly revolutionary element in their philosophy is that

it focuses on the human individual, shifting away from the dogmatized Stalinist interpretation of Marxism-Leninism whose major concern was (and is) with abstract entities embedded in a highly deterministic framework.[28] They take even Marx himself to task for writing at times in a narrow, deterministic vein. For them, Marxism is not a dogma, promulgated once and for all; on the contrary, it requires continuous creative interpretation in theory and application in practice. They conceive of the dialectic as a method of radical critique of everything existing that limits human development.[29] Thus, Yugoslav Marxism undergoes a radical re-evaluation as both theory and method.

In the Yugoslav interpretation it is no longer the collective but the individual who becomes the focus of attention and the fulcrum of Marxist theory. Predrag Vranicki expressed it unequivocally:

> If our desire is to contribute more fully to human liberation, i.e., to the overcoming of various forms of alienation, then socialism must place its fundamental stress on man, and the free personality must be considered a prerequisite to social freedom, in theory and in practice.[30]

Yet, at this point the Yugoslavs establish one of the most complex relationships of Marxist humanist theory: they link the liberation of the individual—his de-alienation—with the liberation of society, since the individual is set in a societal framework. In this, they hark back to Marx's statement in his Sixth Thesis on Feuerbach, that man is the ensemble of social relations, and thus try to connect the two major aspects of Marxism and unite theory and practice, thought and action.[31]

Crucial to understanding this linkage is the Yugoslav view of an underlying continuity in the thinking and writing of the young Marx in such works as *Economic and Philosophical Manuscripts, Critique of Hegel's Philosophy of Right, On the Jewish Question,* and *The German Ideology,* and his later writings culminating in *Capital.* The Yugoslav theorists argue that Marx's later works cannot be understood properly unless one understands the humanist orientation of his early works and his emphasis on the concept of man. Marx's view of man, in turn, cannot be understood apart from the concept of alienation and the problem of how to overcome it in all its manifestations.[32] Human alienation, according to classical Marxist theory, arises from the exploitation of wage-labor by the capitalist who owns the means of production and appropriates the surplus value created by the worker. The classic Marxist "solution" is equally well known, namely to "expropriate the expropriators," abolish private property or nationalize the means of production. But the Yugoslav avant-garde disagrees with this simplistic solution. According to Petrović,

> the problem of de-alienation of economic life cannot be solved by the mere abolition of private property. The transformation of private property into state property (be it a "capitalist" or a "socialist" state property) does not introduce an essential change in the situation of the working man, the producer.[33]

Why should it be so? Because, in Marković's words,

> private property is not the cause but the effect of alienated labor. Abolition of the private ownership of the means of production is only abolition of one possible specific form of the rule of dead labor over living labor. The general structure remains if there is any other social group such as, for example, bureaucracy which retains monopoly decision-making concerning the disposal of accumulated and objectified labor.[34]

Thus, Marković continues, exploitation of labor and resulting alienation obtains not only in capitalist and class society but also in socialist states due to the appropriation of surplus value by "collective capitalists and collective exploiters" as well as by the bureaucracy.[35] But that is not all. According to Veljko Rus, Marxists have been looking in the wrong direction to find the sources of power in society: it is not private ownership, but the division of labor and the accompanying system of roles that is crucial for the distribution of power and goods in society.[36]

The Yugoslav avant-garde has revolutionized Marxist theory by elaborating the phenomenon of *alienation in socialism.* In Marx, the classless society emerges via the dialectical progression of history through different social formations characterized by conflict between the exploiting and the exploited classes. The classless society itself, however, is *without* conflict, exploitation or alienation, according to established Marxist thought. Here again the Yugoslav theorists throw a monkey wrench into the works by questioning this view of communism or classless society as conflictless. It should be obvious that they run into genuine trouble, if we recall why the classless society was desirable to Marx and his followers in the first place. Why have revolutions, why go to the barricades? The classic Marxist answer was: to end exploitation and man's inhumanity to man. The rationale behind the proletarian revolution seemed a most pervasive one in the Marxist view: to end exploitation of man by man, to end human alienation where the products become estranged from the laborer, are appropriated by the capitalist, and rule over work and their creator, acquiring an existence of their own. (A metaphysical concept? Was Marx stigmatized by the tale of the sorcerer's apprentice?) Alienation, exploitation, and, hence, *homo duplex* (the division of man into different spheres or roles), conflict, violence, and war—all of these Marx and his followers attributed to capitalism and class society.

The Yugoslavs agree that the ultimate goal is a classless society, but in their view it will not be wholly without conflict.[37] Conflict, although of a less pernicious nature than that in class society, will continue under socialism and even communism. For one thing, there will be differences of opinion as to ways and means of solving practical problems. The Yugoslavs contend that conflict in socialism will be totally different in nature from that in class society. But this theoretical position is hardly convincing especially since, according to Yugoslav theory itself, alienation (the exclusive hallmark of class society) will also continue. Moreover, the forms of alienation under socialism seem to be twin brothers of those under capitalism, namely, alienation due to commodity production, specialization, division of labor, market, money, hierarchies, bureaucracies, leading to *homo duplex* and the reification of man.[38] Not only do some forms of alienation characteristic of capitalist (class) society survive in socialism, but, surprisingly, *new* forms arise:

> It is true that some of the crudest forms of human alienation have been more or less abolished. But some have survived, and new unsuspected ones have appeared, especially in connection with the creation of new centers of enormous power, which are no longer based on economic wealth as in capitalism, but on unlimited political authority. The increasing power of state and political organizations in some socialist countries has brought to life new kinds of social contradictions on both the national and the international level: new forms of political oppression introduced by bureaucracy; new ways of grabbing the surplus product, even without possessing the means of production; new tensions between rich and poor; new conflicts between nations and countries within the socialist camp, etc.[39]

Marković becomes even more explicit on the fundamental cause of alienation in socialism in his article on "The Power Structure in Yugoslav Society and the Dilemma of the Revolutionary Intelligentsia." He claims that in post-capitalist society there has been an inversion of the relationship between economic and political power: Whereas in bourgeois society political power was based on economic power, in post-capitalist society the "economic power of the techno-bureaucratic stratum, the degree of its control over the means of production and its appropriation of surplus value in the form of privileges is based on its political power and influence in the process of social decision-making."[40]

Marxist critics examining the increasing social and class differentiation in contemporary Yugoslavia, especially since the economic reforms of the 1960s, contend that a new middle class has developed which, according to Milan Kangrga and others, is attempting to transform the proletarian (socialist) revolution into a bourgeois (counter) revolution and thus subvert the achievements of socialism.[41] Ivan Kuvačić draws a further distinction between the "old middle class" of the petty bourgeoisie which he sees as being on the wane, and the "new middle class" which, in contrast, is very much alive and well and growing, feeding off workers' surplus value. As to the social composition of this new stratum, Kuvačić says that:

> The "new middle class" is mutually inter-related and closely linked with the administrative apparatus and partly also with the political elite. Its numerousness and presence in economic, political, administrative, business and other social organizations and especially in the media of mass communications, ensure its power and influence.[42]

According to Kangrga, the middle class has achieved a virtual monopoly over the means of communication by gradually taking over the media based on the principle of self-management—interpreted in its own way.[43] Self-management itself is one of the most original Yugoslav theoretical contributions to Marxist thought. In practice, however, it has been much more problematic, being over-shadowed by both party organs and overbearing managements, on the one hand, and outrageous labor demands, on the other, leading to avant-garde criticism of self-management *practice* (not the theory) as "anti-Stalinist Stalinism" or the "Yugoslav myth." Svetozar Stojanović observes that the Yugoslav Marxist intelligentsia "has the moral obligation to leftwing movements in the world, who include self-management in their programmes, to point out the essential difference between ideological pretensions and the social reality in Yugoslavia."[44]

Furthermore, others point out that science and technology are the precursors of entirely new dimensions of alienation impinging on all social systems, which may eventually replace even capitalism as the primary source of exploitation, reification, and alienation.[45] Stojanović thus concludes that:

> "Today . . . we can no longer believe in the possibility of complete and definite dealienation, which Marx linked with the communist future. There is always going to be the possibility that man's activity and creation [will] be alienated from him."[46]

But what about this communist future? It becomes revolutionized in the Yugoslav reinterpretation of the Marxist *Weltanschauung* in non-eschatological terms. We recall that the goal of Marxism-Leninism is a classless, conflictless communist society. Marx himself distinguished between two stages of the classless society, a lower stage (socialism) and a higher stage (communism). But Petrović reverses Marx's time-honored categories and states that socialism is a higher stage than communism and that "real life" is the highest. The most radical aspect in this revolutionary reconstruction of Marxist-Leninist theory is the avant-garde's insistence that socialism and communism are not the ultimate goals of the dialectic of history, but only transitory stages toward *humanism* and a *human* society.[47]

It is important to re-emphasize that humanism is not about humanism in the abstract, but about *man* and his existence, life, creativity, and freedom. There is thus among Yugoslav Marxist humanists a strong existentialist focus on man as bearing the sole responsibility for his existence and destiny, on man as a being of *praxis.* At the same time, they retain a Marxist framework. Whereas the existentialists are concerned exclusively with the individual and his freedom and responsibility to shape his existence, the Yugoslavs emphasize the need to humanize not only the individual but society as well. This is the circle the Yugoslav philosophers (and not only the Yugoslavs) are trying to square. It is *the* classical problem of political philosophy: how to reconcile individual interest with the social interest or the common good.

3. What Does it Mean to be Human?

Paradoxically, the significance of Marxist humanism lies more in the questions it raises than in the answers it provides. Petrović asks the seminal question: "What does it mean . . . to be a man?"[48] This is the kind of question that was raised by Plato, Aristotle, and Augustine, and that we have scarcely heard since Aquinas, Rousseau, and Kant. Contemporary social theory seems no longer concerned with it. Yugoslav Marxist humanist thought emphasizes the need to reintroduce the ethical, valuational aspect of human concern into our alienated world where science and technology seem to have developed dynamics of their own, overshadowing the human capacity to apply them wisely. The Yugoslavs express the need to concentrate once more on hope and on man, while deemphasizing ideologies, science, technology, collectivities, states, economies. The supreme need in our time, they argue, is to concentrate once again on the most neglected entity—man. Furthermore, in this equation man is not spelled with a capital "M" as some abstract being out in the cosmos, but with a small "m," meaning each individual human being. As Veljko Korać expressed it, echoing Marx and Engels: " . . . a new, human society can be only an association of men where *the freedom of each individual becomes the condition for the freedom of all.*"[49]

The Yugoslavs designate their new philosophy also as socialist personalism.[50] It might more appropriately be termed Marxism-Existentialism. Jean-Paul Sartre, among others, attempted but failed to unite the best elements of Marxism and existentialism. The Yugoslavs, however, have gone a long way toward creating a suggestive admixture of the two philosophies. They have achieved this synthesis on a high level of generalization, at the expense of some specific propositions. And while their definition of man as a being of *praxis* is impressive, it poses more questions than it solves. Petrović is the first to admit this.[51]

Nevertheless, the central and most fertile question, which calls for further research and discovery, new evaluations and orientations, is precisely that dealing with the nature of man and the tension between his existence and essence. Since no man is an island, in order to understand him we must explore his relationship to his fellow men in society and to the world around him. It is this kind of a man-centered paradigm that is called for in a world in which science and technology have run away with human destiny. Today, man seems to lack the capacity to understand these extra-human forces (if he ever did). Yet, if he is to survive and enhance the quality of life on this planet, he must recoup the ability to control these forces by understanding what he is. The Yugoslav Marxist humanists' greatest single contribution to this pan-human enterprise is in redirecting the focus of attention on the nature of man and—perhaps more significantly—on what man should or could be. That the issue of man's essence is a highly complex subject can be gleaned from the questioning by Yugoslav philosophers of Marx's view of the essential goodness of human nature which is corrupted by the social environment. Stojanović contends that "In fact, man's essence includes his destructiveness and not only his creativity, as it appeared to Marx. One can easily say that man is condemned to that duality, to that contradiction of human versus inhuman potentials."[52]

The Yugoslav Marxist humanists reinterpret Marxism by developing not only Marx's philosophy of man but also his "scientific" *method,* the dialectic. In their pragmatic conception, the dialectic does not deal with *laws* of historical development at all, but only with *tendencies* and *probabilities,* which, moreover, can be changed by conscious human action. They see the whole system of dialectical and historical materialism, the stages of society's development, as simply a *model,* not an empirical description of reality.[53] But what happens to Marxist-Leninist theory when it is conceived of as a "model?" Obviously, it can no longer claim to be the exclusive Truth. This is the second key aspect of the Yugoslav avant-garde's revolutionary reinterpretation of Marxist-Leninist doctrine. To them, official Marxism appears as an ossified system of dogma resulting in a narrow positivist interpretation in theory and application in practice. Hence, they emphasize the need for reinterpretation and creative development of a "living" Marxism.

The writings of Marx, Engels, Lenin, and Stalin contain a wealth of contradictory statements, if not different *Weltanschauungen,* in addition to the extremely pliable method of the dialectic itself. Thus, it is perhaps unwarranted to term any of the differing interpretations of Marxism "revisionist," "reformist," "true," and so on. The question of which is the "true" Marxism is beside the point. The accepted view, to differentiate between the "orthodox" and the "revisionist" formulations, has led to a game of devastating critique and opprobrium heaped by one communist regime upon another, degenerating into simple name-calling. Thus, China calls the Soviet Union "renegade," "degenerate," "revisionist," and until recently has hurled even worse epithets at communist Yugoslavia. The Yugoslavs and the Soviets, not to be outdone, describe the People's Republic of China in equivalent terms. The Yugoslavs used to criticize the absurd cult of the individual in Mao's China which dwarfs even Stalin's cult of personality, and deplore Stalinism or state capitalism in the USSR which on close inspection proves to be no better than capitalism.

This harsh judgment passed by one group of communists upon another makes a shambles of the myth of socialist brotherhood and solidarity. It implies tacitly, and sometimes explicitly, that the other group is involved in exploitation, blurring considerably the ideological divide between class and classless society. According to the Yugoslavs, in state capitalism the state takes over the exploiting role of private capital. Under capitalism there is private ownership of the means of production; under state capitalism the state owns the means of production. In either case the worker does not derive the benefits due him. What is needed for a truly classless society, they maintain, is not simply the nationalization of the means of production, but the effective control and management of this nationalized property by the associated producers (workers) themselves. In their view, the nationalized property in the Soviet Union and elsewhere remains in the hands of the state and its bureaucracy, which administers the property for its own benefit.

It is surprising to see the Yugoslav communists echoing some of the most trenchant criticism of the communist system put forward by Milovan Djilas, the leading ideologue in Yugoslavia until his disgrace in 1954 and imprisonment for his book, *The New Class.* Djilas described the communist party elite in Yugoslavia as the new class of privileged administrators of socialized property, possessing greater power than any other class in history. Significantly, some of today's avant-garde are arriving at the same disturbing conclusion about the ideological-political monopoly of the League of Communists for which Djilas and, more recently, Mihajlo Mihajlov were imprisoned. Marković, for one, observes that "basic decision-making regarding the system, its changes, key questions of present policies and especially the entire cadre politics remain in the hands of the Party's top [leadership], outside of the possible sphere of influence by the Party rank and file and the rest of the people."[54]

It is understandable that the League of Communists of Yugoslavia does not sanction such theoretical innovations by its avant-garde Marxist philosophers and that it decided to silence them. Yet the degree to which the League has allowed this creative redefinition of Marxism to exist is a measure of the extent, as well as the possible limits, of liberalization in the country—a measure of how far the system may evolve in the direction of a more *democratic* socialism from its present stage of *socialist* democracy. Marković, like Djilas, Mihajlov, and others before him, minces no words in defining the essential prerequisites for a genuinely self-governing, democratic as well as socialist society:

> What is needed is the existence of strong and free public opinion, and that means: Intensive political life without authoritarian

subordination and manipulation, unhindered circulation of ideas, freedom of public criticism, and independent means of mass communication.[55]

In the words of Vojislav Stanovčić:

> The conclusion follows that a democratic society—which by its principles of organization and way of life allows for the articulation and, hence, also for conflict among differing interests—must have institutional and other means for a continuous resolution of conflicting situations.[56]

This is a far cry from the orthodox Marxist view of the nature of institutions and practices in socialism. The Yugoslav avant-garde gets into serious trouble theoretically, not to mention politically, in advocating institutions and procedures for conflict resolution in socialism, since this is in essence a demand for *politics*, democratic pluralism, and institutions of the state, law, bureaucracies, and the like, the very factors they exorcise as the chief causes of alienation, exploitation, and conflict. They seem to have tied a Gordian knot into the heart of Marxism and to have reopened the central question of the unity of theory and practice which Marx thought he had solved once and for all. The avant-garde is not alone, however, in facing this dilemma. The party itself has turned increasingly toward constitutionalism and socialist legality as the major tools for bringing about direct participatory democracy and the classless society. In many ways the avant-garde seems to be merely holding up a theoretical mirror to social practice.

This may explain in part the considerable tension between the official and avant-garde interpretations of Marxism-Leninism in Yugoslavia. There is a degree of tolerance, but there is also a great deal of suspicion. What seems to have shielded the Marxist humanists as much as anything up to 1975 has been the esoteric and metaphysical contours of their philosophy. It is an extremely complex and difficult school of thought to understand. The avant-garde returned to the early Marx, but they did not stop there. They went back to Hegel, Rousseau, and Kant, and even to the classical philosophers. Their access to Western philosophical works is in itself an indication of the continuing liberalization of the Yugoslav system. Their interest in analytic philosophy, phenomenology, existentialism, personalism, and the philosophy of science, combined with openness, contributed to their reinterpretation of the whole question of what Marxism should be. In their view, it is not important that Marxism be a finished product. On the contrary, they see it as a *process*, a continuing redefinition and creative development of Marxist theory and corresponding application in socialist practice. They believe that, if Marxism is to be a living doctrine, useful to man in guiding his practical activity in solving changing human problems, then the theories must change too. Hence the need, as the Yugoslavs see it, to develop Marxist doctrine in all directions, in accord with the framework of humanism.[57]

There is dispute about the extent to which Marxist humanism is indeed "humanist," as well as "Marxist," for that matter. On the one hand, the orthodox Soviet and some leading Western Marxists claim that there is no relationship whatever between the "young" and the "old" Marx. They often deride Marx for the "youthful fantasies" in his early writings. On the other side, the Yugoslav avant-garde and other Western Marxists see an integral unity and humanist orientation underlying all of Marx's writings. They maintain that the young Marx who was concerned with the human individual and his alienation, and the old Marx whose chief concerns were classes, economic production and surplus value, are in fact one, and that some of Marx's interpreters lost the individual from their purview.[58] It can be argued, however, that there are both humanist and anti-humanist, dogmatic, totalitarian elements in the young and the old Marx alike. Yugoslav Marxism itself, though liberalized, radicalized, and humanized, still labors to a considerable extent under Marxism's generic paradoxes.

In spite of this controversy, the Yugoslav avant-garde's new philosophical orientation is revolutionary, not only for the communist systems themselves, but also with regard to the most pressing needs of our time: humanizing science and technology and dignifying man, probing the quintessential question of the nature of man and what he should or could be, and fostering East-West dialogue, détente, rapprochement, even cooperation. Instead of a nuclear war of mutual annihilation and Armageddon, perhaps we can develop greater understanding and tolerance, if not cooperation, between the two worlds. Marxist humanism seems to embody a philosophical-theoretical framework par excellence for bridging the ideological-conceptual gap between East and West. Why should this be so? Because Marxist humanism dedicates itself openly and unreservedly to the exploration of the phenomenon of man, focusing on man rather than on ideologies, collectivities, state machineries, history, economic systems, science, weapons, and outlived dogmas.

4.   The Avant-Garde and the Party

Like tragedy in triumph, the Yugoslav avant-garde's very attempt to reopen Marxist-Leninist theory and develop it in the direction of a critical philosophy and a humanist creed which could some day bridge the East-West ideological gap sealed their political doom, since the LCY came to see them as a direct threat to its leading ideological role in society. The late President Tito's 1972 Letter to the party, his 1973 address to the first General Assembly of the Federation, the 1973 symposium on "The League of Communists and Theory" sponsored by the LCY's Commission on Ideological Questions, as well as the Tenth and Eleventh Party Congresses, in 1974 and 1978, respectively, all stressed the need to strengthen the LCY's ideological-political unity, reestablish democratic centralism, reinvigorate the party as the leading ideological-political force in Yugoslav society, and oppose both statist-bureaucratic-technocratic tendencies and non-Marxist anarcho-liberal notions.

The point of no return in the ideological confrontation between the LCY and the avant-garde was reached with the letter of March 9, 1973, entitled "No Compromise with the Opposition," from the University Committee of the LCY to communists in the University of Belgrade's Department of Philosophy. The letter asked LCY members to reestablish democratic centralism, and to assert their ideological-political differentiation from, and engage immediately in a "broad and serious political discussion" with, the group of influential academicians who, especially since June 1968, have allegedly been "in open political conflict with the League of Communists."[59]

In a remarkable development for communist states, the avant-garde's two major journals, *Praxis* and *Filosofija*, picked up the LCY theoreticians' challenge. *Praxis'* editorial board expressed its solidarity with the group of academicians at the University of Belgrade and reasserted its self-management, socialist, and anti-Stalinist orientation, and agreement with the politics of brotherhood and unity of the Yugoslav people, as well as its opposition to bourgeois (nationalist) conceptions of society.[60] The President of the Philosophical Society of Serbia, Dr. Staniša Novaković, in a letter to the editor of *Komunist*, LCY's theoretical organ, protested allegations that *Filosofija* was anti-Marxist and anti-socialist and that it constituted a center of counterrevolution. In a separate letter, the chief editor of *Filosofija*, Dr. Jovan Arandjelović, indicated that libel proceedings would be brought against the author of these allegations.[61]

The party waged an all-out campaign, ratified by resolutions adopted at its Tenth Congress, to discredit the avant-garde Marxist theoreticians both morally and ideologically. To this end it declared that the carriers of "new left" views were in reality the "ideological-theoretical 'elite' of the right," attempting to restore bourgeois class society and thus counterrevolutionary.[62] The LCY managed to link the avant-garde Marxists simultaneously with what it called the anarchistic-nihilistic ultra-left, the etatist-dogmatic forces of Ranković, and the ultra-right liberal-anarchic Djilas within the country, and an alleged foreign propaganda campaign against Yugoslavia outside it.[63] It all boils down to one fundamental point—the original sin—of the Yugoslav avant-garde Marxist philosophers: They have challenged the LCY's leading role and thus, according to the party, the class nature of contemporary socialist development and the historic role of the working class and self-management. At a symposium on "the essence and the character of today's extreme left," sponsored by the editorial office of the newspaper *Oslobodjenje (Liberation)* in Sarajevo in conjunction with the Associations for Philosophy and Sociology of Bosnia-Hercegovina, Fuad Muhić called the avant-garde Marxists "spiritual emigrants" (touches of Solzhenitsyn?) and summed up the official party line in the familiar dialectical lingo reminiscent of *Newspeak* in George Orwell's *1984*:

> It needs to be stressed once again: in Yugoslav society there can be no force more left than the LCY; consequently, the appearance of every opposition represents the juncture at which it necessarily turns into the "right."[64]

The avant-garde Marxists thus find themselves in a precarious position, threatened by *Gleichschaltung* from the party, which is jealous of its ideological prerogative and beset by monumental problems including party disunity, ethnic divisions, bureaucratic mismanagement, corruption, speculation, unemployment, and other structural difficulties arising from the development of a market-oriented economy with social ownership. It would be a supreme irony were the political fate of Djilas and Mihajlov, who consider Marxism all but irrelevant to problems of the contemporary world, to be shared by the avant-garde whose chief goal has been to transform a dogmatized, Stalinist conception of Marxist-Leninist ideology into a living Marxism acutely aware of the need to integrate means and ends, theory and action, in the development of a truly human society of humanized social relationships.

The confrontation between Marxist philosophers and party leaders is a classic case of tension between men of thought and men of action. The avant-garde's recasting of Marxist-Leninist doctrine into a method of radical critique of all existing social conditions hindering the free development of the human individual is in a natural state of tension with the party's need for a specific political program geared to solving practical problems of everyday life. The man of action cannot readily turn the philosopher's critical stance, doubts, and uncertainties into decision-making and problem-solving tools. The current impasse, due in great part to the LCY's ascribing to the Marxist humanists a *political* role to which they do not aspire, could be resolved if the party recognized the distinction between, as well as the complementarity of, the roles of the critic and the practitioner. Otherwise, by suppressing its most creative interpreters of Marxism, the LCY may cut itself off from its own intelligentsia and yield once more to ideological somnambulism. The Yugoslav avant-garde seems to have stolen the ideological thunder from the LCY by restoring to Marxist philosophy its Promethean function of radical social critique and critical conscience of a highly institutionalized world.

5. Individual or Social Liberation?

The view of the extreme malleability of human nature has permeated the intellectual climate in communist systems and perhaps also our own. The avant-garde Yugoslav Marxist philosophers are, however, redressing the balance between freedom and determinism through their stress on the volitional aspect of man's thought and action. Though man is bound by time and space, history and society, he is still free to create himself and the world. The relationship between man, society and history is, thus, one of reciprocal influence. In the absence of this voluntaristic aspect of man's capacity to change conditions, the Marxist (and any other) system would be completely predetermined, obviating the need for any kind of active role for man. Man would then need merely to sit back and let History or Fate achieve its predetermined end. The avant-garde maintains, on the contrary, that man should determine his own destiny. Man can do this to a large extent only within society. Hence the Yugoslav emphasis on individual liberation as contingent upon the liberation of society.

The hallmark of some Western utopian thinkers, like the late Herbert Marcuse, is that they shift the focus away from the individual and onto the collective. Most significantly, and unlike the Yugoslav avant-garde, Marcuse seemed quite unconcerned with the humanity of means, preoccupied as he was with his conception of the humanity of goals. The two, however, cannot be divorced. The Yugoslavs, who have had for a generation a radical and disturbing experience with utopianism and who seem to be thoroughly re-evaluating it, point out that unless the ideals of a classless, conflictless, nonalienated, nonexploitative, socialist society, *Gemeinschaft,* are pursued with *humane* means—not in spite of, but in order to enrich the human individual—the socialist end is likely to remain the captive of an ever-distant future. Perhaps the Marxist humanist medium contains, after all, a central message wrapped in a riddle with a challenge to all of us, individually and collectively, whether East or West, North or South, to rise to the full potential of our humanity. The exploration of this quintessential *human* challenge constitutes the subject matter of the present study.

Chapter II · East-West Dialogue and Marxist Humanism

> We offer a dialogue without prejudice or hindrance. We do not ask anyone to stop being what he is. What we ask is, on the contrary, that he be it more and that he be it better. We hope that those who engage in dialogue with us will demand the same of us.
>
> Roger Garaudy, *From Anathema to Dialogue* (1966)

1. Myths and Symbols: Chariots of Man?

The annals of human history teem with a phenomenal variety of omnipresent myths, religions, and symbols. Man in all cultures and historical epochs has tried to cope with the mundane as well as the more esoteric and unknown dimensions of himself and the world. This existential fact in itself may account, at least in part, for the origin of religions, myths, and symbols. But what is the nature and function of myth in human experience?

Mark Schorer has pointed out that myths organize human experience and give it a larger philosophical meaning.[1] Furthermore, Mircea Eliade notes that this larger philosophical meaning has religious connotations, since the living of a myth provides the connection to the Supernatural in that it "re-enacts fabulous, exalting, significant events."[2] Joseph Campbell wonders why man should be beholden to myths:

> And why should it be that whenever men have looked for something solid on which to found their lives, they have chosen, not the facts in which the world abounds, but the myths of an immemorial imagination—preferring even to make life a hell for themselves and their neighbors, in the name of some violent god, rather than to accept gracefully the bounty the world affords?[3]

There is no definitive answer to the question of why man would need the prop of myth. Clyde Kluckhohn relates that psychoanalysts see myth-making as containing mechanisms of ego defense, while Lévi Strauss saw mythology as providing a logical model for resolving contradictions in one's world view.[4] It appears, then, that myths have many functions, among others, providing a larger paradigm to order human experience, relating it to the Supernatural, providing an escape from as well as explanation of the unknown, and resolving contradictions. As Eliade notes, myths contain a yearning for paradise, a Golden Age.[5] Finally, James G. Hart writes that the mythic world is characterized by absoluteness, comprehensiveness, and radicality in its self-disclosure as "the holy."[6]

It is all too easy to deride ancient cultures for their "ignorant myth-making." Yet, modern man, in spite of his moral/ethical relativism, religious atheism, and scientific-technological achievements, remains a myth-making creature. Just like the ancient Greek and other cultures, modern man also creates an entire hierarchy of gods and myths which permeate his whole civilization and culture. Modern man has excavated many an ancient culture, deciphered forgotten languages, and theorized on ancient mythologies, cultures, and symbols. Yet, the jury is still out on the issue of whether modern man understands his own contemporary culture, language, values, myths, and symbols.

We may see Erich von Däniken's *Chariots of the Gods* as creative, imaginative, fantastic, and mind-bending or merely spurious, unbelievable, and a dream. But we need only look in our own cultural-conceptual back yard to find equally fantastic "chariots" of facts, dreams, perspectives, myths, and values which constitute the cultural bedrock underlying entire civilizations. It is as if myths and symbols were chariots of man as well as his idols. There is, of course, nothing wrong with myths and symbols *per se*, except when they become:

(1) Substitutes for reality, precluding further inquiry, new conceptions and orientations, and

(2) A sacrificial altar which seduces man to forfeit not only his freedom of creative thought and action, but his very life and the lives of his fellow men.

Peter L. Berger and Thomas Luckmann contend that man's symbolic universes are like "sheltering canopies" since they provide ultimate legitimation upon protective structures of social organization.[7] Paradoxically, symbolic universes may also contain within themselves the seeds of universal destruction. How is this dialectic to be explained?

We need only take two major symbolic universes—such as "Capitalism" and "Communism"—which are apparently locked in irreconcilable conflict. There have rarely existed two more alienated concepts in the history of the human race; alienated in the sense that both have taken on lives of their own quite apart—or even in spite of—the realities they were originally designed to portray. Each of these concepts subsuming symbolic universes has become the carrier of the most banal, non-negotiable, and supra-rational elements in their respective cultures. The dogmatization of thought which has proceeded apace in both East and West, but especially in the East, can perhaps be best explained by psychiatry, social psychology, and cultural anthropology.

Words, symbols, and concepts, the building blocks of philosophical views and ideologies, are the chief carriers of meaning for modern man. They are the tools with which the human being accedes to an awareness of his own identity as well as the phenomena in the world around him. Man, as pointed out succinctly by Ernest Becker, is a "symbolic animal."[8] In the very act of coining words, man already assigns meaning to the universe.[9] This meaning, according to Becker and Hans Vaihinger in his *The Philosophy of As If*, is basically arbitrary and fictitious. Man's psychological world, which is basically fictitious, becomes real for the human being only through its validation in a social context. The validation of the individual's psychological world is accomplished through his acculturation or humanization, a process by which the individual achieves a sense of identity and relieves his anxiety. This process of acculturation, humanization or socialization of the human individual, that "anxiety-avoiding animal," takes its toll, however, in the form of restrictions on the totality of the world of meaning which leads to man's imprisonment in his own "symbolic mansion."[10]

Both "Communism" and "Capitalism" have, as master symbols,[11] helped perpetuate man's imprisonment in his own "symbolic mansion" and have exacerbated the conflicts in the real world. As extremely ambiguous yet authoritative symbols, they have contributed, to use a pregnant phrase of Harold D. Lasswell, to the "creation of remarkable monuments to human vanity."[12] Like other collective symbols such as nations, classes, tribes, and churches, "Communism" and "Capitalism" have served abundantly man's needs to "indulge his elementary urges for supreme power, for omniscience, for amorality, for security."[13]

2. A Contingent Universe?

It is with some trepidation that students of international interactions approach today questions of war and peace, international tension, crisis diplomacy and multilateral negotiations, the population explosion, ecological implosion, poverty, ignorance, disease, regional integration, and the elusive quest for peace in a world one step ahead of a nuclear Armageddon. We find ourselves wedged between cooperation, interdependence, and conflict on Spaceship Earth in what Norbert Wiener called "a contingent universe."[14] Central to our pursuit of effective interactions for the enhancement of the human condition within a peaceful international framework is an understanding and clarification of myths, symbols, and ideologies.

Despite Daniel Bell's thesis of an end to ideology, ours is an ideological age *par excellence*. As Berger put it:

> Our time is full of visions of the future, loudly and arrogantly proclaimed. Moral self-righteousness is evenly distributed through-out the political spectrum. They all tell us so confidently where it's at today and where, if only they have their way, it will be tomorrow. Yet in fact they know so very little, all these self-confident prophets of doom and salvation.[15]

Lewis S. Feuer notes that the longing for ideology is perennial and universal. Ideology in the contemporary era may very well be the equivalent of ancient myths. Indeed, Feuer believes that myth is one of the three constitutive elements of ideology.[16] More peculiarly, it is invariably a Mosaic revolutionary myth which recreates the drama of the liberation of the Hebrew tribes by Moses. Feuer sees a contemporary revival of ideology based on this Mosaic myth.

It has been pointed out that myths and symbolic universes in general are rooted in the very constitution of man, being products of his ongoing externaliza-tion and attachment of meaning to the cosmos.[17] Ideologies are, furthermore, peculiar interpretations of the mythic representation of reality. Feuer reminds us that an ideology is an "ism" which claims absolute certitude for its tenets, precludes further questioning and inquiry, and fulfills an axiomatic function for a political group as it records final and definitive collective decisions.[18] What characterizes ideologies above all is dogmatism, fanaticism, and unquestioning certitude of true believers. It is not difficult to imagine why ideologies may so readily become justifications for amoral or immoral conduct of the most invidious sort. Here it is apparently not crucial whether ideologies or myths are true or false. That is beside the point. It is sufficient that they are believed and acted upon.

Feuer sees the irrationalization of human life as the basic consequence of ideology. In his words:

> Men's visions have been warped by ideology; their hatreds have been exacerbated; and every anointed elite has felt itself anointed to misuse human beings. Ideological warfare within and among societies has superseded religious warfare; ideologists, like their religious predecessors, have a propensity to think in terms of St. Bartholomew's Days.[19]

Our world, as we well know, is divided into hostile ideological camps. Paradig-matic within this context is the opposition between "Communism" and "Capital-ism," a fierce and potentially fatal conflict, in spite of the fact that social, economic, political, legal, and cultural realities diverge considerably from both ideal types. The confrontation of dogmatized ideologies in the nuclear age has become somewhat of an anachronism, disturbing because of its pervasive link with reality and policy. It threatens to transpose its anachronism onto the human race, which may in the process become an extinct species.

President Eisenhower remarked that "in the thermonuclear age there is no alternative to peace."[20] Peace is, understandably enough, equated with the absence of arms; hence the emphasis on weapons control and disarmament. This is not objectionable in itself, as far as it goes. But it does not go far enough. The Preamble to the UNICEF Charter states a fundamental premise that wars begin in the minds of men and that it is in the minds of men that the defenses for peace must be constructed. This is not antithetical to the politics of peace. But it does point to the complexities of disarming not only the armies but the very minds of men. Is surrender, then, the only alternative to war?

Charles E. Osgood suggests that the appropriate policy for the nuclear age is to be found in GRIT—Graduated Reciprocation In Tension-Reduction. The aims of GRIT are to: (1) Reduce and control international tension levels; (2) Create gradually an atmosphere of mutual trust within which negotiations on critical political and military issues will have a better chance of succeding; (3) Enable the United States to take the initiative in foreign policy; and (4) Launch a new kind of international behavior appropriate to the nuclear age.[21] The key to the successful operation of GRIT seems to be contained in its second postulate, that is, the creation of an atmosphere of mutual trust. The latter, in turn, depends on the possibility of some kind of dialogue between East and West.

The essential features necessary for a genuine dialogue are, according to Anatol Rapoport: (1) An exchange of roles; (2) A recognition that any position whatever has *some* region of validity; and (3) Empathy.[22] As summed up by Fred Warner Neal, coexistence does not necessitate agreement between conflicting ideologies; but it does require a certain amount of scepticism of one's own infallibility and receptivity to learn from others.[23] Crucially, writes Gustav A. Wetter, while *ideological* coexistence between East and West is impossible, peaceful coexistence between *men* of different ideological persuasions "is not only possible but is absolutely required."[24]

One can only agree with Wetter and others that the continuing ideological struggle between East and West should be carried on, if at all, only by intellectual means of free inquiry rather than the physical liquidation of opponents. While Karl Marx held that the arm of criticism could not replace the criticism of arms, it is imperative in the latter part of the twentieth century that the dialogue between men and civilizations proceed by the arm of criticism rather than the criticism of arms.

2.1 The Russian Troika: Sakharov–Solzhenitsyn–Medvedev

One of the most articulate challenges to both East and West originated with the statement entitled *Progress, Coexistence, and Intellectual Freedom* by Andrei D. Sakharov, the Russian nuclear scientist of world fame and winner of the 1975 Nobel Prize for Peace. Sakharov's statement is complemented not only by his later writings but also by those of the exiled Russian Nobel-winning author Aleksandr I. Solzhenitsyn and the noted historian Roy A. Medvedev.

Sakharov states bluntly in his essay that the division of mankind threatens it with destruction:

> Civilization is imperiled by: a universal thermonuclear war, catastrophic hunger for most of mankind, stupefaction from the narcotic of "mass culture," and bureaucratized dogmatism, a spreading of mass myths that put entire peoples and continents under the power of cruel and treacherous demagogues, and destruction or degeneration from the unforeseeable consequences of swift changes in the conditions of life on our planet.[25]

Sakharov's prescription for curing the world's ills is peaceful competition between the United States and the Soviet Union and a four-stage plan of cooperation between the two superpowers. He foresaw in the *first* stage (1960-1980) a growing ideological struggle in the socialist camp giving rise to multi-party systems in certain cases. The *second* stage (1972-1985) would witness the victory of the leftist reformist wing of the bourgeoisie in capitalist countries, the implementation of a program of rapprochement (convergence) with socialism, and attack on racism and militarism. During the *third* stage (1972-1990), the United States and the Soviet Union, having overcome their alienation, would solve the problem of rescuing the poorer half of the world, and implement disarmament. Finally, in the *fourth* stage (1980-2000), the socialist convergence would "reduce differences in social structure, promote intellectual freedom, science, and economic progress and lead to creation of a world government and the smoothing of national contradictions."[26]

Sakharov's four-stage plan of cooperation between East and West seems to have had a measure of success as both superpowers proclaimed détente as their major foreign policy goal. Yet, Sakharov takes no less critical a stance toward the actual practice of détente than Solzhenitsyn or Medvedev. Indeed, Sakharov has come closer in his views on the need for internal democratization of the Soviet Union and the linking of the quest for civil rights with détente to those of Medvedev and Solzhenitsyn, respectively. He expressed this concern in his Nobel Lecture of December 1975:

> Détente can only be of lasting success if it is from the very beginning accompanied by unceasing concern for openness in all countries, for raising the level of publicity, for the free exchange of information, for the unfailing observance of civil and political rights by all countries —in short, if détente in the material sphere of disarmament and trade is supplemented by détente in the spiritual, ideological sphere.[27]

Sakharov maintains in both his Nobel Lecture and *My Country and the World* that genuine détente, disarmament, mutual understanding, and international trust essential to peace are indivisible from civil and political rights, freedom of information and convictions, travel, publicity, choice of residence, and other social, economic, political, and cultural attributes of an open society.[28] Without the relaxation of the political, economic, and ideological monopoly of Soviet totalitarian one-party rule and a guarantee of basic human rights, international on-site inspections of arms agreements, public accountability of authorities, free flow of information, and release of all political prisoners, Sakharov sees détente as only an illusion.

Therefore, he proposes an agenda for internal reform in the USSR, to embrace broadening of the 1965 economic reforms, partial de-nationalization of economic and societal activities, full amnesty for all political prisoners, freedom to strike, public accountability and disclosure of important decisions, guarantees of choice of residence and employment, freedom to travel, ban on excessive party and official privileges, equal rights for all citizens, the right of Soviet republics to secede, a multi-party system, currency reform, and limitation of the foreign trade monopoly.[29] These are far-reaching reforms, indeed. Yet Sakharov underlines that he is an evolutionist and reformist, opposed to violent, revolutionary changes with their attendant mass destruction, suffering, and lawlessness.[30] The key to the proposed reforms is constitutionalism and legality.

Solzhenitsyn and Medvedev could not agree more with Sakharov on the need to democratize the Soviet system. While Solzhenitsyn is more sceptical about the present capacity of the Russian people for self-government, he also argues for legality, openness, and a guarantee of basic civil rights:

> Were we not promised fifty years ago that never again would there be any secret diplomacy, secret talks, secret and incomprehensible appointments and transfers, that the masses would be informed of all matters and discuss them openly?[31]

But Solzhenitsyn, as an artist, writer, and moralist, is bent above all on penetrating the surface level of human rhetoric and political agreements down to their more fundamental ethical or moral level. On this level, Solzhenitsyn is in complete agreement with Sakharov regarding the need for both ideological coexistence and internal relaxation of totalitarian controls within Soviet society. The three major ingredients of a true détente are, according to Solzhenitsyn:

(1) *Disarmament:* not only with respect to war but the very use of violence;

(2) *Guarantees* that agreements will not be broken, which calls for public opinion, a free press, and a freely elected parliament in the USSR; and

(3) *End to ideological warfare.*[32]

Solzhenitsyn, like Sakharov, urges the West to unite and engage in a genuine *bi*-lateral détente with the communist world, that is, a détente based on firmness and unity of purpose, strength in negotiating stance and absolute insistence on international on-site inspections of all agreements. This they oppose to the present disarray, weakness, and unilateral concessions of the West, which is anything but a guarantee for a lasting peace. Solzhenitsyn goes even further than Sakharov in his insistence that genuine peaceful coexistence and détente are incompatible with continuing ideological warfare:

The Communist ideology is to destroy your society. This has been their aim for 125 years and has never changed, only the methods have changed a little. When there is détente, peaceful coexistence, and trade, they will still insist: the ideological war must continue! And what is ideological war? It is a focus of hatred, this is continued repetition of the oath to destroy the western world.[33]

Ideology, as Solzhenitsyn and Sakharov understand it, is one of the major hindrances to genuine East-West dialogue and cooperation. Solzhenitsyn considers ideology to be one of the great scourges of the twentieth century providing justification for evildoing on a mass scale. He sees Marxist ideology as leading the Soviet Union into a double disaster of war with China and destruction, along with the West, in the excesses, ravages, and wastes of advanced industrial civilization.[34] Solzhenitsyn's call is not only for genuine détente coupled with ideological disarmament, but also, and more basically, for a spiritual and moral regeneration and reconstruction in both East and West.

While Sakharov emphasizes the global connections between democratization and détente, and Solzhenitsyn argues for a moral regeneration of both East and West, Medvedev outlines in his essay *On Socialist Democracy* the basic preconditions for a genuine and realistic democratization of Soviet society based on existing structures and societal and party dynamics, including ideology. Although Medvedev rules out any foreign intervention in Soviet domestic affairs as inopportune and counter-productive, he agrees with Sakharov and Solzhenitsyn that a genuine democratization of Soviet society would be beneficial to foreign policy and the preservation of world peace.[35]

Medvedev's outline of democratization as an evolutionary process for the USSR includes guarantees for both majority and minority rights, dissent, opposition, and independent social and political associations, free elections, equality before the law, freedom of conscience and movement, popular control over all government activities, separation of powers into executive, legislative and judicial, de-centralization, de-bureaucratization, and the free development of each individual.[36] Medvedev's outline is almost identical with Sakharov's. Their major difference is with regard to the impetus and source of democratization. Sakharov, seconded to a large extent by Solzhenitsyn, counts on the West to provide this impetus. Medvedev, on the other hand, looks to the "party-democrats," one of the three major groupings within the CPSU itself, to energize democratization in practice and simultaneously revive and develop Marxist-Leninist ideology in the direction of greater openness, democracy, pluralism, and concern for the individual human being.

Characteristically, Medvedev resorts to the writings of the young Marx, the philosophical Lenin, and other Marxist classics to prove that socialism (communism) and democracy are indivisible. He sees the social, economic, political, legal, and cultural monopoly of the Soviet one-party system as products of Stalinism, dogmatism, and the imperatives of a certain stage of political-economic development. Medvedev insists that:

> Only people of limited intelligence identify communism with demands for suppression of dissidence, the prohibition of opposition, and the establishment of a one-party dictatorship.[37]

Like Sakharov and Solzhenitsyn, Medvedev places great stress on ideology. But while Sakharov advocates ideological pluralism, and Solzhenitsyn, in addition, dismisses Marxism-Leninism as a viable blueprint for the future, Medvedev sees a return to original Marxism-Leninism as an essential component for democratizing Soviet institutions and practices. Curiously, where Medvedev cannot find support for his views in the writings of the classics like Marx, Engels, and Lenin, he is not averse to criticizing or even going beyond them. While his theoretical endeavor is an attempt to return to the original Lenin uncorrupted by Stalinist and neo-Stalinist (mis-)interpretations, Medvedev finds Lenin himself wanting in important respects, such as the latter's views on democracy. This leads Medvedev to conclude that:

> . . . Leninism, like Marxism, is not a finished doctrine. As in the case of any other theory, it too is in need of constant improvement and development. Therefore it is wrong to be dogmatic about the universal applicability of Marxism and Leninism, ignoring the fact that any scientific theory or ideology has inevitable limitations.[38]

This is, indeed, a far cry from the run-of-the-mill orthodox interpretation of the nature and function of Marxist-Leninist ideology. It is this conception of an open-ended Marxism which centers its preoccupation on freedom, democracy, pluralism, tolerance, and the all-round development of each individual which promises to be most fruitful for the internal regeneration of communist systems as well as a genuine dialogue between East and West.

2.2 The Christian-Marxist Dialogue

The challenge which Sakharov, Solzhenitsyn, and Medvedev flung to their own society and the world consists more in their succinct summary of major dilemmas of our era than in the specific remedies proposed to alleviate them. The fact that this Russian troika remains largely unheeded only testifies to the fundamental truth of their challenge.

It is a double irony of history that the dialogue between East and West was initiated by the least rational and scientific groups in their respective societies—viewed from the perspective of advanced industrial civilization—namely, Christian theologians in the West and Marxist philosophers in the East. It is a double irony because to the founder of Marxism, religion and philosophy were among the chief manifestations of human alienation, constituting its very rationalization, whereas their practitioners belonged to the so-called bourgeoisie, the "exploiting class." The idea that this latter class could have a genuine interest in alleviating human suffering was foreign to Marx, who insisted on the class nature of all morality.[39]

Among the groups which had organized and conducted East-West dialogue, one of the most significant is the West German Paulus Society founded in the mid-

fifties by the German priest Erich Kellner.   The Paulus Society developed the
Christian-Marxist dialogue on a large scale through conferences at Salzburg (1965),
Herrenchiemsee (1966), and Marienbad (1967).   The Marienbad Conference, sponsored jointly by the Paulus Society and the Czechoslovak Institute of Sociology of
the Czech Academy of Sciences, was the first major Christian-Marxist dialogue
conference to be held in Eastern Europe.   By Easter 1968, the World Council of
Churches took up the Christian-Marxist dialogue at Geneva, where for the first
time in the history of dialogue meetings theologians of the Russian Orthodox
Church participated.   The Soviet-led invasion of Czechoslovakia in August 1968
chilled East-West relations and rendered continued dialogue tenuous and even
dangerous for participants from Soviet bloc nations.   The dialogue between
Marxists and Christians in the West, on the other hand, has increased in intensity.

   The theme that unites Christians and Marxists and constitutes the motive
force of their meetings is the overriding concern with the necessity of East-West
dialogue.   Paradigmatic of this orientation is that a prior of the Augustinian House
of Eindhoven in the Netherlands,[40] a spokesman for the Spanish Communist
Party,[41] a professor of philosophy at the University of Prague,[42] another professor
of philosophy at the University of Poitiers and ex-member of the Politburo of the
French Communist Party,[43] and the Director of the Papal Secretariat for Non-
Believers,[44] all share the belief that dialogue has become more than ever before a
vital necessity of our age and that this new vision should focus on man, the
affirmation of his dignity, and the alleviation of human suffering in its myriad
manifestations.

   In this historic search for a common meeting ground, Marxists and Christians
are drawing on the rich historical, cultural, and philosophical heritage of the past,
and in their focus on man are creating nothing less than a genuine humanist
renaissance.   Both groups have sought to reexamine the basic assumptions
underlying their respective *Weltanschauungen* in search of truths about man and
society, distilling the best features from the doctrines of their intellectual
adversaries and incorporating these insights, whenever possible, into their own
viewpoints.

   Thus, many Christians came to a realization that individual salvation needs to
be supplemented by increased awareness of social responsibility[45] and that neither
the anti-social position of extreme individualism nor the anti-individual position of
Marxism are able to answer the question of how man may find fulfillment in
society.[46] Others have noted that the Gospel contains also a social message[47] and
that, hence, redemption is not simply a private affair.[48] Rather, Christian love
implies social commitment and even revolution,[49] and, perhaps most basically, that
theology "must continually understand itself anew." [50]

   These unconventional views of Christian theologians were matched by the
evolution of equally unorthodox views among Marxists.   Many became painfully
aware that, in spite of Marxist materialism and determinism, man is still
responsible for his actions.[51] Some contend that Marxism embraces pluralism,[52]
and partakes of Christianity's futurist ideal of the millenium.[53] Others see that
Marxists and Christians alike are "forced to concern themselves with the question
of the meaning of human life,"[54] that Marxism is not a fixed system of dogmas,[55]
and that both East and West need to overcome their tragic onesidedness for which
"the Christian symbol is the Inquisition, and for which the Marxist symbol is
Stalinist practice."[56]   Moreover, some Marxists, notably French and Italian, assert
that communism attempts to fulfill the promise, or moral law, of Christianity—that is—love.[57]

   Whatever may be the accuracy of these views, one cannot help but admire the
spirit of openness, inquiry, and reconciliation underlying the Christian-Marxist
dialogue.   It is difficult to imagine a more fundamental and radical departure in the
respective philosophies of both Christians and Marxists nurtured by the most
promising phenomenon of our age—the humanist dialogue.   This dialogue attempts
to come to grips with the practical as well as theoretical questions articulated by
J. Claude Evans, such as: "How do we live in a world that, like it or not, is divided
into Marxist and non-Marxist nations?"[58]   It is a veritable tribute to the human

race and the basic sensibility of the human psyche that proponents of seemingly completely opposite and incompatible ideologies— Judaeo-Christian and Marxist-Leninist—could possibly meet and reason together and learn from each other in order to overcome deep-rooted human alienation within a man-made world of symbols.   The Christian-Marxist dialogue represents, therefore, a fundamental attempt to reappropriate man's alienated symbolic universe by recasting it in the image of the total, whole, complete, realized or humanized individual living in a community of humanized social relationships.

If humanism as a moral stance and intellectual attitude may best be summed up by its openness, empathy, and understanding, then Roger Garaudy's attempt to reconcile Christianity and communism follows in the best tradition of the humanist ethic:

> Indeed, we find it a beautiful thing that man, in his suffering, conceived such dreams, such hopes, conceived the infinite love of Christ. It is this act of faith that proves that man never considers himself wholly defeated. And thus he witnesses to his greatness. This is why we neither despise nor criticize the Christian for his faith, his love, his dreams, his hopes. Our own task is to labor and to struggle, lest they remain eternally distant or illusory. Our task as Communists is to draw near to man in his most glorious dreams and his most sublime hopes, to draw near to him in a real and practical way, so that Christians themselves might find here on our earth a beginning of their heaven.[59]

Garaudy's attempt to reconcile communism and Christianity, perceived as counter-revolutionary and revisionist in the East, and obscure and quixotic in the West, has clearly failed thus far.   There are at least two major reasons for this failure: (1) Internal contradictions as well as conflict between the two ideologies; and (2) Censure and opposition in both East and West.   But this reveals that the essential failure in l'affaire Garaudy may be neither that of the man nor the philosopher but of dogmatized ideologies and their grip on men's minds, East and West.   On top of Garaudy's theoretical difficulties, he suffered a personal tragedy (which may prove to be a greater gain in the future) when he was unceremoniously expelled from the French Communist Party.[60]   This time, as so often in the past, reality seemed to lag very much behind theory, joining its own alienation to that of its conceptualization.   Yet the continuing attempt by French and Italian avant-garde Marxist humanist thinkers to reconcile communism and Christianity is likely to have enormous socio-political, economic, philosophical, and cultural significance transcending national boundaries.

3.   National Communism and Polycentrism

The dialogue between East and West is intimately linked with major political and ideological forces at work in the Soviet Union and Eastern Europe.   Wading through the historical and ideological jungle of Soviet Russian communism in search of the philosopher's stone or at least a key to the understanding of Soviet foreign policy, Winston Churchill, speaking in the House of Commons on October 1, 1939, put it in a nutshell when he stated that:

> I cannot forecast to you the action of Russia.   It is a riddle wrapped in a mystery inside an enigma; but perhaps there is a key. That key is Russian national interest.[61]

Churchill could not have been more correct in his diagnosis.   At the same time, the USSR, along with the other twenty-seven existing communist party states, never gave up its Marxist-Leninist eschatological dream of the ultimate victory of communism in the world.   The end goal of world-wide communism remains as much an article of faith for Russia as for China or Yugoslavia. The *means* to be utilized for the achievement of this end differ widely, however, both spatially and temporally, reflecting the Leninist notion that there are no Marxist tactics, only a Marxist strategy.[62] Basically, it is the necessarily subjective judgment of a particular national interest bounded by space and time and adumbrated by an equally subjective conception of Marxist-Leninist tenets, which continues as the determining motive force underlying the foreign policies of individual communist party states. Their foreign policies have, naturally, reflected domestic policies as well as their relationship to the giants in the communist world, the USSR and China.

The undifferentiated concept of "International Communism" thus appears to be as much a phantom as its corollary, the equally generalized and maligned concept of "International Monopoly Capitalism." It is becoming increasingly obvious that the demands of a particular national interest—Russian, Chinese, Yugoslav, Polish, to name a few—and world revolution and the communization of the world are by no means identical. Indeed, they constitute two major vectors in the intricate web of policy-making considerations for each communist party state. Predictably, those states with an independent power base—notably the USSR, China, Yugoslavia, Cuba, Vietnam, North Korea, Albania and, increasingly Rumania—have enjoyed greater latitude in identifying the interests of the world revolution with their own particular national interest. In the case of the Soviet Union, this identification of the interests of promoting world revolution with the Russian national interest was accomplished by 1928 with the launching of the collectivization drive and industrialization at home.[63] It was reflected in Stalin's theory of "socialism in one country" and the betrayal of the Chinese communists in 1927. The fact that the Comintern, the supposed headquarters of world revolution, functioned as not much more than an appendage to the Soviet foreign office, coupled with Stalin's elimination of the Left opposition headed by Trotsky, were further indices that the ideological plank of world revolution served from the beginning not international but primarily Russian national interests.

Curiously, the myth of Soviet proletarian internationalism—and its corollary, Soviet dedication to spreading communism worldwide—persisted from the time of the conquest of power in Russia by a handful of Bolsheviks in October 1917 until the end of the Second World War. The persistence of the myth was due to the overriding fact that the USSR was the only communist party state in existence. But on June 28, 1948, came the incontrovertible proof of the *national* character of "International Communism." It came in the radical form of expulsion of communist Yugoslavia from the world communist movement by the Communist Information Bureau (Cominform), the successor body to the notorious Comintern or the Third International, headed by the USSR.

The concept of communist proletarian internationalism was so deeply embedded in the minds and psyches of communists everywhere that the natural reaction of the Yugoslav communists to their excommunication from the communist movement was total disbelief at first, followed by utter disorganization and disillusionment with Stalin, though not with communism or socialism as such. At the opposite end of the primordial myth, the Soviet Union found it necessary to justify its action against the Yugoslav communists in apocalyptic terms. These included, next to the Cominform Resolution itself, various forms of pressure up to a full economic boycott, border incidents, and a call to the rank and file of the Yugoslav Communist Party to oust their leaders as revisionists, that is, apostates from the Marxist-Leninist faith.

The Soviet-Yugoslav confrontation was in essence a confrontation between two national interests, two communist movements with independent power bases, two communist parties each with its own integrated cadre, two states in control of their respective armed forces, police, secret police, communications, economy, and society in general. Neal summed up the Soviet-Yugoslav controversy as follows:

> In a sense, the fundamental issue was between two views of Communism: the old, pre-1945 view of Communism primarily in

the interest of the Soviet Union, and the new, post-1945 view of Communism with perforce a national interest to defend and hence loyalties not limited to but in addition to loyalty to the USSR.[64]

The national content of "International Communism" needs to be stressed in spite of its disclaimers in East and West as well as the essentially universalistic appeal of the Marxist-Leninist ideology. Yet, this in no way reduces the importance of ideology as the doctrinal pronouncements by both sides during the Soviet-Yugoslav controversy testify.

The Soviet-Yugoslav break of 1948 ushered in momentous developments in what appeared up to that time as a monolithic and static system of "International Communism." Since 1948, the world has been witnessing the development of a seeming contradiction: national communism and polycentrism, that is, a diversification of world communism. Furthermore, the Soviet-Yugoslav conflict was reenacted in the Polish October of 1956, the Hungarian Revolution of 1956, the Sino-Soviet split of 1960, the Soviet-Albanian split of 1961, and in the Soviet-led invasion of Czechoslovakia in 1968. The substantial difference in outcome in the case of Poland, Hungary, and Czechoslovakia was due primarily to the fact that these countries were unable to withstand—not communism, but Russian national interest.   China and Albania, on the other hand, were able to assert their respective national interests. Yet it would be mistaken to conclude that all we have to deal with from 1948 onward is with particular national interests to the exlusion of ideology. For the particular national interests of the communist party states are inextricably bound up with their respective interpretations of Marxist-Leninist ideology.

The proliferation of communist party states has been accompanied by the proliferation of different conceptions of the Marxist-Leninist ideology. Within the East European framework, the "nationalization of communism"[65] has progressed through five distinct phases: (1) 1945-1947: People's democracy—with institutional and ideological diversity; (2) 1947-1953: Stalinism—institutional and ideological uniformity; (3) 1953-1956: Thaw—institutions and ideologies in flux; (4) 1957-1959: Retrenchment—institutional diversity and ideological uniformity; and (5) 1960 on: Communist pluralism— institutional and ideological diversity.[66] Yugoslavia is the most notable exception to this scheme, though the development of Titoism—the Yugoslav brand of national communism—exerted a manifold influence on the development of East European communist party states and even the USSR. The new communisms that have developed in Eastern Europe—especially after Stalin's death in 1953 and the ensuing period of de-Stalinization punctuated by Nikita Khrushchev's denunciation of Stalin's rule at the Twentieth CPSU Congress in 1956—can perhaps be best characterized by the adjectives "national" and "liberal," although not in the Western sense.[67]

Carl J. Friedrich and Zbigniew K. Brzezinski postulated six features or traits as basic to totalitarian dictatorships, whether fascist or communist:

(1) An elaborate ideology (official body of doctrine);

(2) A single mass party, typically led by one man;

(3) A system of terror (physical or psychic);

(4) A communications monopoly;

(5) A weapons monopoly;

(6) A centrally directed economy.[68]

Despite protestations to the contrary on the part of well-meaning observers in the West and officialdom in the East, these six basic features of the totalitarian model were an accurate description of reality for most of the communist party states up to about 1956. The totalitarian model appears valid even today, although following the Twentieth CPSU Congress in 1956, and especially the Hungarian Revolution at the end of 1956, it becomes a sort of Weberian ideal type against which the post-Stalin policies of the East European communist party states and the USSR can be measured. These post-Stalin policies have inaugurated significant new developments, among them:

(1) Modifications in the centrally directed economies toward decentralization, most pronounced in Yugoslavia, Hungary, Poland, and Czechoslovakia, and increasingly in the USSR itself.

(2) The weapons monopoly in the Soviet bloc continues to be tinkered with by the USSR, but has tended to shift generally in favor of Russia's satellites, especially in the case of Rumania. The Yugoslav and Albanian monopolies have remained intact thus far.

(3) The communications monopoly has remained unchanged, except during the Czechoslovak Spring of 1968 when it was practically erased, but the substantive content which is filtered through it is constantly changing with an overall liberal trend.

(4) The system of physical mass terror has been relaxed, notably in Yugoslavia, but an element of psychic terror, much more difficult to define, continues.

(5) The single mass party has remained, but its leadership has tended in the direction of collective rule and its leading role in society is undergoing questioning and redefinition, quite drastic in the case of Czechoslovakia in 1968 and Poland in 1981, and somewhat less drastic in the case of Yugoslavia.

(6) The official Marxist-Leninist ideology has also undergone change in the liberal, non-dogmatic, socialist humanist direction, particularly during the Prague Spring of 1968, Poland in 1980-81, and in Yugoslavia.

All these changes augur well for a continued liberalization, democratization, and humanization of communist systems. Yet the haphazardness, tenuousness, and reversibility of these changes, coupled with the insecurity of elites and the irrationality of ideological dogma, testify to the continued relevance of the totalitarian framework for an understanding of these systems.

3.1 Metamorphoses of Marxism

Joseph M. Bochenski, one of a group of scholars engaged in pioneering research on philosophy in the Soviet Union and Eastern Europe, points out that parallel with the institutional development of polycentrism in the communist world, there has also been a doctrinal split between the USSR and Eastern Europe.[69] This split represents a radical break with the entire Soviet tradition of dogmatic or Stalinist Marxism-Leninism on the part of East European communist party states, especially Yugoslavia, Czechoslovakia, Hungary, and Poland. This new non-Soviet interpretation of the official ideology is distinguished by its non-dogmatic, non-systematic, and anthropocentric as opposed to the Soviet cosmocentric orientation. In Bochenski's view, it also rejects dialectical materialism and attemps to return to the authentic Marx concerned with man.[70]

Wolfgang Leonhard pinpoints the Yugoslav break with Stalin in 1948 which shattered the monolithic character of world communism as the crucial turning point for the genesis of the new Marxisms.[71] In the Yugoslav case, according to Richard T. De George, Marxism underwent a creative reinterpretation distancing itself from the Soviet model in its critique of Soviet socialism, rejection of the doctrine of *partiinost,* and adoption of self-management and different roads to socialism.[72] Yet in the case of the other East European communist nations, creative reinterpretation of Marxism develops full force only in the third phase, that is, the period of the Thaw, following the death of Stalin and fueled by the de-Stalinization campaign launched at the Twentieth CPSU Congress, and comes into its own in the 1960s.

It is necessary to differentiate from the outset between two major streams of Marxism: the official and the unofficial, or the "scientific" and the "humanistic."[73] It is also important to note that these two major currents are by no means separated by watertight compartments but that they rather interact. Their relationship is somewhat analogous to a plant with offshoots. The offshoots—the unofficial interpretations of Marxism—subsist within the larger system of the plant—the official interpretation. The plant nourishes the offshoots which in turn help sustain the larger system—the plant as a whole. The analogy becomes problematic when we recall that the East European communist party states are highly political-ideological "plants." It is within the power of each plant to simply cut off those offshoots which it deems threatening. On the other hand, the very conception of what is threatening is determined, at least partially, by the plant's growth and its increasing capacity to tolerate more diverse and perhaps ever more obnoxious offshoots. Briefly, there seems to be a complex, symbiotic relationship between the two sets of (re-)interpretations of Marxism, the official and unofficial, with gradations between them. Yet it is incontestable that the official versions of the new Marxisms are far more conservative and dogmatic than the unofficial versions and, in fact, act as a brake on and a limit to the latter's development.

Nevertheless, within the confines of the official Marxist-Leninist ideologies of the East European communist party states there has been a spectacular development of new interpretations and metamorphoses of Marxism. Maurice Cranston identified the major unifying features of these new Marxisms, neo-communism or socialist humanism as: (1) Opposition to bureaucracy; (2) Critique of censorship and police surveillance; (3) Favoring the use of science and technology for improving living standards; (4) Favoring free contacts and dialogue with people in "capitalist" countries; (5) Belief in peaceful coexistence; and (6) Belief in the possibility of reconciling the individual with the economic exigencies of socialism and national-ism with internationalism.[74] The central feature as well as the unifying focus of the new reinterpretations of Marxism within Eastern Europe is their concern with the individual,[75] whereas their overriding dilemma is how to assure the fulfillment of man, the individual human being, in a social or, more specifically, socialist or communist, context.

The renunciation by most of the East European communist party states and the USSR of their totalitarian heritage of Stalinism, even though only partial, made the re-examination if not the reconstruction of Marxism mandatory, while the post-Stalin trend toward liberalization, however fluctuating, made this same quest for justification, rationalization, and prescription possible. The exact date of the origin of this quest for a more humane Marxism is impossible to determine. In the past, Marxism as a science and a faith has had its humanist interpreters already in such men as Eduard Bernstein and Jean Jaurès who insisted on the primacy of the ethical content in Marxism.[76] In more recent times, it was the Hungarian Marxist philosopher György Lukacs who as early as 1923 managed to read Marx's concept of the alienation of labor back to its Hegelian roots of the alienation of man from the Absolute Idea in his *History and Class Consciousness,* long before Karl Marx's *Economic and Philosophical Manuscripts* of 1844 were ever published.[77] Lukacs, who fled in the 1930s before the Nazis to the Soviet Union, had to repudiate his work, but the concept of alienation has been reinstated in the post-Stalin era, particularly in Yugoslavia, as the central unifying concept underlying all of Marx's writings.

It is generally assumed that in order to be able to divine the shape of the future, we must concentrate on the most dynamic forces in each epoch. The new unofficial reinterpretations of Marxism in contemporary Eastern Europe seem to represent such an extraordinary motor force for the future evolution of the new communist societies. The most radical unofficial reconstruction of Marxism is undoubtedly that propounded by avant-garde Yugoslav Marxist philosophers and sociologists, paralleling the not inconsiderable originality of Yugoslavia's official ideology. Among the other communist party states in Eastern Europe, the new unofficial reinterpretations of Marxism have been advanced most consistently in Hungary, Poland, and Czechoslovakia, and to a lesser extent in East Germany and Rumania.

3.2 Marxist Humanism in Hungary, Poland, and Czechoslovakia

Apart from Yugoslavia, it was Hungary under the influence of György Lukacs, Imre Nagy, and the Petöfi Circle in conjunction with the Revolution of 1956 which provided a giant impetus for rethinking Marxist theory and socialist practice throughout Eastern Europe and beyond. One need only recall Lukacs' often tortuous examination of socialist thought and practice, Nagy's reform proposals of 1953, and the Petöfi Circle's intense discussions. Nagy as Premier advocated such far-reaching reforms as the abolition of prison camps, legal guarantees of personal freedom, and freedom for farmers to leave collective farms, tolerance toward the intelligentsia, development of light (consumer) industry, and a thorough demo-cratization of the party as well as the state and society. Following Khrushchev's revelations of Stalin's crimes at the Twentieth CPSU Congress in February 1956, intellectuals both East and West demanded a fuller accounting of indigenous leaderships in the individual East European communist nations. The Petöfi Circle in Hungary was most influential in promoting an in-depth examination of the post-war Hungarian experience. Tibor Déry voiced the new *leitmotif*:

> As long as we direct our criticism against individuals instead of investigating whether the mistakes spring from the very system, from the very ideology, we can achieve nothing more than to exchange evil for a lesser evil. We must seek in our socialist system the mistakes which not only permit our leaders to misuse their power, but which also render us incapable of dealing with each other with the humanity we deserve. The mistakes in question are structural mistakes that curtail, to an entirely unnec-essary degree, the individual's rights and that, again unnecessarily, increase his burdens.[78]

As in Czechoslovakia, Soviet tanks not only crushed the Hungarian uprising, but also put an end to the radical Hungarian re-examination deemed treacherous by the Soviet leadership.

It is, therefore, all the more surprising that there has been a virtual renaissance of Marxist humanist thought in Hungary during the 1960s. Prominent among the various schools of thought is the "Budapest School" founded by Lukacs and developed further by his followers like the sociologists Mária Márkus and András Hegedüs, and the philosophers Agnés Heller and Mihály Vajda.[79] Central to this school is a return to the early Marx and his emphasis on the concept of alienation, combined with a dialectical critique of contemporary social conditions in socialism as well as capitalism.

The whipping boy of the new Marxist critique is bureaucracy in both statist socialism and market-dominated capitalism. An unusual feature of the sociological theories of Hegedüs and Márkus is their critique of the new economic reforms in Hungary and elsewhere in Eastern Europe which rely on the market mechanism. They reject both the bureaucratic statist model of socialism of the Stalinist type and the acquisitive main-road consumption model of the post-Stalin era as alternatives for modernization and social progress. Instead, they propose a third model which would combine economic efficiency with humanism, reduce alienation caused by the division of labor and promote the all-round development of the human individual, offering him the widest choice among life styles. But this is only possible, according to Márkus and Hegedüs, if the rule by the market and state monopolies is curbed by "communities representing a real social force able to dominate both the state bureaucracy and the market."[80]

Predictably enough, the Hungarian CP condemned this "pluralization of Marxism-Leninism" and subjected Hegedüs, Márkus, Heller, Vajda, György Konrád, Ivan Szelényi, and other creative Hungarian Marxist humanist scholars to censure and persecution.[81]

Turning to Poland, the foremost proponents of Marxist humanism seem to be Adam Schaff, Leszek Kolakowski, Marek Fritzhand, Bronislaw Baczko, and Bogdan Suchodolski. Schaff, author of *A Philosophy of Man* and *Marxism and the Human Individual*, expresses the spirit of Marxist humanism in his statement that:

> . . . the central problem of socialism—of *any* socialism, and Marx's socialism in particular—is the problem of man, with its most essential aspect of creating conditions for man's happiness and full development.[82]

In order to develop a new philosophy of man, and of society and their mutual relationship, Polish Marxists, along with their counterparts elsewhere in Eastern Europe, have returned to the writings of the early or youthful Marx to rediscover the fundamental features of Marxist humanism. The return to the early Marx unearthed the evanescent yet ubiquitous concept of alienation in its manifold manifestations. It is this concept of alienation which Baczko considers essential for grasping the central problem of the Marxist conception of philosophy.[83]

Two major schools of thought seem to have developed among Polish Marxists. One concerns itself chiefly with Marx's philosophical anthropology; the other deals primarily with questions of the natural sciences and ontology. There is also a third group which proposes a synthesis between the two via the concept of *praxis.*[84]

To the first group belongs Fritzhand, who in his *The Ethical Thought of the Young Marx* maintains that:

> The Marxist model of the human individual . . . is the active, creative and free man, rather than the "mass man" moulded on a pattern of conformity and uniformity.[85]

Fritzhand's thought mirrors the post-Stalin generation's revulsion toward the dogmatization of Marxism which in its one-sided emphasis on materialism and historical determinism ignored the volitional aspect of human *praxis,* that is, the free creative activity of man in shaping his own destiny within the historical framework of society. Instead, individual responsibility became submerged in the amorphous context of class morality subordinated to History and the "class struggle," which in turn became a pretext for tyranny.

The most prominent Marxist philosopher in the second group is Kolakowski, whose reinterpretation of Marxism has exceeded the limits imposed by the official version of Marxist ideology. Kolakowski wreaks havoc in Marxist epistemology by postulating that "theodicy," or the method of transforming facts into values, a legacy from magical thinking, leads to the dogmatization of Marxist thought.[86] He nevertheless professes the necessity of giving priority to moral values before those of social progress as an antidote to the perversion of Marxism into doctrinaire Stalinism.[87] It is this concern for a humanist ethical grounding of the "science" of Marxism which seems to be the focal point among contemporary Marxist humanists.

The leading proponent in the third group, Schaff, maintains that there is an essential unity between the early Marx of the *Paris Manuscripts* and the mature or later Marx of *Capital.* According to Schaff, the central aim of Marx was to liberate man from alienation of his labor, products, self, and his relationships to other men. The liberation of man would be accomplished through *praxis* —man's active shaping of historical forces *within a social context* which is undergoing incessant change in the direction of a class-less, socialist, and ultimately communist, society. Marx defined the essence of man or human nature as the ensemble of social relations or the entirety of social conditions. Thus, according to Schaff, the liberation of man and the achievement of personal happiness can only be attained by the liberation of society and the achievement of social happiness.[88]

In Czechoslovakia, Milan Prucha, Karel Kosik, Milan Machovec, and Ivan Svitak have propounded Marxist humanism. Furthermore, the Czechoslovak Spring of 1968 as a whole may be termed a giant national socialist humanist renaissance to which Marxism as such became irrelevant in many respects, as it did in the Hungarian uprising of 1956.

The *leitmotif* of the Czechoslovak Spring of 1968 was the attempt to humanize socialism or—as the Czechoslovaks themselves put it—to achieve socialism with a human face.[89] In the process of the Czechoslovak humanist renaissance between Antonin Novotny's ouster in January 1968 and the Soviet-led Warsaw Pact (minus Rumania) invasion in August 1968, many Marxist philosophers—including Svitak—seemed to have, at the time, abandoned classical Marxism altogether in favor of a thoroughly humanist creed beyond both "Capitalism" and "Communism."[90]

As a Marxist humanist, Svitak equated the fundamentals of Marxist humanism with what he perceived as the essence of Marx's *Economic and Philosophical Manuscripts*:

> ... *Communism without humanism is no communism and humanism without communism cannot be humanism.*[91]

As in the Polish case, Czechoslovak Marxist philosophers perceive no conflict between communism, Marxism, and humanism, but hold on the contrary that communism, and hence Marxism, is the most authentic humanism. Machovec seems to add a slight variation to this theme, since he reportedly entertains the idea that there is only one humanism, as against the orthodox Marxist distinction between socialist and non-socialist humanism.[92]

Another singular development in Marxist theory is the nearly universal claim by contemporary Marxist philosophers in Hungary, Poland, and Czechoslovakia that alienation exists also in socialism. The phenomenon of alienation is no longer tied exclusively to capitalist society, the class struggle, and the manifestations of the remnants of "bourgeois" mentality in socialist societies. It is now asserted that alienation, although of an allegedly less pernicious or "non-conflictual" nature, is also generated within the womb of the new, socialist society![93] This is quite an innovation in Marxist-Leninist theory. Furthermore, Schaff seems to contradict his own and the generally accepted Marxist view of the abolition of alienation in communism, when he advances the far-reaching thesis of the inseparability of alienation from the human condition:

> ... as long as various social alienations persist—and these can only be abolished by abolishing society and men themselves—there will exist the social sources and causes of these conflicts.[94]

This cursory review of the unofficial reinterpretations of Marxism in Hungary, Poland, and Czechoslovakia should suffice to indicate the stupendous changes that are occurring in Marxist-Leninist ideology in the direction of a critical, self-conscious Marxism, aware of its Stalinist dogmatization and perversion and bent on a revolutionary reconstruction of the value and the role of man in society.

4. In Search of Man

The current unofficial reinterpretations of Marxism in Hungary, Poland, and Czechoslovakia, and especially in Yugoslavia, are among the most dynamic forces today which in their interaction with official ideologies promise to exert an extraordinarily significant role in the future evolution of communist systems in their own countries and beyond.

The Marxist *Weltanschauung* is a well-known paradox which has been related in the literature filling entire libraries. Like other philosophical systems, Marxism is both a science and a faith, that is, a mixture of facts and values. It is paradoxical that in the contemporary humanist reinterpretation, Marxism is becoming more scientific to the extent that it is abandoning its fixed doctrines and, hence, transcending itself, while its relevance to the contemporary world is increasing in the proportion in which it concentrates on a humanist vision of the future which has very little, if anything, to do with science.

It is also to the extent to which contemporary Marxist philosophers concentrate on the humanist half of Marxist humanism that a genuine dialogue between East and West ceases to be merely a promise and becomes a real possibility. The humanization of institutions and practices in both East and West cannot take place apart from the cultural bedrock from which these worlds draw their inspiration. In the East, and particularly in Yugoslavia, the humanist reconstruction of the Marxist-Leninist ideology constitutes the most promising socio-cultural force not only for the humanization of native institutions and practices but also for a genuine dialogue between civilizations which, until recently, seemed to be worlds of alienated, immanent, frozen concepts locked in deadly conflict.

Crucially, what is at issue is not ideology *per se*, but the future of man. Yet it is part of our dilemma that ideologies, myths, and symbols are inseparable from the human condition. It is impossible to abolish ideologies, myths, and symbols unless one abolishes man as such. However, it should be possible to transform and *humanize* man's symbolic universe so that it serves human beings rather than vice versa. It does not even involve de-sacralizing myths, symbols, ideologies, and other structures constituting man's sheltering canopies. But our nuclear age does call for a radical reconstruction of man's symbolic universes not only for æsthetic, poetic, theoretical, or ethical reasons but because the very survival of the human species is at stake. It is doubtful whether mankind is likely to survive in a world mortgaged by poverty, disease, famine, and pollution, and burdened by ideological dogmas breeding hatred, intolerance, spiritual poverty, self-righteousness, oppression, tyranny, violence, and war.

Marxist humanist thought in the communist world appears as the most promising theoretical and practical bridge between East and West as well as the most realistic indigenous process for the democratization, liberalization, and humanization of totalitarian systems. It is important not only in terms of Marxist theory and socialist practice, but also in terms of international relations, coexistence, and the quest for a lasting peace. As Leonhard writes:

> The fundamental concepts of the humanist Marxists are not only closest to the spirit and to the writings of Marx but, more important, the humanist Marxists are willing and able to apply these concepts independently and open-mindedly to the new problems in our times and our world—including a critical analysis of the developments in the Soviet Union and in Eastern Europe.[95]

But some may still wonder why all this emphasis on the theoretical-philosophical aspects of socialism and communism? Because thought is father to the deed. Garaudy succinctly points out that:

> The philosophical perversions of Marxism have supported its political perversions. If there exists only one "given" reality and one exact reflection of this reality, one man or a group of men can be the depositories of this unique and absolute truth. They will have unlimited authority, since they will bring people this truth "from outside." This is the "theoretical" basis for the single Party and the despotic State.[96]

Marxist humanist thought is, of course, not a panacea. It should not be beyond criticism, either. Indeed, some deny that Marxist humanist thought is humanist at all. Others deny that it is Marxist. But if it is neither humanist nor Marxist, then what is it? Furthermore, is Marxist humanism an antidote to Stalinism? There are those who doubt that. Pavel Kovaly asks:

> Where are the guarantees against the worst excesses of Stalinist theory and practice? So far, Marxist philosophy has not provided a solution to this problem and it is doubtful whether it can ever do so, unless it transcends its own boundaries. The lack of a theoretical formulation of the problem and its application to political theory and practice points to the fact that Marxist philosophy as a whole cannot transcend itself toward its own humanization, unless it changes its own fundamental presuppositions and thus stops being Marxist.[97]

This is, indeed, one of the most important theoretical as well as practical questions confronting us in the latter part of the twentieth century. On its satisfactory solution depends not only the fate of one-third of mankind presently living under communist rule, but also that of the rest of the world. East-West dialogue appears in this context quintessential to a peaceful evolution of both ideologies and people on the planet Earth. In this vital process we have nothing to lose but our dogmatic chains, and we have a world to win—a world of free men and humanized societies.

Chapter III · Titoism: Alternative to Stalinism?

> Marxism is not a doctrine established forever or a system of dogmas. Marxism is a theory of the social process which develops through successive historic phases. Marxism, therefore, implies a creative application of the theory and its further development, primarily by drawing general conclusions from the practice of socialist development and through attainment of scientific thinking of mankind.
>
> *Draft Program of the League of Communists of Yugoslavia* (1958)

1. The Catalyst of 1948

Titoism, or the Yugoslav brand of national communism and the Yugoslav interpretation of Marxism-Leninism, has been designated as the most significant development in Marxism since the October Revolution of 1917.[1] Observers also agree that the Soviet-Yugoslav break of 1948 was instrumental in the Yugoslav communists' search for an independent road to socialism and the attendant ideological reorientation and reinterpretation of Marxism-Leninism.[2] As Wolfgang Leonhard remarked:

> Yugoslavia's break with the Stalin leadership in 1948 was the crucial turning point. The monolithic character of world communism in the Stalinist mold had been broken, and the Stalinist interpretation of Marxism-Leninism was no longer sacrosanct.[3]

Hence, an analysis of the official and unofficial reinterpretations of Marxism in contemporary Yugoslavia must perforce take into account the historic events that transpired, especially in 1948—that veritable turning point in the history of the world communist movement.

The expulsion of communist Yugoslavia from the international communist movement by the Cominform Resolution of June 28, 1948, was the culmination of an indubitably world historic exchange of letters between the Central Committees of the Communist Party of the Soviet Union and the Communist Party of Yugoslavia.[4] Soviet letters reflected in general Stalin's aggressive tone whereas the Yugoslav replies were comparatively mild, defensive but, nevertheless, firm in their defense of Yugoslav independence. This infuriated Stalin, who apparently by that time could not tolerate any form of dissent from his views whatsoever.

Significantly, the Yugoslav communist leadership was accused of an anti-Soviet attitude and nationalism as well as Trotskyism and Bukharinism, that is, both left- and right-wing deviation, revisionism, arrogance, "violation of the equality of Communist Parties," "betrayal of the work done for the international solidarity of workers," and so on.[5] Tito's and Kardelj's reply to the Soviet charges was summed up in their statement that:

> We desire that the matter be liquidated in such manner that we

> prove, by deeds, that the accusations against us are unjust. That
> is, we will resolutely construct Socialism and remain loyal to the
> Soviet Union; remain loyal to the doctrine of Marx, Engels, Lenin
> and Stalin. The future will show, as did the past, that we will
> realize all that we promise you.[6]

The Yugoslav communist leadership completely missed the major thrust of Stalin's demands. The Soviet-Yugoslav controversy did not hinge primarily on the matter of the correct construction of socialism and communism in Yugoslavia, nor the Yugoslav communists' correct interpretation of and loyalty to Marxism-Leninism. It involved, rather, the central question of who shall be in control of Yugoslavia. Was it to be Tito at the head of his indigenous Yugoslav Communist Party, or Stalin, who utilized his own and foreign communist parties as transmission belts for his personal commands?

The fact that Tito was able to withstand not communism but Soviet Russian national interest adumbrated by Marxist-Leninist ideology as defined by Stalin, was due to the overwhelming fact that he had an independent power base. Tito's power base rested on the Yugoslav Communist Party's tight grip on the country following its liberation from Nazi occupation at the end of World War II, the destruction of the pre-war Royalist system of government, and the institution of a hard-boiled police dictatorship. It was also a fact that the Yugoslav communists at the head of the all-Yugoslav national liberation movement freed their country from Nazi occupation with minimal Soviet assistance. In fact, the participation of Red Army troops in the liberation of the Yugoslav capital, Belgrade, put the Yugoslav communists in the embarrassing position of having to explain to the Yugoslav people the generally unfriendly behavior of Soviet officers and men who raped and robbed wherever they went.[7] It became a common joke that the Reds, domestic and foreign, liberated people from everything.

The Soviet-Yugoslav conflict did not originate in 1948. The seeds of this conflict went back to the period between the two world wars, especially the period from 1928 on, which witnessed the complete victory of Stalin over both the Left and the Right opposition domestically, the subordination of world revolution to the Russian national interest, and Stalin's utilization of foreign communist parties as tools of his foreign policy. The Yugoslavs themselves acknowledge that elements of disagreement between them and Stalin went as far back as 1941 and centered around the conception of the character of the Yugoslav revolution.[8]

The Soviet-Yugoslav controversy developed with giant strides in the period between 1945 and 1948. This was the period immediately following the Yugoslav communists' conquest of power in Yugoslavia and, ironically, the very time when they were aping the Soviet system and establishing their own which was, if anything, more Stalinist than Stalin's.[9] However, Soviet aid to Yugoslavia in the form of military and civilian advisers, joint-stock companies, and promised credits for rebuilding war-ravaged Yugoslavia soon turned into their "un-socialist" opposites. They became an imposition of Russian forms in the most rigid manner, infiltration of the Yugoslav Communist Party, the intelligence network, army, police, and economic exploitation. It was basically an attempt by the Russians to turn Yugoslavia into a satellite of Moscow. The Yugoslavs balked at what they perceived as individual Soviet malpractices and complained to none other than— Stalin! The *casus belli* that touched off the Soviet-Yugoslav conflict was a Yugoslav request for a reduction of Soviet military and technical advisers stationed in Yugoslavia.[10]

Stalin could not suffer nor envision such a thing as opposition to his directives by some *parvenu* communists who found themselves in power in a South Slav country. He underestimated the staying strength and misjudged both the nature of the power and the role of Yugoslav communists in post-World War II Yugoslavia. To Soviet charges of nationalism, revisionism, and anti-Soviet attitude, the Yugoslav communist leadership answered that:

> No matter how much each of us loves the land of Socialism, the

USSR, he can, in no case, love his own country less . . . . [11]

In the same letter of April 13, 1948, from the Central Committee of the Communist Party of Yugoslavia to the Central Committee of the Communist Party of the Soviet Union, we also find the historic statement by the Yugoslav communists that socialism in Yugoslavia may have to be built along somewhat different lines than that in the USSR. This constituted the germ of what later became the (in)famous Yugoslav view of independent paths to socialism. It also presaged the Yugoslav critique of Stalinism which A. Ross Johnson has termed "a revolutionary Marxist critique of the Soviet system under Stalin" and the most comprehensive in the communist world. [12]

Unable to bring the Yugoslav communist leadership to heel by an exchange of letters, Stalin decided to apply a drastic measure: excluding communist Yugoslavia from the world communist movement. The Cominform Resolution of June 28, 1948, to that effect, was followed by a tight economic blockade by the USSR and its East European satellites, a suspension of promised credits for the rebuilding of Yugoslavia, and numerous incidents along Yugoslavia's eastern borders. A documentary record of Cominform pressure tactics was compiled by the Yugoslav government and published as the *White Book*. [13] The Yugoslavs did not knuckle under, however. On the contrary, they turned to the supposed arch-enemy of communism, the capitalist West, for much needed aid which was forthcoming (mainly from the United States) without strings and sowing further doubt in Yugoslav minds about the teachings of the motherland of socialism. [14] Not only did Tito turn to the West for essential aid to rebuild the country, but he also concluded in August 1954 a defensive alliance with Greece and Turkey known as the Balkan Pact. Stalin's pressure tactics had failed, but not before they had exacted a heavy toll in human suffering in the neighboring East European "people's democracies," where even prominent communists were jailed and executed for alleged Titoist or national deviation. [15]

The death of Stalin, in March 1953, made a Soviet-Yugoslav rapprochement possible. This in fact came about when Soviet Party Secretary Nikita S. Khrushchev and Premier Bulganin paid a visit to Belgrade in 1955. The result—a joint policy statement of June 2, 1955, called the Belgrade Declaration—was a *de facto* endorsement of Yugoslav policy of independent roads to socialism. Tito scored another victory when the Yugoslav delegation failed to sign the Moscow Declaration of eighty-one communist parties in 1960, referring to the USSR as the leader of the socialist camp and endorsing the Warsaw Pact, and again when the League of Communists of Yugoslavia (so renamed in 1952) was treated at the 23rd CPSU Congress in 1966 for the first time since 1948 as a full-fledged member of the communist bloc. Even more surprising was the fact that at the very time when it was, for all intents and purposes, being re-admitted to the world communist movement, Yugoslavia had become a leader of the nonaligned nations of the Third World. [16] In order to explain this paradox, among others, we must turn to the internal developments in Yugoslavia after 1948, that is, the development of Titoism or Yugoslav national communism, and its theoretical formulation in the most innovative and original reinterpretation of classic Marxist-Leninist teachings.

2.   Titoism

Titoism did not spring ready-made, as it were, from Zeus' head in 1948 as a set of finished doctrines. Yugoslav communists did not even begin to criticize the USSR until a year later. The theoretical justification and elaboration of their own road to socialism emerged gradually over the years, finding its most authoritative expression in the Draft Program adopted at the Seventh Congress of the League of Communists of Yugoslavia in 1958.

The depth of the Soviet-Yugoslav rift of 1948 was reflected in a whole kaleidoscope of differences. These involved divergent views on Trieste, the Yugoslav Partisan effort, the formation of the Yugoslav army, the Yugoslav Five-

Year Plan of 1947, Yugoslav collectivization of agriculture, and Yugoslav foreign policy, particularly the ill-fated attempt at Yugoslav-Bulgarian federation, Yugoslav presence in Albania, and Yugoslav help to the Greek communists. To top it all off, the Yugoslav communists were charged with nationalist revisionism—the heresy of heresies in the communist lexicon. Since they were convinced that they were genuine communists, that is, Marxists and Leninists, it was only natural for them to turn the tables on the USSR and call Stalin's system revisionist. It should be stated from the outset that the Yugoslav communist leadership was more concerned with finding theoretical justification as well as guidelines for their own practical activity within Yugoslavia than calling Stalin names. However, the Cominform action initiated a real soul-searching among Yugoslav communists and eventually led them to a reappraisal of Marxism-Leninism as well as the Soviet and Yugoslav models of building socialism and communism.

The essence of the Titoist reappraisal of Marxist-Leninist theory and socialist practice was put in a nutshell by Fred Warner Neal:

> The essence of Titoism was its independence from and criticism of the Soviet Union. The Titoist system came to involve new socialist concepts and methods, a drastic decentralization of the whole state structure, abandonment of Soviet-type planning, worker-management of industry, a competitive (but not private) economic system and the end of collectivization in agriculture.[17]

The development of communist Yugoslavia falls into several fairly distinct stages: (1) 1945-1950: Period of "administrative socialism" or Stalinism; (2) 1950-1953: The Thaw-Institutionalization of workers' councils in industry and abandonment of collectivization in agriculture; (3) 1953-1958: Decentralization of government and party machineries; (4) 1958-1963: Decentralization of the economy and emphasis on socialist legality; (5) 1963-1971: Further economic and social reforms, emergence of market socialism, federalism, and emphasis on socialist legality and socialist humanism; and (6) 1971 on: Emphasis on ideological unity and the party's leading role combined with institutional diversity.

2.1 Decentralization

Decentralization is the key to understanding Yugoslav developments after 1948 at the level of practice, just as socialist humanism is the key to understanding the same developments at the level of theory. The Yugoslav emphasis on decentralization stemmed from their insights into the nature of the Soviet system. The Yugoslavs inferred from the imperialistic and hegemonistic behavior of the USSR toward Yugoslavia an essentially centralized and bureaucratic deformation of the Soviet system, which they dubbed "state capitalism" or Stalinism (later moderated to "state socialism"). As the Yugoslavs saw it, the fusion of the governmental and the party apparatus in the USSR wielding all decision-making authority in the economy and society resulted in the transformation of the dictatorship *of* the proletariat into a dictatorship *over* the proletariat. Soviet power *of* the people became in effect a power by the bureaucratic elite *over* the people.[18]

The remedy was, logically enough, to be sought in the decentralization of decision-making power in the economy and society. This was the first historic innovation by the Yugoslav communists in the form of workers' councils in industry. Tito himself called this law of 1950 which, at least in theory, turned the factories over to the management of workers, a "revolutionary law" that "contained the fundamental elements of the new general line of the Communist Party of Yugoslavia in the development of socialism in Yugoslavia."[19] It was followed by the abandonment of collectivization in agriculture, reflecting the new doctrine of the long-range socialization of agriculture. This development was reflected in the 1953 Constitution which supplanted the Constitution of 1946. For many reasons, however, the decentralization of the economy did not fully get underway until the late fifties. The promulgation of the Draft Program and its adoption at the Seventh Party Congress in 1958 was instrumental in this development.

The 1958 Draft Program proclaimed the socialization of the means of production as one of its chief goals.[20] This meant not only the *nationalization* of the means of production, which was considered the first step toward socialization and which had already been accomplished in Yugoslavia. In a striking theoretical development, the Yugoslavs asserted that the nationalized means of production would also have to be *socialized,* that is, the effective control over these means of production would have to be turned over to the workers—the immediate producers—themselves. The failure to effect control over the nationalized means of production would lead, as in the case of the USSR, to the alienation of these means in the form of state capitalism. The major aim of this social ownership of the means of production would be to abolish hired labor and thus emancipate labor[21] and overcome the classic alienation of labor in capitalist and state capitalist systems. The kingpin in this new form of social ownership in a decentralized economy would be the workers' councils and their extensions in the polity, the basic self-sufficient territorial units, the communes.

The period after 1963 witnessed further economic and social reforms in Yugoslavia toward "market socialism," reflected in the new Constitutions of 1963 and 1974 as well as the Eighth, Ninth, Tenth, and Eleventh Party Congresses in 1964, 1969, 1974, and 1978, respectively. The 1963 Constitution emphasized in its Article 6 the economic basis of the system of self-management:

> The basis of the social-economic system of Yugoslavia is free, associated work with socially-owned means of labour, and self-management of the working people in production and in distribution of the social product in the working organization and social community.[22]

The Yugoslavs never tire of stressing the economic foundations of their type of "democracy." Political democracy, in their conception, must be subservient to economic democracy. In fairness, however, one should mention that the comprehensive economic reforms of 1965 (sometimes called The Reform) found their equivalent in the political reforms of 1966 when Alexander Ranković, heading the conservative elements within the party, was ousted, and curbs put on the secret police.

The Eighth and Ninth Party Congresses both stressed the need for a more rational deployment of the country's scarce economic resources, especially the need for an investment policy based on the criterion of profitability.[23] The emphasis at the Tenth Party Congress shifted away from investment to increased productivity as the overriding economic goal, while the Eleventh stressed the themes of economic rationality and accountability.[24] All Congresses criticized bureaucratic, etatist (statist), and technocratic forces that allegedly impeded progress and the implementation of economic and social reforms.[25] They took to task equally the bureaucratic-etatist forces which would rather see a return to the earlier type of administrative socialism and the petty-bourgeois liberal and anarchist currents which clamor for the restoration of "bourgeois liberalism" and the multi-party system.[26]

2.2 Democratization

The Yugoslavs have attempted to combine the decentralization of the economy with de-etatization, de-bureaucratization, and democratization in the political sphere, although practice, as elsewhere, has lagged behind theory. Since in the USSR the state bureaucracy under Stalin became a power over the people, the 1958 Draft Program of the party proclaimed that:

> . . . the question of the gradual withering away of the state arises
> as the fundamental and decisive question of the socialist system.[27]

The gradual withering away of the state was to be accomplished by decentralizing the governmental machinery, separating it from the party apparatus, and transferring increasingly greater responsibilities of state organs to local bodies, particularly the commune. Harking back to the young Marx, the philosophical Lenin, and anarcho-syndicalist thought, the Yugoslavs asserted that the commune was to become "not only or primarily a school of democracy, but democracy itself—the basic cell of self-management of citizens in common affairs."[28] With the anticipated withering away of the state, bureaucratic tendencies in the form of conservatism, dogmatism, state-capitalist, and pragmatist revisions of Marxism-Leninism would disappear. So would other reactionary forces holding up progress. The complete withering away of the state would signify or reflect the withering away of the remnants of class antagonisms, the alleged roots of alienation in contemporary socialist societies. It would, hence, usher in the communist era in which the Marxist principle "From each according to his ability, to each according to his needs" would be implemented.

The machinery that was supposed to take over state functions was, according to Yugoslav communist theory, workers' self-management (*radničko samoupravljanje*) bodies in the economy and social self-government (*društveno samoupravljanje*) via delegates in the polity. The idea of workers' self-management constitutes the foundation and the very essence of the Yugoslav communist theory of direct socialist democracy. This idea of direct democracy is inseparable from its economic corollary, that is, the view that the workers themselves ought to manage their factories and dispose of the surplus value of their labor and products as they see fit. The 1958 Draft Program stated this very explicitly:

> In social self-government under socialism, the working people
> should be offered the actual possibility of deciding on the creation
> and total distribution of the social product.[29]

While the 1974 Constitution reaffirmed the commune as "the basic sociopolitical community," it also proclaimed a new unit of workers' self-management more fundamental than workers' councils. In keeping with the spirit that Yugoslavia has entered a new stage in the building of communism understood as Marx's republic of associated labor, the 1974 Constitution characterized the *basic organization of associated labor* (BOAL) as the "fundamental form of association of labour" within work organizations.[30]

Along with the decentralization of the state economic functions, the establishment of a unique form of industrial democracy in the form of BOALs and workers' councils, and emphasis on local government and individual responsibility, the Yugoslavs began tinkering in the 1970s with a complex system of institutions and processes based on the delegate principle of worker representation to sociopolitical bodies from the commune to the autonomous province, republic, and federal assemblies (see Figures 1, 2, 3, and 4). The delegate principle is viewed as transcending the system of indirect and, hence, alienated representation of bourgeois parliamentary regimes in favor of direct democracy. The commune, republic, and provincial assemblies consist of three chambers (Chamber of Associated Labor, Chamber of Communes or Local Communities, and a Socio-Political Chamber) whereas the Federal Assembly has only two chambers (Federal Chamber and Chamber of Republics and Provinces). But it is difficult to see how this is direct democracy when assemblies at all levels have a restricted number of delegates. Even the SFRY Assembly, the highest decision-making body in the land, has only 30 delegates from each republic and 20 from each autonomous province composing the Federal Chamber and 12 delegates from each republic assembly and eight from each provincial assembly in the Chamber of Republics and Provinces.

The Yugoslav communists embarked also upon a democratization of the communist party itself as well as the state machinery for administration, separa-

Fig. 1: Yugoslav Federal Government Organization, 1974 Constitution

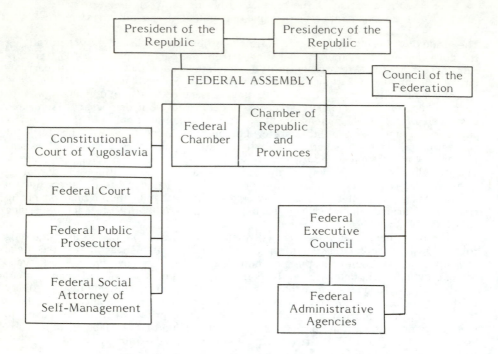

Source: "Constitutional System of the Socialist Federal Republic of Yugoslavia," *YS*, 15, 3, August 1974, p. 119.

Fig. 2: Republic Government Organization, 1974 Constitution

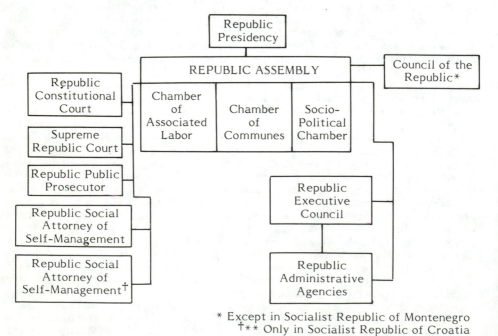

* Except in Socialist Republic of Montenegro
†** Only in Socialist Republic of Croatia

Fig. 3: Provincial Government Organization, 1974 Constitution

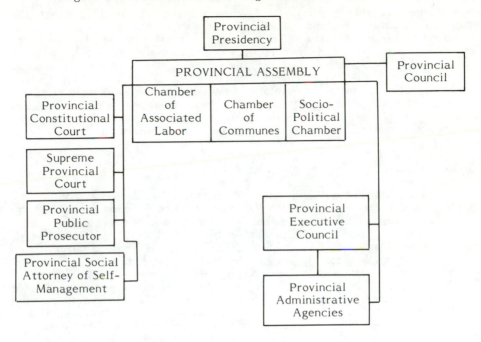

Source: "Constitutional System of the Socialist Federal Republic of Yugoslavia," *YS*, 15, 3, August 1974, p. 91.

Fig. 4: Commune Government Organization, 1974 Constitution

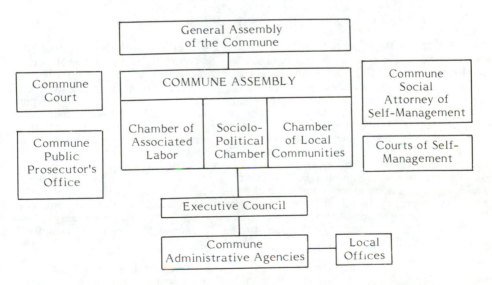

Source: "The Organization and Work of the Commune Assemblies," *YS*, 18, 2, May 1977, p. 5.

ting—at least in theory—party from governmental functions, and even envisaging the withering away of the party. This led to a federalization of administrative organs on the one hand, and the creation of six republic and two provincial communist parties on the other. Not surprisingly, the Tenth and Eleventh Party Congresses stressed unity in the party ranks and envisaged, along with the 1974 Constitution, a revitalization of party influence on all levels of decision-making, ranging from the BOALs to the SFRY Assembly. An example of this re-intertwining of party and governmental functions are the newly created Presidencies, that is, executive organs of the republic, provincial, and federal assemblies, which include the presidents of the Central Committees of the League of Communists of their respective republic, province, or the federation.[31]

2.3 Socialization

The concept of the withering away of the party has caused a good deal of trouble for the Yugoslav communist leadership, ever since its first formulation by Tito in 1952. Tito's remark on the ultimate withering away of the communist party was instrumental in setting off Djilas' train of thought, which led the latter to reject the party and Marxism-Leninism as such, although not socialism.[32] It resulted in adding conspicuously more confusion to the already fluid and complex reality in the minds of those both inside and outside the party.

The concept of the withering away of the party is exceptionally significant because it indicates—in spite of its contradictions, or perhaps thanks to them—the limits of democracy in the Yugoslav experiment with socialist democracy. It also delimits the gulf separating *democratic* socialism from *socialist* democracy. The 1958 Draft Program delineated the circumstances for the withering away of the party as follows:

> The leading political role of the League of Communists of Yugoslavia will gradually disappear in the perspective, as the forms of direct socialist democracy become stronger, develop and expand. This disappearance will proceed parallel to the objective process of the withering away of social antagonisms and of all forms of coercion which historically grew out of these antagonisms.[33]

The 1958 Draft Program linked the withering away of the party (dis)ingenuously with the withering away of social antagonisms or contradictions and the abolition of all forms of coercion, including the state. This interpretation of the withering away of the party was a master stroke for the party leadership. It meant that the party reserved the right as the alleged vanguard of the proletariat to decide when and even if the so-called social antagonisms shall have "withered away," and, hence, when or whether the party should follow in its wake. Such a formulation is disquieting to democrats who may have to wait a very long time for the realization of direct or any other type of democracy. Democratic hopes grew dimmer since the relatively new discovery by avant-garde Yugoslav Marxist philosophers and sociologists that socialism nurtures its own forms of alienation, in addition to those which are allegedly expressions of bourgeois class society. Furthermore, the withering away of social antagonisms, if possible at all, could mean but one thing—the socialization of the individual in a communist, that is, presumably class-less and conflict-less, society according to the communist blueprint. Tito himself adamantly upheld the view that:

> There can be no withering away or winding up of the League of Communists until the last class enemy has been immobilized, until the broadest body of our citizens are socialist in outlook.[34]

It is not obvious, however, whether the socialization of the individual in a conflict-less society would lead mankind to experience a leap from the realm of necessity into that of freedom. It could mean just the opposite: the advent of tyranny à la Huxley's *Brave New World* and possibly even ahead of Orwell's timetable in his distopia *1984.*

While ultimately the party is supposed to wither away, meantime, the Yugoslavs assert by a dialectical summersault, the role and responsibilities of the communists do not lessen but increase.[35] The increasing role and responsibilities of the communists in the period of the transition from capitalism to socialism and communism—that is, in our era—was supposed to manifest itself on the ideological level of state administration. But how are these roles to be kept separate when the League of Communists of Yugoslavia is expected not only to develop as a guardian of socialist morals and the essence of socialism, but also to *act* as a catalyst in the continuing revolutionary transformation of society? In its most far-reaching statement to date, the "Resolution on the Ideological-Political Foundations for the Further Development of the League of Communists of Yugoslavia," adopted at its Ninth Congress in March 1969, the LCY stated unequivocally that the communist vanguard:

> . . . must be a party of the revolution, of the ceaseless revolution-izing of social relationships, of the *abolition of all monopoly, including its own*; it must be a party that keeps moving forward and not one that conserves relationships dating from the early phase of socialism, and fossilizes them.[36]

Surprisingly, the party almost lived up to its quintessential promise of abolishing its own monopoly, at least partially. But the events in Croatia in 1971 and other nationalist stirrings throughout Yugoslavia apparently jolted the top party leadership out of their flirtation with more democratic inner party forms. The Tenth and Eleventh Party Congresses reaffirmed the party's ideological-political and power monopoly in Yugoslavia. Tito was especially careful to place Yugoslavia's continuing institutional pluralization in proper perspective:

> Socio-political organizations are not a transmission of the social role of the League of Communists. But neither can they be parallel political organizations fighting for power or to wield a special kind of influence on the consciousness of men. Each one of them has its own specific role, its tasks in a specific field of societal life and for this it is accountable to its members. It is precisely for this reason that the League of Communists must play the unifying ideological and political role.[37]

While Tito affirmed the party's leading role in Yugoslav society, processes of decentralization, democratization, and liberalization are expanding the totalitarian framework of the system in a nontotalitarian, though not necessarily democratic, direction.

The resolution of the question of the party's monopoly on societal decision-making is likely to coincide with the resolution of the question of the compatibility or incompatibility of socialism (communism) and democracy. This is one of the burning socio-political questions of the late twentieth century. The Czechoslovaks appeared to be only a hair's breadth away from the answer in 1968 before Soviet tanks re-established "normalcy" and ruled both the question and the attempted answer out of order. While the Czechoslovaks were thrown back into Plato's cave, the Yugoslavs are uneasily searching the cave toward the bright-lit exit.

2.4 Nonalignment

Yugoslav communist officialdom has come to regard its conflict with Stalin in 1948 as the consequence rather than the cause of the differences in the internal development of the two countries.[38] It remains a matter of conjecture whether the Yugoslavs would have embarked on their independent road to socialism even in the absence of the fateful events of 1948. The likelihood of a differential development of socialism/communism in Yugoslavia was great, because of the essentially national character of "International Communism." It is a fact, however, that at the time of the Cominform split of June 1948, Yugoslavia was the very prototype of a Stalinist police dictatorship. It can be argued that the seeds for the later Titoist development were present in Yugoslavia in 1948 or even earlier, but this line of reasoning ends very soon in an inconclusive chicken-or-egg argument.

Once they were expelled from the Soviet-led and dominated international communist movement, the Yugoslav communists searched frantically for a theoretical justification of their independent path to socialism. They found it, ironically, in Lenin's theory of the uneven development of—capitalism. According to this theory, the capitalist states develop unevenly, some becoming "ripe" for the transition to socialism and communism sooner than others. The Yugoslav communists now maintained that socialism, too, developes unevenly. Furthermore, since pure capitalism and pure socialism did not exist in the world, the conflict between socialism and capitalism on the level of states was no longer fundamental. Hence, the Yugoslavs declared that the division of the world into military blocs hindered the pursuit of peace and peaceful coexistence of all nations.[39]

As to Stalin's behavior toward Yugoslavia, it represented improper hegemonistic policies and practices and was a gross violation of socialist and democratic principles of independence, sovereignty, equality, territorial integrity, and noninterference in the internal affairs of other countries. The Yugoslav policy of active peaceful coexistence, mankind's only alternative to war and global destruction, was to be based on an unswerving observance of these elementary principles of international law and comity as well as the development of new socialist and more humane relations.[40]

Since foreign policy always reflects the state of domestic policies, argued the Yugoslavs, it was necessary for socialist states to eliminate all etatist-bureaucratic or Stalinist deformations within their own societies, lest they manifest themselves outwardly as tendencies toward domination and hegemony. In line with this reasoning, the Yugoslavs consider the concept of "limited sovereignty" developed by the Soviets to justify their invasion of Czechoslovakia in 1968 as a product of "excessive etatism."[41] What is needed, they claim, is an open, nonpropagandistic, and nonpolemical dialogue within the communist movement. The dialogue should take the form of an ideological-political ferment to democratize the contemporary revolutionary movement and thus reassert its traditional authentic socialist values and principles.[42] According to the Yugoslavs, this dialogue would be based on the fact that:

> Revolutionary ferment in the world, mass movements and the restiveness of the working class, young generations and oppressed nations have a common denominator in aspirations toward emancipation from economic, social, national and any other subjugation of the human personality, towards more human and free relations among men, towards the affirmation of human and democratic content of socialism.[43]

The Yugoslavs concluded that since socialism had become the general form of development of contemporary societies, the international workers' movement should free itself of those undemocratic methods of common action characteristic of the Stalinist era such as monolithism and insistence on the inevitability of a leading center. It should, instead, affirm national independence and the need for a variety of forms and methods in the struggle for socialism.[44]

Tito's statement at the Eighth Party Congress in 1964 on the necessity for independent action in furthering socialist goals on the international plane constitutes the basis of Yugoslav foreign policy of active peaceful coexistence. This policy of nonalignment, though no strict neutrality (witness the pro-Soviet voting pattern of Yugoslavia in the United Nations and elsewhere), and Tito's insistence on unity and an effective voice for the developing nations of the Third World, has increased Yugoslavia's prestige both at home and abroad. As noted by Alvin Z. Rubinstein, Yugoslavia is the only European country accepted as a leader among the nonaligned nations.[45] This observation was corroborated by President Kenneth D. Kaunda's invitation to Tito to preside over the proceedings of the Third Conference of sixty-two Nonaligned Nations in Lusaka, Zambia, in September 1970, and by the election of Yugoslavia to the twenty-five country Coordination Bureau at the Fifth Conference of Nonaligned Nations held in Colombo, Sri Lanka, in August 1976, attended by no less than 106 countries and 11 organizations and movements. Finally, the Sixth Conference of Nonaligned Nations in Havana, Cuba, in September 1979, Tito's last, honored him with a unanimously adopted "Resolution on Recognition to President Tito" as "one of the father-founders of our movement and its first President."[46] The Yugoslav critique of Stalinism in the field of foreign relations had thus achieved equally, if not more, surprising results as in the realm of internal developments in Yugoslavia following the Soviet-Yugoslav confrontation in 1948.

2.5 Socialist Humanism

Already in 1957 Charles P. McVicker pointed to the relative humanism of Titoist socialist democracy as perhaps the most important achievement of the Yugoslav communists' search for their own road to socialism.[47] Today, it is maintained almost universally that the Yugoslavs are the most profound exponents of humanism in the communist camp,[48] and that Yugoslav theory offers a variant of Marxism-Leninism which attempts to pay more attention to the problems of individual rights and human values.[49] These observations refer to the socialist humanist inspiration of contemporary Marxism-Leninism in Yugoslavia. Two basic tendencies in Yugoslavia's development after 1948 contributed to the genesis of Marxist or socialist humanism:

(1) The conception of Marxism-Leninism as both a theory and a method capable of and, indeed, requiring further creative development of theory and verification in practice, that is, unity of theory and practice; and

(2) Focus on the individual human being and his all-round development.

It was Tito at the Fifth Congress of the Communist Party of Yugoslavia—held in Belgrade in July 1948, following the Cominform split—who declared that the false accusations of the Cominform were a grave injustice to the CPY, which had unwavering faith in the science of Marx, Engels, and Lenin. It is significant that even at that time Tito regarded Marxism-Leninism from the practical angle, quoting Lenin (who was quoting Engels) to the effect that:

Our teaching is not a dogma but a guide to action.[50]

A strong case could be built around the thesis that the conception of Marxism-Leninism as a guide to action (which involves the interconnected aspects of justification, rationalization, and theoretical orientation) became the alpha and omega of the official Yugoslav interpretation of Marxism-Leninism after 1948. This view of the need to develop Marxism-Leninism creatively and to apply and test its prescriptions in reality received a comprehensive formulation in the Draft Program adopted at the Seventh Party Congress in 1958 (see quotation at the beginning of this chapter). The Draft Program quoted from the sacred texts of Lenin that:

We do not at all look upon Marx's theory as something finished and inviolable. On the contrary, we are convinced that it has only laid the foundation stone of that science which socialists must move further in all directions, unless they want to lag behind life.[51]

It was this view of Marxism as a living doctrine, perpetually in need of further development and refinement, that made the theoretical innovation of Titoism possible. The need for the development of Marxism as a method for enriching Marxist theory was stressed at the Eighth Party Congress in 1964.[52] The necessity for both a creative elaboration of Marxist conceptions and a critical re-examination of socialist practices was written into the resolution on "Socialist Development in Yugoslavia on the Basis of Self-Management and the Tasks of the League of Communists," adopted at the Ninth Party Congress in 1969.[53] It was reaffirmed by Tito in his address to the Tenth Party Congress in 1974, which claimed that:

> The extent to which the League of Communists performs its leading role is measured by its creative attitude to Marxism. That is the message which emerges from the whole of our rich revolutionary experience.[54]

In sum, the constant revolutionizing or creative development of both the Marxist-Leninist ideology and of socialist practice became something of an article of faith for the communist leadership in contemporary Yugoslavia.

The second tendency which contributed to the development of socialist humanism in Yugoslavia was the emphasis on the individual and the reconciliation of the private with the public interest. It was again Tito who, as early as June 1950, in elaborating on the new law on workers' councils, insisted that:

> Everything built and accomplished in this country has one aim: to bring happiness to our workers, to create better living conditions for them.[55]

Few, if any, could disagree with the intent of this earliest and most profound version of socialist humanism in official circles, but many did and still disagree with the practices as well as the theory adopted for its realization. The focus on the happiness of the individual and the all-round development of every human being is a theme that seems to grow and gain in breadth as well as in depth since its early formulations in the late forties and early fifties. During his visit to the Communist Party of Norway in October 1954, the late Edvard Kardelj, Yugoslavia's foremost communist theoretician (at least after Djilas' disgrace in 1954 and until Kardelj's death in 1979), contrasted the individual's material and moral interests as one of the two basic pillars of democratic self-management in the economy with the centralized, bureaucratic, and inefficient methods of Stalinism. He maintained that initiative and maximum effort on the part of the individual in the economy depended on his individual economic, social, cultural, and material interests.[56] It was on this basis that the Yugoslav system of self-management and socialist democracy was to be built, with the view of reconciling the individual with the public interest.

Throughout Yugoslavia's development there has been a strong emphasis on the socialization of the individual, that is, the creation of the new socialist man. Although the system of physical coercion and terror was relaxed relatively early in Yugoslavia, informal institutions such as sports and professional organizations and schools took on the task of educating the new man, not altogether successfully. The Socialist Alliance[57] has been repeatedly singled out as the major vehicle for socialist self-government, besides BOALs, workers' councils, communes, and the delegate system. The League of Communists remains, however, the only organized ideological and political force both within and outside of the Socialist Alliance with practical ideological-political monopoly in the country. It is this element of totalitarianism that mixes uneasily with the humanist half of socialist humanism. According to Kardelj, humanism in a socialist society must be "concrete" and "effective."[58]   The new Constitutions of 1963 and 1974, along with the 1971 Constitutional Amendrnents, are to be effective guides for the further democratization of the system, insuring socialist legality by, *inter alia,* the creation of Constitutional Courts (unique in communist party states)[59] and the development of workers' self-management in the economy and social self-government in the political sphere.

According to Tito, humanism is an essential ingredient of socialism:

> The whole ideology of Marxism-Leninism is permeated with humanism . . . . A genuinely socialist society must lead to the emancipation of labour, to the genuine emancipation of man, to the full assertion of the human personality.[60]

It is this view of socialism and communism as a humanist enterprise that sounds strange, if not quixotic, to Western ears. We have come to identify communism with "International Communism" and the latter, in turn, with ruthless tyranny, aggression, and oppression. It would be foolhardy to maintain that this stereotype of the communist world is completely outdated today, for it still contains important elements of the truth.   On the other hand, the diversification of "International Communism" after World War II and, especially, the development of the Titoist mutation have added significant new elements to the picture. These new elements, when not ignored, have been poorly understood in the West and, for that matter, also in the East.

3.   Grapes of Wrath

The Yugoslav critique of Stalinism and the concomitant elaboration of the Titoist model of self-managing socialism continue to bewilder observers both East and West, as well as the Yugoslavs themselves. Thus, until recently, Chinese communist criticism that Yugoslavia had sold out to the West and become its Trojan Horse in the communist world was neatly balanced by those Western critiques which see in Titoism a communist Trojan Horse to penetrate Western defenses. Some wonder whether Yugoslavia is really a self-managing democracy or a single-party dictatorship. Others ask themselves whether Yugoslavia's decentralized economy is capitalist or socialist. Many fear for Yugoslavia's territorial integrity and national independence, particularly since Tito's passing away on May 4, 1980.

Even the Yugoslavs are not sure about the nature of their system that has evolved since the economic and socio-political reforms of the 1960s characterized by the four Ds: decentralization, de-etatization, de-politicization, and democratization.[61]   One of the respondents in Sharon Zukin's study of Yugoslav perceptions of Marxist theory and socialist practice admitted that:

> I don't know whether this is socialism. I don't know where we're at, whether it's semicapitalism where we're at . . . .[62]

The confusion as to means and ends, theory and practice of Titoism appears to be widespread among elites, the party rank and file, as well as the masses. This state of affairs is not surprising in the light of the highly unorthodox and contradictory developments in a modernizing society claiming to be socialist.   Paul Lendvai hints at some of these contradictions when he asks such questions as:

> Can a Communist government ever find itself outvoted in parliament and even resign if it fails to get a vote of confidence? In a Communist state, can peasants not only own their land but privately import and operate tractors; can individuals run trucking businesses, restaurants, and motels?   Can a Communist country ever contemplate allowing foreign investments of risk capital and

setting up partnership projects? Can a ruling Communist party admit that it has turned into a break on social development instead of remaining the infallible vanguard and motor of advance toward full communism?[63]

The Titoist model, looking to the West as well as the original texts of Marx, Engels, and Lenin, following the break with Stalin in 1948, mixes generously elements from both East and West. This accounts for the puzzling phenomenon noted by Claire Sterling:

> Top party theoreticians urge a return to doctrinal purity on one hand, yet insist that there is nothing unsocialist about business cycles and bankruptcy laws, or incompatible between Karl Marx and Adam Smith.[64]

The Yugoslavs' enthusiastic adoption of elements of the market mechanism such as profitability, accountability, modern management techniques, rational investment decisions, and capitalist incentives such as reward according to work performed has led Western observers like Paul Sweezy to conclude that Yugoslavia's independent road to socialism is but a peaceful transition to capitalism.[65] If this were the true state of affairs, it would be unique, since the 1971-1972 purges of the Croatian and other republic leaderships, the new Constitution of 1974, and the Tenth and Eleventh Congresses of the League of Communists of Yugoslavia (LCY) left little doubt as to the locus of socio-political and economic decision-making power in the country. According to the 1974 Constitution, the first to acknowledge expressly the party's dominant role:

> ... the League of Communists is the conscious advocate of the aspirations and interests of the working class. It is also the leading organized ideological and political force of the working class and of all working people in the creation of socialism and in the realization of solidarity among the working people, and of brotherhood and unity among the nations and nationalities of Yugoslavia.[66]

Tito himself reaffirmed most emphatically the party's mandate to lead society. This was the substance of the 21st Session of the LCY Presidium, Tito's Letter to the party of September 18, 1972, the new Constitution, and the Tenth and Eleventh Party Congresses. Moreover, after silencing its own avant-garde Marxist humanist theoreticians in 1975, the party reestablished its claim as the sole true interpreter of Marxist-Leninist theory and socialist practice. Yet, Fred Singleton, among others, wonders how the party's monopoly of power can be reconciled with a policy of economic decentralization.[67]

One also wonders how the party's leading ideological-political role can be reconciled with workers' self-management and social self-government. What is the actual relationship between the party, the technical-managerial elites, the governmental bureaucracy, and the masses of peasants and workers? Who is managing whom in practice? Secondly, Yugoslavia has something like 200 wildcat strikes, dubbed "work stoppages," annually. How can workers strike against themselves in a self-managing socialist society based on social ownership? Thirdly, student demonstrations of 1968, 1970, and 1971 in Yugoslav universities raise a similar question to that of workers' strikes. Why should student youth strike in a socialist system which claims them as its most precious national resource? Fourthly, how can communist leaderships in the individual republics and regions become carriers of nationalist aspirations?

Our task here is to elucidate briefly the multiple crises of contemporary Yugoslavia, apart from the question of leadership, that is, the crises of self-management theory and practice, economic efficiency and socialist solidarity, the youth's high expectations and the socio-economic and political realities of everyday life, and the tension between national separatism and communist monolithism, within the broader crisis of communism.

3.1 Party, Elites, Masses: Who is Managing Whom?

One of the major theoretical innovations of the Titoist model has been its attempt to decentralize not only the economy but the governmental administrative machinery as well. From the modest inauguration of workers' councils in 1950 to the most complex institutional pluralization in the 1960s and 1970s culminating in the 1971 Constitutional Amendments, the new Constitution of 1974, and the Tenth and Eleventh Party Congresses in 1974 and 1978, respectively, the major aim proclaimed by the party has been to advance toward Marx's republic of associated labor—communism—by developing direct democracy in the workplace as well as in society at large.

The major institutions of direct democracy in the workplace—those of *workers' self-management*—are: Basic Organizations of Associated Labor (BOALs), Work Communities, and Workers' Councils. In the socio-political sphere, the 1974 Constitution provides such organs of *social self-government* as: Communities of Interest, Local Communities, and Communes, up to the tri-cameral assemblies of communes, republics, and autonomous provinces and the bicameral Federal Assembly, all based on a system of elected delegates with restrictions on terms and the duration of offices. Among other notable institutional innovations, the 1974 Constitution established posts running from communes to the federation for the "social protection of self-management rights and socially-owned property" called "the social attorney of self-management," a sort of socialist ombudsman.[68]

The complexity of the new institutional framework of workers' self-management in the economic sphere and of social self-government in the political sphere is formidable. This complexity is heightened by the fact that the 1974 Constitution attempts to achieve both horizontal and vertical linkages between institutions of direct democracy in the economy and the polity which are to cut across functional, sectional, regional, provincial, and republic lines of governmental organization. On top of its complexity, the new institutional framework is also extremely vague in delimiting *specific* functions, rights, and obligations so that hundreds of laws and thousands of regulations are either anticipated or are already being drafted to flesh out the broad constitutional principles. One of the major new laws passed by 1976 was that on Associated Labor.

Despite this breath-taking institutional fuselage for industrial democracy in particular and democratic policy-making in general, it remains an open question whether reality will bear any relationship to theory. The central question in this context is: Who is managing whom? Jacob Walkin, Bogdan D. Denitch, and Dennison I. Rusinow, among others, all remark that Yugoslavia can no longer be considered a totalitarian system.[69] On the other hand, Rusinow also notes that this fact does *not* guarantee Yugoslavia's evolution toward full democracy. This is, indeed, a unique state of affairs when we have a socialist system which—though nonaligned on the international plane, yet pro-Soviet in its foreign policy stance—is neither totalitarian nor democratic. Walkin suggests that it is "authoritarian."[70] But this designation for the Yugoslav system raises more questions than it solves. What does "authoritarian" mean within the context of a one-party socialist (communist) state?

Perhaps we can learn something about the true nature of this polyphonic socialist society by looking briefly at its major claim, namely, that it is self-managing. There seems to be a surprising degree of consensus among Western and Yugoslav, even party-based, observers on this point. It is that the actual practice of Yugoslavia's self-managing system falls far short of theory. They disagree, of course, on the reasons for this dissonance. Apart from the fact that about half of Yugoslavia's population—the peasantry—remains outside of the self-managing system, the other half—the workers—either do not want to, are incapable of, and/or are prevented from governing by a wide variety of forces. In the official Yugoslav view, these "anti-self-management" forces range from ultra left-wing anarcho-liberal ones which advocate utopian socialism and/or a return to bourgeois democracy and a multi-party system, to techno-bureaucratic managerial elites who understand self-management as their right to manage the workers, to neo-Stalinist and neo-Cominformist right-wing forces of bureaucracy and dogmatism which hanker after the return of "order," a "firm hand," the command economy, and administrative or state socialism.[71]

Tito urged in accordance with this analysis a renewal of the ideological-political leading role of the party in the struggle for socialist self-management. In the opening section of his address to the Tenth Party Congress, Tito claimed that:

> The essence and basic goal of this struggle is to *transform power* [*vlast*] *in the name of the working people into power of the class itself* and of all working people so that workers in associated labor decide directly about the means, conditions, and fruits of their labor and social life generally.[72]

In Tito's conception, the working class was to be led to the end goal of communism by a unified party acting as an integrating and guiding mechanism in safeguarding both socialist achievements and national unity. That's the theory. The practice looks somewhat less auspicious.

Analyzing the practice of social self-government from close up and from the ground floor—the voters' meeting, a basic cell in the self-governing mechanism of the commune—Zukin came to the conclusion that it functions as a transmission belt from top to bottom. The directives flow from the party-governmental Establishment down to the masses, or, rather, to those few among them who care to show up at voters' meetings.[73] The self-governing organs appear to be effectively monopolized by the party and other elites comprising the ruling Establishment. Furthermore, Zukin, Denitch, and others have noted the absence of political institutions for the amalgamation of various local and partial interests, workers' grievances, and the like. These remain within narrow local, republic, or even merely enterprise confines.

For the average citizen under socialism or capitalism the adage seems to remain in force that: "You can't fight city hall!" And Yugoslav sociologists point out that the problem of representation has not been solved yet at any level. This led Zukin to conclude that:

> . . . the apathy of a large part of the population, and the monopoly that their leaders hold over effective political action, comprise a vicious circle in which Yugoslav self-managers are trapped.[74]

The question of whether the party (the League of Communists of Yugoslavia) can lead the self-managers out of the trap or whether it, in fact, may constitute a part of that trap, remains unanswered.

3.2 Strikes: To Each According to His Possibilities?

The Yugoslavs like to point out that their institutions of workers' self-management in the economy are not ends in themselves. They are, rather, means to the end of emancipating the working class from the alienating forces of wage slavery and expropriation of surplus value by capitalists and state bureaucrats. Self-management is to insure that the workers themselves decide on the distribution of the results of their work, including surplus value. The official view since 1950 is that factories belong to the workers.

It is, therefore, all the more surprising that since 1958—the first publicly admitted strike in the Trbovlje mine in Slovenia—strikes have become a regular, though not legally recognized or officially sanctioned, feature of the Yugoslav socio-economic scene. This raises an embarrassing theoretical and practical question for a socialist society: Why do workers—including party members, who manage the factory or mine—go on strike or, in official lingo, participate in "work stoppages" against themselves? And how can a socialist society have more than half a million unemployed at home and allow over one million able-bodied workers to seek gainful employment in the decadent and exploitative bourgeois economies of capitalist Western Europe? What do the workers want? Aren't they good Marxist-Leninists? And what kind of communists are their leaders?

The Yugoslav economic reforms of the 1960s inaugurated policies decentralizing economic decision-making, transferring a great deal of planning, investment, pricing, employment, wages, and other functions to local and enterprise levels. The overriding goal of the Titoist model of market socialism is to increase labor productivity and rationality of investment policies in order to coax out a greater quantity and quality of goods and services at lowest cost. In other words, Yugoslavia has been force-fed the ABCs of economics: how to economize and achieve optimal distribution of scarce resources.

Each enterprise gained a frightful freedom to set its own employment, incomes, and investment policies depending on its profitability and success in market competition with "socially-owned" resources. This led to a number of difficulties since enterprise decisions continued to be made according to political rather than economic criteria. Investment became fragmented along enterprise, local, provincial, and republic lines since each wanted to have their own showcase project regardless of the profitability of the investment. These irrational investment decisions reinforced already strong inflationary pressures and the growing gap between the developed and underdeveloped regions of the country (1975 per capita income for the Republic of Slovenia was over $1,300, that for the Autonomous Province of Kosovo only $360).[75] Inflation on the order of thirty percent and more annually led, in turn, to the reimposition of price controls which distort the actual prices and relative scarcities of raw materials and finished goods and services, and undermine the capacity of the market to allocate resources efficiently.[76]

Strikes are understandable from the vantage point of the average worker's earning power (see Table I). Although Yugoslavia's annual income per capita nearly trebled between 1955 and 1975 to $1,000, over three-quarters of all employed had monthly incomes for March 1975 below 3,800 (new) dinars, which is considered the minimum for a family of four.[77] Furthermore, as the strike in the "Split" shipyard of 1970 showed, the extremely low incomes of 37.6 percent of its 5,000 man-strong work force—below 300 dinars per month in 1969 (though with triple purchasing power over 1975 dinars)—was coupled with lack of housing and a system of remuneration based not on work performed, but on various administrative and traditional ascriptive discriminatory practices.[78] The strikers were also painfully aware of the much higher average monthly income for the shipyard as a whole—1,400 dinars—as well as of the triply higher wages for the same type of work abroad (over 4,000 dinars). They also knew of the fact that while their enterprise, one of the largest in the world, increased output and profits in 1969 over 1968, it realized a lower income in 1969 because of larger tax contributions to communal funds.

This brings us to one of the major socio-economic and political problems in Yugoslavia today: the conflict between economic efficiency and socialist solidarity. The communist leadership insists that the only way to solve Yugoslavia's economic and social problems and improve the workers' living standard is by increasing productivity. It is as if the Yugoslav communists had surreptitiously discovered the Nobel Prize-winning economist Milton Friedman's motto that there is no such thing as a "free lunch." According to Tito:

> Only greater production and labour productivity can assure growth in the living standard, increased employment, the more rapid advancement of the economically less developed areas, the broader and more successful incorporation of our economy into the international division of labour.[79]

TABLE 1. Yugoslav Personal Incomes, March 1975

Income		Percent
In Dinars	In U.S. Dollars*	of Employed
6,000 +	353 +	2.3 %
6,000	353	3.0
5,000	294	3.1
4,500	265	4.7
4,000	235	7.6
→ 3,800	← Minimum monthly income for a family of four†	
3,500	206	12.5
3,000	176	19.1
2,500	147	21.8
2,000	118	9.5
1,800	106	7.5
1,600	94	5.0
1,400	82	2.7
1,200	71	1.2

Source: *"Koliko nam je socijalna politika socijalistička"* ("How Socialist Is Our Social Welfare Policy?"), *VUS*, No. 1241, 21 Feb. 1976, p. 21.

* Official exchange rate, March 1975: 1 U.S. Dollar = 17.0 Dinars. Source: IMF, *International Financial Statistics*, 31, 3, March, 1978, p. 390.

† According to *"Strah nazvan uravnilovka"* ("Fear Called *Uravnilovka*"), *NIN*, No. 1313, 7 Mar. 1976, p. 15.

The Yugoslav emphasis on the socialist (but not communist) principle of: "From each according to his possibilities—to each according to his contribution"[80] has led some Western observers to lament that the Yugoslavs have sacrificed socialist solidarity to the mammon of greater productivity and material self-interest and selfishness of free enterprise capitalism. Thus, Zukin notes that the Yugoslavs have "introduced into socialist ideology not only a rationalization of self-interest but also the elevation of self-interest into a historical necessity in an underdeveloped socialist country."[81]

Yet, the Yugoslav communist leadership objects to charges East and West that they have abandoned socialist or communist solidarity. Thus, Vojo Srzentić, Secretary of the Executive Committee of the Central Committee of the LCY Presidency, noted in an interview on the dangers of the egalitarian principle of *uravnilovka* (wage-levelling) that:

> It is a wrong thesis—found at times—to equate solidarity with or relate it to the *uravnilovka*. Solidarity cannot be a negation of distribution according to work; it is complementary to the principle of distribution according to work and in good measure is the condition for the realization of that principle.[82]

But Srzentić did not stop there. He went on to define *uravnilovka* in a rather unorthodox manner for a communist as the:

> Aspiration of individuals or social groups in society to obtain for their needs more than their work and contribution. To take from those who work better, who create a larger income.[83]

One wonders whether all those who were unjustly expropriated following World War II in Yugoslavia due to the regime's policy of *uravnilovka* are now entitled to compensation? Josip Županov, a noted Yugoslav industrial sociologist, criticizes not only the *uravnilovka*, but also the "spirit of egalitarianism" which is broader than that of the *uravnilovka*. The "spirit of egalitarianism" and its philosophy of "equal stomachs" allegedly lead to anti-professionalism and act as a brake on economic aspirations, productivity, inventiveness, and creativity.[84] In the lead article on "Fear Called *Uravnilovka*" it is pointed out that the "spirit of egalitarianism" pervades Yugoslav society and that it is necessary to break with it and the mentality of "equality in poverty" characteristic of backward, poor, agrarian societies.

If Yugoslav officialdom criticizes the tendency of "equal stomachs," it also censures enrichment by means other than personal labor and the spread of a "petty bourgeois consumer psychology and morality and the race for money which have destroyed so many people."[85] Yet, the "socialist millionaires," and the new affluent middle class—the "*Peugeoisie*"—as well as the general public which today lives better than ever before, seem to have rephrased the official philosophy of greater incomes based on greater productivity into that of: "To each according to his possibilities." The Yugoslav poet Matija Bećković articulates the obvious fact that:

> Yugoslavs make more than they produce, and spend more than they make. How?! Pretty nicely! With magic wands they pull out of soldiers' caps, crochetted beanies, hats, and cylinders that which the modest possibilities of the current stage [of development—O.G.] cannot offer them.[86]　　•

Observers of the Yugoslav scene note that it is a consumer paradise compared to the other communist party states of Eastern Europe and the Soviet Union, not to mention China. They also note a popular consumer psychology and the "struggle for the dinar." But, if the average Yugoslav wages are so low, even below the minimum, how can there be such conspicuous consumption with people owning "two cars apiece, two or three apartments, . . . villas"[87] and so on? Bećković asks rhetorically: "Off what *do* you live, faithful reader?" and goes on to provide a humorous yet realistic answer:

> Per diems, separate maintenance, bribery, graft, contests, kitchen gardens, hens, a half to you—and a half to me? A little renting out an empty room, a little Trieste, a little Sofia? Councils, commissions, analyses, interpretations, extra lessons, supplemental supplements? You rewrite, you rearrange, you recommend? You do a favor so they pay you back, hmmm? . . . Confess! . . . You have an aunt in America, an uncle in Australia, a sister-in-law in Sweden? You save on food? You turn the old one over so it looks like new? . . . Wow! You resell a house they're going to tear down, a crypt, a chauffeur's license? . . . You sold your house and you got an apartment from your enterprise? . . . In wholesale trade you steal a little retail? Or vice versa? . . . You put away cigarettes before the price goes up? . . . You auction off the land of your former work cooperative? . . .
>
> You surely do something! . . . What would you live off, both you, and your little canary, and your piano tuner, and your maid, and your cosmetician, and your dog, and all the others that you carry on your back!?
>
> Whatever you do to work, that's your thing. It's important that you live, that you somehow make ends meet![88]

How are these "un-socialist" activities possible on a mass scale in a socialist system? Zukin, among others, provides insight into this phenomenon in her conclusion that both decision-making and distribution in Yugoslavia still operate along traditional behavioral patterns rather than the official self-management norms. These traditional behavioral patterns and norms include hierarchical relationships, familism, nepotism, connections, ascription, and widespread and many-faceted corruption, along with egotism, duplicity, and irresponsibility. According to Zukin, the traditional norms conflict with the official ideology which stresses material incentives, merit, technological development, profitability, and innovation to such an extent that they endanger both self-management and national unity.[89] Yugoslavia's leading communist theoretician, Edvard Kardelj, concluded that "socially-owned" property belongs to everyone and no one.[90] That is precisely how it is being treated. As Milton and Rose Friedman summed it up:

> When everybody owns something, nobody owns it, and nobody has a direct interest in maintaining or improving its condition. That is why buildings in the Soviet Union—like public housing in the United States—look decrepit within a year or two of their construction, why machines in government factories break down and are continuously in need of repair, why citizens must resort to the black market for maintaining the capital that they have for their personal use.[91]

3.3 Student Demonstrations, 1968: Privileges, Bureaucracy, Unemployment

The Yugoslav communist leadership assures both domestic and foreign publics that the socialist principle of reward according to *work* is only temporary yet essential for building the economic foundations of the higher stage—communism—and the realization of its principle of reward according to *need*. But Yugoslav youth, "fed to the teeth with slogans and blocked from the jobs for which they had been trained,"[92] in its idealism and impatience which it shares with youth worldwide, challenged both traditional norms as well as socialist practice in the name of—Marxist-Leninist theory! The revolt of Belgrade University students in the nation's capital, in June 1968, is instructive in this regard.

Dennison Rusinow notes that students and faculty wore paper badges with symbols and a new name for their institution: "The Karl Marx Red University."[93] University buildings were decorated with pictures of Tito and Marx, while flags and posters proclaimed such demands and slogans as: "We Struggle for a Better Man, Not for a Better Dinar," "There Is No Socialism Without Freedom, No Freedom Without Socialism," "Free Information Media," "More Schools, Less Automobiles," (this one rhymes well in Serbo-Croatian: "Više škola, manje kola!"), "Workers—We Are With You! Our Demands Are Your Demands!," "Work for Everyone, Bread for Everyone," and similar.

The "Political Action Program of Belgrade Students" of June 4, 1968, as well as the "Student Demands Presented to the Serbian Government" of June 3, 1968, outlined five major areas of student demands. These were:

(1) The elimination of privileges and social inequalities in socialism;

(2) Settlement of the problem of unemployment and the determination of job qualifications by qualified experts and technicians;

(3) Removal of bureaucratic forces, rapid development of self-management at all levels, not only in work organizations, democratization of "all socio-political organizations, especially of the League of Communists" and the public information media, and the right to exercise all freedoms guaranteed under the Constitution;

(4) Preventing the disintegration of public property and its conversion into joint-stock property as well as the "estrangement of personal work and the capitalization of individuals and groups," the amassing of luxury and wealth, and speculation with private and publicly-owned housing; and

(5) Reform of the entire educational system in order to assure "equal conditions of education for all young people which is guaranteed under our Constitution."

It is a curious paradox for students to criticize the leadership's policies in a socialist society by pointing out the shortfalls of socialist practice in terms of Marxist-Leninist theory. It is also embarrassing, since the party claims to be the only true interpreter of the Marxist-Leninist ideology and the sole legitimate guide to socio-economic and political practice. According to Rusinow, the authorities pursued a two-pronged strategy in quelling the student revolt. On the one hand, they isolated students from workers by banning further street demonstrations and other activities outside University buildings. On the other hand, they accepted many student demands, especially those concerning material conditions and university reform.[94] Tito himself admitted in a nationwide radio and television address on June 9, 1968, that many of the student demands were justified. In an astute display of statesmanship, Tito called on both students and workers to help *him* in the common cause of implementing the socio-economic and political reforms of 1965 and 1966.

At the same time, the authorities condemned student demonstrations as illegitimate means for partially legitimate ends. They also blamed the humanist intelligentsia—young Marxist humanist professors in the social sciences and humanities at Belgrade University—for instigating student riots and misleading the youth with a New Left ideology in opposition to the party. Veljko Vlahović commented that: "Our extremists have replaced Marx's theses with the thesis of W. Mills [C. Wright Mills]." Mijalko Todorović, Secretary of the Executive Committee, Central Committee of the LCY, concluded at its July 16, 1968, meeting that the New Left and "other reactionary and anti-self-management forces" united in a common platform attacking market socialism and workers' self-management—the two mainstays of Yugoslavia's self-managing socialist system. Nothing could be further from the truth. But the truth was characteristically monopolized by party spokesmen, not least by Tito himself.

In fairness, however, one should add that both the students as well as the governmental and party authorities managed to formulate their respective views in absolute and dogmatic terms of their common ideology. Thus, the student demands, especially in their all-or-nothing initial formulation of June 3, 1968, showed little understanding of the dynamics of economic rationality or the practical policies for reforming an inefficient and wasteful command economy. They failed to understand that their struggle for a better man may be indivisible from the struggle for a better dinar, currency reform, non-inflationary growth, greater productivity, and profitability of the nation's scarce resources.

On the other hand, the authorities also failed singularly to appreciate that their youth was only asking the leadership to fulfill the promises of communist theory—particularly those of equality, unity, solidarity, and democracy—in practical reality. This reality included at the time some 500,000 unemployed at home, almost 1,000,000 able-bodied Yugoslavs forced to seek employment abroad, inflation, low standard of living, bureaucracy, mismanagement, inequalities, and corruption, while the official ideology referred to the building of communism and socialist solidarity, as Zukin notes, "on the side of angels."[95]

3.4 The Croatian Spring, 1971: Socialism in One Republic?

The Croatian crisis of 1971, or the "Croatian Spring," has been called Titoism's "moment of truth" since it involved, according to Rusinow, "the two great unsolved problems of contemporary Yugoslavia: the 'national question' and 'socialist democracy,' the latter particularly including the role of the League of Communists and both including the fundamental nature and purpose of the Yugoslav state."[96] The Croatian communist leadership was charged at the 21st Session of the LCY Presidium meeting at Karadjordjevo in December 1971 with nationalism, separatism, rotten liberalism, and counterrevolution, charges which strangely echoed those made during the Soviet-Yugoslav split of 1948. Only this time the charges were intra-party rather than inter-party. The outcomes were also significantly different.

Dr. Savka Dabčević-Kučar, Miko Tripalo, and Pero Pirker, leaders of the League of Communists of Croatia (LCC), resigned from the Central Committee. According to Singleton, the anti-nationalist purge resulted by mid-January 1972 in the arrest of over 500 people and by autumn 1972 claimed as its victims some of the highest party as well as governmental leaders in all the republics and the federation.[97] Among those forced to resign were Marko Nikezić, President of the Serbian LC, Latinka Perović, the Serbian LC Secretary, Slavko Milosavlevsky, Secretary of the Central Committee of the Macedonian LC, Tone Kropusek, Slovenian Trade Union leader, Mirko Tepavac, Federal Foreign Minister, and Stane Kavčić, Prime Minister of Slovenia. The sweeping purge of party and governmental leaders was instituted by personal directives from the highest leadership circles and, most prominently, by Tito himself. In sum, the 21st Session of the LCY Presidium, Tito's Letter to the party of September 1972, and the Tenth and Eleventh Party Congresses called for ideological purity, a return to Marxism, democratic centralism, and unity in the party's ranks. All this in order to combat alleged petty-bourgeois, nationalist, anarchist, techno-managerial, bureaucratic, statist, dogmatist, neo-Cominformist, and other forces threatening the party's leading role in society and, by implication, socialist self-management.

The obvious question arises: How could the highest-ranking *communist* leaders within the party and governmental structures in Yugoslavia's constituent republics become *nationalist*? And that under the very nose of the all-Yugoslav party leadership? The answer may be gleaned in part from the nature of the Soviet-Yugoslav controversy of 1948 and partly from the dynamics of socio-economic and political decentralization in Yugoslavia in the 1960s. The Soviet-Yugoslav controversy of 1948 brought out clearly the essentially *national* content of international communism. Communism is defined, in effect, as international in form, but national in content. In his critique of Stalinism, Zlatko Čepo notes that:

> Stalin brought a tendency of assuming the leading role in the international communist movement and of imposing Soviet experiences which came into conflict with the *national* interests of individual parties.[98]

Observers note that the decentralization of economic, governmental, and party organizations in Yugoslavia after 1965 led first to particularism and localism. These culminated later in six separate republic communist parties, investments along local, regional, and republic lines, and a separation between party and governmental institutions. The initial impetus for these developments was given by the 1965 economic reform, the ousting of Alexander Ranković and the silencing of the conservative wing of the party in July 1966, the promulgation of the 1969 League Statutes, separating the party from the state, and the 1971 Constitutional Amendments which promoted the federalization of the party and the government.

Rusinow writes that by 1971 Yugoslavia seemed on the road to a confederation of six republics and two autonomous provinces. Federalism developed to the point where federal party and governmental organs were paralyzed because of the new rules requiring consensus on decision-making by regional leaderships.[99] These regional leaderships, especially in the Republic of Croatia, were riding a popular nationalist wave of sentiment. It turned into a tidal wave of popular discontent couched in nationalist-ethnic terms. The communist republic leadership was confident that it could harness national sentiments for socialist ends. But, as Lendvai points out, the ruling party itself became the carrier of "various savage conflicts and multiple contradictions."[100] A split developed not only between the Croatian and the all-Yugoslav party but also within the ranks of the Croatian party between the liberals who favored the "mass national movement" and the conservatives who did not trust it. How could this happen?

According to George Klein, what happened was that a new generation of communist leaders emerged in the republics during the 1960s. These new liberal communists were dedicated to more democratization, decentralization, and economic liberalism—that is, market socialism—and they "assumed the role of representatives in a parliamentary democracy."[101] In an attempt to strengthen their bargaining position vis-á-vis the center—the federal government—the republic leaderships appealed for support to their local constituencies. But it did not work as planned. The leaderships soon became the victims of two dynamics: national-ethnic separatism and communist monolithism.

Thus, on the one hand, the Croatian communist leadership put forward demands in purely national (republic) terms for the reform of the banking, foreign currency, and export-import systems, and contributions to the federal fund for the development of Yugoslavia's less-developed regions. The Croats' exclusive national-ethnic formulation of grievances and proposals charged exploitation by Belgrade, the Serbs, and the federal government. These were also the major grievances which led to the student strike at Zagreb University, in November 1971, which the Croatian communist leadership seemed no longer able to control.

On the other hand, the public, the press, as well as the political leaders, proved to be victims of the dogmatic, totalitarian, and monolithic elements inherent in Marxist theory and socialist practice. This dynamic was manifested, as Rusinow notes, in the public unpreparedness for genuine politics of give and take, leading instead to alarm and partisanship in the form of rival nationalisms. The press characteristically simplified issues, presenting them in a we-they, black-and-white, all-or-none, format—searching for scapegoats and "enemies"—so prevalent in communist systems. And the communist leaders themselves formulated the issues in an uncompromising, non-negotiable, and self-righteous style germane to party meetings behind closed doors.[102]

Djuro Kladjanin, a member of the Central Committee of the LCC, scored the absence of constructive criticism and the resurgence of neo-Stalinism and monopoly of power within the party.[103] And Milka Planinc, who succeeded Dabčević-Kučar to the chair of the Central Committee of the LCC, complained that:

> The method of applying labels, the method of defamation of individuals without argumentation has already penetrated so deeply in some circles that they simply cannot find the strength within those circles to defend themselves against such things. This has made of us a Party of such Stalinist methods as this Party never employed, even in that period that these democrats say was the Stalinist period in the Party.[104]

The rising distrust, recriminations, and incidences of violence among national-ethnic groups in Croatia and elsewhere, coupled with widespread disorganization and ideological confusion within and outside the party's ranks, inertia, and lack of action by responsible organs in the face of domestic socio-economic problems and fear of foreign intervention, all prompted Tito's decisive action at the 21st Session of the LCY Presidium. Croatia's experiment with "socialism in one republic" was outlawed as un-socialist and counter-revolutionary.

4. Reality in Search of Theory

It would be tempting to designate the Yugoslav experiment in self-managing socialism as democratic in form and totalitarian in content—highlighted, especially after the 1971 Croatian Spring and the 1972 crisis of liberal communists in Serbia and elsewhere, by institutional pluralization and ideological re-Stalinization. Tito himself called for a renewed emphasis on *Marxist* education and the *class* nature of socialist legality both within and outside the party and the academic community. The *struggle* for the building of the classless communist society and the *dictatorship of the proletariat* are to intensify. There would be no withering away of the party, nor of the state, for that matter. Yet the system would boast socialist "self-management" or direct participatory *democracy.*

Yugoslav Marxism or the official Marxist-Leninist ideology has become so fluid, eclectic, and contradictory that the party, elites, and masses are equally confused. It might be called solidarity in ignorance or confusion. Half democratic and half totalitarian, wedged between East and West, the Yugoslav experiment remains under the guidance of a party whose revolutionary rhetoric belies its everyday reformist practice. Furthermore, periodically even high-ranking Yugoslav officials are vaunt to remark in private that:

> The party wants to lead—but it does not know where to . . . in fact, the real problem is what to do with the party as such.[105]

Yet, it appears that the more elusive the ideology and the greater the distance between proclaimed ideals and everyday social life, the more vocal and uncompromising the role of that same ideology. Rusinow notes that Yugoslavia after the Tenth Party Congress is returning to Leninism, party unity, democratic centralism, and the re-affirmation of its leading ideological and political role.[106] It has been returning also to the dictatorship of the proletariat and *class struggle*. Presumably, there is to be no return to a Stalinist police state and the commanding role of the party *over* the working class. But where are the guarantees against a return to Stalinism?

Prvoslav Ralić assures us that there is a "qualitative political difference between a leading and a commanding role of the League of Communists."[107] But even the party rank and file is likely to silently disagree with Ralić's assessment, for in the past it has found it extremely difficult to differentiate between the two. In fact, as Lendvai observed:

> The party organizations in the enterprises became increasingly schizophrenic. If they followed the decisions made by the superior organs outside the factory, they lost all real influence over the workers. If they sided with the "irresponsible demands" of the labor force or with the "narrow group interests," they were scolded by their superior party organs for violation of party discipline and for giving in to a backward environment.[108]

This state of affairs is, of course, "dialectical," but that does not lessen the dilemma for the average party *apparatchik*. Living in a modernizing society, torn between traditional ascriptive behavioral patterns and official self-management norms, the party has not been immune to confusion, disillusionment, or the thrall of "petty bourgeois" consumer psychology and the struggle for the dinar. On the one hand, the party and governmental cadre is supposed to lead society in the building of communism. On the other hand, this same cadre is expected to de-professionalize and divest itself of power and privileges in favor of workers' self-management and social self-government. Luckily for the Yugoslavs, they had a *deus-ex-machina* to reconcile the irreconcilable, ranging from nationalist-ethnic rivalries to great inter-regional and inter-republic socio-cultural and economic disparities, market socialism, and the utopian ideal of direct democracy at all levels. That *deus-ex-machina* was—Tito. Alas, Tito is gone. But there may be another remedy, a magic incantation—*samoupravljanje* (self-management/self-government)—sprinkled with "class struggle" and "dictatorship of the proletariat" as the official means to solve all problems.

Rusinow maintains that Titoist myths and symbols had never been more exaggerated or omnipresent than at the Tenth Party Congress. He concluded that it may have been an:

> . . . unconscious reversion to magic in the face of terrifying uncertainties, a parading of icons with their intimations of immortality and divine protection and a conjuring with the personification of unity and stability to frighten away the demons of divisive ethnic nationalisms, political pluralism, and foreign intrigues.[109]

Magic and mythmaking characterized also the Eleventh Party Congress—Tito's "Farewell Congress"—held on June 20-23, 1978. While the Tenth Party Congress was dubbed officially the "Congress of Unity," the Eleventh boasted the ambitious title of "Congress of Action." But the only credible action was the nostalgic chant "Ti-to—Par-ti-ja! Ti-to—Par-ti-ja!" ("Tito—Party!") which reverberated through the Congress halls like magic, recalling bygone days of Partisan glory in World War II, the revolution, and the civil war personified by the aging Marshal, the "rebel who became uncrowned king."[110]   This Congress was premature in at least three respects: (1) Almost a year after the Congress, Tito celebrated his 87th birthday in apparently robust health, although he failed to reach his 88th; (2) It followed the Tenth Congress by a mere four years; and (3) It had little new to say, except to repeat the call for party unity, insist on the need for translating the theoretical program of the previous Congress, the 1974 Constitution, and the 1976 Law on Associated Labor into practice, and to add Kardelj's puzzling notion of a "pluralism of self-management interests."

The myth of party infallibility was duly bolstered by Tito in his Report to the Congress, insisting on the alleged scientific credentials of the Marxist-Leninist ideology:

> Following a critical Marxist analysis of social trends, the League of Communists has arrived at scientific data about the essence of social processes.[111]

Since the party as the avant-garde of the proletariat possesses "scientific" knowledge of social processes, it is only natural that it should be the "leading and guiding ideological-political force in society." Where does that leave the "pluralism of self-management interests?" Could it imply party pluralism? Kardelj's answer was negative, since:

> . . . in socialist *self-managing* democracy, the League of Communists and other factors of organized socialist social, scientific, cultural, and other consciousness and action are formed and organized as a *creative component part* of the self-managing and democratic community of free producers, and not as an alienated political factor in a competitive fight for power over society, social labor, and its product and income.[112]

And why should the League compete, indeed, for power, labor, product, or income in a society in which it has the monopoly on decision-making at all levels? The League does not allow any competitors in theory or practice. Only, it is unclear even to Marxist theorists in Yugoslavia how society can be democratized without a democratization of its avant-garde, which operates on the basis of *democratic centralism,* eschewing pluralism even within the party, let alone the rest of society? Under democratic centralism, the system calls for a Philosopher-King who will interpret the Marxist-Leninist teachings and lay down the party line. The communist party is thus inherently Stalinist. Marx's vanguard, Lenin's party of professional revolutionaries, and Stalin's cult of personality form a unified, logical whole.[113]

Myths, ideologies, and symbolic universes in general function as "sheltering canopies," but they may also contain within themselves mechanisms of self-destruction. While everyone chants about party unity, self-management, and the building of the classless communist society, revolutionary "class justice" is meted out to real and imaginary enemies. These are dutifully branded with such epithets as nationalist, techno-bureaucrats, conservatives, dogmatists, new leftists, petty-bourgeois liberals, neo-Stalinists, neo-Cominformists, and so on *ad infinitum*. Djilas, Mihajlov, and even Marxist humanist scholars at leading institutions of higher learning, their students, and others are ostracized, imprisoned, fired from their jobs or intimidated legally and extra-legally for their temerity to ask questions about the theory and practice of Yugoslav socialism (see Chapter X). What kind of socialism is it which silences even its internationally known *Marxist* philosophers and sociologists?

The continuing incantation of outlived slogans of the official ideology bears less and less relationship to practical reality. Yet, as Lewis S. Feuer pointed out:

> The contribution of ideology is to imperil human reason, and by so doing, to render men's problems insoluble.[114]

Thus, the socio-economic, political, and cultural problems of mankind in the latter part of the twentieth century bear remarkably little relationship to dogmatized ideologies of either "socialism" or "capitalism." East and West, the central question is how to assure the greatest good for the greatest number of people and the minimum decent standard of living for all. Yet, instead of concentrating on real problems and seeking their solution, ideologists—like Don Quixotes—wield slogans against non-existent windmills on levels of abstraction removed from real life. Ideologists thus trap both themselves and others in closed circles of enchanted universes of discourse. For instance, in the economic sphere, increasingly it is no longer a question of whether to plan or not to plan, but *how* to plan and *where*. In the socio-political sphere, the salient question world-wide is not between direct and representative democracy, but of responsiveness and responsibility of private and public decision-making bodies. And, in the cultural sphere, the realization is growing that party programs and market forces are no substitutes for individual freedom and creativity.

The time is ripe, therefore, for a *positive* transcendence (*Aufhebung*) of the Marxist *Weltanschauung*. What is needed is an in-depth examination of the claims and disclaims of Marxism as the only scientific and humane road to individual and societal development. This calls for an analysis of the Marxist-Leninist world view to determine whether it is, indeed, humanist, democratic, and liberal in essence. Or, is it merely dogmatic, totalitarian, and anti-humanist, and as such brooks no hope for a radical de-alienation of both men and societies? No group of Marxist scholars has done more to illuminate the essential features of Marxist-Leninist theory and socialist practice than the avant-garde Yugoslav Marxist humanist philosophers and sociologists.

Marxist humanists throughout Eastern Europe and the USSR have sought to renew Marxist theory and to expose socialist practice to critical scrutiny in order to rid both theory and reality of the vestiges of Stalinist dogmatism and dictatorship, and the consequent alienation of societies and men. They understand that this effort requires, in the words of Leonhard's *Three Faces of Marxism*:

> . . . the abolishment of one-sidedness and monolithic character, the development of several schools of Marxism, the supplementation of Marxism by the findings of hitherto neglected Marxist theoreticians, an objective study of recent developments in modern capitalism, a critical analysis of the experiences of the socialist countries (with a clear differentiation between etatism and socialism), and greater emphasis on the problem of man and the problem of alienation.[115]

Tito and his League of Communists were adamant in protecting at all costs what they understood to be the achievements of the socialist revolution. The question still remains: What is to protect people from a revolution capable of devouring its own children? Apparently we live in a world of omnipotent ideologies and impotent men. While the party in Yugoslavia is in search of a role, reality is also conspicuously in search of theory. Since people East and West yearn for happiness, our task remains to search for man.

Chapter IV · Yugoslav Marxism Discovers Man

To be radical is to grasp things by the root. But for man the root is man himself.

Karl Marx, *Contribution to the Critique of Hegel's Philosophy of Right* (1843-1844)

1. Unexplored Territory

Marxism has been defined as constituting not only a political program but also a mode of social criticism and an "ambience of culture."[1] In the previous chapter we examined Yugoslav Marxism chiefly from the point of view of a political program. The major task is, however, to illuminate the much more evanescent nature of Yugoslav Marxism as a critical philosophy and a cultural milieu as well as to gauge the dissonance between theory and practice.

Yugoslav Marxism as a creative socialist humanist enterprise and a critical philosophy is largely unknown in the West due to its comparatively recent development and the fact that relatively few works by Yugoslav Marxist philosophers have been translated thus far. Yugoslavia, as Arnold Künzli put it, remains an intellectual continent yet to be discovered.[2] At the same time, there can be little doubt that Yugoslav Marxism, especially in its avant-garde formulation, represents a new and significant, a *sui generis,* development in the interpretation of Marxist-Leninist teachings. Thus, A. J. P. Taylor writes in a review article that Yugoslavia stands out among communist countries for its active school of Marxist "revisionists" whose writings are "as puzzling as theology to the unbeliever."[3] George Zaninovich notes that the most interesting development in Yugoslav ideology is the growth of a vital debate on the meaning and application of Marxist theory.[4] Albert W. Levi and Howard L. Parsons agree that contemporary philosophy and sociology in Yugoslavia represent a genuine renaissance of Marxist thought as well as a revolutionary reinterpretation of Marxist doctrine.[5]

The development of Yugoslav Marxist philosophy has paralleled, in general, the development of the ideological and institutional infrastructure of Titoist Yugoslavia. It is possible to distinguish at least six major periods which are, of course, not watertight (there is considerable intertwining and overlap): (1) 1945-1950: Period of Stalinism; (2) 1950-1953: The Thaw— Critique of Stalinism following the Soviet-Yugoslav split of 1948; (3) 1953-1958: Back to Marx— Return to the "original" or "young" Marx conceived as a humanistic philosopher; (4) 1958-1963: Creative Marxism—Redefinition of Marxism as both theory and method; (5) 1963-1975: Marxist humanism—Emphasis on the social individual and revolutionary *praxis* in the pursuit of de-alienation, liberation of man, and participatory democracy reflecting the new conception of Marxism as a radical critique of everything existing; and (6) 1975 on: "Underground" period—Ouster of the "Belgrade Eight," closing of the journals *Praxis* and *Filosofija,* and the regime's attempt to silence the avant-garde (see Chapters X-XI).[6]

Basically, the period between 1948 and 1963 may be characterized as a period of considerable confusion and intense searching on the part of Yugoslav Marxist philosophers and sociologists for theoretical justifications and practical guidelines to fill the intellectual void left by Stalinism. It is not until the early 1960s that we witness the first definite contours of the new revolutionary reconstruction of classical Marxism-Leninism by avant-garde Yugoslav Marxist philosophers.

Following the 1960 Bled discussions, at which the theory of reflection was laid to rest, the year 1963 represents perhaps a turning point in the development of Yugoslav Marxism, paralleling the promulgation of the 1963 Constitution for the Socialist Federal Republic of Yugoslavia. It saw the publication in Serbo-Croatian of a two-volume study entitled *Humanism and Socialism* based on discussions held by the Croatian Philosophical Society devoted to the "Humanistic Problems of Socialism."[7] In the same year, an international philosophical symposium on "Man Today" was held in Dubrovnik in which philosophers from both East and West took part.[8] Also, 1963 saw the founding of regular colloquia on "Marx and the Contemporary Age" sponsored jointly by the Yugoslav Institute for the Study of the Workers' Movement and the Institute of Social Sciences in Belgrade.[9] Most important, the First International Summer School of the University of Zagreb on the island of Korčula opened in 1963, organized by avant-garde Yugoslav Marxists of the Zagreb review *Praxis*. The Korčula Summer School became an annual international event drawing some of the best known philosophers and sociologists from Europe and America, Marxist as well as non-Marxist. The themes of the International Summer School sessions ranged from "Progress and Culture" (1963), "The Meaning and Perspectives of Socialism" (1964), "What is History?" (1965), "Creativity and Reification" (1967), "Marx and the Revolution" (1968), "Power and Humanity" (1969), to "Hegel and the Contemporary Age; Lenin and the New Left" (1970), "Utopia and Reality" (1971), "Freedom and Equality" (1972), "The Bourgeois World and Socialism" (1973), and "Art and the Modern World" (1974). There was no School during 1966 (ouster of Ranković) and none since 1974.[10] The proceedings of the Korčula Summer School were covered regularly in the Zagreb review *Praxis*.

The first Serbo-Croatian edition of the journal *Praxis*, the exponent of a new, radical Marxism of all-out criticism, deep concern for alienation, and dedication to socialist humanism, appeared in September 1964.[11] The first international edition of *Praxis*, published in English, French, German, and Italian, was launched a year later. It soon became a veritable international forum of Marxist dialogue with such figures as Erich Fromm, Herbert Marcuse, Ernst Bloch, John Lewis, Thomas Bottomore, and many others participating.[12] The advanced theoretical level and sophistication of articles published in *Praxis* made it one of the most reputable and controversial journals among the intelligentsia not only in Yugoslavia but in the communist world at large. Its full significance is yet to be appreciated by Western intellectuals.

Among significant publications, in 1964 we have *Man Today* (I: Man and Freedom, II: Man and Technique, and III: Man and Peace) covering the proceedings of the international philosophical symposium in Dubrovnik of 1963, and the two-volume *Marx and the Contemporary Age* based on the First Scientific Gathering on "Marks i savremenost" held in Belgrade and Arandjelovac, December 17-21, 1963, and in Novi Sad, June 1-5, 1964. In 1965, the proceedings of the Second Korčula International Summer School were published under the title *The Meaning and Perspectives of Socialism*. In the same year, one of the foremost avant-garde Marxist philosophers in contemporary Yugoslavia, Gajo Petrović (University of Zagreb), published his seminal work *Filozofija i Marksizam*, translated into English in 1967 as *Marx in the Mid-Twentieth Century*.[13] In 1966, the Serbian Academy held a symposium "On Socialist Humanism" in the Yugoslav capital of Belgrade from December 19 to 21, while the Institute of the Philosophy of Science at the University of Zagreb founded a new "Journal of Synthesis of Science, Art and Social Practice" entitled *Encyclopædia moderna*.[14] In the same year, articles by leading Yugoslav Marxist philosophers—Petrović, Mihailo Marković, Rudi Supek, Predrag Vranicki, Veljko Korać and Danilo Pejović— appeared in *Socialist Humanism*, edited by the late Fromm.[15]

The year 1968 was highlighted by a meeting of Czechoslovak and Yugoslav philosophers on the topic of "Present-Day Socialism" held in Opatija from December 5 to 7 and expounding such themes as "What is socialism?," "What is the relationship of socialism to democracy?," and "What is the relationship of Stalinism to socialism?"[16] In 1969, articles by Petrović, Korać, Marković, Milan Kangrga,

Mihailo Djurić, Supek, Miladin Životić, Danko Grlić, Ljubomir Tadić, Branko Bošnjak and Andrija Krešić, together with documents tracing the development of the journal *Praxis*, appeared in *Revolutionary Praxis* (in German), edited by Petrović. The year 1969 also saw the publication of *Man and History* by Vranicki, one of Yugoslavia's foremost authorities on the esoteric concept of alienation, and *Man and Values* by Životić.[17]

As Marković notes in his assessment of Marxist philosophy in Yugoslavia, the official reaction against the June 1968 student demonstrations also slowed the activity of the *Praxis* group, increasingly the target of regime criticism. Nevertheless, the period between 1968-1975 saw, *inter alia*, further Korčula Summer Sessions, a whole series of publications in *Praxis'* pocketbook edition, and the institution in 1971 of annual Winter Philosophical Meetings together with the journal *Filosofija* and the Serbian Philosophical Society.[18] But the political climate entered an ice age after the 1971 Croatian crisis which later also sealed *Praxis'* doom. Increasingly, students and professors attending Korčula or the Winter Philosophical Meetings were subjected to harassment, searches, confiscation of papers and conference tapes, and even imprisonment. Thus, according to Marković's account, at the last Winter Philosophical Meeting in February 1974, Dragoljub Ignjatović, a poet, was arrested and sentenced to three and a half years of imprisonment for his speech delivered at the meeting.

These are only highlights of some of the major events, meetings, and publications during the 1960s and early 1970s. They allow us some insight by themselves into the beginnings and development of avant-garde Yugoslav Marxist humanist thought.

1.1 Schools of Thought

Yugoslav philosophy since the end of World War II—that is, since the communist conquest of power in Yugoslavia—has been predominantly Marxist. Until recently, Yugoslav Marxist philosophy had all but ignored the not inconsiderable pre-war philosophical tradition of the South Slav peoples embodied in the works (chiefly in Latin and Italian) of such thinkers as P. P. Vergerije, Matija Hvale, Jakob Štelin, Juraj Dragišić, Benko Benković, and Rudjer Bošković. These date from between the fifteenth and the eighteenth centuries. Works of the nineteenth and twentieth centuries by Franjo Marković, Djuro Arnold, Albert Bazala, Petar Petrović Njegoš, France Veber, Božidar Knežević, Branislav Petronijević, and others remain equally in need of serious assessment. A notable exception is Svetozar Marković, generally considered the first South Slav theorist of socialism, whose centenary of death was commemorated in 1975 by a number of symposia and publications.[19]

Yugoslav Marxist philosophy has largely ignored its non-Marxist heritage and is, therefore, the poorer for it. On the other hand, Yugoslav Marxism gradually outgrew many of its "Stalinist" prejudices which automatically disqualified all non-Marxist thought from serious consideration. Thus, we find among contemporary Yugoslav Marxist philosophers a considerable influence by European and American philosophies, particularly existentialism, phenomenology, pragmatism, personalism, and to a lesser extent analysis, positivism, and philosophy of science.

The Soviet-Yugoslav break of 1948 and the ensuing processes toward decentralization, democratization, and liberalization in Yugoslav government, politics, economy, and culture, provided a favorable climate for the rethinking of Marxist-Leninist teachings and facilitated the development of a creative and more humane Marxism. The key to the understanding of contemporary Marxist philosophy in Yugoslavia is its focus on man, the individual human being and his possibilities for liberation from various forces and conditions impeding his free, creative development. According to Petrović, it is the *problems of man, praxis*, creativity, freedom, alienation, technique, science, and the arts that have advanced to the center stage of philosophical discussions in Yugoslavia. Avant-garde Yugoslav Marxist thinkers consider their interpretation of Marxism-Leninism as "authentically Marxist, creative and non-dogmatic."[20]

Perhaps the single, most cogent statement of the new Marxism in contemporary Yugoslavia can be found in Petrović's assessment in his *Marx in the Mid-Twentieth Century*. In this work, Petrović ranges over problems of Marxism versus Stalinism, the "young" versus the "old" Marx, the continuity in Marx's thought, dialectical materialism and Marx's philosophy, Marx's concept of man, freedom, alienation, *praxis*, philosophy and politics in socialism, and other themes. Petrović notes as the major achievement of Yugoslav Marxist philosophy:

> . . . the discovery that man, who was excluded from the Stalinistic version of Marxist philosophy as an abstraction, is in the center of authentic Marxist philosophic thought.[21]

The road from Stalinism to Marxist humanism has proved to be a long and arduous one which the avant-garde Yugoslav Marxist thinkers are still traveling. The key problem for Yugoslav Marxists has been to redefine communism as a realized humanism and to restore man to the center of the drama of historical materialism, that is, the transition from capitalism to socialism and communism. The cosmology of this humanist enterprise came to include all the major sinews of the Marxist-Leninist faith. The avant-garde's quest to de-ideologize and de-dogmatize Marxism focused particularly on the category of *praxis*, the unity of theory and practice, and the concept of alienation. It required a redefinition of what is human and historical as well as a rethinking of the very nature of both humanism and communism. In their preface to the two-volume study on *Humanism and Socialism*, Bošnjak and Supek conceptualized the major task for Yugoslav Marxist thought to be the concrete development of humanistic problems in socialism. The editorial board of the study on *Marx and the Contemporary Age* remarked that the basic purpose of the new colloquia on Marxism was to consider and encourage the study of current questions in Marxism and contribute to the development of socialism in the world, especially in Yugoslavia.

Among many currents and trends, two major schools of thought stand out in contemporary Yugoslav Marxist philosophy:

(1) The first group concerns itself predominantly with Marx's philosophical anthropology and is bent on a reinterpretation and further creative development of Marx's teachings in light of the humanistic writings of the youthful Marx of the *Economic and Philosophical Manuscripts* of 1844. Most of the philosophers and sociologists in this group are centered at the University of Zagreb in Croatia and have been the initiators of the radical Marxist review *Praxis* and the International Summer School on the island of Korčula.

(2) The second group has concentrated its attention on the problems of the philosophy of science in an attempt to reconcile the Marxist dialectic and historical materialism with the findings and methodology of twentieth-century science. The philosophers and sociologists in this group are, for the most part, at the University of Belgrade, in Serbia.

It should be pointed out from the outset that the two groups or schools of thought are less far apart than it might seem at first. Yugoslav Marxist philosophers and sociologists may in this respect be unique among their East European counterparts. Most of the Yugoslav Marxist scholars of both schools share a common concern and analytical approach as well as a theoretical framework whose goal is to integrate or synthesize Marx's anthropological orientation with the Marxist dialectic and historical materialism. In addition, both schools are aware of the need to draw on the rich Western cultural heritage as well as contemporary findings in the humanities, social, and natural sciences. The overriding concern, constituting the most distinctive feature of Yugoslav Marxism, is expressed succinctly by Marković of the University of Belgrade:

> One of the most fundamental problems in contemporary philos-
> ophy . . . is how to make humanism a dialectical philosophy and
> dialectic a humanist method.[22]

Marković continues by stating that the dialectic cannot be separated from Marx's humanist inspiration and that the central problem in Marx's philosophy remains the question of the place of man in the universe.[23] Vranicki of the University of Zagreb carries Marković's novel conceptualization of the dialectic a step further, and practically revolutionizes it, by noting that the question of the dialectic reveals itself fundamentally as the question of man and of what it means to be fully human.[24]

Yugoslav Marxist philosophers and sociologists of the radical bent comprised the mainstream in contemporary Yugoslav Marxist thought, with only a small minority of imperturbable dogmatists—*diamatchiki*—at least until the silencing of the avant-garde in early 1975. The actual state of Yugoslav Marxist philosophy and social sciences was and is, of course, much more complex than the above division into schools of thought and openness in outlook would indicate. Apparently many, East and West, have underestimated both the staying power of the *diamatchiki* and the executive reach of the League of Communists of Yugoslavia. These two jointly inherit the avant-garde's whirlwind. Yugoslav Marxism, like so much else in Yugoslavia, remains in a veritable state of flux. Furthermore, there are important individual and group differences even among avant-garde Yugoslav Marxist thinkers on problems of the scope and nature of philosophy and science, freedom and determinism, the theory of reflection, dialectical materialism, and other topics, apart from their relationship to the powers that be.

1.2 Marxism versus Stalinism

It is of paramount importance that the dialectic or the "scientific" method-ology of Marxism-Leninism was redefined by Yugoslav Marxist philosophers as essentially a method of critique *and* of revolutionary practice.[25] This redefinition of the dialectic provided the Yugoslav Marxist philosophers with the tool necessary for a re-examination not only of capitalism and state capitalism (Stalinism) but also of socialism. The new conception of the dialectic as a method for enriching Marxist theory and guiding socialist practice has helped Yugoslav Marxists to recapture some of the humanist inspiration of Marx's thought. It has also contributed to their view of Marxism as an open-ended and creative enterprise rather than a system of frozen dogmas or final and unchallengeable truths. Avant-garde Yugoslav Marxist philosophers have consequently developed a conception of the role of philosophy as critical social conscience necessarily independent of and not subservient to the state and politics. This epochal reconceptualization of the scope and role of Marxist philosophy, predictably enough, finally drew official condemnation from the communist Establishment (see Chapter X).

Stalinism has been defined by the authoritative *Small Political Encyclopædia* as a "bureaucratic deformation of socialism and pragmatist and dogmatic revision of basic scientific tenets of Marxism and Leninism."[26] Yugoslav Marxist philos-ophers have gone to some lengths in contrasting their view of socialist-humanist or creative and authentic Marxism with the "revision" of Marxist theory and the "deformation" of socialist practice in the Soviet Union and elsewhere. Vranicki states that Marxism is in its essence creative thought which consists of three elements: materialism, dialectic, and humanism. Stalinism, on the other hand, represents not only dogmatism and revisionism, but also a deformation of socialist relations, personality and culture in general and Marxist theory in particular.[27] Yugoslav Marxism holds that Stalin's cult of personality was neither the cause nor simply the form of the deformation of the socio-political system in the Soviet Union but rather its expression and consequence![28] Both Stalinism and the cult of personality (of the Leader) are condemned by Yugoslav Marxists as deformations of socialist thought.[29]

In spite of the virulent condemnation of Stalinism by Yugoslav Marxists, there have been relatively few thorough-going studies on the phenomenon of Stalinist revisionism. This is understandable considering the sensitivity of the topic, particularly in its bearing on Yugoslav-Soviet relations. Thus, Vranicki's critique of Stalinism as not deserving the title of socialism—not even that of state socialism —in his book on *Marxism and Socialism* (1979), drew an official protest by the Soviet ambassador in Belgrade. And Stojanović could not publish his *History and Party Consciousness*—an allusion to Lukacs' *History and Class Consciousness*—in Yugoslavia at all. Vranicki terms Stalin's system one of "state capitalism," with unlimited power of a state-party monopoly in all spheres of life, culminating in a "divinization of the party, the state and the leader." Stojanović, like Vranicki, also echoes Djilas in concluding that Marxism was Leninized and Stalinized in the USSR, and that the Soviet system developed into a new class society, or statism, in which a new statist class disposes collectively of the means of production.[30]

Apparently for reasons of censorship, the Yugoslavs have not yet discovered Solzhenitsyn's *magnum opus* and its devastating critique of Marxist theory and socialist practice in such works as *The First Circle, Cancer Ward, The Gulag Archipelago, Letter to the Soviet Leaders,* and *Lenin in Zürich.* Yet, some of the more enterprising Yugoslav Marxist sociologists and philosophers have, nevertheless, delved into an analysis of Stalinism, which they hold responsible for the dogmatization of thought especially in the social sciences. Supek, Professor of Sociology at the University of Zagreb, bases his critique of Stalinist revisionism ingeniously on that of the prominent French Marxist philosopher Roger Garaudy. Garaudy's critique of Stalinist dogmatism is without doubt one of the most far-reaching advanced by any Marxist philosopher.

Garaudy's critique of Stalinism, adopted by Supek, merits extensive restatement. Supek expounds Garaudy's views, point by point, in his chapter on "Dogmatism or Revisionism?" It runs as follows:

(1) Stalin impoverished dialectical materialism by reducing materialism to three traits and dialectics to four traits. By separating the dialectic from materialism, that is, method from theory, Stalin failed to realize their essential unity and consequently substituted dogmatic materialism for dogmatic idealism.

(2) Since the category of practice (the link between theory and method) determines the historical character of human action, the return to a vulgar materialism and extreme determinism signifies a regression to a naturalistic or mechanistic conception of reality.

(3) The elimination of the category of practice and, hence, of creative and self-creative human activity (*praxis*) led Stalin to a positivistic interpretation of science and philosophy.

(4) The positivistic orientation of Stalinism led, in turn, to a mechanical understanding of the relationship between the "base" and the "superstructure" in the form of economism and historicism, that is, extreme economic and historical determinism, since the category of human *praxis* was extirpated.

(5) The inability of Stalinism to interpret the relationship between social products and ideas dialectically resulted in the misinterpretation of basic social phenomena characterized by anti-humanism.

(6) The false thesis of the withering away of the superstructure in the historical movement of the base eventuated in the utterly misguided attitude of cultural isolationism toward the heritage of the "bourgeois" past.

(7) Finally, Stalinism rejected Marx's theory of alienation together with Hegel's dialectical method, since it contained a humanist critique of statism as well as a critique of the positivistic
submission of the human personality to the collective or society.[31]

Yugoslav Marxist philosophers have rejected for the most part extreme
historical determinism as inadequate for understanding man and society. Kangrga,
Professor of Philosophy at the University of Zagreb, cites Marx's own critique in
The Holy Family of the conception of history as an abstraction which acts on the
world stage:

History does not do anything, she does not "possess" great riches,
she does not "fight battles!" On the contrary, it is real, living man
who does all that, who possesses and who fights; "history" does not
avail herself of man as a means to realize her ends—as if she were
some separate person—instead, she is nothing but the activity of
man who pursues his own ends.[32]

Yugoslavs take even Marx himself to task for his tendency to write at times as an
extreme determinist, which is in direct conflict with his belief expressed in the
Eleventh Thesis on Feuerbach that the point is not only to interpret the world but
to change it. Yugoslav Marxists have generally rejected the notion of freedom as
the awareness of necessity, advanced by Hegel and Engels, both on theoretical and
practical grounds, as leading to socio-political conformism. The epistemological
theory of reflection, propounded by Lenin in his *Materialism and Empirio-
Criticism*, suffered the same fate as Marx's historical determinism and Engels'
deterministic conception of freedom: it was supplanted by the category of *praxis*,
that is, human practice, defined as the relatively free and creative ability of man
to fashion himself and the world.[33]

Yugoslav Marxists explain the degeneration of Marxist philosophy under
Stalinism as a result of three groups of factors:

(1) Marx's theory became the official ideology of victorious
labor movements, which facilitated the tendency among Marxists
to become apologists rather than critics of their socialist societies,

(2) Socialist revolutions occurred in relatively backward
countries, in which the tasks of capital accumulation, industrialization, and urbanization had not been accomplished, and which led to:

(3) The necessity to establish a centralized system and an
authoritarian state structure in order to accelerate industrialization and further economic development.[34]

The result was the emergence of state, political, and military bureaucracies,
the strengthening of the state *apparat* and centralized economic decision-making
organs, all of which led to state capitalism, that is, a bureaucratic revision of
socialism. In the Stalinist bureaucratic system of state capitalism, problems of coal
and steel supplanted the problems of man, as Marković aptly put it.[35] The original
Marxist conception of more humane social relationships was superseded by the goal
of economic production. In this sense, contends Pejović, Professor of Philosophy at
the University of Zagreb, Stalinism was only a continuation of the bourgeois
Weltanschauung.[36] Instead of trying to deal with the phenomenon of alienation,
Stalinism denied that alienation existed in socialism. Instead of liberating man by
developing forms of self-government, Stalinism had enslaved man by its bureaucratic-etatist structures.

In order to overcome the anti-humanism of Stalinism, Yugoslav Marxist
philosophers postulated the need for returning to the "original" Marx and the

further creative development of Marx's thought as both theory and practice. The Yugoslavs found the clue to the "authentic" interpretation of Marx's thought in his early writings, particularly in his *Economic and Philosophical Manuscripts* of 1844, *On the Jewish Question, Contribution to the Critique of Hegel's Philosophy of Right, Theses on Feuerbach,* and *The German Ideology.* The majority of Yugoslav Marxist philosophers now maintained that it was impossible to understand Marx's thought correctly without paying close attention to Marx's basic humanist inspiration that underlies *all* of his works.

There are two major aspects to the Yugoslavs' humanist reconstruction of Marx's and Engels' teachings (with precious little reference to Lenin):

(1) Marx's thought has been redefined as both theory and method, with emphasis on Marxism as a *method* of social criticism. Marxism, according to Petrović, is a theory that contains unsettled questions and which thus remains incomplete and unfinished. It is the task of socialists to develop Marx's humanistic thought further in all directions.[37] Marx's thought is conceived as basically self-critical. The dialectic, its method, is essentially a method of criticism and of revolutionary *praxis* aiming at the unity of theory and practice. Marxism is, therefore, an "always critical social and political philosophy or it is nothing at all."[38]

(2) Marxism and hence socialism and communism have been linked by Yugoslav Marxist philosophers to Marx's humanism. It is contended that socialism which runs counter to man and which does not consider *the human being as the first, only, and highest value* is no socialism at all! [39] This conception of socialism in turn called for superseding Marx's—and especially Engels'—deterministic conception of freedom.

These two aspects constitute the basis of the revolutionary reconstruction of the Marxist-Leninist intellectual heritage by avant-garde Yugoslav Marxist philosophers and sociologists.

2. The Missing Link: Man as Praxis

Yugoslav Marxist philosophers agree on the basic premise that man has the capacity to transform himself and the world around him through relatively free and creative action. Although human action is circumscribed by economic and historical factors, still the human being retains degrees of freedom expressed in a relatively open-ended sphere for creativity and is, therefore, morally responsible for his actions.

Yugoslav Marxist philosophers found it necessary in their critique of Stalinism and the resulting humanistic reconstruction of Marxism to focus on a long-neglected entity in the communist world: man. As a result, Yugoslav Marxists embarked on a redefinition of Marxism-Leninism by developing what they consider as the essential ingredient in Marxism which was missing in Stalinism: Marx's philosophy of man. As early as 1963, Marković hailed the prospect of the development of a general philosophy of man and the elaboration of the concept of alienation as well as the means for the all-encompassing liberation of man as a renaissance of Marxist humanist thought.[40] Yugoslav philosophers have pointed out that socialist societies have often gone to the extreme of collectivism in their attempt to uproot the "capitalist" evil of individual egoism. The shift in emphasis from the isolated individual to an abstraction called the collective was, however, contrary to the humanistic inspiration of "original" Marxism, since it often led to the vindication of group but not of social interests.[41]

Perhaps more than any other contemporary Yugoslav Marxist philosopher, Petrović has concerned himself with the elaboration of an authentic Marxist humanist philosophy of man. Petrović notes that Stalinism regarded man as an economic animal, a concept which is "equally strange to the young and the old Marx." On the contrary, Marx did not regard man either as merely a "rational animal," "toolmaking animal," or "economic animal," but rather as *a being of praxis*. As a being of *praxis*, man's essential possibility and nature is free creative activity. It is this possibility of man's acting in the world which alone can bring about Marx's imperative of changing it. Marx's humanism is conceived as superseding the traditional opposition between materialism and idealism, since it constitutes their synthesis or, in Marx's own words, their unifying truth. Petrović cites approvingly from Lenin's *Philosophical Notebooks* the notion that man is not completely determined either economically or historically, for:

> Man's consciousness not only reflects the world, it also creates it.[42]

Petrović's basic thesis is that Marx's concept of man as a free creative being of *praxis* who is bent on overcoming his alienation forms a bridge and expresses the essential unity between Marx's early and later works. Marx's thought is basically a *revolutionary humanism,* a critique of man's alienated condition in the inhuman world of capitalist society, as well as a prescription for the overcoming of this alienation and the realization of a "free community of free men" via socialism.[43] Marx's philosophy is thus a philosophy of revolutionary action aiming at the unification of theory and practice and the liberation and reintegration of man, his return to himself, or, as Marx put it:

> . . . a *restoration* of the human world of human relationships to man himself.[44]

Korać, Professor of Philosophy at the University of Belgrade, has defined Marx's thought as a new humanism whose goal is universal human emancipation and whose premise is the conception that the root of man is man himself.[45] In order to understand Marx's humanism, contend Yugoslav Marxists, it is necessary to understand the essence of man, and the essence of man cannot be understood apart from the category of *praxis*, that is, man's free creative activity. Avant-garde Yugoslav Marxism postulates the revolutionary thesis that the conception of *man as praxis* constitutes the solution to the riddle of history. Man as *praxis* is conceived as the key to the achievement of a more humane world, a world in which the individual has become socialized and society individualized. Immanent in these twin processes is the new revolutionary conception of freedom advanced by Yugoslav Marxist philosophers. It is man as *praxis* that constitutes the missing link between the dogmatic Stalinist conception of Marxism, socialism, and.communism, on the one hand, and authentic Marxism, that is, Marxist humanism and humanistic socialism, on the other.

2.1 Marxism as the Humanization of Social Relations

Contrary to the Stalinist redefinition of socialism as the development of the productive forces of society, Yugoslav Marxists assert that economic development *per se* was never the final goal for Marx's socialism. The final goal of socialism and communism is *a revolution in human relations* and the humanization of both the individual and society.[46] The humanization of social relationships is based on the discovery by Yugoslav Marxism that man is a being of *praxis,* for whom humanism is the only true goal.[47] The aim of socialism, accordingly, can only be man and the all-round development of his personality and creative abilities. The development of the individual person can, however, take place only in the context of society; hence the need for the humanization of social relations.

Yugoslav Marxist philosophers maintain that the twin goals of socialism—that is, the socialization of the individual and the individualization of society—can be achieved only by overcoming the phenomenon of alienation, especially economic alienation, which is defined as the alienation of the surplus product of one's labor. The goal of socialism at the level of the individual is to reintegrate the individual's split personality—*homo duplex*, the division of man into an egoistic individual and a moral person, a citizen—into a whole or total man. In order to realize this goal, it is necessary, according to Yugoslav Marxists, to *humanize work* by returning to the workers the power of decision-making in the enterprises, especially the power to decide on the final disposition of the surplus product. Workers' *self-management* thus becomes the Yugoslav answer to alienation as well as the definition of Marxist or socialist humanism.

Self-management is supposed to be the means by which the human being outgrows his alienation, or reduction to a mere means, characteristic of labor in capitalist societies. A free, self-governing human community is, according to the Yugoslavs, one that negates simultaneously "both the egoistic individual and the alienated institutionalization of society."[48] This free human community is allegedly the negation of politics and of political society, which are held responsible for the suppression and alienation of man.

In addition to the need for overcoming alienation generated by the remnants of "bourgeois" mentality and conditions prevailing in class society, socialists are confronted with the task of overcoming alienation generated by socialism as well. Avant-garde Yugoslav Marxist theorists thus advance the novel thesis of alienation in socialism. Primary forms of alienation in socialism, according to Yugoslav Marxists, are hierarchy, bureaucracy, the state, localism, particularism, national narrowness, chauvinism, market relations, fetishism of commodities, specialization, and the existence of *homo duplex*.[49] The remedy proposed for the elimination of alienation in socialism is the withering away of the state, bureaucracy, and politics, and supersession of the division of labor, the market, and commodity production. These are to be replaced by workers' self-management and social self-government and the development of new, more humane social relationships. Thus, Marković concludes that we may speak meaningfully about real historical progress only to the extent that social relations become increasingly human.[50]

2.2 Communism as a Transition to Humanism

The major distinguishing features of avant-garde Yugoslav Marxism elaborated thus far consist in:

(1) The redefinition of the dialectic, the methodology of Marxism-Leninism, as both theory and method, with emphasis on the dialectic as a critical method and Marxism as radical social critique of all existing conditions whether in capitalist, state capitalist, or socialist societies; and

(2) The redefinition of historical materialism and economic determinism in the spirit of the humanistic thought of the young Marx of the *Economic and Philosophical Manuscripts* of 1844, whose central concern was the de-alienation and liberation of the human individual via the humanization of social relationships in a socialist—that is, communist—community of free men.

By defining the dialectic as essentially a method of critique of everything existing, Yugoslav Marxist philosophers have achieved the seemingly impossible: the radicalization of Marxist thought. By insisting that Marxism-Leninism as a theory contains unresolved questions, Yugoslav Marxists have created an *open-ended Marxism*, one that may, and indeed does, require further elaboration or theoretical development as well as verification in practice. These steps alone might suffice for Marx, were he alive today, to note laconically once more that: "All I know is that I am not a Marxist."[51] But avant-garde Yugoslav Marxist theorists seem to be on firm ground, even when they advance their most far-reaching thesis—that Marx never looked upon socialism and communism as a definite socio-economic formation or as the ultimate goal of historical progress. Marx and Engels stated very explicitly in *The German Ideology* that:

> Communism is for us not a stable state which is to be established, an *ideal* to which reality will have to adjust itself. We call communism the *real* movement which abolishes the present state of things.[52]

Marx and Engels were less explicit on what communism as a "real movement" was to consist of except the ubiquitous class struggle. Beyond the class struggle, that is, the transition from capitalism to communism, Marx and Engels give us very few pointers into the future. Yugoslav Marxism does Marx one better by maintaining that the true and only aim of the period of transition from capitalism to socialism and communism as well as of communism itself is—*humanism.* According to Petrović:

> Communism, in fact, is the "transitory period" from capitalism (and class society in general) to humanism . . . .[53]

At the same time, Petrović insists that communism, socialism, and humanism, although not identical, are not essentially different. He also reverses Marx's traditional sequence of socialism as the lower phase of communism, and humanizes both by adding that "real life" is even a "higher" phase than communism![54] Petrović rounds out his reconstruction of Marx's philosophy by stating that, according to Marx:

> . . . *communism is in essence the emergence of humanism.*[55]

Avant-garde Yugoslav Marxism has revolutionized Marxist-Leninist theory by defining communism, its end goal, as the emergence of humanism. The avant-garde's conceptualization of humanism is based on Marx's concept of man that the root of man is man himself, that it is man as a being of *praxis,* as a relatively free creative being, who is the key to the solution of the riddle of history. Marx's conception of man was, however, that of a social individual, for the individual, as Marx put it in his Sixth Thesis on Feuerbach, is nothing but the ensemble of social relations.

Socialist practice had emphasized the need for the socialization of the individual, class struggle, and his obligation to sacrifice himself for the collective. Yugoslav Marxist philosophers are for the most part critical of this practice and have stood the Marxist conceptualization corresponding to it on its head: it is the *individual,* not the collective, which is at the center of Marx's philosophy of the radical de-alienation and liberation of man. Korać conveys this radical reorientation of avant-garde Yugoslav Marxist humanist thought well:

> . . . practice has indeed become far separated from Marx's social-ist theory . . . : where there is no freedom of the personality, there is not and cannot be any freedom for "the people."[56]

On the other hand, assert the Yugoslavs, in an attempt to square the circle and reconcile the individual with society, individual liberation is possible only within the societal framework and through the simultaneous liberation of society.

Avant-garde Yugoslav Marxism has come to recognize that at the core of the problem of individual and collective liberation and the reconciliation of the private with the public interest is the many-faceted question of—*freedom.* What is novel and significant in respect to this classic dilemma is the fact that Yugoslav Marxist philosophers have connected the question of freedom with the question of man's essence, which they have found to lie in *praxis*—man's free creative activity and the goal of that activity—the overcoming of alienation or the estrangement of man in what Marx once called a "soulless" universe. Petrović maintains that:

> As a being of praxis, man is a being of freedom. There is no freedom without man, and there is no humanity without freedom.[57]

Yugoslav Marxism has thus opened up the question of individual freedom and responsibility, the Achilles' heel of Marxist-Leninist teachings. The opening up of the question of freedom is another distinguishing feature of Yugoslav Marxism, and in the long run perhaps the most significant one.[58] By redefining Marxist methodology as a method of radical social criticism, and Marxist theory as a prescription for and guide to the humanization of both the individual and society, Yugoslav Marxist philosophers have at the same time *radicalized* and *humanized* Marxism-Leninism. By restoring man to the center of both Marxist theory and socialist practice, and by its radical reconceptualization of the essence of man as freedom or liberation via *praxis*, Yugoslav Marxism may truly be said to have *discovered* man.

2.3 Socialist Personalism and Freedom: A Copernican Revolution in Marxism

The avant-garde's philosophy of man as a being of *praxis*, of freedom and responsibility, gradually evolved into a philosophy of *socialist personalism*. This constitutes a Copernican revolution in Marxism. Classical Marxism centered its preoccupation on the liberation and de-alienation of society and the collective, while bracketing the individual and his self-realization. Thus, in orthodox Marxism-Leninism, it was the society or the collective in theory, and the absolute state in practice, which represented the focal point and the end goal of individual and social action. Avant-garde Yugoslav Marxist philosophers and sociologists have revolutionized Marxist-Leninist theory by placing the all-round development and self-realization of the human *individual* in the center of the dialectic of history and social transformation. According to Stojanović, Professor of Philosophy at the University of Belgrade:

> Marxist personalism treats the good of the personality as the highest goal of all social endeavor, and demands that it be the central concern of social development and that its dignity be respected above all else.[59]

Stojanović's view of Marxist or socialist personalism is seconded by Supek, who sees the liberation of the human personality as the "true meaning and goal of the socialist order." Petrović notes: "There can be no free society without free personality."[60] But what about the socialist transformation, class struggle, and the role of the party, the state, and other institutions in socialism? It is noteworthy that Marković considers socialist institutions as "only means to the creation of a better and more humane society and to guarantee more liberty to the individual, and not an end in itself, an alienated power lording it over men."[61] Crucially, socialist personalism has been intimately intertwined with the idea of freedom.

Gary C. Shaw and David Myers note that Marx's epistemology was influenced not only by materialism, but idealism as well, especially that of Kant. They detect a Kantian element in Marx's notion that the human subject actively participates in cognition.[62] Hence, knowledge is a joint product of objective reality and human "revolutionary," "practical-critical" activity, as hinted at by Marx in his First Thesis on Feuerbach.[63] This means that man is not simply a passive recipient of external knowledge and data, existing somewhere out there outside of human sense perception, according to Engels' and Lenin's copy theory of knowledge (theory of reflection). Rather, man is an active participant in the very act of knowledge-creation. Marković writes:

> Old theories (of the Greeks, Spinoza, Hegel, Engels), according to which freedom is essentially knowledge of necessity, are no longer tenable as they stand because they reduce freedom to conformism and voluntary slavery.[64]

While Kant distinguished between the real world of *noumena* inaccessible to human perception and the apparent world of *phenomena* knowable by man, Marx did not. Yet, both in Kant and Marx, the synthetic nature of knowledge due to man's active participation in cognition affirms the potential for human freedom. This activist epistemology is congenial to the avant-garde's notion of man as a being of *praxis*, a creative and self-actualizing being.

While, in his Sixth Thesis on Feuerbach, Marx defined the essence of man as the ensemble or totality of social relations, Zagorka Pešić-Golubović, Professor of Sociology at the University of Belgrade, maintains that the human personality cannot be so defined without taking personal determinants into account.[65] Golubović notes that what is needed is a new understanding of both the individual human personality and society as products of much more complex forces, both social and individual. She outlines three groups of factors responsible for the development of the human personality: (1) biological and psycho-physiological; (2) social and cultural; and (3) personal. She finds that while the philosophical theory of individualism is insupportable, personality is not simply socially determined, either. Rather, the human personality itself is an active factor co-determining its development. From her study emerges the rather widely accepted view among avant-garde Yugoslav Marxist philosophers and sociologists of the mutual interrelation of the individual and society. Golubović's notion of man and human essence as a "reservoir of infinite possibilities" is representative of avant-garde thinking. She caps her vision of the future-oriented human being in an intersubjective world by the suggestion that the Marxist theory of class struggle needs to be supplemented by a theory of human motivation.[66] This leads Petrović to conclude that the de-alienation of social relations is a precondition for individual human self-realization, but that the free human personality is the precondition for the de-alienation of social relations.[67] Yugoslav Marxist humanism thus keeps returning to its new focal point of individual and societal *praxis*: man.

Vojan Rus, Professor of Philosophy at the University of Ljubljana in Slovenia, develops Petrović's idea of the relationship between individual and societal de-alienation further by stating that socialism can function only when the majority of people develop their personality and individuality. He also provides a definition of this new socialist personality:

> Socialist personality can be only a unity of rich contradictions, of various contradictory and strongly connected basic human traits within the totality of the same individual.[68]

Richard T. De George and others have observed that problems of the individual, long submerged in Marxist writings, are beginning to surface in the communist world.[69] The avant-garde Yugoslav conception of the human individual is strikingly un-Marxist in that we are no longer dealing here with a mass man, a member of a social collective, nor with an individual who is supposed to become completely de-alienated in the future communist society. Rather, what emerges is a view of man as a *project* and a *process* with no end in sight. As Petrović, Stojanović, and others note, man is an open-ended process, characterized by complexity, contradictory drives, and freedom.

In contrast to Marx's overoptimistic view of human nature as essentially good, Stojanović and Marković counterpose a view of human nature riddled with paradoxes and opposite tendencies. They observe such antinomies as man's quest for freedom and escape from responsibility, universal-national, creativity-destructiveness, self-sacrifice-lust for personal power and domination, love-hate, rational-irrational, among others.[70] The major question arises then, according to Marković, which of these contradictory traits of human nature should we strive to develop and actualize?[71] Obviously, the positive ones: man as a rational, creative, sociable, self-actualized being of *praxis*. But Yugoslav Marxist humanism has still not resolved the problem of the tension between its positive conception of man, on the one hand, and freedom, on the other. Its model excludes failure and/or the development of other dubious or ambiguous qualities of human nature, such as asociability, imperfection, ignorance, bungling, and the like. As rational children of eighteenth century Enlightenment, avant-garde Marxist humanists appear to have little, if any, use for unenlightened children. Thus, even their liberal Marxism contains a strong element of intolerance, self-righteousness, non-acceptance of ambiguity and hence—terror. Plato's Philosopher-King rears his imperial head. Marković is willing to admit that Marxism lacks a fully developed philosophical theory of freedom which could simply be taken over by contemporary Marxist thinkers.[72]

Zivotić, Professor of Philosophy at the University of Belgrade, claims that the task of non-dogmatic philosophy is to fight for a personalistic humanism defined as a community of liberated personalities.[73] But what are to be the criteria for this fight? What is to prevent society from imposing on the individual society's rather than the individual's conception of what is truly human and desirable? Tadić, Professor of the Philosophy of Law at the same university, is aware of "soulless Marxism" which can put men in new chains. He maintains that Marxism as the theory and practice of freedom can exist and develop only within a societal framework in which individual freedom is not subordinated to the freedom of the community as an absolute.[74] This is, of course, easier said than done. Especially in view of the fact that "despotic socialism" creates, according to Radojica Bojanović, an authoritarian personality syndrome and an alienated mass which are hardly conducive to the humanization of socialism.[75]

Avant-garde theorists oppose an autonomous and creative personality characteristic of mature communism to collectivism and the phenomenon of the mass man in primitive communism and statist or bureaucratic socialism. For Stojanović, the principles of Marxist personalism, humanistic hedonism, and stimulatory material compensation for labor are the proper attributes to be found in mature communism.[76] Other avant-garde theorists, however, take a dim view of Stojanović's "stimulatory material compensation for labor," since they see this notorious market principle—currently the official policy in Yugoslavia's market socialism—as leading to growing social differentiation, inequalities, a new class society, and the twilight of the socialist ideals of equality and solidarity. According to Marković:

> Socialism cannot permit mass unemployment, increase in social differences outside certain limits, increase in the lagging of the backward and undeveloped, stagnation and even decline of production, dangerous disproportion and instability, and drastic forms of disharmony and anarchy.[77]

Paradoxically, elsewhere Stojanović is in complete agreement with Marković regarding the pernicious nature of social inequalities, unemployment, privileges, and the like. The question still remains whether socialism can afford freedom? Or, is socialism's overriding concern with egalitarianism and solidarity incompatible with civil rights and individual freedom? Marković himself recognizes that:

> ... in the name of socialism bureaucracy has robbed him [the worker] of some of his traditional rights: to organize, to move freely, to have his own press, to meet and express critical opinions in public, to struggle for the improvement of his working and living conditions, to demonstrate and to strike. Most of these rights are recognized in the constitution, but abolished in reality.[78]

The epochal question for socialism thus emerges in the form: How can a closed society allow the free development of its individual members? Can the conception of man as a being of *praxis* be operationalized under the watchful eyes of the secret police, press censorship, and thought control? How can a one-party state allow genuine workers' self-management and social *self-government*? Can socialist personalism be personal as well as socialist? Or, are they irreconcilably opposed, excluding one another? If man is an autonomous, free, creative, and self-actualizing being of *praxis*, can his "bourgeois" freedom *from* be abridged in the name of a superior socialist or communist freedom *for*? Tadić and Golubović maintain a rather novel view for Marxists and communists that *negative* freedom is an important precondition for *positive* freedom. Does not this insight come rather late in the history of the world communist movement, built on the self-abnegation and forced sacrifices of countless millions of human lives? It may come rather late, but apparently still too soon even for the League of Communists of Yugoslavia, which must feel haunted by Tadić's words that

> ... for free action to be possible at all, it is necessary for negative freedom to exist as well, that is, freedom from pressure and violence.[79]

But, if man is free, he is eminently responsible. Marković himself maintains that responsibility is but another face of freedom.[80] Consciousness and freedom of human action raise the question of moral responsibility, of ethics. Does socialism need ethics?

3. The Watershed: Kant's Categorical Imperative

It is notable that a *moral* protest against Marxist-Leninist moral/ethical relativism forms the common denominator of such diverse critics of communism as Milovan Djilas, Mihajlo Mihajlov, and Aleksandr I. Solzhenitsyn. While Mihajlov and Solzhenitsyn are Christian in their ethical and religious orientation, Djilas is atheist. Yet, all of them subscribe to a vision of *ethical* non-Marxist socialism.[81] Theirs appears to be a revolt against Marx's and Engels' dictum according to which communists do not propagate any kind of morality at all—since it is just another bourgeois fetishism—and Lenin's view that for communists morality is that which serves to advance "the interests of the class-struggle of the proletariat."[82] "The philosophy of a savage," as a character in Solzhenitsyn's novels would put it. Predictably, the absence of ethical criteria led to an inversion of means and ends, and the genesis of a phantasmagorical communist universe. The building of the communist utopia has proceeded according to the laws of distopia:

> So that prisons may forever disappear, we have built new ones. So that frontiers between States may crumble, we have surrounded ourselves with a Chinese Wall. So that work may become in the future a rest and pleasure, we have introduced forced labor. So that not a drop of blood may ever be shed, we have killed, killed, without respite.[83]

Avant-garde Yugoslav Marxist humanist thinkers are acutely aware of the ethical and axiological dilemmas of socialism. This was the implicit starting point for their rigorous critique of Stalinism. Yet, curiously, the avant-garde is divided on the need to develop a Marxist ethics as such. The Yugoslav avant-garde has thus arrived at a crucial watershed. Either it will develop a Marxist ethics which cannot circumvent Kant's categorical imperative to treat each individual human being as an end rather than a means, or continue to subsume individual moral responsibility under the mantle of the dialectic of history and the continuous revolutionizing of society.

It is the latter stance which is propounded by Kangrga, who believes that there is no such thing as a socialist ethics or morality. More important, he sees no need to construct one. For Kangrga, morality is one of the essential limiting aspects of man in bourgeois class society. To be a citizen as a moral person means to remain an egoistic individual, a man "reduced to a member of bourgeois society," on the one hand, and abstract political emancipation, on the other.[84] This semblance of morality, according to Kangrga, amounts simply to a confirmation of one of the forms of human self-alienation. What Marx really had in mind was the transcendence of morality as such by revolutionizing the underlying alienated social conditions which give rise to it. Kangrga thus disagrees openly with Kant's conception of man as a moral being. Instead, he claims that a moral stance can only consist in the continuous revolutionizing and negation of given social conditions. Kangrga thus reduces morality and ethics to Marx's Promethean concept of the "ruthless critique of everything that exists."[85]

It is curious that Kangrga fails to realize that in an important sense his stand only begs the question. For Marx's "ruthless critique of everything that exists" is meaningless without an ethical/axiological Archimedes point which would orient its critique. If this critique is exercised from the standpoint of socialist personalism which focuses on man and his all-round free development, we are back to the starting point. Supek writes that what is needed is a special *philosophy of life* which would deal with the premises for human self-realization. And it is this philosophy of life which ought to become the basis of communist ethics and aesthetics.[86] In Stojanović's view, no society can function without a normative minimum.[87] But this is to challenge Kangrga's major assumption head-on.

Among Marxist humanists, it is Stojanović and Marković who have been exploring most vigorously the ethical potential of Marx's thought. There is a consensus that a Marxist ethics has not yet been constructed. Yet the need for constructing one is not universally accepted, as mentioned above. Nevertheless, Stojanović sees Marx as belonging in the great European humanist ethical tradition. Marković notes that a cultural and moral revolution is no less important than the political reconstruction of society.[88] Both Marković and Stojanović take to task the principle that the end justifies the means. According to Stojanović:

> The end can morally justify the means only if the means do not morally disqualify the end.[89]

He points out that Marx himself held the view that "the end which requires bad means is not a good end."[90] This radical view of the means-ends relationship constitutes perhaps the most significant watershed separating socialist personalism from communist totalitarianism. Curiously, Marković and Stojanović do not realize the Kantian gap which separates their humanist vision of socialism from Marxist-Leninist theory and communist practice. They consider their vision as authentic, genuine, or true socialism, while relegating communist dictatorship, inhumanity, and malpractice to Stalinism, bureaucracy, and statism. This occurs in spite of the fact that both are keenly aware of the phenomenon which Stojanović calls, "the finalization of means and the instrumentalization of ends," prevalent in communist practice, where immoral means tend to replace humanistic ends.

In a stance which is practically indistinguishable from ethical socialism, both Stojanović and Supek erect new ethical rules governing the relationship between the individual and the revolution and its avant-garde, the communist party. For them, it is personal dignity which sets the limits for an individual's self-sacrifice for the party or the revolution. According to Stojanović:

> The revolutionaries cannot sacrifice their dignity to the revolutionary cause, because it is inseparable from the moral nucleus of the personality.[91]

Personal dignity is inalienable and indivisible. This is equivalent to Kant's Second Copernican revolution. It is a far cry, indeed, from the orthodox Marxist-Leninist view of the expendability of individual human lives, let alone dignity, in the building of the classless communist society, and the irrelevance of morality/ethics in the ubiquitous class struggle. This new Marxist categorical imperative focusing on personal dignity appears diametrically opposed to the requirements of expediency associated with class struggle. How can socialist personalism be reconciled with the intensification of the class struggle so prevalent as a political and action slogan in communist systems? And how can the new emphasis on personal dignity be reconciled with the many forms of violence practiced as "social prophylaxis" in the name of socialism and communism? Marković himself realizes that:

> Violent repression of heresy and dissent has become part of everyday life in these countries—the theory of the necessary intensification of class struggle in the process of development of socialism, far from explaining anything, is logically absurd: socialism by definition means the transition period in which men evolve towards a non-violent classless society.[92]

Class struggle appears to carry no implicit or explicit ethical criteria to guide or evaluate human action. It represents, rather, the faceless amoral process, advocated by Kangrga, of the continuous revolutionizing of social conditions, destruction of the old, and building of the new, and the devil take the hindmost. It is the kind of process in which Stalinism exalted in its legendary ruthlessness. Stojanović considers the Stalinist morally condemned on three counts: (1) immoderate use of violence; (2) absence of moral scruple; and (3) use of violence against comrades-in-arms. But this position also raises more questions than it solves. For instance, one might ask what is "moderate" violence? What are moral scruples, and is violence toward the majority of the people—who are not comrades-in-arms within the revolutionary organization or the party—acceptable or justified? Stojanović indicates that permanent revolution may all too easily be replaced by permanent terror. And the thin line distinguishing red terror from white terror fades into insignificance. It leads Stojanović to conclude:

> When a communist responds in kind to the enemy's sadistic brutality, how are we to distinguish one from the other? Red terror which reacts in this manner against white terror imperceptibly changes its own color in the process, despite its proclaimed humanistic goals.[93]

Stojanović is critical particularly of Stalinist *partiinost* ("party-mindedness") which demands unconditional obedience and moral prostration from the individual revolutionary under the guise of "self-criticism." He contends that in the Soviet Union such innocuous "self-criticism" ended ten years later with mass murders. And even today, continues Stojanović, Stalinist *partiinost* leads to the spectre of a "revolution which humiliates its children." Hence, Stojanović insists on the fundamental ethical rule that the revolutionary's personal dignity may never be (ab-)used as a means to a revolutionary goal.[94] Stojanović has thus elaborated an impressive *ethics of humanistic reciprocity,* based on mutual respect between the revolutionary and his party. The central problem remains, however, since such an ethics still begs the question of the ultimate basis of, or criteria for, justification of ethical action.

Marxism in general and Yugoslav Marxism in particular stand before the epochal task of elaborating an ethics which does not subsume the individual under the historical dialectic, the revolution, or the classless society. As De George notes: "Marxist-Leninist ethics has come into its own, but it still has, it seems, a long way to grow."[95] His assessment of Soviet efforts to build a Marxist-Leninist ethics holds equally for the analogous efforts by Yugoslav Marxist theorists. It is the great merit of these avant-garde theorists to have reformulated Marxism as socialist personalism and thus focused attention on the existential component of man's life, thought, and action. They discovered the phenomenon that man as a being of *praxis* is a rather special creature which by his self-consciousness and ability to create and conceptualize bears "objective cosmic responsibility" for himself and his actions.[96] But this also means, according to Rus, that it is only *man's* purpose in the universe which is continuously in question, both in a cosmic and a functional sense. As the only self-negation of nature, man creates himself and his world. Thus, man's deepest purpose is, indeed, self-creation. With man as the center and pivot of individual and societal action, Yugoslav Marxism dons a distinct existentialist-phenomenological garb.

3.1 Marxism, Existentialism, Phenomenology: A Hegelian Triangle?

Orthodox Marxists accuse the Yugoslav avant-garde theorists of left-wing radicalism and collusion with existentialism, phenomenology, the Frankfurt School, and other "alien" bourgeois philosophical trends. According to Seweryn Żurawicki, the *Praxis* group considers its main task to "bring Marx closer to Husserl, Heidegger, Adorno and others . . . ."[97] Is there substance to Żurawicki's charges? An attempt to broach this question should also clarify the relationship between avant-garde Yugoslav Marxism and major contemporary Western philosophical currents such as existentialism and phenomenology.

It is apparent that the Yugoslav conceptualization of socialist personalism— focusing on man as a free, conscious, self-conscious, and creative being of *praxis*—carries a strong existentialist and phenomenological moment. Yet, the relationship between Yugoslav Marxist humanism and existentialism and phenomenology is much more complex. Avant-garde Yugoslav Marxist theorists show an extraordinarily open mind and willingness to learn from other philosophical orientations. But openness, receptivity, and learning are one thing. Wholesale acceptance or capitulation are another. Yugoslav theorists find much that is suggestive and fascinating in existentialism and phenomenology. At the same time, they are highly critical of both. While Yugoslav Marxist thinkers are obviously sympathetic to existentialism's concern for the individual, his freedom, dignity, and creativity, they also point out its subjectivism, ahistoricism, individualism, and lack of social action.

Pejović notes that existentialism attempted to transcend abstract idealism, and thus arrived at much more fundamental structures of man's historic being. Yet, existentialism limits itself to locating the basis of man's self-alienation in the individual's isolated and "worrysome existence." It overlooks the fact that the problems of individual existence manifest also a social dimension and that, consequently, a social revolution is needed for the transcendence of alienation and the genesis of real humanism.[98]

What about the relationship between Marx and Heidegger? Petrović gives Heidegger credit for stating that the Marxist view of history is superior because of Marx's insight into the phenomenon of alienation which, according to Heidegger, "reaches with its roots back to the homelessness of contemporary man." Man's true home, as understood by Heidegger, is man's historic Being. Among Yugoslav Marxist humanists, Petrović and Životić have developed the first tentative outlines of a Heideggerian Marxism in their attempt to explore the ontological roots of Marxist humanist thought. Thus, Petrović advances the thesis that Marxism cannot be understood apart from the thought of the revolution. Yet, the thought of the revolution is but the expression of the true essence of man's Being, or "Being in its essence."[99] Životić goes even further in his contention regarding the basic similarities between Marx and Heidegger. In his view, Marx and Heidegger considered the existing world and man's Being as thoroughly alienated. Their solutions were also similar: the question of truth of an authentic free Being was to be sought in the revolutionary act of opening up toward new possibilities of human self-realization. Both thinkers were thus fighting against human self-alienation in a technological world which forgets man's Being, by insisting on the essential distinction between work (labor) and creation (creative activity)—the fundamental-ontological standpoint. In sum, concludes Životić, both Marx and Heidegger insisted on a future-oriented utopian vision as the only credible ontological basis for understanding man's Being.[100]

While Yugoslav theorists find Heidegger's ontology captivating, it also disappoints them in its passivity, nihilism, and acceptance of the status quo. Petrović observes that while Marx prescribed a ruthless criticism and revolutionizing of all existing social conditions, Heidegger is content to merely sit back with conscious reflection (*besinnliches Nachdenken*), neutral toward the world of things, and open for secrets.[101] Elsewhere, Petrović summarizes the relationship between Marx and Heidegger as consisting in diverse interpretations of the meaning of Being. For Heidegger, the meaning of man's Being is *temporality*, whereas for Marx it is free creative activity or *praxis*.[102]

Above all, Yugoslav theorists find Heidegger's concept of man's Being as a Being-towards-death (*Sein-zum-Tode*) and its resolution in Nothingness both disturbing and self-defeating. It leads all to easily to Sartre's *Nausea* and *No Exit*. For Kangrga, man's realization and consciousness of the inescapability of death need not lead to defeatism or the notion of the meaninglessness of life. On the contrary, says Kangrga, this realization should serve as an *"impetus for action."*[103] In what sense? In the sense that man is a historical being whose trace is never extinguished provided he leaves his own creations behind. Yugoslav Marxists thus contrast man's active, historical, and social roles in Marxism with Heideggerian passivity and existentialism's isolated individual condemned to freedom and impotence in an asocial universe.

Avant-garde Yugoslav Marxist theorists appear even more receptive to phenomenology than to existentialism. This is understandable from the standpoint of their efforts to develop a new epistemology, transcending both positivism and Engels' and Lenin's theory of reflection. The avant-garde's approach to knowledge is phenomenological, more than Kantian. Phenomenology attempts to transcend the gap between knower and the known, subject and object, as well as the antitheses positivism—neo-Kantianism and idealism—realism. The Yugoslavs, like Western Marxists, find Husserl's phenomenological method of eidetic reduction—*epoché*—especially attractive. Epoché aims to return man to the eide or essences, that is, to knowledge of things-in-themselves (*"zu den Sachen selbst"*) unadulterated by excess valuational and other extraneous baggage. While Marković considers Husserl's *epoché* to be misleading, and the notion of pure immediacy to be only "an illusion"—since everything is mediated and filtered through human sensation and perception[104]—others may not be so easily dissuaded.

Vladimir Filipović, Professor of Philosophy at the University of Zagreb, observes approvingly that for Husserl the notion of phenomenon is that of an object of perceptual reduction which discovers its more or less hidden essence or *eidos*. Hence philosophy, like mathematics, is pure *eidetic* science, and as such is a "strong critical science" open to new questions regarding human existence.[105] Husserl's quest for original essences via radical intuitionism and man's practical immersion in the *Lebenswelt* appears to fascinate those relatively few among avant-garde Yugoslav Marxist theorists who have dared enter his phenomenological world. Kasim Prohić of the University of Sarajevo in Bosnia-Hercegovina finds that Husserl's *Crisis of the European Sciences and Transcendental Phenomenology*, the major work of the late Husserl, contains many relevant themes and questions which occupied Marx as well. Among these are the meaning of historical events, the crisis and the fetishization of the sciences and the *Lebenswelt*, intersubjectivity, and the radical and growing problems of individual authenticity and human Being-ness. Within this context, Prohić sees the phenomenological *epoché* as a quest for the discovery of man's authentic Being, his true life and image.[106]

It is not accidental that Yugoslav Marxist theorists feel drawn to Husserl's phenomenological method. This method emphasizes the human act of knowing and promises to tear the veil away from reality and discover the underlying essence. For Marxist revolutionaries, the return to the *Ding-an-Sich*, to things-in-themselves or the real thing, is a much needed reassurance that their quest for truly revolutionizing the world's social conditions will be meaningful. Apart from that, the knowledge that they are really dealing with essences or *noumena*, rather than mere Kantian *phenomena*, is likely to feed not only their enthusiasm for revolutionary transcendence of the existing world and its false consciousness, but also to morally justify the means as well as the proclaimed ends. Phenomenology may thus lend itself curiously to a radicalization of Marxism. This is precisely what Western proponents of phenomenological Marxism like Paul Piccone, William McBride, and Enzo Paci point out.[107]

Whereas Marxism may be radicalized via phenomenology, it is less certain whether it can also be de-dogmatized and humanized. Instead of transcending the dichotomy between idealism and realism, phenomenology seems to reduce itself by its subjective radical intuitionism to a self-righteous idealism which claims to have discovered the Method for reaching the *noumena,* essences, or *eide.* It dispenses with Kant's humility in distinguishing between *phenomena* and *noumena,* which leaves human beings with the assurance of the possibility of error and a realization that man is not God and that there are realms of knowledge and realities which he may be unable to conceptualize or enter. Hence, in their exaggerated notions of consciousness and self-consciousness and a Faustian quest for Absolute Knowledge at any price, Marxism, existentialism, and phenomenology may, indeed, form a Hegelian triangle. Within this triangle, existentialism is excused by its tragic conception of man condemned to freedom, the irreversibility of his death and non-existence, and the unbridgeable gulf separating the real from the ideal this side of eternity.

3.2 Critique of the New Left and the Frankfurt School

Avant-garde Yugoslav Marxist theorists have been accused also of New Left radicalism and sympathy for the Frankfurt School. What is the actual relationship between them? As could be expected, avant-garde theorists find many congenial aspects in Western New Left thought. Above all, they share the New Left's ruthless critique of both capitalism and bureaucratized or Stalinist socialism, as well as its anti-positivism and desire to revolutionize existing social conditions in the name of a de-alienated classless community—*Gemeinschaft*—of free men. Marković lauds the progressive characteristics of Western counter-culture, such as solidarity, feeling of equal human rights, demand for unfettered self-expression, reintroduction of the principle of joy as opposed to realism, and the spirit of true universalism.[108] Both the New Left and the Yugoslav avant-garde are adamantly opposed to the varied forms of human exploitation, whether under capitalism or state socialism. Their joint ideal is genuine socialism defined as both individual and societal liberation. Trivo Indjić suggests that socialism ought to encourage and adopt this counter-culture if it wants to outstrip liberal "bourgeois" culture and overcome its own repressive culture.[109]

It would thus appear at first that avant-garde Yugoslav Marxist humanist thought is in complete agreement with Western New Left views. But such is not the case. In fact, the Yugoslav avant-garde offers a rather trenchant critique of other important aspects of Western New Left thought. Paramount within this framework is its critique of the New Left's "romantic utopianism," ahistoricism, subjectivism, lack of an organization or program, and the underestimation of the role of the proletariat. Paradoxically, Marković criticizes the New Left for disputing *everything* in a society which amounts to disputing "even what in existing historical conditions, at least for a time period, should be preserved in the new society."[110] The same charge has been leveled against avant-garde Yugoslav Marxists by the communist Establishment! According to Marković, the New Left's stance can lead to a revolution in thought only or to its preliminary catalytic phase, at best, since it fails to specify what can really be transcended. He is also critical of the New Left's—especially students'—distrust of all political institutions. For Marković, a total negation of the Establishment by the New Left is hardly any negation at all. And he points out that even in a new social organization, some institutions and functions of the state would have to survive.

While the Yugoslav avant-garde shares the New Left's antipathy toward positivism, dogmatism, technocracy, and bureaucracy, it criticizes the New Left's extremely negative view of science and technology. Thus, Marković notes that Theodore Roszak in his *The Making of a Counter Culture* "confuses technology and technocracy" throughout and "advocates a return to pre-industrial, agricultural, tribal society."[111] This version of Rousseau's return to nature is clearly unacceptable to avant-garde thinkers. For them, there appears to be too much anarchism in the New Left's mixture of anarchism and Marxism. While Stojanović expresses understanding for some of the New Left's asceticism, collectivism, and leveling egalitarianism, and their fascination with the Maoist "cultural revolution," he condemns this *Weltanschauung* as "primitive communism."[112] Stojanović considers the Maoist "cultural revolution" as a permanent fixation on the initial phase of the revolution, an immature and primitive phase which, according to Marx himself, constitutes a "regression to the *unnatural* simplicity of the poor and wantless individual."[113] This individual, Marx concludes, has not only not transcended the bourgeois framework of the full development of productive forces in capitalism, but has not even attained it yet.

The most devastating critique by avant-garde Yugoslav Marxist humanists concerns, however, that part of the New Left and its counter-culture which withdraws into the occult and/or a drug sub-culture. The avant-garde considers this aspect of the New Left not only harmful, but a potent new form of total self-alienation. Mystical cults, drugs, and altered states of consciousness are seen as an inverted and absurd form of the realization of Marx's ideal of human liberation and all-round development of man's sensual potential. This form of pathological or pseudo-de-alienation is rejected by the avant-garde. Marković leaves no doubt as to the undesirability of this New Left conception of a new world and a new culture needed to overcome alienation:

> The new culture and the new world cannot be based on a bohemian, parasitic life-style, on infantile irresponsibility, sexual promiscuity, on a rediscovery of the myths of primitive and backward social structures, on other-worldliness and drugging of the senses. This is an antithesis of the seriously ailing world. Sometimes it is unclear which is the sickest society: that of the official "establishment" or that of the opposing culture.[114]

Much of the Yugoslav avant-garde's critique of the Western New Left is applicable also to the Frankfurt School. Again, one should point out that the affinity between the Yugoslav avant-garde and the Frankfurt School is, if anything, even greater than between it and the New Left. Yet, the avant-garde is bent upon preserving its own autonomous vision and critical stance, differentiating itself from other philosophical currents. Marcuse as an original thinker bridging the New Left and the Frankfurt School attracts the avant-garde's attention. The Frankfurt School's "critical theory of society" is respected, and the avant-garde appears to be seriously studying such works as Marcuse's *One-Dimensional Man* and *Eros and Civilization*, Jürgen Habermas' *Theory and Practice*, C. Wright Mills' *The Sociological Imagination*, and works by other authors in the Frankfurt School tradition.

While the Yugoslav avant-garde is receptive to the Frankfurt School's emphasis on dialectics, critique of positivism, bureaucracy, capitalism, Stalinism, ideology and false consciousness, and the search for a rational unity between theory and practice, it is critical of the School's ahistoricism, subjectivism, utopianism, Freudianism, and exclusive emphasis on *negative* dialectics. Thus, Tadić criticizes the late Marcuse for his excessive "objectivism" and overestimation of the repressive functions of technological rationality. He also takes a dim view of Marcuse's transposition of the revolutionary utopia into the sphere of subjectivity and uncertainty, abandoning the proletariat as the revolutionary subject and transferring the impetus for change outside of or onto society's borders.[115] Tadić considers Marcuse's attempt to synthesize psychoanalysis and Marxism as problematic. He is especially bothered by Marcuse's idealization of the satisfaction of uncultured Eros and his opposition of Orpheus and Narcissus as symbols of the "Great Refusal" to Prometheus as the prototypical hero of the "performance principle" and culture. This aspect of Marcuse's *Weltanschauung* grates conspicuously against the Yugoslav avant-garde's Promethean vision of Marxism and its central concept of man as a being of *praxis*. Pejović concludes that Marcuse's attempt at a philosophical interpretation of Freud and integration with Marxism brings Marx and Freud too close.[116] Pejović notes the discrepancies between Marx's and Freud's views of human nature and conflict resolution, especially Freud's critique of Marx's overoptimistic view of human nature. He consideres Freud's view as overly pessimistic and Marcuse's as overly optimistic in its expectations of future possibilities for man.

Other avant-garde theorists, like Vojin Milić, Professor of Sociology at the University of Belgrade, observe that the Frankfurt School has failed to investigate contemporary forms of social structure and social organization and that Marcuse and Adorno equate their critical theory with utopia. Milić claims that a truly revolutionary theory must provide "a historically realistic answer to the question about a revolutionary subject," and utopia fails in this regard.[117] Thus, according to Abdulah Šarčević, Professor of Philosophy at the University of Sarajevo, Adorno's negative dialectic, in spite of all its strengths, still ends up providing a naive picture of a "contemporary Kierkegaard."[118]

It is Petrović's critique of the Frankfurt School in the work of one of its most promising younger exponents—Habermas and his *Theorie und Praxis*—which is the most far-reaching and whose full theoretical and practical import have gone largely unrealized by even the Yugoslav avant-garde. Petrović asks the seminal question: whether a "critical theory of society" reduced to sociology can adequately comprehend human alienation and offer standards for overcoming that alienation. According to Petrović, alienation cannot be overcome by a Marxism understood as merely a politically inspired philosophy of history. It necessitates a Marxist anthropology and ontology as well. Crucially, Petrović observes that alienation is always human alienation and asks:

> Is revolution something which concerns only "social conditions" and not also the "nature" of man? If this is the case, then we really may need merely a "critical theory of society," and no ontology and anthropology, as a theoretical basis for abolition of alienation.[119]

It is also unclear to Petrović how a sociology "freed from philosophy and rooted in the existing state of affairs, can ever be a 'critical theory'." He concludes that Marxism is not merely a non-philosophical "critical theory," philosophy or scholastic ontology and anthropology but the thought of the revolution. The major challenge that the New Left, the Frankfurt School, and other would-be social engineers and social critics face is contained in Petrović's capsule question:

> But what if the "social order" is not quite so external to man? And what if the revolutionary abolition of alienation means also a change in the essence of man?[120]

Stojanović makes it even clearer when he sums up the quintessential dilemma confronting the revolutionary:

> If he wants to remain faithful to himself, he must change not only the world, but himself as well.[121]

4. Marxism as a Critique of Socialism

Even this cursory expedition to discover Yugoslavia as an intellectual continent makes it clear that avant-garde Yugoslav Marxist humanist thought is a major, creative, powerful, *sui generis* reconstruction of the entire Marxist-Leninist *Weltanschauung*. As such, it is not reducible to either existentialism, phenomenology, Kantianism, personalism, intuitionism, pragmatism, analytical philosophy, the Frankfurt School—or to Marxism-Leninism, for that matter. Rather, avant-garde thought constitutes a fascinating novel elaboration of the classics of Marxism as well as a synthesis of some of the most important philosophical currents in the great Western intellectual tradition. We still lack an adequate understanding of this new school of thought, let alone a name for it. Let us then summarize briefly the major thrust of avant-garde thought.

While Lenin maintained that there can be no revolutionary movement without a revolutionary theory, Marković notes that there can be no revolutionary theory without a theory of man and human nature.[122]   Avant-garde Yugoslav Marxist humanist thought has grown anthropological, ontological, and axiological roots, in addition to a phenomenologically-oriented dialectical epistemology.   The avant-garde's motto has been from the beginning Marx's notion contained in his Postscript to the Second edition of *Capital,* according to which the dialectic "cannot bear to have anybody as a tutor . . . it is essentially critical and revolutionary."[123]   Yugoslav theorists have taken Marx's injunction seriously and concluded that Marxists can no longer rest content with a simple repetition or quotation-mania of sacred texts.   Rather, it is incumbent upon contemporary Marxists-revolutionaries, in Rus' opinion, to develop the Marxist dialectic independently in unexplored areas, applying it to unresolved problems.[124]   To these avant-garde theorists, Marxist philosophy is the thought of the revolution.   As such, it must deal with contemporary problems in the widest, eighteenth-century sense of the term "philosophy."   Hence, revolutionary Marxist philosophy must embrace all aspects of human thought, knowledge and action, the humanities, social and natural sciences, social organization, politics, economics, law, individual freedom and societal liberation.   Stojanović and Pejović contend that those who really want to be creative interpreters of Marxist theory and socialist practice, and thus think and act in the spirit of Marx, must go *beyond Marx,* although that does not mean without Marx.[125]   As Golubović summed it up: we live in an era of technologically advanced industrial civilization—with new problems as well as novel vistas for human self-realization—hence Marx's perspective can no longer be our own.[126]

Crucially, the Yugoslav avant-garde claims that Marxism is *critical* thought par excellence, or it is nothing at all.   What is extraordinary in the avant-garde's basic stance is that for them the major task for Marxist philosophers and sociologists living in socialist systems is to be its critics, rather than apologists for and ancillaries to the state and politics.   Stojanović scores the Janus-faced attitude of numerous Marxists who are radical critics of capitalism, but apologists for socialism.[127]   Marxism must be a critique of "*all* existing societies."   Avant-garde Marxist humanist theorists base their view of Marxism as a critique of socialism on Marx's conception of the role of philosophy as "ruthless criticism of all existing conditions," which is not afraid of its findings or of conflict with the powers that be.[128]

As a result, avant-garde thought has trained its sights on a Marxist critique of its own socialist society.   Their devastating critique of bureaucracy, market economy, rising inequalities, stratification, the genesis of a new middle class, unemployment, party and state monopoly of decision-making and communications in Yugoslavia finally brought down upon them the wrath of the communist leadership.   According to Gerson S. Sher, the major reason for the suppression of the *Praxis* group and the ouster of the "Belgrade Eight" was their attempt to institutionalize criticism.[129]   Yet, Ludvik Vrtačić may be closer to the heart of the matter when he observes that the avant-garde's initial critique of Stalinism—not only sanctioned but instituted by the party itself—gradually developed into an "autonomous" critique of everything that exists, including the League of Communists of Yugoslavia and its work.[130]

Sher's and Vrtačić's notions point in the right direction, but do not exhaust the nature of the controversy between avant-garde theorists and the party.   The essence of this controversy lies deeper, in the fact that Yugoslav avant-garde Marxist humanists have revolutionized Marxist-Leninist theory by insisting on a creative reconstruction of Marxist theory and critique of socialist practice independently of the party.   In so doing the avant-garde has created a Gramsci-like open-ended Marxism and *reopened the central question of the unity of theory and practice in socialism.*

According to Tadić, the disjunction between theory and practice constitutes "the most significant unsolved problem of the socialist revolution."[131]   The avant-garde is confident that its radical critique and creative development of Marxist theory as the thought of the revolution is able to close the gap between theory and practice.   Avant-garde theorists are convinced that if only socialist practice would be redirected according to their theoretical blueprint, then society would be truly launched on the road to a classless communist future. Yet, paradoxically, their critique of socialist practices and institutions has opened up a Pandora's box of unresolved, contradictory, and perhaps insoluble problems in both the practice and the theory of socialism and communism. Our study is dedicated to an exploration of this unique phenomenon.

Avant-garde Yugoslav Marxist philosophers still suffer from a strong dose of ideological thinking, although their Promethean effort to de-ideologize and de-dogmatize Marxist-Leninist theory has already sprung a surprising number of ideological chains. As Dobrica Ćosić remarks: "Modern man is Sisyphus whose stone is ideology."[132] Ideological thinking appears to function as a kind of sixth sense for its adherents in their Faustian quest to know all the mysteries of the universe. This phenomenon would be relatively harmless were it not for the fact that the enchanted world of ideology becomes a substitute for everyday reality. According to the late Hannah Arendt:

> . . . ideological thinking becomes emancipated from the reality that we perceive with our five senses, and insists on a "truer" reality concealed behind all perceptible things, dominating them from this place of concealment and requiring a sixth sense that enables us to become aware of it.[133]

It is also well known that epochal truths require epochal interpreters who possess Absolute Knowledge. Yet, ". . . from absolute knowledge to absolute power is only one step," remarks Tadić.[134] In fact, Tadić characterizes the charismatic-bureaucratic leadership, which relies on a mystical mission or Providence, or on Absolute Knowledge, as "a special type of Cæsaropapism." Tadić's view is corroborated by Krešić's analysis of the phenomenon of the "cult of personality," in which the latter concludes that the centralization of economic and political power in an omnipotent and omniscient top politician-economist is the quintessence of "political papism" or Stalinism.[135]

Thomas Molnar distinguishes between two types of Marxist intellectuals: (1) the "unreconstructed ones" who see the Soviet experience as a deviation from authentic Marxism, and (2) the "penitent ones" who realize the unrealistic nature of Marxist aspirations.[136] To which type do the avant-garde Yugoslav Marxist humanist intellectuals belong? To both. Or, rather, they appear as a bridge between the two camps. Whether their efforts can be sustained theoretically and practically is an open question. On the one hand, the avant-garde has rediscovered philosophy in the classic sense as critical thought. On the other hand, the avant-garde finds it difficult to transcend the historical-ideological-utopian perspective of the enchanted universe of Marxist-Leninist discourse. And yet, the avant-garde's return to philosophy is turning out in accordance with Molnar's expectations as a return to man, individual freedom, and common sense.[137]

Avant-garde Yugoslav Marxism has undoubtedly discovered man. It is less certain whether it can also liberate and humanize him, as well as society. The Yugoslavs are aware of this dilemma, as shown by a commentary on the symposium "On Socialist Humanism:"

> By merely looking for salvation through the "law" [of historical progress—O.G.] we do not always arrive at humanism, neither do we by a mere appeal to humanism arrive instantly also at its realization.[138]

Contemporary Yugoslav Marxism may, indeed, call itself Marxist or socialist humanism. It remains to be seen, however, whether, or to what extent, it is truly humanist in orientation. Even more questionable is the assumption that socialist humanism represents the only "true red" humanism. The compatibility of humanism and Marxism has become one of the most important questions of our time, in no small measure thanks to avant-garde Yugoslav Marxist philosophers and sociologists.

In approaching the question of the compatibility or incompatibility of humanism and Marxism, we must concentrate on two major strands of issues on the basis of which Yugoslav Marxism claims to be the only genuine humanism and authentic Marxism: (1) Man's estrangement or alienation in class society; and (2) Man's dealienation and liberation in socialism and communism. An examination of this cosmology of issues will help illuminate the avant-garde's conception of man as a being of *praxis*, the key to the liberation of both the individual and society. It will also clarify such ambiguous and unresolved questions as: What is man, what is *praxis*, and what is the nature of the relationship between the human individual and *praxis*, freedom, society, the economy, law, politics, the party, and the state? Can the antithesis between the individual and society, private interest and common good, scarcity and utopia, be resolved or at least reconciled?

Chapter V · The Concept of Alienation

> Alienation is apparent not only in the fact that *my* means of life belong to *someone else*, that *my* desires are the unattainable possession of *someone else*, but that everything is *something different* from itself, that my activity is *something else*, and finally (and this is also the case for the capitalist) that *an inhuman power* rules over everything.
>
> Karl Marx, *Economic and Philosophical Manuscripts* (1844)

1. A Time to Re-Live Marxism?

Bertram D. Wolfe notes that it was Marx's merit to ask "large questions," although he gave us "shallow, oversimplified, dogmatic answers."[1] Yet, ideas have a way of taking on a life of their own. A case in point is the avant-garde Yugoslav Marxist philosophers and sociologists who have been transforming Marxist-Leninist ideology into a critical philosophy in the classic sense, as explored in the previous chapter. For them, both the questions and the answers regarding the human condition are becoming increasingly more complex. This fact has socio-economic, political, philosophical, and cultural significance of the first order, not only in terms of Yugoslavia but for Marxist studies generally.

The avant-garde's very attempt to create a living, nondogmatic, and open-ended Marxism collided with the party's (the League of Communists of Yugoslavia) view of its legitimacy as the sole true interpreter of Marxism-Leninism. The party's silencing of its own avant-garde raises serious questions with regard to the unity of theory and practice in socialism, not only in Yugoslavia but generally (see Chapters X-XI). Can socialism, defined as the practice of Marxist-Leninist theory, accommodate human creativity and freedom? Is it possible to reconcile socialism with democracy? Can the diverse forms of alienation—individual, socio-economic, political, cultural, spiritual—be overcome in socialism? Can Marxism outgrow its theological (in the narrow sense), positivistic, nineteenth century, pre-Einsteinian and pre-Heisenbergian view of man, society, and the universe?[2] Is a non-dogmatic Marxism possible? Can socialism be made safe for children and other living things? Is Marxism a humanism?   In Svetozar Stojanović's classic formulation of the socialist dilemma:

> Can dictatorship lead to democracy? Coercion and violence to freedom? Class struggle to classless society? Is it true that uniformity can generate variety? Is it reasonable to believe that stateless society, the self-governing community will originate from absolute state power? How is the socialist revolution, which is part of prehistory, to lead humanity to the beginning of its real history? Can the creation of new life and the education of new man be the work of revolutionaries who themselves belong to the old world? Who is to educate the educators?[3]

The paradox crowning both Marxist theory and socialist practice has led Western scholars like Paul Piccone to observe that:

> The most pressing problem facing any serious Marxist today is the crisis of Marxism, seen not only on a *practical* level dealing with the degeneration of the Soviet Union, but also on the theoretical level, since it would be abstract and idealistic to suppose that a fundamentally sound Marxism could have resulted in the unsound consequences that it has had: something must have been wanting in Marxism from the very beginning. And it is precisely the locating of this original flaw which must allow an analysis of Stalinism and its consequences.[4]

One does not have to be a Marxist, or a socialist for that matter, to agree with the substance of Piccone's analysis as well as his proposed remedy that Marxism needs to be re-lived, dialecticized, and reconstituted as both theory and *praxis* if it is to provide viable *"alternative institutions"* and a "new science and a new culture fit for human beings."[5]

Humanist and phenomenological reconstructions of the Marxist *Weltanschauung* may well be among the most promising attempts in our century to fashion a living, creative, and nondogmatic Marxism which could once again live up to its Promethean ideal as a radical critique of all existing social conditions which hinder the free development of all human potentialities whether in capitalism, state capitalism (Stalinism), or socialism (communism). The Yugoslav avant-garde's contribution to this pan-human enterprise is unique as it involves a radical reconstruction of the entire universe of Marxist-Leninist discourse. Central to this radical transvaluation is the avant-garde's emphasis on the concept of alienation within Marx's philosophy of man.

If Marxism needs to be re-lived as critical theory, especially in the humanist and phenomenological senses, in order to become relevant again, it is essential, as Piccone writes, that we:

> ... penetrate the categorical formulations in which it has become entrapped and go back to the constitutive pre-categorical foundations which gave rise to it.[6]

Possibly the most crucial category in Marxist-Leninist theory is the esoteric concept of alienation, a concept which, according to some, lacks any definite content. As Troun Overend remarks:

> Sociologists have not at all been clear *among themselves* as to what they *mean* by the concept alienation and, ipso facto, what social phenomena(non) *is* alienation.[7]

The writings of the Yugoslav avant-garde are pregnant with fascinating, unorthodox and in part even "un-Marxist" insights into phenomena clustered around the concept of alienation—the missing link in socialism with a *human* face—as well as possible remedies.

2. Essence versus Existence

The Yugoslavs developed the Marxist conception of man in the form of man as a being of *praxis*, that is, a free, creative, and self-creative (self-actualizing) being. However, as Gajo Petrović cautions, the definition of man as a being of *praxis* does not solve all our problems. On the contrary, many questions only begin once we have defined man in this way.[8]

The postulate that man is a being of *praxis* or, in Mihailo Marković's terms, "a potentially free, creative, social rational being, able to develop further its nature, to create new own senses, powers, abilities,"[9] was conceived as the active ingredient in Marx's philosophy of man counterposed against alienating social forces and conditions. Marx's philosophy of man and his concepts of alienation and de-alienation were thus interpreted as forming a unified whole. According to Petrović, Marx's conception of man cannot be separated from his "humanistic theory of alienation and de-alienation."[10] Yugoslav Marxist philosophers and sociologists have come to regard the problem of alienation as the central problem confronting man in *all* societies. Furthermore, the Yugoslavs claim that Marx's conception of the causes and effects of alienation constitutes the essence of his thought on man and society.[11] Thus, Rudi Supek states that Marx's theory of alienation represents both a critique of bourgeois society and classical political economy as well as a theoretical and methodological unity of his research on society, and as such is simply contemporary sociology.[12] Stojanović notes that the concepts of alienation and de-alienation are "the most general synthetic-critical categories in Marx's humanistic theory," while Marković considers "disalienation" as the key concept in Marx's humanistic philosophy.[13] According to Predrag Vranicki, the problem of alienation is the central problem not of capitalism (which can allegedly only exist as alienated, that is, whose essence is alienation) but of socialism—whose very *raison d'être* is the progressive overcoming of alienation.[14]

But what is alienation? Marx conceived alienation, note Petrović and Stojanović, as a split or contradiction between "man's real 'nature', or 'essence', and his factual 'properties', or 'existence'."[15] It follows that socialism and communism must attempt to narrow this gap between man's essence and his existence by emancipating and liberating man from inhuman conditions. A major Yugoslav theoretical innovation in this regard is their insistence that man's de-alienation can never be complete or absolute, since its consummation would result in a sort of *"perpetuum immobile,"* leaving no room for further improvement, humanization, and progress.[16] And it is struggle, work, sacrifice, and the solving of problems, writes Jovan Djordjević, which are the preconditions of every humanity of man and society, and which thus constitute his basic human precondition.[17]

Yugoslav Marxist philosophers also like to point out that the concept of self-alienation applies solely or uniquely to man. Only man can be alienated in the proper sense of the term, that is, only man can exist as something other than his/her potentiality or essence. But the very concept of alienated man implies that man can change and become real, whole, total, integrated, and de-alienated since, as Milan Kangrga meditates, if man were given once and for all time, he could not possibly be alienated from this givenness, which would constitute his essence.[18] This point also highlights one of the essential paradoxes of Marxist-Leninist theory and its dialectic—the clash between economic-historical determinism and Marx's appeal to philosophers (and the proletariat) in his Eleventh Thesis on Feuerbach to change the world.

Marx conceived man's essence, according to Petrović, as his "historically created human possibility (i.e., real possibility as against 'mere possibility')."[19] This "historically created human possibility" would be realized by none other than man acting in time and space, history and society, that is, by *praxis*. The aim of this *praxis* would be to liberate and humanize asocial man dominated by private interest by emancipating labor from exploitation, returning decision-making power to the people and thus humanizing social relationships and vindicating the general or public interest. The end goal, viewed as a process of *approximation,* would be the full realization of the individual in a genuine community, or as Veljko Korać put it, in a "new, human society."[20]

Marković stresses that the basic concepts for Marx are *nature,* which is humanized by human *praxis,* and *man,* who becomes natural through the all-round development and affirmation of his faculties.[21] The humanization of nature and the naturalization of man constitute Marx's own definition of humanism and communism in his *Economic and Philosophical Manuscripts* of 1844 (the "Paris Manuscripts"). Communism, states Marx, with the angel of medieval theology and dogmatism looking over his shoulder, is therefore "the solution of the riddle of history and knows itself to be this solution."[22]

3. The Roots of Marx's Concept of Alienation

Avant-garde Yugoslav Marxist philosophers have embarked on an exciting journey to discover the early Marx as well as Feuerbach and Hegel, with occasional references to Rousseau and Kant. Yet, for an in-depth understanding of Marx's concepts of the whole man, the duality between man's essence and his existence as well as his concept of the community (*Gemeinschaft*) versus society (*Gesellschaft*) one must go beyond Feuerbach and Hegel to Rousseau, the Enlightenment, and even further back, to Plato and Aristotle.

Even a cursory glance at the Western intellectual heritage as reflected in the history of political philosophy reveals that the concept of alienation did not originate either with Hegel, Feuerbach, Marx, Rousseau, or the eighteenth century Enlightenment. The concept of alienation is embedded in a much more fundamental framework of the disjunction between fact and value, is and ought, means and ends, existing reality and human ideals. This duality between *is* and *ought* weaves like Ariadne's thread through the whole Western cultural tradition. Some—like Erich Fromm in his *Sane Society*—have traced the *concept* of alienation back to the *Old Testament* prophets' notion of idolatry, whereas István Mészáros in his *Marx's Theory of Alienation* traces the *term* "alienation" back to St. Paul's Epistle to the Ephesians 2:12 in the *New Testament*. Suffice it here to draw attention briefly to such philosophical systems as those of Plato, Aristotle, Hobbes, Rousseau, and Kant which antedated Hegel, Feuerbach, and Marx, as well as later writers, particularly the exponents of psychoanalysis, existentialism, and phenomenology.

Thus, Plato's Allegory of the Cave in his *Republic* is a dramatic illustration of man's alienated condition, that is, of man's inability to grasp the real world—the world of *Being* or ideal Forms—since he can only perceive the reflections or shadows of the real things during his mortal life in a material world of *Becoming* or appearances. In Plato's universe the disjunction between essence and existence, between the world of Being and the world of Becoming, seems to be built into the human constitution. It is only the Philosopher-King who may aspire to lead men out of the dark Cave into the Light.

Aristotle's works, especially his discourse *On the Soul,* contain a similar duality between *matter* (potentiality) and *form* (realization or actuality) within his unique synthesis. It finds perhaps its most elaborate expression in Kant's dichotomy between *phenomena* (the world as it appears to us) and *noumena* (the real world) as the duality between *is* and *ought* reflected in his two most famous works, *The Critique of Pure Reason* and *The Critique of Practical Reason.*

In Hobbes, the duality between is and ought can be traced to his conception of the *state of nature* versus *civil society*. In the Hobbesian state of nature man is alienated since it is a state of perpetual war of every man against every man, with the result that man is in "continual fear, and danger of violent death; and the life of man, solitary, poor, nasty, brutish, and short."[23] It is for this reason that men conclude the social compact, transfer their sovereignty, and found civil society.

Rousseau continues Hobbes' duality between the state of nature and civil society, but in his valuation stands Hobbes on his head. For Rousseau, man is free in the state of nature and quite happy, while in civil society he becomes corrupted, enslaved, and thus totally alienated. While Hegel may have coined the term "alienation," Rousseau had already discussed it abundantly in his discourses "On the Moral Effects of the Arts and Sciences" (1750) and "On the Origin and Foundation of the Inequality of Mankind" (1755). Rousseau indicted the whole Enlightenment tradition by maintaining that the progress of the arts and sciences had merely corrupted and enslaved man by luxury and profligacy, substituting commerce and money for morals and virtue.[24] He then went on to trace the origin of moral or political (not natural or physical) inequality among men to the foundation of private property consecrated by civil society and laws which:

> . . . for the advantage of a few ambitious individuals, subjected all mankind to perpetual labor, slavery, wretchedness.[25]

Rousseau was to elevate his philosophy of protest—a critique of social conditions enslaving man—into a veritable mystique for revolutionaries of all ages, from the French to the Russian (Bolshevik) Revolution and beyond, through his formula that:

> From great inequality of fortunes and conditions, from the vast variety of passions and of talents, of useless and pernicious arts, of vain sciences, would arise a multitude of prejudices equally contrary to reason, happiness, and virtue.[26]

Crucially, Rousseau's indictment of the corrupting influences of civilization, civil society, the state, and laws was canonized by Marx and Engels into their indictment of "bourgeois" or *class* society and the state as the embodiment of the alienated political power of the people. The necessity for the withering away of the state, the return of decision-making power to the people, and the imperative of direct democracy adopted by Marx and his followers reflected Rousseau's notions on the alienation of natural man in civil society, the idea that men were naturally good, that sovereignty was inalienable and indivisible, and that the general will could not be represented.[27]

Rousseau's account of the origins of society, the state, and laws as justifications and adumbrations of private property and inequality surfaced in the writings of Marx, Engels, Plekhanov, Lenin, and others as the doctrine of the economic base and social superstructure and the *class* nature of society founded on private property. Rousseau's concept of the natural man (the "noble savage") in a happy state of innocence and ignorance whom society and private property corrupted was transposed by Marx into his notion of the whole man rent asunder by specialization, whose labor was expropriated and who grew alienated to the extent that in his human functions he became an animal while in his animal functions remained human.[28] To Rousseau's description of the "assembly of artificial men and fictitious passions" in civil society, Marx posited the notion of both the worker and the capitalist as thoroughly alienated in their dehumanized, reified property relations mediated by money—the quintessence of man's self-alienation.[29]

Finally, modern philosophy and sociology as well as Marx and his followers are indebted to Rousseau's timeless formulation of the essence of alienated man in civilization in his resounding phrase that:

> ...we have nothing to show for ourselves but a frivolous and deceitful appearance, honour without virtue, reason without wisdom, and pleasure without happiness.[30]

Jean-Jacques Rousseau, called the father of Romanticism and "the supreme humanist,"[31] left to posterity a merciless—but largely unexamined—critique of civilization, questioning the unbounded rationalism and optimism of the Enlightenment and the modern conception of science and technology as progress by invoking the standpoint of man and the paradox that:

> Man is born free; and everywhere he is in chains.[32]

3.1 The Hegelian Legacy

Yugoslav Marxist philosophers have come to acknowledge Marx's intellectual indebtedness to Hegel's speculative philosophy and Feuerbach's anthropological naturalism as the philosophical sources of Marx's humanism. Hegel's and Feuerbach's philosophical systems are considered as the highest achievements of consciousness in class society in the form of philosophy.[33] To the Yugoslavs, the dialectical triad of Hegel-Feuerbach-Marx represents the transformation of abstract thought about the world into practical humanism. Feuerbach's anthropological naturalism is credited with the role of transformer of Hegel's speculative philosophy into Marx's dialectical materialism.

It is possible to distinguish at least five key areas of the Hegelian legacy which were transposed by Marx and Engels into their system of historical and dialectical materialism:

1.   First of all, Hegel's concept of externalization or objectification (*Entäusserung*) and its corollary self-externalization (*Selbstentäusserung*) became in Feuerbach's and Marx's terminologies estrangement or alienation (*Entfremdung*) and reification (*Verdinglichung*).   Yugoslav Marxists give credit to both Hegel and Feuerbach for being the first, along with Marx, to give an explicit elaboration of the concept of alienation, which was later to enter as a key concept into philosophy, sociology, and psychology.[34]

2.   But Hegel's concept of objectification or externalization cannot be understood apart from his concept of the unfolding of Reason or the Absolute Notion through time, which proceeds via the dialectic of its objectification and estrangement and the supersession or transcendence of its estrangement through self-consciousness and its final realization as the Absolute Idea, Spirit or *History*. It was Feuerbach's achievement, in turn, according to Marx, to show that the Absolute Notion itself was a form of human self-alienation.   Hence, what was needed was to stand Hegel on his head and assert that the realization of the *Spirit* was none other than the realization of—*man*.[35]   Andrija Krešić maintains that while Hegel interpreted history as the progress of the *concept* or notion of liberty, history was in reality the "advancing of the *praxis* of man's liberation."[36]

Hegel's speculative philosophy—which alienated man by transferring his essence to an abstract concept of Spirit—was allegedly brought down to earth by Feuerbach's anthropology, which contended that it was man who originated concepts, not vice versa.   Marx completed the process begun by Feuerbach and revolutionized traditional philosophy by advancing the thesis of the realization, supersession, or transcendence of philosophy: The disjunction between the real world of man (his essence) and the world of appearances (his existence) would be transcended by *praxis*.   By reducing Hegel's metaphysical world to a perceptible one and revolutionizing the latter, metaphysics is realized or made concrete and the preoccupation with the world beyond becomes once more the *praxis* of this world, concludes Vanja Sutlić.[37]

3.   Hegel's dialectical *method* of thesis-antithesis-synthesis—by which Reason or Spirit unfolds in the process of universal History—was adapted by Marx to more concrete goals such as the abolition of class society, the state, exploitation and alienation of man, and the institution of a classless and conflictless communist association of free men.   The dialectic as adapted by Marx, says Marković, was a "new method of thought"—a method of social criticism which attempted to discover "inner limitations, tensions and conflicts."[38]

4.   Hegel's concept of *self-consciousness* metamorphosed into Marx's concept of *socialist consciousness* and the notion that the communists represented the vanguard of the working class or the proletariat, itself the most conscious of the social classes in history.   Marx's conception of the *new man*—liberated and humanized, living in a de-alienated community or free association of immediate producers (workers)—was linked with the idea of the socialized individual imbued with proper socialist consciousness.[39]

5.   Finally, Yugoslav Marxist philosophers agree that the concept of *alienated labor* constitutes the essence of Marx's concept of alienation.   It is also pointed out by some that the *idea* of alienated labor can already be found in Hegel.[40]

In Hegel's system, especially in his *Phenomenology of Mind,* labor or work was conceived as a process through which alienated man attains to his liberation. Hegel's concept of work as a means to, and process of, liberation forms the foundation of Marx's concepts of *praxis* and of human essence defined as free, creative, and self-creative activity.   But Hegel's concept of labor was that of alienated (estranged) labor, since it was undertaken within an alienated historical framework, a framework of conflict between the Lord (Master) and the Bondsman (Slave).   Hegel drew a picture of this conflict between Master and Slave as a life and death struggle for "recognition."   Man could aspire to Absolute Knowledge only by attaining full self-consciousness which, in turn, could only be attained through the process of being "recognized" by another self-consciousness:

> Self-consciousness exists in itself and for itself, in that, and by the
> fact that it exists for another self-consciousness; that is to say, it
> *is* only by being acknowledged or "recognized."[41]

Hegel thus posited History as the human struggle for recognition which resulted in the antithesis of the Master and the Slave. Acting in a Darwinian universe (my term, not Hegel's), the man who risked his life in the fight for recognition became Master over the man unwilling to risk his biological life in turn. Yet the Master himself is faced with an existential impasse since: (1) He is unhappy with, and uncertain of, his status as Master because he must be recognized by an *equal*, that is, another Master; and (2) He is unable to transcend his role of pseudo-Master because he only fights and does not work. Hegel's solution, which became central to Marx, was to advance the thesis that man could attain to the realization of himself *qua man*, that is, to a true knowledge of his autonomous self-consciousness, only through *work*:

> Thus precisely in labour where there seemed to be merely some
> outsider's mind and ideas involved, the bondsman becomes aware,
> through this rediscovery of himself by himself, of having and being
> a "mind of his own."[42]

It is therefore the Slave who is destined to become *the* Master, redeemed by his work for the pseudo-Master. In Alexandre Kojève's interpretation, man surpasses dialectically his initial condition of dependent self-consciousness of the Slave through the negative-negating activity of work and appropriates the essential reality of the autonomous self-consciousness of the Master.[43]

Marx seems to have merely generalized the Hegelian metaphysic regarding the conflict between Master and Slave into the conflict between exploiting and exploited *classes* in all epochs, climaxing in the life and death struggle between the capitalists and the wage-earning proletariat in the so-called *bourgeois* social formation. He also adopted the Hegelian outcome of this historic (class) struggle: The proletariat, the exploited class, was destined to overcome the alienation of both classes, regain its self and the world by producing and reappropriating them. For Marx, this reappropriation of the world and the true humanity of man would be consummated by a proletarian revolution and the expropriation of the expropriators (the negation of the negation). Significantly, the means by which man would overcome his alienation and reappropriate himself and the world around him were the same for Marx and Hegel: work, labor, *praxis*. Marx himself saw Hegel's discovery of the concept of man's liberation through work (labor) as his major theoretical contribution:

> The outstanding achievement of Hegel's *Phenomenology*—the dia-
> lectic of negativity as the moving and creating principle—is, first,
> that Hegel grasps the self-creation of man as a process, object-
> ification as a loss of the object, as alienation and transcendence of
> this alienation, and that he, therefore, grasps the nature of *labour*,
> and conceives objective man (true, because real man) as the resul·
> of his *own labour*.[44]

3.2 The Concept of Alienated Labor

The authoritative *Small Political Encyclopaedia* reflects the general consensus among Yugoslav Marxist scholars that the alienation of labor and its products defined as economic alienation forms the basis for all other manifestations of alienation in society. Alienated labor is construed as the source of all other forms of alienation, be they economic (exploitation), political (domination by the state, bureaucracy, politics), cultural (ethno-centrism and national chauvinism), spiritual (religions, ideologies, myths), or human (reification of man—man treated as means rather than end).[45]

According to Petrović, Marx identified four major aspects or characteristics of the phenomenon of alienation in the section on alienated labor in his *Early Manuscripts:*

    (1)   Alienation of the products of labor;
    (2)   Alienation of the labor process or the process of production;
    (3)   Alienation of man's essence or of man from himself; and
    (4)   Alienation of man from his fellow men or the species.[46]

Marx also adds a fifth category, which Petrović does not list specifically:

    (5)   Alienation of nature from man.[47]

Marx conceived of the phenomenon of the alienation of labor in terms which simultaneously cover all its ramifications under the five aspects mentioned above. This fact alone lends Marx's concept of alienated labor not only its controversial character but reflects also its extreme complexity. The concept of alienated labor is, furthermore, one of the major concepts in Marx's philosophical-sociological system that remains unresolved. The Yugoslavs are quick to point out the necessity for answering Marx's own unanswered question on alienated labor formulated at the abrupt ending of his *First Manuscript,* indicating only a general direction for its resolution.[48] Marx wrote that:

> We have taken as a fact and analyzed the *alienation* of *labour.* How does it happen, we may ask, that *man alienates his labour*? How is this alienation founded in the nature of human development? We have already done much to solve the problem in so far as we have *transformed* the question concerning the *origin of private property* into a question about the relation between *alienated labour* and the process of development of mankind. For in speaking of private property one believes oneself to be dealing with something external to mankind. But in speaking of labour one deals directly with mankind itself. This new formulation of the problem already contains its solution.[49]

Marx presumed that the object of labor was the realization or objectification of the species life or species being of man, that is, man as a *generic* or social being. Alienated labor, on the other hand, was an activity that frustrated man's creative potential to achieve this species life, which Marx also equated with "productive life" or "life producing life."[50] In his view, class society was dominated by capital or "dead labor" ruling over the workers' live labor. This domination of capital over live labor resulted in the appropriation by capital of the *surplus value* created by live labor (based on the labor theory of value of Adam Smith, David Ricardo and other classical economists adopted by Marx and his followers). The appropriation of the surplus value of labor meant the alienation of the products of labor from their creator, the worker, and amounted to his *exploitation* (another category that became sacrosanct and untouchable in the Marxist metaphysic).

The Yugoslavs hence insist that the abolition of *wage-labor* represents "the fundamental aim of a proletarian revolution."[51] They regard the wage-labor relationship of capitalist society as an alienated, dehumanized, and reified framework within which the workers' products are constantly alienated. Wage-labor itself is considered as an expression of the alienation of the labor process, since the end of the process of production is mediated by a commodity—money—which acquires a value and an existence of its own, independent of true human needs. It is this medium of money which, according to Marx, acts as a transformer of all values into their opposites. Through the mediation of money, genuine human relationships degenerate into artificial, alienated commercial relationships defining "bourgeois" society. This degeneration of human relationships into mediated, commodity relations constitutes the alienation of man from his fellow men, since he no longer regards man as an end in himself but merely as a means toward the realization of other, mediated ends. But the alienation of man's sociability also reflects his *self-alienation* (alienation from his true self or essence) since the essence or nature of man is that of a *social* being. According to Vranicki, contemporary bourgeois society—in spite of its considerable technical and economic achievements—remains a society dominated by the wage-labor relationship and commodity production in which man is inescapably reified and alienated.[52]

The exploitation of labor by the capitalist was, however, only one horn of the dilemma of alienation as Marx saw it. The other source of the alienation of labor was to be sought in the very *division of labor* and specialization. The Yugoslavs have rediscovered this aspect, and contend that the major aim of socialism is to overcome the inhumanity of the division of labor (manual versus mental) and the mechanization and fragmentation of man by transforming the worker into a man whose essence is totality or wholeness.[53] This is imperative since, according to Milić, modern industrial society alienates and mutilates man by remolding him into a mere function.[54]

It is significant that the Yugoslav interpretation of the concept of alienated labor turns at this point into a contemporary psychology and sociology of work, and a very critical one at that. Yugoslav philosophers and sociologists are contributing much to our understanding of the effects on man of mechanization, automation, specialization, and the increasing fragmentation of tasks and functions characteristic of labor in modern industrial production. Supek, for instance, covers such issues as the bureaucratic-statist conception of man, the humanization of work as the immediate task of the socialist revolution, the effects of the division of labor, and ways to eliminate the consequences of monotonous and partialized work. He examines also the trend toward less professional education, the significance of professional awareness at the level of the work force, the role of workers' councils, the compounding of all problems connected with the humanization of work due to increasing automation, the dangers of bureaucratic omnipotence, and the need for humanizing both production and consumption.[55] What modern man needs, asserts Supek, is no less than the humanization of industrial work and its concomitant re-evaluation in intellectual, moral, and socio-cultural terms. The contemporary division of labor in modern industrial society—epitomized by the assembly line— goes against the very grain or nature of man and results in his de-spiritualization or psychic numbness. Man, the integral or whole human being, is reduced by the industrial mode of production to a mere partial being, a worker. In Marx's words:

> Production does not only produce man as a *commodity*, the *human commodity*, man in the form of a *commodity*; in conformity with this situation it produces him as a *mentally* and *physically* dehu-manized being . . . .[56]

The Yugoslavs have come to recognize that the problems of modern industrial production caused by the extreme division of labor, specialization, automation, and mechanization, and the resulting dehumanization of man and his alienation exist equally in socialism as well as in capitalism.[57] Hence, for them, the *humanization of work* emerges as the foremost task for the socialist revolution. This returning of human significance to production can be achieved, argues Supek, by creating new objective or physical, and more importantly, also subjective conditions for work as a framework for more humane social relations informed by enlightened socialist consciousness.[58] The failure to humanize work and achieve more humane social relations leads inevitably to the alienation of man from himself (his essence) as well as from his fellow men. The consequent alienation of labor in its various forms of exploitation, division, specialization, automation, mechanization, and fragmentation feeds into the complex of the alienated man—*homo duplex*—divided against himself, society, and nature.

3.3 Homo Duplex

Marx's sociological theory of alienation finds its most critical expression in the end product of the various forms of alienation—the phenomenon known as *homo duplex*, that is, man divided into various parts, roles or spheres: man as a selfish private individual, a virtuous citizen, an exploited wage-earner (or an equally alienated exploiter), a sometime father, husband, lover, and so on. In sum total, *homo duplex* is the quintessence of an impoverished and alienated being squatting outside both himself (his essence) and the world, to use Marx's vivid metaphor. Vranicki contends that *homo duplex* is the end result of the reification of man in the bourgeois framework of the wage-labor relationship and commodity production, whose manifestations can also be found in politics, the state, religion, the market, money, and mass culture. However, while socialism has—presumably—eliminated the wage-labor relationship, it has nevertheless retained the system of commodity production, which also leads to alienation. Hence, Vranicki terms the problem of alienation due to continuing commodity relations the central problem of socialism.[59]

In spite of Vranicki's insight, most Yugoslav theorists continue to hold the more orthodox view that it is basically modern industry in capitalist or bureaucratic (state capitalist) societies which is responsible for splitting man into a moral public person and a selfish private individual. This splitting of the integral human personality into conflicting spheres is perceived as the basic alienation and dehumanization of man in *class* society.[60] Supek traces the roots of this division—true to a long-established metaphysic—to the break-up of the primitive community due to the division of labor, barter, and the creation of private property and social classes, which represent at the same time the alienation of man as a social being and his separation, suppression, and isolation. Supek thus revives Rousseau's and Engels' notions of the disintegration of the human community and the concomitant alienation of human sociability which run parallel to technological and economic development.[61] All the different forms of alienation—economic, social, political, cultural, spiritual—converge in the quintessential form of *human* alienation, a state in which man is split into a duality and his relationships with other men are transformed into mediated, reified commodity relations. Viewed in this perspective, concludes Danko Grlić, Marx's critique of bourgeois political economy emerges as essentially a critique of inhuman relationships prevailing in class society.[62]

But a critique of social relations, according to Marx's Theses on Feuerbach, brings us back to the phenomenon of *man.* The Yugoslavs defined man as a being of *praxis,* an integral, total or whole human being who cannot be split up into separate parts, spheres or roles. The fact remains, however, that man has never attained yet to his full potentiality of *homo integralis*—the total, whole, or integral man. Petrović attempts to resolve this paradox when he notes that Marx, unlike Engels, thought that man had thus far always been alienated, but that he need not remain in that condition.[63] The key to man's liberation and reintegration as a total, self-actualized, being has to be sought in man's *generic* being—or essence—which is that of a *social* being.

The Yugoslav avant-garde maintains that, according to Marx, the essence of man as a social being is *labor* in the form of free creative activity or *praxis* and—since labor takes place within a social context—the nature of social relationships. The *humanization of social relations* and the cosmology of problems that it entails is thus seen as the key to the simultaneous de-alienation and liberation of man and society. It would herald the return of man from alienated conditions of power politics, the state, bureaucracy, exploitation, division of labor, false consciousness, pretended morality, artificial family, and physical, moral and spiritual poverty to himself as a free, creative, and self-creative being of *praxis.* In order to achieve this historical *novum*, what is needed, according to the avant-garde, is not simply a political, economic, moral or social revolution but rather "a total humanist revolution."[64] A total humanist revolution is considered necessary since alienation is not restricted to any particular sphere of human activity. Rather, the fundamental form of human self-alienation, according to Petrović, has to be sought in that special "sphere" constituting the relationship between the various spheres into which human activity is split up.[65] Curiously, and unsuspected by the avant-garde, Stalin's angel of medieval theology smiled again.[66]

4. De-Alienation as the Outgrowing of Commodity Relations

Avant-garde Yugoslav Marxist philosophers and sociologists have attempted to answer the second question on the nature of alienated labor asked by Marx at the end of his *First Manuscript*. The upshot of their efforts is a rather unique reconstruction of the ultimate goal of socialism and communism as the outgrowing, supersession, or transcendence of reified market relations and dehumanizing commodity production, which itself is highly problematic.

One of the cardinal findings of the avant-garde in terms of Marxist studies as well as socio-economic and political theory may well be their reassessment of the nature of alienated labor and private property. Probing into pre-categorical meanings of Marx's concept of alienated labor, the Yugoslavs discovered that he considered private property as the consequence or *effect* of alienated labor and not its cause! Marković contends that the basic question for Marx was that of the *"nature of labour"* rather than the question of private property. He points out that, contrary to those Marxists who claim that exploitation is a phenomenon restricted to capitalism, exploitation can also take place under socialism by *"collective capitalists and collective exploiters"* as well as the *bureaucracy,* which retains decision-making monopoly in a statist system.[67]

Furthermore, Stojanović and Marković note that both *self-governing groups* and the *workers* themselves can function as exploiters! These are rather novel ideas in Marxist-Leninist theory. Indeed, they are likely to revolutionize both Marxist theory and socialist practice. According to Stojanović:

> In Yugoslavia alienation in socialism is treated exclusively as a consequence of statism. Yet alienation can appear in self-government as well, not only because of the activity of oligarchic groups, but also because of the behavior of *entire self-governing groups* toward society. Alienation of the means and products of labor from society can be accomplished by individual self-governing groups as well.[68]

But how is it possible that workers can function as exploiters in a socialist society? Marković's answer to this question is intriguing:

> Under the conditions of commodity production, self-management does not yet have *universal* human character. While producing for the market, competing, and trying to maximize their income, workers necessarily come into conflict with other workers and sometimes even assume the role of exploiters.[69]

Private ownership of the means of production constitutes, therefore, only *one* of the possible forms of exploitation and alienation. The essence of exploitation, according to Marković, must be sought in the rule of accumulated, objectified, or dead labor (capital) over living labor and its appropriation of the surplus value created by live work.[70] Krešić states the point graphically:

> The worker in the state factory, just as his comrade in the private capitalist-owned factory, feels the *alien* force of capital opposing him, irrespective of the differentiation between the state employer

and the private capitalist, and regardless of the colour of the state flag.[71]

Nicholas Lobkowicz has pointed out that the notion of private property as a consequence or effect of alienated labor robs the concept of alienation of its original realistic connotation. It reduces alienation to "merely a *psychological* fact which would seem to be socially relevant in a very remote way, namely, the worker's uneasiness about and dissatisfaction with his labor."[72] Yet, the avant-garde maintains that Marx never reduced the problem of de-alienation and liberation of man to that of the abolition of private property.[73] Marx himself termed the mere abolition of private property as "crude communism" and the social form of simplicity and poverty corresponding to it as an "unnatural" state in which man has "not only not surpassed private property but has not yet even attained to it," and in which man's reduction to the role of worker would be extended to all men (and women?) instead of abolished.[74]

The basic question remains, then, that of the *nature* of labor and its de-alienation and humanization and the consequent reintegration of the whole man into a free community (*Gemeinschaft*) of free men. Since the alienation of labor and the fetishism of commodities (production for production's sake, and the like) are characteristic of every system of commodity production, not just of capitalism, Marković advances the thesis that the "gradual supersession of reified market relations" should be the central task of socialism.[75] The outgrowing of commodity relations can be achieved, according to the avant-garde, by orienting production to human needs rather than for profit, and by self-management of associated producers in the economy and self-government in politics. The dove-tailing of the Marxist solution of alienation into two spheres—self-management in the economy and self-government in politics—may, however, rekindle the very *dualism* of an alienated world which it aims to transcend! Furthermore, the dilemma confronting socialist theory and practice in Yugoslavia, apart from the question of profitability and its relationship to truly "human" needs and the feasibility of direct mass participation in self-government, concerns the role of the party, the bureaucracy, and the state which constitute embarrassing concentrations of alienated political, economic, and socio-cultural power in the country. The avant-garde is aware of this dilemma. According to Božidar Jakšić:

> ... the domination of political centers of power projects itself in the absolute ideological and political monopoly of the Party apparatus.... [76]

It has led Stojanović, among others, to note a curious dualism:

> Even a superficial glance at the real centers of social power in our country can show that a "self-governing, self-managing *society*" exists only in ideology, while a vivid dualism exists in practice— self-managing *groups* in the base and a rather strong statist structure above them.[77]

This kind of socio-economic and political configuration naturally gives rise to new forms of conflicts and *alienation in socialism*. The avant-garde's major contribution and the *casus belli* for their suppression was the attempt on their part to deal with these problems in good faith, but at times independently of both the party and the Marxist-Leninist ideology as defined by the party. Paradoxically, Marxist theoreticians, including the avant-garde, continue to expect socialist *politics* to de-alienate politics, Yugoslav constitutional *law* to transcend bourgeois law, the new communities of *interest* to vindicate the public interest, the party of *professional* revolutionaries to deprofessionalize itself and, together with the *state*, lose its independent governing function over society and gradually "wither away!" *Quo vadis*—to Camelot? The rationale for this Marxist categorical imperative in the great utopian tradition is summed up by Zagorka Pešić-Golubović, the lone woman member of the ousted "Belgrade Eight":

> The state *cannot replace the revolutionary movement of workers.*
> Thus Marxist analysis unmasks the role of the state and defines it
> for what it is in its essence: as an instrument of class struggle in
> the hands of the ruling class that preserves its own interests. The
> state becomes this even in socialism if it grows into *a force above*
> *the revolutionary working class.*[78]

As to the central task of socialism—that of outgrowing reified commodity
relations—the avant-garde realizes that this is easier said than done. The
fundamental dispute in contemporary Yugoslavia, according to Marković, centers
namely on the very question of how to reconcile the exigencies of increasing living
standards via greater commodity production with the ideal of creating new, more
humane ("socialist") social relations or, in a nutshell, economic rationality with
socialist humanism.[79] Here, too, the socialist dilemma is exacerbated by the
imperatives of the Marxian dialectic regarding commodity production as summed
up by Stojanović:

> . . . in order for social products to lose their character as
> commodities, it is necessary, according to Marx, that they
> exist in abundance.[80]

Surely, there are at least two alternative valuations of this projected state of
abundance. Would the superabundance of commodities not make them relatively
valueless, and since man, according to Marx, is a material being, would this not
also amount to a devaluation of man? Alternatively, could the superabundance of
commodities and their production and consumption come to dominate all other
aspects of human life to such an extent that man would again be reduced to the
lowest common denominator of Rousseau's "assembly of artificial men and fictitious passions?"

These philosophical, political, socio-cultural, and economic dilemmas are
illustrative of the critical juncture at which both the Yugoslav avant-garde and the
party have reopened the basic question of the unity of theory and practice in
socialism, which Marx thought to have solved once and for all. The problem stated
in its most basic form concerns the disparity and conflict between the efficiency of
means and the rationality and humanity of goals or, as we stated at the outset—the
disjunction between existence and essence, is and ought, fact and value. Is it
possible that the avant-garde did not tie a Gordian knot into the heart of Marxism
after all? Has it merely rediscovered late in the twentieth century the sheltered
existence of a vital paradox in the lengthening shadows of an outlived ideology?

5. The Hamlet Theme

Marx's concept of alienation may well represent an attempt on the part of
Marx, the intellectual, to socialize his own self-alienation, as Robert Tucker
argues.[81] At the same time, the concept of alienation goes further than either the
concepts of the socialization of the individual or that of the individualization of
society would indicate. It reflects a much more fundamental dilemma confronting
human existence, namely the dichotomy between reality and man's aspirations. As
such, the concept of alienation merges into the concepts of man's potential for
self-development, growth, and the improvement of debasing conditions in the real
world, material as well as human and spiritual.

Avant-garde Yugoslav Marxist philosophers are groping their way to the
realization that there may not be a final reconciliation between these two worlds,
the world as it is and the world as it could or should be and that, furthermore, the
consummation of a definite union between the two may not even be desirable. As
Stojanović implies, Marx's conception of a complete and definite de-alienation in

the communist future is today no longer tenable. What is more, *all* systems, whether socialist, capitalist or Stalinist, are confronted in the contemporary world with the phenomenon of *super-alienation:*

> . . . today the greatest and most important form of alienation is encountered not in the production of means to life, but rather of means to death. We are all witness to superalienation: human creations are now revolving around the earth, threatening not only individuals or classes, but humanity as a whole. The apocalyptic "revolt of things" against their creator—the anthropological form of the Last Judgment—is in sight. A cynic might say that the definitive disappearance of alienation may coincide with its irreversible triumph.[82]

The Yugoslav avant-garde has begun to outgrow some of Marx's ideological blinders in their consideration of the phenomenon of alienation in the modern world. Marx's concepts of alienation and exploitation as exclusive products of *class* society and the *capitalist* mode of production are brought into question by alienation in socialism as well as the modern phenomena of science, technology, superorganization, bureaucracy, and commodity production epitomized by the assembly line. The Yugoslavs are beginning to discover that alienation and exploitation of man due to capitalism may be dwarfed by the alienation and exploitation which modern technology, automation, the industrial mode of production, specialization, rationalization, organization, and bureaucracy exact from him equally in socialism as in capitalism and state capitalism.

Grlić and Abdulah Šarčević point out that modern technology tends to become the master of man, exploiting man and turning him into an appendage to the machine, dehumanizing him as well as his world.[83] The ubiquitous fact remains, muses Jure Kaštelan, a noted Yugoslav poet-philosopher, that a new reality—a world of machines—has grown up separating man from nature.[84] It would seem that this new reality, a world of gadgetry, has as little to do with capitalism as with socialism or state capitalism as its immediate cause. The avant-garde is well aware that even socialism and communism tend to degenerate from the ideal of the creation of a new *human* community into the secular quest for a simply *affluent* society.

Surprisingly, some Yugoslav Marxist philosophers are slowly beginning to question even Marx's view of society as the only source of man's alienation and unhappiness known as the *institutionalist fallacy*—the view that if only social institutions were set right, man would be liberated. Thus, Petrović wonders whether the Frankfurt School's critical theory of society is really capable of assessing the phenomenon of *human* self-alienation and offering ways of transcending it. According to Petrović, the revolution does not concern only social conditions but also the very nature of man. He asks:

> But what if the "social order" is not quite so external to man? And what if the revolutionary abolition of alienation means also a change in the essence of man?[85]

Petrović concludes that for a genuine de-alienation it is necessary to change both external conditions and the "inner" man.[86] This is a rather novel conceptualization of the imperatives of the socialist revolution. In the orthodox Marxist view, the revolutionaries had simply to change the underlying material conditions in order to de-alienate man. The Yugoslav avant-garde, on the other hand, poses a new imperative for Marxist theory and socialist practice: the change in man's essence is a precondition for social change and vice versa.

Even more disturbing within this context is Milić's penetrating afterthought which remains unanswered:

> Finally, are all the roots of human alienation in society? Or, are

some of them perhaps immanent in the basic anthropological structure of man, that being who is capable of forming a conception of infinity and who, precisely because of that, is conscious of his inescapable death and of the limitations on his personal aspirations?[87]

Bonjour, tristesse. On closer scrutiny, the avant-garde discovered that man is not only mortal, but that he is considerably more complex than Marx's overoptimistic evaluation of human nature and its essential goodness would admit. Thus, Marković notes,

> . . . there are in man internal contradictions between positive and negative, good and evil, rational and irrational, desire for freedom and reluctance to assume responsibility, creative and destructive, social and egoistic, peaceful and aggressive.[88]

This leads Stojanović to conclude that:

> *The contradiction between essence (in Marx's sense) and existence belongs to the essence of man.*[89]

At this point, the Yugoslav avant-garde seems to have left both Marx and his intellectual heritage far behind, but not the spirit of the dialectic, according to which the realization of the Marxist program of a more humane future can only be achieved by transcending or superseding Marxism itself.

But it is Milić who best sums up the basic universal truth contained in the esoteric concept of alienation and illuminates its true nature. The concept of alienation emerges as a reflection of man's ambitions, aspirations, goals, ends, and values frustrated by the most varied limitations of everyday life, or, in Husserl's phenomenological terms—the *Lebenswelt*. The concept of alienation thus constitutes nothing less than the *theme of Hamlet*—of man's awareness of his conflict-ridden existence—and testifies to the limitations but also to the grandeur of that being of animal drives and angelic aspirations.

Further, the concept of alienation reflects a double mystery. It appears simultaneously both Sphinx-like and inexhaustible, linked via an asymptotic relationship to infinity and eternity. In sum: a quintessential paradox. The most exhaustive media for its expression and comprehension, surpassing even political theory, philosophy, and the social sciences, may be the more esoteric genres of human creation such as art, literature, sculpture, poetry, and music.[90]

But what about a potential resolution of the paradox of alienation on the individual and societal levels? Did Rousseau perchance create, along with his ideal construct of the noble savage and the societal genesis of the original sin—human corruption—also a new mythology which found itself alienated and metamorphosed into the Hegelian and Marxist systems? Was the Hegelian legacy in some way merely an adumbration and a more consummate restatement of the Rousseauan metaphysic, scientized by the dialectic, and further entrapping Marx and his followers? Does the Rousseauan-Hegelian-Marxian chain on alienation constitute the original *theoretical* flaw which inexorably leads to socialist malpractice, especially in its obtuseness toward the living human individual, warts and all, in the name of higher, yet abstract and perhaps unrealizeable ideals, such as the classless, conflict-less, non-alienated, non-exploitative communist society brimming with brotherhood, equality, and absolute freedom? In brief, is Marx's utopia the ultimate source of socialist distopia?

There is an important consensus among Western thinkers concerning the neo-Platonic and Rousseauan roots of Marx's utopian dream of perfect harmony and unity of civil and political society. This consensus points out that Marx's *theoretical* utopia leads to its direct opposite—distopia, dictatorship, and totalitarianism—in everyday *practice*. In Leszek Kolakowski's reassessment of the socialist idea:

The dream of perfect unity may come true only in the form of a caricature which denies its original intention: as an artificial unity imposed by coercion from above, in that the political body prevents real conflicts and real segmentation of the civil society from expressing themselves.[91]

If this is true, whence the appeal of the neo-Platonic, Rousseauan, and Hegelian roots of Marx's distopia? Karl R. Popper and Friedrich A. Hayek, among others, see the appeal of these intellectual precursors of Marx in the nostalgia for a closed, tribal society based on natural emotions and the immediacy of a closely-knit primitive community.[92]   This pristine original community, or primitive communism, underlies socialism's continuing appeal, East and West. What is still poorly understood is that the attempt to create this utopia must perforce end with forced labor camps and prisons of Hitler's or Stalin's Gulags.   But what has philosophy to do with concentration camps? Apparently, more than we realize. According to André Glucksmann, the *enfant terrible* of the May 1968 French student demonstrations and the exponent of "La nouvelle philosophie," such philosophers as Fichte, Hegel, Marx, and Nietzsche systematized earlier currents of thought, combining the monopoly of force with the monopoly of knowledge, which leads with an iron logic to the totalitarian state.[93]

The Yugoslav avant-garde (and not only the Yugoslavs) is still blissfully unaware of the fateful links forged among such thinkers as Plato, Machiavelli, Hobbes, Rousseau, Fichte, Hegel, Nietzsche, Freud, and Marx, on the one hand, and Marx, Engels, Lenin, and Stalin, on the other. In fact, most Yugoslav theorists sever the totalitarian link between Stalin and Lenin, and they simply dismiss any possible relationship between authentic Marxism and Stalinism. Even Marković is willing to admit only that the Stalinist conception of the party's socio-political monopoly has its basis in Lenin but not in Marx.[94]

It is therefore all the more surprising that some avant-garde theorists have rediscovered Hegel as an arch-Stalinist!   Thus, Dragoljub Mićunović criticizes Saint-Simon and Comte as advocates of systems, organizations, and the technocratic transformation of society. But he reserves special ire for Hegel as "the first to provide a philosophical justification for bureaucracy as a universal estate." Krešić takes this idea a step further in his analysis of absolute political dictatorship as the "total politicization of the spirit." He concludes that: ". . . Stalinism represented a faithful *realization* of Hegelian idealism, particularly concerning Hegel's philosophy of the state."[95]

We may have to begin to ask some disturbing, if not metaphysical, questions which would both exhaust and transcend the Marxist metaphysic, although not be limited to it. Do the phenomena associated with the concept of alienation belong to that rhapsodic realm which some have dubbed the"heart of darkness?" And if so, whose heart? Solzhenitsyn, one of the few who came back from that heart of darkness, hailing from the first circle, reminds us that:

If only there were evil people [or *classes*?—O.G.] somewhere insidiously committing evil deeds, and it were necessary only to separate them from the rest of us and destroy them. But the line dividing good and evil cuts through the heart of every human being. And who is willing to destroy a piece of his own heart?[96]

The heart that throbs in alienation may be the very heart of man in its flight of creativity, imagination, and phantasy, wedded to man's essential will to live. But, if that is true, then the resolution of the paradox of alienation may have to be sought along altogether different, post-Rousseauan, post-Hegelian, and post-Marxist, lines.   In this crucial twentieth century enterprise, it would seem imperative that Hegel's notion that the owl of Minerva flies only at dusk be metamorphosed and transcended in an integral sense by the humanist and phenomenological aspiration: that the dove of spirituality, love, and peace begins its journey at dawn.

5.1   A Rumor of Angels

It has been noted that Marx's concept of alienation appears to be religious in nature. This is the more baffling since Marxism-Leninism subscribes to a view of "scientific" atheism. Yet, Thomas J. Blakeley finds a curious affinity between medieval Scholasticism and contemporary Marxist-Leninist philosophy, particularly in the Soviet case. Both schools of thought strive toward a system of belief, a total *Weltanschauung.* The major difference between them is that contemporary Soviet philosophy fails to even pose the question of the relationship between faith and knowledge.[97] It would seem that Marxism-Leninism has translated philosophy into faith, or, more precisely, into a secular religion akin to Eric Voegelin's conception of modern Gnosticism. The major aim of Gnosticism, or civil theology, according to Voegelin, is the "immanentization" of everyday experience, the divinization of man, and reduction of the Absolute and its incorporation into man.[98] In Marxism-Leninism, it is the liberation of the proletariat via the socialist revolution which becomes the new Absolute. The Marxist view of the divinity of man finds its most consummate expression in the Promethean conception of man who, according to Joseph M. Bochenski, stands alone in a hostile world without God, summoned to the heroic task of an "eternal revolution," remaking both himself, society, and the universe.[99]

It is precisely this Promethean conception of man which is elaborated most consistently in the writings of the Yugoslav avant-garde. It can be summed up in Vojan Rus' words that man is the only being who, to our knowledge, is capable of living in the way of Prometheus. According to Rus, it is man's ability to conceptualize and become aware of his future which enables him to confront the aimless flow of this future and to fashion the world in his image.[100] Yugoslav Marxist humanist thought has thus developed a new focal point for Marxist theory and socialist practice: Protagoras' man as the measure of all things. From a totalitarian denial of man in orthodox Marxism to a romantic—if not narcissistic —preoccupation with the human individual in Marxist humanism is a long way indeed. Yet, there is trouble in paradise. Romanticism may invite despair.

The point is that the avant-garde discovered not a perfect and essentially good being—an angel—but rather a very imperfect and fallible man. Marković and Stojanović note that *evil* can no longer be excluded from a Marxist conception of *human essence* and *human nature.*[101] In fact, Supek writes that:

> With his first step into history, man appears as a contradictory, divided and unhappy being.[102]

Can this be considered a sort of *felix culpa,* a glorious sin, to be redeemed, as Lobkowicz and others intimate? Not quite. This becomes clear from Petrović's view, which is even more disconsoling, since he believes that self-alienation may exist in a classless society as well! More important, he sees no easy way out of the theoretical circle in which de-alienated social relations are a precondition for individual liberation, whereas free human personalities are a precondition for social liberation. The only way out of this dilemma, maintains Petrović, is by way of revolutionary *praxis* through which man changes both social relations and his own nature.[103] That is—back to Prometheus.

Marx W. Wartofsky, among others, has expressed uneasiness with the direction of Yugoslav avant-garde, especially Petrović's Platonistic or Heideggerian Marxism, and its "existentialist characterization of man as essentially alienated, or divided being."[104] It is, indeed, enigmatic that the Yugoslav conception of man as a being of *praxis,* cast in the image of Prometheus, turns out to be that of a mortal god. Avant-garde thought appears to be suspended between a utopian and a positivistic conception of the human potential. There can be no final resolution to the human dilemma, no final abolition of human alienation, imperfections, weaknesses, or woes. In Rus' words:

Man shall never be able to escape from the dialectic of lasting contradictions within himself and the world.[105]

Is Yugoslav Marxist humanism a Heideggerian Marxism, then? Whereas Heidegger appeared content with the contemplation of the secret of man's Being-towards-death, the Yugoslav avant-garde rebels against Heideggerian nihilism and passivity. At this point, some students of the late Heidegger might contend that *Sein-zum-Tode* is characteristic of Dasein, and not of "man." But this view does not stand up under closer scrutiny. While Heidegger distanced his exploration of the meaning of Being from anthropology, psychology, and biology early in his work, *Sein und Zeit*, he defined Dasein as "an entity which is in each case I myself; its Being is in each case mine." Heidegger then went on to question his own definition as well as to extend it to include Others in the "who" of Dasein. Speaking about "Being-towards-death and the everydayness of Dasein," Heidegger even accused Dasein of covering up the fact of one's Being-towards-death. It also becomes clear that Dasein, Being-towards-death, and dying all purport, in the final analysis, to the individual "I," or man, even if Heidegger himself eschewed the latter term. But there is no ambiguity in his contention that: "Dying, which is essentially mine in such a way that no one can be my representative, is perverted into an event of public occurrence which the 'they' encounters." And Heidegger concludes:

> Factically one's own Dasein is always dying already; that is to say, it is in a Being-towards-its-end. An it hides this Fact from itself by recoining "death" as just a "case of death" in Others—an everyday occurrence which, if need be, gives us the assurance still more plainly that "oneself" is still "living."[106]

There is a consensus among avant-garde thinkers that man's essential Being is not to be found in a passive contemplation and waiting for the dark night of death and Nothingness, but in action, in an active transformation and constant revolutionizing of existing social conditions, including man himself. As Petrović meditates:

> Man is man not when he passively and patiently awaits the inescapable burden that time brings us, but when he acts and fights to realize his real human individual and social Being.[107]

But what about the Heideggerian preoccupation with death? Does not the logic of avant-garde thought lead to the question of the universal leveller? According to some, death has no sting. Significantly, death is considered by some, if not most of the avant-garde, as having no theoretical or practical relevance. According to Milan Kangrga, death, far from establishing the meaninglessness of life, is an impetus for action. And, he wonders, how can people possibly fear death as a crossing into Nothingness and not be afraid of the "Nothingness" of everyday life which unfolds continually before us?[108]

Avant-garde thought thus finds itself in a curious existential impasse. On the one hand, it continues the Gnostic immanentization of everyday experience and the reduction of God to man in the image of Prometheus. On the other hand, it has declared the finiteness and mortality of man. Quite an unenviable position. For, while orthodox Marxists vacated the throne of God long ago and replaced Him by the proletarian revolution, the avant-garde seems to be genuinely atheistic. How does one live without God? What can possibly give meaning to the perennial struggle of a being, which while Promethean, is condemned to die? These are some of the unusual questions which were explored in a no less unusual three-hour debate between Branko Bošnjak, a Marxist philosopher, and Mijo Škvorc, a Jesuit theologian and philosopher, in an Open Forum at Zagreb University's Student Center on March 28, 1967, before a packed audience. The dialogue was based on a critique of Bošnjak's book, *Philosophy and Christianity.*

Bošnjak concluded in his book that there was no final purpose or reason for man's existence as a cosmic phenomenon in the sense of man as a totality or Being.

It is the only logically consistent position for an atheist. Man exists in spite of, and in the face of, his finitude and Nothingness. For a Marxist, there can be no escape into religion since Marxist humanism "excludes every religion" because it is allegedly a "complete humanism."[109] But it was Škvorc, not Bošnjak, who took the offensive and whose questioning unfolded in full view Bošnjak's tragic stance. For, according to Škvorc, how can one possibly insist that life is worth living when "Being is condemned to Non-Being, life to destruction, work in its final consequence to meaninglessness, [and] our thoughts to emptiness . . .?[110]

Škvorc then went on to delineate a Christian view of man's being and essential nature which turns out to be surprisingly humanist. Apparently, the few remaining Yugoslav non-Marxist philosophers and theologians have also been strongly influenced by the prevailing humanist framework. In Škvorc's vision, man emerges as Pascal's irreplaceable human being, one which has full meaning and justification, a being which is not a "what" but a "who." Further, man's essential being is seen in the world of values, his capacity to love and be loved, his ability to wonder and to comprehend the world at all, as well as by his transcendence and faith in God who is the "fullness" of love. To convey some of the meaning of man's humanity, transcendence, and immortality, Škvorc quotes the following lines by the poet Dobrica Cesarić:

> U suton, kada prve zvijezde i kada prve lampe sinu,
> kad ljubavnik o dragoj sanja, a pijanica o svom vinu,
> ja tiho hodam pored kuća u kojima se svjetla pale.
> Sva zla i nevolje i sumnje na jednom budu posve male.
> I smiješim se u meki suton od zapaljenih zvijezda svecan
> i osjetim dubinu svega i da je život vječan, vječan.[111]

> In the twilight, when the first stars and first lamps light up,
> when the lover dreams of his loved one, and the drunk of his wine,
> I walk in silence past homes where lights are turned on.
> All evil, misfortune, and doubts grow suddenly altogether small.
> And I smile into the tender twilight festive with glowing starlight
> and sense the depth of all things and that life is everlasting,
>   everlasting.

Škvorc's gifted exposition of a Christian humanist perspective apparently left its imprint on Bošnjak. In a later dialogue between Marxists and Christians, Bošnjak was to discuss the question of death seriously. As related by J. Claude Evans, Bošnjak, quoting Bertrand Russell's "maybe" to the question of life after death, maintained that one must have an open attitude toward this question. It is one of the remarkable traits of the avant-garde. Bošnjak concluded that the essence of man was to be found outside of the dilemma of religion and atheism in man's capacity to wrestle with ultimate questions. In a world in which man is a mortal being, one would always find a relation between philosophy and religion focusing on the question of man's essence.[112]

It is as if from afar Yugoslav Marxist humanism were becoming conscious of a rumor of angels, of a subterranean and/or heavenly pulsating reality without words, concepts without images, esoteric territories and voyages of no return, of that realm where no man has set foot, and where, Solzhenitsyn would say, "only the soul gives a groan." Should one conclude that for avant-garde Yugoslav Marxist humanists not only God had failed but man as well? Is atheism really an alternative to religious faith? Roger Garaudy doubts that:

> The true alternative to a religion that is the opium of the people is not positivist atheism, because positivism is not only a world without God but a world without man.[113]

Could it be the world of the relentless class struggle, wars, revolutions, tyranny, idolatry, dogma, ecological imbalance, and interplanetary pollution? Could it be that time which the poet Hölderlin described as "meagre" or "inadequate" and which led T. S. Eliot to ask:

> What are the roots that clutch, what branches grow
> Out of this stony rubbish? Son of man,
> You cannot say, or guess, for you know only
> A heap of broken images, where the sun beats,
> And the dead tree gives no shelter, the cricket no relief,
> And the dry stone no sound of water. Only
> There is shadow under this red rock
> (Come in under the shadow of this red rock),
> And I will show you something different from either
> Your shadow at morning striding behind you
> Or your shadow at evening rising to meet you;
> I will show you fear in a handful of dust.[114]

The way out of this existential impasse may be through hope, faith, and love.

5.2   The Principle of Love

The Yugoslav avant-garde has developed an eminent philosophy of man and of action in the form of *praxis* as free, creative, and self-creative activity. Avant-garde thought thus approaches Hannah Arendt's conception of the centrality of the *vita activa* and of action in human affairs. It appears to share with her the conviction that "men, though they must die, are not born in order to die but in order to begin."[115] On the other hand, the avant-garde's conception of man in the image of Prometheus, the rebel or revolutionary, remains inherently tragic.

As Jack Jones writes, Marx transferred the hierophanic faith in human omnipotence to the idea of man and later to that of the worker and the proletariat, convinced that the revolution would overcome the repression of natural by cultural reality. Marx failed to realize that the phenomenon of culture is "inherently sacrificial."[116] In the case of Yugoslav avant-garde theorists, they have arrived at a curious juncture of tension and paradox between reality and utopia. On the one hand, the avant-garde looks at revolution as *"a radical transcendence of the essential internal limit of a certain social formation,"* to recall Marković's formulation.[117] On the other hand, Petrović claims that a de-alienated human personality is a precondition for society's de-alienation and liberation. This leads to the following quandary: How can the revolution possibly transcend the "essential internal limits of a social formation," when its individual members continue to exist as self-alienated? The non-utopian and tragic nature of the avant-garde's philosophy of man as *praxis* is highlighted by the fact that the Promethean activity of man comes to resemble that of Sisyphus, who must forever push his stone to the top of the mountain. In the end, this Sisyphus is metamorphosed into a mortal Hamlet who knows that he must die. But this is the ultimate in classical Greek tragedy. Nor is man's dreary striving lightened in avant-garde Marxist humanist thought by either humor, forgiveness, tolerance, ambiguity, or love.

That Marxism-Leninism lacks humor or the capacity of merriment and laughter may be compensated for by the rich traditions of native folklore and humor, at least in the Slavic orbit. But the reason for this lack of humor and the ability to laugh at oneself is apparently due to the fact that Marxist-Leninist thought takes itself too seriously. After all, it subscribes to the Enlightenment's optimistic faith in reason, progress, science, and the self-sufficiency of rational man. The Yugoslav avant-garde, while critical of positivism, seems to be continuing the Enlightenment tradition, unaware of the ambiguities inherent in both human knowledge and action. In order to retrieve humor, joy, and laughter, Marxism may have to discover the notion of *ambiguous* knowledge and action. It would have to admit that man is not only mortal and imperfect, but also less than omniscient and omnipotent. The Yugoslav avant-garde has yet to discover the full meaning of Heisenberg's principle of indeterminacy/uncertainty and of Einstein's theory of relativity for human affairs. According to Mark Reader and Donald J. Wolf:

> No matter how comprehensive or definite our science, religion, or philosophies—and no matter what their content—each must remain partially uncertain as long as it is made by, and attached to, people who can neither fully limit nor control (and consequently comprehend) the universe at large. This is so largely because the knowledge of anything is always dependent, either directly or indirectly, upon instruments that are attached to imperfect human beings.[118]

Heisenberg's principle of indeterminacy in quantum physics translated into human affairs leads to the *principle of tolerance* articulated so well by Jacob Bronowski:

> Every judgment in science stands on the edge of error, and is personal. Science is a tribute to what we can know although we are fallible.[119]

Apart from tolerance, the Yugoslav philosophy of man as a being of *praxis* is as unaware of the fact of the irreversibility of human action as of its ambiguous character. Yet, Arendt reminds us that it is only through the faculty of forgiving, a "constant release from what they do," that men can remain free agents. One can understand the avant-garde's emphasis on life as opposed to death which echoes Steinbeck's lines in *The Grapes of Wrath:* "They got to live before they can afford to die." But, it is Arendt, again, who points out that without forgiveness men remain chained to a recurring process of *re-acting* against an original trespass. This is certainly a curse and a kind of death, but it is more than that. It is the absence of a real freedom to act:

> The freedom contained in Jesus' teachings of forgiveness is the freedom from vengeance, which incloses both doer and sufferer in the relentless automatism of the action process, which by itself need never come to an end.[120]

The absence of such concepts as tolerance, forgiveness, humor, and the ambiguities of action point to a much more fundamental malaise, perhaps the basic *ontological-axiological flaw*, in the Marxist-Leninist *Weltanschauung*, even in its avant-garde formulation. This fundamental flaw is that Marxism-Leninism is a loveless universe. Not only is love absent, but its opposite—hate—is the cornerstone of its foundation. It is the relentless and eternal hate of everything and everybody who opposes or even doubts the march of history in the form of the proletarian revolution and its elusive goal of a classless society. But a world without love is also a world without man.

While Arendt advocates respect in lieu of love, Karl Menninger recommends personal responsibility and accountability for both ourselves and others.[121] But personal responsibility and accountability seem impossible without ethics, values, and a normative *ought*. The Yugoslav avant-garde, along with Marx, thus find themselves in what Lobkowicz would call "a hopeless dilemma":

> If ideals play no genuine role in history, it hardly is meaningful to speak of a revolutionary practice and, in fact, to be a revolutionary or even "progressive" at all. Practice in this case is as little "revolutionary" as biological evolution or the movement of stars. On the other hand, if there really exists a truly "revolutionary, critical-practical activity," as Marx suggests in the first of the "Theses on Feuerbach," then not only must it be possible to be guided by some ideals but moreover there must exist some norms,

an *ought* which transcends existing reality more radically than the "consciousness of existing *Praxis*" to which Marx in the *German Ideology* reduces all theoretical consciousness.[122]

It is this search for an *ought*, for values, and a genuine ethics, which represents a Kantian watershed for avant-garde Marxist humanist thought as explored in the previous chapter. But if the avant-garde ever consciously adopts and develops a genuine ethics, Kantian or otherwise, it will also affirm the *principle of love.* For, in the vast emptiness and desolation of space, to even speak about man is to affirm a value. Yet, it is difficult, if not impossible, to affirm man as a value if he is simply an irresponsible, purposeless, meaningless, querrulous, warlike, scurrilous, presumptuous, and death-bound speck of cosmic dust. As the great scientist Carl von Linné wrote: "I turned around me through nature, history and spirit, and I saw the trace that someone passed there. I said, God passed there."[123] If there is ultimate meaning to man, it must be metaphysical. Yet this is not the crucial difference between a Marxist and a Christian. This crucial difference centers, rather, in the notion of personal responsibility for one's actions, in forgiveness, and love. Lionel Trilling articulated this distinction between a communist and a Christian well:

> . . . You and I stand opposed. For you—no responsibility for the individual, but no forgiveness. For me—ultimate, absolute responsibility for the individual, but mercy. Absolute responsibility: it is the only way that men can keep their value, can be thought of as other than mere *things*.[124]

We saw that the avant-garde, in contrast to orthodox Marxism, considers man responsible for his actions. But if man is responsible, he is utterly alone. There remains only Milan Mirić's plaintive refrain:

> Man's true season can be measured only by decay. Only from this insight was it possible to conceptualize that the season and unseason of man's fate have no likelihood of being separated in that fate, nor can the cleared path be really reconciled in a happy synthesis, the appearance of a human permanence in which the season of unseason and the unseasonness of season were not a soundless countdown on the stopped watch of our separate destinies.[125]

In avant-garde thought, man appears at first as a radiant Prometheus in action. Yet, soon the night falls, the fog seeps in, and the "dust of death" settles on the mortal figure of Hamlet bound to the inescapable limits of that action.[126] But is not this conceptualization of death-bound man the expression of the most consummate, basic, and supreme form of human self-alienation? Finally, the avant-garde's Hamlet bears a heavy cross. While Paul's injunction to men was to "walk in love" in the spirit of Christ (Ephesians 5:2), the avant-garde's prescription for men is to "walk in anger." Always seeking, fighting, hating, never resting, and never coming home.

Defiance in the face of death may be heroic, but does it enhance life? This question leads us directly from the wuthering heights of the spirit down to an exploration of the economic sphere of man's material life which Marxists everywhere consider, proximately or ultimately, to be the fundamental source of man's self-alienation.

Chapter VI · Market Socialism: What Price Equality?

The worker emerges not only not richer, but emerges rather poorer from the process than he entered. For not only has he produced the conditions of necessary labour as conditions belonging to capital; but also the value-creating possibility, the realization [*Verwertung*] which lies as a possibility within him, now likewise exists as surplus value, surplus product, in a word as capital, as master over living labour capacity, as value endowed with its own might and will, confronting him in his abstract, objectless, purely subjective poverty.

Karl Marx, *Grundrisse* (1857-1858)

1. What is Market Socialism?

Paul A. Samuelson notes that in economics Marxism has too often tended to be "the opiate of the Marxists."[1] While Marxists themselves disagree on the precise meaning of such key concepts as the labor theory of value and surplus value, they all agree that it is all true. This led Samuelson to conclude that:

> Obscurity in a bible is no defect: as Oscar Wilde said, " . . . to be understood is to be found out."[2]

The rediscovery of the *Grundrisse* substantiates the view of the philosophical, psychological, and sociological nature of Marx's purportedly scientific economic theories. As David McLelland has pointed out, the *Grundrisse* are every bit as Hegelian as the *Economic and Philosophical Manuscripts* of 1844 and other works of the young Marx.[3] But the fact that Marx's economic theories should suddenly emerge as putatively metaphysical is, of course, not sufficient grounds to dismiss them as irrelevant or false. An examination of Marx's thinking on economics is called for even more in the light of the present renaissance of Marxist thought, East and West, which tends to ignore Marx's economics in favor of his psychology and sociology.[4]

It is, again, the Yugoslavs who, paradoxically, provide the most comprehensive re-assessment, questioning, and development of Marx's economic thought. Curiously, however, the roles of the party and the avant-garde Marxist philosophers and sociologists seem to be reversed in this important area of socialist theory and practice. It is the party which emerges as far more open-minded and innovative in the economic sphere than its Marxist humanist critics. This openness is not to be equated *prima facie* with the success of the party's thinking and practice, but rather with its radicality. What has emerged in Yugoslavia in the 1960s under the rubric of market socialism is bewildering to both supporters and critics of the Yugoslav road to socialism. Avant-garde theorists appear less sure of themselves in this area, although they continue to hold on to their vision of equality, self-management, and socialist solidarity as superior to what they perceive as the increasing inequality, social differentiation, embourgeoisement, the rise of a new middle class, and new ways of appropriating the surplus value and exploiting the worker, even without the existence of private property. The Yugoslav model of market socialism, combining elements of planning and the market mechanism, holds great fascination for economists, East and West, and not without good reason. For here is a historic attempt by a communist leadership to utilize, as the avant-garde would put it, capitalist means to achieve socialist/communist ends.

The sceptics are legion. But what is market socialism? In her assessment of the roles of planning and the market in Yugoslav economic thought, Deborah Milenkovitch distinguished five major periods: 1945-1949, 1949-1953, 1953-1961, 1961-1965, and 1965 on.[5] The first period, 1945-1949, as we had occasion to observe earlier, was the period of the command economy on the Soviet model. The subsequent periods were characterized by abandonment of collectivization and central planning in agriculture (1953), followed by the dismantling of central planning of production details (1950-1954), and of investment (1961, 1965 on). At the same time, the banking system became autonomous (1965). With the passage of the 1971 Constitutional Amendments, Yugoslavia entered a new phase of overall social guidance or "indicative" planning, linked with "self-management planning" via social compacts and self-management agreements.

But the party's decentralizing reforms caused serious economic difficulties in the early 1960s which seemed to combine the worst of both worlds—planning and market. This was due to the fact that, while introducing market elements into the economy, centralized administrative controls were retained and often strengthened. Dennison I. Rusinow described three clusters of factors responsible for the new economic problems: (1) economic; (2) social and political; and (3) technical. Among economic factors, Rusinow noted the following:

(a) Investment and saving remained under centralized administrative and political control;

(b) The tax system was taking from profitable producers and areas and giving to unprofitable ones—a positive disincentive to economic rationality; and

(c) Inflationary pressures—due to the investment system—forced the regime to continue price controls.[6]

Among social and political factors, he singled out technical incompetence, disinterest of the majority of workers in self-management, and retention of decision-making by managers and party bureaucrats, whereas the major technical problem remained "how to undo a command economy without chaos and breakdown."

Rusinow concluded that decentralization and profit orientation by themselves did not amount to a market economy, and that Yugoslavia's compromise economic model was "inherently unstable and eventually untenable."[7] He observed also that Yugoslavia's laissez-faire socialism, in leading to monopoly, maldistribution of income and other inequalities, would necessitate the same kind of government intervention to redress imbalances as in the capitalist West.

There is precious little advice in Marx's own writings on how to run a socialist economy. This is, indeed, one of the great dialectical contradictions in Marx's system of thought. Beyond the injunction to abolish private means of production and that the associated producers organize their exchange with nature on a rational or planned basis, Marx left future socialist societies bereft of any practical guidelines.[8] The Yugoslavs and others are attempting desperately to fill this gap. The central question in Yugoslavia and, increasingly, in other socialist systems is that of the right mixture of planning elements and the market mechanism in determining the answers to the three basic questions of economic organization of any society: (1) *What* is to be produced; (2) *How* are goods and services to be produced; and (3) *For whom*?

John E. Elliott reminds us that Marx had a centralized, authoritarian, hierarchical side as well as a decentralized, democratic, anarcho-syndicalist side, and that his vision of economic coordination implied a "blend of plan and market, or at least the provision of a *socialist equivalent* of market exchange."[9]   But this very issue of the correct blend of plan and market has bedevilled the Yugoslavs and others ever since.

1.1 The Reform of 1965

The Yugoslavs have since 1945 played both ends of the spectrum of plan and market. However, Joel Dirlam and James Plummer indicate that the economic reforms of 1965 represented "a kind of doctrinal watershed."[10]   The Yugoslavs themselves have come to refer to the cluster of economic and socio-political innovations of 1965 as simply the *Reform.* At least theoretically, the Yugoslav communist leadership opted in 1965 for expanding the role of the market. A brief summary of the major planks of the 1965 economic reforms reflects their unprecedented scope:

(1)   Abandonment of central planning of investment;

(2)   Elimination of taxes on enterprise profits;

(3)   Enterprises given complete control over the use of profits;

(4)   Enterprises permitted to lend money at interest;

(5)   Creation of profit-making banks paying dividends to share-holders;

(6)   Firms allowed to sell bonds to the public;

(7)   Expansion of private enterprise encouraged;

(8)   Various forms of nonlabor income sanctioned;

(9)   Foreign capital invited to share Yugoslav profits;

(10)   Toleration of an unemployment rate as high as 20 percent.[11]

As mentioned in Chapter III, the major aim of the economic reforms of 1965 was to achieve a more rational allocation and use of scarce resources, commonly known as *the* economic problem and definition of economics *par excellence.* The official view is that the economic reforms of the 1960s have worked, increasing economic efficiency and the general standard of living. This view is corroborated by such economic indicators as per capita income which rose to $1,000 in 1975 from $375 in 1955, increase in real income, consumer credit, and personal savings following the Reform (Table 2).

Critics of the Reform point, on the other hand, to the two most deleterious consequences of the new economic policies: unemployment and inflation (Tables 3, 4).

Indeed, avant-garde Marxist humanists and others find it difficult to square such facts as over half a million unemployed at home, one million working abroad, curtailment of free social services such as medical care, etc., and the continuing gap between developed and underdeveloped regions within Yugoslavia with socialist solidarity and equality. The regime justifies its policies of economic efficiency and distribution of material rewards according to work performed on the principle that equality in poverty consonant with wage-levelling (*uravnilovka*) is hardly any equality at all.

But the student demonstrations of 1968, 1970, and 1971, the Croatian crisis of 1971, and avant-garde criticism have contributed to a re-assessment of economic means and ends. Since 1971, there has been a renewed concern with the need for overall coordination of economic and financial activities, that is, with planning. The 1974 Constitution and the Tenth Party Congress laid down comprehensive new guidelines for planning and coordination ranging from the BOALs to the federation.

TABLE 2. Real Income, Consumer Credit and Personal Savings, 1952-1981

Index/Year	1952	1962	1965	1967	1968	1969	1970	1971	1972	1973	1974	1975	1976	1977	1978	1979	1980	June 1981
Index of Real Income* (1976=100)	33	48	63	76	79	84	90	95	95	92	97	97	100	102	108	108	100	93
Consumer Credit† (billions of dinars)	.05	1.8	3.8	2.5	4.2	4.8	6.8	6.9	6.2	8.0	12.3	18.5	31.9	39.7	49.6	55.4	54.9	51.8
Personal Savings† (billions of dinars)	.04	1.5	3.5	7.5	9.7	12.9	16.8	21.2	24.9	31.3	40.3	52.5	70.6	90.0	125.3	152.3	162.8	174.9

Sources: Savezni Zavod za Statistiku, Indeks, 30, 12 Dec. 1981, pp. 5, 43, 54; Statistički godišnjak Jugoslavije, 1981, pp. 83, 95, 96.

*1965 and 1978-81 figures are my re-computations with 1976=100; the Yugoslavs revise figures continuously, and change base years and other concepts frequently—in the December 1981 issue of Indeks, the base year is 1980=100.

† End of year.

TABLE 3. Unemployment, 1952-1981

(Yearly average, in thousands)

Index/Year	1952	1962	1965	1967	1968	1969	1970	1971	1972	1973	1974	1975	1976	1977	1978	1979	1980	Sept. 1981
Job-Seekers (Registered)	45	237	237	269	311	331	320	291	315	382	449	540	635	700	735	762	785	817
Unemployment Rate (In Percent)*	2.5	6.7	6.1	7.0	7.9	8.2	7.7	6.7	6.9	8.1	9.0	10.2	11.4	11.9	12.0	11.9	11.9	12.0

Employed in West Germany†	NA	24	64	98	100	226	389	469	472	466‡	473	419	390	377	370	367	357	NA
Worker Emigration (Net)	NA	14	140	296	401	572	783	923	1020	1100	1035	940	870	825	800	790	770	NA
Total Employment§ Socialized Sector	1734	3318	3662	3561	3587	3706	3850	4034	4210	4306	4514	4758	4925	5148	5383	5615	5798	6013
Employment in Private (Service) Sector	50	68	79	95	100	84	85	90	95	93	91	91	92	96	103	109	117	123

Yugoslavia's Total Population, Mid-1980: 22,344,000

Sources: *Statistički godišnjak Jugoslavije*, 1981, p. 81, and *Indeks*, 30, 12 Dec. 1981, pp. 4, 43, for job-seekers, total employment, employment in the private sector, and total population; *OECD Economic Survey of Yugoslavia, 1981*, p. 55, for Yugoslav worker emigration (net), 1968-80; earlier figures in the *1978 Survey*, p. 59; Bundesanstalt für Arbeit (Nürnberg), "Amtliche Nachrichten der Bundesanstalt für Arbeit," various issues through No. 4, April 1981, p. 535, for Yugoslav workers employed in West Germany.

Note: NA = Not Available.

* Job-Seekers (Registered) as % of Total Domestic Labor Force Outside Private Agriculture (Total Employment in Socialized Sector + Registered Job-Seekers); excludes Yugoslav workers abroad.

† June.

‡ January; subsequent figures are not strictly comparable with those of preceding years due to change in the accounting method.

§ Excludes private agriculture (4 million private farmers, 1971 Census); includes "Employment in Private Sector" (mostly services).

TABLE 4. Inflation, 1952-1981

Index/Year	1952	1962	1965	1967	1968	1969	1970	1971	1972	1973	1974	1975	1976	1977	1978	1979	1980	June 1981
Consumer Price Index (CPI)* (1976=100)	8	14	22	29	31	33	37	43	50	59	72	90	100	115	131	158	206	296
Average Nominal Monthly Income (in dinars)	92	242	501	787	862	990	1173	1432	1676	1938	2477	3060	3535	4198	5075	6113	7368	9711
Index of Real Income* (1976=100)	33	48	63	76	79	84	90	95	95	92	97	97	100	102	108	108	100	93
Total Money Supply† (billions of dinars)	*	*	*	*	*	*	*	*	*	*	*	*	206.5	251.1	315.3	375.1	461.6	506.0
Cash Only† (billions of dinars)	.5	2.8	5.1	7.9	9.5	11.9	14.9	18.4	23.5	29.0	34.8	41.9	49.1	58.3	75.0	90.7	116.0	124.4
Demand Deposits† (billions of dinars)	*	*	*	*	*	*	*	*	*	*	*	*	157.4	192.8	240.3	284.4	345.6	381.6

Sources: Savezni Zavod za Statistiku, Indeks, 30, 12 Dec. 1981, pp. 42, 43, 54; Statistički godišnjak Jugoslavije, 1981, pp. 83, 96, 202, 211; and earlier issues.

* 1965 and 1978-81 figures are my re-computations with 1976=100; the Yugoslavs revise figures continuously, and change base years and other concepts frequently—in the December 1981 issue of Indeks, the base year is 1980=100.

† End of year; 1976-81 figures for Total Money Supply and Demand Deposits are from the December 1981 issue of Indeks—not comparable with earlier figures due to new accounting method.

Self-management agreements and social compacts are to be major tools for coordinating policies among self-managing units in the economy and society. At the same time, price formation is to be transferred increasingly to self-managing units. There is to be a stricter enforcement of new accounting rules which would restrain enterprises from excessive investment or distribution of wages which cause illiquidity problems and inflation. Real wages are to rise only as fast as productivity increases. Yet, the continuing flow of manpower from agriculture, added to the return of workers from abroad, have made the problem of employment "acute," according to the 1976 OECD *Economic Survey of Yugoslavia*. The *Survey* also notes that Yugoslavia's balance of payments deficit of ca. $1 billion continues to be a major constraint on domestic economic policy.

By 1981, unemployment became, if anything, even more acute, reaching 12 percent of the total employment in the socialized sector (excluding Yugoslav workers abroad as well as underemployment in private agriculture). As to the balance of payments, deficits became chronic, with the trade balance in the red by $6.3 billion in 1979, and imports continuing at twice the value of exports, leading the post-Tito leadership to declare a 30 percent devaluation of the dinar by June 6, 1980 ($1 U.S. = 27 Dinars).

While inflation subsided to 9-10 percent per annum in the first half of 1976, the growth of industrial production also slowed down to 1.1 percent, endangering Yugoslavia's projected annual growth target of 5.5 percent during the 1976-1980 Medium-Term Economic Plan. In order to stimulate domestic demand and revitalize industrial production, a package of new measures was passed in May 1976, among them:

(1) A more liberal consumer credit policy;

(2) Selective reductions in the sales tax for several consumer items;

(3) Partial relaxation of investment restrictions; and

(4) Special incentives to stimulate residential construction.[12]

Faced with high unemployment, and, hence, the imperative for economic growth to provide jobs, the regime has followed expansionary fiscal and monetary policies since 1976. The Yugoslav economy has grown at a respectable six percent per year, resulting in higher employment in the socialized as well as the private (service) sectors. Private agriculture, on the other hand, has been losing an estimated two percent of its work force annually—the single major cause of continued high unemployment, and labor migration abroad.

In addition, the Yugoslavs have since 1971 been turning their attention to the possibilities of long-range indicative planning. A series of studies have already been completed covering long-range social and economic development, 1971-1985. The major themes of this long-range planning are: (1) Goals and self-management; (2) Growth in the standard of living; (3) Growth in production and labor productivity; (4) Humanization of work; (5) Changes in the population structure and growth of employment; and (6) Regional development and problems of urbanization.[13] The discussions by Yugoslav economists of long-range planning underline the fact that Yugoslavia is entering a new, higher stage of development based on *qualitative* factors, such as increase in labor productivity, technical and scientific cadres, industrialization with emphasis on energy, raw materials, dynamic branches such as organic chemistry and the construction industry, economies of scale, and a better inter-branch and inter-regional integration of production.[14] In one word, the overall theme of long-range planning seems to be consonant with short-run policies: to increase economic efficiency and rationality in the allocation of scarce resources.

But, apart from the avant-garde's lament that problems of coal and steel are replacing problems of man under market socialism, there are serious problems in terms of coal and steel themselves. These problems center on the ambiguous relationship between plan and market and the difficulties of utilizing elements of the market mechanism in an economy based on "social ownership" rather than private property. Chief among these is the problem of prices, without which there can be no rational allocation of scarce resources in any system, socialist or capitalist.

1.2 The Role of Central Planning and the Market

The new Yugoslav Constitution of 1974 attempts to combine an all-Yugoslav market—understood as free pooling of labor and free sale of goods and services—with a system of social planning via self-management agreements and social compacts "concerning economic development of interest to the country as a whole."[15] The rationale for this unique combination is as follows: A unified Yugoslav market operating on the basis of demand and supply is expected to lead to increased productivity of labor, greater rationality of factor inputs (land, labor, capital, management/entrepreneurship), modernization of the economy, increasing the quantity and quality of outputs and their competitiveness in both domestic and international markets. On the other hand, the system of social planning is expected to correct the imbalances created by the market which, in reality, is hardly unified at all, in addition to its structural imperfections. In brief, the Yugoslavs are attempting to combine the best elements of the market mechanism with conscious planning and direction, a goal which is increasingly challenging economic policymakers both East and West.

Supporters and critics of market socialism wonder whether the Yugoslavs are trying to create a "triangular square," as Ludwig von Mises writes:

> A socialist system with a market and market prices is as self-contradictory as the notion of a triangular square.[16]

Indeed, Mises, Friedrich von Hayek and other adherents to the Neo-Austrian School and its critique of market socialism insist that in the absence of private property, entrepreneurship, and a realistic price system, economic calculation is impossible under socialism.

How does Yugoslav market socialism stand up under the Neo-Austrian critique? It appears that both supporters and critics of the Yugoslav economic model have proclaimed the advent of market forces somewhat prematurely. Apart from property relations (to be discussed below), prices are the lifeblood of the market mechanism. How are prices determined in Yugoslavia's market socialism? By the impersonal forces of supply and demand? Not quite. The 1976 OECD *Economic Survey of Yugoslavia* noted the following curious price structure:

(a) One-third of the producer prices were free of control—determined at enterprise level;

(b) One-third were subject to adjustments on the basis of automatic formulæ related to world market prices or adjustments made jointly by producers and industrial consumers; and

(c) One-third were subject to direct government control at federal, republic, provincial or communal levels.[17]

The price structure in Yugoslavia is, in other words, a patchwork of controlled and free market prices. The next major question would be: how rational is this price system? What are its underlying principles? The major underlying principle of the price system is, not surprisingly, Marx's unproved assumption of labor as the only source of value. The application of Marxist accounting principles has led, as Dirlam notes, to public admission by Yugoslavia's leading economic weekly, *Ekonomska politika*, that "no one knows what cost is" and that "Yugoslav firms go into the international market like Alice into Wonderland."[18]

The theoretical postulate of labor as the only source of value underlies the rapid rise in unit labor costs of Yugoslav products, which, like American products, have been pricing themselves out of international markets. Thus, the *1979 OECD Economic Survey of Yugoslavia* notes that Yugoslavia has lost market shares in most Western markets since the early 1960s due to three factors: (1) rapid rise in unit labor costs; (2) exchange rate policy; and (3) protectionist measures in foreign markets, especially since 1973. A new comprehensive trade and tariff agreement in February 1980 between the European Economic Community (EEC) and Yugoslavia lowered tariff barriers for many Yugoslav products and extended a five-year, low-interest, $250 million loan to Yugoslavia. Nevertheless, the Yugoslavs found it necessary by June 1980 to devalue their currency, which has been "floating" since July 1972 (in effect pegged to the U.S. dollar, and, hence, depreciating with the latter), as well as to secure a "stand-by" loan of 340 million Special Drawing Rights (SDRs) from the International Monetary Fund.

Dirlam and Plummer found that, in general, most Yugoslav firms seem to draw up their investment, sales, and pricing policies on a short-run, almost *ad-hoc* basis.[19] Due to the involuted accounting rules, Yugoslav firms do not show wages as cost nor do they include opportunity costs of capital in arriving at the price. There are also major structural problems. Chief among these is the high concentration in most Yugoslav industries, leading to oligopolistic and monopolistic price setting. According to Dirlam, 48 percent of the products were sold in 1970 by five or fewer independent producers, and 65 percent by ten or fewer.[20] When workers' self-management with its bias toward distributing profits in the form of higher wages is added to this configuration, it becomes clear why the wage-price inflationary spiral is proving to be much more intractable in Yugoslavia than in the capitalist West. This dynamic led Dirlam and Plummer to conclude that:

> ...the market structures in Yugoslavia do not enforce enough economic discipline to allow *free* workers' management to operate without resulting in intolerable inflation. Those workers' councils which operate in concentrated markets can and will use their power to obtain inflationary price and wage increases.[21]

The Yugoslavs are aware of this phenomenon which they call "group ownership" and "privatization of income." Thus, M. Aćimović points out that in Yugoslavia's capital, Belgrade, no less than 455 organizations of associated labor and work communities exceeded in their January 1980 disbursements the income distribution guidelines set by the 1979 Resolution on Economic Policy.[22] That Resolution called for incomes to be frozen at the November 1979 level until March 1980. Aćimović added that the fight for economic stabilization—the country's chief economic goal since the Eleventh Party Congress—calls for decisive action by all socio-political and self-management forces. In Zagreb, the capital of Croatia, the picture is similar. According to M. Predragović, in the organization "Family and Home," the average monthly income was 42,000 dinars as compared to the republic average of 6,600 dinars. He was surprised also at the large wage differential in Zagreb on the order of 1:14, and concluded that in such enterprises as "Family and Home," characterized by group ownership, very little was invested for further growth, the creation of new jobs, and, hence, for the strengthening of the society's material basis.[23]

That wage-price spirals and resulting inflationary price increases can be self-defeating is as obvious as it is difficult for some to fathom, East and West. Table 4 above tells the story more eloquently than any words could: Between 1971 and 1980, average monthly nominal income more than quadrupled, while real income remained nearly unchanged. The attempts by Yugoslav authorities to step on the inflation tiger's tail in early 1976, slowed its pace only at the price of greater unemployment, price controls, and slower production.

While Yugoslavia's leading economists and even party theoreticians like Kardelj inveigh in favor of more efficient management of social capital, higher labor productivity, and greater rationality of investments, they overlook a basic fact. And that is the above mentioned problem in cost accounting. Egon

Neuberger and Estelle James were perplexed that:

> Under the Yugoslav system, it is not possible to calculate implicit
> wages or capital costs and compare them to each other or to
> material costs in order to determine a rational input mix. Neither
> is it possible to analyze the contributions of labor, management,
> risk taking, monopoly power, etc. to the "profitability" of various
> enterprises.[24]

If that is true, how can there be a rational price structure? And without a rational cost and price structure, how can there be rational allocation of resources and meaningful investment criteria? In addition, as Svetozar Pejovich, Eirik Furubotn, Armen Alchian, and Warren Nutter observe, the firm's pricing policies are directly related to the nature of property rights in an economy.[25] There is a consensus that a socialist version of a capital market is necessary for the proper functioning of the market in market socialism. Yet in Yugoslavia, financial instruments cannot be transferred or sold, which impedes the free flow of investment funds. While fixed-debt owned assets (bonds and saving accounts bearing interest) are permissible, private ownership of equity shares is not.

Apart from this, both labor and capital factor markets are hampered by ethnic/national and local pressures which impede their mobility. As to land, users pay very low rents to local government authorities, which contributes to the uneconomic use of that factor input. At the same time, as Dirlam, Plummer, and others have noted, there seems to be a great deal of speculation in housing, and the sale and resale of land claimed by individuals as nominal lessees.[26] Like other socialist states, Yugoslavia has a chronic housing shortage, particularly acute in urban centers, which George F. Klein has diagnosed as leading to social deviance due to the lack of privacy.[27] Such deviance may range from sexual behavior to construction of housing without a permit. It has also led to the phenomenon of "wild settlements" or shanty towns on the outskirts of cities, built by peasant-workers and others.

The Yugoslavs have only recently begun to probe the causes of the housing shortage and the fact that some, especially the young and newly-married couples, have to wait for years for an apartment, while paying exhorbitant rents for sub-letting a room in the meantime. In an article on "The True Price of Housing," one of Yugoslavia's leading economists, Branko Horvat, sums up the rationale for the introduction of economic rents and the need to stimulate housing construction. In Horvat's view, rents are too low since they fail to include costs for amortization, maintenance, and future construction.[28] Gavrilo Mihaljević goes a step further by suggesting that the true economic rent for housing can be determined only by the market forces of supply and demand—and that these forces operate presently in their purest form in the area of sub-letting. Mihaljević argues also for the introduction of zoning laws and the valuation of property based on location.[29]

Slovenia, Yugoslavia's most advanced republic, was the first to draw up a social compact for the transition to economic rents, which mandates a quadrupling of rents between 1978-1982. The Yugoslavs are beginning to realize that uneconomic rents, expensive building permits, and high taxes, especially on private homes, have resulted in a situation where those privileged enough to have an apartment pay more for heating and electricity, or even cigarettes, than for rent, while others cannot obtain an apartment at all.

The private sector, mainly in agriculture and services, is severely circumscribed by its fundamental rules of less than 10 hectares of land and maximum of 5 employees in private businesses. This sector may be undergoing change, in spite of the traditional socialist/Marxist aversion toward it. The regime seems to be tolerating more private entrepreneurship for the sake of increasing output, providing services, and employment. Apart from burgeoning private catering establishments, which Paul Lendvai and others see as succeeding where socialist ones fail,[30] there are interesting new developments in industry. Wilson and Denton relate that in 1968 four individuals investing 2 million new dinars (about $160,000), rented a textile factory from a commune in Croatia and equipped it. Besides 120 women employees, they were also to work in the factory and be remunerated "up to the rate of interest payable to the banks but without guarantee, i.e., their position will be roughly that of preference shareholders."[31]

Another interesting experiment is the starting of a private factory in Slovenia in 1975, producing agricultural machinery. The factory, nicknamed "Typhoon," which employed 60 workers and seven apprentices in 1976, was organized by two brothers, one a private craftsman, the other a farmer, along with 23 workers. The brothers provided more than 2 million dinars in machines and buildings, while the workers contributed labor. A ten-year agreement was signed at the end of which the two brothers were to be repaid their original investment. When the investment ratio became 10:90 in favor of the workers, then the original firm would become a Basic Organization of Associated Labor (BOAL) managed by the workers. During 1975, the workers' average monthly income was 3,590 dinars and was expected to increase during 1976. The brothers realized an income of 800,000 dinars on their investment as the firm's managers. The weekly *NIN* which covered the story, refused to go out on a limb with any final assessment of this unusual development, which is hardly distinguishable from capitalism.[32]

In a striking new development in the communist world, the Yugoslavs have thus developed a new hybrid form of business organization called a Contractual Organization of Associated Labor (COAL), which they consider as a transitional form between private enterprise and associated labor. The 1979 World Bank (IBRD)-sponsored study of the Yugoslav economy draws attention to the fact that the first COALs were established—predictably—in Slovenia, which boasted up to thirty COALs by the end of 1976.[33] Since then, COALs have apparently sprung up in other republics as well. Thus, by 1979, there were ten COALs in Serbia, with another 15 on the drawing boards. A brief account in the April 2, 1979 issue of *Ekonomska politika* reports that these COALs employed between 10-50 workers (average: 30), with an initial capital of between 200,000 and two million dinars, and employing 4-15 people.

With the passage of the new Law on Contractual Organizations in 1978, the COALs have received official sanction and encouragement. The regime seems to be seriously interested not only in the growth of COALs, but also of what it calls the "small economy" of the private (service) sector. It is acknowledged widely that Yugoslavia's service and handicrafts industries in the private sector are weak and incapable of meeting the growing demand for services of an increasingly industrialized economy. The Yugoslavs admit that the "small economy" could provide employment opportunities for many of the nation's unemployed, particularly Yugoslav "guest workers" returning from abroad with accumulated savings, but no job. In the Belgrade area alone, 4,500 additional workers are needed for servicing radio, television, record-player, and other electronic equipment.[34]

But in order for the private sector to live up to society's expectations, it would be necessary for society to abandon its widespread aversion toward the former, embodied in high taxes and contributions to various funds, discrimination in credit and foreign exchange, frequent changes in government regulations, lack of business space and manpower, and the inability of small business to provide social insurance and other fringe benefits comparable to the socialized sector.[35] Above all, it would presuppose a reversal of cultural discrimination against any and all "private" enterprise, which for a generation has been equated with "capitalist" greed, exploitation, and alienation. Such cultural discrimination, combined with the regime's promises to the private sector in the past—made and then just as regularly broken—have put the private service sector in the same category with private agriculture: to be avoided at any cost. Hence, it is not surprising that those returning workers who dare to invest their savings in a small business of their own, like an auto-body shop, cannot find any co-workers, skilled or unskilled. As Robert Nisbet intimates, if we are to retain a free and stable society, the concept of "private" must again become as honorable as that of "public," in all walks of life.[36] No more appropriate advice could be offered to the Yugoslavs as well.

But the "Typhoon" and COALs are exceptions to the rule in the Yugoslav mixture of private and public sectors. In general, the private sector remains characterized by regime suspicion and extreme instability. George Macesich's example of an instance of discrimination against the private sector when the government raised taxes on private businesses sevenfold in May 1962, driving some 10,000 craftsmen out of business by the end of that year, appears fairly typical.[37] More representative of the Yugoslav economic scene, outside of agriculture, is the self-managed firm based on "social ownership," dubbed by Western economists "the Illyrian firm."

1.3 The Illyrian Firm

Horvat summed up the dilemmas of the Yugoslav economy as follows: plans/economic policy inexpertly formulated, rules of economic activity constantly changing, state obligations not performed. The result: an extremely unstable economy and extreme uncertainty in decision-making.[38] The Yugoslav economic model appears to be still far removed from either rational planning or effective operation of the market. Dirlam and Plummer concluded that the Yugoslav economy's allocative efficiency could be improved by decreasing exchange and price controls and penalizing business incompetence.[39]

But what about inflation and unemployment? There is a growing consensus that an unregulated labor-managed economy contains strong inflationary pressures of the cost-push type. How could that be? The primary culprit for inflationary pressures in the contemporary Yugoslav economy appears to be none other than the self-managed firm based on "social ownership." Lendvai writes:

> Perhaps no other society is so income-orientated as this supposedly socialist one. But the structural defects in the investment, banking, and price systems channel the scramble for money in the wrong directions—into distribution instead of profit-making.[40]

The original theoretical flaw can be traced back, not to Stalin or Lenin, but again to Marx himself, who in *Capital, Grundrisse,* and elsewhere maintained adamantly that labor was the only source of value. In Volume I of *Capital,* Marx inveighed that:

> . . . the value of each commodity is determined by the quantity of labour expended on and materialized in it, by the working-time necessary, under given social conditions, for its production.[41]

From this basic premise followed Marx's assumptions, adopted by Yugoslavs and others, that since only labor created value, then interest, rent, and profit as payments to capital, land, and entrepreneurship were unsocialist and amounted to exploiting live labor.

Consonant with this tradition, the labor-managed firm has, predictably, developed a myopic preoccupation with distribution and a corollary bias in favor of increasing wages. To understand the important issue of resource allocation by the labor-managed firm, a body of theory has arisen dealing with the Illyrian firm. Benjamin Ward, Evsey Domar, and others have found that the Illyrian firm behaves like a producers' cooperative. The major rule for the Illyrian firm is to maximize workers' income, that is, wages per worker. This, however, may lead to the firm's reluctance to hire new workers, lest wages/dividends per worker be diminished. Among Ward's other important theoretical findings on the model firm in Illyria were:

(1) A change in the fixed costs of the competitive Illyrian firm leads to a change in output in the same direction;

(2) A change in price to the competitive Illyrian firm leads to a

change in output in the opposite direction.[42]

Translated into everyday English, the first theorem implies that if a new tax, e.g., is levied on the Illyrian firm, increasing its fixed costs, it would increase production. Following the second theorem, an increase in the free market price for the firm's product(s) would cause the firm to decrease output. Both of these findings are diametrically opposed to economic rationality and the behavior of the capitalist firm.

But there are other problems in Illyria with regard to market imperfections, monopoly and oligopoly, investment, entry and exit of firms, labor mobility, government intervention, and management procedures within the firm. Thus, Ward found that the Illyrian firm might have a negatively sloped supply curve and that an Illyrian monopolist would produce less while charging a higher price than its capitalist counterpart.[43] In terms of investment, Ward observed that the Illyrian firm may have a bias toward capital-intensive investment, while Pejovich and Furubotn noted that the labor-managed firm is likely to prefer present consumption to higher future returns from investment.[44] Furubotn and Pejovich advanced the thesis that the worker-investors, who have no transferable rights in the firm's capital, only *usus fructus* or the right to use, are likely to prefer personal savings to investment in their firm.[45] This is admitted by Yugoslav observers like Mitja Kamušić who call the phenomenon "privatization of accumulation."[46]

While investment should seek its highest return, in Yugoslavia this is not so. Yugoslav authorities chide the BOALs, who under the 1974 Constitution have primary responsibility for investment and income decisions, for preferring investment in their own basic organizations to outside investment. The late Edvard Kardelj condemned this investment preference as "a kind of exploitation of other basic organizations, for those who closet themselves off with 'their' accumulation, into 'their own' basic organization, deprive others of the required resources and thus prevent or obstruct their development."[47] Ward and others concluded that decentralized investment may be a weak link in Illyria and that, hence, the government may have to take a more active role in investment decisions for the economy as a whole.

Another hallmark of the Illyrian firm is that it cannot fail. It can have losses, default on outstanding bills, overdue bank loans, tax obligations, and even wage payments. As Laura D'Andrea Tyson remarks, in 1961, 1967, and 1969-1972, some 10-30 percent of the socialized sector was at the brink of bankruptcy due to multiple defaults, that is, non-repayment of debts—the so-called "illiquidity problem." Her remedy appears simple on paper: "enterprises must be compelled to bear the risks of financial irresponsibility."[48] Actually, in Yugoslavia, all—from the consumer, to the Illyrian firm, to the various levels of government—have been living beyond their means by incurring vast debts, domestic and foreign.

Yugoslav officials complain ritually of irresponsible investments by enterprises. Yet they have contributed in no small measure to such uneconomic investments, fueling inflation, by easy money and credit policies reflected in money supply growth far in excess of the growth in productivity, and by negative real interest rates which have encouraged careless borrowing and spending of such manna from heaven. The results of such policies were predictable: a quadrupling of the cost of living between 1972-1980 (measured by the CPI), stagnating productivity and real incomes, shortages, inability to plan ahead or even to determine costs and profits, and a foreign indebtedness surpassing $14 billion by 1980. The Yugoslavs realize that their policy of cheap money has contributed to inflation.[49] However, they have yet to act on this insight.

The major single problem of the Illyrian firm appears to be its inability to accumulate capital. A continuing debate in Yugoslavia centers precisely on this question of how to build mechanisms for capital formation and investment into BOALs in particular and the economy in general.[50] What is puzzling is that some, like the Organization for Economic Cooperation and Development, praise Yugoslavia's alleged annual growth rate of six percent for 1973-1978, which compares favorably with that of 2.5 percent for the OECD nations, while others, like Ljubo

Sirc, claim that nearly ten percent of Yugoslav economic output is waste, and, more important, that "the economy cannot finance its own development and is forced to incur ever larger debts at home and abroad."[51] Indeed, in the period between 1973-1978, Yugoslavia borrowed $7.1 billion abroad, while Yugoslav workers abroad sent home some $11.4 billion. Thus, Yugoslav migrant labor and the capitalist West have been financing the Yugoslav experiment in market socialism. As the irrepressible Svetozar Vukmanović-Tempo, a former Politburo member, put it at the Eleventh Party Congress in 1978: "And instead of singing hymns, better that we get on with an analysis of the sources in society that lead to all this."[52] Yet, it is precisely Marxist economic analysis, muses Sirc, which precludes real solutions to Yugoslavia's economic woes.[53]

Milenkovitch wrote that free entry of firms into the market is a major requirement for efficiency in Illyria, yet the Yugoslavs have given relatively little attention to the problem.[54] This is not surprising, since individual entrepreneurship is still suspect to Marxist theory, if not socialist practice. It is true that Yugoslav economic theory considers the firm as such, and more recently its basic unit—the BOAL—as a "collective entrepreneur." But this conceptualization of entrepreneurship is highly dubious, for in the final analysis some *one* must make the decision. It has led Horvat to draw up five new principles of organization for a self-managed enterprise in order to maximize democracy and efficiency:

(1) Polyarchy: creation of sufficiently small and homogeneous work groups;

(2) Bodies or individuals who make decisions bear responsibility for them;

(3) Execution of decisions a matter of expertise, not democracy;

(4) Separation of the value, interest sphere from the sphere of expertise; and

(5) Institutionalizing control over enterprise management.[55]

As things stand, there is little in terms of entrepreneurial incentives in Illyria. Neuberger and James write that:

> . . . no value is placed on differential amounts which the member may have contributed to the firm's capital stock through previous collective saving and investment.[56]

Ward and others point out that the prohibition of individual equity holdings and direct sharing in profits is another major factor constraining entrepreneurial motivation.[57] Dirlam and Plummer noted that individual initiative of entrepreneurial types was curbed by the difficulties in removing incompetent subordinates, while Ichak Adizes examined the wide disparity between authority and responsibility, contribution and inducements to the Yugoslav executive and the need for risk-taking which has led to the novel phenomenon of "contractual management."[58] In sum, concludes Sirc, a self-management system based on social ownership is incompatible with responsible entrepreneurship.[59]

All these factors have led Western economists to assess the Illyrian firm as less efficient than its capitalist counterpart. A consensus has also emerged among Yugoslav and Western economists that the unregulated labor-managed firm contains a built-in inflationary dynamic. The phenomenon of wildcat strikes so prevalent in Yugoslavia is seen by some as exacerbating this inflationary dynamic by exacting wage increases independently and/or in addition to those adopted by self-managing bodies in the enterprise. And yet, the social-psychological and political aspects of workers' self-management, apart from the question of efficiency, are seen as highly desirable. Thus, Gudrun Lemân sums up the advantages of labor-managed enterprises as:

(1)   Strengthening personal initiative and responsibility;

(2)   Shortening lines of authority: decisions made on the lowest possible level;

(3)   Immediacy of decision-making; and

(4)   Training for business-like thinking and transactions.[60]

In sum, self-management in the economy would appear to be a giant educational enterprise.   But, as Adizes has observed, there are limits to this educational enterprise. These limits appear to be economic efficiency, on the one hand, and socialist equality, on the other. The crises of economic efficiency and socialist solidarity are, in turn, but harbingers of a larger institutional, theoretical, and practical crisis of communism.

2.   Fear Called Uravnilovka

A consensus has emerged in Yugoslavia and elsewhere which holds that there is an inherent contradiction or conflict between economic efficiency and social(ist) equality. Western observers like Sharon Zukin see the socialist project of equality and solidarity in Yugoslavia being replaced by market competition and resulting social differentiation, individual, class, and regional inequalities. In her view, Yugoslav self-managers find themselves a generation after the revolution in the midst of the "struggle for a dinar."[61] The socialist project seems to have yielded to the brutal reality of economic rationale.

Apart from students and youth, avant-garde Marxist humanist philosophers and sociologists have been the most vocal critics of the increasing social differentiation and inequalities in contemporary Yugoslavia. Although the avant-garde is opposed to the levelling egalitarianism of the *uravnilovka,* they still find that the present inequalities and laissez-faire market relations are incompatible with the socialist project of more humane social relations, that is, individual and social de-alienation and liberation. Ivan Kuvačić contends that the associated workers cannot possibly become free under the pressure of the market mechanism which transforms social property into group property and the amassing of wealth on the basis of privileged positions within the system of the division of labor and power.[62] Mihailo Marković concurs in this assessment by stating that where there is a "socialist market," there are also likely to be "socialist capitalists." This state of affairs is as incompatible with socialism and its principle of self-management as are unemployment, growing social inequalities and strikes, as pointed out by Milan Mirić.[63]

The re-appearance of capital on the scene, this time in the form of privatized group ownership, is especially ominous to the avant-garde who consider it, in established Marxist fashion, as the harbinger of exploitation, alienation, and class society. Marković and others argue, therefore, for the need to stop the enrichment and the formation of a new middle class of petty-bourgeois socialist stock-holders.[64] Miroslav Radovanović outlines four conflicting tendencies of socio-economic development in contemporary Yugoslavia:

(1)   Private or petty-bourgeois ownership;

(2)   Corporate or techno-managerial ownership;

(3)   State or politocratic ownership; and

(4)   Social or self-managing—communist ownership.[65]

Radovanović blames private, corporate, and state ownership about equally, but reserves particular ire for the so-called petty-bourgeois drive and mentality which "feels and works solely in the category of personal calculus and private interest." Interestingly, this "petty-bourgeois" orientation is condemned equally by the avant-garde and the party, although neither may, in fact, know what they are talking about.

There can be no doubt, however, on one point: the extent of social differences in contemporary Yugoslavia which have developed in giant strides during the 1960s, paralleling the social and economic reforms. Srdjan Vrcan catalogued the social inequalities of a systematic and structural nature under four headings:

(1) Material production and reproduction of society in the world of work;

(2) Political domination;

(3) Division of labor into intellectual and manual; and

(4) Total social distribution of all benefits and achievements of civilization and culture.[66]

In another article, Vrcan distinguished between three major sources of social differentiation:

(a) Town-country: the major part of poor in Yugoslavia are rural poor;

(b) Private sector: enrichment of large private enterprises; and

(c) Social sector: power and influence unevenly distributed.[67]

Vrcan found that social differences and inequalities in Yugoslavia exist in practically all fields, from the general position of families, housing conditions, possibilities for training and education, choice of profession and health and social protection, to social power and influence. Vrcan put actual income differences on a scale of 1:30. Some of the sources of extra income were overtime and part-time work, travel expenses for official trips, allowances for use of cars, special rewards, provisions, advertising, representation allowances, and similar. But the most disturbing aspect, according to Vrcan and others, was the fact that these social differences and inequalities appeared to be systemic, cumulative, and self-perpetuating.

This has led the avant-garde to condemn both the bureaucracy and its privileges and the unregulated market and the greed of petty-bourgeois socialist *nouveaux riches* who compete in appropriating other people's labor. The official "glorification of competition" is equally abhorrent to the avant-garde. Miladin Životić sums up the avant-garde's concern for socialist humanism:

> If only material incentives ("the law of income") and not moral and ethical motives as well played a role in our society, we should build up a rich society, but a society in which only the relations of "naked interest and soul-less cash payment" (Marx) would exist.[68]

The avant-garde thus never tires of reminding the communist leadership that socialist humanism should not be sacrificed to the mammon of increased production and economic efficiency, lest they lose both socialism and efficiency understood in a broader context. As Životić concludes: "The kind of Communism we achieve depends on what our socialism is like."

The avant-garde has thus stated openly what may be a basic contradiction in market socialism: the reliance on increased material incentives, competition, reward according to work performed, leading to greater inequalities of income and status versus the socialist project of cooperative, humanized social relations, individual self-realization for the poor and the weak as well as for the mighty, equality and solidarity. In brief, can socialist/communist ends be achieved by capitalist means?

2.1 How to Lose the Surplus Product Without Really Trying

While the avant-garde—along with some Western observers like Albert Meister and Zukin—deplores the increasing social differentiation and inequalities in Yugoslavia, the communist leadership is worried about the opposite trend—*uravnilovka* and the spirit of egalitarianism and their effect on productivity. Meister noted the paradox of Yugoslavia as a socialist country without an incomes policy or limits on wages and, hence, wage scales of 1:20 even within the same working collective.[69] On the other hand, in the mid-1970s, the regime became concerned with the egalitarian trend and wage-levelling to a scale of 1:2 or 1:3 which Vojo Srzentić, Secretary of the Executive Committee, Central Committee of the LCY Presidency, called inadequate for stimulation of initiative among top cadres and for increasing labor productivity. Indeed, Srzentić concluded that:

> The *uravnilovka* de-stimulates the fight for greater productivity and, viewed as a whole, is a regressive tendency. It draws toward the average, inhibits initiative, fails to encourage creativity and the development of work capabilities, and leads to a levelling of the results of work. Hence, it is understood that it exerts an influence on irrational business conduct and irrational allocation of social resources.[70]

Another leading article entitled "Fear Called *Uravnilovka*," summed up the leadership's view that it is necessary to part ways with the *uravnilovka* as the mentality of a poor, backward, agrarian society. It also noted an interesting fact: the insistence on an equal distribution of goods and services—"since we all have equal stomachs"—was not only equality in poverty, but necessitated a redistributive model of the state and an all-powerful bureaucracy.[71]

And yet, the political leadership finds it important to point out that the current principle of distribution according to work is not its ideal, but only a necessary evil in the transition stage from capitalism to communism. This means that the regime itself remains committed to egalitarianism, if not the *uravnilovka*, in the long run. But, is it possible that the *uravnilovka*, in the short or the long run, may be economically dysfunctional, resulting in the loss of the surplus product and misallocation of resources? Even the avant-garde is aware of the fact that the crucial question is the *price* to be paid for the reduction or elimination of inequalities.[72]

The first question which arises in this connection is the extent of the *uravnilovka* as a cultural norm within Yugoslav society. There is a consensus that egalitarianism/*uravnilovka* is widespread. Perhaps the most exhaustive study of the scope of the *uravnilovka* in contemporary Yugoslavia is that by Josip Županov, University of Zagreb, one of the country's leading industrial sociologists, entitled "Egalitarianism and Industrialism." Because of its unusual findings, it requires a more detailed restatement. What Zukin found in her study regarding the predominance of traditional values and behavior over official self-management norms is substantiated by Županov, who finds a three-way split among cultural values in Yugoslavia: *personal enrichment* on the individual level, the *heroic image* on the national level, and *egalitarianism* on the societal level.[73] If Županov's distinctions hold water, it would mean that Yugoslavs prefer enrichment for themselves, but socialist solidarity and egalitarianism for others. It recalls Mises' classic formulation of the welfare principle:

> What those people who ask for equality have in mind is always an increase in their own power to consume. In endorsing the principle of equality as a political postulate nobody wants to share his own income with those who have less.[74]

According to Županov, the egalitarian syndrome is as widespread in Yugoslavia as it is economically dysfunctional. He isolates seven interrelated elements which constitute the egalitarian syndrome:

(1) Perspective of limited goods as the cognitive component;

(2) Redistributive ethics;

(3) Norm of egalitarian distribution;

(4) Obsession about the private enterpreneur;

(5) Anti-professionalism;

(6) Intellectual *uravnilovka*; and

(7) Anti-intellectualism.

What Robert Nozick, Hayek, and others observed as an inherent conflict between *equality of opportunity*—which given unequal abilities leads to unequal results—and *equality in distribution* without regard to contribution, is realized also by Županov.[75] Županov sees the cognitive roots of the egalitarian syndrome in the conception of a zero-sum game or limited goods perspective of closed agrarian communities for which equality means an equal distribution of limited goods among all members of the community. What is disturbing to Županov and others is that this redistributive ethics leads to a strong centralized political apparatus of the state, bureaucracy, and the concentration of both economic and political power. Županov corroborates in all essentials Hayek's conclusion that:

> The principle of distributive justice, once introduced, would not be fulfilled until the whole of society was organized in accordance with it. This would produce a kind of society which in all essential respects would be the opposite of a free society—a society in which authority decided what the individual was to do and how he was to do it.[76]

But what does egalitarianism have to do with *economic* efficiency? Apparently, egalitarianism and its redistributive ethics have greater economic impact than Marxists, socialists, and communists have been willing to admit. First of all, Županov observes that egalitarianism limits not only nominal incomes but income aspirations as well. Secondly, it considers enrichment akin to crime, especially by a private entrepreneur. Egalitarianism is particularly suspicious of entrepreneurship, observes Županov, since entrepreneurship undermines the egalitarian conception of equal capabilities and threatens to expose the lack of efficiency in many work organizations, especially in the socialized tertiary sector.[77] The widespread Yugoslav bias against entrepreneurship and the view of riches as illicit is corroborated by other observers like Adizes in his description of "contractual management." In one instance, a professional manager closed a contract with a firm on the verge of bankruptcy according to which he was to be given a free hand in decision-making and receive a bonus. But the spirit of the *uravnilovka* was so strong in the party and trade unions which claimed that his bonus would amount to exploiting the workers by his expert, specialized knowledge, that the manager voluntarily returned half of his bonus and bought the city of Skoplje in Macedonia an ambulance with a portion which remained.[78]

Whereas Yugoslavia's long-range socio-economic plans concerning economic growth call for a greater reliance on professional cadres and the application of the newest scientific and technical know-how, Županov notes that the egalitarian syndrome is biased against professionalization and intellectual work as such.[79] The economy's need for better and more professional cadres is in direct contradiction to the offical ideology of de-professionalization in all walks of life. The avant-garde's branding of Županov's findings as a "positivist-functionalistically oriented sociology" which supports the *status quo* appears light years away from an adequate understanding of the dilemma.[80] Županov can only note ironically that anti-managerial declarations have become "signs of proper social upbringing" in contemporary Yugoslavia.

Županov sees the intellectual *uravnilovka* as harboring a bias against entrepreneurship, innovation, and creativity, and he gives actual examples of inventors being socially ostracized, fired, ignored, deprived of proper remuneration, and discriminated against by their collective. All these trends have discouraged innovation and reduced the number of patents. Županov sums up the result of the collective repression of innovators by quoting Robert McNamara's observation that: "Brains, like hearts, go where they are appreciated," adding, "and where they are utilized."[81] The spirit of the *uravnilovka* appears to be that universal levelling by the masses of everything that is excellent and superior, which Alexis de Tocqueville, Ortega y Gasset and others have described as the tyranny of the masses.

Županov concluded in his study, which draws on the findings of many independent sources, that the egalitarian syndrome was dysfunctional in an industrial society. Industrialism emphasizes progress, intensive development, acquisitive ethics, continuous growth of aspirations, development of the tertiary sector based on initiative, increasing professionalization of jobs, emphasis on the creative potential of labor, and creative organizational, monitoring and informational activities—the exact opposite of the anti-professionalism and levelling egalitarianism of the *uravnilovka*. To top it off, Županov saw egalitarianism in the economic sphere leading directly to authoritarianism in the political sphere.[82] There is, therefore, an inherent contradiction in the avant-garde's stance which argues for greater economic equality as well as more political liberalization. This point has not been lost on party theorists like Kardelj, who points out that the avant-garde's utopian vision could be realized only by re-creating a giant repressive administrative apparatus, and, hence, contributing to the growth of a new statism and Stalinist dogmatism.[83]

2.2 Private Property, Alienated Labor, and Income

Apart from the *uravnilovka*, another major Marxist legacy is haunting the Yugoslavs: the dilemma of private property. This is the more surprising since private ownership of the means of production was abolished in Yugoslavia following the revolution in 1945. Yet, a generation later, the 1974 Constitution states that:

> Socially-owned resources may not be used for appropriating the surplus-labour of others, or for creating conditions for such appropriation.[84]

In other words, the new Constitution warns the self-managers not to exploit their fellow workers with socially-owned property. Is this provision in the new Constitution simply a poor joke?

It is one of the greatest curiosities that both the avant-garde and the party have come to be concerned with the phenomenon of exploitation under socialism. In the previous chapter, we had occasion to review major statements by the avant-garde on this subject. Briefly, Marković, Stojanović, and others consider that the abolition of private property does not eliminate all forms of exploitation and alienation. Apart from the bureaucracy and the new middle class, there can be also collective exploiters and collective capitalists who appropriate surplus value under socialism. Even self-managing groups can function as exploiters. This led Marković to conclude that the essence of exploitation was not to be found exclusively in private property, but in the rule of objectified, dead labor/capital over the worker and his live labor.

In pursuing these ideas further, the avant-garde developed the concept of group ownership and other forms of privatization of social ownership. Thus, Radovanović notes that there has been an expansion in the concept of ownership which now includes, besides social ownership, also petty-commodity production, group ownership, corporate-sharing, private-capitalist, state-financial, money-financial (private, group, state), and trading-profiteering (with money capital, farming and construction land, buildings, etc.).[85] What they all have in common, except for social ownership, is the appropriation of unpaid labor, surplus value, and, hence, exploitation. Aleksander Bajt thinks that:

> ... the proclamation of ownership as social (state) does not by itself create social ownership in the economic sense. If the surplus product is appropriated by a stratum of people—for example a state bureaucracy or state hierarchy—economic ownership nevertheless remains private and can even be class ownership, although it is proclaimed constitutionally as social.[86]

But how can social ownership degenerate into group and other privatized and allegedly exploitative forms of ownership under socialism? Both the avant-garde and the party seem to point in the same direction—market socialism. In Marković's view, self-managing groups, while competing under market conditions, can end up exploiting other workers, whereas Rudi Supek points to the phenomenon of "twice-alienated capital" which first became state and then group capital.[87] Radomir Lukić claims that there are two major forms of exploitation in contemporary Yugoslavia:

(1) on the basis of private property; and

(2) one that is unique to a socialist, self-managing society.[88]

The first type of exploitation Lukić sees in the uses and abuses of the private—especially the service—sector, highlighted by resale, usury, and other middlemen services of a vast array of speculators, rentiers, and other "businessmen." But, Lukić sees a "new kind of exploitation" in the socialist sector and exploitation between self-managers. Characteristic among these is exploitation of seasonal labor in socialized agriculture and services. Further, there is partial exploitation of lower strata of workers within individual self-managing organizations and between different economic organizations within the same or different economic branches. Finally, Lukić notes the conflict between the economy and other parts of society, especially the state, and points to the increase in illegal exploitation ranging from corruption, bribery, unjustified price increases, machinations and speculation, to outright criminal acts such as theft and forgery.

All this has led to a state of affairs in which everyone accuses everyone else of exploitation:

> Agriculture claims that it is exploited by industry, industry—that it is exploited by banks and trade, producers of raw materials that they are exploited by the producers of final products, etc. And vice versa. The underdeveloped claim that they are exploited by the developed, and vice versa. Small firms claim that they are exploited by big ones and vice versa, the big ones claim that they carry the small ones on their backs.[89]

In sum, everyone in Yugoslavia claims not only that he is exploited, but that this is an actual, definitive and factual, rather than a purely imaginary, condition. But, if everyone is so sure that they are being exploited, one would expect that they know the precise meaning of the term "social ownership." Yet this is not the case. *Actually, no one knows the precise meaning of "social ownership!"* According to Horvat, there is disagreement in everything but the fact that social ownership "implies self-government, that it is a new social category, that if it is a legal concept, it does not imply an unlimited right over things characteristic of the classical concept of property, and that it includes property elements of both public and private law. . . ."[90] Of course, it is also based on the labor theory of value which has proven untenable under careful examination by such Western economists as Samuelson, Blaug, Böhm-Bawerk, and Mises. Marx attributed all value creation to labor. Contemporary Yugoslav economists, including Horvat, follow suit to the extent that they maintain that labor ought to receive all income.[91] But this is as irrational as ascribing all value creation and/or income to capital or any other single factor input. Thus, Marc Blaug concluded that Marx could have transformed values into prices in the same irrational way had he operated with a *capital* rather than a labor theory of value.[92]

Another major dilemma concerning private versus social ownership noted by both Yugoslav and Western observers is the question whether market socialism leads necessarily to a privatization of social ownership. Županov in the East and Milenkovitch in the West noted the transformation of social into group ownership. Thus, Milenkovitch observed a privatization of income streams from socially-owned resources in the sense that the working collective, rather than society, received the returns to land and capital, in addition to labor.[93] This is also seen by the avant-garde as leading to increasing inequalities among social strata, as well as between unequally endowed working collectives and regions.

But it is difficult to conceptualize how it could be otherwise. Collective ownership—if not a contradiction in terms, as Hannah Arendt put it[94]—can only be operationalized in the form of satisfying concrete human wants, if it is individualized. The individual use of goods and services is a "direct negation" of collective or social ownership, to use a Marxist/Hegelian term. Every working collective has a natural need to appropriate a portion of the socially-owned resources. That it may be appropriating capital and rental income as well, is due more to Marx's labor theory of value perpetuated in Yugoslav theory and practice than to its selfishness. Yugoslav communists thus find themselves on the horns of a self-imposed dilemma: if they continue to subscribe to Marx's labor theory of value, they will have exploitation, and if they reject that theory and pay interest, rent, and profits to suppliers of those factor inputs, they will also have exploitation by definition.

Marx and Engels seem to have had the last laugh, after all. As Marx said in the *Grundrisse* and elsewhere: capital confronts labor as alien and labor opposes capital as alien. But, is it not curious that even in socialism people should possess a Midas' touch: private initiative and entrepreneurship, when combined with labor, land, and capital, turns socialized property everywhere into private property.

2.3 How Socialist are Strikes, Privileges, and Unemployment?

While the avant-garde condemns privileges and unemployment, it is split on the issue of work stoppages or strikes under socialism. According to Mirić, unemployment, increasing social differentiation as well as strikes, are incompatible with the principle of self-management, whereas Svetozar Stojanović and Neca Jovanov urge the legalization of the right to strike as a basic precondition for socialist democracy and conflict resolution under socialism.[95]

Western observers like Dirlam, Plummer, Neuberger, James, Zukin, and Lendvai all note the anomaly of the absence of institutions for conflict resolution in socialist Yugoslavia. As summed up by Dirlam and Plummer:

> Leaning heavily on nonexistent sentiments of mutuality, Yugoslav economic and political theory largely ignores the possibility of conflicts of interest among individuals or groups once socialism is achieved, as does guild socialism and orthodox Marxism.[96]

While abolished in theory, conflicts, including industrial ones in the form of strikes, are very much alive in real life. Yugoslavia averages some 200 work stoppages annually. None of these wildcat strikes are strictly legal or illegal. Yet they persist in that grey, formless twilight of socialist legality. Nebojša Popov holds that strikes in contemporary Yugoslavia result from two major causes:

(1) Distribution of personal income; and

(2) Malfunctioning of self-management.[97]

Popov concluded that strikes would persist as a natural consequence as long as wage-labor relationships existed in the economy.

We are back, of course, to square one: Marx's labor theory of value. Given its premises, it is not surprising that the Illyrian firm is oriented toward maximizing income per worker in an income-oriented society. But, as Blaug and others have demonstrated, even a socialist society will be unable to live up to Marx's labor theory of value, since its need to invest will necessarily involve withholding a portion of the whole product from distribution to labor and consumption.[98] This means that if a socialist society wanted to further capital accumulation and investment needed for future economic growth, it would nesessarily have to "exploit" labor. Furthermore, as Nozick has pointed out, there will be exploitation in any society, including the socialist one, "in which those unable to work, or to work productively, are *subsidized* by the labor of others."[99]

The absence of private property rights and the Marxist preoccupation with distribution rather than production has led to apparently less than efficient utilization of non-labor factor inputs, especially capital, land, and entrepreneurship. The regime has, in effect, acknowledged these deficiencies by emphasizing the need to conserve and enlarge capital. In Kardelj's words:

> . . . the efficient management of social capital, i.e., of the materialized labour of workers, creates more favourable conditions for a higher productivity of living labour and thereby also better conditions for the general advancement of society.[100]

But if social capital increases labor productivity, this entails that capital, and not only labor, is productive. Yet, the Yugoslavs fail to draw the conclusion that suppliers of capital should receive proper reward, especially under conditions of risk and uncertainty. This leads to the conception of capital as something self-generating by a natural or supra-natural force. Thus Yugoslav socialists and others continue to treat capital as manna from heaven, to which Nozick likens John Rawls' conception of distributive justice taking place behind a veil of ignorance.[101] It seems to be, indeed, ignorance, but ignorance of fundamental economic principles and equally basic principles of human nature.

Given Marx's labor theory of value adopted by the Yugoslav communist leadership, it should not be surprised by labor militancy in self-managed enterprises, even if the self-management mechanism functioned as conceived. But, the avant-garde as well as Western observers have pointed out that there are other sources for labor unrest as well. Chief among these are unemployment and the threat of unemployment, privileges, and distribution according to norms other than work, in addition to traditional behavior patterns of corruption, bribery, theft, and the like.

Indeed, one of the principal causes of labor unrest and social conflict generally in Yugoslavia may be the widespread notion that everyone steals from everyone else. While the private sector is usually singled out under the socialist double standard of morality, even avant-garde theorists admit that the socialist sector is no better. If we are to believe Kuvačić: ". . . undoubtedly the greatest number of people in the socialist sector lives off someone else's labor."[102] It is the old accursed theme of exploitation which—real of imaginary—may be one of the main stumbling blocks not only to economic efficiency, realistic wage scales, and greater productivity, but also to rational and impartial conflict resolution under socialism. That privileges exist is an open secret. All of these are woven by the avant-garde and the party into a scenario true to Marx, according to which privileges mean exploitation, exploitation means class enemies, and class enemies deserve what is coming to them: the self-righteous ire of primitive irrationality combined with the coercive instruments of a modern, all-powerful state. While Marx looked at the capitalist as the incarnation of the devil, the avant-garde blames the bureaucracy and petty-bourgeois class mentality for all evils.

When it comes to unemployment, both the avant-garde and the party realize that this is a real problem and a major source of inequality. But, while the avant-garde has condemned unemployment as "unsocialist," it has not offered any practical solutions. Apart from inflation and raising productivity, unemployment remains a major headache for the Yugoslav communist leadership. One may sympathize with the avant-garde's moral outrage against unemployment, excessive social differences, privileges, and the like, but it will take more than moral indignation to solve these problems. The regime finds itself in an unenviable position on these matters, since it condemns privileges and wealth amassed on a basis other than personal labor, while opposing the *uravnilovka* as economically dysfunctional. But those East and West who attribute the high rates of unemployment in Yugoslavia exclusively to the operation of the market mechanism overlook another major source: the continuing stream of excess agricultural manpower into cities and industries.

2.4   The Phenomenon of Peasant-Workers: Love's Labors Lost?

Agriculture has been not only the Achilles' heel of socialist economies, but also the stepchild of Marxist economic and socio-political theory. One need only recall Marx's own viewpoint on the idiocy of rural life and the need to overcome what he called the "foundation of every division of labour... the separation between town and country."[103] Now, apart from programmatic statements by the party and occasional references to agriculture and the peasantry by the avant-garde, the plight of Yugoslav agriculture and the low incomes, social prestige, and power of the peasantry have been almost uniformly ignored.

In his prize-winning study on modernization and agrarian change in Yugoslavia, Heinz Kontetzki drew up a picture of systematic discrimination against agriculture and the peasantry. Kontetzki saw the peasantry driven into socio-cultural and political isolation. The majority of the peasantry is outside of the socialist sector. Although it comprises almost half of the population, it is excluded from the self-management system and is woefully underrepresented in the party and other socio-political organs. It is the least integrated of all social sectors in Yugoslavia. It suffers from lack of education, social, medical, and cultural services as well as a socio-cultural lag. All this has led, in Kontetzki's analysis, to a state of affairs in which the agricultural sector contributes to the overloading and a latent disintegration of the Yugoslav socio-political system.[104] How did this situation come about?

It is no secret that Marxist theory and socialist practice in Yugoslavia and elsewhere set up industrialization as the supreme economic goal. Agriculture was to foot the bill. This policy orientation led to the collectivization of agriculture. Although agriculture was mostly de-collectivized in Yugoslavia, it continued to receive the lowest priority in terms of investment, technical, and scientific innovation as well as prestige, while suffering low prices and high taxes. This socialist bias against agriculture spread into development theory and policy practiced in the Third World. But, forced industrialization at any price and the concurrent neglect of agriculture proved counterproductive to such an extent that there has been a re-assessment. The Soviet model of development planning turned out to be misleading for many countries. Derek T. Healey shows that planning often led to a "wastage of the all-too-scarce resources of the developing countries".[105]

But agriculture is more than just land and crops. It also means people. In Yugoslavia, the modernization process of transition from agriculture to industry has been personified, so to speak, by a new middle layer of peasant-workers wedged between agriculture and industry. What or who are these peasant-workers? In 1969, there were more than five million peasant-workers, almost one quarter of the total population, and more than half of the peasantry.[106] Stipe Šuvar and Horst Günther saw rapid industrialization, on the one hand, and slow urbanization, on the other, as major immediate causes for the formation of peasant-workers.[107] Many peasants in Yugoslavia have not completed the transition from agriculture to non-agricultural occupations. Indeed, they continue to live on the land, eking out a meagre living from their small parcel of land or garden. At the same time, they commute for work to cities or mining/industrial centers. Their daily or weekly migrations are necessary because of the lack of living quarters in the cities and their extremely low incomes. Suvar, Joel M. Halpern, and George W. Hoffman agree that these peasant-workers are the carriers of a new, mixed life style in Yugoslavia, contributing to the phenomenon of the urbanization of villages and the ruralization of towns.[108]

The peasant-workers are the cultural battlegrounds for conflicting norms and values: traditional and modern. Apart from a relatively small group of people in Slovenia and Croatia who combine the best features of city and rural life—as farmers-workers—most of the peasant-workers are torn not only by subsistence and the question of economic survival, but by conflicting norms and values. The traditional peasant norms of the land, patriarchal extended family, cooperation, honor, ascription, and the like are being challenged directly by modern norms of the city, industrialization, the nuclear family, competition, material status, efficiency, and professionalization. The regime may now be having second thoughts on its negative orientation toward agriculture, judging by the priority accorded to agriculture under its 1976-1980 development plans dubbed the "Green Plan." But it appears to be too late. The material discrimination against agriculture was compounded by cultural discrimination. The result: a virtual exodus from the land of the youth, the able, the intelligent, the adventurous, and the entrepreneurial types into cities and industries. And on the land remain the old, the women, children, the handicapped, and those without hope, which further diminishes agriculture's ability to compete in the modern division of labor or even to sustain the remaining agricultural population.

The regime foresees in its long-range socio-economic plans the increasing socialization of agriculture and looks forward to the efficiency of mechanization, technical know-how, and economies of scale associated with large units. The actual growth in agricultural production during the 1976-1980 Medium-Term Economic Plan was 2.5 percent. The 1981-1985 Plan calls for continued priority investment in agriculture in order to achieve a 3.5-4.0 percent growth rate. Highly-placed officials like Kiro Gligorov, member of the CC of the LCY, admit that agricultural development has lagged behind, resulting in the first trade deficit ever in agricultural products.[109]

Apart from low productivity, agriculture is plagued by a massive flight of both manpower and capital into non-agricultural endeavors. As Klein points out, land abandonment is common in Yugoslavia, even in fertile regions, since the ten hectares limit on land ownership is too low to provide a standard of living expected by the population.[110] As a result, 600,000 hectares of land remain fallow or inadequately farmed; 40,000 hectares are lost every year to sprawling cities, weekend homes, roads, artificial lakes, and industrial plants, as well as to storms, floods, and erosion; private savings are invested outside of agriculture and the remaining investments are geared to short-term profits, and, hence, inefficient; growth in mixed households from 39 percent in 1960 to 60 percent in 1978; and an aging agricultural population.[111] It is only unclear how such an agriculture can be the cutting edge of economic growth and stabilization in the new Medium-Term Economic Plan, 1981-1985, by producing food staples for export.[112]

And where have all the young farm-hands gone? They went to the factories, mines, and towns. But many cannot find work and hence must travel on, hoping to find bread in foreign lands. Apart from a certain pathos—a whole civilization based on a close symbiotic relationship to land and nature and bound with an umbilical cord of tradition to the past, is dying out—the official neglect of agriculture has obviously retarded capital formation, overall economic development, and thus industrialization itself. The revolution of rising expectations, modernization, industrialization, and mass production and consumption are the powerful forces dominating our century. Yet, an entire civilization connected with the land may die out without a whimper. It is leaving behind bewildered people, among them the army of peasant-workers whose transitional life style is perceived as marginal by their fellow men:

> The character of the worker-peasants as a middle layer is high-lighted by the fact that in the city they are not considered as workers and on the land are no longer considered as peasants. To the city industrial worker they are "ignorant, backward and uncul-tured," whereas to peasants they are lost souls since they had left the circle of peasant traditions and views.[113]

The peasant-workers thus share the predicament of the elderly in our era which considers the latter too young to die, yet too old to be socially relevant. Should we not conclude with Shakespeare that here we really may have love's labors lost?

3. Humanizing the Economy

While the party is worried about the price of socialist *equality*, the avant-garde is questioning the price to be paid for economic *efficiency*. There is a consensus among the avant-garde that the price for economic efficiency and the market mechanism has been too high. Such consequences of market relations as unemployment, privileges, increasing social differentiation and inequalities, the growing gap between the developed and underdeveloped regions, materialism, and the petty-bourgeois mentality of socialist millionaires and *nouveaux riches* are seen as incompatible with the socialist project of equality, solidarity, and humanized social relationships. The avant-garde thus mounted a radical critique of alleged insufficiencies of individual and social relations in market socialism centering on three major economic contradictions:

(1) Industrial development, market, commodities, technical ex-perts, subordination of man to technology versus human objec-tives of socialism;

(2) Increasing need for specialization of labor versus the "whole man"; and

(3) Need for firm, inflexible organization to employ efficient management techniques versus a new community of free association of producers.[114]

Throughout its critique of contemporary socialist practice in Yugoslavia, the avant-garde harkens back to the vision of the young Marx and his philosophy of man with its emphasis on individual and social de-alienation and liberation via *praxis*. Yet the avant-garde's critique itself is torn between the ambiguities and contradic-tions inherent in Marx's and Engels' economic, socio-political, and philosophic vision. Thus, while most scholars, East and West, admit that central planning was the central aspect of Marx's economic thought, both the party and the avant-garde in Yugoslavia diverge from this consensus. Indeed, to planners further East, the Yugoslav conception of the need for efficient allocation of resources via the market mechanism is highly embarrassing. Avant-garde Yugoslav Marxist philos-ophers and sociologists, condemned in the East, may appear at first as its ideological allies in the sphere of economics with their critique of market relations. But the avant-garde's stance is much more complex in reality.

The avant-garde's basic question with regard to market socialism is whether the socialist project of more humane social relations among men will become submerged in reified market relations between things. Concurrently, Supek notes that a technologically advanced society, combining planning and market, should not imply retaining commodity-money relations and the capitalist quest for profits. Rather, it ought to imply "free regulation of diverse human productive (creative) forces and needs in the realm of social exchange."[115] In other words, the avant-garde is not opposed to any and all uses of the market mechanism in socialism. Most consider the use of some elements of the market as a necessary evil in the transition stage from capitalism to communism. Surprisingly, a few among the avant-garde, like Stojanović and Županov, are willing to admit that the market has considerable positive functions. Thus, Stojanović notes that "the market can unmask parasitism and introduce effective selection and stimulation," and otherwise promote economic growth.[116] Županov is even more critical of those who see in the market, the consumer society, and commercialism only unmitigated evil:

> When commercialism is attacked head-on, it only shows a lack of understanding of the market mechanism. The market is actually a daily plebiscite of a great number of people regarding the value and usefulness of various goods and services.[117]

Following Marx's own dichotomy between profits versus human needs, capital versus labor, economics versus man, the avant-garde is concerned lest the party's preoccupation with economic *means*, productivity, efficiency, and the market, result in a displacement of socialist *ends*, solidarity, equality, and humanism. Supek and others point to a growing ideological vacuum in contemporary Yugoslavia, which is increasingly filled by such unsocialist phenomena as "old bourgeois habits, parvenu socialist traders and speculators, embourgeoised socialist managers, a commercial life style and the chase for [a higher living] standard above all in one's own home and on that same commercialized and privatized basis . . . ."[118] What the avant-garde laments, along with Zukin and others, is that the prospect for a revolutionary social transformation and the quest for de-alienated, humanized social relationships has yielded to the secular quest for a simply *affluent* society and a de-humanized "struggle for the dinar." No one seems concerned any longer with the ultimate aim of abolishing wage-labor, restoring human significance to production, reconstituting the individual worker as a "whole man," liberating him from the idiocy of over-specialization and the division of labor, transcending commodity-money relations, establishing genuine control over surplus value by associated immediate producers and thus liberating both society and men. What about the problems of man? Are they divisible from coal and steel? Is it posssible to transcend the division of labor and commodity production?

3.1 Transcending the Division of Labor and Commodity Production

Perhaps no other group of Marxist thinkers has done so much in bringing to light the ambiguities inherent in Marx's concepts of exploitation and alienation as the Yugoslav avant-garde. The avant-garde as well as the party have come to recognize that exploitation can exist in socialism even without private ownership of the means of production. Yet, as we mentioned in Chapter V, the other prong of Marx's theory of exploitation rested on the notion of the division of labor and specialization attending commodity production or the capitalist mode of production for exchange.

While Marx ascribed alienation of labor and the fetishism of commodities to *capitalism* alone, Marković maintains that they are characteristic of "*every* commodity production."[119] The avant-garde has, thus, come to realize that the production of commodities, specialization, and the division of labor are characteristic of the *industrial* mode of production and not just of capitalism. In Gajo Petrović's formulation:

> Some forms of alienation in production have their root in the nature of contemporary means of production and in the organization of the process of production so that they cannot be eliminated by a mere change in the form of managing production.[120]

At the same time, the avant-garde insists that in order to abolish class exploitation, it is necessary to abolish capital and wage-labor and "overcome commodity production and the market as the basic regulator of production."[121] Is it possible that the avant-garde, along with Marx, would like to eat their cake and have it, too, when it comes to science, technology, the division of labor, and commodity production?

This dualism in Marx's thought is nowhere more explicit than in his lauding the benefits of science, technology, and the division of labor as instrumental in bringing about material affluence, while condemning this very process as alienating live labor and reducing man to the status of an appendage to the machine. The avant-garde follows here in Marx's footsteps. Thus, while Marković exalts technology on the one hand as a "condition of human freedom," he condemns it on the other as destroying all natural, patriarchal, and idyllic relations, introducing cool methodical calculation and efficiency as the basic value.[122] Kuvačić observes that the extreme division of labor and the total organization of modern industrial production lead to "absolute reification."[123] Živojin Denić, Vojan Rus, and others conclude that specialization, division of labor, and organization will be necessary even in a developed socialist society, yet these will no longer be alienating but liberating forces within the framework of social ownership.[124] Other members of the avant-garde disagree, pointing out that technology, division of labor, and specialization have the same alienating effect in socialism as in capitalism, and that participation in workers' councils has "no effect upon alienation at work."[125]

Some among the avant-garde thus substantiate Western observations that the dilemmas of science, technology, division of labor, specialization, and commodity production are not problems inherent in capitalism, but in the industrial mode of production prevalent East and West. This does not mean that the problems associated with humanizing work and the workplace are less real or urgent. But it would appear to mean that here, too, Marx's notion of exploitation is reduced to what Nozick calls "the exploitation of people's lack of understanding of economics."[126]

The avant-garde continues to subscribe to Marx's view of commodity production for exchange and profit rather than for immediate use and fulfillment of human needs as both exploitative and peculiar to the capitalist mode of production. Surprisingly, party ideologues like Kardelj dismiss the notion of the market and commodity production as sources of inequalities and capitalist relations:

> . . . specific forms of the market and of commodity production have accompanied all social systems since man became able to produce not only for himself, but for others as well. And it was not the market which determined the character of production relations, but the other way around—it was production, that is, class relations, which determined the character of the market.[127]

Yet, the avant-garde seems to be closer to the heart of Marx's metaphysic regarding production and exchange. It was the capitalist's production for exchange which alienated both the product itself and the laborer's human essence incorporated in it during the ill-fated process of production. The more the worker produced, the greater was the value of the world of things, commodities, and the lesser became his own human value as a species or social being (*Gattungswesen*). It was this process which Marx equated with "human servitude" and which resulted in the infamous inversion between persons and things, that is, in reified relations between persons and social relations between things.[128] To remedy this reification, according to the avant-garde, it is necessary to abolish capital and wage-labor and transcend commodity production. For the avant-garde, the abolition of wage-labor emerges as the fundamental aim of the proletarian revolution. But how can wage-labor be abolished in a society without private property, a society in which everyone has been reduced to the status of a hired hand at the mercy of either the state or self-interested collectives?

Some Yugoslav theorists admit that labor is a commodity under socialism and that most people are bound to the wage-labor relationship. Zagorka Pešić-

Golubović writes that:

> The existence of hired labor does not automatically end when the
> classical State, as a centralized organ, ceases to have the mono-
> poly over all decisions and continues to make only the vital ones,
> while it delegates the power to make some of the decisions in
> connection with the organization of production and the distribution
> of the products of work to the enterprises (primarily, as we said, to
> the organs of the State within the enterprises, such as the directors
> and the management); in fact, such a complex system of depend-
> ence increases the workers' insecurity and the feeling of power-
> lessness.[129]

Yet, Golubović's formulation only re-introduces Marx's dualism between the state
and the individual, capital and labor, in a new form, which, like its predecessor(s),
brooks no hope for easy resolution or is, indeed, insoluble as such. It leads others to
such acrobatics as to maintain that while labor is still a commodity and while the
worker still sells his labor power under socialism, this is no longer exploitation or
alienation, since he has a say in setting its price.[130]
    But the Hegelian dialectic demands complete capitulation from its practi-
tioners. Consequently, Slaven Letica boosts his view of the de-alienated essence of
hired labor under socialism by his patently un-Marxist conclusion that:

> Commodity-labor power not only does not negate the socialist
> character of our society, but it (of itself) represents the only
> fragment of complete freedom in capitalism as well, that is, the
> only fragment of economic "democracy."[131]

The dialectic has thus triumphed once more, at the expense of both common sense
and Marxism. Yet, Marx's and Engels' "butterfly" formula, the vision of the
liberation of man from the stupefying vise of fragmentation, overspecialization,
division of labor, reduction to a commodity to be stamped, measured, valued in
purely monetary terms and exchanged, remains as much a challenge for socialism
as for capitalism.

3.2 To Each According to His Needs?

    Both the party and the avant-garde are critical of violations of the socialist
principle of reward according to work. As Zukin found in her study, the official
ideology of self-management with its emphasis on productivity, rationality, efficiency, scientific and technical expertise, and reward according to personal effort
is one thing. The reality is quite another. In actual practice, traditional norms and
values resting on nepotism, collusion, ascription, connections, bending the rules,
corruption, speculation, and the like often dominate both production and distribution.
    Tito himself sharply condemned the accumulation of wealth independently of
personal effort and sacrifice. He singled out particularly three categories of
misdemeanor in the economy:

(1)   Those who engage in corrupt behavior for the benefit of their
      collective;

(2)   Those guilty of petty and major thefts; and

(3)   Big-time operators "who joined forces with various people in
      our foreign trade."[132]

As a result, campaigns aimed at examining the sources or origins of wealth gained
new momentum, although news media continue to lament the extremely slow

progress of this process of socialist accounting. The slow pace of the process, on the other hand, might corroborate the presupposition that the phenomenon of legal and extra-legal enrichment is quite widespread.

The avant-garde, which bears no great love for the regime's "heavenly" principle of reward according to work, has been in the forefront of criticizing its abuses. The avant-garde maintains that this socialist principle of "to each according to his work" is honored more in the breach than in practice. Radovanović sees the actual distribution of material and non-material values and goods proceeding in line with the following criteria:

(1)   Social-class position;

(2)   Employed or member of the reserve army of labor;

(3)   Market and systemic position of the branch and the particular enterprise;

(4)   Valuation of labor power on the market for unqualified labor;

(5)   Supply and demand of a particular kind of skill;

(6)   Born in the developed North-West or the less developed South-East;

(7)   Size and strength of private property;

(8)   Social origin and all forms of inheritance;

(9)   Merit, evaluated by like-minded colleagues;

(10) Needs—as desired, understood, and evaluated by a narrow group;

(11) Possibilities of selling the same labor product several times;

(12) Social threat;

(13) Level of skill and work contribution;

(14) Agreement and the employer's good will;

(15) Work contract; "You to me—I to you";

(16) Bourgeois-legal contract.[133]

Radovanović also notes various "cumulative-symbiotic" forms of "reward according to work." All of this leads to the impression of the extremely subjective criteria and bases of determining reward according to performance.

Yet the avant-garde would not be satisfied even if the socialist principle of distribution operated as intended. This would still be very far from the communist principle of: "From each according to his abilities, to each according to his *needs*." The avant-garde holds that this egalitarian principle cannot be postponed until the arrival of full communism. Some Yugoslavs retain their good humor even when it comes to this sensitive topic. Thus, at a symposium on "Social Inequalities in Socialism", Vladimir Milanović recalled a joke in which a boy was asked what communism was. He replied that it was the social order visible on the horizon. But when asked about the horizon, the boy replied: "The horizon is the line which increasingly recedes as we approach it."[134]

It is this vision of communist solidarity, equality, and humanism receding into a distant future which is alarming to the avant-garde. Market socialism and bureaucracy are held to be the primary culprits. The avant-garde is split, however, when it comes to determining the precise meaning of the communist principle of distribution according to needs. While this principle is commonly thought to be synonymous with solidarity and equality, Marković notes that for Marx:

... the principle of a communist distribution of goods was neither strict equality of share, nor amount of work, but human needs.[135]

This raises the rather practical question of *who* is to decide on the nature and scope of human needs? That this may be a rather complicated affair can be gleaned from Supek's intimation that human needs will be determined by the free exchange of goods and services.[136] No one mentions that human needs are subjective and that they change over time.

Županov noted that egalitarianism in the economic sphere leads to authoritarianism in the political sphere. It leads to the arbitrary power of a central bureaucracy and the state, the very factors criticised by the avant-garde. But it is Stojanović who characterizes Marx's principle of distribution according to needs as an illusion, since:

> People's needs will undoubtedly always exceed the possibility of satisfying them.[137]

Marković and others attempt to circumvent this obvious difficulty by holding that the thrall of material goods will yield in the future to non-material aspirations. These, of course, presuppose material abundance. But this common presupposition may not be warranted in terms of either efficiency or equality.

In terms of efficiency, Stojanović, along with Županov and others, points to the need for incentives and adequate material compensation for personal initiative and effort. According to Stojanović, the violation of the human propensity toward increased comforts, personal differentiation, and material rewards consonant with effort leads to "universal indifference to work, low productivity, material privation, and spiritual apathy."[138] Stojanović equates collectivism and ascetic egalitarianism with the morality of underdeveloped or immature communism, which Marx himself dismissed as a "regression to the *unnatural* simplicity of the poor and wantless individual."[139]

If there is to be equality and socialist solidarity in the communist future, it would mean for the avant-garde equality in affluence rather than in poverty. But the economic question still remains: who is to foot the bill? The avant-garde's classic answer is: society. But society is an abstraction or, at best, a very high level of generalization. Once this concept of society is operationalized, it turns out to rest on individuals. That means that we are back to Stojanović's question: how to motivate individuals to produce? Or, is universal affluence going to fall simply as manna from heaven?

Apart from efficiency, there is the equally complex question of equality from the standpoint of equity or justice. Characteristically, Marxists, socialists, communists, and increasingly others, East and West, equate justice with equality. There is also a tendency to view equality of opportunity and equality of outcomes as synonymous. But that is misleading. As Hayek, Nozick, and others observe, if we treat different people equally, the result will be inequality in outcomes, given differences in abilities and effort. Some Yugoslav theorists have come to realize that Marx's principle of distribution in communism fails to take account of personal effort. It leads Stojanović to remark that:

> With two equally capable people the principle of distribution according to need would actually favor the person who had invested less effort in developing his capabilities.[140]

How is this to be squared with justice and equality? Some, like Lukić, go even so far as to conclude that the attempt by a poorer individual to take from the richer without compensation amounts to exploitation.[141] But Stojanović stops short of condemning the redistributive principle. His solution is, rather, to advocate the con-joining of the two principles of distribution according to work *and* needs. Thus, the principle of distribution according to work would be supplemented by:

(a) Measures to insure real equality of opportunity such as equal pay for equal work; and

(b) Broadening the area of distribution according to needs to include free schools, child care, medical and general social insurance, free cultural goods and similar.[142]

This distributive ethics grafted onto self-management is seen as combining economic efficiency and socialist solidarity/equality. Stojanović thus seems to have developed a promising new synthesis. What is surprising is that this new socio-economic synthesis is much more democratic than socialist. It reflects some of the best thinking not only in the tradition of American pragmatism, but European democratic socialism as well. The only question is: how Marxist is this new synthesis?

3.3 Man as an Economic Animal and as a Being of Praxis

As explored in Chapter IV, the avant-garde's conception of man is that of a being of *praxis,* a free, creative, and self-creative or self-actualizing being, rather than merely an economic animal subject to exploitation and alienation by powerful yet uncontrolled economic forces under capitalism or Stalinism. It is understandable, then, that the introduction of market socialism in Yugoslavia posed a novel theoretical challenge to the avant-garde. They have attempted to grapple with this theoretical challenge, following in the footsteps of the young Marx.

Thus, the avant-garde found that under market socialism, production became once more the end of man, rather than man the end of production. Tadić noted that while in capitalism the individual was subsumed under private property, in socialism man became an abstraction under socially-owned property. In either case, this economic determinism did not "leave much room for human freedom."[143] In its critique, the avant-garde re-creates Marx's vision of the need to transcend commodity production, that is, production for exchange and profits rather than for direct use and human needs, the imperative of transcending the division of labor and wage-labor relations, and abolishing capital or the rule of objectified labor over live labor. Marković summarizes the major dilemmas of contemporary socialism as follows:

> If socialism does not wish to enter history as a form of social organization which successfully secures retarded industrialization, it must show and show *now* how it is possible to organize production for human needs, and not for profit, how remuneration can be correlated to work, and not to mere success on the market, and, finally how the rule of objectified things over live labor can be abolished.[144]

Up till now, neither the avant-garde nor the party have been successful in satisfactorily solving Marx's Faustian dilemmas. But neither have they raised the question of whether the king wears any clothes at all. Are these real dilemmas amenable to practical or, at least, theoretical solution, or are they bogus dilemmas?

The second problem mentioned by Marković—that of linking remuneration effectively to work performance rather than arbitrary market valuation—appears real enough. But, as Županov and others have noted, the failure of proper remuneration of personal effort and initiative is due in contemporary Yugoslavia more to the lack of operation of the market forces of demand and supply than to their arbitrary and injudicious valuation. Thus, Županov writes that the inadequate valuation of intellectual labor in particular "does not derive from the existence of a market for intellectual services, but rather from the fact of its negation."[145] Županov's is a rather unorthodox view among Marxists, including the Yugoslav avant-garde, who continue to subscribe to Marx's conclusion that the market is incompatible with justice and equity. But this raises another serious dilemma for the avant-garde, since if the market is barred from determining remuneration, who or what shall take its place? The bureaucracy is excluded by definition as a new exploitative class, separate from the social interest.

The first dilemma mentioned by Marković is a corollary to the second. It is the socialist imperative of organizing production for human needs rather than for profit. The roots of this dilemma reach back to Marx's notion that the capitalist mode of commodity production for exchange is *solely* for profit rather than satisfying real social wants by producing use values for personal consumption. The sin of profit is compounded in Marx's view by the universal prostitution of labor embodied in alienated products, which in the form of capital come to rule over live labor, on the one hand, and become exchange values in a market dominated by money—the quintessence of human alienation—on the other. Marx equated this state of affairs with something akin to primordial sin:

> The exchangeability of all products, activities and relations with a third, *objective* entity which can be re-exchanged for everything *without distinction*—that is, the development of exchange values (and of money relations) is identical with universal venality, corruption.[146]

Only it is difficult to see how a future communist society could abandon the division of labor, commodity production, exchange, and money unless it wanted to regress to a simple, small barter economy in which individuals, while perhaps social, would produce exclusively to satisfy their own separate private interests. It also remains for the avant-garde and others to learn the common fact of economic life, which the party has been learning in spite of Marxist theory, that unless production is organized in such a way as to result in an efficient allocation of society's scarce resources *and* profit, production will be neither scientific, efficient, nor will it satisfy human needs, whatever these may be. Western observers like Paul C. Roberts and Matthew A. Stephenson contend that the polycentric nature of the modern economy is such that exchange cannot be transcended and that, hence, "Marxian exploitation, if it is not a purely intellectual construction, is merely a fact of life."[147]

The third dilemma recalled by Marković regarding the possibility of abolishing the rule of objectified things/dead labor/capital over live labor remains one of the most vexing for Marxist theory and socialist practice. The lack of the proper valuation of capital in socialist accounting and its resurrection as privatized group property under socialism were elaborated above. But the roots of this controversy reach further back to Marx's metaphysics, which is, indeed, inseparable from his economics.

According to Marx, objectified labor or capital comes to dominate the worker's live labor under capitalism. But the avant-garde found that capital continues to dominate live labor under socialism as well, in the form of privatized group property, exploitation by the bureaucracy, and the like. We have already dealt with the aspect of the exploitation of labor by capital above. But what about the phenomenon of the alienation of labor? It appears that many among the avant-garde, following Marx, confuse alienation and objectification. Petrović would protest, claiming that Marx distinguished between these phenomena, separating alienation from objectification, the latter defined as "the process of projecting human potentialities through man's productive activity into external objects."[148] But, Marx's own writings are replete with instances of a methodical confusion and con-joining of alienation and objectification. Some among the avant-garde have come to realize what Marx disclaimed—namely, that science, technology, and machinery as embodied capital will confront labor as alien under socialism as well. Marx himself wrote that:

> In machinery, objectified labour confronts living labour within the

labour process itself as the power which rules it; a power which, as the appropriation of living labour, is the form of capital.[149]

Neither Marx nor the avant-garde have provided a credible explanation—practical or theoretical—how this alienation of labor and domination of capital over the workers is to be abolished in the communist future. But the greatest contradiction concerns the fact that Marx and his followers, after writing tomes on the need to de-alienate labor and thus free the creative potential of the human individual, conclude that labor/work cannot liberate man after all, since it remains a realm of necessity. Thus, on the one hand, Marx held out the promise that in the future communist society, from a mere means of life, labor would become the prime necessity of life, while maintaining, on the other, that the realm of freedom "lies beyond the sphere of actual material production" and labor.[150] In Hannah Arendt's view of Marx:

> The fact remains that in all stages of his work he defines man as an *animal laborans* and then leads him into a society in which this greatest and most human power is no longer necessary. We are left with the rather distressing alternative between productive slavery and unproductive freedom.[151]

Could it be that the avant-garde may have to settle for a new communist man, half free and half slave? Free in his spare time outside the process of production, but still a slave within production itself? The avant-garde subscribes to Marx's view of the need to abolish or, at least, reduce toil, labor, work to a minimum of socially necessary labor. In Marković's words:

> The basic condition of human liberation in all its forms is liberation from toil, and the gradual increase of free time—this presupposes technological progress.[152]

But, in the absence of agreement on what constitutes basic human needs, how will the associated producers determine what constitutes socially necessary labor time to be embodied, i.e., alienated in goods and services for their satisfaction? And, will not technological progress come to dominate man even under communism in the form of objectified, dead, alienated labor, capital, machinery, superorganization, and bureaucracy ruling over live labor?

Finally, the avant-garde echoes Marx in its complaint that in capitalism everything has a price. Marx's critics, on the other hand, point out that in socialism nothing has a price. This has not led to priceless things in socialism, but rather to things devoid of value and a corresponding treatment of valueless things in a system of social ownership in which property belongs to everyone and no one. While in capitalism private owners of the means of production were engaged in conspicuous accumulation/capital formation, in socialism the associated producers are preoccupied with conspicuous consumption/distribution. Since socially-owned resources belong to no one, it is not surprising that no one should be particularly concerned with saving, capital accumulation, and augmentation of socially-owned resources. As Milton and Rose Friedman remind us: "If there is no reward for accumulating capital, why should anyone postpone to a later date what he could enjoy now? Why save?"[153] Marxist accounting principles with their one-dimensional focus on labor as the only source of value complement this reckless discounting of capital along with land and entrepreneurship.

The avant-garde's concept of man as a being of *praxis* also becomes more problematic, since man is surrounded in socialism by a world of valueless things. But if man's material world has become radically devalued, does not this lead to a devaluation of man himself, since he is, after all, a material being? Man is, of course, more than just a material being or a *homo œconomicus*. But, whenever Marx's followers (as in the case of the avant-garde) are vaunt to prove that man is more than just a material being, they are forced by sheer logical consistency to abandon the economic sphere and seek an explanation of man's nature and behavior elsewhere. Thus, the avant-garde's concept of man as a free, creative, and self-creative being of *praxis* represents an ideal which is not reducible to matter alone nor determined by economic forces. This raises serious questions with regard to Marx's economic determinism.

At the same time, the avant-garde sees the economic sphere everywhere as limiting man and contributing to his alienation and enslavement. This predicament of the avant-garde is firmly anchored in Marx's and Engels' views. According to Marx and Engels, humanity's leap from necessity into freedom will occur in the future communist society by abolishing or, at least, reducing the sphere of toil and harnessing the forces of science, technology, and nature within a framework of universal affluence. Communist liberation is, thus, the liberation of man not only from the curse of useless and exploited toil, but also from economics and its chief problem of scarcity as such. Man would finally have the opportunity for unhindered all-round development of all his faculties in the new realm of freedom—of free time.

Neither Marx nor the avant-garde mention one of the major problems of utopias: the absence of challenge and resulting boredom. The strange thing about the communist utopia is that it may turn out to be a very realistic distopia: a society of inverted values and helpless people frustrated by the rationality of false happiness in a world in which any fluctuation from the consensus would be considered criminal. In the meantime, we are left with such practical problems as how to construct a viable new economic theory as a guide to socio-economic practice this side of paradise.

4. Toward a New Economic Theory

It has become fashionable among some youth and intellectuals, East and West, not only to dismiss economics along with science and technology as irrelevant, but to consider them positively harmful to human self-realization. Among avant-garde Yugoslav theorists, the conviction has grown that the economic rationality of the market and commodity production are incompatible with socialist humanism, a view that is shared by the New Left elsewhere.

Some—like Galbraith, Heilbronner, Harman, Bowen, and Boulding in the West—conclude that capitalism is in a crisis, that economists must become social philosophers, that planning is necessary, if not unavoidable, and that the growth and consumption ethic should be replaced by an ecological and self-realization ethic, and the glut of useless private goods by essential public goods.[154] But the Yugoslav experiment in market socialism warns us from an unbounded new faith in planning as a cure-all for social and economic ills. It is possible to misplan and misplan badly. The Yugoslavs have learned the painful truth that planning can be more wasteful, inefficient, arbitrary, and inhumane than the market mechanism. They arrived at the juncture where they might subscribe to Friedman's dictum that: "Attempts to use government to correct market failure have often simply substituted government failure for market failure."[155] On the other hand, the Yugoslav experience suggests also that in the absence of perfect competition, the market cannot be a perfect guide to economic rationality, let alone socialist humanism. This has led Horvat to note that the dilemma of plan *or* market is a false one:

> The market is only one—and until now the most efficient—of the planning mechanisms, and the plan is the precondition for the proper functioning of the market.[156]

It may come as a surprise to Western intellectuals, economists, and statesmen that a group of *communists* should lecture them on the benefits of the free market and the disadvantages of government regulation of the economy. Indeed, it is party theorists like Kardelj, and not the avant-garde, who have come to question all the major sinews of the Keynesian economic theory prevailing in the West which holds that a society/economy can spend its way to prosperity. To these theorists, the Keynesian prescription of eliminating unemployment by increasing total aggregate demand via government and consumption spending based on public and private borrowing, respectively, and the concurrent expansion of the money supply, appears increasingly suspect.

While their failings in the economic sphere are legion, the Yugoslav communists should be credited with trying out Keynesian policies to the hilt and acknowledging quite candidly that the latter lead to both greater inflation *and* greater unemployment—or *stagflation.* In the area of monetary policy, for instance, the Yugoslavs have tried their Keynesian best: they increased the money supply and credit, both public and private, far in excess of productivity increases, and found that the resulting inflation was merely debasing their currency. As to the currency—the dinar—the Yugoslavs have done everything in their power to stabilize it: from exchanging 100 old dinars for one new dinar; allowing the dinar to float in international currency markets and to depreciate along with the U.S. dollar; to devaluing the dinar repeatedly. Yet, all to no avail.

Nor can anyone fault Yugoslav officials for not attempting an *incomes policy,* that is, wage and price controls, recommended by some as a radical cure for inflation. In the area of prices, for one, the Yugoslavs really explored all the possibilities: the command economy in which all prices are centrally administered; farming out price-setting among different sectors; and freezing prices, e.g., from August-October, 1979, and again in June 1980, following devaluation. The most conspicuous results of freezing prices temporarily, that is, short of returning to administered prices, have been the growing bottlenecks and shortages of various commodities such as coffee, sugar, and building materials, held back by suppliers unwilling to release stocks, waiting for the next price increase.[157] But you can still obtain everything on the black market—as in the "good old days" of the command economy (which most Yugoslavs would rather forget)—at outrageous prices. This state of affairs is hardly conducive to a rational allocation of scarce resources, since all economic calculation becomes, indeed, impossible. It is true that Yugoslav Economic Policy Resolutions aimed at freezing wages have been poorly enforced, not least because of the obvious doctrinal difficulties and foot-dragging by bureaucrats. But, even if a wage freeze were in effect, people could always moonlight (as the regime complains), change job classifications (resulting in higher pay), or simply borrow.

The Yugoslav experience thus converges with the thinking of the "new economists" in the West, who call for a radical redirection of our attention from the Keynesian emphasis on the *demand* side to *supply* side economics. The new economists blame Keynesian economic theory—which has dominated U.S. economic thinking and policy since the New Deal—for creating a giant, unproductive governmental bureaucracy and an expensive and obscure regulatory maze, which has hamstrung private initiative, investment, and economic growth, and encouraged the growth of "welfare" programs (benefitting mostly the affluent middle class) and wasteful consumption. They call for America's re-industrialization to be achieved through fiscal and monetary restraint, along with new measures to stimulate saving, investment, productivity, and thus real growth in employment and incomes.

Above all, new economists like Friedman and William E. Simon, former U.S. Secretary of the Treasury, emphasize what the Yugoslavs have been learning surreptitiously—that there can be no real economic growth without profitable enterprises, and that, hence, *profit* should be sought after and regarded as a "social blessing," rather than a curse and a stigma denoting greed, exploitation, and alienation.[158] Yugoslav party theorists like Dušan Bilandžić, University of Zagreb, are critical of the practice, East and West, through which "losses are socialized while profits are nationalized."[159] Bilandžić warns that the transfer of profits from profitable enterprises to those incurring losses is counterproductive and only encourages "the spirit of parasitism."

The Yugoslav experiment also corroborates Peter F. Drucker's contention in his *Managing in Turbulent Times* (1980) that no one, not even Exxon or Mobil, really makes any money in inflationary times. Least of all in a self-managed economy in which, argues Sirc, the workers sacrifice their general interest as consumers by indulging their sectional interest as producers.[160] In fact, what self-managers in Yugoslavia distributed to themselves in wages and bonuses between 1972-1980, beyond corresponding increases in productivity, was nullified by the rising cost of living. To complete the paradox of self-management socialism, the self-managers' power of decision-making concerning the distribution of the "surplus product"— whether in the form of wages, investments, or contributions to various funds—was effectively expropriated by the government's inflationary monetary and credit policies. In Sirc's view, Yugoslav self-managers were thus forced to save for future investment and growth.[161]

The self-defeating nature of wage-price controls, and of inflationary fiscal, monetary, and credit policies is dawning slowly on the Yugoslavs (and others), although the regime is unable to extricate the country from its economic difficulties while it continues spellbound to Marx's metaphysic—which passes for economic science—and the Frankenstein of labor militancy. On the other hand, the Yugoslav experience would also indicate that we need an entirely new economic theory to cope with problems of economic organization in the latter part of the twentieth century.

Take for instance the central economic dilemma of stagflation. The Yugoslavs have rediscovered the quaint common sense adage that there can be no stable economic growth if incomes and consumption exceed production.[162] This insight challenges, however, the one-sided interpretations of the causes of inflation and unemployment in the West, where government blames business and labor, and business and labor blame government as well as each other, and everyone blames everyone else. In reality, each segment of society—business, labor, government, producers, and consumers—bears a part of the overall responsibility. The conclusion follows that if inflation and unemployment are to be solved, they will require the joint effort of all.

It appears then that such observations as by Blaug that the two schools of economic thought, free enterprise and planning, may finally be approaching a reconciliation, are not altogether utopian.[163] The Yugoslav economic model is hardly without major and minor faults, but whether we like it or not, its problems and prospects may represent to an alarmingly great extent the problems and prospects of societies and economies, East and West. The major challenge of the Yugoslav model, as we have learned, is how to combine the best elements of the market with social planning in a world of imperfect information and scarce resources. The dilemma of increasing productivity—all but abolished in New Left and avant-garde thought—emerged as the major single problem for the Yugoslav leadership.

Marcuse or Galbraith would be clearly embarrassed, as is the avant-garde, by the party's emphasis on the need to increase productivity, science, technology, and economic rationality in the allocation of scarce resources, even if it means living with the market mechanism. Can we conclude, then, that the Yugoslav avant-garde's insistence on the need to rehabilitate the socialist goals of more humane social relations and individual self-realization is so much empty chatter? On the contrary. With the success of economic development, scientific and technical know-how, and the rational allocation of resources, the question of the *quality* of life will increase in significance and problems of man promise to become more acute than problems of coal and steel.

But the question of the quality of life and of what constitutes humane goals and a richer life for each individual cannot be solved on the basis of Marx's or the avant-garde's dualism counterposing man versus economics. The ignorance of economic rationale will not lead to the abolition of economics, but to the material impoverishment of people. And one does not have to subscribe to Marx's economic determinism to realize that man is, among other things, a material being and a *homo œconomicus* and that the negation of *homo œconomicus,* far from enthroning *homo humanus,* will result in the negation of an integral aspect of *homo sapiens.* Hayek, co-winner of the 1974 Nobel Prize in Economics, remarked in 1944:

> It may sound noble to say, "Damn economics, let us build up a decent world"—but it is, in fact, merely irresponsible. With our world as it is, with everyone convinced that the material conditions here or there must be improved, our only chance of building a decent world is that we can continue to improve the general level of wealth.[164]

The "no-growth" schools of thought are, thus, both misleading and enlightening. They are crassly misleading when seen against the terrifying backdrop of world hunger, poverty, and want which cannot be cured by words from the Club of Rome promising a stationary economic state. They are enlightening when they draw attention to the *quality* of outputs and economic growth. Increasingly, both private and public decision-makers in the economic sphere are confronted by choices between different products, inputs, and technologies. These choices are never absolutely clear or unambiguous, but the stakes appear to be increasing, while the margin of error is decreasing.

An example of these relatively novel dilemmas are externalities such as air and water pollution, soil erosion, noise, and less measurable esthetic effects. These notorious diseconomies are only slowly being incorporated into cost calculations by individual private or public enterprises, East and West. If these costs are not taken into account, mankind will find itself denuding the planet of energy, raw materials, clean air, water, and livable space in an act of unwanted and unforeseen suicide. The nuclear arms race may turn out to be less dangerous than conventional pollution and so-called peaceful uses of atomic energy in nuclear reactors and dumping of radioactive wastes in the air, soil or oceans. Voices in the wilderness cry: why not develop non-polluting and virtually inexhaustible solar energy?[165] Do we merely lack the requisite technology, or are we too timid in our vision?

One can only agree with the avant-garde that science, technology, and economic rationality, when left to themselves, bereft of conscious evaluation and direction, will ensure neither equality, efficiency, nor a more humane world in which man is not simply an extension of the machine. On the other hand, one must disagree with Marx and the avant-garde when it comes to their view of science, technology, and economic rationality as value-laden. If science, technology, and economic rationality had values independently of man, then not only the quality of human life, but man's very survival would be in doubt. Our only hope is that science, technology, and economic rationality are instrumental *means* which can be used by man for diverse *ends.* But if that is true, then the avant-garde's conception of man as a being of *praxis,* a free, creative, and self-creative being which is called to determine its own destiny, emerges as quintessential in the enterprise of evaluating means and ends toward a more humane future.

This enterprise of evaluating means and ends leads us directly to the socio-political realm and the examination of the art and science of politics. Does Marx's utopia wane in this sphere, or does it simply metamorphose into luscious new forms?

Chapter VII · Self-Management and the Party: The Quest for Totalitarian Democracy

> Human emancipation will only be complete when the real, individual man has absorbed into himself the abstract citizen; when as an individual man, in his everyday life, in his work, and in his relationships, he has become a *species-being*; and when he has recognized and organized his own powers (*forces propres*) as *social* powers so that he no longer separates this social power from himself as *political* power.
>
> Karl Marx, "On the Jewish Question" (1843-1844)

1. The Model of Totalitarian Democracy

It is commonly assumed that the twentieth century is dominated by science, technology, rationality, and bureaucracy. And that irrational myths, utopian beliefs, and religious systems are withering away. This view is shared widely, East and West. Yet, Maurice Duverger and Eric Voegelin, among others, have observed a curious phenomenon of the rise of political religions or secular faiths attending the twilight of traditional religious belief systems.[1] In the West, this search for a new secular faith found expression during the 1960s in the New Left, the counterculture, and the more diffuse student demonstrations and alienation of the youth and intellectuals from the prevailing mechanistic, materialistic, positivistic, and hierarchical socio-economic and political system. It has led to a questioning of the basic valuational, human, economic, social, political, and cultural foundations of Western civilization. At the center of this questioning has been the very nature and basic assumptions underlying the Western democratic form of government.

In their report to the Trilateral Commission on the governability of Western democracies, Michel Crozier, Samuel P. Huntington, and Joji Watanuki noted that the current pessimism about democracy in the West concerned the sense of purpose rather than the rules of the game.[2] Intellectuals, youth, and others are increasingly questioning the very purpose of the democratic form of government. The formal democratic processes appear to many no longer satisfactory by themselves. What is demanded is that they be infused with new content. Could the West be on the road to totalitarian democracy? This is one of the burning questions of our age. It is still open. One thing is certain. The Yugoslav odyssey provides us, again, with the most comprehensive insight into these uncharted political seas. For the Yugoslavs have attempted now for more than a generation to achieve just that: totalitarian democracy.

But what is totalitarian democracy? Since there is a high emotional charge attached to both "democracy" and "totalitarianism," let alone their conjunction, a brief terminological explanation may be in order. There are, first of all, those who would discard the use of both terms. Others question the adequacy or relevance of the concept of totalitarianism. The new conventional wisdom holds that modern-day communist political systems can no longer be classified as totalitarian, or some would say, even authoritarian.

John H. Kautsky argues that we would do better simply to compare communi~t with non-communist systems, institutions, and processes.[3] Yet, William A. Welsh cautions that while communist systems no longer boast monolithic elites, this "should not be interpreted as disagreement over fundamental goals."[4] And Joseph LaPalombara stresses the fact that social scientists should be careful in applying concepts such as political pluralism in their analysis of communist systems. In LaPalombara's view, pluralism in the political sense should not be confused with "pluralistic" or "diverse" in the cultural, ethnic, or economic sense. He concludes that whatever the nature of the communist systems, it excludes political pluralism since they do not accept the legitimacy of open alternative associations or competing allegiances organized as a political opposition.[5]

We identified in Chapter II Friedrich and Brzezinski's model of totalitarianism as consisting of an official ideology, a single mass party, a system of terror, communications and weapons monopolies, and a centrally directed economy. We also stated that it was a model or an ideal type, the increasing deviation from which seemed to characterize actual reality in the Soviet Union and Eastern Europe. In the case of Yugoslavia, we saw in Chapter VI that the economic reality of market socialism diverged considerably from the command model of a centrally directed economy. But the jury is still out when it comes to the other equally important ingredients which make up the totalitarian model.

Western observers of the Yugoslav socio-political scene like Jacob Walkin, M. George Zaninovich, Dennison I. Rusinow, and Bogdan D. Denitch agree tha the Yugoslav system can no longer be considered totalitarian. While Walkin ca.ls it authoritarian, Rusinow disagrees, holding that it is a "polycentric polyarchy involving a network of elites," rather than a party autocracy.[6] Zaninovich even questions whether we can classify Yugoslavia as a communist party state.[7] This is a rather sweeping and overwhelming consensus. In addition, Denitch claims that the official interpretation of Marxism in Yugoslavia as an open system means that it is not a totalitarian ideology. At the same time, Denitch admits that there is a direct contradiction between the participatory norms of self-management and the hierarchically-organized party and state structures.[8]

Fred B. Singleton writes that according to the 1974 Constitution, the majority of Yugoslav citizens may participate in the various structures of self-management. Yet he wonders whether they really exercise power, since:

> The state and party both stand above the system of self-manage-
> ment at the grass roots, and are able to intervene to impose
> decisions from outside.[9]

The Yugoslav communist leadership insists that its system of workers' self-management in the economy and social self-government in the polity is the most democratic system of government the world has ever known. But even such a sympathetic veteran observer of the Yugoslav experiment in direct participatory democracy as Fred Warner Neal concluded that it was half democratic and half totalitarian, half in the West and half in the East.[10] How is it possible that some observers can easily gain the impression that the Yugoslav system is a totalitarian one-party dictatorship, while others consider it a promising model of worker participation and direct democracy?

1.1 Rousseau's General Will

A consensus exists among such thinkers as Stephen Miller, David Levy, and Jacob Talmon in the West and Milovan Djilas, Mihajlo Mihajlov, and Leszek Kolakowski, who hail from the East. It holds that Marx's utopia leads necessarily to the socialist distopia. What does that mean? According to Miller:

> . . . Marxian thought, owing to its utopian belief that man can leap
> from the realm of necessity to the realm of freedom, inevitably is

only "realized" through totalitarian regimes.[11]

Levy concurs in this view by pointing to the intimate connection between the Marxist theory of total liberation and the socialist/communist practice of total coercion.[12] Talmon draws attention to the striking similarity between the Jacobin and Marxist conceptions of utopia. Both emphasize a complete harmony of interests based on Rousseau's conception of the inalienable, indivisible, and always "correct" general will.[13]

In the East, Djilas voiced the concern that the communist pursuit of the utopia of a perfect or classless society resulted in dogmatism and human suffering.[14] This view is corroborated by Kolakowski, who terms despotism a "desperate simulation of paradise."[15] It led Mihajlov to conclude that Yugoslavia has reached a historic crossroads. It would either develop in the direction of a democratic, multi-party socialism, or revert to Stalinism.[16] The idea cost Mihajlov his freedom. He was sentenced once more in 1975. This time it was seven years of imprisonment at hard labor, plus four additional years of silence. While released in 1977, and visiting the United States since 1978, another warrant for his arrest is pending already in Yugoslavia. Could Mihajlov be right? Why does a "polycentric polyarchy" find it necessary to jail Yugoslavia's Mihajlovs? Is it possible that the Yugoslav system of workers' self-management and socialist democracy contains elements of Stalinism in the form of dogmatism, intolerance, and terror?

Patrick O'Brien pointed out that even Khrushchev's far-reaching administrative reforms ending the Stalinist terror did little to change the fundamental institutions of Soviet society. Hence, we have confused "de-Stalinization" with "liberalization."[17] But the reverse may also be true. In the Yugoslav case, there can be no doubt that a multi-faceted liberalization has taken place, whether one looks at the economy, governmental, legal, or cultural frameworks. Yet, while there has been a considerable liberalization in all spheres, this does not amount to a complete de-Stalinization. Elements of Stalinist dogmatism, monolithism, and intolerance remain in both the avant-garde's critique and the official Marxist-Leninist ideology, as well as in socialist practice.

In order to understand the roots of Stalinism, one must excavate not only Stalin, Lenin, Marx, and Engels, but Rousseau and Plato as well. This may seem presumptuous at first. What do Plato and Rousseau have to do with Stalin and the rest? More than is commonly supposed. For it was Plato who in his *Republic* and other writings put forth not only the organic conception of the perfect society, but supplied it with its king-pin, the concept of the infallible and omniscient Philosopher-King. In Rousseau's *Social Contract*, Plato's Philosopher-King merely changed his name to that of Legislator/Sovereign who was both above and beyond the reach of the law, while called to give men a constitution and equitable laws.[18]

As we mentioned in Chapter V, Marx and his followers adopted Rousseau's notion of the essential goodness of human nature which was corrupted by inequitable social institutions. They also adopted Plato's and Rousseau's concept of a benevolent, omniscient, and omnipotent Philosopher-King or Legislator-Sovereign in the form of the communist party as the vanguard of the proletariat. Finally, they internalized Rousseau's conception of the ideal society as an organic whole, boasting a unity or identity of interests. This identity of interests—the common good—Rousseau called the *general will*. The general will—or Sovereignty—was inalienable, indivisible, and could not be represented.[19]

At first, a general will which cannot be represented or delegated appears incompatible with the idea of a Philosopher-King or Sovereign. Rousseau solved this contradiction ingeniously by maintaining that:

> The general will is always right, but the judgment which guides it is not always enlightened.[20]

He maintained that the "will of all" did not amount to the "general will." It meant that people's decisions reached by immediate or direct democracy were not necessarily in their best interest. But if the people could not be trusted to arrive unaided at the common good which they wanted, who would lead the way? Plato's answer was: The Philosopher-King. Rousseau's answer was: The Sovereign-Legislator.

Rousseau defined the Sovereign in the same terms in which communists define their party. The Sovereign had no interests contrary to the individuals who compose the body politic: "The Sovereign, merely by virtue of what it is, is always what it should be."[21] What if you happened to disagree with the general will, the Sovereign's expression of the common good? According to Rousseau, you would be "forced to be free."[22]

It was thus that Jean-Jacques Rousseau, a foremost intellectual figure of the Enlightenment and the father of Romanticism, laid the theoretical foundations for totalitarian democracy. Rousseau was also in search of utopia, a new perfect social order, in which harmony would reign, the individual would become once more part of a primordial, mystical, organic whole ("back to nature") devoid of egoism, exploitation, inequality, servility, corruption, alienation, and de-humanization. Both individuals and society would be liberated by changing human nature, abolishing conflicts and inequalities, and transforming society into a terrestrial paradise. Particular interests and wills would be subordinated to the general will and the public interest. How could Rousseau's utopian vision lead to dictatorship?

In his brilliant study on the origins of totalitarian democracy, Jacob L. Talmon concluded that:

> The very idea of an assumed preordained will, which has not yet become the actual will of the nation; the view that the nation is still therefore in its infancy, a "young nation," in the nomenclature of the *Social Contract*, gives those who claim to know and to represent the real and ultimate will of the nation—the party of the vanguard—a blank cheque to act on behalf of the people, without reference to the people's actual will.[23]

In the hands of Marx and his followers, Rousseau's general will metamorphosed into the conception of the *class* nature of history and reality, and the communists' monopoly on both truth and action. The dualism of *homo duplex* in class society, the artificial separation of man into private and public spheres, would be abolished. All intermediate associations or organizations standing between the individual and the state would have to go. The state itself would eventually "wither away." Reality would be revolutionized. In the end, there would be free men organized as a free association of immediate producers in a new classless community of humanized social relationships. Political messianism thus came of age.

In Yugoslavia, both the party and avant-garde Marxist humanist thinkers are enthralled by Rousseau's and Marx's utopian vision. Edvard Kardelj contends that the party has the task of leading the fight for "progressive social positions" in all fields.[24] Najdan Pašić claims that the formal division of power and sovereignty, seniority and subordination are fading within self-managing institutions, whereas the party "retains a certain monopoly: that of representing the long-term interests of the workers, while confronting its views in a democratic procedure with others."[25]

Rousseau's general will is reflected in Andrija Krešić's notion that self-management by the workers cannot be mediated by anyone.[26] The utopian quest for total liberation is echoed by Dragomir Drašković, who maintains that the associated producers/workers must rule over all the conditions, results, and the organization of labor or the *totality* of material and social relations without which individual and class liberation are impossible.[27] Krešić sums up the most intimate sinews of the new secular theology of the abolition of politics as a separate sphere of man's activity in his statement that the majority of the suppressed population storms the political heaven in order to subdue it.[28] In Rudi Supek's view, the program is clear: What is needed is to bring about a truly *radical* change in the entire system.[29]

As noted earlier, the avant-garde maintains that what is needed is a total humanist revolution, rather than just tinkering with the political, economic, social, moral, and other spheres. But a call for a total revolution may be not only utopian but reactionary as well. As Neil McInnes writes, total revolutions exist only in the imagination:

> Indeed, any partial change—a reform or even a very considerable revolution—would fall so far short of total change as to cut a pale figure alongside the eucharistic miracle of transsubstantiation. In this way, mock-revolutionary absolute idealism can lead to conservatism.[30]

Of greater human concern is the fact that absolute idealism in the form of the utopian quest for total revolutions may require total solutions like Hitler's "final solution" to the Jewish question, which was anything but moral, democratic, or humanist. Some voices among the avant-garde question Marx's notion of the illegitimacy of particular interests. In his critique of Stalinism, Jovan Mirić noted that:

> Every political totalitarianism presents itself as the alleged defender of the *general* interest from particularistic tendencies.[31]

It is as if the avant-garde was becoming aware of Rousseau's afterthought that " . . . the pretext of the public good is always the most dangerous scourge of the people."[32]

1.2 Praxis and Self-Management

Both exponents and critics of the Yugoslav experiment in workers' self-management agree that self-management is a distinct feature of the Yugoslav scene. Ghiţa Ionesco called self-management the "most characteristic and genuine element in the Yugoslav structure of socialism."[33] Even Djilas, a stern critic of the Yugoslav system and the institution of workers' councils, conceded that these forms had the potential of becoming the carriers of genuine democratic self-goverment.[34]

The official Yugoslav view, that of the communist officialdom, considers the institutions of workers' self-management and social self-government as the essence of the new system of direct socialist democracy in Yugoslavia. They are the key to the future development of the system, destined to replace all the alienating forces and institutions, primarily the state, law, bureaucracy, and politics. Kardelj, while presiding over the Commission for Constitutional Questions of the 1963 Constitution, stated that self-management was the "basic principle" of the Yugoslav socio-economic and political system, while Mijalko Todorović called self-management the "historical aspiration of the working class."[35] These views were reenforced by the 1974 Constitution, and the Tenth and Eleventh Party Congresses.

Avant-garde Yugoslav Marxist philosophers, sociologists, legal and political theorists have elaborated the concept of self-management reflecting a cosmology of problems, questions, uncertainties, and attempted solutions which rival in their complexity the esoteric concept of alienation and the problems associated with it. The Yugoslavs agree that self-management and direct democracy constitute the answer to the phenomena of alienation. They share the view of Miroslav Pečujlić, who sees Yugoslavia as a giant experimental social field pioneering a new futuristic social system.[36] The essence of this new social system is a quest for a radical transcendence of all classical political institutions. Thus, Mihailo Marković calls for the supersession of such institutions as the state, political parties, army, political police, and the security services. For Marković, in order to abolish alienation in post-capitalist societies, bureaucracy itself will have to be transcended.[37] And Svetozar Stojanović posits the basic social choice in the contemporary era as that between self-managing socialism and bureaucratic statism, rather than between socialism and capitalism.[38]

Dragutin Leković sees in self-management the essential element of communism in its lower phase of socialism, while Predrag Vranicki maintains that self-management and direct democracy are the seeds of the historical *novum* (communism).[39] The Yugoslavs thus conceive self-management as nothing less than, to borrow a famous Hegelian phrase, the rose of the future in the cross of the present. It represents the means by which to traverse the difficult road from capitalism and state capitalism to socialism and communism.

Most problems associated with the concept of self-management are by and large unintelligible, at least from the Yugoslav Marxist perspective, without a thorough insight into the problems summed up by the concept of alienation. We examined in Chapters V and VI some of the major aspects of the concept of alienation, and found that Yugoslav interpreters see the alienation of labor as the root cause of all the other forms of alienation, be they economic, political, cultural, spiritual, or human. They found that the end result of the alienation of labor within the framework of the capitalist wage-labor relationship was the total alienation of man, *homo duplex*, in a dehumanized world of reified commodity relations.

The proposed remedy was to de-alienate and liberate man, reappropriate the surplus product of his labor, humanize production and consumption, supersede market relations, and return man from alienated conditions to his real self as a generic (social) being. *Praxis*—man's creative and self-creative activity—was conceived as the key to his de-alienation and liberation, and return to his essence (social being). Yugoslav theorists thus closed the conceptual gap between man's alienation and estrangement due to alienated labor and man's de-alienation and liberation via *praxis* or de-alienated labor, following Marx's postulate that

> The supersession of self-estrangement follows the same course as self-estrangement.[40]

The Yugoslav reformulation of Marx's concept of the essence of man as a being of *praxis*, and of *praxis* as the means for the de-alienation and liberation of man from inhuman conditions, raised more questions than it solved. Nevertheless, the major achievement of avant-garde Yugoslav Marxism was this very focus on man and the restoration of man to the center of the drama of historical materialism. The avant-garde found that man as *praxis* was the missing link between Stalinism—which continued the classical dehumanization and alienation of man—and authentic socialism or socialist humanism—for which the realization of the individual was the only legitimate goal. By their conception of man as a social being, the avant-garde connected the question of individual liberation with that of the liberation of the entire society. And this conception of man as a social being as well as a being of *praxis*, a creative and self-creative (self-actualizing) being, forms the basis of the Yugoslav concept of self-management.

Why, then, would the Yugoslav concept of self-management come under the rubric of totalitarian democracy? Because it carries the implications of Rousseau's general will and Plato's Philosopher-King. Supek proposes that a major goal of self-management would be to integrate "man-the-citizen with man-the-producer; to do away with that dualism between 'public existence' and 'private existence,' equally characteristic of representative democracy (especially with the strengthening of the state and bureaucracy) and of statist socialism."[41] Would this mean that the individual would finally make his own decisions regarding his individual and social existence? Not necessarily. Someone else may have to decide for him. As Marković put it:

> To be sure, the individual's acquisition of the right of decision-making does not at all guarantee that he will decide in the general social interest, or even in his own, personal interest, for he must be rather rational to judge his interest correctly.[42]

Since the individual's will may be neither rational nor enlightened, it could not guarantee his or society's best interests as expressed in Rousseau's general will. But, if the individual could not be trusted to make optimal social or individual decisions, who could? And, if there were many divergent particular interests, who would determine which among them, if any, were in accord with the common good? The avant-garde advanced an answer in the great utopian tradition:

> While there are a multitude of clashing particular interests of various enterprises and economic branches, various regions and nationalities—a particular force is needed which will mediate, arbitrate, and direct in the name of the general interest, although the general interest has not yet been constituted.[43]

What particular force would it be which would know the society's true general interest? Could it be the state, the party, bureaucracy, or professional politicians?

1.3 "Withering Away" of the State, Bureaucracy, and Politics

Both the avant-garde and the party consider self-management as the means for overcoming all forms of alienation in society and man. Djordjević and Vranicki write that self-management has the task of overcoming both major forms of alienation, that is, *economic* alienation based on private or state ownership of the means of production and *political* alienation due to the continued existence of the state, law, bureaucracy, and politics.[44] Of the two forms of alienation, the economic is considered more important and fundamental.

The Yugoslav answer to the query whether the state, bureaucracy, or professional politicians would determine the general interest is a resounding "no." The Yugoslavs consider, namely, the "withering away" of the state, law, bureaucracy, and politics as a precondition for any genuine and complete de-alienation and liberation of man, as well as for the creation of a communist community or free association of immediate producers.

They base their demand for the withering away of political institutions on Marx's, Engels', and Lenin's conceptions of the state, law, and politics as forces of oppression, instruments of class rule and exploitation. Supek claims that general social interests become sacrificed under capitalism to particular private interests through the state which, as a tool of the ruling class, becomes a source of bureaucracy and contributes to the further atomization of society.[45] To Vranicki, the state is but the political expression of the society based on wage-labor and private ownership of the means of production.[46] Hence, the institutionalization of the political power of the people in the state represents its alienation and transformation into an instrument ruling over the people.

Curiously, this Marxist vision of the capitalist state was carried over by the party and the avant-garde to the role of the state under socialism. Thus, the Yugoslavs maintain that, in addition to alienation caused by the state in capitalist society, the state can become equally oppressive in socialist society. Krešić characterizes limited self-management as a "square circle," since

> . . . workers' self-management under the tutelage of the state cannot be a new production relation in which exploitation of the workers is no longer known.[47]

Zagorka Pešić-Golubović voices the concern widespread among the avant-garde that the socialist state comes to resemble increasingly the classical state under capitalism by acquiring a "monopoly of social power."[48] Ljubomir Tadić wonders about the fateful inversion between means and ends in socialism, where authoritarian means metamorphose into ends, resulting in the freedom of the socialist state order rather than a socialist order of freedom.[49]

This led Marković to conclude that it was in the nature of the state to become a "modern leviathan, an alienated power, basically independent of the people."[50] Under socialism, the state could become the exploiter of the surplus value created by workers when dead labor (capital) continued to rule over live labor. The only way to abolish exploitation, argued Marković, was to ensure that the associated immediate producers (workers) regulated production and disposed of the surplus product of their labor. With workers' self-management, the necessity for the state and professional politics would also disappear.[51] In Supek's view, the introduction of self-management represented not only the conquest of the state by that first revolutionary act, but also its liquidation or immediate withering away.[52]

But what about the Weberian postulate of the routinization of the revolution and the bureaucratization of charisma? Echoing Trotsky's critique, both the party and the avant-garde consider bureaucracy as socialism's number one enemy. They are concerned lest the bureaucratization of the state under socialism lead to what Trotsky called the "triumph of the bureaucracy over the masses."[53] Yugoslav theorists maintain that the phenomena associated with the term "bureaucracy" are, like the state, remnants of class society. While realizing that bureaucracy thrives on socialist as well as on capitalist ground, they insist that it is a *political* (class) phenomenon whose chief source is the state. Bureaucracy is connected with hierarchy, political power, and the state as in Djordjević's study on bureaucracy and bureaucratism.[54]

The Yugoslavs have come to regard, in a rather sweeping manner, all problems associated with the state as expressions of bureaucratic *etatism* which they consider one of the major forces impeding the development of worker's self-management and social self-government.[55] Radomir Lukić and Marković maintain that bureaucracy is responsible for exploitation of the proletariat when it holds a monopoly of decision-making power in society, particularly in the form of deciding on the distribution of the surplus product. Hence, Lukić continues, the relationship of the proletariat toward the bureaucracy is the key problem of the power and authority of the proletariat, while the major task of the socialist state becomes not to strengthen itself, but rather build a free society in which there will be no need for the state.[56]

Having identified bureaucracy (and, hence, the state) as one of the "greatest enemies of socialism," Tito, in his speech of June 26, 1950, heralding the establishment of workers' councils in Yugoslav industry, quoted Lenin's prescription of the means to fight bureaucracy:

> A fight to the finish against bureaucracy, and complete victory over it, will only be possible if the *entire population has a share in the administration.*[57]

The Yugoslavs adopted Lenin's postulate on popular participation in the administration of society as the key to de-alienation and liberation of man and his labor. The corollary to this postulate of self-administration was the simultaneous withering away of alienated forms of government embodied in the state, bureaucracy, and politics.

Vranicki expressed the Yugoslav consensus that the state must begin to wither away already in the first stage of communism—that is in socialism—and that it was undialectical to separate the two stages.[58] The Yugoslavs rely on the writings of Marx and Engels, but also on Lenin's *State and Revolution,* in which he maintained that the seizure of power and the state by the proletariat must be followed up by the gradual supersession of the state. Why? Because the state only mirrors class antagonisms:

> . . . this proletarian state will begin to wither away immediately after its victory, because in a society without class antagonisms, the state is unnecessary and impossible.[59]

The concept of the withering away of the state is quite different from its abolition. Marx, Engels, and Lenin maintained that only the bourgeois state is abolished, while the proletarian state simply withers away.[60]   This alleged withering away of the state has been challenged by Richard Adamiak as a misleading myth camouflaging a statist ideology.[61] Undaunted, the Yugoslavs claim that the withering away of the state, bureaucracy, and politics will proceed concurrently with the development of new forms of self-government. The goal of these new forms of self-management/self-government is to transcend the estrangement or alienation of the political power of the people, return this alienated power of decision-making to the workers and thus, in Engels' terms, replace the government of persons with the "administration of things." Since political power embodied in the state bureaucracy, political parties, and the like rules over the people in favor of propertied interests of the few (echoing Rousseau), its reappropriation by the majority in the form of direct self-government constitutes the de-alienation of man and the return of his alienated *political* powers to himself as *social* powers (see this Chapter's epigraph).   As Miladin Životić put it, the negation of the alienated institutionalization of society would be the negation of *political* society and political institutions as "instruments of power over man." The proletariat, whose function is to bring about universal human emancipation, abolishes those institutions whose function is to rule over men.[62]

The liberation of man and his de-alienation in communism entail, according to Boris Ziherl, a transition from governing in society's name, that is, from socialist statehood, to a system of social self-government based on social ownership of the means of production.[63] The task of the socialist state in this process of developing new forms of social self-government would be to abolish "its own independent functions in the process of production, trade, and distribution," concluded Todorović.[64] We are back to square one: the fundamental aim of the proletarian revolution. In Krešić's view, it is the abolition of wage-labor and capital, and the restoration of human significance to production.[65]

Is it possible for the state, bureaucracy, and politics to wither away? Are workers' self-management and social self-government radically new institutions beyond the state, bureaucracy, and politics? How are different interests to be reconciled under socialism? Does the utopian quest for unanimity and harmony of interests demand Stalinist monolithism and dictatorship? In brief, is the socialist utopia compatible with freedom?

2.   Self-Management as the Emancipation of Labor

Marx once described the state as "the intermediary between man and human liberty."[66]   He concluded that proletarians, in order to assert themselves as individuals—that is, to re-appropriate themselves and the world—would have to abolish the existing societal organization in the form of alienated labor and its supreme expression, the state.[67] This is echoed by the avant-garde:

> . . . revolution is legitimate *all the time* because the state rule is never just and never serves the interests of the oppressed bulk of the people.[68]

The state, law, and politics were for Marx and Engels expressions of the alienated power of the people resting as superstructures on the material foundation of equally alienated exploitative production relations.[69] It is significant that they conceived of socio-political institutions and practices as deriving from prevailing economic conditions. This forms the basis of the Marxist-Leninist doctrine of the economic base and the socio-political superstructure.

Yugoslav Marxist theorists build their conception of self-management and the de-alienation and liberation of man in socialism precisely on this basic Marxist framework of the primacy of the economic sphere in social life. The search for new democratic institutions of social self-government thus becomes synonymous, in Yugoslav perspective, with the search for new democratic and non-exploitative relations in the sphere of economics or material production. The socialization of the means of production is, according to Djordjević, the first act in the true humanization of man, representing the overcoming of *economic* alienation.[70]

However, the mere socialization of the means of production, while necessary, is not a sufficient condition for man's liberation, the Yugoslavs argue, because private property, according to Marx, is not the cause but rather the *effect* of alienated labor. The emancipation of *labor* constitutes, therefore, the true goal of socialism and of the proletarian revolution, contend Djordjević and Krešić.[71] The realization of freedom in the realm of economics—the primary goal of social-ism—Vranicki terms as the precondition for the attainment of all the other human freedoms.[72]

The avant-garde and the party thus returned to Marx's conception of alienated labor as the basis of all forms of human alienation and posited self-management by workers in economic enterprises as the solution to the problem of alienation. Vranicki maintained that the concept of self-management must be viewed in the perspective of Marx's conception of man since self-management was essentially the process of outgrowing the various forms of human alienation characteristic of bourgeois society.[73] Workers' self-management, stated Vranicki, constitutes the negation of both the bourgeois society and of the bureaucratic-etatist forms of the early phase of socialism.[74]

The emancipation of labor via self-management means to the Yugoslavs simultaneously:

(1) Freeing of labor from exploitation by the capitalist, state capitalist, bureaucracy, or other collective exploiters;

(2) Humanization of work, or the restoration of human signif-icance to production;

(3) Withering away of the state, law, bureaucracy, and politics; and

(4) Transcendence of all forms of alienation, be they economic, political, cultural, or spiritual; culminating in:

(5) De-alienation and liberation of man, the reintegration of his split personality, and return to himself as an integral social being.

The aim of self-management is conceived as the emancipation of man and the reinstatement of the whole man in all his dignity in a de-alienated community of (economically) free men.

Yugoslav theorists consider the organization of and control over production by workers' self-management as the basis for the development of the whole man in society in which freedom within the sphere of production, according to Marx, consists in the rational management of the material exchange with nature by the associated producers.[75] Man would allegedly supersede his economic and political alienation due to wage-labor (alienated labor) and its expressions in the state, bureaucracy, politics, and false consciousness once he reappropriated his object-ified essence and organized production relations on the basis of self-management. The development of communism, concluded Vranicki, was thus the realization of the historic rights of the working man, the supersession of all institutions which thought and acted for him, and mostly against him, and the establishment of a society in which the administration of people would be supplanted by the adminis-tration of things.[76]

The emancipation of labor or the abolition of wage-labor via the socialization of the means of production and self-management became in Yugoslav perspective the solution of the riddle of history and the answer to Marx's own unanswered question on alienated labor posed at the end of his *First Manuscript* (1844). Socialism, reiterated Djordjević, began to solve the age-old contradiction between labor and capital, the producer and his submission and domination by the product, production and consumption, and between the real man and the abstract citizen. Socialism began to solve, Djordjević assured us, all these contradictions in favor of man.[77] Seen by Vranicki, self-management and direct democracy constitute the historical axis of socialism, that is, those seeds, elements, and relations which are the essential characteristics of the new social order of communism.[78]

The avant-garde maintained that, in addition to emancipating labor by abolishing the exploitative framework of the wage-labor relationship, self-management represented also the precondition for the humanization of *work*. The humanization of work, contended Supek, depended on *social* determinism, that is, on social production relations, and on *natural* determinism, that is, the ways in which man used his labor power whether in harmony with his personal requirements as a producer or not. The way to humanize work, continued Supek, was to create new objective (physical) and subjective (human relations) conditions for work which would strengthen the worker's socialist consciousness.[79]

Organizations of associated labor, workers' councils, and self-management of enterprises thus emerged as the most immediate and effective forms for the emancipation and humanization of labor since they represented the framework of human relations concerned with production.

2.1 Basic Organizations of Associated Labor (BOALs)

The 1971 Constitutional Amendments and the 1974 Constitution set up the basic organization of associated labor (BOAL) as a new socio-economic relation and a "fundamental form of association of labour."[80] The BOALs are conceived of as the basic cells in a society-wide integration of labor. Their basic goal is to transcend the wage-labor relationship, stimulate productivity, and provide a framework for deciding over surplus value created by the associated producers.

There are three organizational forms of associated labor:

(1) Basic organization of associated labor;
(2) Work organization; and
(3) Composite organization of associated labor.

The BOAL is an autonomous, income-earning part of the work organization. Work organizations are of two types: (1) individual or (2) associated. The individual work organization is a small, integral unit. No BOALs can be set up within it. On the other hand, the associated work organization consists of two or more BOALs. Workers in the BOALs can decide for their work organizations to join into composite organizations of associated labor via self-management agreements. Mihajlo Velimirović indicates that the workers within BOALs constitute the subjects taking decision, whereas their work organizations are the subjects associating in a composite organization.[81]

Yugoslav theorists thus view the BOAL as the basic cell in the system of self-management. The chief characteristic of the BOAL, maintains Vladimir Bakarić, is its capacity to create independent value.[82] The BOAL's chief motivation is expected to be its willingness to coordinate its income-earning activities with other organizations of associated labor, beginning with its own work organization, of which it is a part. The BOAL is, of course, the fundamental constitutive unit of Marx's republic of associated labor.

Our discussion in Chapter VI highlighted the crucial place given to the notion of surplus value in Marxist thought. The BOAL is the Yugoslav solution to the dilemma of exploitation based on the alienation of surplus value. In Slaven Letica's analysis, the BOAL is the association of the integral man, that is, of man the decision-maker or manager and his labor power or potential. Letica sees the BOAL as the definitive resolution of the antagonism between the individual and the market. While the worker still sells his labor power on the market, he now allegedly unites the roles of the seller and the buyer in determining the price of his labor power. This signifies the return of the alienated wage worker to himself as a de-alienated, humanized, social being. Letica insists that it also means the beginning of the process of development of the intrinsic value of labor power and the whole man.[83]

But there is trouble in paradise. The question has arisen among self-managers within BOALs of just what constitutes surplus value, and how much income the associated producers should dispose of. The regime emphasizes the norm of distribution according to work performed. It appears also that the major *economic* reason for setting up BOALs was the regime's concern with increasing labor productivity. But why BOALs?

In Kardelj's view, the BOALs make it possible for workers to follow the movement of their past labor along with social capital and thus motivate them to increased responsibility for their own and the BOAL's contribution to productivity. But Kardelj also chides the BOALs for egoism, for preferring investment in their own basic organization to outside investments. There is also the problem of covering deficits in other BOALs. Here, Kardelj recommends what amounts to a capitalist remedy for socialist ills. A prosperous BOAL which lends money could demand from another BOAL running deficits to "remove the weaknesses in its operations within a certain time limit, or that the business organs or workers responsible for the situation be removed, and other measures along these lines."[84] Thus, the tendencies of some to live at the expense of others would be curtailed.

Another dilemma haunting the BOALs is the question of disposable or net income. As Velimirović notes, the new social relationships set up within BOALs are essentially income relationships.[85] Hence, the question of how workers are to manage the production and distribution of income. As we saw in Chapter VI, Yugoslav theory holds that all income produced belongs to the workers. But, there is an important qualification. What official spokesmen mean by income is "net income," rather than total income. Thus, the workers in BOALs decide independently only over a part of the total income left over after various social obligations in the form of tax contributions to local, communal, insurance, and other funds have been met.

When speaking of net income, regime spokesmen, like Kardelj, like to invoke the Marxist-sounding notion of the alleged "class substance of income." Why the need for this quasi-ecclesiastical phraseology? Because even net income does not belong to the workers. It cannot be distributed for current consumption. We know the reason for this: it is the necessity to invest a portion of this net income. This, urges Kardelj, will increase the common productivity of labor and contribute to the rational management of scarce resources. It is unclear how this unromantic socio-economic position of the workers is supposed to "do away with all the remaining vestiges of wage-labour mentality among the workers."[86] Especially, since socially-owned property belongs to everyone and no one. Who cares?

Even more disturbing in terms of Marxist theory and socialist practice is the fact that it may be impossible to determine or measure surplus value. Paradoxically, it is not the avant-garde, but official party spokesmen, who raise precisely this point. Kardelj writes that due to the complex processes of modern industrial production, involving the contributions of science, technology, organization, socially-owned property, and associated labor, it is impossible to determine the exact quantity and quality of an individual's contribution to the social product.[87]

But, if an individual's contribution to total value cannot be measured, how can surplus value ever be determined? And without a precise delimitation of surplus value, how can the individual wage-earner ever be compensated and the surplus value be returned to him? Unless the surplus value is returned to the worker, he will continue to exist as an alienated, de-humanized, exploited, and impoverished being dominated by estranged capital lording it over him! Is the worker, then, destined to continue to live in a state of exploitation and alienation of his labor power under socialism as well?

2.2 Workers' Councils

The 1963 Constitution listed the following basic principles as the "inviolable foundation of the position and role of man" in a socialist society:

(1) Social ownership of the means of production;
(2) Emancipation of labor;
(3) Self-management;
(4) Equality of rights, duties, and responsibilities conforming to constitutionalism and legality; and
(5) Economic and social security of man; among others.[88]

These five major principles of human rights laid down in the 1963 Constitution, and reaffirmed by the 1974 Constitution and the Tenth and Eleventh Party Congresses, all reflect the Yugoslav concept of economic democracy and its central place in socialist democracy. The Yugoslavs maintain that these principles actually represent a fusion of economic with political democracy. This interpretation is reflected also in the *Small Political Encyclopædia*, which differentiates between four basic forms of social self-government:

(1) Self-management in enterprises;
(2) The *opština*;
(3) The power structure;
(4) The Socialist Alliance.[89]

Self-management in enterprises means primarily the BOALs (called economic or work units before 1971) and workers' councils in industry, and self-managing bodies in other institutions. *Opština* (*opčina* in Croatian) refers to local government and is synonymous with the Yugoslav concepts of the local community (*mesna zajednica*) and the commune (*komuna*). The power structure implies the system of delegates and assemblies (*skupštine*) at all levels of government, communal, republic (or provincial), and federal. And the Socialist Alliance of the Working People of Yugoslavia is defined as the broadest political form of people's self-government.

Apart from BOALs, Yugoslav theorists consider the workers' council as the basic form of self-management by the immediate producers in economic enterprises and as such the basis of all the other forms of workers' self-management and social self-government. The Yugoslavs admit frankly that Marx did not talk specifically about workers' councils, which became of such paramount importance in their system.[90] They realize that the concept of workers' councils is an old revolutionary idea, but reserve to themselves the distinction of having elaborated it most thoroughly.

Lenin is given credit for introducing workers' councils (soviets) into the Soviet Union as new forms of social organization, and for warning that the state must begin to wither away immediately. Vranicki claims that the "council" (soviet) became the symbol for the supersession of bourgeois civilization, the symbol for a world without exploitation, classes, the state, bureaucracy, politics, private ownership of the means of production, national hatred, and conflict. The council came to stand equally, contends Vranicki, for the negation of the bureaucratic-etatist forms of the first stage of socialism.[91]

Both the avant-garde and the party agree that the year 1950 signifies a veritable turning point in Yugoslav socialism, or, as Vranicki put it, a "new historical milestone."[92] On June 25, 1950, President Tito declared that

> Today in this country the factories, mines, and the like are going to be managed by the workers themselves. They themselves will determine the methods and volume of work, they will know why they are working, and the purposes for which the results of their labor will be used.[93]

For a considerable period, however, workers' self-management in Yugoslav industry remained more of a promise than a reality for manifold reasons. Živan Tanić distinguished two periods in the early development of the unique institution of workers' councils: (1) 1950-1956, during which most workers' councils existed more or less only on paper or their functioning was merely a formality; and (2) From 1956, a period of democratization of the councils, rise in interest and interaction between them and the workers (producers). Tanić concluded that, in spite of the trend toward democratization, undemocratic forms persisted; yet workers' self-management had become increasingly independent.[94]

The fact that in the 1950s the workers' councils were only nominally "self-managing" for the most part was corroborated by early studies like Jiri Kolaja's observation of two Yugoslav factories in 1959. Kolaja found a general lack of interest on the part of workers in their council since it was unrepresentative. The council worked, namely, in close cooperation with management. On the other hand, Kolaja found degrees of interaction between the four major organizations in both factories, that is, management, the workers' council, labor union, youth organization, and, in the background, the League of Communists. The conclusion of Kolaja's study: the major function of both workers' councils was to inform and to educate.[95]

The educational function of the workers' council is, of course, not antithetical to their *raison d'être*, which includes the humanization of work and the development of greater awareness in the worker, as Supek pointed out, of the nature of his activities in the working collectivity.[96] This educational-participationist function of the workers' councils remains an integral element of their broader self-managing functions. It seems particularly important in a society which has to train a continuing influx of illiterate, semi-literate, and unskilled youth and other workers of peasant background. But worker management has its educational-participationist value even in developed, modern industrial societies. David Tornquist equated this function of the workers' councils with social adventure in that "workers' management allows a man to get more than money out of his job."[97] Tornquist found great variation in the degree of development and functioning among workers' councils in Yugoslavia. His general finding remains valid up to the present.

There are indications, however, that in the 1960s the councils began to develop more according to their original blueprints. Denitch points to the economy as a crucial turning point for the councils' acquisition of at least minimal enterprise autonomy.[98] Some workers' councils and their boards of management apparently acquired sufficient autonomy to ignore resolutions of various party and state organs, deciding instead on the basis of sectional commercial interests, as indicated by Singleton.[99] This development of the workers' councils is attested to by criticism from different quarters.

On the one hand, critics of the regime's policies like Djilas and Nenad Popović dismiss self-management and workers' councils as a new myth and a smoke screen, respectively.[100] Djilas claims that the workers' councils are dominated by party members and that, at any rate, their scope of the single firm is extremely narrow. Hence, they cannot solve any of the important social or national problems. At the same time, Djilas admits that workers' self-management "can be used as a handhold by those who identify socialism with social justice and human freedom."[101]

Criticism diametrically opposed to that of Djilas and Popović is voiced by none other than Kardelj, who complains that workers' councils are becoming too independent. In his Report to the Eighth Session of the Central Committee of the League of Communists of Slovenia on October 13, 1969, Kardelj bore down on a recent tendency among workers' councils, especially those in Slovenia, to "turn the workers' council into some sort of institution of formal democracy, instead of it being an institution of socialist production relations in which the working class, i.e., working man will play the leading role."[102] Kardelj did not elaborate on his critique of workers' councils as institutions of formal democracy, but one may conjecture that he had in mind either or both: (1) the possibility of the workers' councils going beyond the narrow scope of the firm in their deliberations, that is, practicing politics; and (2) the possibility that workers' councils were becoming really self-managing, independent even of the party.

The most comprehensive critique of self-managing institutions and practices, including workers' councils, in Yugoslavia has flowed from the pens of avant-garde Marxist philosophers and sociologists. The avant-garde found to its surprise and dismay that workers' self-management in the enterprises was reproducing all the ills associated with capitalism, including the privatization of socially-owned property, egoism, sectionalism, power politics, and new hierarchical relationships. How could that come to pass?

Golubović contends that self-management has been reduced to discussions about income, that work organizations function on the principles of decentralized etatism, and that workers are reduced to hirelings in socialism, since the state delegates only minor decision-making functions, and even those primarily to the state organs, like directors and management within the enterprise.[103] Even party spokesmen admit that something unusual has happened to self-management bodies. Stipe Šuvar writes that the traditional oligarchic system of power has reproduced itself within self-managing organizations in the form of informal groups as centers of social power.[104] In his April 19, 1979 address to a special meeting of the CC of the LCY, the late Tito lamented the fact that:

> In places, concealing themselves behind alleged self-management forms, narrow groups are trying to pull strings, and are placing self-management organs, assemblies and delegations before accomplished facts.[105]

Ivan Kuvačić sees these informal groups as powerful extensions of the bureaucratic apparatus hiding behind the legal façade of workers' councils, while Pečujlić adds that these informal groups monopolize management and distribution, escape control, and impose their own narrow interests.[106] Thus, the avant-garde maintains that bureaucracy and etatism do not wane, but merely migrate from one place to another, from the federation to the republics, communes, enterprises, and self-management bodies. What that means, concludes Supek, is that hierarchical relationships and authoritarian power structures are reproduced within the system of workers' self-management.[107]

Marković sees the assumption of control over workers' councils by small oligarchic groups such as managers, heads of administration, and political functionaries as a new form of class struggle.[108] Supek blames the alienation of self-managing institutions and practices on their routinization. He sees the dynamics of democracy in managing enterprises as greatest at the beginning, that is, at the point of introduction of self-managing institutions. Soon, however, self-management becomes "a routine activity, in which the technical problems of running business predominate over problems of participation of the members and social problems in general."[109]

Another major problem of workers' self-management in Yugoslavia has been the absence of responsibility, proper distribution of power within the enterprise, and institutions for conflict resolution. Both Kardelj and Branko Horvat emphasize that personal responsibility has not been precisely defined in self-managing bodies and that the separation of responsibility from decision-making has led to irresponsibility, inefficiency, and a negation of self-management.[110] The Yugoslavs are slowly beginning to realize that, as Stephen M. Sachs put it, " . . . responsibility that is defined only collectively means that no one can be held responsible in practice . . . ."[111] This lack of responsibility among both the managers and the managed dovetails with the Marxist conception of socially-owned property.

How can there be proper responsibility when, as Lendvai points out, some self-managers can neither read nor write?[112] And how can there be proper responsibility in a system in which Gerry Hunnius finds that

> The director has great influence but little legal authority, and hence, little clear-cut responsibility, while the workers' council has

legal authority but lacks influence.[113]

Ichak Adizes described the vast chasm between authority and responsibility, and between contribution and inducements for Yugoslav executives, which has led to the phenomenon of "contractual management."[114] It has also led to a thorough rethinking of the entire Marxist framework of the nature and role of self-managing institutions in socialism.

Veljko Rus reemphasizes the importance of the institutions of self-management in spite of the emergence of other vital social issues in Yugoslavia, such as the student movement, unemployment, emigration, and nationality conflicts. Rus' criticism turns around two basic issues: the division of labor and private ownership of the means of production, and their respective influence on the distribution of power and goods in society. Rus' conclusion is that the division of labor is more important than ownership, and that in order to limit bureaucratization of self-management institutions, one should concentrate more on the relationship between active and passive power, which depends crucially on the division of labor within an organization.[115] Rus maintains that the collectivist model of self-management, built on the premise of conflictless participation, is misleading in at least three respects:

(1) It considers all conflict and opposition as a class enemy to be excluded from the social fabric;

(2) Its goal should not be to protect specific interests but to "deny the interests of the working class, of meritocracy and intellectuals as separate interests;" and

(3) It cannot be an efficient instrument for negotiation, reconciliation, or contractual agreements if it is not based on a bargaining process.[116]

Western observers like Joel Dirlam, James Plummer, Egon Neuberger, Estelle James, Sharon Zukin, and Bogdan Denitch all note the absence of institutions for conflict resolution in Yugoslavia. Neuberger, James, and Zukin note that the director and his staff or the enterprise *aktiv* (basic LCY cell)/Establishment dominate self-management bodies in enterprises.[117] Others point out that the solidary conception of society conceived as a harmony or unity of interests could exacerbate conflicts between workers and management by ignoring them. Hence, the wildcat strikes on the Yugoslav scene. All this led Benjamin Ward to conclude that Illyria may be institutionally as well as economically unstable.[118]

As to the ideal of workers' participation in self-management, the actual practice leaves much to be desired. Jakov Blažević reports that worker membership in workers' councils declined from 76.2 percent in 1960 to 67.6 percent in 1971.[119] More disturbing is the actual composition of workers' councils (see Table 5). Observers East and West note that white collar and skilled workers are overrepresented on the councils, and so are party members who constitute one-third of council membership as opposed to six percent in the general population, while blue collar, unskilled, and women are underrepresented. Sidney Verba and Goldie Shabad observed political stratification within workers' councils in which party members and other well-to-do Yugoslavs predominate. They concluded that

... the dispersion of decision-making into decentralized institutions—be they workers' councils in factories or self-governing councils in towns and neighborhoods—does not automatically mean a more equitable dispersion of decision-making power to a greater number of citizens as advocates of participatory and industrial democracy argue.[120]

Sachs writes that the level of participation by the average worker is low and

TABLE 5. Yugoslav Workers' Councils, 1952-1979

Year	Workers' Councils	Membership in Workers' Councils		
		Total	Women	Youth
1952	4,646	105,018	13,401	NA
1953	4,758	105,540	13,817	9,175
1954	5,324	115,479	12,520	8,936
1956	5,989	124,204	15,983	13,807
1957	6,314	128,607	19,987	19,798
1958*	26,620	305,844	49,329	19,465
1960	28,023	336,899	57,370	25,372
1962	24,408	323,834	56,430	23,641
1964	17,064	348,533	107,328	38,896
1965†	6,746	149,404	25,915	15,674
1966†	6,809	150,389	26,510	14,841
1968	15,700	346,918	105,057	31,578
1970	15,333	339,857	105,506	46,899
1972	15,081	343,653	110,668	46,365
1976	22,151	344,839	91,455	46,663
1979	29,833	445,730	129,679	57,896

Source: *Statistički godišnjak Jugoslavije*, 1981, p. 79.

* Since 1958, data include elected members of councils in organizations of associated labor in public affairs (government).

† Refers only to BOALs in the economy.   NA = Not Available

that a high degree of alienation remains in the workplace. Sachs conducted interviews in 1972-73, asking workers a few days after a workers' council meeting what had transpired there. The answers were less than felicitous. Workers, regardless of age, sex, education, or length of employment in the enterprise, did not know what happened at the meeting. Moreover, they saw the workers' council meeting as none of their business, as a job concerning only members of the council itself.[121] This is, of course, not much different from the actual practice of popular participation anywhere, East or West.

Dirlam and Plummer concur that worker participation is often little more than an empty ritual, that only a third of the workers' council members care to examine detailed documents submitted to them, and that even in Slovenia (which boasts the highest literacy, skills, and technology) they would hesitate to question complex technical proposals put forward by management.[122] Yugoslavs themselves admit that the director and the management board often dominate workers' councils, since management controls the information flow and the latter, writes Aleksander Bajt, requires professional knowledge. Thus, in Bajt's view, "workers' decision making is frequently reduced to choosing among alternatives presented by managers, and with preferences strongly influenced by managers."[123]

On the other hand, some Yugoslavs score the "rather naive ideology contained in legislation and political propaganda" which advocates "direct participation in administrative work as indispensable to safe-guarding the interests of the workers" as only complicating self-management practice.[124] Others see a more fundamental malaise in workers' self-management practices: the absence of workers. They note with concern that the workers' desire for participation in self-managing institutions, including workers' councils, is dwindling, while the drive to earn is increasing.

How can this lack of interest on the part of workers in self-management be reconciled with the Marxist notion of worker solidarity? As a self-manager told Jovan Mirić, he worked for money, not for solidarity.[125] There is also evidence that the socialist ideal of universal participation/direct democracy/self-management may hinder, rather then help, the development of the whole man. Adizes found that many workers no longer wanted to be in self-management bodies because it hurt their family life. The reason: interminable meetings without compensation lasting up to eight hours held after working hours, including Sundays.[126] Contrary to the self-management ideal, Sachs found that the workers had no organizational support in disputes with administrators or technocrats. Furthermore, many were reluctant to voice "their real opinions, contradict directors, or complain about conditions or policies because they were afraid of losing their jobs."[127]

What about unions which protect workers' interests in the West? It is an open secret that unions are merely party and governmental transmission belts in communist systems. Hence, it is not surprising that in Yugoslavia many workers expect their workers' council and other self-management bodies to act as unions in their behalf, protecting the workers' interests. Zukin complains that one of her respondents seemed to be confusing self-management with trade-unionism.[128] But, there is nothing accidental about it. The workers' conception of workers' councils as a substitute for the "company" unions is reflected in the greater interest shown in council meetings dealing with such traditional trade union concerns as take-home pay, working conditions, housing, recreation, and vacations. When workers' councils and other self-managing bodies turn into "company" councils, the workers protest by the only quasi-legal means left to them—wildcat strikes.

David A. Dyker dismisses the notion of effective participatory management in Yugoslav enterprises.[129] In this, he is seconded by Marius J. Broekmeyer in the West, and Veljko Rus in the East, who maintain that despite 25 years of self-management, the actual distribution of power has remained essentially unchanged in Yugoslav enterprises.[130] At the same time that the system fails to bring about effective worker participation, notes Dyker, it does insure trade-union rights to workers. As a by-product, he sees workers' councils contributing to the cost-inflationary dynamic prevalent in the Yugoslav economy.

Even more perplexing is the conclusion by Rus, Tom Baumgartner, Tom R. Burns, and Dusko Sekulić that direct worker participation in self-managed enterprises does not amount to the full liberation of work nor to political emancipation. This is so since genuine liberation and emancipation presuppose the effective political control of the larger institutional system, that is, the levers of political power.[131] Moreover, Ellen Turkish Comisso contends that workers' control does not eliminate bureaucracy, alienation, or inequality, either. On the contrary, it may foster them. Comisso is led to believe that the major socio-political consequence of workers' control is organizational change—a continuing demand to reorganize workers' control. Hence, workers' councils emerge as basically destabilizing factors whether in a planned or a market economy. Indeed, she sees workers' councils as transforming a planned economy into a market system, and vice versa. While plant-level democracy and socialism are not necessarily utopian, argues Comisso, there is a paradox in that workers' councils may contribute to structural strains in a polity, which aggravates the process of trade-offs in the pursuit of societal goals.[132]

The very model of universal participation in workers' councils and other self-managing bodies may be misleading, if not counterproductive. Thus, in Zukin's study an important question was posed by some Yugoslavs as follows:

> Who would you prefer to make the decisions in a hospital . . . the surgeon or the janitor?[133]

Josip Obradović found that workers actually ranked self-management last or next-to-last as a source of job satisfaction. Pay, working conditions, job interest, promotional opportunities, all ranked higher. The most paradoxical finding was that participants in self-management were more alienated than non-participants.[134] Their alienation was ascribed to excessive expectations.

Rus came to the conclusion that what was needed was not an equalization of power among diverse groups within the enterprise, but rather making power more responsive. This obviously flies in the face of such Marxist tenets as equality in participation, supersession of hierarchical relationships, ending the separation between labor and management, and abolishing power, separate interests, bureaucracy, and politics. Instead, Rus calls for a division of power, checks and balances in the form of a functional and professional rather than political polycentrism:

> Our goal should be not to weaken management's responsibilities but to develop countervailing mechanisms which would guarantee the equilibrium between influence received and influence exerted and would provide for the orderly adjustment of conflicts of interest.[135]

Conflicts of interest under socialism? But their admission would shatter the Marxist-Leninist myth of socialist solidarity, the assumption that the proletariat has only one true interest which the party defines and guides to its realization. It would also mean heightening the division of labor, professionalization, and reestablishing the old hierarchical order of the rulers and the ruled, all expressions of class divisions, exploitation, and alienation characterizing the capitalist social order. Rus concedes that the roots of the problems associated with self-management may lie in the rigid system of basic societal values which oscillate between "abstract 'revolutionary radicalism' and 'occasional compromise'," and which put the blame of shortcomings on social practice rather than on accepted ideals.[136] It is true that the Yugoslavs consider their new system of self-management as being still in its early stages of development. Zoran Polič writes that, in the final analysis, self-management is not a goal in itself but rather a method through which the goal of new socialist relations and the full affirmation of the individual can be reached.[137] But means cannot be divorced from ends. And the question remains whether utopian goals necessitate Stalinist means even when the road to hell is paved with good intentions.

2.3 Local Communities

The Yugoslav conception of direct democracy dovetails into workers' self-management in the economic sphere and social self-government in the political sphere. We saw above that BOALs and workers' councils, primary organs of workers' self-management in the economy, harbor many contradictions both in theory and practice. This is the more disconcerting as Yugoslav theorists are vaunt to boast of self-management as genuine economic democracy, even if political democracy may still be in its infancy. Some avant-garde thinkers question, however, this traditional Marxist dualism between economic and political democracy. Stojanović maintains that economic democracy is only a myth, since it cannot develop without political democracy.[138]

But how can one measure political democracy? Western democratic tradition holds that political democracy is intimately intertwined with the multi-layered fabric of human rights. It considers the relationship of the state and social system to the individual and his free exercise of all his rights as the scale for measuring the extent of political democracy. Surprisingly, some Yugoslav Marxist theorists concur, at least partially, in this view. Jovan Mirić argues that the major characteristic of a democratic political system is pluralism of *thinking and action,* rather than merely institutional pluralism.[139] What is the extent of pluralism of thought and action in the Yugoslav model of self-managing socialism?

Apart from BOALs and workers' councils, the Yugoslavs conceive of the local community as a basic cell of self-management/self-government, linking the economic with the political and social spheres. The 1963 Constitution introduced local communities (*mesne zajednice*) to supersede the earlier housing communities in cities and local committees in rural localities. They are seen as an integral part of the commune or *opština* which is to transfer more and more of its governing functions to local levels. In 1978, there were some 12,654 local communities in Yugoslavia (see Table 6). In the master plan of the capital city of Belgrade, local

TABLE 6. Local Communities in Yugoslavia, 1978

SFRY	Community Councils	Total Council Membership	Communities with Conciliation Councils	Number of Conciliation Councils	Conciliation Council Membership
Total	11,330	235,323	9,928	11,526	52,578
City	1,596	54,402	1,469	1,580	8,677
Village	8,093	138,499	7,006	8,189	34,806
Mixed	1,641	42,422	1,453	1,757	9,095

Source: *Statistički godišnjak Jugoslavije*, 1981, p. 108.

communities are to include from 5,000 to 15,000 people.

Smaller local communities have proved to be more desirable. In cities, the optimal size of local communities is about 10,000 people. They are financed by individual taxes (*samodoprinos*), grants, enterprise and commune budgets, and other sources. In 1970, they held over 50,000 meetings with more than 150,000 agenda items. Of major concern were: child care, adult welfare and health care, construction and maintenance of public utilities, education, and culture. Also, social and recreational life, consumer supply, health facilities in settlements, other questions concerning the standard of living, national and civil defense, cooperation with enterprises and other organizations, and the like.[140]

Since 1971, local communities conclude social compacts and self-managing agreements with organs of the commune, enterprises, institutions, and communities of interest. Increasingly, they resort to referenda on various issues. In brief, local communities are to bring decision-making power to the people on issues which affect their daily lives. This direct decision-making is expected to facilitate the formation of common interests between citizens and enterprises, and to reduce conflicts of interest.[141] Local communities thus emerge in Yugoslav theory as one of the three integral areas of direct democracy in the commune, in addition to work organizations and other basic socio-political organizations. To Leon Geršković, local communities represent the basic cells of territorial self-government, while to Bogdan Pilić they are the most basic cells of political organization in the *opština*.[142]

But the Yugoslavs do not stop there. They claim that the local communities are a new form of self-managing institutions devoid of "any elements of power or coercion."[143] The 1974 Constitution concurs in this view that local communities do not exercise political power. Rather, they represent a "specific type of community of interest."[144] At the same time, some Yugoslavs admit that in certain communes there are strong tendencies for local communities to develop as outposts of the organs of power.[145] Other observers, East and West, warn that the real structure of power within the commune and local communities is vastly different from the formal model of self-government. How do local communities actually function? To answer this question, one has to look at voters' meetings, the basic decision-making body within local communities.

Geršković maintains that if direct democracy is to take hold within self-managing bodies in the political sphere, then it must be affirmed in such basic organizations as local communities and communities of interest. Yet he admits that voters' meetings remain bureaucratic and undemocratic.[146] A most intimate look at the local power structure in Yugoslavia is that by Zukin, who observed the proceedings of voters' meetings in the capital area. Apart from the local community's very narrow scope of competence, Zukin found that the political actors were stratified into several levels under self-management while the much-heralded scope of "initiatives from below" was hierarchically determined.[147] The actors were stratified into the Establishment, issue activists, citizen-Partisans, and unmobilized masses. In the 10,000-strong local community with 4,000 of voting age, some 40 people, usually the same ones, attended voters' meetings, against a backdrop of mass indifference/apathy, with most people considering politics boring or uninteresting.

Zukin saw the apathy of the masses complemented by the *aktiv*/Establishment's monopoly over political action. While the citizen-Partisans' demands for social equality and justice regarding unemployment, income, housing, standard of living, and the like were too broad to be resolved at the local level, the self-managers never received any feedback to their proposals from higher organs. Some Yugoslav social researchers admit that voters have no influence on their representatives, nor are the latter always informed about opinions of their constituencies. As a respondent in Zukin's study put it: " . . .it's all managed from the top down."[148]

A general feeling of lack of political efficacy seems to pervade the Yugoslav political scene even at this level of participation closest to the average citizen. The curious thing is that this feeling of political impotence extends to party members as well. Some 50,000 members left the party in 1970 alone, according to Zukin.[149]   Where have all the party members gone? What happened to socialist solidarity?   And whence this inordinate concentration of economic and political power, which renders even ordinary party members impotent? How is it possible that the Yugoslav attempt to establish a conflict-less social system leads, instead, to a conflict-prone society?

2.4   The Commune

If self-managers are unable to influence decisions directly at the level of voters' meetings in local communities, can they do so at the level of the commune? What constitutes a commune, to begin with?   The Yugoslav concept of the commune grows organically out of that of the workers' council, of which it is in one sense an extension.   The *Small Political Encyclopædia*, as we saw, ranked the *opština*, or commune, second among the four basic forms of social self-government.

Yugoslav Marxist theoreticians have traced the intellectual antecedents of the commune back to Marx's *Civil War in France*, Lenin's *State and Revolution*, and other Marxist classics.   Kardelj points out that Marx proclaimed the Paris Commune of 1871 in his *Civil War in France* as that political form in which it would finally be possible to achieve the full emancipation of labor.[150]   Vranicki quotes Lenin's *Future Tasks of Soviet Power* on the concept of self-management of producers in workers' councils organized as communes with the responsibility for the organization of production as well as the end products and their distribution.[151]

The Yugoslavs distinguish among three basic aspects of the commune:

(1)   As a form of political-administrative organization of territorial units;

(2)   As a socio-economic community responsible for the distribution of the surplus product; and

(3)   As a basic cell of social self-government responsible for the integration, coordination, and harmonization of individual interests and the interests of particular collectivities with the general interests of society.

Kardelj advanced the thesis that the commune would outgrow its political functions and concurrently strengthen its socio-economic functions.[152]   The commune as the basic socio-economic self-governing unit of society is seen destined to transcend the alienated institutions of government embodied in the state, bureaucracy, and politics. The commune is thus allegedly the carrier of the new form of classless society, along with BOALs, workers' councils, local communities, communities of interest, and other self-governing bodies.   The 1963 Constitution held that: "Self-government by the citizens in the commune is the political foundation of the uniform social-political system."[153]   In the 1974 Constitution, communes are "both self-management communities and the basic socio-political communities, based on the power of and self-management by the working class and all working people."[154]

The Yugoslavs use the terms *komuna* (commune) and *opština* (in Serbian) or *općina* (in Croatian) interchangeably, which may indicate the essential nature of the Yugoslav commune as basically a decentralized unit of local government or administration. Jack C. Fisher maintains that the Yugoslav emphasis on *komuna* or *opština* follows a distinction between a socio-economic community and a political-administrative form of organization. A commune, in Fisher's view, is "a unit that is economically and socially as well as administratively homogeneous."[155]

The development of Yugoslav communes accelerated with the adoption of the Law on the Organization of Communes and Districts in 1955 and the promulgation of the 1963 Constitution.   Since 1955, the *opštine* or *komune* expanded both territorially and in the sphere of functions increasingly delegated to them at the expense of districts (*srezovi*) and the republics. While the communes expanded in territory and population, their number shrank from 1,479 in 1955 to 500 in 1969, increasing to 527 by 1981 (see Table 7). The distinguishing features of the communes were assessed by Kardelj as:

(1) Independence of action in the sphere of economic development; and

(2) Organic connection with workers' councils and other democratic forms of social self-government.[156]

Article 96 of the 1963 Constitution stated that the communes' major functions were to:

Provide the material and other conditions necessary for the work and development of the productive forces; guide and coordinate economic development and the development of the social services; determine and distribute the means for common communal requirements; create the conditions required to satisfy the material, social, cultural and other common needs of the citizens; coordinate individual and common interests with the general interests . . . .

In the 1970s, however, following the 1971 Constitutional Amendments and the 1974 Constitution, more and more of the commune's governing functions were to be delegated to BOALs, workers' councils, local communities, communities of interest, and other self-managing bodies. The new delegate system is expected to provide for a much closer linkage between the various levels of self-management/self-government. The Commune Assembly, its highest decision-making organ, is composed, as of 1974, of three chambers: (1) Chamber of Associated Labor; (2) Chamber of Local Communities; and (3) Socio-Political Chamber. Delegates are elected to a 4-year term, with a limit of two consecutive terms, with both delegates and delegations subject to recall.[157] The new electoral system is seen as transcending the traditional system of political representation in capitalist states. That's the theory. What about actual practice?

Šuvar in the East and Hunnius in the West observe a considerable difference between the nominal and the real structure of power in the commune. Both agree that although the Assembly (*skupština*) is in theory the highest decision-making organ in the commune, in practice the real power is often lodged in informal groups or a combination of formal and informal decision-makers.[158] This fact was admitted even by Tito in his Report to the Eleventh Party Congress:

There are still quite a few instances when decision-making on various socio-economic and political issues is concentrated within the communal committee, and sometimes various informal groups or individuals make the decisions themselves in the place of the competent organs and organizations.[159]

What about workers' participation in decision-making? Šuvar admits that worker participation ends, as a rule, at the level of their work organization, and that within political organizations workers are mainly passive members.

The positive aspect of the commune consists in its role as a unit of decentralized decision-making within a basically highly centralized system at the republic and federal levels. Yet, while decision-making in the commune is decentralized, it does not necessarily mean that it is democratic. The commune is supposed to be a system of direct democracy, but its highest body, the *opština skupština* (Commune Assembly)—usually referred to simply as *skupština* (Assembly)—consists of *delegates* elected to its Chambers (see Table 8). Furthermore, while the people vote for delegates, the nominating process is guided by the party

TABLE 7. Yugoslav Communes, 1957-1981

Year	SFRY	Bosnia & Hercegovina	Montenegro	Croatia	Macedonia	Slovenia	Serbia		
							Total	Kosovo	Vojvodina
1957	1,441	191	36	299	86	130	699	80	201
1958	1,193	191	28	278	73	122	501	65	161
1959	1,103	134	28	275	73	92	501	65	161
1960	839	134	28	275	73	89	240	28	57
1961	782	122	20	244	73	83	240	28	57
1962	751	122	20	230	73	66	240	28	57
1963	581	106	20	111	61	66	217	28	49
1964	577	106	20	111	61	62	217	28	49
1965	577	106	20	111	61	62	217	28	49
1966	516	106	20	111	32	62	185	22	44
1967	510	106	20	111	32	60	181	22	44
1968	501	106	20	104	32	60	179	22	44
1969	500	106	20	105	30	60	179	22	44
1970	500	106	20	105	30	60	179	22	44
1971	500	106	20	105	30	60	179	22	44
1972	500	106	20	105	30	60	179	22	44
1973	500	106	20	105	30	60	179	22	44
1974	500	106	20	105	30	60	179	22	44
1975	510	106	20	114	30	60	180	22	44
1976	508	106	20	112	30	60	180	22	44
1977	512	106	20	112	34	60	180	22	44
1978	515	109	20	112	34	60	180	22	44
1979	516	109	20	113	34	60	180	22	44
1980	516	109	20	113	34	60	180	22	44
1981	527	109	20	113	34	65	186	22	50

Source: *Statistički godišnjak Jugoslavije,* 1981, p. 586. Data for 1957-58 are from the 1979 *Statistical Yearbook,* p. 588.

TABLE 8. Delegates to Commune Assemblies, 1953-1978

Year	SFRY	Bosnia & Hercegovina	Montenegro	Croatia	Macedonia	Slovenia	Serbia		
							Total	Kosovo	Vojvodina
1953	81,460	9,076	2,037	14,613	4,776	6,743	44,215	NA	NA
1957	68,933	9,688	1,525	17,560	5,041	5,441	29,678	3,774	8,588
1963	42,994	7,146	1,311	9,432	4,022	3,803	17,280	2,248	3,972
1965	41,445	7,160	692*	9,448	2,814	3,803	17,528	2,261	4,021
1967	40,279	7,188	1,343	8,868	2,822	3,723	16,335	2,083	3,953
1969	41,002	7,636	1,379	9,078	2,760	3,591	16,558	2,127	3,953
1974	49,071	10,229	1,599	12,183	3,249	1,506†	20,305	2,430	4,812
1978	50,022	10,916	1,758	11,482	3,898	1,435†	20,533	2,430	4,914

Source: *Statistički godišnjak Jugoslavije*, 1981, p. 79.

*   Only half of the representatives elected in 1965 are shown.

†   Refers to delegates elected to the Socio-Political Chamber.

NA = Not Available

and its transmission belts, primarily the Socialist Alliance and the trade unions. It has led avant-garde theorists like Stojanović to conclude that:

> To build up an integral system of self-government it is necessary to have a developed and democratic system of political organization and activities. But our socio-political organizations, despite declarations to the contrary, still are the transmissions of the League of Communists. And in the League of Communists itself, democracy is still in its infancy.[160]

The avant-garde and the party are equally concerned about the lack of democratic processes within self-managing institutions, their bureaucratization and alienation. Milentije Popović thinks that bureaucratic logic is the end result of the underdevelopment of self-government in the commune. He sees direct democracy in the commune reduced to the activities of the Assembly and its political organs, while local communities and other forms of citizen participation remain underdeveloped.[161]

The Yugoslavs also worry about the commune's lack of integrative functions and its tendency toward independence and autarky. Damjanović notes the contradiction inherent in the concept of self-government and independent communes, and the problems associated with maximum freedom and autonomy, on the one hand, and coordination and social direction in the national and international frameworks, on the other.[162] The 1974 Constitution calls for cooperation between and association among communes. They can associate in regional communities, communities of communes, urban communities, and may even cooperate with local communities in other countries, national and international agencies and organizations, within the framework of republic and federal policies. Yet the communes seem to be drawn in the opposite direction, toward self-sufficiency or autarky, enclosing themselves within republic or local confines.

Radivoje Marinković and Tomac score the communes' tendency to become communities of exclusive self-interest, subordinating economic development exclusively to their own interests. They conclude that in order to promote the integrative role of the communes and prevent social atomization, production must be organized according to an overall social plan.[163] Rus rounds out the criticism of the communes by concluding that "re-integration on the level of micro-group, cooperative or local communities is anti-human and unsupportable provincialism."[164]

The fate of the communes in Yugoslavia seems to be intimately linked to that of workers' councils and workers' self-management. Considering the fact that BOALs, workers' councils, local communities, communes, and communities of interest are postulated as the most basic forms of Yugoslav socialist democracy, their importance for the future development of the Yugoslav system and of Yugoslav Marxism can hardly be exaggerated.

2.5 Communities of Interest

Among the most recent innovations in the Yugoslav theory of self-management/self-government are communities of interest. The Yugoslavs maintain that the realization of direct democracy in the socio-political sphere must begin at the level of local communities and communities of interest. What sort of a political animal is a community of interest?

A community of interest is a self-managing association which unites consumers and producers in both economic and non-economic areas of concern. There are five basic communities of interest in the non-economic sphere: education, science, culture, health, and social services. In all these areas, communities of interest are to replace the role of the state by permitting users and suppliers of various services to decide directly on financing and distribution. According to the 1974 Constitution, communities of interest establish their own assemblies con-

sisting of recallable delegates elected by working people, organizations of associated labor, and other self-managing organizations and communities.

The major rationale for establishing communities of interest, holds Blazević, is
to provide the citizen with a full accounting of just how much he is paying for what
services.[165] This citizen-monitoring function is expected to contribute to the most
rational economic use of scarce resources. It is also expected to bridge the gap
between the consumers and the suppliers of various services, and thus eliminate or
reduce conflicts of interest.

Speaking at the 20th Assembly of the Standing Conference of Towns in
Herceg-Novi on October 4, 1974, Kardelj outlined the concept of the communities
of interest as "a new organizational mechanism, in terms of both democracy and
self-management, which will go a long way toward improving the effectiveness of
our system of self-management." Kardelj saw three major aspects of communities
of interest:

(1) Socializing certain functions or democratizing the jurisdiction
     of the state by integrating social interests in a specific field;

(2) Horizontal integration of self-management; and

(3) Organization of large self-managed systems.[166]

Communities of interest are thus expected to contribute to the transcendence
of market relationships and the withering away of the state in accord with the
Marxist tenet that workers should dispose of surplus value (even if surplus value
cannot be determined). The communities of interest are expected, however, to fit
into the framework of commune and republic assemblies. Furthermore, state
organs will retain supervisory control and inspection, insuring that the decisions
made by communities of interest are "in keeping with a spirit of solidarity."[167]

While *non-economic* communities of interest are organized on a territorial
basis, *economic* communities of interest are to run along functional lines. This is
of major importance in a society in which self-managing institutions and economic
enterprises are delimited by ethnic-national boundaries, reducing economic efficiency as well as socialist and any other kind of solidarity. Both the avant-garde
and the party are aware of the fact that functional organization runs counter to
the prevailing ethnic-local-republic trend. As Pečujlić remarks: economic integration usually stops at local or republic levels. And Vojan Rus claims that
communities of interest often have less self-managing content than the assemblies
and socio-political organizations.[168]

The 1974 Constitution calls for the establishment of communities of interest
in such diverse fields as pension and disability insurance, housing, communal
activities, power production, water management, transportation, communications,
and various spheres of production. Communities of interest may combine into
larger communities, associations, or federations, and establish other forms of
mutual cooperation. In brief, communities of interest are to be the most important
institutions of self-government in the socio-political sphere besides local communities and communes. It is also apparent that the potential scope of the
communities of interest, especially in terms of functional integration, may be
broader than that of the communes. Delegates of communities of interest are to
participate in the appropriate socio-political bodies of the commune and republic
assemblies.

Along with BOALs and communities of interest, the 1971 Constitutional
Amendments and the 1974 Constitution provided for new procedural devices of
interest aggregation, articulation, and bargaining. These devices are *self-management agreements* and *social compacts.* They are to be utilized by all self-managing
institutions, from BOALs to communities of interest. In Časlav Strahinjić's view,
self-management agreements and social compacts are new types of legal relations,
moral and legal, but with the legal element allegedly withering away.[169]

Self-management agreements serve primarily to determine mutual rights, obligations, and responsibilities with regard to the division of labor, pooling of labor and resources, production and distribution of income among workers in basic and other organizations of associated labor, communities of interest, etc. Social compacts, on the other hand, are to regulate socio-economic and other relations of broader general interest by organizations of associated labor, economic chambers, communities of interest, and other general associations. The trade unions are expected to have greater initiating and monitoring functions regarding self-management agreements and social compacts. Disputes are to be settled by internal arbitration, courts of associated labor, economic or regular courts. Yet the legislation involved is said to be withering away.

More critical is the fact that the party's guiding role is to intensify parallel with the system's phenomenal institutional pluralization. How can the party's quest for socio-economic, political, and ideological monopoly be reconciled with market socialism, constitutionalism, socialist legality, and institutions of direct democracy ranging from BOALs to the federation?

3. Direct Democracy, Constitutionalism, and the Party

The Yugoslav conception of man as a being of *praxis* forms the foundation of the concept of direct democracy. The Yugoslavs consider self-management via BOALs, workers' councils, local communities, communes, and communities of interest as the emancipation of labor. And that, in turn, means the outgrowing of class institutions of the state, law, bureaucracy, and politics resulting in the de-alienation and liberation of man and society.

On closer inspection it becomes obvious, however, that the Yugoslav self-managing institutions from BOALs to the system of assemblies at communal, republic, and federal levels, including the leadership of the broadest form of social self-government, the Socialist Alliance, are *representative* forms of government rather than instances of direct participation of all the citizens in common affairs, that is, direct democracy (see Table 9). Stojanović admits that direct democracy is an unattainable ideal, a Weberian ideal-type, or as he terms it a "limiting concept."[170] Stojanović concludes that the problem of democracy will, hence, always remain open-ended because of the inescapable necessity for *mediation* and *representation* even in post-socialist forms of society's development. Marković deplores the misleading Yugoslav "myth of direct democracy," which insists that workers will decide in the future directly all key questions of social development, obviating the need for any kind of indirect, representative democracy.[171]

There is a consensus among the avant-garde and the party that the present Yugoslav institutional system combines both direct and representative democracy. Official spokesmen see in the *delegate system* the means for the final supersession of representative political institutions. Central to the delegate system is Rousseau's conception of the general will as inalienable, indivisible, and incapable of representation. Thus, Tomac claims that the delegate system demands that the power of the working people remain inalienable.[172] According to Milan Matić, the principle of delegation implies that the power and sovereignty of the people are not held in trust or carried over onto representatives, but exercised directly by delegates elected by self-managing institutions.[173]

If these delegates were allowed to decide freely on societal issues, the Yugoslav system would indeed approximate direct democracy. In reality, the Yugoslav system is a quest for totalitarian democracy. This becomes apparent from the Yugoslavs' own description of the nature of the delegates' "imperative mandate." The Yugoslavs hold that delegates and delegations cannot be allowed to act contrary to the general interest or the common good. In Djordji Caca's view, the delegation cannot relegate all rights and responsibilities to a delegate. The delegate, continues Caca, must desist from all autarchic, partial, particularistic, or egoistic positions in favor of the general interest.[174] And Angel Čemerski chides those delegates who represent the exclusive interests of their own delegation, organization of associated labor, or community, since such behavior is allegedly a

TABLE 9. Delegates to Federal, Republic, and Provincial Assemblies, 1953–1978

Year	Federal Assembly	Republic Assemblies						Provincial Assemblies	
		Bosnia & Herce-govina	Monte-negro	Croatia	Mace-donia	Slo-venia	Serbia	Kosovo	Vojvo-dina
1953	554	196	122	263	182	194	291	120	185
1957	587*	217	150	278	191	205	310	165	190
1963	670	400	254	440	340	400	440	270	349
1965	670	399	254	438	340	400	440	270	350
1967	670	394	254	437	335	400	440	270	350
1969	620	399	254	440	333	285	437	269	345
1974	308	320	135	355	240	262†	340	190	245
1978	308	320	165	355	250	262†	340	190	245

Source: *Statistički godišnjak Jugoslavije*, 1981, p. 79.

* Elections for the Federal Assembly were held 23–26 March 1958.

† Refers to the number of delegate positions, rather than actual delegates to the Chamber of Associated Labor and Chamber of Local Communities.

regression to a system of political representation.[175]

The late Kardelj maintained that the delegates cannot build socialism spontaneously, since

> The essence of the delegate system is not to be found in a broad formal democracy, or in hundreds of thousands of elected delegates, nor in the frequency of their meetings, but rather in the direct expression of the will and interest of the working people.[176]

Hence, Tito added, the party "must be present wherever self-managers take decisions, and it must be an inner driving force of the system and not above or beyond it." And, Tito boasted at the Eleventh Party Congress: "the League of Communists has become incorporated into the basic cells of society."[177] Tito was right, judging by the growth in the number of basic party organizations: from 15,825 in 1971 to 47,212 in 1977, as well as the increase in overall League membership to 1.8 million by 1980. It is the party, then, which continues in the role of carrier of Rousseau's general will and whose task is to inform the delegates concerning society's true interests.

The actual results of the delegate system and the "imperative mandate" have fallen below expectations. On the one hand, party members have proven singularly inept in interpreting the general will applied to particular circumstances. Hence the call for accountability and responsibility for decision-making which continues to resound in the Yugoslav press, especially since the Eleventh Party Congress. On the other hand, delegates and delegations have become mired in confusion and indifference. The Yugoslavs admit the fact that the delegates have become "lazy," some even at the time of the system's genesis in 1974. Major problems of the delegate system, according to a 1978 Gallup-type poll among Belgrade citizens, reported by Dragan Jovanović, were:

(1) Lack of worker and citizen interest to become involved in the activities and processes of delegate decision-making;

(2) Inadequate linkage of delegations and delegates with workers and citizens;

(3) Lack of timely information;

(4) Hierarchical (forum- and director-like) decision-making;

(5) Excessive influence of executive-political and administrative organs;

(6) Slow harmonization of various interests;

(7) Underdevelopment of self-management relations;

(8) Laziness of both functionaries and delegates in carrying out their duties; and

(9) Lack of precisely defined responsibilities.[178]

Tito boasted in his April 19, 1979 address to a special meeting of the CC of the LCY that in the 1978 elections some 800,000 members of delegations were elected, along with another 53,000 delegates to assemblies of socio-political communities, and that more than three million people were involved directly in political decision-making through the delegate system. Yet, curiously, in the capital, few citizens know their delegate even to the Commune Assembly. Moreover, 67 percent of those polled knew nothing about their delegation, whether it worked or how. Some 40 percent thought that the delegation existed only on paper.

To top it off, no less than 31 percent of delegation members themselves in the poll declared that they knew nothing of the work of their delegation! While Jovanović concluded that the delegates have failed due to the sheer complexity of the system, Gavriel D. Ra'anan provides the clue to the real source of failure:

> . . . in effect, Yugoslavia has professionalized governance at the top, powerless, amateur, pro forma representation at the base, and a powerful, centralized, party apparatus supervising and running the system as a whole.[179]

Surprisingly, some avant-garde thinkers have begun to question aspects of direct democracy, such as the alleged non-political nature of delegates and the desirability of quick rotation. Thus, Jovan Mirić wonders what delegates are if not *political* mediators and, above all, representatives of *particular* interests?

> The system of self-management not only does not render political representation and mediation superfluous, but, on the contrary, it can develop only on those assumptions. *Only political total-itarianism renders political (and all other) mediation superfluous. It knows best all interests and methods for their resolution!*[180]

Mirić concluded that the concept of unity of interests is a misleading fiction, and that only representative democracy is possible.[181]

Vojan Rus criticizes both the quick rotation of delegates and direct elections conceived as exclusive means of participatory democracy as potentially dysfunctional. Instead, Rus sees indirect elections preferable in certain cases such as the election of representatives to the SFRY Presidency by republic assemblies. And a constant turnover of delegates in commune, republic, and federal assemblies may jeopardize the continuity and synthetic role of those bodies. Much more important for continuing democratization of self-managing institutions would be to establish more democratic electoral practices and press coverage, and a plurality of candidates for each elective position. As things stand, Rus sees a continuing suppression by the media of initiatives and criticism not officially sanctioned.[182] Stojanović concludes that in the absence of genuinely free elections to commune, republic, and federal legislative bodies, or even within the party, one can only speak of *formal* self-management, that is, self-management in name only.[183]

Even if direct democracy were possible, the self-managing or truly democratic character of it in the Yugoslav framework would remain problematic because of its interlocking relationship with the League of Communists. During the Stalinist era in Yugoslavia, 1945-50, this issue did not exist. The party was dominant, ruling through various transmission belts such as the state and party machineries, sports, educational, and economic associations. The issue of direct democracy versus party monopoly was born together with the establishment of workers' councils in industry, the first form of workers' self-management, in 1950. But, since workers' councils existed mostly on paper during much of the 1950s, the issue, while it did exist, was still not a major one. Only in the 1960s did the relationship between different forms of workers' self-management or direct democracy and the socio-political and ideological monopoly of the party become extremely complex and problematic. This was true especially after the promulgation of the 1963 Constitution, the 1965 economic reforms, and the ensuing socio-political reforms, such as the attempt to divorce the party from the machinery of government.

From the party's vantage point, the problem can be stated in a nutshell as the dilemma of how to preserve socialism and communism while at the same time attempting to further revolutionize existing social relationships and develop more effective forms of social self-government and direct democracy within a framework of constitutionalism and legality. The party's problem is, then, briefly, how to preserve socialism while developing democracy. The party sees itself as the ideological midwife mustering all "progressive" forces for the development of socialist relations and combatting two major trends impeding self-management: (1)

bureaucratic-etatism and (2) *bourgeois-liberalism* and *anarchism.*

Yugoslav Marxist theorists maintain that even organs of self-management in socialism tend toward bureaucratization. The forces allied with bureaucratization of self-management institutions are characterized as bureaucratic-etatist forces consisting chiefly of those who advocate a return to administrative socialism ("state capitalism") and who oppose the development of a market economy and concurrent economic and social reforms. These forces are also blamed for clinging to outdated ideals of early socialism such as:

(1) General equality and absolute justice (supposedly attainable only in communism);

(2) Identification of the working class with manual workers exclusively;

(3) Speed in the execution of decisions; and

(4) Greater unity of goals and action.[184]

The League of Communists argues, on the other hand, that what the society needs now is ideological unity on a new basis which is democratic and dynamic, and which should be established by people's self-government, guided by the party.

The second phenomenon which party spokesmen take to task is that of bourgeois-liberalism and anarchism, whose exponents are credited with advocating the end of all planning and social direction in the economy, favoring the unfettered operation of the market mechanism (economism), and the establishment of a multi-party system. Tito made it clear that socialist democracy "does not mean democracy for [these] antisocialist elements . . . ."[185]

3.1 The Paradox of the Party

The difficulty of establishing a new ideological unity on a *democratic* basis is due to the League's continuing conception of itself as the *leading ideological force* in society. Thus, according to Kardelj, who cites the *Communist Manifesto,* the *communists* are "that section of the working class and workers movement, capable of *thinking on behalf of the whole* and of *seeing further than the working class masses.*"[186] It amounts to Plato's Philosopher-King or Rousseau's Legislator-Sovereign. So long as this conception of the party's role persists, it is less than meaningful to talk about pure and unadulterated *direct democracy* or *self-management/self-government,* because of party guidance in all forms of workers' self-management and social self-government.

The party's continuing monopoly over social life has led to a far-reaching critique by avant-garde thinkers. The avant-garde considers the current Yugoslav practice as a hybrid consisting of self-managing institutions in the base and a strong power structure above, dominated by party and other elites, primarily bureaucrats and technocrats. Antun Žvan and Golubović write that present institutions of self-management have not brought political decision-making power to the people:

> Our present condition is as follows: it is not the associated workers who decide about the existential issues of their own state but it is the other way around—it is the state which decides about these issues of the disunited producers' associations, restricted within their factories.[187]

It has led Marković to observe that the problem of the alienation of political power after the socialist revolution has not yet been solved in theory or practice.[188] Marković considers the party in post-capitalist—that is, socialist—

societies as "an even more important center of alienated political power than the state." Alienation in socialism can allegedly be remedied only by a radical supersession of bureaucratism and a withering away of the party.[189]

Some avant-garde thinkers have connected Stalinism with communist monolithism and party monopoly. Muses Supek:

> ... the deformation of socialism which is called stalinism and which is sometimes very naively reduced to the term "cult of personality," has its roots in a definite conception of the state, of the avant-garde role of the communist party, of the monolith nature of the political system, an extremely centralized one, with all the ensuing consequences, such as: bureaucratism, etatism, full control of ideological trends, especially of cultural creation, that is to say, complete subjugation of the intelligentsia; briefly, it has its roots in an absolutistic conception of rule "from above" or "over the people" in the name of the working class and the workers in general."[190]

Avant-garde thinkers are thus beginning to realize that Stalinist dogmatism and the cult of personality may stretch back to Lenin and his conception of the party. Milan Mirić notes that Stalin's personal contribution to Stalinism has been overrated, while the possibilities for bureaucratization and institutional thinking ushered in by Lenin's work are forgotten.[191] In Kresić's view, Stalinism or "political papism" consists in a centralized mechanism of political economy at whose apex is the all-powerful and omniscient top politician-economist—the source of all authority and knowledge. It is the figure of God in human garb.[192]

The avant-garde thus launched a radical critique of both bureaucracy *and* party monopoly. Dragoljub Mićunović outlined the following measures in the struggle against the bureaucratization of society:

(1) Direct citizen control over public affairs;

(2) Freedom of criticism of the work of governmental bodies;

(3) Right of prosecution and removal of office-holders in the event of abuse of office;

(4) Executive bodies to function publicly; and

(5) People to be informed.[193]

Pesić-Golubović considers the principle of free elections essential to a human community and the development of the individual's inner sources of motivation. Tadić concurs in the principle of free elections and the voluntary association of producers at all levels of society, "without any tutelary influence by 'higher authorities' . . . ."[194] In Marković's view, professional politics and bureaucracy as a ruling stratum can be overcome only by direct participatory democracy, on the one hand, and the possibility of challenging and criticizing all practical activity, including that of the leaders, on the other. Above all, Vranicki calls for the abolition of the party monopoly over public opinion.[195]

All this has led the avant-garde to insist that the party itself must become more democratic, along with other social institutions. Stojanović and Marković believe that socialist democracy can develop only if all institutions from BOALs to the federation are constituted on a self-managing basis. In Marković's vision, this calls for

> a pluralism of less formal political groups and loose political organizations without party apparatuses, hierarchy, and unquestioned loyalty to the leadership instead of to the people.[196]

Stojanović holds that genuine democracy is impossible in self-managing institutions without democracy in the party. What about the party's insistence on *unity* of thought and action? Tadić observes that monolithism in thought would have to be eliminated in order to achieve genuine unity in action.[197] The socialist dilemma of the *single alternative* is exposed by Danilo Pejović and Marković, who note that freedom of political choice is possible only with regard to at least two alternatives.[198] This has led some Yugoslavs, like Stevan Vračar, to ask: "Would it not be more natural to have two parties, both of which struggle for socialism?"[199]

This Djilasist solution—a multi-party system—is clearly unacceptable to the party. Curiously, it is rejected by most avant-garde thinkers as well, who argue not for a multi-party system, but for a system without parties. They would prefer to see the withering away of the state, bureaucracy, and political parties, including the communist party. Lukić theorizes that political parties are destined to "wither away," replaced by direct decision-making which converts every citizen, in one sense, into his own political party.[200] How realistic are the calls for the withering away of the League of Communists?

Saddled with the Hegelian albatross of "Absolute Knowledge" and Marx's injunction that the communists represent the vanguard of the proletariat, the party must lead, even when it does not know where to go. As Marko Nikezić, himself a communist, once pointed out, communists need to free themselves of a certain conservatism which substitutes a renewal of ideology and the party for solutions to changing societal needs.[201] What about this ideology and its central method—the dialectic? Is it a reliable compass for the party's leading role? Not so. The dialectic can be and has been used to accuse the party and its individual members of both left-wing and right-wing deviation.

If the party ventures into unexplored territory, following Marx's call to transform the world, it can be accused of adventurism, lack of scientific orientation, infantilism (Lenin), that is, left-wing deviation and revisionism. On the other hand, if the party sticks to proving its revolutionary theoretical armor in the fire of everyday practice and hence adjusting theory to it, it can be accused of pragmatism, conservatism, petty-bourgeois slovenliness, *khvostism*—following instead of leading the masses—that is, right-wing deviationism.

The communists are fond of distinguishing between "objective" and "subjective" conceptions of truth, reality, and the like. But, Kuvačić and Stojanović have pointed out that the distinction between objective and subjective truth was instrumental in the Stalinist manipulation of people—including communists—forming the basis on which the individual could be accused, tried, and sentenced even without being aware of his guilt. It led to a new *homo duplex*, a revolutionary with a split consciousness, a Prometheus in front of the enemy and a weakling in front of the party, concludes Stojanović.[202] Furthermore, this unlimited *partiinost*, or the party as the carrier of objective truth, led to the justification of any and all party actions, whether correct or incorrect, moral or not. It could also lead to the destruction of the very self-respect, dignity, and authenticity of the individual revolutionary-communist. Stojanović and Supek conclude that a revolutionary can sacrifice everything to the party and the cause except his dignity, which is the moral nucleus of his personality.[203]

Stojanović observes that the major danger for a revolutionary movement is the finalization of the revolutionary organization itself. From a mere vehicle to revolutionize social relationships, the Stalinized communist party becomes an end in itself, wielding a total monopoly of socio-economic and political power. Thus, the revolutionary organization can enslave both its own members and society as a whole. It thus becomes a source of new forms of alienation in socialism. It represents an infamous "finalization of means and the instrumentalization of ends."[204] Stojanović concludes that utopian goals may be responsible for the emancipation, alienation, and tyranny of the means:

> An organization which stubbornly tries to realize utopian goals is driven to the pursuit of politics at any cost. The more difficult it finds the goals to achieve, the more terrible will be the means

which it will employ.[205]

This involution/inversion between revolutionary goals and Stalinist means constitutes a strong undercurrent in avant-garde thought. Mihailo Djurić has noted also the paradox of the apparently most humane political programs leading "straight to the most cruel political praxis."[206]

Does the conception of an infallible and omniscient party necessitate a leader, *Führer, vozhd,* called to lead the proletariat to the promised land? Could that be the reason why the official mythology in communist party states projects the party leaders—Stalin, Tito, Mao, Castro, Ho-Chi-Minh, and the rest—larger than life? Stojanović writes that:

> For its rank and file and for the society as a whole, the organization is under these circumstances identified with the bearer of absolute truth, including absolute moral truth. An organization of this kind, which finds its embodiment in the leadership, acts under the illusion of possessing absolute knowledge which comprehends absolute historical necessity. How can this leadership be anything but arrogant, conceited and intolerant?[207]

Even if its leadership is dethroned, the party remains infallible. It continues to serve as an altar at which individuals and groups, including communists, have to be sacrificed in order to preserve the purity of the secular faith and the unchallenged authority of its high priests. Curiously, the idol worship encloses both the victim and the executioner within its iron gates. Truly, the owl of Minerva flies only at dusk, as Hegel said. Yet this creature of the night portends darkness, not light. It is an evil omen.

The party, if it wanted to become genuinely democratic, would have to trade Minerva's owl for a dove which begins its flight at dawn, ushering in a new day and a new age of understanding, love, and peace. And the albatross of Absolute Knowledge would have to metamorphose into an eagle unafraid of free flight, soaring into unexplored distances. It would be a very different party, very human and fallible, as before, but no longer hiding behind the terrible mask of infallibility and perfection. If it knew not where to lead the nation, it would admit it openly and ask for help. It would act as an equal partner, rather than The Master, in the quest for a more humane future.

Following the Croatian crisis of 1971, official spokesmen increasingly emphasize the *class* nature of socialist democracy and self-management as expressions of the *dictatorship of the proletariat.* But the avant-garde has voiced reservations about these concepts, which in the past were used to justify the party's unlimited mandate. Gajo Petrović writes that the conception of the transition period from capitalism to communism as a dictatorship of the proletariat is a "very dangerous theory, which can be used, and actually has been used, for antisocialist purposes." How? Because, according to that conception, inhumanity, unfreedom, and violence can be justified as the best or only possible "dialectical" road to socialism.[208]

In Tadić's view, vulgar Marxism harbors the seeds of Stalin's cult of personality and the Stalinist perversion of the socialist society. It petrifies the dictatorship of the proletariat into a dictatorship of the charismatic-bureaucratic type, while perverting the Marxist theory of the withering away of the state into a theory of the strengthening of the state in socialism and the intensification of the class struggle.[209]

Since 1971, the League of Communists has also re-emphasized Lenin's conception of the need for party unity based on *democratic centralism.* Some avant-garde thinkers interpret it as an ominous sign of a possible return not only to Leninism, but to Stalinism as well. Stjepan Pulišelić points out that the insistence on democratic centralism in the past led to bureaucratic centralism and a serious infringement of democracy.[210] Others conclude that what the party needs is just the opposite of democratic centralism. According to Stojanović, there is a need for the development of genuine inner party democracy which can mature only if the party recognizes the legitimacy of an active *minority* free to "openly advocate changes in the officially adopted party policies."[211]

Hence, it appears that for democracy to survive within and outside the party, centralism would have to go. It would be replaced not by anarchy, but by cooperation and consultation. The avant-garde is slowly becoming aware of the fact that the party may have to be de-Leninized, if not de-Marxified, in addition to shedding its Stalinist deformations. Lenin's and Stalin's notions of the party wielding unlimited economic, political, and ideological monopoly in society are challenged by the avant-garde.

Yet, avant-garde thinkers are relatively unaware of Marx's contribution to the totalitarian conception of the party. They do not seem to realize fully that Marx's persuasion that the communists are called by History to lead humanity to an earthly Jerusalem, and that they possess the exclusive knowledge summed up by Rousseau's general will, constitutes the Marxist roots of Stalinism. No one—not even the communists or their party—is called by History to do anything. Even Marx remarked that History did not do anything. Furthermore, history can only be meaningful if human lives have meaning. But if human lives are continually sacrificed along the way to utopia, how can they possibly have a secular meaning? And if they were sacrificed for a truly religious, transcendental meaning, it would contradict the communist stance that life after death does not exist, let alone have meaning.

Lendvai writes that by promoting economic decentralization and political liberalization, the party may commit institutional suicide.[212] But the historical record would seem to indicate otherwise. In the past, the party survived. But people died. Regardless of whether they belonged to the party or not. The party claimed their lives as well as their souls. Can a communist party, then, simply wither away?

The avant-garde is waiting for the party to wither away. According to Tito, however, the party would wither away only when the last class enemy had been eliminated.[213] But that shall never be. For the Marxist-Leninist party presupposes *class enemies*, domestic and foreign. As Solzhenitsyn observed about the Soviet communist leadership, it could not live without enemies as a pretext for tyranny:

> "The enemy will overhear"—that is your excuse. The eternal, omnipresent "enemies" are a convenient justification for your functions and your very existence. As if there were no enemies when you promised immediate openness. But what would you do without "enemies?" You could not live without "enemies"; hatred, a hatred no better than racial hatred has become your sterile atmosphere. But in this way a sense of our single, common humanity is lost and its doom is accelerated.[214]

Let us suppose that a communist regime could round up, at any point in time, all the adult population and determine who was or was not a class enemy. Even if the regime got rid of all present class enemies, its job would never be done. For each newborn babe would represent a potential class enemy. The party could never be sure of an individual's allegiance until s/he was fully socialized, attaining the prescribed level of socialist consciousness. Cruel future. Irony of history. Our science and technology used in the manner of Orwell's *1984* or Huxley's *Brave New World* may very well assist the party's conquest of individual consciousness to an unprecedented degree. And for those relatively few bold or foolhardy incorrigibles, beyond the pale of socialist reeducation, there would always be prisons, insane asylums, forced labor camps, death or exile, in addition to social ostracism, loss of prestige, job, family, friends, and other sophisticated administrative measures in the arsenal of socialist legality and "class justice."

Yugoslav media are saturated, especially since 1971, with references to an intensification of the *class struggle* against enemies of the state and alien ideas. This, too, is suspect to the avant-garde, who are well aware of where it all leads: the suppression of heresy and dissent as defined by the party. Marković cautions that

> . . . the theory of the necessary intensification of class struggle in the process of development of socialism, far from explaining anything, is logically absurd: socialism by definition means the transition period in which men evolve towards a non-violent classless society.[215]

In spite of the party's tampering with self-managing institutions, one can perhaps no longer talk of pure and unadulterated party *monopoly* in the organs of self-management, either, because of the latter's tendency toward independence. This, too, is a hallmark of the Yugoslav quest for totalitarian democracy. Because of its essentially utopian character, it remains a quest rather than a reality. The democratic self-management trends are basically irreconcilable with party monopoly of decision-making. What we have, then, is a fluid situation in which self-managers and the party appear to pull in opposite directions: popular direct democracy and totalitarianism. In actual practice, we find a great spectrum in which these two elements—self-management and the party—mix uneasily and in variance with such circumstantial factors as levels of decision-making, government, sections of the country, personalities, local customs, levels of education, literacy, and the standard of living.

Paradoxically, it is necessary at times to defend the party against its Marxist critics. Not because of their criticism, but rather because of their Marxist assumptions according to which self-management democracy is impossible unless the party withers away. It should be clear by now that:

(1) The party is not going to wither away;
(2) The party cannot wither away; and
(3) There is no need for the party to wither away.

But if democracy is to become a reality within self-managing institutions, then the Marxist-Leninist premises of the party would have to be transcended (*aufgehoben*). This would not mean a simple rejection by the party of its Marxist-Leninist heritage. It would, rather, represent a positive transcendence /supersession of that heritage, retaining its best elements, such as the party's coordinating function in society, and rejecting its Stalinist perversions.

It is also apparent that this would no longer be a *communist* party, but a *social democratic* one, dedicated to furthering realistic goals and aspirations of a *democratic* socialism rather than pursuing the utopia of a *socialist* democracy. This would call for a genuine freedom of thought as well as of action, a separation of powers, checks and balances, pluralism, including at least the possibility for the formation of other, socialist and non-socialist, political parties, a polycentrism of power and influence, the aggregation and articulation of different interests, and institutional means for conflict resolution. This is rejected by the party as *political* representation based on *class* interests in a *bourgeois* parliamentary system of rule. The choice before the party would thus appear to be: socialism *or* democracy. The problem with this choice is that the party's conception of socialism is utopian, while its conception of democracy is totalitarian.

3.2 Is There a New Exploiting Class?

The party gained a new lease on life in the Stalinist mold even before the Croatian crisis of 1971, the 1971 Constitutional Amendments, the 1974 Constitution, and the Tenth and Eleventh Party Congresses in 1974 and 1978, respectively. The party acquired this new Stalinist lease on life by insisting on the class nature of socialist democracy, dictatorship of the proletariat, and the need for democratic centralism and class justice in the face of alien ideas, domestic and foreign enemies, and the appearance on the domestic scene of a new exploiting class composed of bureaucrats, technocrats, nationalists, separatists, petty-bourgeois liberals, and others.

But it is not the party which has been in the forefront of elaborating the theory of a new exploiting class in contemporary Yugoslavia. This role has been filled admirably by avant-garde thinkers who let loose the Marxist ideological thunder of a new exploiting class and new class enemies, which in the end boomeranged, costing them their freedom. Is there a new exploiting class in Yugoslavia?

We saw in Chapter VI that the avant-garde considers market socialism to be in direct contradiction with socialist humanism, solidarity, equality, and humanized social relationships. Following in Marx's footsteps, the avant-garde saw the market as well as the state, bureaucracy, the party, and professional politics as sources of alienation in socialism. Srdjan Vrcan summed up the avant-garde consensus that

> The free functioning of the market economy presumes a continuous existence of a certain systematic social inequality on the one hand, and a constant perpetuation and deepening of the existing social inequality on the other.[216]

Vrcan's view is seconded by Marković, who holds that the market undermines worker solidarity in self-managed enterprises, which can result in the workers' assumption of the role of exploiters.[217] Stojanović attributes this alienation of self-governing groups in socialism to the continuing dominance of oligarchic groups and ossified state structures. He concludes that individual self-governing groups can also function as exploiters by alienating/appropriating the means and products of labor from society.[218]

All this has led some members of the avant-garde to claim that Yugoslavia remains a class society. In Božidar Jakšić's formulation, the Yugoslav power elite is composed of four subgroups:

(1) Techno-bureaucratic structure in economy and state administration;
(2) Political apparatus of the power centers;
(3) The financial oligarchy; and
(4) The propaganda apparatus.

In his view, the power elite rules over the working class and the peasantry via an instrumentarium of ideological, political, economic, and cultural manipulation.[219]

The avant-garde has developed a sweeping thesis of a new multi-layered exploitative class, consisting of a new middle class of the red bourgeoisie (*Peugeoisie*), technocrats, and managers in the economy, interlocked with party and state bureaucrats and professional politicians in the socio-political sphere. Golubović writes that power in Yugoslav society is in the hands of the political and industrial bureaucracy, while technocrats are gaining in influence. Marković adds to this configuration a proliferating group of socialist millionaires or socialist great capitalists nurtured by market socialism.[220]

While Kuvačić distinguishes between three basic groups or layers in Yugoslav society—bureaucracy, the middle class, and working class—Vrcan and Lukić outline four circles or social layers. Vrcan sees the following:

(1) First circle living outside the world of politics, at the bottom of the social pyramid with incomes considerably below the average;

(2) Second circle is in the middle of the existing social pyramid, acting in politics mostly with its feet as interested watchers-fans;

(3) Third circle members live and participate in the world of

politics as activists and functionaries who popularize and apply
political decisions and who enjoy significantly higher than
average incomes and a high degree of social security; and

(4) Fourth and narrowest circle consists of decision-makers in
leading socio-political structures, "the nucleus where the
greatest social power and influence is concentrated."[221]

Lukić offers a complementary breakdown of the Yugoslav social structure into four
large social layers:

(1) The passive poor: rural and urban, beggars, the wayward, and
all others bracketed out of society;

(2) Lower layer: people who barely maintain a minimum for
existence and who are often exploited—rural poor, unskilled,
and unemployed workers—the proletariat;

(3) Middle layer: majority of the population; and

(4) Higher layer: high incomes—rich peasants, craftsmen, service
operators, rentiers, professionals, bureaucrats, technocrats, as
well as speculators and plunderers.[222]

Lukić sees a major conflict between the lower (and to an extent the passive
poor) and the higher layer. His solution to this conflict is unique among the avant-
garde: raising material production and the general standard of living. It is an un-
Marxist solution. To most avant-garde theorists, what is needed in a situation of
class inequalities and conflict is genuine Marxist analysis and class solutions.

What is the Marxist shape of this new exploiting class? The avant-garde has
spared no effort to outline the major characteristics of a new middle class, which
appropriates surplus value in socialism. Kuvačić distinguishes between the old and
the new middle class.[223] The old middle class, which predominates in the private
sector, consists of craftsmen, caterers, and providers of other services, owners of
means of transportation, and some professionals. The new middle class, lodged in
the socialized sector, is composed of employers in business, offices, trade, and
numerous social services. This new middle class is, furthermore, interlocked and
intertwined with the governmental apparatus and partly also with the political
elite, especially in the area of mass communications.

The growth of the new middle class is predicated primarily on speculation, on
what Thorsten Veblen termed the attempt to gain something for nothing. The new
middle class, according to Kuvačić, has even developed its specific ideology based
on nationalism, technical progress, growth in the standard of living, private
initiative, and anti-egalitarian social differentiation.

In Kuvačić's view, the introduction of the market mechanism destroyed the
monopoly of the central administration. However, monopoly then simply migrated
to the republic and local levels, where the prosperous middle class forged an
alliance with republic and local bureaucracies. According to Pečujlić, this has led
to the formation of miniature monopolies or states writ small, which "force
working people to serve narrower centers of power, cliques, guild interests, new
men of power and privileges."[224] In Supek's view, this monopoly is especially
pronounced in the mass communications industry, which in spite of the self-
management ethic, is more concentrated than its counterpart in modern capitalist
states.[225]

All this has led the avant-garde to consider the new middle class, along with
state hierarchies and the party bureaucracy, as a new exploiting class. Milan
Kangrga writes that the new middle class exploits the workers by appropriating
surplus value, manipulating the media, and generally interpreting self-management
in its own interest.[226] But how can anyone appropriate surplus value under

socialism, where private property has been abolished?

The avant-garde's response to this dilemma, adopted by the party, is that alienated labor, not private property, is the source of alienation. While the means of production were nationalized, says Marković, they never really became social property but "remain alienated from the producers and fully at the disposal of the new ruling elite."[227] How is that possible? We have to recall here the Yugoslav distinction between private, nationalized, and socialized property. As we saw in Chapter VI, the avant-garde observed a re-privatization of socialized property under market socialism. Hence, Mijo Biličić concludes that the new middle class in contemporary Yugoslavia is based on privatized social ownership as well as small private ownership.[228] Privatized social ownership refers, of course, to individual, group, state, and other infringements of social ownership. The avant-garde blames market socialism for fanning the fires of localism, bureaucracy, greed, and egoism, contributing to the breakdown of socialist solidarity and equality, and the growth of horizontal and vertical differentiation and inequalities.

Curiously, the party joined the avant-garde critique of the new middle class. Kardelj admitted that workers can function as exploiters, and that the major conflict in Yugoslav society was that between workers' self-management, on the one hand, and state ownership and technocratic-bureaucratic monopoly, on the other.[229] But Kardelj's proposed remedy was the opposite of that propounded by the avant-garde: a closer adherence to the laws of the market, greater responsibility regarding production and distribution, and a realization that it is impossible to determine the exact contribution by an individual to income, and hence absolute justice in distribution.[230] As mentioned before, if an individual's contribution to total income cannot be determined, neither can surplus value. But if surplus value cannot be determined, how can exploitation be measured? And if one cannot measure exploitation, how can one talk about a new exploiting class?

3.3 Reservations for Thought and Action

It is impossible not to be moved by the existential pathos in Milan Mirić's Marxist humanist politico-literary tract entitled *Reservations.* In it, Mirić sums up the growing consensus among the avant-garde that the intelligentsia and the working class in contemporary Yugoslavia live in separate reservations. The intelligentsia is allowed to think independently, but its freedom of thought never extends to freedom of action. Hence, it remains a freedom of the reservation.[231]

As to the working class, it, too, finds itself in a reservation, its self-managing functions confined within the walls of individual factories. The only social group outside of these reservations is the bureaucracy—the sole actor on the socio-political scene. Mirić concludes that these new social relations of a reservation have strenghtened the power of the bureaucracy and brought socialism as a truly human community, rather than just an institutional set-up, into question.

Mirić's views are echoed by Pešić-Golubović, who sees the working class atomized, restricted to individual factories and institutions, unable to unite social forces, and thus contributing to the old hierarchies and stratifications. At the top of the pyramid are the state and party mechanisms, whose political power is absolute:

> The political power of the State and party mechanism is a condensed version of their economic power, of their role of arbiters in all social activities: it is the power to superimpose the official ideology over all other ideologies and to control them; the power to set all organs of the State in motion against disloyal citizens and groups.[232]

Thus, the avant-garde sees political power as very much alienated in socialism. Both individuals and classes appear rather powerless. Marković sees the root cause of this political alienation in the fact that the self-management system is localized, atomized, and disintegrated, confined to the micro-level, whereas classical institutions of power such as the bureaucracy, state, party, and professional politics continue to dominate the macro-level. Marković expresses the avant-garde consensus in his view that these two types of socio-political structures, self-management and the state-bureaucracy-party, are basically incompatible.[233]

Jakšić holds that workers' self-management is not only imprisoned within the walls of individual factories, businesses, and institutions, but also weighed down by the techno-bureaucratic structure, one of the four subgroups in the power elite. The power elite dominates and manipulates the working class within the system of self-management, which has been transformed into an ideology.[234] Supek sees the real triangle of power in statist socialism composed of the party leadership, government, and the army-police leadership. Its political-ideological transmission belts are:

(1) The party organization in the political sphere;
(2) The trade unions in the economic sphere; and
(3) Socio-cultural organizations in the ideological sphere.[235]

On the other hand, self-managing socialism is characterized by the withering away of all political organizations and the transfer of all decision-making power to the associated producers. But self-management cannot remain confined to the micro-level. Instead, it must extend from the BOALs to the federation. In Marković's view, the structure of integral self-government would encompass three levels:

(1) Workers' councils in factories, services, and all types of local communities;

(2) Intermediary organs: horizontal, coordinating entire regions, and vertical, integrating branches of activity; and

(3) Institutions of self-government of the global society.[236]

The avant-garde holds that as things presently stand, workers have very little influence in social self-government. Marković notes the decline in the number of worker delegates to the Federal Assembly from eight percent in 1958 to six percent in 1963, to a mere one percent in 1970, whereas Blažević claims that the percentage of workers in republic Chambers of Associated Labor declined from nine percent in 1968 to only one percent in 1971-72.[237] It is true that in the 1970s, the regime tried to draw millions of Yugoslavs into broad participation via the delegate system. Yet the system itself has remained carefully orchestrated by the party. Apart from ideology, this brings up also the issue of the party's representativeness of Yugoslav society.

Students of participation and political equality, East and West, are perturbed by the fact that the League of Communists has become a party of the "haves" in what Sidney Verba, Norman H. Nie, and Jae-On Kim call a "dominant institutional system" in which party affiliation is "both a necessary and sufficient condition for very high levels of regular political activity." They also point out that while the party is the key to regular political activity as well as membership in self-government organs, party membership is "not distributed equally across social groups in Yugoslavia," but rather tends to draw on the higher socio-economic strata in society.[238] Their finding is corroborated by Baumgartner, Burns, and Sekulić, who conclude that the resulting social composition of the party has turned it into a party of managers and professionals, rather than workers and peasants.[239] On the other hand, the fact should not be overlooked that the party threw its doors wide open in the 1970s, achieving a great turnover as well as increase in the number of new party members in the wake of the 1971-1972 nationalism crisis. Nevertheless, the party remains the principal means of social advancement in Yugoslav society, and, as such, a continuing source of careerism, which, in Ralph Pervan's impression, has proved irresistible even to Yugoslav youth organizations, as the latter follow the party's role model.[240]

Zvan surmises that workers cannot influence the reform or social events which are carried out by the political bureaucracy in the name of the working class. This renewal of Stalinism, of bureaucrats ruling in the name of the working class, Zvan holds responsible for the failure of socio-economic reforms and the present-day crisis of socialism:

> That failure reflects the crisis of its practice, and I would suggest, the double crisis of its theory. The crisis of practice has been expressed as the power of bureaucracy to liquidate reforms, to prevent any new, fresh ideas to develop within socialism. That twofold theoretical crisis has been reflected by the theoretical scope of the suggested reforming concepts, and by an almost absolute insufficiency of theoretical understanding of the crisis on the part of top bureaucrats.[241]

It all boils down to one fundamental point. And that is that the workers' *social* power has become *politicized* once more under socialism, where as alienated political power it dominates the working class through classical institutions of the market, the state, party, law, bureaucracy, and politics. This has led the avant-garde to the conclusion—propounded already by Rosa Luxemburg—that the alienation of political institutions of the state, party, and bureaucracy constitute the greatest danger to the working class after the socialist revolution. Marković sums up this epochal socialist dilemma as follows:

> ...for Marx the ultimate goal of a communist is a *radical economic and political democratization*: a full freedom of develop-ment for each *individual* (not class or party, or any other mediator among individuals). However, it is not at all clear how to dismantle organized political power once it has been established on a new ground.[242]

Both the avant-garde and the party remain committed to Marx's goal of abolishing political power. But, what if abolishing professional politics, the state, party, bureaucracies, and political power should turn out to be possible only in the imagination? Could this utopian quest lead to a fairy-tale land in which both thought and action would be inverted, trapping the rulers and the ruled alike? Could it lead to the presumption that partial interests and conflict are un-socialist and their protagonists merely class enemies? Could self-management thus be reduced to a myth veiling the artificial smooth surface of a solidary conception of society? And how would direct democracy be reconciled with a system in which, if we are to believe Marković:

> ...basic decision-making about the system, its changes, key questions of current politics, and, especially, the entire cadre policy remains in the hands of the party's top [leadership], outside of the possible sphere of influence of party members and the rest of the people.[243]

4. Toward Socialist Politics?

Communist party states are well known for denying the existence of different group interests and conflict in socialism. One need only recall Stalin's formulation of the theory of "non-antagonistic" contradictions in socialism. The Yugoslavs, both within and outside the party, admit the existence of different interests and their conflict in socialism. Yet the Yugoslav admission of conflict in their society is hedged in by the Marxist conviction that conflicts are the expression of exploitative class relations and, hence, unsocialist. It thus behooves the party and self-managing institutions to eliminate them.

In Gerškovič's view, as long as there are sources of conflictual relations, so long will there also remain the need for political power for their solution.[244] And political power, in the Marxist lexicon, is itself an alienating force. The circle is thus closed: alienation—class relations—conflict—political power—alienation. Both the avant-garde and the party have been searching for ways to cut this Gordian knot and attain release from an enchanted framework.

The avant-garde has been in the forefront of this search. First came a realization of growing social inequalities, conflicts, and strikes in contemporary Yugoslavia. Markovič saw three basic contradictions:

(1) Conflict between ruling bureaucracy and powerless working people;

(2) Constant war between various strata and factions within the bureaucracy; and

(3) Particularist tendencies versus centralist (anti-nationalist) countermeasures.[245]

The avant-garde thus observed a gathering storm of conflict turning into a major crisis of socialism. The major symptoms of this new crisis, according to Mihailo Popović, were:

(1) Continuous accumulation of problems which remained, in general, unresolved;

(2) Serious lack of responsibility ranging from work organizations to institutions and forums on the republic and federal levels; and

(3) Characteristic lack of social criteria and effective social control over the behavior of economic, political, and other subjects.[246]

Yugoslav sociologists found the curious phenomenon of increasing interest differentiation in their society, on the one hand, and the absence of institutions for conflict resolution, on the other. This led Vladimir Arzenšek to formulate the hypothesis of the prevalence of insoluble and unrealistic conflicts in socialism. In his view, the rigid social structure which prevails in socialism leads to the accumulation of tensions, unrealistic conflicts, and their disruptive consequences. Arzenšek concluded that the low level of toleration of conflicts in socialism and their inadequate institutionalization prevented their resolution and thus resulted in "diffuse, intensely affective [i.e., emotional], and insoluble conflicts."[247] In an earlier paper, Arzensek found that in Yugoslavia deviant structures are regarded as results of a lack of socialization, the work of class enemies, or the society's scarcity of resources. He noted that instead of institutionalizing conflicts, the monolithic nature of the social system substituted criticism and self-criticism characteristic of ideological struggle.[248]

Arzenšek's views are supported by other Yugoslav sociologists, who also assert that the problem of institutionalizing conflict is a relatively neglected area of research in Yugoslav sociology. Why? Zdravko Mlinar sheds some light on this question. He contrasts two institutional models of socio-economic and political organization: a conflict-less model versus a model incorporating conflict. The basic values of the conflict-less model are: collectivism (socialization), equality, social harmony, unity, social security, radicalism (revolutionary, new), future (long-term perspective), conscious (planned) direction of development, symbolic (moral rather than material) reward, loyalty, and intolerance. Mlinar concludes that the undifferentiated organizational structure of the conflict-less model precludes the institutionalization of conflict. This at the very time when conflicts in the economy and the political sphere have proliferated, due to the introduction of workers' self-management and decentralization of political decision-making.

On the other hand, Mlinar holds that a second set of values is contributing to a revival of conflicts: individualism (individual initiative), inequality (differentiation), necessity of conflicts (transcendence of social harmony), unity as a synthesis of differences, risk (uncertainty), reformism (tradition), present-orientation (pragmatism), spontaneity (freedom of initiative), material rewards, non-political values (professionalism, effectiveness), and toleration (openness). Mlinar concludes that Marx's thesis of the withering away of conflicts in socialism due to economic development is mistaken and that, instead, there begins a process of the institutionalization of conflicts.[249]

The avant-garde and the party have become especially concerned with the phenomenon of wildcat strikes. Kardelj himself admits that conflicts are inevitable in socialism and that there is a need for democratic mechanisms for conflict resolution. Yet he retains the Marxist presumption that work stoppages—the regime's pseudonym for wildcat strikes—are unsocialist, representing a breakdown in the democratic mechanism for conflict resolution, self-management, and socialist consciousness. Kardelj observes that work stoppages in self-managing socialism no longer have the same historical or class function that they have in capitalism.[250] Nevertheless, the regime refuses to legalize strikes.

Disagreeing with Kardelj, Jakšić holds that strikes are "the most significant evidence of social conflict," which indicates that Yugoslavia remains basically a class society in search of full socialist consciousness.[251] In Nebojša Popov's view, it is the regime and its ideology of monolithism which prevent the manifestation of social contradictions and their democratic resolution.[252] The basic socialist dilemma, according to Stojanović, consists in the fact that the regime denies that any conflict could be *socialist* in character. Hence, there is a tendency to *suppress* conflicts rather than allow for their resolution through democratic processes. Instead, observes Stojanović, all conflicts are reduced to antagonistic contraries like state ownership—privatization of ownership, statism—anarcho-liberalism, unitarianism—nationalism, all of which are opposed to pure socialist orientations as defined by the party.[253]

The equation of all conflict with class enemies leads to a fateful inversion, summed up by Veljko Rus as follows:

> . . . conflict and the use of power are justified as a means for settling accounts with class enemies and with vestiges of capitalist society. However, this logic has its own paralogical inversion: everybody who is in conflict and everything which is overcome by the use of force is classified as a class enemy or something which must be excluded from social activity.[254]

Popović and Supek think that self-management itself has become a mythology concealing the real shape of conflicts in socialism. In Popović's view, the self-management mythology prevents a realistic assessment of the system's strengths and weaknesses. And the anti-bureaucratic psychosis contributes, on the other hand, to scrapping of administrative institutions essential to the proper functioning of self-management and social planning. It leads Supek to conclude that self-management is "the strongest ideological stereotype" today in Yugoslav society.[255] Or, as an educated Yugoslav remarked half-jokingly to this author, self-management slogans are similar to advertising in the West: everyone mouths them, but few take them seriously. Yet ideologies and myths can acquire an existence of their own, independent of people but influencing their behavior.

Stojanović, Stanovčić, and Rus shatter the Marxist myth that conflicts of interest among interest groups are the exclusive hallmark of capitalist class society by maintaining that they are very much in evidence in socialism as well.[256]

In his path-breaking study on *Interest Groups and Political Power*, Jovan Mirić questions the fiction of the unity of interests of the working class, abolition of politics, and the alleged non-political nature of delegates. Instead, Mirić holds that the system of self-management is a *political* system *par excellence*, since democratic decision-making is political in essence. Mirić is particularly critical of the view which equates a system's democratic quality with total harmony, homogeneity, and monolithism, instead of seeing it as an appropriate political framework for the articulation of a rich diversity of interests and human competition. Total absence of conflict, social peace, and harmony are likely to prevail only in a monolithic system of political totalitarianism:

> Political totalitarianism carries all the marks of despotism: in front of it, all are equal, too, there is no reason (or possibility!) for conflicts, *there is nothing to contest or fight for since everything is determined and known.* Social peace and harmony prevail! But it is a harmony of suffering which excludes even the possibility of choosing an alternative form of serfdom.[257]

In a puzzling theoretical innovation, which strikes one as thoroughly un-Marxist, party theorists like Kardelj and Šuvar have come to acknowledge the fact that there are contradictions and conflicts of interest within the working class itself, which is allegedly composed of different layers. This prompts Šuvar to conclude that socialist self-management is anything but a calm system and conflict-less development.[258] Apparently, such conflicts of interest can be a boon to a party which claims to *know* the workers' *true* interests. That is the precise basis on which Kardelj builds up his notion of the party's essential leading role in interpreting the "pluralism of self-management interests." In Kardelj's thinking:

> ... the League of Communists has become one of the strongest pillars of democracy of a new type—a democracy of pluralism of self-management interests. This means that the League of Communists has lost also its character as a classical political party which fights for its political monopoly in competition with other political parties.[259]

Stanovčić expresses the new socialist dilemma most clearly when he observes that the development of social relations on a *democratic* and *humanist* basis *presupposes* the possibility of the formation of *partial* and *group* interests which come into conflict as long as there is—not capitalism—but the attempt by people to monopolize or appropriate for themselves existing values.[260] These existing values—or in David Easton's terminology "valued things"—are all those things people seek: goods, privileges, positions. But what about the general interest? Mirić provides a definition of the general interest unique among the avant-garde:

> The general interest consists in the creation of such social and political conditions in which particular [interests] can be articulated, defended, and realized, without domination and outside pressure.[261]

Stanovčić argues for the necessity of introducing into existing political institutions such practices and instruments which can deal with situations of conflicts of interest.[262] What kinds of practices and instruments for conflict resolution should be established in socialism?

Marković advocates a conscious policy of abolishing bureaucracy and securing economic rationality while developing socialist humanism. He sees the need for "a pluralism of flexible *ad hoc* political organizations which would represent various different interest groups" to replace the alienated power of permanent party and state bureaucracies.[263] Marković, Supek, and others also call for the withering away of the party with the concomitant development of self-management. Marković is aware of the need for central coordinating institutions, but wonders how a synthesis can be achieved between direct and representative democracy. In his view, socialism could profit by adopting some principles of liberalism (liberal or bourgeois democracy) such as:

(1) Rotation: true vertical replacement of office-holders;
(2) Division of powers: separating the judicial, executive, and legislative branches;
(3) Elected leaders: instead of professional functionaries;
(4) Decentralization: Thomas Jefferson's idea of dividing the country into self-governing units based on the notion of pluralism.[264]

Above all, Marković considers the existence of a strong, free public opinion, intense political life without authoritarian subordination and manipulation, unhindered circulation of ideas, freedom of public criticism, and independent means of mass communication as essential preconditions for genuine self-government. Marković concludes that political organizations "may not have a monopoly of political power and assume the role of a higher force in relation to organs of self-management."[265]   Stojanović concurs in this analysis by stating that pluralism should replace artificial political unanimity. In his view, trade unions should be allowed to enter the political stage, the party should democratize itself, and "existing socioeconomic organizations must be on an equal status with the League of Communists."[266]   Yet, the avant-garde's solution to party monopoly—in Stojanović's enscription—that the party become the "initiator of the socialist movement," in reality only begs the question, since the party claims to be doing just that: initiating as well as guarding the revolution.[267]

Both the avant-garde and the party are vaunt to cite classics of Marxism in support of the idea of self-management. The avant-garde has also dug up Lenin's remarks on the danger of the executive power of the bureaucratic *apparat* ossifying and turning into a power alienated from the workers. No one seems to be aware of the other, anti-self-management, trend in Lenin's writings which emphasizes party monopoly of decision-making. Lenin also wrote that:

> To govern you need an army of steeled revolutionary Communists. We have it, and it is called the Party. All this syndicalist nonsense about mandatory nominations of producers must go into the waste-paper basket. To proceed on those lines would mean thrusting the Party aside and making the dictatorship of the proletariat in Russia impossible.[268]

Does that mean that the Yugoslavs, in order to remain Leninist, must choose between self-management and the party, that is, direct democracy and party monopoly?   Not necessarily. As we have seen, the Yugoslavs chose a third possibility: totalitarian democracy. It is another ideal type, democratic in form, but totalitarian in content, combining institutional pluralization with ideological re-Stalinization. Yet this is an unstable solution.

The phenomena of constitutionalism and legality, an incipient separation of powers among branches of government, and workers' self-management coexist uneasily with the party's mandate to guide the self-managers toward the common good.   The recognition that conflicts among interest groups are growing in socialism along with democratization processes is in direct contradiction with the Marxist-Leninist ethos of the withering away of all contradictions in communism. Both the party and the avant-garde refuse to acknowledge, with few exceptions, that the need for the establishment of institutions and practices to deal with these conflicts, in fact, constitutes a demand for *politics*!

The Yugoslavs do not seem to realize that their demand for conflict resolution as well as for the full democratization of socialist institutions is not only a demand for *politics*, but also for *democratic pluralism* and for corresponding *institutions* of the state, law, bureaucracy, and government. But how can these institutions develop in socialism when they are considered as forms of alienation, exploitation, and dehumanization?

The Yugoslav answer to this conundrum seems to be: subordinate politics and all institutions to the general will. But no one, not even the party, knows the general will. Hence politics, while abolished in theory, is very much alive in actual practice. This calls for continuous reorganizations of the party, state, and other structures, on the one hand, and vigorous ideological incantations akin to a magic rain-making dance, on the other. Thus, politics waxes, while the general will remains as elusive as ever. It is, after all, a search for utopia. Robert Nozick summed up this search ingeniously as follows:

> One persistent strand in utopian thinking ... is the feeling that there is some set of principles obvious enough to be accepted by all men of good will, precise enough to give unambiguous guidance in particular situations, clear enough so that all will realize its dictates, and complete enough to cover all problems which actually will arise. Since I do not assume that there are such principles, I do not assume that the political realm will wither away.[269]

Western observers are impressed by Yugoslav institutional developments, particularly the unusual quest for constitutionalism and socialist legality. Winston M. Fisk points out that Yugoslavia may be developing into a communist *Rechsstaat* concerned with the protection of legal rights of individuals and containing degrees of independence between the legislature, judiciary, and the executive via the processes of the institutionalization of politics and increasing use of public law.[270] Yet, William Zimmerman, Singleton, and George Klein contend that since 1971 there has been a recentralization of both the party and the state, with no sign of the party withering away or of a real separation between the party and the state.[271] Even such sympathetic observers of the Yugoslav scene as Gary K. Bertsch and Robin Alison Remington admit the interlocking nature of the party and the state at the highest levels: between the LCY Presidium and the SFRY Presidency.[272]

Hunnius and Robert Sharlet draw attention to the gap between theory and practice of self-management with respect to the principle of rotation of delegates. In theory, the principle of rotation implies the participation of the greatest possible number of people in self-government. In practice, however, this principle functions somewhat akin to a game of musical chairs, with a recycling of elites from one decision-making area or socio-political organization to another.[273] Following at once in Marx's and Djilas' footsteps, Šuvar criticizes the new middle class for usurping self-management and converting the Yugoslav experiment into "petty-bourgeois socialism." In Šuvar's estimate, there are some 7,000 professional politicians in socio-political organizations, in addition to about 5,000 elected members of representative bodies. This loosely aggregated, hierarchically-organized grouping of elites, which is "turning in its own circles," dominates decision-making in the communes, provinces, republics, and the federation, constituting "relatively independent centers of political power."[274] This is not a novel phenomenon. It is the manifestation of the standard interlocking set-up between the party, the state, trade unions, and other economic, socio-political, and cultural organizations typical of communist party states.

Beneath the level of top decision-makers who are recirculating, rotation does take place. But this can lead to some unexpected consequences. The problem is that the frequent rotation of delegates in legislative bodies impairs their decision-making ability, since they lack the time to develop the expertise necessary for dealing with complex technical issues. Lenard J. Cohen concluded that rotation thus encouraged greater reliance on an expert bureaucracy.[275] The strengthening of bureaucracy, however, is in direct contradiction to the official ideology and the avant-garde critique.

The central role of the party and its intertwining with all other institutions is articulated for the first time in the 1974 Constitution. Nor is the party's role conceived, as at the Ninth Party Congress, as merely educational and ideological. Instead, the party is to be the nucleus of both self-management thought and action. This, too, is theory. What about reality? In the past, communists found themselves outvoted at times in self-managing institutions. As Lendvai reports, on December 7, 1966, the entire Slovene communist government resigned following the defeat of its bill in the social-health Chamber of the Republic Assembly.[276] The bill requested an increase in workers' contributions to health services. Illusions may have power. According to Lendvai, the regime's introduction of self-management represented at first an illusion of power. Soon, however, the illusion of power turned into a power of illusion.[277] There are people within and outside the party who take self-management seriously and who find it difficult to reconcile party monopoly with self-management.

The system seems to call for a *deus-ex-machina*, a supreme Philosopher-King who knows Rousseau's general will. Fortunately for the Yugoslavs, they were convinced that they had such a figure in Tito. But who will interpret self-management now that Tito is gone? The avant-garde has come close to realizing that what their society needs is not the abolition of political power, but its limitation and institutionalization. Significant in this context is Stojanović's after-thought that nothing substantive has been done in Yugoslavia to set up limits or checks and balances to the party's political monopoly.[278] In this enterprise, however, the "classic" texts of Marx, Engels, and Lenin are more misleading than enlightening. Instead, both the avant-garde and the party might profit by looking more closely at Western political theory, whose major concern has been how to limit power.

Western democratic theory seeks a realistic institutional framework for dealing with the question of power, its uses and abuses. Central to this tradition is James Madison's eminently un-Marxist notion in the *Federalist* (No. 51) that ambition must be made to counteract ambition:

> The interest of the man must be connected with the constitutional rights of the place. It may be a reflection on human nature that such devices should be necessary to control the abuses of government. But what is government itself but the greatest of all reflections on human nature? If men were angels, no government would be necessary. If angels were to govern men, neither external nor internal controls on government would be necessary. In framing a government which is to be administered by men over men, the great difficulty lies in this: you must first enable the government to control the governed; and in the next place oblige it to control itself.

This calls for an institutional model which incorporates a separation of powers between different branches of government, a system of mutual checks and balances, independent means of communication and information, a comprehensive Bill of Rights, and other substantive and procedural constraints. Such is the nature of *the institutional imperative.*[279]

But this would be unacceptable to the party, since it would challenge its monopoly on truth. O'Brien noted that the party elite, vested with the authority and monopoly on truth, is "the sole reconciler of conflicting interests" and decides which interests are to be ignored.[280] And LaPalombara observed that the idea of autonomous groups, organizations, and competing allegiances crystallized in an organized political opposition was contrary to Marxism-Leninism, whether in the Soviet, Yugoslav, or Chinese version.[281]

What, then, prevents self-management from becoming a genuine democratic means of decision-making? Is it the party? Not really. It is, rather, idolatry. It is the party's conception of itself as the executor of the will of History. It is, as Talmon pointed out, the incompatibility of an all-embracing and all-solving creed with liberty:

> The two ideals correspond to the two instincts most deeply
> embedded in human nature, the yearning for salvation and the love
> of freedom. To attempt to satisfy both at the same time is bound
> to result, if not in unmitigated tyranny and serfdom, at least in the
> monumental hypocrisy and self-deception which are the concomi-
> tants of totalitarian democracy.[282]

It appears, then, that the Marxist quest for utopia in the political sphere may
lead to distopia, as it did in the economic sphere. And for the same reasons. In the
economic sphere, the end result of the quest to de-alienate man led to the mocking
reality of all men and women reduced to the status of hired hands in a system in
which property belonged to everyone and no one. In the political sphere, the quest
to abolish politics leads to a new *homo duplex*, an individual afraid to voice his real
opinions in public life, which increasingly subverts his private life by politicizing all
life. Marx seems to have had, again, the last laugh: politics would, indeed, be
abolished in the communist future, but at the price of everyone's compulsory
participation in it. Thus we arrive finally at a socialist Camelot with all the
earmarks of the totalitarian state, which recalls Bernard-Henri Lévy's definition:

> A state is totalitarian when, by dilating the political, it claims to
> have annulled and abolished it; when, by multiplying the centers of
> domination, it dissolves the image of the Master; when it proclaims
> simultaneously that "everything is political," and that "the age of
> politics is at an end."[283]

There is only one problem marring Marx's triumph. And that is the question of
the necessity for economic development, industrialization, urbanization, the development of the market mechanism (*economic rationality*), along with increasing
inequalities, differentiation of interests, conflicts, and politicization in socialism
(*the institutional imperative*). How are these phenomena to be reconciled with the
utopian vision of a new human society and non-alienating, non-exploitative social
relations (*socialist humanism*)? This question reopens the socialist dilemma at the
very juncture where Marx thought to have closed and solved it once and for all.

Chapter VIII · Is Marxism The Only Humanism?

> Communism as a fully developed naturalism is humanism and as a fully developed humanism is naturalism. It is the *definitive* resolution of the antagonism between man and nature, and between man and man. It is the true solution of the conflict between existence and essence, between objectification and self-affirmation, between freedom and necessity, between individual and species. It is the solution of the riddle of history and knows itself to be this solution.
>
> Karl Marx, *Economic and Philosophical Manuscripts* (1844)

1. Yugoslav Marxism-Existentialism

Albert W. Levi writes that " . . . the Marxist enigma—and the issue of humanism and terror which lies at its center—is the most fateful question of our age."[1] As indicated at the end of Chapter IV, the question of the compatibility or incompatibility of humanism and Marxism is linked to the major issues of alienation, de-alienation, and liberation via socialism and communism. On this basis, Yugoslav theory claims to be authentic Marxism and the only genuine humanism.

Before one can answer the question of whether Marxism is the only humanism, it is necessary to establish whether Marxism is, indeed, a humanism, and if so, of what kind and/or to what degree. Communist officialdom in the East maintains that Marxism/socialism/communism is the only humanism. After more than half a century of socialist malpractice, it is surprising that Western Marxists and others share this conception. Thus, Howard L. Parsons insists that Marxism is "the most powerful and influential humanism to appear on the face of the earth."[2] George E. Novack contrasts the basic irrationalism, subjectivism, ahistoricism, and pessimism of Western existentialism with the scientific, rational, objective, historical, and confident method of social change and political action boasted by Marxism.[3] And John Hoffman is concerned with distinguishing the true humanism of scientific Marxism/socialism from revisionist conceptualizations, especially that of Yugoslav *Praxis* theorists.[4]

Critics of the Marxist *Weltanschauung* deny that it is humanist in content. Henryk Skolimowski argues that Marxism as a social model remains far removed from humanistic ideals even after a century of "improvement."[5] Richard T. De George notes that the humanism implied in Marx's and Engels' *Communist Manifesto* is "a class humanism concerned with classes rather than individuals," and that it "requires a violent overthrow and abolition of a portion of humanity, namely the class of the bourgeoisie."[6] Paul C. Roberts and Matthew A. Stephenson also observe the pervasiveness of the notion of violence in Marxism. They conclude that Marx " . . . does not rely on humanism as the method by which to reach a humane communism."[7]

Other observers see a split in Marx's humanism in two spheres: ideals versus principles. George L. Kline is willing to admit a humanism of ideals in Marxism, but denies it a humanism of principles. Kline argues convincingly that Marx's humanism of ideals, which relegates the humanist ideal of fulfilled human beings to the future, does not preclude Leninism, Stalinism, and the misuse of human beings in the present. This leads him to conclude that:

> Only a present-oriented ethical humanism, a humanism of principles, which respects living individuals, can, with theoretical consistency, exclude the recourse to anti-humanist means in the service of a humanist ideal.[8]

Is avant-garde Yugoslav Marxist humanist thought an ethical humanism based on a humanism of principles?

Yugoslav Marxist theory shifted its focus and emphasis from the collective to the individual and his de-alienation, liberation, and all-round development in a social context. This, in itself, constitutes a Copernican revolution in Marxism, as summed up in Chapter IV. The radical reorientation of avant-garde Yugoslav Marxism resulted in a new *Weltanschauung* or philosophy of life as well as a new paradigm or basic frame of reference, perhaps best summed up by Predrag Vranicki:

> If our desire is to contribute more fully to human liberation, i.e., to the overcoming of various forms of alienation, then socialism must place its fundamental stress on man, and the free personality must be considered a prerequisite to social freedom, in theory and in practice.[9]

The Yugoslav avant-garde seems to have achieved considerable success in combining elements of existentialism with Marxism. This complex enterprise has been tried by others. Prominent among them was the late Jean-Paul Sartre, whose attempt to combine the two philosophies in his *Critique of Dialectical Reason* failed to satisfy either existentialists or Marxists. Walter Odajnyk saw Sartre's early attempts to unite the best elements of Marxism and existentialism ending in his forsaking existentialism for Marxism.[10] To Raymond Aron, Sartre's muddling-through achieves confusion rather than synthesis since:

> Marxism cannot be renewed by going back from *Das Kapital* to the *Economic and Philosophic Manuscripts,* or by trying to achieve some impossible reconciliation between Kierkegaard and Marx.[11]

While Odajnyk criticizes Sartre for forsaking existentialism for Marxism, the Soviets and others press the opposite charge that he forsakes Marxism for existentialism. According to Thomas J. Blakeley, Soviet charges against Sartre's *Critique of Dialectical Reason* boil down to his stress on individual liberty and practice which the Soviets interpret as "bourgeois individualism."[12]

Are Marxism and existentialism fundamentally incompatible, then? Odajnyk found that the major difference between the two philosophies lay in their respective conceptions of the individual. While Marxism lost the individual in a materialistically determined world, existentialism lost the individual's vital connection to society.[13] But this seems to point to complementarity as well as contradiction. Nicola Abbagnano and Nicholas Lobkowicz underline the complementarity. They see both Marxism and existentialism as one-sided. The one-dimensionality of Marxism is reflected in its exclusion of aesthetic, ethical, and other considerations, whereas the one-dimensionality of existentialism consists in considering nature and the world as part of man instead of vice versa.[14] The common denominator between existentialists and Marxists is their quest to overcome alienation.

How does avant-garde Yugoslav Marxism fit into this framework? By its rediscovery of man and his restoration to the center of the drama of dialectical and historical materialism, avant-garde Yugoslav Marxism redefined itself as *Marxism-Existentialism.* Yugoslav Marxism-Existentialism incorporated in its *telos* the existentialist focus on man, his alienation, reification, and fragmentation in modern industrial society, his individual responsibility for shaping himself and the world in a never-ending process of becoming, and his supreme problem of freedom. Some avant-garde thinkers even defined communism as the "full realization of individualism."[15]

Avant-garde Yugoslav Marxism agrees fully with atheistic existentialism that there is no God, Creator, or supra-human force in the universe. It considers man to be alone and that it is up to him what he makes out of his life. As sketched in Chapters IV and V, man in avant-garde thought is both free and responsible. Unlike existentialism, however, the avant-garde places man in the context of society, and postulates his *social* being as the essence of man. Existentialism sees the lonely individual condemned to freedom and the necessity of choice in an unfriendly or, at best, neutral universe. Hence the idea of the "absurd." Yugoslav Marxism, on the other hand, postulates the dawning of a new age—communism—and the possibility for man's progressive de-alienation and liberation by the emancipation of labor, humanization of work, economic freedom, *praxis,* self-management, and direct democracy.

The most significant achievement of avant-garde Yugoslav Marxism, constituting its major existentialist and humanist elements, is undoubtedly its *"unbracketing" of the human individual* and, hence, of the classic dilemma of reconciling the individual with the social interest. The focus on the individual and his freedom and dignity became the starting point for Yugoslav *socialist personalism* or Marxism-Existentialism:

> The starting basis of our self-governing socialist system is man, his personality, his social position, material prosperity, freedom, creative labour and all-round development.[16]

The avant-garde's revolutionary reconstruction of Marxist-Leninist doctrine in the light of the humanistic writings of the early Marx resulted in a de-emphasis, weakening, modification and, in some cases, a total rejection of the Leninist heritage. R. N. Carew-Hunt singled out five major contributions of Lenin to Marxist theory:

(1) Strategy and tactics of revolution;
(2) Dictatorship of the proletariat;
(3) Role of the party;
(4) Strategy and tactics of communist parties; and
(5) Doctrine of capitalist imperialism.[17]

How do the Yugoslavs look at Lenin's contributions? Briefly, they:

(1) Maintain that revolution is only one of the ways to advance the interests of socialism and the proletariat, and that socialism can also be attained via parliamentary, socio-democratic, evolutionary, and other ways.[18]

(2) Consider the doctrine of the dictatorship of the proletariat as a "very dangerous theory, which can be used, and actually has been used, for anti-socialist purposes."[19] But, note that the party (the League of Communists) disagrees.

(3) Are reexamining the role of the party in conditions of social self-government, attempting to democratize and remake it into a "leading ideological force" in society.[20] Since 1971, however, the LCY has been returning to unity, democratic centralism, and Leninism.

(4) Have called for the democratization of communist parties, dialogue, equality, and non-interference in the internal affairs of other socialist states, independent paths to socialism, and "socialist pluralism."[21] The Brezhnev doctrine of limited sovereignty is seen as an example of "excessive etatism."

(5) Regard capitalism as the major source of imperialism, but point out that Stalinism or state capitalism also manifests imperialist-hegemonist tendencies.[22]

The Yugoslavs have thus significantly altered, abandoned, or are rethinking many of Lenin's major theoretical innovations. The party, however much it may have initiated the trend, has obviously lagged in this enterprise. It is primarily avant-garde theorists relying on the writings of the early Marx, the philosophical Lenin, and contemporary thought who have most consistently reinterpreted and developed Marx's thought in a humanist framework. With its quintessential focus on the individual, his de-alienation and liberation, Yugoslav Marxist theory, especially in its avant-garde formulation, can perhaps be best characterized as Marxism-Existentialism.[23] To the extent that it has become existentialist, Yugoslav Marxism has also become humanist, since existentialism's basic preoccupation with man and his self-realization is also the nucleus of any genuine humanism.

2. Humanism

Erich Fromm commented that our age was witnessing a veritable renaissance of humanism in various ideological systems which is a reflection of the growing threats to mankind by nuclear annihilation and submission to political institutions.[24] That a humanist renaissance could take place even in the communist world appeared until recently as a near impossibility. Yet, observers of the Yugoslav scene claim that humanism is a deep commitment of Yugoslav communism.[25] This is particularly true of avant-garde Yugoslav Marxist philosophers. Ludvik Vrtačić admits that the idea of humanism "stands in the forefront of their efforts."[26] More specifically, it is human fulfillment and equality which constitute the focus of concern for *Praxis* Marxists, in the view of Gerson S. Sher.[27]

Yet, even as recently as 1968, H. J. Blackham could write off Marxism-Leninism as a deviant from the humanist tradition because of its dogmatism, class-orientation, metaphysic, and opposition to the open mind and the open society. Blackham concluded that the communists and the churches were least likely to advance the humanist tradition.[28] But the fact is that it has been precisely Christian theologians and avant-garde Marxists who initiated a humanist Christian-Marxist dialogue. In the case of Yugoslavia specifically, Marxist-Leninist doctrine underwent a revolutionary humanist reconstruction in light of Marx's early writings and a critique of Stalinized socialist practice.

While Blackham, an atheistic humanist, dismissed Marxism-Leninism as a humanist force, Jacques Maritain, an exponent of integral (Christian) humanism, observed as early as 1938 that:

> There is in this socialist humanism a great urge towards truths which cannot be neglected without grave detriment, which are highly relevant to the sense of human dignity.[29]

Our task here is to distill these truths as well as the falsehoods inherent in Marxist or socialist humanism as advocated by avant-garde Marxist philosophers and sociologists in Yugoslavia. But, first, we must define humanism. Webster's provides the following panoply of meanings:

(1) Devotion to the humanities;
(2) Devotion to human welfare: interest in or concern for man;
(3) A doctrine, set of attitudes, or way of life centered upon human interest or values; (a) A philosophy that rejects supernaturalism, regards man as a natural object, and asserts the essential dignity and worth of man and his capacity to achieve self-realization through the use of reason and scientific method—called also *naturalistic humanism, scientific humanism;*
(b) Religious Humanism; and
(c) A philosophy advocating the self-fulfillment of man within the framework of Christian principles—i.e., Christian or Integral Humanism; and

(4)   New Humanism.

Marxist humanism in Yugoslavia falls most clearly into categories (2) and (3) (a), that is , naturalistic or "scientific" humanism.   Gajo Petrović terms Marx's thought a "revolutionary humanism," while Mihailo Marković sees Marxism as a "humanism of *praxis*."[30]

J. P. Van Praag, President of the International Humanist and Ethical Union, remarked at its 1966 Congress in Paris that there are in a sense as many humanisms as there are humanists.[31]   His statement mirrors the similar observation made often about Marxism and Marxists.   In the broadest conceptualization, humanism is perhaps best described as an attitude of mind, a quest for value and for man's reintegration in the universe based on his own life and work.   In the words of the 1973 Humanist Manifesto II, humanists urge the "recognition of the common humanity of all people."[32]   Central to the humanist quest is the dignity, fullfillment, and self-realization of each individual within a free, open, democratic society based on reason, intelligence, moral equality, economic well-being, and transnational community.

Van Praag advanced four postulates of humanism with respect to its view of the nature of man and the world:

(1)   The world exists, I exist and I recognize both existences;
(2)   The world is whole and dynamic;
(3)   All men have the same sense organization and mental structure; and
(4)   Men participate in their reality and cannot escape from it.[33]

Humanism, broadly defined, is thus a pragmatic conception of the world and of man's existence and full responsibility for his actions in it.   Humanism is, hence, existentialist in essence.   But, its existentialism is optimistic rather than pessimistic.   Humanism believes in man and his capacity to change and improve conditions in the world.   It considers both man and the world as complex, but not absurd.   It thus opposes nihilism and nihilistic existentialism.

At the same time, atheistic humanism claims that there is no existence for man beyond this earthly one and that, hence, he should concentrate all his efforts on the development and enrichment of his life in the here and now.   This deeply tragic view of man as a mortal Hamlet condemned to the absurdity of acting in the face of his mortality and nothingness is shared by the avant-garde, as explored in Chapter V.   Humanism does not claim to provide final answers to any questions, and regards the process of living as life's purpose.   Its outlook is basically anthropocentric and open.   Its central concern is man, the open mind, open society, open heart, and open hand.[34]   Humanism is thus devoted to the full realization of man in this world, which implies the all-round development of the human individual in a humanized social context.   Enjoyment and endurance are said to be major distinguishing traits of humanism whose supreme goal is—man.

In Blackham's view, humanism is neither simple materialism nor abstract idealism.   It is, rather, their "fertile combination."[35]   Gerald Wendt contends that the goals of humanism are: (1) Existence; (2) Health and long life; (3) Mental health; (4) Dignity; (5) Growth; (6) Creativity; and (7) Endurance through centuries.[36]   According to Wendt, the essential ingredients of humanism are empathy, understanding, liberty, equality, and fraternity.

It becomes obvious even from this cursory review that humanism is an extremely broad conceptual framework which can encompass both Christians and atheists, democrats and communists.   Contrary to Marxists and others, humanism does not have to deny God in order to affirm man.   Jerome D. Frank, Eda LeShan, and Horace M. Kallen are critical of the failure of Humanist Manifesto II to acknowledge the more esoteric areas of human experience such as intuition, the sense of the mystical, or even differences in beliefs.[37]   The world-famous Russian physicist Andrei D. Sakharov signed Manifesto II with two important reservations:

(1) I do not consider it correct from the philosophical and ethical point of view to contrapose religion and humanism, religion and scientific knowledge. Furthermore, I do not consider such a contraposition to be relevant in our time.

(2) I believe that the Manifesto does not sufficiently reflect the most urgent contraposition of our time—between humanism and false theories and pernicious practices, based on the concepts of class struggle, dictatorship, ideological monism, and intolerance and contempt for the rights of the individual.[38]

Maritain believed that humanism must both glorify God and dignify man, and that it may not be "*manichean,*" like Marx's humanism.[39] On the other hand, humanism may not forfeit man for idol worship. The primary purpose of humanism, in the words of Van Praag, is to "formulate a basis for a humanist practice in everyday life," rather than simply to attack religion.[40] Finally, Paul Kurtz points out that tolerance is "a fundamental normative principle of humanism," and that "any philosophy that contradicts the principle undermines ethical humanism."[41] The humanists' high view of man has led critics like Os Guinness to conclude that "optimistic humanism, like idealistic Marxism, is really a Christian heresy."[42] But even Guinness does not call for the abolition of humanism; on the contrary:

What is needed is a stronger humanism, not a weaker one. We need a concern for humanness that has a basis for its ideals and the possibility of their substantial realization.[43]

Humanism is linked also with life experiences, sensation, perception, observation, reality, and truth. But the humanist conception of truth is not that of Absolute Knowledge or Truth, as in the Hegelian and Marxist systems of thought. The epistemological justification of tolerance essential to humanism is contained in the postulate formulated by Kurtz that: "No one individual or group can claim a monopoly of truth or virtue." Hence, no man or group of men, in or out of power, can be considered "all-wise or all-good."[44] This conception of truth is diametrically opposed to that of Plato's Philosopher-King, Rousseau's Legislator-Sovereign, Hegel's Absolute Notion, and Marx's view of communists as the vanguard of the proletariat. Jacob Bronowski formulated the *principle of tolerance* as the corollary to Heisenberg's principle of uncertainty/indeterminacy as follows:

There is no absolute knowledge. And those who claim it, whether they are scientists or dogmatists, open the door to tragedy. All information is imperfect. We have to treat it with humility. That is the human condition, and that is what quantum physics says.[45]

The humanist conception of knowledge and truth is, therefore, that of *doxa* or opinion—knowledge of reality which can and, indeed, must undergo change, development, and improvement in order to correspond to changing reality and/or our improved understanding of that reality. The relative nature of human knowledge was summed up perceptively by the great American pragmatist and humanist, William James:

The fundamental fact about our experience is that it is a process of change. For the "trower" at any moment, truth, like the visible area round a man walking in a fog, or like what George Eliot calls "the wall of dark seen by small fishes' eyes that pierce a span in the wide ocean," is an objective field which the next moment enlarges and of which it is the critic, and which then either suffers alteration or is continued unchanged.[46]

James' formulation of the human experience of knowing is a remarkably accurate statement of the contemporary conception of epistemology. It contradicts both logical positivism and eighteenth century rationalism, and their conception of science as Absolute Knowledge, of which Marx's thought was also a victim.

Humanism is concerned with man and all that affects him. A humanist conceptualization of Marxism would, therefore, have to reveal itself in a preoccupation with the human individual (Marx's anthropology or philosophy of man). Humanism would also have to be reflected in the Marxist conception of man's relationship to the world and the nature of his knowledge about the world (Marx's dialectical materialism or epistemology).[47] In both instances, conclusions would have to be based on observation, experience, facts, and humanist values.

It is common knowledge that Marxism denies the separation between facts and values, or the logical gulf between "is" and "ought." Yet, in an examination of Marx's anthropology and epistemology, it is necessary to bear in mind that "ought" statements cannot logically be deduced from "is" statements. We shall thus guard against the *naturalistic fallacy.* This separation of science from ethics in no way implies that science cannot help us in choosing alternative courses of action. It asserts, however, that science cannot (yet?) give us answers regarding either final questions about the meaning of the universe or the purpose of human life. Nor can science tell us what we should or ought to do. Science can illuminate the causes and consequences of alternative possibilities and choices, but it is men who must choose among the alternatives.

Contrary to the Yugoslavs and others, the conception of science as value-free does not imply value relativism. It simply contends that the realm of ultimate values and value choices is outside the scope of science. As Max Weber remarked:

> We are far removed . . . from the view that the demand for the exclusion of value-judgments in empirical analysis implies that discussions of evaluations are sterile or meaningless.[48]

In fairness, however, one should point out that the fact-value controversy is far from settled. Furthermore, there are not two, but at least *three* basic approaches to this question represented by exceptional scholars in all three camps.

Thus, among those who deny the separation between fact and value, besides Marx and his followers, are also neo-Marxists and neo-Freudians like Karl Mannheim, Herbert Marcuse, C. Wright Mills, and Fromm. Surprisingly, to this camp belong also intuitionists and naturalists like Eric Voegelin, Maritain, Leo Strauss, and Harry V. Jaffa who, while recognizing the fact-value dichotomy, contend that science includes values, ontology, and metaphysics by definition. In the second group we find those like Arnold Brecht, Hans Reichenbach, Bronowski, and Felix Oppenheim who maintain with Max Weber that there is a logical gulf between "is" and "ought," between statements of fact and statements of value. Finally, the third group—which includes Immanuel Kant, John Stuart Mill, John Dewey, Michael Polanyi, Ernest Becker, Kenneth Boulding, Norbert Wiener, Abraham Kaplan, Thomas Kuhn, and Abraham Maslow—points to the viscosity of the two categories of fact and value and/or offers connecting links between them.[49]

The conception of science as value-free is a blow to the "scientific" character of Marxism. But it does not diminish the humanist or moral value of Marxist thought as a protest against inhuman conditions that enslave societies and men. And it is this latter aspect of Marxist thought which is, indeed, its least perishable and, perhaps, most significant aspect. The conceptual distinction between science/facts and ethics/values is of prime importance in any assessment of Marxist thought. Marxism characteristically fuses these two distinct kinds of knowledge. Significantly, Marxism pronounces its conception of man, his morals, ethics, purpose, and meaning, as Absolute Knowledge derived from rigorous empirical observation. Marxism calls this philosophical paradigm "Science." It is precisely this *scientizing of value judgments,* that is, giving its values the status of an incontrovertible Science with a capital "S," that is at the root of the anti-humanist, dogmatic, and totalitarian dimension of Marxist thought. It represents also a major source of the ambiguities and paradoxes inherent in the Marxist *Weltanschauung*. In Gordon Leff's view:

> It [Marxism as a doctrine] claims to be a science yet regards its truths as transcendental; it upholds the inexorability of change while remaining frozen in its century-old categories; it asserts the conditional nature of all outlooks and claims exemption for its own; it condemns pragmatism but makes success its criterion; it denounces metaphysics while labouring under its own metaphysical presuppositions.[50]

Avant-garde Yugoslav Marxism, while liberalized, radicalized, and humanized, still labors to a considerable extent under *Marxism's generic paradoxes*. The Yugoslav avant-garde has already performed a giant task of submitting many ambiguities in Marx's thought to critical scrutiny. Yugoslav theoreticians have journeyed further than any group of Marxists, East or West, on the road of highlighting and rendering explicit pre-existing ambiguities in the Marxist framework. They have thus contributed most to a humanist reconstruction of the entire Marxist world view. Yet, the writings of the avant-garde also mirror the basic *duality* in Marxism, that is, the close intertwining of *humanist* and *anti-humanist* (dogmatic and totalitarian) aspects. It is this duality in Marxism which enables the avant-garde to interpret Marxism as a realized humanism, genuine democracy, and all-round emancipation, de-alienation, and liberation of man. Critics of Marxism can derive from the same duality an equally convincing view of Marxism as absolute dehumanization, enslavement, dictatorship, and ruthless totalitarianism.

Both the exponents and critics of Marxism as humanism have a case. In order to assess the humanism and anti-humanism of Marxism, and specifically Yugoslav Marxism-Existentialism, it is necessary to delve, even if briefly, into the basic assumptions underlying the Marxist universe and the cosmology of problems that they entail. We can provisionally divide the Marxist *Weltanschauung* into two broad spheres dealing primarily with: (1) Problems of man, values, ethics/morals, and philosophy; and (2) Questions of science, the dialectic, materialism, history, economic and historical determinism, class struggle, and utopia.

3. Marx's Philosophy of Man

Marxism as a philosophy of moral protest has proved much more challenging and durable than its shaky and often grossly inaccurate "scientific" analyses and predictions. As Paul A. Samuelson remarked concerning Marx's "law" of the declining rate of profit and increasing poverty of the working class in capitalism:

> The purported laws—as, e.g., the law of the declining rate of profit and the immiserization of the workers—are not cogently derivable from Marx's own conceptual schema.[51]

This led Mark Blaug to conclude that Marx's major work, *Capital,* represents actually "a long drawn-out *petitio principii.*"[52] Marx's method is to assume consistently at the outset of his argument what needs to be proved. But if Marxism's "scientific" predictions and laws have turned out to be so unreliable and misleading, why do intellectuals and statesmen, East and West, North and South, continue to subscribe to them? Can Marxism be relevant to the needs and aspirations of individuals and societies in the late twentieth century?

To the extent that Yugoslav Marxism-Existentialism focused on man and his well-being, it began to reorient itself in the great Western humanist tradition. But, Yugoslav Marxism, by defining man as a being of *praxis*, raised more questions than it solved. The redefinition of man as a being of *praxis* is undoubtedly the major humanist contribution of Yugoslav Creative Marxism. On the other hand, the Yugoslav conception of man as a being of *praxis* labors under significant anti-humanist as well as humanist *a priori* notions of their mentor Karl Marx. In order to assess the Yugoslav reconstruction of Marx's philosophy of man, we shall concentrate briefly on five key problem areas.

3.1 Man as a Being of Praxis

A general consensus has grown, East and West, which regards the concept of *praxis* as central to the "Belgrade School" or *Praxis* school of thought in contemporary Yugoslavia. Is *praxis*, then, really the way to revolutionize, transform, and humanize Marxist theory and socialist practice? What, in essence, is this concept of *praxis*?

It should be clear from the analyses in the preceding chapters that the Yugoslav concept of *praxis*, especially in its avant-garde formulation, is a comprehensive notion akin to a world view. It includes simultaneously individuals, societies, and nature. Significantly, and parallel to the dialectic, *praxis* is both a process or method and an ideal, norm, or goal. This undoubtedly contributes to its complexity and resulting confusion and controversy. For *praxis*, like the classical Greek ideal of the good life or happiness, may be all things to all people. And since people differ in their values and aspirations, it is likely to mean also different things to different people. Could *praxis* imply tolerance, diversity, pluralism, and freedom? Yes, if we mean by *praxis* a process or method. No, if we mean by *praxis* an ideal, norm, or goal. How is this contradiction to be resolved?

There can be no doubt that the concept of *praxis* as process or method constitutes the major humanist contribution of avant-garde Yugoslav Marxist humanism. It was this concept of *praxis* understood as man's continuing revolutionizing, changing, and humanizing both himself and the world which led the avant-garde to restore man to the center of the historical drama. The avant-garde defined man's essential capacity as a free, creative, and self-creative being, open toward the future. Man as a free being can remake both himself and society in a never-ending process of becoming. Vranicki concluded that:

> In this historical openness, man does not have to be always rational and conscious of this process, yet he feels it spontaneously as the development of his being, his infinite possibilities, since he can never be defined ultimately.[53]

Clearly, then, the avant-garde's concept of *praxis* as process or method is the corollary to the Promethean conception of man cast in the role of the freedom fighter, rebel, or revolutionary. Yet, the avant-garde's concept of *praxis* as man's unfettered, free development of all his capabilities conflicts with the Marxist conception of positive freedom in *praxis* as ideal, norm, or goal.

While *praxis* as process means unfettered, free human activity, creativity, and choice, Marković cautions that:

> It would be odd to say that a choice was free even though it was made on the basis of false assumptions. Ignorance is incompatible with freedom, although its negation, knowledge, is only its necessary (and not a sufficient) condition.[54]

The consensus among the avant-garde is that action is *not free* unless it leads to a *positive* result—*praxis* as norm—which entails rationality understood as the realization of the Marxist socio-economic, political, and cultural program for a more humane future. But freedom to do only what is right, apart from the difficulty or impossibility of determining this category, is no freedom at all! It is the absolute, unconditional (though perhaps "benevolent") tyranny of Plato's Philosopher-King, Rousseau's Legislator-Sovereign, and Marx's avant-garde (the communists) which allegedly knows the scientific laws of society's development (Absolute Knowledge). Hence, the avant-garde's conception of *praxis* as norm is totalitarian:

it excludes the freedom to do one's own thing. Jacob Talmon concluded that in a totalitarian democracy:

> Liberty will be offered when there will be nobody to oppose or differ—in other words, when it will no longer be of use. Freedom has no meaning without the right to oppose and the possibility to differ.[55]

But what about the concept of *praxis* as norm? Is it rational, unified, realizable? On the surface, *praxis* as an ideal includes rationality, creativity, freedom, intentionality, sociality, and individual self-realization. Yet, as Western scholars have pointed out, conflicts between the different individual components within *praxis* cannot be resolved by reference to *praxis* itself. David A. Crocker argues that what is needed is a meta-ethical theory of justification of *praxis* which would include some priority or weighting principles. This is imperative in order to resolve conflicts internal to *praxis* such as:

(1) Intentional action need not be creative, social and/or rational action; I can act on purpose and for the purpose of realizing norms which are the opposite of *praxis*;

(2) The minimal freedom of absence of external and internal constraints can conflict with the maximal freedom of self-fulfillment;

(3) My freedom and optimal individual self-realization may conflict with yours or with the aims of my group—not only in the short run but also, unfortunately, in the long run; and

(4) In circumstances in which it is impossible to realize fully each and every one of my distinctive talents (compatible with *praxis*) we find another possible conflict within *praxis*.[56]

It would appear, then, that the avant-garde's concept of *praxis*, like so much else in the Marxist *Weltanschauung*, is half democratic and half totalitarian, harboring both humanist and anti-humanist elements. The concept of *praxis* as process—freedom—is irreconcilably juxtaposed to the concept of *praxis* as end goal—communism. And from this enchanted universe there is no theoretical or practical way out but by reconstituting the very parameters or basic underlying assumptions. If man is really to be free, he must be allowed all options, including those entailing ignorance, error, and foolishness. Without freedom, there can be no responsibility. And without the capacity of choice and responsibility, there can be no ethical grounding for man's actions. And without ethical grounding of one's actions, one can live either as a beast or a superman, but not as a man.

3.2 Man's Egoism Under Capitalism and Homo Duplex

Avant-garde Yugoslav Marxist philosophers accept Marx's concept of man as an integral or whole being who is fragmented, atomized, reified, alienated, exploited, and dehumanized in capitalist society. In Veljko Korać's formulation:

> . . . the society of private property was nothing more than a society of merciless exploitation, dehumanization, and the deformation of man . . . .[57]

There is an important *a priori* in Marx's concept of man. It is Marx's counter-position of the egoistic man in capitalist society to man's essential, *generic*, or species being, which can allegedly be realized only in a classless communist society. Yugoslav avant-garde theorists continue to subscribe to Marx's metaphysical proposition of the socialization and humanization of egoistic man, and the consequent remodeling of man into a new creature under proper socialist conditions, as an article of faith. The Yugoslavs claim, along with Marx, that man's egoism is a product of his alienation in class society and that his socialization will entail his liberation from egoism.[58] Yet, there is no evidence, scientific or otherwise, which would indicate that the new socialist man, now or in the future, is or is likely to become, any less egoistic than his counterpart under capitalism. Indeed, the evidence seems to point in the opposite direction: the resurgence of new, possibly even more virulent, forms of egoism under socialism.

Avant-garde Yugoslav thinkers as well as the regime are slowly becoming aware of the return of egoistic man under socialism. Only, this time with a vengeance. It is not only critics of Marxist theory and socialist practice like Milovan Djilas, Nenad Popović, and Mihajlo Mihajlov who point out the emergence of a new class of the privileged or *nouveaux riches* in socialism, but even leading exponents of Yugoslav Marxist humanism like Marković, Ivan Kuvačić, Svetozar Stojanović, Miahilo V. Popović, Rudi Supek, Miroslav Radovanović, Mijo Biličić, and Zoran Vidojević.[59] Surely, this is an epochal development in socialism, if egoism continues to rear its ugly head. After all, if egoism cannot be abolished in socialism, what possibilities remain for rearing the new selfless man in communism? What is the shape of this new egoism in socialism?

It is the avant-garde, again, which mounted the most comprehensive critique of the new market relations, embourgeoisement, enrichment, privileges, loss of socialist solidarity and socialist consciousness in contemporary Yugoslavia. According to Marković and Stojanović, self-governing groups in Yugoslavia sometimes act as "collective capitalists."[60] This new phenomenon is based on an alleged "profiteer mentality" and "petty-bourgeois capitalism" and consumerism.[61] This led the avant-garde to lament, in Kuvačić's words, that: " . . . private interest, whether personal or group, is becoming increasingly the basic motor force of social development."[62]

How could private or group interests revive in socialism? The avant-garde and the party point to the market as well as self-management. These new institutions have allegedly not been immune to abuse by individuals or groups, nor have they been able to guarantee equality and solidarity. Both the avant-garde and the party lament the emergence of separate individual and group interests. Even Edvard Kardelj had to admit that working class solidarity is unable to abolish selfishness:

> The selfish desire to live, if possible, at someone else's expense cannot be abolished even by the feeling of working class solidarity.[63]

This led some observers to conclude that the very notion of working class solidarity in contemporary Yugoslav society is illusory. Jovan Mirić noted that:

> Our working class is disunited regarding its interests. Hence, it is illusory to talk about its solidarity. Class solidarity may, indeed, be the object of theoretical debates, but hardly also of realistic understanding.[64]

While most Marxist thinkers in Yugoslavia still cling to the view articulated by Branko Horvat that " . . . socialism is not based on individual egoism,"[65] this assumption is belied by the realities of everyday life. In reality, individual and group egoism continue unabated in socialism. The forms may differ somewhat from those in capitalism, but not the essence. Avant-garde thinkers like Popović and Stojanović, as well as leading journals such as *Ekonomska politika,* point to egoism and irresponsibility among self-managing groups and enterprises which apply one criterion to income distribution to themselves and another to their contribution to communal funds, or insist on self-management principles to make faulty investment decisions but appeal to socialist solidarity and central organs when facing bankruptcy.[66]

The phenomenon of pressure groups appears also widespread in contemporary Yugoslavia. And one of their strongest motives seems to be the acquisition of privileges. This is, of course, in direct contradiction to the official ideology of socialist solidarity. The quest for privilege also runs counter to egalitarianism, which Josip Županov considers as the central norm or cultural value in Yugoslav society. Yet, Radovanović observes that individuals or groups oppose privileges only so long as they themselves are excluded from the circle of the privileged.[67] This behavioral phenomenon lends credence to Oliver Wendell Holmes' observation that the passion for equality "seems to me merely idealizing envy."[68]

It appears, then, that Yugoslav socialism has not bred egoism out of its citizens. The emergence of interest groups in Yugoslavia, especially after the economic reforms of 1965, and the trend toward independence and assertion of egoism or self-interest among Yugoslav BOALs, workers' councils, communes, and economic enterprises, is telling evidence that egoism and Marx's egoistic and alienated man thrive under socialism as well as, if not better than, under capitalism.· Whether communism can bring forth a non-egoistic man remains yet to be seen, but one can hardly make any "scientific" predictions based on past experience.

Some Yugoslav theorists have criticized Marx's concept that man is an intrinsically good, constructive, creative being who is debased by class conditions into a selfish, dehumanized, alienated being, functioning, in Marx's words, as a "belly." Thus, Stojanović and Marković admit that Marx underestimated man's capacity for irrationality, submission, enslavement, aggression, and destruction.[69] In the avant-garde's conception, man emerges as a good deal less rational, benevolent, and unspoiled in his natural state or essence than Marx believed him to be. Indeed, Marković criticizes Marx for excluding evil from his conception of human essence and human nature, relegating it to "a historically transient phase of alienation," whereas evil lies very deep in human nature itself.[70] On the other hand, Marković continues to cling to the utopian expectation of a radical change or "mutation" of human nature in the future.[71]

Stojanović has also pointed out that socialism's preoccupation with uprooting egoism has often led to the other undesirable extreme—collectivism.[72] And collectivism has not led to socialist solidarity and equality, but to group or collective egoism. Biličić can only conclude that egoism and particularism are more internalized in the human psyche and that they possess a greater resiliency or vitality than commonly assumed.[73]

While socialism has not bred egoism out of its citizens, it has tended to breed out another human quality: responsibility. Kardelj admits that personal responsibility has not been sufficiently developed and refined in theory or practice.[74] If Prvoslav Ralić is correct in assuming, according to the well-known ethical maxim, that the sense of responsibility constitutes the measure of man's humanity,[75] then Marxist theory and socialist practice confront one of their most important failings. The socialist dilemma is reflected in the contradiction between socialist solidarity and collective action versus individual self-realization and personal responsibility. How could a political system of totalitarian democracy under party tutelage and an economic system based on socially-owned property engender *personal* responsibility? Could collectivism and socialist solidarity be simply a cover for individual selfishness, unmitigated private interest rationalized in terms of the public good? Once more, the socialist framework seems to beg the moral question. As Friedrich A. Hayek summed it up:

> Only where we ourselves are responsible for our own interests and are free to sacrifice them has our decision moral value. We are neither entitled to be unselfish at someone else's expense nor is there any merit in being unselfish if we have no choice.[76]

In sum, to the extent that Yugoslav Marxism concerns itself with man's egoism, alienation, and division into a moral citizen and a selfish private individual, it points to a very real problem of the *humanum*. But to the extent that the avant-garde follows Marx's dictum that capitalism is the root cause rather than a possible aggravating condition of egoism, *homo duplex*, and alienation, it is dogmatic, close-minded, and simply misguided—and hence—anti-humanist.

3.3 Alienated Essence of Man: Private Property and Alienated Labor

Avant-garde Yugoslav Marxist philosophers humanized Marx's doctrine not only by their reformulation of the essence of man as a being of *praxis*, but also by their insistence on the necessity for man's de-alienation and liberation. The Yugoslavs found the alienation of labor, its exploitation, division, specialization, fragmentation, and automation to be the source of all other forms of alienation. At the same time, Yugoslav theorists still accept uncritically Marx's *a priori* postulate that the alienation of labor and its exploitation are due to the capitalist mode of commodity production and appropriation of surplus value. Hence, they regard the *socialization* of the means of production as the precondition for the emancipation of labor and man's liberation. This dogmatic *a priori* is adhered to even by those like Marković who have otherwise shown that Marx in his *Early Manuscripts* considered private property not as the cause but as the consequence of *alienated labor*.

Curiously, the avant-garde admits that contemporary socialism remains a society of commodity producers leading to alienation in socialism. Stipe Šuvar contends that socialism is still tainted by characteristics inherited from capitalist class society.[77] And while remnants of private property, class antagonisms, and particular interests remain, along with commodity production, there can be no genuine de-alienation and liberation of man. Private property continues to be regarded as a *bête noir* by the avant-garde and the party. Only isolated voices among the avant-garde can be heard occasionally questioning the basic Marxist assumption regarding private property. Thus, Danko Grlić criticizes Marx for his excessive emphasis on the importance of production and asks:

> How, then, can we justify the statement that private property is the one negative determining feature of human freedom and of the authenticity of human life as a whole?[78]

More disturbing is the fact that both the avant-garde and the party are beginning to realize that surplus value cannot be determined. Leading government spokesmen like Kardelj as well as economists like Ivan Maksimović admit that it is impossible to determine precisely the exact contribution to the social product by any individual producer.[79] But, if an individual's contribution to the social product cannot be measured, neither can surplus value be determined. And without a precise delimitation of surplus value, how can one measure exploitation and alienation? The Yugoslav view of the indeterminacy of surplus value differs from the prevailing Western critique which holds that:

> Nothing in the three volumes of *Capital* persuades us to believe that every worker of equal skill generates an identical amount of surplus value no matter what equipment he works with or what kind of output he produces. And when we drop this assumption, the entire house that Marx built comes tumbling down.[80]

The Yugoslav conception of the indeterminacy of an individual worker's contribution to the social product is obviously an antidote to the inflationary wage demands of the labor-managed enterprise, dubbed the Illyrian firm. But, it seems to undermine another dimension sorely needed in socialism: personal effort and responsibility. Within an economic system in which property belongs to everyone and to no one, and in which personal contribution to the social product is considered indeterminable, what is to motivate individuals to produce efficiently?

The absence of responsibility has already been noted. The lack of rational economic decision-making and risk-taking are equally endemic. The search for the causes of inefficiencies in the Yugoslav economy has led *Ekonomska politika* to conclude that:

> ...no economic system can yield rational economic results in which risk is not borne by the person or organ which makes business decisions.[81]

We are back to square one: the difficulty of assigning the locus of responsibility in market socialism and workers' self-management. Western observers note that the lack of responsibility, initiative, risk-taking, and rational economic decision-making in socialism derives from the absence of a truly competitive market and private property rights. According to D. R. Denman, private ownership generates a responsibility for the optimal productive use of a society's scarce resources which socialized ownership cannot duplicate.[82] But what about the Yugoslavs' introduction of elements of the market mechanism into the economy? Does not that augur well for economic efficiency and a better allocation of resources? Warren G. Nutter, for one, would disagree. In his view, markets without private property are an illusion:

> Markets without divisible and transferable property rights are a sheer illusion. There can be no competitive behavior, real or simulated, without dispersed power and responsibility. And it will not do to disperse the one without the other.[83]

Indeed, one of the most unusual results of the Yugoslav experiment with the market mechanism and self-management has been the privatization of socially-owned property and the reconstitution of private, individual or group, property. Thus, Županov in the East and Deborah Milenkovitch in the West wonder whether efficient production in a decentralized market economy necessitates private ownership.[84] Milenkovitch writes that:

> The concept of "social ownership" of productive factors, always vague, in fact proved vacuous. Gradually, certain members of society increased their effective rights over social property.[85]

The regime itself has walked a tightrope between two opposite socio-economic, political, and cultural trends: egalitarianism/*uravnilovka* versus personal enrichment apart from personal effort. Kardelj declared that egalitarianism in income distribution was harmful and that the societal goal should be income distribution based on performance:

> ...egalitarianism most certainly has nothing in common with social justice. On the contrary, it usually nurtures parasitic attitudes and irresponsibility.[86]

While Kardelj and Mika Tripalo called for an end to parasitism, Stojanović pointed out that parasitism arises in a system without competition.[87] But competition as a value contradicts collectivism, egalitarianism, the *uravnilovka,* and socialist solidarity. And egalitarianism is so deeply entrenched as a central cultural value in Yugoslav society that it has resulted in an inability and/or unwillingness to confront and deal with its contradictory demands.

On the one hand, the regime encourages income differentiation and material rewards based on work performed. On the other, it frowns on personal enrichment as illegitimate. *Ekonomska politika* considers differences in incomes of individuals and organizations as a necessary stimulus for greater labor productivity.[88] Yet, Radovanović maintains that some collectives exploit a portion of the working class, while Kuvačić scores the phenomenon of "unnatural differentiation" and conspicuous consumption in socialism.[89] Vukašin Pavlović concludes that both excessive social differences and the *uravnilovka* constitute "particular forms of exploitation of someone else's labor."[90]

Once more, there appears to be no theoretical or practical way out of this socialist dilemma: private property and initiative, responsibility, risk-taking, and economic efficiency *or* socially-owned property and lack of initiative, irresponsibility, inefficiency. The dilemma has only been compounded by the fact that maldistribution of wealth continues under socialism, socially-owned property is privatized, and the central societal value of egalitarianism in the economic sphere leads to authoritarianism in the political sphere. Furthermore, the rationale for the socialization of private property leads necessarily to the imperative for the socialization of work capabilities as well. And even socialist economists realize that the socialization of work capabilities in the form of income levelling is inefficient since it overlooks the stimulatory function of private ownership.[91] Marx's magic circle thus appears to be closed. It is only uncertain where within this circle there remains any room for man as a being of freedom.

Marx postulated the basic antagonism between labor and capital as an *a priori* principle, rather than a relationship which was to be examined empirically. The Yugoslavs took Marx's category of the capitalist and broadened it to include the state, bureaucracy, and other "collective exploiters." Yugoslav theorists thus contributed to our understanding of the nature of capital and labor in socialism. But their insistence on Marx's *a priori* notion of the necessarily exploitative nature of capital, whether in capitalist, state capitalist, or socialist societies, has not contributed to a clarification of these issues. It has simply continued their obfuscation.

On the other hand, some avant-garde thinkers are becoming increasingly aware of the fact that the division of labor is a factor more important than ownership for the distribution of power and goods in society.[92] The Yugoslavs have also advanced our understanding of the problems associated with modern industrial production characterized by the assembly line, automation, mechanization, fragmentation of tasks, dull, monotonous work, and man's "despiritualization" by pointing to the need for the humanization of work. Significantly, the Yugoslavs found that problems associated with commodity production, the market, money, and the like, are as severe under socialism as they are under capitalism. Marković concludes that there is serious antagonism between the exigencies of economic rationality and socialist humanism, that is, between the need for economic development, industrialization, urbanization, and the market mechanism, on the one hand, and the equally pressing need for a new non-exploitative and non-alienated or human society of humanized social relationships, on the other hand.[93]

To the extent that avant-garde Yugoslav Marxist philosophers and sociologists developed the cosmology of problems concerning alienation under socialism, which belies Marx's *a priori* of the necessity of abolishing private property as the cause of alienation, they humanized Marxism. But, to the extent that capital and private ownership of the means of production continue to be regarded as *a priori* exploitative and alienating forces, Yugoslav Marxism remains chained to Marx's basically religious categories of *capital = sin, evil* and *labor = good, grace* which is dogma and not science and, hence, anti-humanist.[94]

3.4 Means and Ends

Avant-garde Yugoslav Marxist philosophers humanized Marxism most distinctly and pervasively in their consideration of the means-ends continuum. Indeed, they revolutionized Marxism-Leninism by viewing the dilemma of means and ends as a *continuum* rather than a *dichotomy.*

Marx formulated one of his most perniciously anti-humanist *a prioris* in his early writings, 1843-1844. This *a priori* is an outgrowth of his apocalyptic Hegelian notion of the life and death struggle between capital and labor, and the necessity of an equally opprobrious strategy for winning the phony struggle. Thus, Marx in his *Contribution to the Critique of Hegel's Philosophy of Right* maintained that:

> For a *popular revolution* and the *emancipation of a particular class*
> of civil society to coincide, for *one* class to represent the whole of
> society, another class must concentrate in itself all the evils of
> society, a particular class must embody and represent a general
> obstacle and limitation. A particular social sphere must be
> regarded as the *notorious crime* of the whole society, so that
> emancipation from this sphere appears as a general emancipation.
> For *one* class to be the liberating class *par excellence*, it is
> necessary that another class should be openly the oppressing
> class.[95]

This invidious *a priori* of Marx, reflecting a ruthless, self-righteous, and
fanatical *Weltanschauung*, forms the cornerstone of the element of totalitarianism,
terror, and anti-humanism in Marx's thought which runs through *all* of his writings.
Gustav Wetter in the West and Stojanović in the East have challenged, explicitly or
implicitly, Marx's notion of the proletariat as a *general* class destined to bring
about *universal* human emancipation and liberation. Thus, Wetter questions Marx's
claim that the proletariat has not suffered particular, empirically determinable
wrongs, but wrongs *in general*, and wonders whether the proletariat can be anything
more than just another *particular* class with particular interests?[96] And Stojanović has pointed out the intimate connection between Marx's revolutionary collectivism and totalitarianism:

> Only a ruling class that speaks the language of collectivism, while
> at the same time protecting its own interests above all, can
> guarantee any durable *hypostatization* of "general" interests and
> suppression of personal and group interests. This is how revolution-
> ary collectivism degenerates into statist particularism. Totalitar-
> ian practice is rationalized by a totalitarian interpretation of
> Marx.[97]

From Marx's notion of the notorious crime of the capitalist class against man
("the proletariat"), world, and nature, it was but one step for Marx and Engels to
proclaim in their *Communist Manifesto* that the proletariat should disavow all
morals, and to Lenin's equally ruthless moral/ethical relativism which postulated
that *the only moral act* was that performed in the service of the proletariat and its
cause (as interpreted, of course, by its avant-garde, the communist party leadership).[98] It was this principle of ends justifying any and all means which became the
ideological basis of communist ruthlessness, terror, anti-humanism, and totalitarianism. It led to the intemperate use of deception, lies, inhumanity, and violence
on a scale unmatched in previous history.

Some Western Marxists turned away in disgust from the spectre of Stalinist
inhumanity and violence. But others, like Maurice Merleau-Ponty and Herbert
Marcuse, resorted to clichés and dialectical somersaults to rationalize the use of
violence. Marcuse and other New Left spokesmen, including some of the Frankfurt
School, maintained that "revolutionary" violence—that is, violence that advanced
the cause of socialism and their view of justice, humanism, and the new classless
society—was justified. On the other hand, violence perpetrated by Western
bourgeois regimes in defense of the *status quo* was "reactionary" and unjustified.
Marcuse went even so far in his "Repressive Tolerance" as to advocate the
suppression of "reactionary" thought, speech, and criticism.[99] And Merleau-Ponty
concluded in his *Humanism and Terror* that:

> All we know is different kinds of violence and we ought to prefer
> revolutionary violence because it has a future of humanism.[100]

It is this view of the necessity and even the desirability and moral justification of murder, lies, cheating, and all the rest in a Machiavellian *Realpolitik* philosophy that has undergone a radical and deeply humanist questioning on the part of Yugoslav theorists. Thus, Petrović dismisses Marcuse's notion of "revolutionary tolerance" as wrong in principle and harmful in practice. Only pure tolerance as such can contribute to universal human liberation. And he warns of the dangers inherent in a Stalinist interpretation of the "dictatorship of the proletariat," which paints an idealized future, but insists on advancing in the opposite direction in the present.[101] Stojanović considers Merleau-Ponty himself a victim of the adventures of the dialectic, and the Moscow trials of the 1930s a tragic mockery of any and all justice, rather than the expression of "revolutionary" justice.[102] Both Stojanović and Tadić score the Marxist conception of "objective" necessity and "historical" significance as misleading, pseudo-objective, and justifying Stalinist terror. Tadić concludes that:

> From the time of the Moscow trials all socialist alternatives to the Stalinist course of the "strengthening of the state" were proscribed and persecuted as the most grievous offense "against the people and the state," while *criminal law* and sophistically interpreted "class law" assumed a place of honor in the system of all-encompassing state law. From this time forward, the path to the enforced slave labor of the concentration camps and the martyrdom of citizens and producers was thrown wide open and justified and sanctified on the basis of "objective necessity."[103]

It is as if the avant-garde were becoming aware of Tolstoy's dictum that:

> The difference between repressive violence and revolutionary violence is only the difference between cat shit and dog shit.[104]

Thus, Arif Tanović, Grlić, Veljko Vlahović, Marković, Stojanović, Petrović, and Djordjević insist that there must be an integral link between means and ends, and that human ends cannot justify inhuman means.[105] In Stojanović's vision:

> The end ought to be the constitutive as well as the regulative principle of the means. *Causa finalis* must be operative in *causa efficiens.* What else is realization of the end but the application of means?[106]

The failure to integrate means and ends in a humanist framework leads more often than not to the despicable reality of dehumanized means and unattainable ends. In Vlahović's summary:

> Marx's thought and past experience in the fight for socialism teach and warn us that if humanist ends are left entirely for the future, then the means become transformed into ends while the ends themselves are never arrived at.[107]

Avant-garde theorists have become aware to a surprisingly great extent (for Marxist-Leninists) of the necessity for building the new socialist man and the classless society with *humane* means, lest socialist ideals themselves become, in Miladin Životić's words, "an instrument of tyranny."[108] The avant-garde's deeply humanistic ethical orientation has led to extensive criticism, East and West. In the East, Soviet and other Marxists take the Yugoslav avant-garde to task for revisionism and worse. What is surprising is the *extent* of criticism from Western intellectuals. Thus, Sharon Zukin belittles the *Praxis* group's theoretical contributions since she sees their thought as predominantly ethical and overly conciliatory.[109] More vitriolic criticism comes from Hoffman who ridicules Petrović's ethical orientation which opposes inhumanity, unfreedom, and violence in principle. In Hoffman's view, Petrović's "abstract" ethics has nothing to do with Marx:

> Marx . . . neither supported nor opposed "inhumanity, unfreedom
> and violence" at the level of abstract principle. There could be
> occasions when violence was essential to the success of revolution
> and circumstances when it was wholly unnecessary.[110]

Now, it is important to understand that, with few exceptions—notably Ivan
Supek—the avant-garde is not pacifist. Yugoslav theorists do not oppose any and
all use of force. What they criticize is "surplus violence" in revolutionary struggle
and violence which becomes an end in itself. Thus, Marković observes that:

> Once violence becomes a value in itself it turns against those who
> use it: after killing their oppressors men continue to kill each
> other. Such a reversal of means and ends renders the whole
> process of liberation a typical Hegelian *false infinity*: endless
> repetition of the same contradiction.[111]

Crucially, the avant-garde has come to question Marx's, Engels', and Lenin's
moral/ethical relativism, especially with regard to the revolutionary organization
itself, that is, the party. The avant-garde came to be preoccupied with the
question of how to prevent, in Marković's words, the "rapid alienation of the
revolutionary avant-garde" in socialism,[112] a question which Western Marxists and
would-be revolutionaries tend to overlook completely. Stojanović notes the
perplexity of the revolutionary means ossifying into inhuman ends, the revolutionary organization itself becoming a monolithic structure, imprisoning not only
society but even the revolutionaries themselves:

> The emancipation of revolutionary means and their finalization is a
> form of alienation: Revolutionary activity and its creations escape
> the control of the revolutionaries and begin to rule over them.[113]

Hence, concludes Stojanović, the revolutionaries are confronted with the cruel
spectacle that their movement recreates the same kind of evil against which they
rebelled in the first place.

How can the revolutionary organization emancipate itself and come to
dominate its members and society at large? What does it take to transform a
Prometheus in front of the enemy into a weakling in front of the party? What are
the causes for this new socialist *homo duplex*? Supek and Stojanović think that the
new *homo duplex* is the result of the total negation of the authentic personality of
the individual revolutionary. The party demands from the revolutionary complete
ethical prostration. But, instead of leading to genuine socialist solidarity, ethical
prostration becomes a major ethical antinomy characterizing revolutionary existence:

> The testimony of an ethical prostration turned into a purely formal
> ritual—into its opposite: true solidarity into false testimony of
> unanimity, the "consolidation of our ranks" into general suspicious-
> ness and distrust, "monolithism" into general reserve or even
> conspiracy; every apostle adopted the part of Judas.[114]

How can the fateful split between the revolutionary and his organization be
remedied? Stojanović believes that the split can be remedied only by the principle
of complete mutuality between the revolutionary and the party, which calls for
mutual respect, solidarity, loyalty, and recognition. Stojanović thus calls for the
renaissance of a new ethical principle to govern the relationship between the
revolutionary, the party, and society. This *ethics of humanistic reciprocity*
—which in reality only begs the question—seems to be the closest any Marxist has
ever come to the recognition of Kant's categorical imperative. Thus, Stojanović's
call for a new respect for Marx's categorical imperative is Kantian more than
Marxist:

Marx's "categorical imperative that all conditions must be revolutionized in which man is a debased, an enslaved, an abandoned, a contemptible being" should apply, before anything else, to the communists themselves.[115]

In sum, to the extent that Yugoslav Marxism-Existentialism concentrated its attention on man's supreme existentialist dilemma of means and ends, postulating the necessity for humane means, constitutionalism, legality, respect for the *individual,* as well as basic human rights and the dignity of man, it may truly be said to have revolutionized and humanized Marxist thought. Crucially, the avant-garde engendered a radical break with Marx's, Engels' and, especially, Lenin's moral/ethical relativism. To the extent, however, that the avant-garde continues to view reality through the distorted prism of class struggle and opposition between labor and capital, it carries within itself the seeds of anti-humanism and terror, limiting itself to a partial, socialist, humanism.

The avant-garde's signal contribution to theory and practice in late twentieth century, East and West, is their raising the quintessential question of history. But, it is not a question posed by history. It is a question posed by and for man. This quintessential question was formulated by Albert Camus, one of the greatest humanists of all time:

> Does the end justify the means? That is possible. But what will justify the end? To that question which historical thought leaves pending, rebellion replies: the means.[116]

3.5 Representative Democracy and Political Freedom versus Direct Democracy and Economic Freedom

Avant-garde theorists can be credited with reviving and throwing new light onto problems of politics, interest groups, conflicts, and political representation, as well as the important connection between political and economic freedom. The Yugoslavs advanced our knowledge of some of the possibilities for more direct participation and representation, especially in industry. But, they failed to live up to their proclaimed ideal of direct democracy. As we found in the previous chapter, even such basic organs of Yugoslav workers' self-management and social self-government as the BOALs, workers' councils, local communities, communes, and communities of interest are instances of *representative* rather than direct democracy. Furthermore, the *delegate system* is burdened with the *positive conception of freedom* which considers the delegates' choice free only if it accords with the party's definition of the public interest (Rosseau's general will).

Both the avant-garde and the party seem to be unaware of the contradiction between their call for genuine self-management and direct democracy, on the one hand, and the Marxist imperative for only one outcome or end product of self-management choice, on the other. Thus, Markovic's recipe to emancipate self-management from the grip of bureaucracy and manipulation by the technostructure, by providing self-managers with independent access to data, alternative proposals by management, and the right to elect, re-elect, or replace the manager,[117] is incompatible with the *positive* conception of freedom and truth, according to which there can only be one correct or enlightened socialist decision.

Even more embarrassing to both the avant-garde and the party has been the resurgence of interest groups and conflicts in socialism. Following in Marx's footsteps, the avant-garde and the party concluded that conflicts were "unsocialist" and that the remedy was to abolish the remnants of the state, law, politics, bureaucracy, and other reified and alienated political institutions. But the Yugoslavs, like Marxists elsewhere, may in this area be merely fighting windmills. As Jack Gray summed it up:

> Economists have pointed out that the idea of marginal utility is

missing from Marxist economics. In the same way, and in a close psychological relationship, the idea of legitimate conflict and competition is missing from Marxist politics. The market place, whether for goods or ideas, is irrational and dangerous.[118]

Kardelj admits that it is not realistic to expect the withering away of all social conflicts, and that the socialist revolution and self-management need new institutions and mechanisms for democratic conflict resolution.[119] Yet, Kardelj's and the avant-garde's demand for institutions for conflict resolution in socialism is basically *un-Marxist,* since it presupposes the continuation of conflicts and, hence, of class relations, exploitation, and alienation in socialism and communism.

Furthermore, some avant-garde theorists see the aggregation and articulation of different interests and, hence, their conflict, as a necessary precondition for the evolution of self-management and direct democracy in socialism. Thus, Jovan Mirić writes that it is wrong to consider conflicts of interest as deviant behavior. On the contrary, only in a free political community is it possible to articulate different interests.[120] As to the reality of interest groups in Yugoslav society, Damir Grubiša notes that every enterprise in a system of self-management constitutes a particular interest group which opposes other interest groups in the marketplace.[121] Yugoslav theorists have come to realize not only that there are different interest groups in socialism, but also that self-management does not eliminate the element of power either within an enterprise or in the relationship between enterprises. All this led Kardelj to formulate his thesis of the "pluralism of self-management interests," while retaining the classic Marxist-Leninist notion that only the party expresses "a specific, but socially and historically very significant form of the interests of the working class and, hence, of the interests of all working people and society . . . ."[122]

While most Yugoslav theorists continue to call for the *abolition of power* within enterprises and the larger society, Veljko Rus, Arzenšek, and Mirić call for its *institutionalization,* even if indirectly.[123] The avant-garde is slowly beginning to realize that what is needed is not the abolition of power, but its *institutionalization, dispersion, and limitation.* Marx's intellectual heritage constitutes a major barrier to rational understanding in this area, since its utopian premise has always been to abolish power and its carriers, primarily the state, political parties, administrative bureaucracies, and the like. This "anti-bureaucratic complex" has reached such proportions in contemporary Yugoslavia, according to Popović, that it has resulted in the abolition of even those forms and elements of the administrative substructure vital to societal development.[124]

Indeed, Supek remarks that self-management itself has become the strongest ideological stereotype in Yugoslav society which renders a realistic analysis and assessment of social and political conflicts difficult. Why? Because conflicts are reduced to only two categories: (1) those strengthening self-management; and (2) those in opposition to self-management.[125] This dichotomy, combined with the dominant notion that all conflict is "class conflict" and hence "unsocialist," leads logically enough to the suppression of all conflicts instead of their democratic resolution. In Stojanović's view:

As the official politics believes itself to be the standard of socialism, any criticism of it becomes *by definition* an attack on socialism.[126]

The Yugoslavs' humanist contribution in the field of politics consists, then, in their questioning of Marx's utopian framework which is devoid of interest groups, conflicts, and mechanisms for democratic conflict resolution. In the field of industrial relations, the Yugoslavs made their most creative contribution with the institution of the workers' council, its educational and informational role, in its attempt to humanize work or, at least, production relations, and its promise to become a genuinely self-managing institution. They failed in this area to the extent that institutions of workers' self-management function as a façade behind which the League of Communists and the enterprise power structure continue to determine policy. Yugoslav attempts to democratize their institutions and practices, whether at the macro level of social self-government or the micro level of workers' self-management, suffer from the peculiar contradictions inherent in the quest for totalitarian democracy, explored in the previous chapter.

But, if political freedom and direct democracy remain elusive for the Yugoslavs, what about economic freedom? Is it really true that the question of freedom constitutes the Achilles' heel of the Marxist system? The Yugoslavs, like other Marxists, never tire of pointing out what to them is the abstract and false character of political freedom in the West, which allegedly fails to incorporate economic freedom. Marković claims that classical bourgeois liberalism fails to resolve concrete questions associated with individual freedom (abstract humanism), whereas socialism attempts to realize individual freedom practically (real or socialist humanism).[127]

In the West, adds Životić, liberal ideals concerning freedom of thought, speech, press, association, and behavior have become simply a "moralistic embellishment of the existing reality; they live only in rhetorical phrases of contemporary political pragmatists, in phrases which contribute to the maintenance of the existing order and not to its change."[128] Životić thus implies that Western liberal ideals have become a rationalization of existing institutions and practices as well as malpractices—or ideology—and opposes socialist humanism to both capitalism and Stalinism. This is the accepted Yugoslav view. However, there are dissenters who point to a similar tendency toward institutionalization of socialist ideals and their transformation into ideology or false consciousness in socialism. Thus, according to Veljko Rus, fundamental socialist categories such as "the emancipation of labour, democratic socialism, social equality, etc." are becoming increasingly "abstractions since their immutable generality has transformed them into abstract symbols, that is, they have become indifferent to a concrete content of conflict."[129]

Crucially, the avant-garde is beginning slowly to realize that the socialist promise of economic freedom is illusory without political freedom. Thus, in Marković's view, alienation continues as long as there are social groups with a monopoly of either economic or political power which leads to exploitation or political hegemony, respectively.[130] In this, the avant-garde echoes Lord Acton's warning on absolute power which corrupts absolutely, as well as Friedman's proposition that "the greatest threat to human freedom is the concentration of power, whether in the hands of government or anyone else."[131] Marković and Stojanović conclude that Marxism has not yet superseded liberalism in the question of political power and individual rights and freedoms. Indeed, Marković contends that:

> In the authoritarian forms of government, in socialism, we come up against a far higher degree of political alienation than we had in certain liberal societies.[132]

And Stojanović calls the notion that economic democracy can be developed without political democracy "a myth."[133]

Most Yugoslav theorists, however, adhere to the view that while the question of man is the question of freedom, it remains, in the final analysis, the question of man's material existence. The Yugoslavs are bothered by the economic realities under socialism where, as Kostas Axelos pointed out, the will for power and appropriation could reconstitute themselves even after the abolition of private property.[134] They have come close to realizing Weber's dictum that bureaucracy would triumph ultimately in socialism and that:

> The expropriation of all the workers would be retained and merely brought to completion by the expropriation of private own-
> ers ....[135]

Yet, avant-garde thinkers abhor the mere suggestion that private property, free enterprise, and the market have anything to do with political or economic freedom. Hence, Friedman's insistence on the free market as an "offset" to the concentration of political power would probably strike Yugoslav theorists as odd, if not completely mistaken.[136]

In sum, Yugoslav Marxism-Existentialism has contributed to a humanist frame of reference by exploring the interweaving of economic and political freedoms, the necessity for assuring the individual a concrete economic or material basis, and the preconditions for his genuine emancipation, all-round liberation, development, and enjoyment of material, political, æsthetic, cultural, spiritual, and other freedoms. On the other hand, Yugoslav Marxist theory and socialist practice remain profoundly anti-humanist to the extent that they consider economic freedom in the form of socially-owned property as primary and all-important, and political and all other human freedoms as expendable. As to the question of individual versus social liberation, the real-life issue is summed up in Marković's statement:

> The real issue is whether radical individual emancipation is feasible without radical change of the whole social structure.[137]

It is the classical dilemma of two mutually exclusive world views of the yogi and the commissar, of change from within versus change from without, the individual versus the social environment, *physis* versus *nomos.* The conservatives' dilemma is reflected in their dogmatic answer to Marković's question in the form of an unequivocal "yes," and the socialists' dilemma in the equally close-minded and dogmatic answer as an unequivocal "no."

4. The Dialectic: Scientization of Philosophy?

Avant-garde Yugoslav Marxist philosophers recast, radicalized, revolutionized, and humanized not only Marx's philosophy of man, but also the "scientific" methodology of Marxist thought, the dialectic, and economic and historical materialism connected with it. In this enterprise, the Yugoslavs have so far shown considerable success in reshaping and humanizing the dialectic as a method of inquiry.

However, the dialectic in the Marxist system is not simply a method. It is also a comprehensive theory, philosophy, and *Weltanschauung* which lays claim to Absolute Knowledge or Science of exceptionless "laws" of economic and historical development of societies. The Yugoslavs have slowly begun to question this crucial anti-humanist and dogmatic aspect of the Marxist faith. Thus, Petrović pointed out that dialectical materialism and its theory of reflection contradict Marx's humanist conception of man as a being of *praxis*.[138] If man is completely determined by economic and historical factors, then he can hardly be held responsible for his actions, and Marx's imperative to change the world becomes an absurd call on automatons to cease their programmed existence and act independently on the basis of free choice.

Yugoslav theorists have tried to surmount the deterministic aspect of the dialectic by relying on Marx's Third Thesis on Feuerbach, the Lenin of the *Philosophical Notebooks,* and other Marxist classics which claim that men are shaped by circumstances, but that circumstances are also shaped by men. The Yugoslav answer to Marx's economic and historical determinism which pervades his writings was, of course, the conception of man as a being of *praxis*, a relatively free, creative, and self-creative being. The Yugoslavs thus humanized the dialectic to the extent that they connected it with the phenomenon of man as a being of *praxis*. *Praxis*, however, has turned out to be an extremely broad category as complex as the dialectic. It has failed to a considerable extent to deal with the *generic* paradoxes inherent in the concept of the dialectic both as theory and method.

4.1 The Nature of the Dialectic

The dialectic is conceived in the Marxist *Weltanschauung* as a scientific method *par excellence*, capable of predicting the laws of historical development of human societies. Among the major constituent elements of the dialectic are a view of totality, *Gestalt*, or wholeness linked to History, unity of opposites, negation of negation, and the transformation of quantity into quality, and vice versa.

Yugoslav Marxist philosophers have only recently begun to admit that Marx's theory contains important non-empirical, metaphysical, *a priori* and *a posteriori* notions. The avant-garde sees nothing unusual in this. Staniša Novaković holds that there can be no knowledge without metaphysical propositions, and that we cannot hope to draw a sharp dividing line between empirical statements in the sciences and metaphysical statements beyond scientific testability in philosophy. Indeed, Novaković concludes that metaphysical presuppositions often advance the scientific enterprise. And they are crucial in their capacity to relate the sciences to humanistic values.[139]

What are these non-empirical, *a priori* and *a posteriori* notions? Marković's list includes the following:

(1) An *a priori* philosophical vision;
(2) A view of historical situations in their totality;
(3) A conceptual apparatus of social critique which distinguishes between structures which exist (such as concepts of commodity, surplus value, capital, class, state, law, politics, ideology) and those which are not yet but can be created (such as species being, *praxis*, human production, community, freedom, history, communism); and
(4) Dialectical notions of *negation* and *ideal* which emphasize discontinuities, disfunctions, and internal conflicts.[140]

These non-empirical, a-scientific, *a priori* and *a posteriori* notions are part of the *telos* of the dialectic, and mirror its essentially *philosophic* rather than *scientific* nature. The dialectic thus constitutes a comprehensive *paradigm*, in Thomas Kuhn's sense, with the distinction that the philosophic *a prioris* which it brings to the paradigm turn it into a predominantly *philosophic* method of inquiry. This raises an important question as to the testability of dialectical propositions: how does one prove or disprove a philosophic statement? By another philosophic statement, empirical propositions, hypotheses, testing, verification or refutation, reality, experience?

The avant-garde concentrated its attention elsewhere. Marković posed the central question for Yugoslav Marxist humanism as the problem of how to transform humanism into a dialectical philosophy and the dialectic into a humanist method. The avant-garde humanized the dialectic as a method by recasting it into a method of radical social *criticism* of *all* societies, whether capitalist, state capitalist, or socialist, and by linking it to Marx's humanism, that is, to the central question of man and the need for his de-alienation, emancipation, and liberation. The Yugoslavs thus humanized the dialectic to the extent that they conceive of it as a method which must reflect the unity of theory and practice focused on the well-being of man. They even made the dialectical method more scientific by connecting it with their conception of open-ended Marxism as a humanism of *praxis*, change, creation, and development.

Yet, the Hegelian dialectic in Marx's system remains a quasi-scientific technique of circular or pseudo-reasoning. The dialectic is characterized by its abandonment of the rules of formal logic, substituting for them the accordion-like flexibility of dialectical "logic." Whereas the rules of formal logic postulate that an entity cannot be itself and its opposite, *in toto*, at the same time, dialectical logic thrives on collapsing mutually exclusive categories, called the unity of opposites. It is also fond of entertaining the simultaneous birth and death of different notions embedded in the same concept, called the negation of the negation, and so on. The dialectic thus creates a make-believe world in which things are continually in a state of flux, of becoming. In a sense, the dialectic has only ghosts to deal with, concepts which change while being analyzed, categories that have an eerie Alice-in-Wonderland quality of stretching and contracting. The greatest contradiction concerns the elusiveness of concepts which are, nevertheless, marshalled toward a predetermined historical end. On the positive side, the dialectic is capable of illuminating complex, interdependent, and dynamic phenomena. Yet, it lacks touchstones for judgment. While capable of high internal logical consistency, the dialectic remains, nevertheless, a technique of reasoning which tends to offer as proofs the very factors or concepts it started out to prove.[141]

The plasticity, pliability, and lack of formal logic in dialectical reasoning appears to be at the root of the relativizing element in the dialectic with regard to both facts and values. Stojanović in the East and Lobkowicz in the West note the curious phenomenon that the dialectic enables one to press contradictory charges of left-wing and right-wing deviationism concerning *a single act.* Thus, Stojanović observes that the dialectic allows the party leadership to accuse a revolutionary not only of sabotage for failing to carry out party decisions, but for overzealousness as well.[142] In sum, concludes Stojanović, the dialectical notions of "objective" meaning and "objective" responsibility for both the intended and the unintended consequences of one's actions constitute a trap used by the Stalinized party to ensnare the individual revolutionary.[143] Lobkowicz sees the dialectic as a method with which the party elite rationalizes the practical measures of its everyday power politics, calling analogous developments reactionary or revolutionary depending on whether they do or do not accord with the party's current policies.[144] It has led Guinness to conclude that:

> . . . with only relativism or dialectic underlying modern principles, no about-face is unthinkable, no moral somersault impossible.[145]

If the dialectic can be used to prove opposite propositions, does not that call for a Philosopher-King who possesses Absolute Knowledge and, hence, can decide between right and wrong? And does not this, in turn, imply totalitarianism, intolerance, and terror, and, from the standpoint of the party or the Philosopher-King, the necessity for the suppression of differences of opinion and criticism? In Solzhenitsyn's masterpiece, *The First Circle*, Stalin asked his confidant, Abakumov, about the mood of the young people. Abakumov merely gestured, but said nothing. For, if he replied "Good," he could be accused of political blindness. And, if he replied "Bad," he could be taken to task for not believing in the future![146] Stojanović admits that the party—cast into the role of the revolutionary subject—represents an Absolute in relation to which everything else may be defined as an "anti-subject."[147] The dialectic as a method of reasoning binds the practitioner with its invisible chains to the sacrificial altar within a closed universe. And the victimizer is bound to be himself victimized.

To the extent that Yugoslav Marxists fail to admit the logical viscosity and non-scientific nature of the dialectic, they are bound to be imprisoned by their own creations. In this, the avant-garde continues the traditional Marxist scientization of philosophy, lending the Marxist *Weltanschauung* a scientific halo. On the other hand, to the extent that the Yugoslavs redefined the dialectic as a method which must concern itself with empirical facts of a changing reality, flux, and development, they lent it aspects of a genuinely scientific methodology.

4.2 Economic Determinism

One of the major *a priori* elements in Marx's dialectic as theory is economic determinism, the conception of the primacy of economic factors in social development. Yugoslav avant-garde theorists weakened the deterministic element in

Marxist thought by their conception of man as a being of *praxis*. They insist that the ecomonic factor is "only in the last analysis the decisive social factor which determines directly or indirectly all other social phenomena."[148] The Yugoslavs point out that Marx conceived of the economic base and the social, political, legal, and cultural superstructure not as independent of each other, but as *interdependent*. They are fond of quoting Engels' letter to a friend in which he admitted that he and Marx were partially to blame for over-emphasizing the economic factor in social life which led some younger Marxists to misunderstanding and the creation of "surprising nonsense."[149] Engels maintained in his letter to Joseph Bloch that:

> According to the materialist conception of history, the *ultimately* determining element in history is the production and reproduction of real life. More than this neither Marx nor I have ever asserted. Hence if somebody twists this into saying that the economic element is the *only* determining one, he transforms that proposition into a meaningless, abstract, senseless phrase.[150]

Hence, Živko Surčulija claims that economic determinism, fatalism, and automatism of social development are foreign to Marxism.[151] Western observers like James J. O'Rourke advance the notion that Marx is not guilty of "historical determinism" since historical laws apply only to "supra-individual entities in the formation of their general types of economic and social structure."[152] Yet, Max Weber remarked that the materialist conception of history and the attempt to explain everything by economic causes alone did not suffice even within the economic sphere itself.[153] And, Stojanović reminds us of the paradox that in socialist revolutions the party first establishes its predominance in the political sphere, and only thereafter in the economic sphere.[154]

Some avant-garde thinkers take even Marx, Engels, and other Marxist classics to task for writing at times in an overly deterministic vein. According to Grlić:

> . . . one cannot rely completely even on Marx, who inevitably, placed far more importance on production than would be necessary today after all that has been served up to us in the name of the development of the forces of production, if that is, we wanted to untangle certain knotty issues and cure some of the ulcers of our society.[155]

Petrović concurs in Grlić's view, adding that the economic factor is likely to lose its predominant role in the future with the de-alienation of man and the creation of a classless society.[156]

The avant-garde's most pervasive critique has been directed at the Soviet and other dogmatic, positivist conceptions of the dialectic as the realization of technology, economic rationale, and production. The basic failure of positivist dialectic and historical materialism, or "diamat," in Životić's view, is that such a dialectic becomes a theory of reality excluding man and human *praxis*. To the avant-garde, the authentic dialectic must be based on the theory of freedom, alienation, and de-alienation. And the goal of such a dialectic is personalistic humanism, that is, the realization of a community of liberated personalities.[157]

Yugoslav Marxism-Existentialism, in contradistinction to Stalinist positivism, conceived man as a being of *praxis*, freedom, creative activity, choice, and responsibility, rather than simply an economic animal or mass man. Furthermore, the Yugoslavs postulated as the end goal of communism not mere economic development, increased commodity production, industrialization, and material abundance, but, more importantly, the necessity of developing new humane social relations in a free community of immediate producers which has transcended economic rationality and attained to socialist humanism. If the essence of communism, according to Axelos, lies in its attempt to set total technique in motion for the conquest of the world,[158] then the avant-garde's is a non-communist vision. For, the avant-garde considers the realization of communism as mere technology, technique, or production as a continuation of the bourgeois *Weltan-schauung* and, hence, a betrayal of its humanist ideals.

While the avant-garde claims that authentic Marxism has nothing to do with economic or historical determinism, an important problem remains. And that is Marx's claim that the future classless society would transcend the framework of alienation, exploitation, economic rationale, and scarcity, and leap from the realm of necessity into the realm of freedom. This utopian element in the Marxist world view is unusually deterministic, couched in eschatological language. To Hannah Arendt, it was clear that life and necessity are so intimately intertwined that "life itself is threatened where necessity is altogether eliminated." She concluded that the abolition of necessity would not lead to freedom, but only to a blurring of the dividing line between freedom and necessity.[159]

To the extent that Yugoslav Marxist theorists evolved a more comprehensive and synthetic view of the interplay of economic with non-economic factors in social life, they muted the deterministic aspect of the dialectic and contributed to a more accurate and humane understanding of the significance of economics for society and man. To the extent, however, that the Yugoslavs continue to adhere to the view of the primacy of the economic sphere and the justifiability of sacrificing all other spheres of life to it, their dialectical materialism remains doctrinaire and anti-humanist. But, the opposite proposition also holds: to the extent that the avant-garde dismisses economic rationale and the imperative for optimal allocation and use of scarce resources, it remains under the spell of Marx's dialectic, whose economic determinism promises, paradoxically, deliverance from scarcity and economics as such in a leap from total enslavement to total liberation.

4.3 The "Law" of Historical Class Struggle

Merleau-Ponty advanced the *generic* anti-humanist thesis of Marxism as a pessimistic view of "our starting point—conflict and struggle to the death" and, hence, as containing an irrepressible "element of violence and terror."[160] It is this view of the dialectical progress of History via class struggle that constitutes perhaps the most notorious *a priori* notion in Marx's system of thought canonized into a "law" by the pliable dialectic. The notion of class conflict is taken for granted by most Yugoslav Marxist philosophers and sociologists, as well as the party. After all, it grows organically out of Marx's *a priori* principles that the interests of the capitalist are always opposed to those of society, that the landlord of necessity exploits society, and that the capitalist represents the worker's non-existence and vice versa—a purely Hegelian notion.[161]

We pointed out that the conflict between labor and capital in Marx's system reflecting the basically religious categories of absolute good versus absolute evil is not conducive to impartial empirical investigation of their relationship. Rather, it precludes any factual examination by postulating *a priori* the ubiquitousness of their conflict as a historical law—the "law" of class struggle. This has led some observers, East and West, to comment that socialism has missed out on some 50 years of development of modern capitalism. In De George's view, Marx failed to take into account such phenomena as compromise, collective bargaining, coopera-tion, and the state as possible mediators between labor and capital, which have since altered the capitalism of his day.[162] Instead of good will, Marx put forward, according to Roberts and Stephenson, the concept of violence and class struggle as mediators between different interests in society, which implies Leninism and Stalinism.[163]

The Yugoslav communist leadership has reemphasized, especially after the 1971 Croatian crisis, the 1974 Constitution, and the Tenth Party Congress, the need for the intensification of ideological and class struggle. Tito and Kardelj made it clear, and most avant-garde theorists take it for granted, that the class struggle has not come to an end, and that the Yugoslav foreign policy orientation of active peaceful coexistence does not mean "class coexistence."[164] Indeed, both Tito and Kardelj launched a vituperative criticism of those, inside and outside the party, who advocate "alien" ideas and "bourgeois" notions of the end of ideology, classes, and the class struggle in Yugoslav socialism. Kardelj bore down on those who equate democracy with "freedom to fight for different opinions." What was needed, insisted Kardelj, was to recognize the *class* nature of socialist democracy. In accord with this conceptualization of the class substance of present socialist society, Tito advanced the thesis that socialist self-management democracy was actually "a specific form of the dictatorship of the proletariat." And, for good measure, Tito assured everyone that the state will not wither away as long as the working class exists.[165] For the Yugoslav communist leadership, class struggle and the dictatorship of the proletariat are permanent features in the socialist advance toward a classless society.

Avant-garde thinkers have begun to question these seminal assumptions regarding the permanency of the class struggle and the ubiquitous need for a dictatorship of the proletariat. Thus, Petrović, Krešić, Tadić, and Pejović note that in the past these doctrines have led to Stalin's cult of personality, bureaucracy, etatism, and socialist malpractices. Krešić wonders whether the class struggle actually intensified between the working masses and political institutions. His conclusion is that in Stalinism the conflict between the official politics and society and the revolution was presented as the class struggle between the proletariat and the bourgeoisie.[166] Tadić regards the doctrine of the regime's unlimited mandate in Stalinized or vulgar Marxism as the seed for Stalin's cult of personality, which converts the dictatorship of the proletariat into a charismatic-bureaucratic type, while perverting the theory of the withering away of the state into its opposite—the strengthening of the state and the intensification of the class struggle.[167] Pejović concurs in the view that the notion of the intensification of the class struggle, that is, of the organs of oppression, is hardly conducive to the withering away of the state.[168] As to the dictatorship of the proletariat as a guide or compass for the revolution, Milan Mirić concludes that it no longer points anywhere.[169]

While taking class struggle for granted, Yugoslav theorists began a searching reexamination of the nature of conflict, struggle, exploitation, and alienation in socialist societies. In this process, the avant-garde became increasingly aware of the fact that new forms of alienation can exist in socialism, alongside the classic forms of alienation embodied in the state, law, bureaucracy, politics, and private ownership of the means of production. Veljko Rus, Stanovčić, Kuvačić, and Jovan Mirić point to the reality of conflicts of interest in socialist societies due to the formation and articulation of particular and group interests in the processes of democratization.

Kuvačić and Supek contend that science and technology today have become powerful new instruments of domination and exploitation which, according to Supek, are possibly supplanting capitalism in this function.[170] Marković found that besides the capitalist, there can be such exploiters in society as the bureaucracy and other "collective exploiters." Rus showed that the entire self-management model based on conflictless participation was grossly misleading, underrating the division of labor as a factor which empirical investigations have shown to be more important for the distribution of power and goods in society than ownership itself.

The avant-garde has thus begun to challenge the basic *a priori* in Marx's thought that conflict is a *class* phenomenon—that it arises from the exploitation of labor (the proletariat) by capital which finds expression in warring classes, recurring and increasingly greater economic crises, increasing pauperization of the proletariat leading to the negation of the negation, the expropriation of the expropriators, that is, a proletarian revolution and the socialization of the means of production. Marković, for one, has questioned the Stalinist practice of inventing ever new enemies to justify the Establishment's unlimited mandate in the class struggle and the suppression of all dissent.[171] Yet, avant-garde theorists continue to subscribe to Marx's bizarre notion that the state is a *class* institution used by the ruling class in its own interests. Some among the avant-garde, like Zagorka Pešić-Golubović, voice the demand for *class* justice, understood as the right to equality and freedom, to replace the notion of lawfulness derived from law as an instrument of the state.[172] On January 28, 1975, the "Belgrade Eight," including Pešić-Golubović, were on the receiving end of *class* "justice," when they were suspended from their teaching duties at the University of Belgrade.

By insisting on the necessity of reconciling private interests with the public interest, and by focusing on the dependent role of labor in the labor-capital relationship, Yugoslav theorists advanced our knowledge of their dynamics. By broadening the categories of class conflict, exploitation, and alienation to encompass phenomena in socialist societies, the Yugoslavs scattered the impact and humanized somewhat the original Marxist *Weltanschauung* concerning the conflict between labor and capital. They also raised serious questions with regard to the viscosity of such notions as class struggle and the dictatorship of the proletariat as instruments of tyranny over the proletariat in Stalinism or statist socialism. Yet, the Yugoslavs' continuing incorporation of the "law" of class struggle and "true" dictatorship of the proletariat into the *telos* of Marxist theory, including socialist humanism, remains the single most profound source of the element of violence, terror, and unmitigated anti-humanism in Marxist thought.

4.4 The Party as the Executor of the Will of History

It is not coincidental that whenever communist regimes suppress basic rights on a large scale in campaigns featuring terror, violence, and lawlessness, they invariably try to justify this by reference to the class struggle, the dictatorship of the proletariat, and the need to defend the achievements of the socialist revolution from the machinations of foreign and domestic enemies. Yet, it is not the workers and peasants—the proletariat—but, rather, the communist party as the alleged vanguard of the proletariat which assumes everywhere the role of the executor of the will of History. What are the implications of this phenomenon for Marxist theory and socialist practice, especially in terms of liberalizing, humanizing, and democratizing the Marxist-Leninist intellectual heritage?

Avant-garde Yugoslav theorists have challenged a number of commonplace Marxist-Leninist assumptions concerning the party. They have criticized the lack of democracy and freedom of discussion within the party which relies on democratic centralism, ideological unity, and monolithism leading to a monopoly of leadership. The avant-garde concluded that if the party is really to lead socialist society toward a more democratic and humane future, then the party itself would have to become a more democratic institution. The party monopoly of thought and action would have to yield to a pluralization of decision-making and execution, both within and outside the organization.

Thus, Stojanović calls for an end to monolithic centralism and monopoly of leadership, and for a radical reform of the party. A genuine democratic reform of the party, according to Stojanović, can be achieved only by the institution of genuine public opinion within the party and, hence, of an active minority with the right to "openly advocate changes in the officially adopted party policies."[173] In Tadić's view, it is imperative that monolithism in thinking be abandoned in favor of genuine unity in action. This calls for a democratization of the communist movement, without which there can be no effective struggle against Stalinism and the cult of personality.[174] In addition, Marković stresses the fact that institutions of self-management/self-government must be independent of any political party, including the League of Communists. The continued monopoly of either economic or political power in statist socialism leads to new forms of alienation, the rule of bureaucracy, politocracies or partocracies over the proletariat. Hence, Marković concludes with a call for the withering away of the party:

> The radical supersession of bureaucratism involves, therefore, not
> only the transformation of the organs of the state into the organs
> of self-government, but also emancipation from the tutelage of the
> party. At first the party should reduce its functions to purely
> educational and theoretical ones. At a later stage it should "wither

away" completely.[175]

It is curious, however, that even those among avant-garde theorists who have been most vocal in their critique of the party, do not propose a multi-party system, but, like Stojanović and Kangrga, call on the party to become truly the initiator and carrier of the communist revolution. Even more puzzling is the fact that whenever the avant-garde criticizes the party, it criticizes the phenomenon of the *Stalinized* party in *etatist* socialism, as if the *communist* party could be anything but Stalinist and statist. The Yugoslav avant-garde has only partially begun to criticize the fundamental *Leninist* assumptions of the communist party. Somehow, the avant-garde expects the party to become a democratic institution, while remaining communist. Moreover, the avant-garde ascribes centralism, monolithism, elitism, dictatorship, and terror in the party's thought and action to Stalin rather than Lenin. And no one mentions Marx or Engels. Yet, it is Lenin's moral/ethical relativism combined with Marx's and Engels' conception of their doctrine as Science or Absolute Knowledge, and of communists as the vanguard of the proletariat, which constitutes the Stalinist seeds of totalitarianism and terror in Marxism-Leninism, as well as the party.

The new conventional wisdom in the West holds that Marx and Engels had nothing to do with the party; that the party is Lenin's brainchild. While Lenin's organizational genius in welding together an effective decision-making and executive unit of professional revolutionaries cannot be gainsaid, the inspiration for a command-type, quasi-military, quasi-religious sect was provided by Marx and Engels in their *Communist Manifesto*. In the *Manifesto*, Marx and Engels maintained that the communists were "the most advanced and resolute section of the working-class parties of every country," and that they understood *better* than the proletarian mass "the line of march, the conditions and the ultimate general results of the proletarian movement." As early as 1848, Marx and Engels claimed for the communists "scientific" knowledge of the laws of society's development. This was not some ordinary, incomplete, and fallible knowledge, but Absolute Knowledge of Plato's Philosopher-King:

> The theoretical conclusions of the communists are in no way based on the ideas or principles that have been invented, or discovered, by this or that would-be universal reformer. They merely express, in general terms, actual relations springing from an existing class struggle, from a historical movement going on under our very eyes.[176]

Not only did Marx and Engels claim, in effect, that the communists knew Rousseau's general will, but, also, that the communists had "no interests separate and apart from those of the proletariat as a whole." This notion parallels Rousseau's conception of the Legislator-Sovereign. As we recall, Rousseau's general will was indivisible and incapable of representation. Hence, the general will was indentical with the Legislator-Sovereign. And, whoever disagreed with the general will *as defined by* the Legislator-Sovereign would be "forced to be free," that is, be reeducated or, at least, dealt with administratively.

The communist party is thus bound to act in a *Stalinist* way since it is imprisoned within the dialectic which demands that it act as the executor of the will of History, leading the proletariat to the promised land. Since it is armed with the "science" of dialectical and historical materialism, it is assumed that the party cannot err. It is always individuals— including party members—who must shoulder the blame for disastrous consequences of mistaken policies whether in the political, economic, legal, spiritual, or cultural spheres. Grlić is one of the few who recognizes the element of terror deriving from the concept of the legislator or law-giver cast in "the role of the most progressive state order, higher historical justice, the carrier, guarantor, and guardian of the achievements of the revolution and historical reason."[177] Stojanović agrees that the party's socio-political monopoly derives from the party's conception of itself as the vanguard and carrier of historical progress, which has epistemological as well as axiological implications. The party's claim to an avant-garde monopoly also explains the fact, writes Stojanović, that the party is neither willing nor able to enter into coalitions with other groups or parties on an equal basis.[178] It is the conception of the party as omniscient and infallible which is at the root of Stalinist malpractice and terror.

The party's chief weapon against both friend and foe has been its ideology, particularly the dialectic and its distinction between "subjective" and "objective" reality, truth, action, and its consequences. Stojanović notes that the distinction between the "subjective" or intended and the "objective" or unintended consequences of action enables the Stalinized communist party and its leadership to incriminate the individual revolutionary for aiding the enemy whatever the nature of his action. Utilizing the dialectic, the party's policies, right or wrong, are always presented as necessitated by "objective" conditions. The party leadership can thus play upon the individual communist's loyalty to the cause, and belief in the infallibility of the party, and subject him to moral degradation and the loss of individual dignity. Stojanović concludes that in this way, "the communist fighter in fact becomes caught in the web of party subjectivism."[179]

Unlimited *partiinost* in the form of democratic centralism, monolithism, and the sacrifice of the revolutionary's dignity leads to the phenomenon of *homo duplex* in socialism. According to Stojanović, this new *homo duplex* does one thing and thinks differently and negatively about it, while to Radovanović, *homo duplex* characteristically has two or more opinions about everything, one public and the other private.[180]

Avant-garde Yugoslav theorists can thus be credited with raising a number of embarrassing questions regarding the Stalinist heritage of the communist party. They have tried to recast the institution of the party into a more democratic, liberal, and humanist mold. But, they have yet to explore fully Marx's, Engels', and Lenin's contributions to Stalinism and the Stalinized party. The avant-garde's most effective humanist challenge of the Stalinist elements in the party is their questioning of the artificial unity, monolithism, monopoly, and omniscience of the party. Communists/Marxists, East and West, have attacked the avant-garde most virulently for this sacrilege. To them, the avant-garde is denying the party's leading role in society as well as the scientific nature of Marxism-Leninism. In Hoffman's view:

> This link between science and the Party was forged explicitly by Lenin in *What is to be done?*, where he argues that socialism as a science cannot arise spontaneously from within the ranks of the workers but must be brought in from the outside. It is no wonder that his views have incurred the wrath of praxis anarchism.[181]

Communist leaderships, including Yugoslavia's, could not agree more with Hoffman. Budislav Šoškić sums up the Yugoslav leadership's view when he contends that the role of the League of Communists is irreplaceable in the "development of ideology as a synthesis of scientific-socialist thought, concrete historical interests, goals, and experiences of the working class which it gains in its self-activity through self-management practice."[182] Yet, another Western Marxist questions Hoffman's and Šoškić's thesis. It is none other than a leading French "dissident" Marxist philosopher, Roger Garaudy, who reminds us that:

> The philosophical perversions of Marxism have supported its political perversions. If there exist only one "given" reality and one exact reflection of this reality, one man or a group of men can be the depositories of this unique and absolute truth. They will have unlimited authority, since they will bring people this truth "from outside." This is the "theoretical" basis for the single Party and the despotic State.[183]

Garaudy's is an epochal judgment on the relationship between philosophical assumptions and political (mal) practices, Absolute Knowledge and totalitarianism, a monolithic party and dictatorship. The full implications of Garaudy's statement remain yet to be elaborated and understood by Marxists and non-Marxists alike, whether East or West, North or South.

4.5 Non-Eschatological Communism?

The most unusual, radical, humanist, and revolutionary reconstruction of Marx's dialectic of the formation of the classless communist society is perhaps the Yugoslav avant-garde theorists' reformulation of dialectical and historical materialism into a non-eschatological vision.

Vranicki, Djordjević, and Marković maintain that the view of communism as an eschatological (pre-determined) end is a conception completely alien to Marxism.[184] Marković contends that the laws of historical progress are not "laws" in the proper sense of the term, but only "tendencies" which require certain conditions for their actualization, conditions which, in turn, can be changed by man. In Marković's view, Marxism emerges as something distinctly novel and "un-Marxist," in the narrow sense of that term. Namely, the view of Marxism not as a set of empirically proven historical laws predicting future developments with scientific precision, not even an empirical description of reality, but "a model, the symbolic expression of an idealized structure."[185]

The view of Marxism as a *model*, and of Marx's exceptionless historical laws as *tendencies*, makes room, of course, for the quintessential Yugoslav conception of the dynamic role of man in shaping historical circumstances and his destiny—the concept of man as a being of *praxis*. Crucially, *praxis* as process is an open-ended enterprise which, according to Grlić, cannot end in some non-conflictual perfection and restfulness.[186] Instead, *praxis* implies a continuous revolutionizing and changing of individuals, society, and the world. Pejović is thus able to contrast Stalinism and its positivistic realization of philosophy as technology and total organization of all spheres of life with socialist humanism, whose goal is to revolutionize man and social relationships. This revolutionizing of man and social relationships is, in turn, possible only if Marxists revive the Promethean function of their philosophy.[187] It is thus, writes Životić, that creative Marxism can become that *tertium quid* between positivism and its demands for factual consistency, on the one hand, and existentialism and its demands for authentic being, on the other hand.[188] In the final analysis, what is needed, assert Petrović and Zdravko Kučinar, is for Marxist thought to transcend itself and the framework of bourgeois society of which it is a reflection, and thus realize itself.[189]

In the avant-garde's conception, socialism and communism become transformed from ultimate goals into transitory phases of society's development, following Marx's own cryptic non-communist dictum that:

> Communism is the necessary form and the dynamic principle of the immediate future, but communism is not itself the goal of human development—the form of human society.[190]

Marx did not specify what the form of this future human society would be in real life. But the Yugoslavs do. It would be a *human* society of humanized social relationships based on social ownership and control of the means of production, workers' self-management, and direct democracy or social self-government. The goal of this new human society would be first and foremost—man, the human individual, his all-round development, progressive de-alienation, emancipation, and liberation.

While Tito claimed that the emergence of communist society was "historically inevitable,"[191] avant-garde theorists disagree. To them, the advent of a free association of immediate producers or classless community of free men as Marx's Republic of Associated Labor is neither assured nor certain. Marković distinguishes between two stages of the communist revolution: (1) the first abolishes class society and exploitation by the bourgeoisie or the bureaucracy; and (2) the second abolishes commodity production.[192] If we accept Marković's categories, the communist revolution has not been achieved anywhere, not even in its first stage. Furthermore, even in socialism and communism there would still remain differences of opinion and presumably also conflict. Some avant-garde theorists maintain that democratization is impossible without the formation, differentiation, and articulation of various interests in society and, hence, conflict between them. While most avant-garde theorists join in Marx's utopian call for a social order without the state, parties, bureaucracies, and politics, they stop short of expecting the withering away of all difficulties and conflicts. In Djordjević's view:

> A society without politics is not a societal form without a norm, a program, or new conflicts, struggles, and difficulties.[193]

In a theoretical innovation likely to be disturbing to utopians, East and West, the avant-garde also holds out the prospect of permanent human self-alienation even in the classless society. Vojan Rus, Petrović, and Grlić contend that the very concept of *praxis* implies that man as a creative and free being can never be completed or ultimately defined. In Rus' view, the humanistic ideal of man's self-realization is, hence, bound to remain always ahead of actual practice and of man's present being and essence.[194] Hence, adds Petrović, it is impossible to abolish all forms of alienation once and for all. Self-alienation can, therefore, exist in a classless society as well.[195] *Praxis* as process, according to Grlić, does not mean a final end or result, a blessed life in this or another world, but rather a *constant change in the future*.[196]

To Marxists and utopians everywhere, this non-utopian, non-eschatological feature of avant-garde Yugoslav Marxism may equal or exceed the impact of Toffler's *Future Shock*: modern man's loss of compass and resulting fear in a world of ubiquitous and upsetting flux, change, impermanence. This phenomenon was recognized by Kierkegaard and immortalized in his *Fear and Trembling* and *The Sickness Unto Death*. Yet, others will discover that the avant-garde's step away from utopia is a step away from totalitarianism and terror. As Stephen Miller remarks:

> From time to time we are obliged to listen to sages who warn us of radical transformations. More disturbing than the threat of future shock is the persistent hope in utopian change.[197]

In the Yugoslav avant-garde's perspective, communism emerges primarily as a means for the continuing humanization of man and society rather than a predetermined and non-improvable final end. In Mihailo Djurić's concise summary:

> . . . a society governed by general agreement and harmony would no longer have a history (if we define history as social process with far-reaching, but never completely foreseeable consequences). In such a society there would be no need or opportunity to create anything new, to change established practices in an area of communal life, or to seek better, more suitable forms of social organization.[198]

Non-eschatological communism may, hence, be termed the institutional equivalent to the Yugoslavs' conception of Marxism as a humanism of *praxis*, that is, practical humanism. On the other hand, the avant-garde still suffers from a Marxist blind spot in its utopian neglect of *the institutional imperative*, calling for the abolition of power, the state, bureaucracy, law, parties, and politics, instead of their institutionalization, dispersion, and limitation.

To the extent, then, that Yugoslav Marxism-Existentialism no longer regards communism as an eschatological end, but as a process or means in whose *telos* is incorporated the focus on man and his liberation and well-being, and in its concentration on the humanity of means as inseparable from the desirability of ends, it has become *Marxist* or *socialist humanism,* partaking of the great Western humanist tradition. To the extent, however, that socialist practice lags behind Marxist theory, and to the extent that socialist/communist ideals even within a non-eschatological framework are divorced from reality and the true nature of man, non-eschatological communism remains an anti-humanist orientation.

5. Humanism and Marxism

We may conclude that Marx's humanist and anti-humanist *a priori* notions strongly color both his anthropology and epistemology. Many of these notions remain unchallenged by avant-garde Yugoslav Marxist philosophers and sociologists. Thus, one of the most notorious among Marx's *a priori* notions, taken for granted by the Yugoslavs, is his presupposition of an ubiquitous struggle between labor and capital, and the class nature and origin of conflict. On the other hand, avant-garde thinkers revolutionized and humanized Marxism-Leninism by their discovery of alienation in socialism, including conflict, and by their focus on man as a free agent, shaping historical forces in a world not completely determined by either economic or historical factors. Most distinctly, the avant-garde is guided by a vision of communism not as an end goal which justifies any and all means, but as a transition stage to the real goal, a genuinely human society.

Yugoslav Marxism-Existentialism remains hostage to Marx's *generic* paradoxes nurtured by his *a prioris* set in the framework of the eighteenth century rationalist-positivist conception of the dialectic and Science as Absolute Knowledge. The avant-garde has only recently begun to question this positivist conception of science, which is that of a Scientist-Technologist rather than a Scientist-Creator. The Yugoslavs are slowly beginning to realize that scientific knowledge itself is "something *human, imperfect* and *incomplete,*" that Marxist theory is simply a *model* rather than an empirical description of reality, and that Marx's historical laws are *tendencies* only. Novaković maintains that the distinction between the Scientist-Creator (SC) and the Scientist-Technologist (ST) implies two concepts of science and humanism:

> . . . for the SC knowledge is always *doxa;* he admits ignorance but not authority; for the ST, however, knowledge is always *episteme;* he denies ignorance, but accepts authority. So for the SC scientific knowledge is also something human, imperfect and incomplete, while for the ST it is something super-human, perfect and complete.[199]

This led Dobrica Ćosić to advocate *imaginative scepticism* as "one of the richest and most satisfactory forms of humanism today, if not the only true form of humanism."[200] The avant-garde's view of Marxist theory as a radical critique of everything existing combined with the concept of *praxis,* and of man and society as open-ended projects, constitutes a remarkable new perspective of a non-eschatological communism. Indeed, the avant-garde theorists' major humanist contribution to Marxist theory and socialist practice is their opening-up both theory and practice to the dilemmas and needs of societies and men in late twentieth century.

Petrović sums up the avant-garde's humanist inspiration in his remark that the major need today is to develop Marx's ideas further in all directions, rather than simply to conserve them. This calls for a broad and open discussion in which intelligent critics of Marx's thought may contribute more than its limited, dogmatic proponents.[201] The basic task of contemporary, anti-dogmatic, open, total, revolutionary Marxism, writes Surčulija, is a reconstruction of the unity of theory and practice, or "a living, open Marxism."[202] In the avant-garde's view, there is a need for a constant renewal of both theory and practice in search of a truly human community of liberated personalities. This is imperative, since, as Stojanović remarks:

> Marxism must relentlessly confront the reality of socialism with the ideals of humanism, unmasking newly constructed myths, fetishes, taboos, and sacred tenets in order to contribute thereby to the willingness of the people to continue their revolutionary activity. Socialist society, too, easily falls prey to ideological self-deception.[203]

And yet, avant-garde Yugoslav Marxism remains torn between *humanist* and *anti-humanist* aspects of the Marxist *Weltanschauung*. Even the Yugoslav concept of man as a being of *praxis* is contradictory, juxtaposing the imperative of *free* choice in *praxis* as process with the totalitarian demands of *positive* freedom in *praxis* as norm or end goal. This helps to explain the ease with which Marxism has been labeled respectively as a humanist and anti-humanist creed, as well as science, philosophy, religion, ethics, myth, ideology, and utopia. Our finding is that there are elements of all of these in Marxism generally and in Yugoslav Marxism particularly. It is, hence, impossible to render an unequivocal judgment on Marxism telescoped into a short sentence or summary. All we can say is that Marxism, especially Yugoslav Marxism-Existentialism, is *a humanism*, though a *partial, socialist,* one, hemmed in by its Hegelian-Rousseauan-Marxist *a priori* notions. The extreme contention by the Yugoslavs and others that Marxism is the only genuine humanism does not hold up on either count. It is not the only humanism. Nor is it a pure, unalloyed, genuine humanism, but one that fuses important elements of anti-humanism in the form of dogmatism, violence, and terror within its confines.

According to some Western observers, there is also a problem with the humanist half in Marxist humanism. And that is that the avant-garde's optimistic humanism is ultimately romantic and thus lacking a realistic basis. Guinness notes that:

> Optimistic humanism is strong in its stress on the aspirations of man but weak in its understanding of his aberrations. Accordingly, it lacks a base for the fulfillment of the former and its solutions to the latter are deficient; thus its ultimate optimism is eternally romantic.[204]

Guinness concludes that optimistic humanism is an "idealism without sufficient ideals," proposing instead the Christian view of man's sinfullness rather than smallness as the proper Archimedean point for human self-realization via salvation.[205]

But the Christian prescription for man's salvation is antithetical to the avant-garde's concept of man as a rebel or revolutionary, called to remake both himself and the world. Caponigri and De George note that Marxist humanism shares with the new humanism an orientation toward wholeness as well as the myth of man's auto- or self-creation.[206] The avant-garde's optimistic humanism is undergirded by scientific atheism. Yet, Blakeley considers Marxist-Leninist scientific atheism a basically pessimistic orientation regarding the soundness of the human character and man's capacity to adapt to and control his environment.[207]

On the practical side, as Bertram D. Wolfe and Karl R. Popper have pointed out, Marxism fails to deal with the most profound problem of social life—the problem of *power*—while concentrating almost exclusively on the question of private property.[208] While the avant-garde retraced Marx's steps to the concept of alienated labor, it continues Marx's utopian quest for the abolition of power rather than its institutionalization and limitation. Yet, even the "new philosophers" in France like Bernard-Henri Lévy have come to recognize that power is a necessary precondition and essential ingredient in any organized society, rather than "the result of class societies and their perverse machinations."[209] And Hayek wonders about the fateful inversion between Engels' notion of the administration of things and unlimited power over men:

> It is one of the ironies of history that socialism, which gained
> influence by promising the substitution of the administration of
> things for the power over men, inevitably leads to an unbounded
> increase of the power exercised by men over other men.[210]

Thus, the avant-garde remains in the grip of Marx's ideology, reinforced by the
Hegelian dialectic, Rousseau's general will, Plato's Philosopher-King, Absolute
Knowledge, and the Enlightenment conception of science as Absolute Truth. All
this contributes undoubtedly to a sense of fanaticism shared by the avant-garde and
the party. As Lewis S. Feuer argues:

> Ideology exacerbates political fanaticism; for the ideologist pre-
> sumes that he has the warrant of a world-destiny; the ideological
> myth has exalted him as a hero, and an alleged science provided
> the credentials.[211]

On the theoretical side, as legions of analysts from Tucker to Leff, John A.
Hutchison, Wolfe, and Popper have shown convincingly, Marxism tapers off into
religion, myth, and *utopia.*[212] This aspect of Marxism would not, in itself, be
objectionable, but for the fact that its religion, myth, and utopia are not
recognized as such by its practitioners. On the contrary, these aspects are
canonized into "objective" truths based on allegedly rigorous empirical analyses of
facts or—Science. It is when utopia becomes a substitute for reality or a pretext
for its unconditional transformation—and when in the name of its lofty, yet
unattainable, ideals living human beings are sacrificed—that utopia turns into its
opposite and becomes the road to hell on earth, though paved with good intentions.
David Levy concludes that " . . . the worm of totalitarianism . . . lurks in the bud of
every utopia."[213]

Hutchison thus sees the real danger of communism not in its atheism, but in its
idolatry or "passionate attachment to a false god."[214] Ludwig von Mises called
socialism a religion of self-deification in which the inflated Ego glorifies itself as
"infinitely good, omnipotent, omnipresent, omniscient, eternal."[215] Avant-garde
theorists are not completely unaware of the human propensity toward idolatry, of
installing man as a prosthetic god on the vacated throne of the Almighty. Thus,
Mirić reminisces:

> Having lost God as meaning, he [man] attempted feverishly to
> replace Him with his own self, attempting to enthrone on the
> vacant place the human individuum who would be capable of
> traversing loneliness in a self-actualizing effort, filling *Nothing-*
> *ness* with himself, that is, with his meaning realized in the process
> of self-actualization.[216]

Yet, idolatry is an unhappy solution to the dilemma of man's estrangement and
unhappiness, and his quest for meaning and faith. This is so since idolatry is
equivalent to the Hegelian notion of a "false infinity," an endless repetition of the
same contradiction.

Axelos, among others, has noted Marx's penchant for nothingness, reflected in
his ubiquitous concepts to abolish, annihilate, and transcend. Indeed, Axelos terms
the Marxist vision an advanced form of magnificent, *planetary nihilism* which relies
on total technique to transform the world.[217] Yet, the avant-garde's Marxist
conception of the world suffers not so much from nihilism as from *oversimplifi-*
cation. Leff, for one, charges Marxism not with determinism, but *reductionism,*
the tendency of Marxist thought to reduce and simplify reality progressively to an
idealistic, yet simplistic, skeleton which no longer resembles real life.[218]

In brief, avant-garde Yugoslav Marxism remains heir to Marx's *generic*
paradoxes which cloth it with an anti-humanist, dogmatic, and totalitarian garb.
At the same time, Yugoslav Marxism-Existentialism has begun to question many of
these Marxist *a prioris,* explicitly or implicitly. Hence, its *humanist* orientation

cannot be dismissed as simply another "tactic" in the ideological struggle between the two worlds. The Yugoslavs have already succeeded in humanizing Marxism to a considerable extent. The question of whether they can transform the Marxist *Weltanschauung* into a genuine humanism, or humanism in all its aspects, can properly be addressed only to avant-garde Yugoslav Marxist philosophers and sociologists themselves. But, there can no longer be any doubt that the contemporary renaissance of humanism has found among the Yugoslav avant-garde able and devoted disciples and practitioners. Levi concludes that:

> With the writings of the youthful Marx, Marxism asserts a valid claim to membership in the great humanist tradition of Western culture. With the best of Lukacs' efforts this claim is deepened and enlarged. And with the spirit of the philosophy and sociology of contemporary Yugoslavia, it has reached a point where it offers valid hope for the slow humanist transformation of the entire Marxist world.[219]

Yet, there still remain important doubts regarding Yugoslav Marxist humanism. These concern not only the viability or theoretical sophistication of Marxist humanist thought, but also the chances for its survival in a social system which once more insists on the "scientific" correctness and ideological purity even of academic discourse. As Pavel Kovaly reminds us, past attempts to humanize Marxism were crushed both in philosophy and politics.[220] In the East, the communist party has thrown the book at some of its most prestigious Marxist humanist intellectuals. This leads De George to point out that " . . . their freedom and their creativity may be short lived . . . ."[221] Or, as we observed in the opening chapter, the avant-garde's only future may, ironically, be their past.

Even more disturbing than party censure is Western ignorance of this unique school of thought, whose major promise to liberalize, humanize, and democratize an entire civilization and culture may be stillborn. Paradigmatic of this colossal ignorance, envy and/or opposition among Western intellectuals to the *Praxis* school of thought is Hoffman's summary misjudgment that:

> For all its leftist phraseology, the theory of praxis is surprisingly uncritical. Its philosophy is positivist, its politics are anarchist, and its economics . . . are characteristically naive and superficial in their relation to the capitalist system.[222]

On the other hand, some Western observers tend to err in the opposite direction of considering Marxist humanism as a panacea or cure-all. Thus, Wolfgang Leonhard maintains that "Marxist theory today is most effectively represented by the humanist Marxists—branded by the Soviet leadership as 'deviationists' and 'renegades'."[223] So far, so good. But, Leonhard's overly optimistic view of Marxist humanism leads him to conclude that:

> The humanist Marxists see socialism as a living, free, pluralistic society, based economically on the self-management of producers (including workers' councils in the factories) and characterized politically by legally insured democratic freedoms for its citizens, and by free discussion between various groups.[224]

This assessment of Marxist humanism, while informed and well-intentioned, ignores completely the anti-humanist, dogmatic, and totalitarian elements which constitute an integral part of Marxist humanist thought.

Finally, there is a third group of Western scholars, including Kovaly, Kline, and Antón Donoso, who believe that Marxism may have to transcend itself in order to become humanistic. To Donoso, socialism with a human face may well have to be "non-Marxian."[225] To Kovaly, the way to transcend dogmatic Marxism is by concentrating on ethical problems and, in general, problems of man. Marxists, East and West, thus face the quintessential question formulated by Kovaly as follows:

> Where are the guarantees against the worst excesses of Stalinist theory and practice? So far, Marxist philosophy has not provided a solution to this problem and it is doubtful whether it can ever do so, unless it transcends its own boundaries. The lack of a theoretical formulation of the problem and its application to political theory and practice points to the fact that Marxist philosophy as a whole cannot transcend itself toward its own humanization, unless it changes its own fundamental presuppositions and thus stops being Marxist.[226]

Crucial to a humanization of Marxist theory and socialist practice would be the recognition of Kant's categorical imperative, that is, the need to develop a genuine ethics. On this epochal issue, the Yugoslav avant-garde is split, although most theorists recognize the intimate bond between means and ends which calls for a present-oriented ethical humanism. And, in Kline's view, only such a humanism of principles or ethical humanism can stand as a bulwark against Stalinism.[227] Avant-garde Yugoslav Marxism thus confronts a crucial watershed: either it will transcend itself and thus cease being Marxist or it will remain imprisoned within the enchanted universe delimited by Marx's dogmatic *a priori* notions. The epochal choice in the late twentieth century is: humanism *or* Marxism.

Chapter IX · Toward a New Humanism

> Science has changed man's standpoint and relationship to his native planet and the cosmos, the limits of the universe have been extended, but man's nature, his basic human questions and needs have remained unchanged in the givenness of the human organism: walking, health, hunger, and thirst, cold, loneliness, joy, grief, toothache, passions, madness, and death.
>
> Jure Kaštelan, *"Pjesnik i svijet stroja"* (1963)

1. Praxis and Alienation

Robert C. Tucker has written about the phenomenon of the deradicalization of Marxist movements in the contemporary era.[1] One could assert that in the case of Yugoslavia we have witnessed, especially during the 1960s, just the opposite trend: a radicalization of Marxist theory and socialist practice and, hence, of the Marxist movement in Yugoslavia. According to Lewis S. Feuer, Western Marxism has undergone a "bifurcation into two ideologies—managerial middle-age and alienationist youth."[2] Yugoslav Marxism-Existentialism, especially in its avant-garde formulation, would appear within the context of both Western and non-Western Marxism as without doubt a Marxism of "alienationist youth."

Marxism of "alienationist youth" rebels against dogmatism, bureaucracy, and a deterministic conception of history, and stresses ethical consciousness, voluntarism of action, and the metaphysic of revolution, relates Feuer. Feuer's description of Western Alienationist Marxism fits like a glove Yugoslav Marxism-Existentialism, with its emphasis on creativity, humanism, self-management, *praxis*, revolution, de-alienation, and liberation. As a Marxism of "alienationist youth," Yugoslav Marxism-Existentialism has thus become eminently relevant not only to its own and other communist societies, but also to the alienated youth, intellectuals, and student movements, East and West. Thus, a pamphlet of the radical student movement in France expressing the malaise, alienation, and revolutionary ethos of alienated Western youth which stated that:

> We have been led to question all exploitative societies, all organizations, and tackle such general problems as state capitalism, bureaucratic management, the abolition of the state and of wage-slavery, war, racism, "Socialism," etc.[3]

could have been written by avant-garde Yugoslav Marxist humanists.

The questions raised by avant-garde Yugoslav Marxist philosophers and sociologists, those of the roles of the individual and society, party and the state, self-managing organs such as workers' councils and communes, as well as their acute awareness of the conflict between economic rationality and socialist humanism are the burning questions of the contemporary era both East and West. Curiously, an element of utopianism regarding the institutional imperative is also gaining ground, East and West, reflected in the demand for the abolition of the state, hierarchies, bureaucracies, parties, and politics.

The significance of Yugoslav social practice and its avant-garde Marxist theory lies, then, precisely in raising these crucial questions and delving into dilemmas of modern alienated man. On the one hand, Yugoslav Marxism is significant because it tries to combine socialism/communism with democracy, and thus reestablish the unity between theory and practice, means and ends, is and ought, which has consistently eluded Marx and his followers. It is in this area that Yugoslav Marxist theory, with its model of totalitarian democracy, has shown considerable sophistication, perhaps more so than its East European or even Western Marxist counterparts and student manifestoes. It is true that Yugoslav Marxism remains heir to many of Marx's generic paradoxes deriving from his *a priori* notions, especially those of class struggle and the class nature and origin of conflict. At the same time, the reality of everyday socialist practice provides Yugoslav Marxists, in and out of power, with sobering experience, although it does not necessarily dampen their revolutionary rhetoric.

There seems to remain a radical disjunction between Yugoslav Marxist theory and socialist practice. In this sense, Tucker is correct in characterizing contemporary Marxist movements as being in a stage of deradicalization. In spite of its *revolutionary rhetoric*, much of everyday Yugoslav *practice* has actually been *evolutionary.* The revolutionary concepts of Yugoslav Alienationist Marxism such as de-alienation, liberation, self-management, direct democracy, socialism, communism, and humanism have turned out to be piecemeal and at times not too successful *reforms* of an increasingly democratic and basically evolutionary nature.

It is this aspect of *reformism*—widespread in all of Eastern Europe, although not as intense as in Yugoslavia—which led observers like Karl Reyman, Herman Singer, and William E. Griffith to conclude that East European revisionists have "introduced the corrosive element of democratic socialism into the heart of communism."[4] Alas, what Charles Gati calls the "golden age" of experimentation in Eastern Europe during the 1960s, particularly from 1964 to 1968,[5] yielded to normalization and retrenchment under Soviet hegemony and the Brezhnev doctrine of limited sovereignty within the socialist commonwealth.

The element of reformism in contemporary Yugoslav communism is rather strong. In essence, it is, indeed, democratic socialism with emphasis on democracy as *process, means, praxis, self-management.* This trend was especially strong during the 1960s, culminating in the resolutions adopted at the Ninth Party Congress in 1969 and the 1971 Constitutional Amendments. To most outside observers, Yugoslavia appeared on the threshold of genuine democratic socialism. Mihajlo Mihajlov could thus observe that Yugoslavia was the first nation to reach a historic crossroads where it could choose either democratic, multi-party socialism, or revert to Stalinism.[6]

But the Yugoslavs chose a third option: combining elements of democracy and totalitarianism, institutional pluralization and ideological re-Stalinization. Yugoslavia's *socialist* democracy thus remains distinct from Western *democratic* socialism—as practiced in Great Britain and the Scandinavian countries, and elements of which are increasingly evident elsewhere, including Western Europe and the United States. As delineated in Chapter VII, the League of Communists' continuing ideological-political monopoly and supervision of self-management institutions and practices at all levels from the BOALs to the federation remains the monkey wrench in Yugoslavia's socialist democracy. This has prompted a reassessment among some Western observers who, along with Marius Broekmeyer, now admit that economic democracy of self-management—such as it is—does not necessarily lead to political democracy.[7] Avant-garde theorists have reached similar conclusions. In Svetozar Stojanović's summary:

> To get to the roots of the situation in Yugoslavia one must deal with the ruling communist organization. The Yugoslav society today remains a political society *par excellence.* The Party is the fundamental factor of power, legitimacy, continuity and change. In a situation of this kind, there is no possibility for a genuine

democracy within the society as long as democracy is in its infancy within the ruling party.[8]

On the other hand, the party is undergoing a continuous self-searching concerning its future role in society's development, attempting to democratize itself. During the 1960s, the party even attempted to divorce itself from the machinery of government. This led Western observers like Denitch, Zaninovich, Rusinow, and Walkin to conclude that Yugoslavia can no longer be classified as totalitarian or even as a party autocracy.[9] Duncan Wilson goes furthest in his unlikely claim that Yugoslavia may be considered as an open, pluralistic society.[10] Yet, Fred Singleton and Paul Lendvai note the contradiction between industrial democracy and a single totalitarian party, and Lenard J. Cohen refers to the leadership's abandonment of the experiment with political competition in direct popular elections for regional and federal legislative assemblies first tried in 1967.[11]

With Tito's Letter to the party of September 1972, the 1974 Constitution, and the Tenth and Eleventh Party Congresses, the party resumed its uncompromising revolutionary rhetoric which hardly contributes to a real diminution of its all-powerful role in Yugoslav society. Yet after so many reforms and course changes over the past generation, it is not surprising that the party rank and file, as well as the masses, are bewildered. Kardelj himself admitted that even the party "sometimes shows signs of hesitation as to how much of social responsibility it should assume."[12] In view of the dialectic's flexible logic, can the ordinary party *apparatchik* be blamed for not rushing headlong into unexplored territory, whether in theory or in practice? Would it not be more realistic to assume that even party members have come to have second thoughts concerning revolutionary rhetoric? Especially in view of the fact, pointed out by Veljko Rus, that revolutionary rhetoric can be more misleading than enlightening, concentrating as it does on the shortcomings of socialist practice instead of questioning the basic revolutionary ideals.[13]

One of the most important questions today is whether Yugoslav communism may be undergoing a process similar to the experience of West European social democratic movements at the turn of the century at the time when their revolutionary socialist rhetoric seemed to increase in proportion to the successes (and failures) of their evolutionary and democratic practices.[14] This prompted Bernstein, the founder of Western democratic socialism, to observe that social democrats would make much more rapid and palpable progress in attaining their socialist objectives if they concentrated more on democratic practice and less on revolutionary rhetoric, and if:

> . . . social democracy could find the courage to emancipate itself from a phraseology which is actually outworn and if it would make up its mind to appear what it is in reality today: a democratic, socialistic party of reform.[15]

Yet, in spite of the breathtaking institutional pluralization of self-management/self-government, the League of Communists of Yugoslavia is not a "democratic, socialistic party of reform." It remains a communist—that is, Marxist-Leninist—party based on democratic centralism, which excludes intra-party democracy, and the conception of vanguard of the proletariat and the sole representative of society's true interests (Rousseau's general will), which excludes genuine pluralism of thinking and action or democracy outside the party—indeed, excludes all other parties, whether socialist or not. To sympathetic observers of the Yugoslav socio-political and economic scene, Kardelj's last call for enacting the new socio-political principles of the system of delegates and a "pluralism of self-management interests" might appear as another solid indication of Yugoslavia's evolution toward *democratic* socialism. Yet, Tito himself repeatedly warned the Western world ever since the 1948 Soviet-Yugoslav split not to make out of Yugoslavs what they are not. They are communists. Tito and Kardelj lost no opportunity to remind both East and West of the *class* nature of Yugoslav democracy and the imperative for continuing ideological and class struggle.[16]

Vladimir Kusin writes in his assessment of East European reformism that "the essential contention is between communism and democratic socialism of the reformist variety."[17] Western analysts have difficulty judging both the Yugoslav and West European varieties of communism. Jean-François Revel is one of the few who realize that in regard to the increased autonomy of West European communist parties from the Soviet Union, we have mistaken de-Russification for democratization, whereas in reality those parties remain Marxist-Leninist and, hence, Stalinist.[18] The same is true of the Yugoslav League of Communists. Unlike the Yugoslavs, some Eurocommunists, notably the Italians, are even willing to renounce the notion of the dictatorship of the proletariat and other cherished tenets of the Marxist-Leninist faith. Yet, Revel is sceptical whether these verbal manifestoes mean anything unless they lead to "an open and avowed transition from a Marxist-Leninist character to a reformist and social democratic character."[19] On the other hand, Peter C. Ludz writes that the Soviet leaders consider democratic pluralism, combined with anti-Stalinism, as the major challenge of Eurocommunism. Ludz concluded that Eurocommunism, which draws heavily on Yugoslav theory and practice, sharpened the crisis of legitimacy throughout Eastern Europe and the Soviet Union.[20]

Avant-garde Yugoslav theorists and the party take quite different approaches to the phenomenon of Eurocommunism. Stojanović hails Eurocommunism as the genesis of a truly "democratic" socialism/communism, distinct from the reform-oriented, liberal, democratic socialism as well as from authoritarian, statist communism. But he cautions that for such a democratic communism, which emphasizes democratic means, to be credible, it would have to abjure violent revolution and the "dictatorship of the proletariat."[21] In contrast, party theorists like Kardelj have a less romantic notion of Eurocommunism. Kardelj regarded Eurocommunism as simply a specific form, way or method of advancing the socialist (communist) cause in the specific conditions prevailing in Western Europe at present. And he laughed out of court those social democratic leaders who equate Eurocommunism with a victory of the social democratic, reformist wing of the workers' movement over the revolutionary, communist wing.[22]

In the case of Yugoslavia, both the party and the institutional framework seem to be undergoing continuous change, reorganization, and reform, yet the underlying essence—the party's veto on all societal decision-making—remains the same in theory, even if sometimes it is breached in actual practice. The League of Communists itself balks, of course, at any intimation that it may in fact become a party of reform, since this would amount to the greatest sin among true believers in the "science" of Marxism-Leninism, namely that of *revisionism*.

2. Beyond Capitalism and Socialism?

Leszek Kolakowski calls Yugoslavia the first revisionist state with the first revisionist communist party.[23] Yet, it is difficult to designate Yugoslav Marxism, or any other Marxism for that matter, unequivocally as revisionism, because the Marxist-Leninist intellectual heritage is so rich in contradictions and because its very methodology, the dialectic—a quasi-scientific, but essentially philosophical tool—allows phenomenal flexibility and extrapolations of past doctrines. The very term "revisionism," like those of "capitalism" and "communism," has been used not only to designate deviation from the true, normal, and desirable; it has also served as a vehicle employed with great gusto and, alas, resulting in human tragedy, of calling one's opponents dirty names and rationalizing one's own narrowmindedness, self-righteousness, and ignorance, leading with an iron logic to a demand for the elimination of "evil" forces impeding progress.

The Yugoslavs not only deny that they are revisionists, but claim that the Soviet Union and especially Red China are the arch-revisionists while they, the Yugoslavs, are the exponents of genuine Marxism and authentic socialism. The

Yugoslavs see in the USSR what they call state capitalism or etatistic, bureaucratic socialism, and, until recently, scorned the absurd cult of the individual in Mao's China. In contradistinction, the Yugoslavs assert that it is the self-managing and democratic aspect of their socialism based on socialized property and popular participation in decision-making which alone can lead to a true socialist community of free men in the classless communist future.

Malcolm Macdonald has pointed out that revisionism may actually claim *orthodoxy*, since it attempts to unite theory and practice and thus remain in agreement with "the spirit and intent of Marx."[24] It is precisely this standpoint which avant-garde Yugoslav Marxists claim as their own, namely, the necessity to reinterpret Marxist dogma in light of the humanistic writings of the early Marx and to develop Marx's thought further in a humanist direction as a guide to socialist practice. The Yugoslavs are frank in admitting that their practice (not to mention that of other socialist states) has lagged behind theory. Mihailo Marković sums up the Yugoslav experience as follows:

> Only in the light of Marx's humanism one can have an overall critical view of the whole, half a century long history of socialist society, and only comparing the present-day reality with Marx's humanist project one can fully grasp how much the former is still far from the latter and how little resemblance there is between present-day bureaucratism and Marx's free associations of producers who themselves regulate production and all social life.[25]

The by now almost proverbial Yugoslav pragmatism and frankness in assessing their strengths and weaknesses has led some observers to consider the writings and debates of avant-garde Yugoslav Marxist philosophers as expressions of a unique, new "candid Marxism."[26] Indeed, while the term "revisionist" may be misleading, the uniqueness of Yugoslav Marxism, especially in its avant-garde formulation, presses on us the question not only of labelling, which is relatively easy, but also of understanding this novel variant of Marxism.

The major significance of Yugoslav Marxism-Existentialism lies undoubtedly in its humanist aspects, its preoccupation with the human individual and the existentialist dilemma of reconciling private with the public interest and means with ends. Avant-garde Yugoslav Marxism thus seems to be modeling itself more in the image of the great social democrat and humanist, Bernstein, than in that of the ruthless organizer and revolutionary, Lenin. The whole emphasis in contemporary Yugoslavia on self-management, democratization, liberalization, direct democracy, constitutionalism, socialist legality, and the concern with means mirrors Bernstein's truly revolutionary thesis that:

> To me that which is generally called the ultimate aim of socialism is nothing, but the movement is everything.[27]

Yet, both the avant-garde and the party have difficulty in admitting the Bernsteinian element in their concern with the priority of means, movement, *praxis.* Both the party and the avant-garde consider Bernstein's preference for the movement over socialism's ultimate goals to be counter-revolutionary. According to Rudi Supek, Bernstein's motto is characteristic of pseudo-revolutionary movements[28] such as Western social democracy. In Stojanović's view, Western social democracy with its conception of the welfare state degenerates to the point where it becomes largely incorporated into the capitalist system, whereas the workers' movement is reduced to "the struggle for a high standard of living, access to the educational institutions and use of the exclusively bourgeois arsenal."[29]

It is, therefore, surprising to find some avant-garde theorists who disagree even in part with this conventional Marxist wisdom concerning Bernstein. Thus, Marković holds that Bernstein's reformist thesis does contain a revolutionary element since:

> ...if a movement is socialist at all, it must by itself possess a revolutionary character and not only *prepare* for a future event which alone will be regarded as revolution.[30]

Marković seems to be on firm theoretical ground since Marx himself underlined the importance of practical action as opposed to merely theoretical programs. In his letter of May 5, 1875, to Bracke, Marx wrote that: "Every step of real movement is more important than a dozen programmes."[31]

On the other hand, Marx as well as Lenin opposed economism and reformism, or the general subordination of the goals of the proletarian revolution to social democratic tinkering with the existing system. Both Marx and Lenin insisted that without the communists as their vanguard, the working class could only develop "trade-union consciousness" rather than revolutionary socialist consciousness. True to the classics, Kardelj also maintains that the workers cannot be left to their own devices in self-managing institutions to decide spontaneously on various issues. What they need is the League of Communists to steer them in the proper direction.[32] Only it is difficult to see how this tutelary role of the party can possibly be reconciled with Marx's own dictum that: "The emancipation of the working class must be the work of the working class itself."[33] A point which avant-garde theorists have raised repeatedly with somber personal consequences.

Nevertheless, Yugoslav Marxism-Existentialism has developed great concern for the means as well as the ends of the socialist movement. The Yugoslavs discovered that "Unanimity Does Not Always Signify Equality," that "The Existing Legal and Political System Limits Society's Development," and that socialist development via institutions of self-management/self-government must proceed within a framework of democratization and constitutionalism.[34] Nation-wide discussions in Yugoslavia on the 1971 Constitutional Amendments, the 1974 Constitution, and the 1976 Law on Associated Labor indicate that the emphasis is increasingly on the reality and substance of self-managing institutions and practices, rather than merely on their proper outward form.[35]

The avant-garde's revolutionary reconstruction of the end goal of Marxism-Leninism raises a whole new series of questions with respect to both major contemporary social formations—"capitalism" and "socialism." It appears immediately that both "capitalism" and "socialism," in practice though not in theory, contain more "socialistic" and "capitalistic" features than their exponents are willing to admit. To begin with, as Ralph K. White notes, there is an international misunderstanding regarding the very terms "socialism" and "capitalism." "Socialism" has been largely misinterpreted by equating it with government ownership of the means of production, rather than with government regulation of industry and business in general and concern for social welfare. Hence, White relates, visitors to the United States, especially those from the developing nations, are surprised at the extent of socialism in America.[36] Furthermore, even such staunch advocates of free enterprise as Milton Friedman and Friedrich A. Hayek balance their call for competition with the concept of a guaranteed floor or minimum income (negative income tax).[37] By the same token, visitors to socialist Yugoslavia are surprised at the extent of its capitalism reflected in a decentralized economy with emphasis on sales and profit, unemployment, lack of and misuse of public funds for the development of poorer regions, inflation, rising cost of living (pauperization of the proletariat?), lack of adequate housing, recreational facilities, education, and medical care.[38] It would appear that "capitalism" and "socialism" are in important respects not that far apart after all.

Indeed, exponents of convergence theories who claim that both East and West are confronted increasingly with basically the same dilemmas, not those of "capitalism" or "socialism," but those of *advanced industrial societies,* can find ample justification for their theories in the development of Yugoslav institutions and practices. The oversimplified conception of convergence between the two systems of capitalism and socialism which tends to reduce this phenomenon to a fifty-fifty proposition is, of course, the easiest to state, but the most difficult to substantiate. Like so much else in the real world, the theory (or theories) of convergence, whose value is chiefly heuristic, reflect(s) a complex living mosaic in which the colors, shapes, and even the overall framework itself remain unfinished.

Among Western theorists, Daniel Bell and John Kenneth Galbraith have propounded most consistently the theory of the rise of post-industrial society, the planning and organizational imperatives, and East-West convergence. In Bell's view, a complex society inevitably becomes "a planning society." Why the need for planning in an affluent, technically-advanced society? Because, even the affluent post-industrial society cannot escape new scarcities of information, coordination, and time.[39] According to Galbraith, Western economies already contain elements of planning by technostructures of the dominant corporate sector in a new industrial state.[40] The problem is that planning by the corporate, union, and governmental sectors is partial, haphazard, and uncoordinated. What is lacking is over-all planning which would reflect the public purpose and the common good. Hence, Galbraith calls for the establishment of a "public planning authority" and the replacement of the market by comprehensive planning.[41]

Exponents of the virtues of the market mechanism and free enterprise as the best means for both economic well-being and personal freedom, like Friedman, are forced to concede that the idea of government intervention has become fashionable even among Western businessmen and intellectuals. In fact, Friedman argues that:

> . . . the two groups that threaten the free market most are businessmen and intellectuals, but for opposite reasons. The businessman is in favor of free enterprise for everyone else but not for himself . . . . The intellectual is just the other way. He is strongly in favor of free enterprise for himself but not for anyone else.[42]

Bell notes that the socialist ethic of "equality of result" is superseding the liberal ethic of "equality of opportunity," with a resulting communal ethos, politicization of decision-making, and a populist demand for complete levelling.[43] Could the future post-industrial society based on applied science, advanced technology, superorganization, and bureaucracy, and bent on universal egalitarianism or *uravnilovka*, endanger both individual liberty and privacy?

Alexis de Tocqueville remarked that the demand for equality would result in a concentration of power and that private rights of individuals would be endangered by the designs of an all-powerful government.[44] How uncanny that more than a century since Tocqueville spoke about the dangers of the popular quest for egalitarianism in America, in another part of the world—of all places in communist Yugoslavia—an industrial sociologist would echo Tocqueville by holding that egalitarianism in the economic sphere leads necessarily to authoritarianism in the political sphere. And that a lack of understanding of this dynamic constitutes a major source of continuing tension and conflicting demands made on the body politic.[45]

Avant-garde Yugoslav thinkers approach theories of post-industrial society and East-West convergence with great caution. On the one hand, the avant-garde welcomes the scientific-technological revolution as the necessary material basis for self-management and the liberation of man from toil. Miroslav Pečujlić thus sees automation, cybernetics, and the scientific-technological revolution as a corollary to the new socio-political system of self-management and workers' control over production and, indeed, as its scientific and technical, rather than purely moral, vindication.[46] In Pečujlić's vision, self-management is made mandatory by the new relations of production, which create the phenomenon of the "collective worker" due to increasing emphasis on science and technological know-how rather than simply on individual labor. The avant-garde thus looks to science and technology as that long-sought-after means to liberate man from the drudgery of unpleasant, exploitative, and alienating work. In this, the avant-garde harkens back to Marx, who maintained that:

> . . . to the degree that large industry develops, the creation of real wealth comes to depend less on labour time and on the amount of

labour employed than on the power of the agencies set in motion during labour time, whose "powerful effectiveness" is itself in turn out of all proportion to the direct labour time spent on their production, but depends rather on the general state of science and on the progress of technology, or the application of this science to production.[47]

This, of course, is the prerequisite for the material basis of abundance in the future communist society, in which necessary labor time would be reduced to a minimum, thus opening up vistas for man's enjoyment of free-flowing, creative, and self-creative activity—*praxis*—in his free time. In Supek's view, the future technologically-advanced society would be not only polycentric, but "polymorphic" as well, that is, it would combine both planning and market elements.[48] And Marković foresees that man would finally be able to relax about efficiency by mastering it and relegating it to machines.[49]

But this idyllic picture of a technically-advanced civilization is counterbalanced in the avant-garde's view by the costs of science, technology, and industrial development. And these costs are enormous. While the scientific-technological revolution seems to be a prerequisite for a classless communist society, it represents at the same time its greatest potential enemy. For one thing, the avant-garde points out that technology, bureaucracy, organization, and economic development become ends in themselves, endangering the socialist ideal of a new human society of humanized social relationships. According to Marković, one of the principal dangers of the East-West technological race is that socialist societies might lose their socialist consciousness and become simple consumer civilizations like the capitalist West.[50] Danilo Pejović sees the coexistence of capitalism and socialism based on the same alienating, positivistic machine technology, resulting in the caricature of socialistic capitalism and capitalistic socialism.[51] And Supek writes that one of the central tasks in both capitalist and socialist societies is the struggle against bureaucracy, which allies itself with technology.[52]

In terms of economics and ecology, the avant-garde proposes an end to the limitless exploitation of man and nature, to be replaced by a more careful husbanding of both human and natural resources. Thus, Supek prefers a "stable society"—one which has established a harmonious equilibrium with nature and its own development potential—to a rapacious "consumer society," bent on unlimited production and accumulation of material goods.[53] Yugoslav theorists thus share Rudolf Bahro's assumption that the economic principle of profit maximization in existing socialism represents "an essentially quantitative progress leading into a bad infinity."[54] They would also subscribe to his thesis of the need for a reconciliation between culture and nature, as well as general human emancipation via a cultural revolution.

Yugoslav theorists speak in an even more critical vein of possible East-West convergence. Ivan Kuvačić considers the theory of convergence itself as more of an ideological manipulation than a scientific theory.[55] Nenad Kecmanović maintains that over the long run self-managing socialism is the final goal of genuine convergence, since it transcends the alienated framework of both state capitalism in the West and etatist socialism in the East.[56] The avant-garde's conclusion is, hence, that not only capitalism or socialism, but an entire civilization based on the exploitation of man and nature, subordination of man to production for production's sake, domination, and social Darwinism, is in crisis, endangering the very survival of the human species.[57] The solution to this universal alienation is to be found in the return of man as a being of *praxis* to a de-alienated community of immediate producers—a *Gemeinschaft* which has transcended economic rationality and attained to socialist humanism.

Paradoxically, the avant-garde's revolutionary theory is constantly undermined, and at times defeated, by the complexities of everyday life. Marxist theory and socialist practice seem destined, as it were, to dwell in two distinct worlds, that of the ideal, of "ought," and that of the real, of "is." Its high ideals of humanism, socialism, communism, self-management, direct democracy, de-alienation and liberation, advanced by the avant-garde and the party, still seem far from their realization, if indeed they are realizable at all. A perceptive Yugoslav expressed the paradoxical relationship between ideals and practice through a folk tale in which:

> An angel once said to the devil, "I will defeat you by endowing every individual with high ideals," to which the devil replied, "I will win in the end, for I will institutionalize the ideals."[58]

It is, indeed, the institutionalization of Yugoslav Marxism's revolutionary ideals which seems to weaken and, at times, to defeat them. Milentije Popović, the late President of the Constitutional Commission in Charge of Drafting the Amendments, admitted that the workers' councils, in spite of their self-managing outward form, remained in essence administrative-bureaucratic in nature, preventing the workers from exercising their constitutional right of deciding on the distribution of surplus value. Popović argued that the chief goal of the new Constitutional Amendments would be to eliminate this conflict between etatism and self-management on all levels, be they workers' councils, communes, republics, or the federation.[59] But as the Tenth and Eleventh Party Congresses have shown, there is no final reconciliation in sight between "is" and "ought." And how, indeed, can self-management be reconciled with party monopoly, democracy with totalitarianism, individual responsibility with social ownership, reality with utopia?

3. Significance of the Yugoslav Experiment

The disjunction between ideals and practice in Yugoslav reality does not invalidate the fact that Yugoslav Marxist theory and socialist practice remain, nevertheless, the most radical, liberalized, and humanized among communist party states. Yugoslav theory and practice—with their emphasis on liberalization, democratization, decentralization, socialist legality and Marxist humanism, their critique of Stalinism and insistence on independent roads to socialism, equality and non-interference in the internal affairs of other countries, and active peaceful coexistence between different socio-economic systems—have had a far-ranging impact on other East European communist party states, the USSR, China, as well as on the newly independent and developing nations of the Third World, and the increasingly autonomous West European communist parties.

Many of Yugoslavia's reformist measures, chiefly in the field of economic decentralization, emphasis on profitability, economic rationale, quality of products, and the demand for more consumer goods, have been adopted in practice, though not always admitted in theory, by both East European communist party states and the Soviet Union. Poland, Hungary, and Czechoslovakia seem to have advanced furthest in the field of economic reforms à la Yugoslavia. Thus, Hungary adopted a New Economic Mechanism (NEM), and by 1979 expanded its economic decentralization program based on profit maximization as the "principal criterion for success in any individual factory," with each enterprise accountable to its own workers for production.[60] During the revolution in Hungary and the near-revolution in Poland in 1956 as well as in Czechoslovakia in 1968, workers' councils on the Yugoslav model were among the first institutions to be established. When the Hungarian, Polish, and Czechoslovak attempts to liberalize and humanize communism were crushed, it was again the workers' councils which the respective party leaderships, under Soviet tutelage, were most adamant in abolishing or emasculating. These facts testify to the revolutionary nature and wide popularity of workers' councils in Eastern Europe as genuine instruments of worker participation in decision-making. In general, the more relaxed "goulash communism" that followed the de-Stalinization campaign in Eastern Europe and the USSR since 1956 bears considerable resemblance to the Yugoslav penchant for muddling through.

Nor can the influence of Yugoslav wildcat strikes on popular opinion in Eastern Europe be discounted, although the Polish labor movement has clearly surpassed

Yugoslavia both in size and the scope of its demands. Polish labor toppled Gomulka in 1970, spawned the "Workers' Defense Committee" ("KOR") in 1976 (restructured as "The Committee for Social Self-Defense" in 1977) and the "Movement for the Defense of Human and Civil Rights" in 1977, and by 1980 engaged in nation-wide action demanding not only an independent labor movement ("Solidarity") in Poland, but civil and political rights such as freedom of speech, press, and association as well. Roger E. Kanet notes that political groupings such as "KOR" in Poland and "Charter 77" in Czechoslovakia, which are the result of modernization and increased differentiation of socialist societies in Eastern Europe, call for a restructuring of socialist politics, since

> The ultimate goals of these groupings include the right to dissent, the accountability of state officials to society, the right to organize politically, and the creation of a pluralistic political system in which all groupings—not merely the official party elite—will have an opportunity to share in the policymaking process.[61]

The Yugoslav critique of Stalinism is of particular significance in the East European and Soviet framework, because it shattered the myth of party infallibility and denounced Stalin's personality cult and the bureaucratic-dogmatic malpractices of Stalin's system long before Khrushchev acknowledged Stalin's misdeeds at the Twentieth CPSU Congress in February 1956. It is, therefore, not too farfetched to maintain with Dan N. Jacobs that the communist world has been shaped since 1948, and definitely since 1956, more by the Yugoslav than the Soviet experience.[62] In the realm of foreign policy, the Yugoslav example seems to have inspired especially Rumania, which since the early 1960s has enjoyed more latitude than ever before in its pursuit of a more independent foreign policy within the Soviet bloc. Thus, the new polycentrism in Eastern Europe found dramatic expression when Rumania, although a member of the Warsaw Pact, failed to participate in the Soviet-led invasion of Czechoslovakia in August 1968, and refused to accept the COMECON plan which would have relegated Rumania to the role of granary for the Soviet bloc. Significantly, however, Rumania's liberalization or pluralization in foreign policy was combined with a tightening of the party's control domestically. De-Russification did not entail democratization.

One of the greatest triumphs of the late Marshal Tito's foreign policy has undoubtedly been Yugoslavia's reconciliation with China, following Tito's 24-day tour in August-September, 1977, to the USSR, North Korea, and the People's Republic. This is all the more unusual since these two communist party states have for a generation accused each other of revisionism. Mao Tse-tung's passing from the scene and the continuing Sino-Soviet rivalry made the Sino-Yugoslav rapprochement easier. We are thus witnessing the monumental development of post-Mao China taking a new look at Yugoslav theory and practice. This leaves communist Albania in the position of odd man in both Europe and Asia, calling the great communist triangle of USSR-China-Yugoslavia arch-revisionist.

The influence of Yugoslavia's example within the Soviet bloc and the communist world at large has been matched, or even surpassed, with respect to its influence in the Third World. Alvin Z. Rubinstein relates that the Yugoslav model of nation-building has found a receptive audience among the developing nations who "admire the Yugoslav success in forging the essentials of a modern state."[63] Again, it is the now almost proverbial Yugoslav pragmatism in nation-building, with its emphasis on local government, self-management, workers' councils and, not the least, its relative success in socialization and integration of multiple nationalities and ethnic groups into a state and nation (compared with civil war during World War II), that appeals to the leaders of the Third World, whose countries are beset by problems and dilemmas similar to those which still occupy the Yugoslavs. Nor has Yugoslavia's successful maneuvering between the superpowers escaped the attention of other nations. We can conclude that the Yugoslav experiment in liberal and humanistic socialism and its foreign policy of non-alignment is likely to continue to have important repercussions in influencing the internal and external affairs of its East European neighbors, the USSR, and other communist party states, as well as enjoying wide respect, if not admiration, among the developing nations of the Third World.

Western observers like Andrzej Korbonski and Christopher Cviić argue that Yugoslav influence on Eastern Europe declined in the 1960s, due to Yugoslavia's internal problems of nationalism, inflation, unemployment, and mass emigration to the West.[64]   There is some truth to this contention.   Yet East European intellectuals as well as their leaderships, especially in the Prague Spring of 1968, seem heavily indebted to the Yugoslav experiment, as do the Hungarian economic decentralization measures of the 1960s and 1970s. Paradoxically, while Yugoslavia's influence in the East may be declining, it appears to be gaining ground in the West, particularly in the organized labor's quest for industrial democracy and the West European communist parties' increasing independence from Moscow.

Co-determination has become the watchword for labor-management relations in Scandinavia, Britain, and West Germany. By 1980, even the United States moved in this direction, when Douglas Fraser, President of the 1.4 million-strong United Auto Workers, was appointed to the board of directors of the ailing Chrysler Corporation. Other UAW leaders like Raymond Majerus and Donald Ephlin also pledged to work for the extension of industrial democracy throughout America. And the Second Conference of European Communist and Workers' Parties of June 29-30, 1976, in East Berlin, attended by representatives of 29 European communist parties, vindicated the Yugoslav principle of independent paths to socialism advanced a generation ago. In fact, as Kevin Devlin notes, the new principles of consensus governing inter-party relations is a *de facto* recognition of the independence, equality, and autonomy of all communist parties.[65] Thus, Western labor movements seem to be inspired in important respects by the Yugoslav quest for industrial democracy. And West European communist parties appear to be equally impressed with the Yugoslav foreign policy of non-alignment and independence from Moscow.

One can only agree with William Zimmerman that Yugoslavia's foreign policy has been an "enormous success."[66] For some, it has been too successful. Tito accomplished in the field of foreign affairs what few statesmen representing small nations could hope to do successfully—sitting on several chairs at once: a leader in the councils of the non-aligned nations of the Third World, a tacit ally of the Soviet Union and the communist world, and a somewhat more dubious ally of the West in East-West dialogue. To Laurence Silberman, former U.S. ambassador to Yugoslavia, American foreign policy toward Yugoslavia is misdirected, since it is based on two false assumptions:

> The first is that our *only* important interest there is to sustain Yugoslavia's independence from the Soviet Union. The second is that we foster that independence by providing bilateral support to the Yugoslav government, without regard to notions of reciprocity.[67]

A more realistic U.S. foreign policy stance toward Yugoslavia, continues Silberman, would rest on genuine reciprocity, requiring that the Yugoslavs heed America's bilateral and multilateral concerns. Yet, it is obvious that Yugoslavia's foreign policy grows out of weakness, not out of strength.   Hence, it is understandable that the basic motivation of Yugoslav foreign policy-makers with regard to the superpowers, United States, USSR, or China, is suspiciousness and opportunism. And, while not exactly moral, most observers agree that this policy orientation has worked—at least for the Yugoslavs. The Yugoslavs' cautionary approach toward East-West détente, particularly US-USSR rapprochement, is based on the Yugoslav leadership's fear of a Soviet-American deal at the expense of Yugoslavia. Considering the geo-political history of the region and the nature of East-West relations in the nuclear age, Fred Warner Neal proposed a US-Soviet "mutual non-intervention understanding" concerning post-Tito Yugoslavia.[68]

Paradoxically, when we turn to assess the significance of the Yugoslav experiment and, especially, its avant-garde Marxist theory to the domestic scene, we find even fewer clear-cut and unambiguous answers. This may be due to at least three factors at work in Yugoslavia: (1) Ideological fatigue supplemented by rampant materialism; (2) The fluidity of the Yugoslav situation, that is, the rapidity of changes, economic and social reforms, open borders, constitutional developments, party reorganizations, etc; and (3) The complexity of the new doctrines associated with Marxist humanism.

Andrew György has observed that communism in Eastern Europe after 1956 passed rapidly into a period characterized by an "all-pervasive spirit of material-ism" coupled with "ideological fatigue and indifference."[69] Yugoslavia seems to represent no exception to this trend but for the fact that in Yugoslavia it started even earlier. The new trend of the pursuit of wealth and privileges, and the devil take the hindmost, in Eastern Europe and Yugoslavia, belies the alleged purity and truthfulness of the socialist ethic as superior to its capitalist counterpart. Egoism, that well-worn blight of capitalism, seems to have been reborn and is flourishing in socialism in the form of an ubiquitous *blat* (payoff, blackmail, and bribe) which is accompanied by "reduced effort, tremendous absenteeism, and the embezzlement of public funds," dishonesty and, in one word—alienation. Milovan Djilas and Nenad Popović have described this phenomenon as the crisis of the new class of privileged administrators of socialized property in Yugoslavia.

The fluidity of the Yugoslav situation, punctuated by the promulgation of the 1963 and 1974 Constitutions, the economic reforms of 1965, the ouster of Alexander Ranković in 1966, the elections of 1967, the successive devaluations of the currency and further economic and social reforms, the re-centralization of the party, institutional pluralization, emigration, the silencing of some of the country's leading Marxist scholars, and ideological re-Stalinization, have contributed to widespread ideological apathy, on the one hand, and relative incomprehension, on the other. Nation-wide discussions of everything, including the future role of the party, duly reported in a largely self-censored press, have not dispelled confusion. Nor have the complex doctrines of Marxist humanism and socialist legality. And the past seems to provide no consolation. A 1960 poll by the Yugoslav Institute of Social Science in Belgrade of 3,889 university students on basic principles of Marxism revealed that half of the students either gave no answer, did not know, or thought that Marx's works did not contain concrete principles and statements![70]

The complexity of avant-garde Yugoslav Marxism-Existentialism does not augur well for or contribute to easy comprehensibility. That the avant-garde's reconstruction of Marx's thought is widely misunderstood in their native country, including its leadership, is evidenced by the inconsistent charges advanced against the journal *Praxis* and its contributors. The communist Establishment's early attacks on *Praxis* intensified during 1966 and 1968.[71] Among the major charges advanced against *Praxis* were that:

(1) It opposed workers' self-management and, hence, Yugoslav socialism in general;

(2) It was an advocate of etatism;

(3) It was centrist in orientation and defended economic and political centralism;

(4) It was an enemy of economic reforms;

(5) It was an enemy of the market economy and of monetary-commodity relations;

(6) It defended the thesis of the necessity of establishing a multi-party system;

(7) From its standpoint of radical criticism of everything existing, it interpreted Marx in an inexact manner;

(8) It was unitarian; and

(9) It represented in its ideological activity modern or contemporary anti-communism.[72]

Toward the end of 1968, the editorial board of *Praxis* finally wrote a detailed refutation of major charges brought against the journal. *Praxis'* editors showed point by point that the charges against the journal were unsubstantiated. They went on to state with renewed vigor that creative Marxist humanist thought ought to become the conscience of the contemporary age as well as the basic perspective for the socialist society of the future.[73] It was the 1971 Croatian crisis, student demonstrations at Zagreb University, and the spectre of national-ethnic separatism on the eve of Tito's departure from the Yugoslav socio-political scene which accelerated the party's resolve to silence the avant-garde—ironically, the staunchest defender of Yugoslav national unity.

Yet, avant-garde Yugoslav Marxist philosophers and sociologists may not be hoping quite in vain regarding the prospects for their fledgling Marxist humanist thought. Support for this view can be gleaned from the same student poll on basic principles of Marxism mentioned above. One-third of the student body identified these principles with the "humanization of relations among people, equality among people, human solidarity, mutual assistance, and freedom of the human personality." This is, indeed, the heart of avant-garde Marxist humanist thought. Furthermore, the avant-garde's humanistic reconstruction of Marxism-Leninism with its emphasis on de-alienation and liberation of man and the creation of a new *human* society may turn out to be, despite its paradoxes, one of the most incisive analyses and approaches into the technological future, East and West. It may, thus, open up vistas and possibilities whose relevance is likely to transcend artificial barriers of creed and nation.

4. Science, Technology, and Freedom: Alienation Unbound?

It seems likely that the revolutionary reinterpretation of Marxism-Leninism by contemporary avant-garde Yugoslav Marxist philosophers and sociologists will go down in history primarily for its recasting of Marx's philosophy as a radical critique of everything existing which limits human development, or in Zdravko Kučinar's terms, as a "critical conscience" of a highly institutionalized world.[74]

Our increasingly rationalized, bureaucratized, institutionalized, and dehumanized technological world, East and West, is in dire need of constructive criticism guided by a humanist vision. The contemporary era and civilizations which have witnessed over the last half century or so an unparalleled progress of science and technology, economic development, industrialization, rationalization of all spheres of life, and superorganization, have spawned a cosmology of problems which seem to dwarf our "benign" dilemmas of an earlier age dominated by "capitalism" and "socialism." What seems to be at stake today is no less than the very existence, as well as the quality of life, of modern man. Science and technique, the erstwhile obedient tools of man, seem to acquire increasingly an existence and a dynamic of their own, independent of human control, and tend to subordinate man and his human values to the exigencies of technological, purely calculatory, organizational, narrowly "rational" and amoral "technological reason." Jacques Ellul's technological society, Zbigniew Brzezinski's technetronic society, and Theodore Roszak's technocratic society are all expressions of this domination of technique over man and his resulting total alienation.

The ethos of science, according to Bell, is the new ethos of the post-industrial society, just as the Protestant ethic was the ethos of capitalism and socialism the ethos of Soviet society.[75] Indeed, Richard Kostelanetz sees the power of new technologies and shared technological awareness as possibly "the greatest ecumenical force in the world today."[76] Futurologists like Herman Kahn, William Brown, and Leon Martel feel comfortable with the new technologies, which they consider instrumental in solving key problems of the near term such as population, economic growth, energy, raw materials, food, pollution, and thermonuclear war. But, even the optimists are aware of the curious "Faustian bargain" which man has struck with science and technology. Kahn and his colleagues contend that there is no turning back.[77] Man seems to be destined to accumulate more knowledge and powers.

On the other hand, critics of science and technology point out that the crucial question concerning man and the quality of life is somehow lost in the shuffle. Science and technique are increasingly encroaching upon the private lives of individuals, East and West. B. F. Skinner's proposal for conditioning of human behavior and good riddance to man *qua* man is abhorrent to those who believe in human freedom and dignity.[78] Even more perplexing are the issues raised by genetic engineering and new advances in bio-medicine which confront the human species with alluring visions of playing God in curing incurable diseases, creating new life, and changing human nature. It is in this area more than any other in which it becomes clear, as June Goodfield writes, that the scientific enterprise has ceased to be purely scientific and has become moral and political as well.[79] The human race thus stands suddenly at the crossroads of our common destiny. Even optimistic futurologists are led to wonder:

> What kind of a life will a genetically engineered, vital-organ-replaceable, mental-state-adjustable, computer-robot-assisted human being want to live? Will he find satisfaction in the postindustrial era?[80]

The pessimists want to put the genie of science and technology back into the bottle before it emancipates itself from man and becomes his Master. Erich Fromm's hope for the humanization of technology, Herbert Muller's warning to cage the Frankenstein of science and technology by subordinating them to essential human values, and Herbert Marcuse's attack on the one-dimensionality, totalitarianism, and basic irrationality of the seeming rationality of advanced industrial society, with his quest for a new sensibility and aesthetic ethos to help liberate man, testify to the major dilemmas and new challenges to man as he approaches the year 2000.[81] The underlying theme of all these writers, as well as of modern philosophical thought in general—mirrored in existentialism, phenomenology, humanism, Marxist humanism, and critical theory—is the preoccupation with the twin threats to human existence posed by modern means of mass destruction and the total reification and dehumanization of man in advanced industrial society. And these dilemmas are likely to intensify in the post-industrial era. East and West, philosophers and scientists like Norbert Wiener, Ernest Becker, Andrei D. Sakharov, and Nikolai M. Amosoff have joined their voices in warning mankind of the dangers inherent in a civilization run rampant in an attempt to convince it of the need to subordinate technological reason to human values.[82]

Avant-garde Yugoslav Marxist philosophers and sociologists have contributed to our grasp of these human dilemmas of late twentieth century. Thus, Kuvačić points out that scientific and technological progress are increasingly becoming instruments of domination and exploitation of man, that modern industry based on total organization leads to "absolute reification," and that privileged groups in Yugoslavia tend to sacrifice social for technological progress.[83] The dilemma of modern man with respect to the choice of means and ends, values and techniques, is summed up by Marković:

> This philosophy of success, this obsession with the efficiency of means, followed by an almost total lack of interest for the problem of rationality and humanity of goals, are the essential characteristics of the spiritual climate of contemporary industrial society.[84]

The avant-garde has become aware of the fact that technological rationale must be differentiated from "reasonableness," echoing Marcuse, Muller, Fromm, and others, East and West. The Yugoslavs are discovering that what is possible for technique and economic rationality is not always desirable from a human standpoint. Furthermore, they maintain that the goal of socialist humanism is not simply the realization of an affluent and technically advanced, but also, and above all, of a *human* society and a civilization which puts its primary emphasis on man rather than technique. Hence, Pejović claims that while Stalinism was merely a "realization of philosophy as technology" resulting in total organization and institutionalization of all spheres of life, the real aim of socialism is to bring about a "revolution in human relations and a turnabout in man himself."[85] It is, therefore, necessary, continues Pejović, to revive the Promethean function of philosophy in its role of a radical search for the de-alienation and liberation of man.

The avant-garde has called most consistently for the humanization of work as the primary task of the socialist revolution. While the exploitation of labor may recede into the background due to the increased emphasis on machinery, organization, and innovation, nevertheless, the division of labor, its specialization, fragmentation, atomization, and alienation are likely to increase. According to Živojin Denić, the social division of labor will continue even after the abolition of commodity production.[86] This is all the more disquieting since, in Dragomir Drašković's view, the socio-psychological dilemmas and negative consequences of the atomization of work cannot be remedied by a purely intellectual valorization of work, be it in the form of expanding the worker's roles, rotation, or knowledge of the entire technical process.[87] Marković concludes that narrow specialization and excessive division of labor lead to partial, fragmented human consciousness, and an atomistic approach to reality in a world in which the old dichotomy between physical and mental work has been replaced by the creative work of a few and drudgery for the vast majority.[88]

The Yugoslavs have thus opened up the cosmology of problems at the center of which lies the question articulated by Muller in his *Children of Frankenstein,* of what technology has done *to* as well as *for* people. Yugoslav theorists are engaged in elaborating and assessing the impact of modern technology on man, and their writings are a rich source of insights into the relationship between technology and human alienation. Marković articulates the alienating nature of technology as follows:

> Owing to the influence of a number of objective and subjective factors technology everywhere seeks to destroy all natural, patriarchal and idyllic relations; everywhere it mercilessly breaks up the variegated spontaneous links between people and tends to repress all other relations between man and the world except cool methodical calculation and skills developed to perfection.[89]

While realizing the full alienating impact of technology on man, most Yugoslav thinkers are agreed in their view of the necessity of technological, scientific, and economic development which, however, should take place within a "humanistic context."[90] The Yugoslavs thus warn us not to fall into the false dilemma of *man versus technique,* science, civilization, and culture. Science, technology, and an affluent society emerge in the avant-garde's *Weltanschauung* as *necessary,* but *not sufficient,* conditions for the true humanization of society and man. The Yugoslavs therefore posit the need for the humanistic and technical-scientific intelligentsia to work together, rather than against each other, if they want to achieve a more humane society.

Some avant-garde Yugoslav Marxist philosophers have begun also to delve into the relatively unexplored problem areas of philosophy of science and the relationship of epistemology to science and technique. Supek maintains that our "technological transformation of nature has obviously surpassed the limits of the [merely] human world" due to the power of man's analytical-instrumental intelligence.[91] Yet, surprisingly, the very achievements of the analytical-instrumental intelligence seem to contribute to its defeat because:

> Through its gradual mastering of relationships in the physical

world, the analytical-instrumental intelligence comes into conflict with its original matrix—with the very structure of human conceptualization since it is forced to transcend both its traditional space-time coordinates (with the theory of relativity and non-Euclidian geometry) and its modes of perception (with Bohr's correspondence principle and Heisenberg's principle of indeterminacy in the field of quantum physics).[92]

Technology, according to Supek, has thus created, with the help of instrumental intelligence, a "transhuman" world. It may be more germane, however, to designate Supek's "transhuman" world as a non-human or a-human world, since the word "transhuman" may mislead one to believe that our world is somehow super-human, that it has already fulfilled all the requirements of the human psyche, mind, and constitution, and that it is pressing beyond that. Whereas in reality our technological world is a thoroughly non-human or a-human one, relatively unconcerned with human values. It is the very need to reincorporate human values into our technological universe which seems to become increasingly the number one problem for the human race. As Becker pointed out, in this a-human world, we have allowed science to be spelled with a capital "S" and have allowed expedience to triumph over man's controlling vision:

> Why have we allowed Science to be spelled with a capital "S"; allowed quantities and things to get the ascendancy over man; allowed the sheer accumulation of data to block out our human vistas; allowed ourselves, in sum, to continue to wallow without direction or vision . . . .[93]

Not only has man become lost in the labyrinth of his own creation, but, moreover, he seems to show a tendency to escape from the dilemmas engendered by it. The escape from freedom, responsibility, and moral choice has been noted as a pathological trait of modern man. Fromm described this phenomenon graphically in his *Escape From Freedom*. The avant-garde has also dealt with the problem of man's freedom and responsibility and concluded that the spreading phenomenon in the modern world of man's escape from freedom constitutes another "form of man's self-alienation."[94]

Social engineers like Skinner assure us that freedom will become a superfluous commodity in the well-organized and peaceful society of perfectly conditioned human beings *Beyond Freedom and Dignity*. This might, indeed, happen to mankind in spite of repeated warnings contained in such anti-utopias as Huxley's *Brave New World* and Orwell's *1984*. In fact, if we are to believe Roland Huntford, such a brave new world of social engineering already exists in embryonic form in—Sweden. Now, Sweden is considered by many as the prototype of an ideal social organization of the future, combining socialism and democracy, affluence and personal freedom. But Huntford points out that material comfort and security in the Swedish welfare state have been purchased at a heavy price of absolute conformity and uniformity. He concludes that the choice before mankind is between technological perfection in a superorganized, bureaucratic system with outward trappings of democracy, on the one hand, and personal liberty, on the other.[95]

And what is this thing called "freedom," anyway? There is a widespread cynicism among Western youth and intellectuals concerning freedom. Is "freedom" but another word for "nothing else to lose?" Or, does it constitute the essential humanity of man? Is freedom necessary and liberating, or merely a ballast and a burden, to be shed like a tortoise's shell or a snake's skin in exchange for security, peace, and material happiness? Can the past be understood, the present lived, and the future hoped for in the absence of freedom? Roger Garaudy muses that:

> The past is where things are irrevocably done, the place of finished projects, frozen and crystallized into facts, where one, and only

> one, possibility has triumphed. In retrospect, it appears to us as
> the sphere of necessity. But the future is the home of what
> remains to be done, the home of a plurality of possibilities for
> which we are responsible. It is the locus of freedom. Between the
> closed past and the open future, the present is the time of decision,
> the time of man.[96]

Science, technology, and freedom thus seem to have become major indices with which we can measure the total alienation of man in contemporary advanced industrial civilization, a civilization in which alienation, to quote Becker:

> ...seems to be *the* word that characterizes our time, or better,
> the one that tries to come to grips fumblingly with the problem of
> man in our time. It seems to be the concept wherewith man is
> trying to lay hold of the knowledge he needs in order to free
> himself.[97]

James A. Ogilvy advances the thesis of a fateful inversion between nature and technology/politics, in which the latter have replaced the former as an alien environment. In his view, the arguments offered in defense of advanced industrial civilization based on technology (centralization of resources), economics (economies of scale), professionalism (specialization), and politics (professional politicians)—"all point toward the centralized State with its bureaucracy, its myths of power, its Eleatic logic of control of form over matter."[98] What is needed, argues Ogilvy, is just the opposite: a decentralization of people, technology, and politics, which leads to a pluralized and multi-selved many dimensional man capable of paraconsciousness (symbolic consciousness, intuition, and affective sensitivity), paratechnology, and decentralized, multi-valued, pluralistic parapolitics.

Alvin Toffler contends that we are presently at the threshold of a new age of synthesis—the third wave—cresting atop the spent waves of agricultural and industrial civilization. This new "practopian" age, claims Toffler, is "neither the best nor the worst of all possible worlds, but one that is both practical and preferable to the one we had."[99] Twenty-first century democracy in Toffler's *practopia* is based on minority power, semi-direct democracy, and decision division. Culturally, third wave civilization favors a democracy of shared minority power; experimentation with more direct democracy; transnationalism and a fundamental devolution of power; the crack-up of giant bureaucracies; a renewable and less centralized energy system; legitimate options to the nuclear family; less standardization and more individualization in the schools; environment-consciousness; and restructuring the world economy on "a more balanced and just basis."[100] Third wave cultural values thus bear a remarkable affinity to the Yugoslav avant-garde's Promethean quest for a new civilization and culture "fit for human beings."

It was Marx's great merit to have placed man in a social context and to have looked at man's world and creations through the prism of human needs, though marred by *a priori* notions. It is an even greater merit of avant-garde Yugoslav Marxist philosophers and sociologists to have recast Marx's philosophy of man and his methodology and epistemology into a humanistic philosophy and a non-positivistic science shorn largely of its teleological and suprarational overtones. Finally, the avant-garde deserves credit for subordinating both to a guiding vision—that of the de-alienation and liberation of man, the human individual, within the context of a free community of free men, and to have begun to question many of Marx's anti-humanist *a prioris.*

5. Toward a Kantian Christian Humanism

Albert Camus observed that "Man is the only creature who refuses to be what he is."[101] It is this rebellious streak in human nature which remains man's ultimate hope for the improvement of his lot, his self-development, de-alienation, and liberation, as well as the most reliable guarantee that he will refuse to subordinate himself to inhuman conditions, institutions, and practices which seem to have mortgaged his past, dominate his present, and endanger his future. As Milan Mirić writes:

> The limits are given, and we in them also, but it is likely that we can be men only insofar as we do not accept either the limits or ourselves bound within them.[102]

Avant-garde Yugoslav Marxist philosophers and sociologists revived the Promethean function of their philosophy as a radical critique of existing structures, institutions, and processes. In returning to Marxist dogma the creative thunder of radical social criticism, guided by a humanist vision whose goal is the freedom, creativity, and all-round development of man, the avant-garde created a humanist philosophy receptive to man and dependent on a continuous and genuine dialogue. The development of Yugoslav Marxism-Existentialism is thus of signal importance for a genuine dialogue not only among Marxists but also among people everywhere concerned with the future and the well-being of the human species and of each individual, whether East or West, North or South.

One can only agree with the prominent Marxist humanist Garaudy that dialogue has become "an objective necessity of the age."[103] It has perhaps become clear that the future cannot be shaped in a world rent asunder by dogmatized ideologies, which in their tendency to neglect real human needs constitute possibly the supreme expression of man's alienation within a man-made world of symbols. As Peter L. Berger notes, moral self-righteousness abounds across the entire political spectrum, yet history has been a stream of blood. The times hence call for humility and compassion, which Berger sees as "the only credible motive for any actions to change the world."[104] And Stojanović reproves crime committed in the name of revolution as no less opprobrious than that committed in the name of counter-revolution. Hence, the Marxist revolutionary stands before the epochal choice between barbarism and socialism.[105]

Genuine dialogue between men and civilizations is thus an absolute and primary order of the day if our complex technological world is to survive and remedy its blemishes and resolve once more to dignify man rather than his machines, techniques, sciences, or ideologies. It is therefore of utmost importance that the new dialogue concern itself with man and real human needs, rather than with false dilemmas of an earlier age dominated by "capitalism" and "communism." What is needed, then, is a genuine *humanist* dialogue which would assimilate in its perspective the richness of human thought and technical, scientific, and cultural achievements. It would combine man's vision with science and technology, and dedicate itself to a truly human future, striving toward the elimination of want, misery, and suffering in their myriad manifestations. Christians and Marxists, democrats and communists, liberals and conservatives, people of all nations, races, and creeds, could find in this truly revolutionary pan-human enterprise the most progressive, humane, and challenging task of all epochs.

It is, indeed, late in the historical drama of our rediscovery of man—our common odyssey. Man has become progressively alienated from God, himself, nature, the world, and his fellow men to the extent that today he stands as the arbiter of his destiny, having acquired immense knowledge, fashioned powerful tools, and created a new world. Yet his wisdom and understanding have not kept pace with the forces he has released from the womb of nature. And we have arrived at the point where Arthur Koestler remarks that: "Nature has let us down, God seems to have left the receiver off the hook, and time is running out."[106]

Today, as at no time before in history, man faces his destiny. He may be close to Teilhard de Chardin's omega point of *Christogenesis*. Both science and philosophy indicate that it is high noon in the history of man, civilization, technology, science, and culture. But, if he is not careful, the high noon may turn out to be midnight. We are beginning to realize with Koestler in his *Darkness at Noon* that there may be an error somewhere in the calculation.[107] Man may miscalculate himself into oblivion.

Is there any hope for man? The humanist's answer to the human dilemma is—man. It is said that man holds the key to his destiny. The kind of world that he lives and will live in depends on human *praxis*, his activity, creativity, and enlightenment. Humanists urge man to take as a guide for his *praxis* the humanist ideals of Horace, that nothing human is alien to him; Protagoras', that man is the measure of all things; Kant's, that man should always be the end and never a means; and Marx's, that man is not an abstract being squatting outside the world but that he is the human world, society, and the state. There can be no doubt that the most pressing need of contemporary man is the *humanization* of himself and his alienated world. The most important question for man today is thus not revolution, capitalism, socialism, communism, and the like, but the *humanum*—the nature, means, and goals of man.

We are thus back to the opening question of this modern odyssey: what is man? Paradoxically, this question may be unanswerable within a framework which limits itself to the physical world and man as a purely physical or social being. A framework of ethics, values, and metaphysics appears to be essential. In fact, some theorists contend that the contemporary crisis of civilization, East and West, reflects a lack of firmly grounded values, morals, and a corresponding religious faith. According to Bell, the absence of a transcendentally grounded ethic, a public philosophy, and a sustaining religious faith are at the root of the contemporary cultural crisis of capitalism. With the disappearance of the Protestant ethic and religious faith, only unbounded hedonism and vulgarity are said to remain. In Bell's view, the rationalism and efficiency needed for the proper functioning of the capitalist system of mass production and consumption are in direct contradiction with modern cultural trends of hedonism, self-realization, and instant gratification.[108]

If a transcendent ethic and a religious faith are waning in the West, they were uprooted long ago by the exigencies of the class struggle and dialectical materialism in the East. We may thus be witnessing a fateful East-West convergence of a third kind. At the heart of this cultural or value convergence is the Nietzschean death of God and the loss of absolutes. Curiously, as Bell notes, the death of God implies a dissolution of social bonds among people and, hence, the death of society as well. And he cautions that: "Where religions fail, cults appear."[109] Esad Ćimić, one of Yugoslavia's leading authorities on the sociology of religion, concurs in the view that atheism can reappear as "a theology without God" or a "negative theology."[110] And Bernard-Henry Lévy proposes that totalitarianism can become the "religion" of the state, with idolatry replacing atheism. In Lévy's conception, the totalitarian state merely secularizes religion, substituting profane beliefs, abolishing politics, and repressing dissent, in its quest to dominate "the lives and passions of men." Hence, concludes Lévy, the atheist state is a "barbarian State."[111]

Francis A. Schaeffer writes that synthesis has triumphed on both sides of the Iron Curtain. East and West, people no longer seem aware of fixed moral/ethical categories. Schaeffer locates the source of this moral/ethical relativism in—humanism:

> Beginning from man alone, Renaissance humanism—and humanism ever since—has found no way to arrive at universals or absolutes which give meaning to existence and morals.[112]

But, if men no longer have any absolute standards by which to judge human actions, expediency and cynicism are likely to carry the day. Moreover, Schaeffer claims that society itself becomes absolute if there are no absolutes by which to judge society.[113] And the end result is arbitrary action or expediency of situational ethics, sociological law, and power politics. Is there a need for absolute standards in the post-industrial society? Will not the post-industrial society supplant unreliable human judgment and decision-making by scientifically-programmed computers? Infallible cybernetics rather than human error and misjudgment?

Kahn and his team of futurologists conclude that:

> The postindustrial world we foresee will be one of increased abundance, and thus hopefully of reduced competition; it will be one of greater travel and contact, and thus possibly one of diminished differences among its people. But it will also be one of enormous power to direct and manipulate both man and nature; and thus its great issues will still be the very questions that confront us now, though enlarged in range and magnitude: *Who will direct and manipulate, and to what ends?*[114]

The question of how we should live and govern ourselves is thus likely to remain with us and even intensify in the post-industrial era. And this in spite of the rise of Bell's new scientific-technical elites or society's future mandarins. While the choices confronting mankind seem to be increasing in their complexity and magnitude, the loss of absolutes leaves the field wide open for unprecedented manipulation by the new mandarins or Philosopher-Kings, East and West.

Schaeffer argues that the Christian consensus has waned and that this void is being filled increasingly by manipulative authoritarian rule.[115] Could the East-West convergence end up in a new form of totalitarian manipulation of people in the post-industrial era beyond capitalism and socialism? What about freedom? Will not people rebel against authoritarian or totalitarian manipulation, East and West? This merely begs the question, since Tocqueville observed over a century ago that " ... liberty cannot be established without morality, nor morality without faith."[116] In a world without absolute guides in morals or faith, liberty itself may be the casualty. At present we seem to be bound with the same bonds which Tocqueville articulated:

> Has such been the fate of the centuries which have preceded our own? and has man always inhabited a world like the present, where all things are out of their natural connections, where virtue is without genius, and genius without honor; where the love of order is confounded with a taste for oppression; and the holy rites, of freedom with a contempt of law; where the light thrown by conscience on human actions is dim, and where nothing seems to be any longer forbidden or allowed, honorable or shameful, false or true?[117]

But if ultimate values are important, so are tolerance and compassion, if not love, toward all men, including dissenting voices. It may be that the socialist and similar experiments in social engineering are doomed to fail because they have undertaken to change society and man even before they have understood man and social phenomena. As the Russian scientist Amosoff reminds us in his *Notes From the Future*:

> Apparently, economics and ideologies do not yet create happiness. Basically, people are all the same. "They live, dream, love, bear children, grow old and die. Perhaps they don't even *want* immortality?"[118]

While it may be contestable whether there is such an entity as "human nature," it seems likely that man has to understand the human condition continuously anew. According to the late Leo Strauss, thinking constitutes the humanity and wisdom the proper end of man.[119] History suggests, however, that the human experience has been one of ubiquitous struggle, disappointments as well as triumphs, old problems yielding to new ones, and that there have been very few, if any, wise men. Even the proverbial wise man of antiquity, Socrates, claimed that all he knew was that he knew nothing. At the same time, one cannot overlook the fact that man—as Karl R. Popper put it—is the creative and problem-solving animal *par excellence,* who alone among creatures is aware not only of his inescapable death, but also of his potential:

> A higher animal may have a character: it may have what we may call virtues or vices. A dog may be brave, affable, and loyal; or it may be vicious and treacherous. But . . . only a man can make an effort to become a better man: to master his fears, his laziness, his selfishness; to get over his lack of self control.[120]

Crucially, man finds himself at the insterstices of two worlds: the known and the unknown. Kant envisioned man as an appearance or *phenomenon,* as well as an intelligible being or *noumenon.* Even more perplexing, Kant's dualism rests on another: that of nature and freedom. Hence, there are also two sets of laws coexisting in the world: laws of nature and laws of freedom. In one of the more poetic passages of his *Critique,* Kant writes that:

> Man . . . who knows all the rest of nature solely through the senses, knows himself also through pure apperception; and this, indeed, in acts and inner determinations which he cannot regard as impressions of the senses.[121]

Thus, Kant's Copernican revolution in epistemology consisted in refuting the Humean empiricist notion that our knowledge rests on experience alone. Instead, Kant maintained that knowledge arises from the joint action of sensibility and the understanding, where the former provides objects or intuitions and the latter supplies concepts or meaning. The resolution of the Kantian dualism is possible only via the *principle of tolerance,* reflecting the essential incompleteness, ambiguity, and imperfection of man and his artifacts, including knowledge. The conception of man as a free, creative, and self-creative being—which recalls the Yugoslav avant-garde formulation—gives rise to the imperative for ethical conduct. In this reaffirmation of the moral "ought," independence, and freedom lies the essential resolution of the Kantian dilemma, as well as the reconciliation between science and ethics.[122]

It appears, then, that man remains our last frontier and central challenge. The Kantian vision of man as *phenomenon-noumenon* acquires new meaning in one of the most spectacular and controversial hypotheses of psychophysical interactionism advanced by Popper and the Nobel laureate John C. Eccles: that the non-physical self-conscious mind is the pilot or programmer of the physical brain. This would imply, in Kantian terms, that the *noumenal* aspect of man determines the *phenomenal.* Moreover, Popper conjectures that the self-conscious mind reveals "a personality, something like an ethos or a moral character."[123] This would signify, in turn, that the human mind is the carrier of the Kantian categorical imperative, or the "moral law."

The most daring proposition by Popper and Eccles is that the self-conscious mind—which develops in relationship with World 3 influence (culture)—provides the integrating function in actively seeking, organizing, modifying, and "reading out" from the immense variety of data stored in the physical brain. Eccles postulates that the *liaison brain*—certain areas of the cerebral cortex in the dominant hemisphere—is in direct contact (liaison) with the self-conscious mind. Significantly, the self-conscious mind directs and controls the brain by providing neurophysiological synthesis. Hence, Eccles concludes that "the unity of conscious experience is provided by the self-conscious mind and not by the neural machinery of the liaison areas of the cerebral hemisphere."[124] Should the Popper-Eccles hypothesis of psychophysical interactionism prove correct, social as well as natural scientists will have to forge entirely new paradigms for understanding man, society, and nature.

What Nicholas Rescher calls the "divine discontent"—and Kant sketched as the transcendental employment of reason in search of freedom of the will, the immortality of the soul, and the existence of God[125]—constitutes at the same time the creative spark in the human race and the best guarantee for continuing exploration and increase in knowledge. But we should never forget that it is *human* knowledge we are talking about, which by its nature is limited and imperfect. As Weber admonished: "Fundamental doubt is the father of knowledge."[126] The riddle of man's nature, origin, and destiny moves Eccles to exclaim that:

> Our coming-to-be is as mysterious as our ceasing-to-be at death.
> Can we therefore not derive hope because our ignorance about our
> origin matches our ignorance about our destiny?[127]

On the other hand, man seems to have already reached the stars, uncovered hitherto unknown secrets of the atom, and acquired the capacity to create new life forms in the laboratory. The implications of genetic engineering, for instance, are so vast, largely unexplored, and fateful for the human race that science or knowledge by itself can no longer be considered a reliable guide or an unadulterated boon and blessing for mankind. Man is at the threshold of being able to play God, as Goodfield intimates, but without the wisdom, love, or mercy commensurate with the task. Hence, there is an urgent need in late twentieth century for a reconciliation between science and ethics, physics and metaphysics.

In this vital twentieth century enterprise, it is necessary to reaffirm the moral "ought" or Kant's categorical imperative as a guide to knowledge and action. And, in reaffirming the moral "ought," perhaps we can also reaffirm our love for man—this fallible and imperfect, yet unique and irreplaceable creature at the apex of God's creation. A paradigm based on the *principle of love*—a Kantian Christian humanism—could provide a fascinating blueprint of inquiry into the furthest reaches of the human odyssey.

The Bible states that wisdom is paramount and that we ought, therefore, to acquire wisdom. But it adds that whatever else we might acquire, we should acquire *understanding* (Proverbs 4:7). Understanding, based on knowledge and leading to wisdom, may prove to be the philosopher's stone and the key which opens the heart of man and the universe, that golden fleece which man has sought since time immemorial. The capacity of understanding, of *Verstehen*, has today become not only desirable but essential for the very existence and the quality of life of the human species. In the Judaeo-Christian tradition, understanding means forgiveness and love. And for the humanist, it implies tolerance. By nurturing such a *humanist dialogue of understanding*, we might possibly recover the coveted prize of anthropogenesis—the key to the solution of the riddle of man and the universe.

Chapter X · Prometheus Bound: Silencing the Avant-Garde

Various paths of philosophy and literature of our era seem to lead to the same age-old lost home, the one from which we started out: myth. The "difficulty" consists in the fact that the mythic world can no longer return; no one even tries to reestablish it, nor would he succeed in doing so since it is "timeless." However, both philosophy and literature reveal today more consciously than ever before their most intimate longing—to return a primeval world to man in which he could live his only fleeting life in a more humane way.

Danilo Pejović, *Sistem i egzistencija* (1970)

1. For the Good of the Cause?

The attempt by the Yugoslav government and the communist party to silence their leading avant-garde Marxist humanist philosophers and sociologists illustrates the inherent conflict between Marxist ideals and socialist/communist practice, as explored in this modern odyssey. The embryo of this conflict was apparent to Engels who, in his letter of December 18, 1889, to Herson Trier, raised the following question regarding freedom of discussion in the workers' movement:

> The workers' movement is based on the most stringent critique of the existing society. Criticism is its life force; how can it, then, avoid criticism of itself and tend to forbid discussion? Do we demand from others freedom of speech for ourselves only in order to destroy it in our own ranks?[1]

Or, as Branko Bošnjak put it in a nutshell almost a century later: "Does our society need creative Marxist criticism or only an apology of the existing [state of affairs] ?"[2]

Communist officialdom in Yugoslavia insists that theirs is the freest country the world has ever seen. As the members of the 35-nation Conference to review the implementation of the 1975 Helsinki Accords convened in Belgrade, Tito declared that there were no human rights violations in Yugoslavia. Moreover, writes Dragan Bartolović, Yugoslavia had not only achieved, but even surpassed the requirements concerning freedom delineated in the Final Act of Helsinki.[3] Yet, since 1971, the Yugoslav regime intensified its crackdown on all dissent. Anyone who even dared question publicly the regime's flowery description of basic human rights and freedoms prevailing in contemporary Yugoslavia ran the risk of being labeled an enemy of the state and of self-managing socialism.

Thus, Živojin Radović, an engineer, was sentenced during 1977 to two and a half years of imprisonment by a Sarajevo court for his remark in a café that there would be greater freedom in Yugoslavia after President Tito dies. In the fall of 1976, Viktor Blažić, a journalist, was sentenced in Ljubljana to two years for stating in a review that freedoms were restricted in Slovenia. At the same time, Franc Miklavčić, a judge, was sentenced to five years and eight months for a secret private diary outlining a democratic system for Slovenia and for a March 1976 article in *Zaliv* (Trieste), a literary-cultural review, in which he defended Edward Kocbek's assertion to the same journal that the Yugoslav Partisans (communist-dominated National Liberation Front) executed some 12,000 Slovenian "home guards" when these were handed over to them at the end of World War II by British and American allied forces.[4] Finally, Vitomir Djilas, a lawyer and cousin of Milovan Djilas, sent a letter to the editor of *Politika*, a Belgrade daily, in which he asked:

> I am interested in knowing whether we in Yugoslavia can also fight for democratic society (truly democratic), whether there is now the possibility of free speech and freedom of the press here, or does fear of arrest and repression still exist?[5]

The answer to Djilas' inquiry was swift: accusation in the controlled press of being a "provocateur" in the pay of foreign powers, arrest on March 14, 1977, and sentencing on May 6, 1977, to two and a half years of imprisonment for "hostile propaganda."[6] His letter, of course, was never published.

In view of these and other violations of basic human rights in Yugoslavia, it is somewhat ironic that the Conference to review the implementation of the Helsinki Accords convened in the Yugoslav capital of Belgrade during 1977-78. On June 15, 1977, the opening day of the preparatory conference, Frank Osvald, a Czech-born reporter for Radio Denmark, was deported from Belgrade for attempting to contact a group of Jewish women who were prevented by the police from staging a demonstration outside the conference building. The women were arrested at their local hotel, taken to the Belgrade airport, and flown out of the country.[7] Yet, the U. S. Commission on Security and Cooperation in Europe omitted Yugoslavia altogether from its August 1977 Report to Congress on the implementation of the Helsinki Accords by the Soviet Union and East European nations.[8]

Many people, East and West, were also disappointed by the failure of the closing document covering the Belgrade Conference to deal substantively with or even mention progress toward greater freedom, openness, and human rights in the communist world. It seems that, increasingly, the West may be willing to sign just about anything which has "détente" stamped on it. The voices of those like Sakharov, Solzhenitsyn, Laqueur, and Moynihan who caution that genuine East-West détente, arms limitation, reduction of tensions, and cooperation are impossible without greater democratization, openness, international inspection to insure compliance with arms agreements, and respect for human rights, are simply ignored.[9]

Could the Western world be moving toward what Jean-François Revel calls Finlandization—a kind of self-censorship by the European Left, pusillanimity, and lack of vigorous criticism of Stalinism in theory and practice?[10] Finlandization appears to stalk the American Left, some students, youth, and intellectuals as well. And, can they be held to task when Gerald R. Ford, a Republican President, refused to meet the exiled Russian Nobel laureate Solzhenitsyn, for fear that it might damage U.S.-Soviet détente? Or, when President Jimmy Carter welcomed Tito during the 30th anniversary year of the United Nations Declaration of Human Rights as a "true friend" of the United States and a symbol of Eastern Europe's yearning for freedom and independence?[11] Even a conservative like Ronald Reagan, the Republican contender in the 1980 U.S. Presidential elections, was forced to apologize for suggesting a restoration of official U.S. relations with Taiwan, for fear of alienating the People's Republic of China. Increasingly, the assumption seems to be that whoever declares independence from Moscow is *ipso facto* a champion of freedom and a friend of the West. Yet, Tito's break with Moscow and particularly Stalin in 1948 did not imply a break with communism. On the other hand, it is true that while Yugoslavia's rhetoric of espionage, subversion, and imperialism is aimed at the West, its guns point to the East. And, to show their commitment to human rights, a national amnesty was declared in November 1977, freeing Mihajlo Mihajlov and Miklavčić, among others.[12]

Few seem to have noticed, however, that the 1977 Yugoslav amnesty was less comprehensive than it appeared on the surface. Mihajlov pointed out to members of the U.S. Congress and the U.S. Helsinki Commission that of the 218 political prisoners affected by the amnesty, only about 30 were freed, while others merely had their sentences reduced somewhat. Congressman Edward J. Derwinski of Illinois entered Mihajlov's testimony into the *Congressional Record* on August 1, 1978. Curiously, the U.S. State Department's *Report* to Congress on human rights practices in Yugoslavia, published on February 8, 1979, failed to record the discrepancy concerning the amnesty (see Chapter XI).[13]

2.   Prometheus Bound

It is within this framework that the regime's crackdown on its Marxist intelligentsia must be understood. Their case, more than any other, highlights the generic paradoxes inherent in both Marxist theory and socialist practice. The socio-political and philosophical drama enacted in Yugoslavia in the 1970s concerns the regime's attempt to silence its avant-garde theorists at the country's leading institutions of higher learning. The government's showcase was the expulsion of eight Marxist philosophers and sociologists from the University of Belgrade, the closing of the two radical Marxist journals, *Praxis* and *Filosofija*, and ending the International Summer School on the Adriatic island of Korčula as well as the Winter Philosophical Meetings in Serbia. The Dean of the Faculty of Philosophy (Social Sciences) at Belgrade University, Dr. Sima Cirkovic, resigned in protest just prior to the dismissal of the "Belgrade Eight"—Professors Zagorka Pešić-Golubović, Trivo Indjić, Mihailo Marković, Dragoljub Mićunović, Nebojša Popov, Svetozar Stojanović, Ljubomir Tadić and Miladin Životić.

The Marxist scholars—seven men and one woman—were suspended from their teaching duties for alleged "activities contrary to the aims and practices of Yugoslavia's socialist society, basic constitutional principles and policies of the Communist party" by the Parliament of the Republic of Serbia which, ironically, first had to change the law governing universities in Serbia, so that the university professors could be fired on political grounds.[14] Such action, infringing university autonomy, was unknown in the "reactionary" pre-war Kingdom of Yugoslavia, which, in this respect at least, was beyond reproach. Thus, Lazo M. Kostić, a legal scholar on the Law Faculty at Subotica, was not prosecuted at all for his critique of the Royal Constitution from the standpoint: *in dubio pro populo.* Moreover, one of his students, who defended the freedom of the press in an essay contest, received the King's St. Stephen Award.[15]

To observers, East and West, the ill-fated action by the Serbian Parliament appeared unconstitutional under both the federal and republic Constitutions, as it contradicted the country's basic principle of self-management. Under self-management, all hiring and firing in economic, educational, and cultural institutions are the exclusive prerogative of self-managing bodies or councils. But the party and the government found a way around that principle. The Serbian Parliament changed the Law on Higher Education governing universities in Serbia twice during 1974, packing the University's Joint Council with government appointees and allowing the Parliament to suspend professors directly when the latter's activities "threaten society's interests."[16]

Under the new law, the eight professors had to submit to a reevaluation of their "moral and political qualifications to continue teaching" in the Faculty of Philosophy at the University of Belgrade. To that effect, eight five-member committees composed of forty well-known Yugoslav scholars were formed in March 1974. Their reports to the Faculty Meeting on July 1, 1974 not only rejected all accusations against the "Belgrade Eight," but praised them for outstanding scholarly and educational achievements. The committees' reports were overwhelmingly approved at that Faculty Meeting: 150 for, none against, and one abstention. On July 5, 1974, even the Faculty Joint Council, composed of twenty members each from within the University and those delegated by the government and various scholarly organizations and institutions, approved the reports.

In order to provide a cooling-off period and facilitate a normalization of relations and dialogue between them and the government, the eight professors expressed their willingness to reduce their teaching loads and/or take temporary leaves of absence for research, writing or lecturing abroad, beginning in the fall of 1974. Their major precondition was that the government stop persecuting and jailing their student supporters for "disseminating hostile propaganda." As the regime's persecution of students continued, however, the eight scholars declared at the November 21, 1974, meeting of the Faculty of Philosophy that they could not let their students down nor accept charges of being anti-socialist and anti-self-management, or remain silent in the face of changes in the law infringing university autonomy and self-management, and endangering freedom of research and inquiry. They would, hence, continue teaching.[17]

The League of Communists of Yugoslavia responded: *Komunist,* the League's theoretical organ, launched in January 1975 renewed attacks on the "Eight" for their activities which were allegedly "contrary to the essential principles of Marxism, to the ideological and political foundations of the League and to the self-governing society."[18] On January 28, 1975, the Serbian Parliament, utilizing the new law, dismissed the professors from their teaching posts. They were supposed to remain free to engage in research at other institutions and/or to retire, while continuing to draw salaries until they found alternative employment.[19] It was an indication of how far Titoist Yugoslavia had evolved from the Stalinist prototype of a police state toward a more humane, liberal, and democratic system of socialist humanism. But, especially since 1971, this humanism increasingly meant democracy, freedom, and basic human rights only for those the party considers Marxist.

The "Belgrade Eight" appealed in vain to the Constitutional Court of Yugoslavia on July 3, 1975, through their lawyer Srdja Popović. The Court rejected their appeal at the end of May 1977. Popović himself was sentenced to one year of imprisonment on March 10, 1976, for spreading "hostile propaganda," since he agreed with the views of one of his previous clients, the poet Dragoljub Ignjatović, at an earlier trial in April 1974. Ignjatović's sentence for a critical paper delivered at the last Winter Philosophical Meeting of February 1974, at Divčibare, was suspended by the Serbian Presidium in September 1975. Yet, his lawyer, Popović, whose sentence was suspended on May 26, 1976, was still barred for one year from practicing law.[20] This, of course, makes a shambles of Yugoslavia's advance toward socialist or any other kind of legality, let alone a *Rechtsstaat* or socialist humanism. In early 1976, the International League for Human Rights circulated a petition among members of the American Bar Association, addressed to Tito, and defending Popović's constitutional right to express his opinion.

As to the avant-garde's major journals, all copies of issue 1-2, 1974, of *Filosofija,* containing the proceedings of the 1974 Winter Philosophical Meeting, were seized by the police without any warrant or court procedure at the publisher, before their release to the public. In February 1975, *Praxis* was also forced to close. The editorial board of *Praxis,* given the ultimatum radically to alter or abandon the periodical, chose to close it.[21] The 1975 and 1976 Korčula Summer Schools with the theme "Socialism and Human Rights" were banned. So was the February 1975 annual meeting of the Yugoslav Sociological Association, scheduled for Opatija, because two of the papers were by Marković and Pešić-Golubović.

The case of the "Belgrade Eight" set the precedent for the regime's crackdown on intellectuals both in and out of academia. The government pressed similar drives at other institutions of higher learning, notably at Ljubljana University in Slovenia, the University of Sarajevo in Bosnia-Hercegovina and, more delicately, at the University of Zagreb, in Croatia. According to Rudi Supek's Presidential letter of February 20, 1976, to members of the Yugoslav Sociological Association, besides the eight professors at Belgrade, under attack were also four at Ljubljana—V.

Arzenšek, T. Hribar, J. Jerovšek and V. Rus—, two at Sarajevo—B. Jakšić and Esad Čimić—, and another six along with M. Djurić at the Faculty of Law in Belgrade. But the party's witch hunt for Marxist class enemies appeared to be much wider, encompassing *Praxis*-sympathizers and others as well. The regime's aim seemed to be, in Supek's view, no less than the "elimination of a particular Marxist orientation from our society."[22]

The regime's mounting campaign against avant-garde Marxist scholars and intellectuals in general focused on banishing this embarrassing conglomeration of home-grown critics from all public media. In their Appeal of October 20, 1975, to the Presidium of the Socialist Republic of Serbia, the "Belgrade Eight" complained of "systematic violation of our civil and academic rights."[23] Among them: Confiscation of passports in 1972 from Životić and Indjić; discontinuation of publications by avant-garde theorists such as the banning of high school textbooks in *Logic* by Marković and *History of Philosophy* by Životić; withholding from sale of Golubović's book *Man and His World* published in 1973 by Prosveta, and failure of the Zagreb publishing house Naprijed to print her *Family as a Human Community*; attack by political forums and the press on the same publisher for merely intending to publish Tadić's *Philosophy of Right,* and another publisher Liber for planning to print his *Authority and Contestation,* written in 1972. Marković's book *Preispitivanja (Reassessments)* was banned outright on November 15, 1972, by the Belgrade District Court because of a chapter which contained "false and distorted arguments causing alarm among the population."[24] By December 1975, the same fate awaited Čimić's *Man at the Crossroads,* whose author was dismissed from the Faculty of Philosophy at the University of Sarajevo.[25] Further, no Yugoslav publisher dared print Stojanović's *History and Party Consciousness.* And Liber probably regretted publishing Predrag Vranicki's *Marxism and Socialism,* which drew an official protest from the Soviet ambassador to Belgrade. Even during the "liberal" 1960s, such protest led to the censure of publishers and/or dismissal of journal editors, a ban on publications, and imprisonment of their authors—as in the case of Mihajlov's *Moscow Summer.* For the same reason, Djilas was imprisoned the second time, although his *Conversations With Stalin* never appeared in Yugoslavia. And the blacklist goes on, encompassing radio, television, and public appearances by avant-garde theorists in general.

In December 1975, Tadić, Životić and Mićunović were fired also from the Institute for the Study of the International Labor Movement in Belgrade. With that, it appeared that the only place remaining in Yugoslavia where *Praxis* theorists could possibly be active professionally was the Inter-University Center for Post-Graduate Studies in Dubrovnik. Although the Center boasts some 83 member institutions from all over the world, it is formally still considered to be an extension of the University of Zagreb. This provided Yugoslav authorities with a new avenue via an ultimatum from the Federation of Yugoslav Universities to exclude from the Center's activities all scholars who are barred from teaching in other Yugoslav universities.[26] The move was clearly aimed at all the ousted *Praxis* Marxists, whose ranks may still be swelling. On January 12, 1978, ten *Praxis* Marxists—Supek, Petrović, Životić, Golubović, Ćosić, Popov, Stojanović, Mićunović, Tadić and Marković—petitioned the SFRY Presidency and the Federal Assembly to lift the requirement of "moral-political suitability" as a prerequisite for employment in the public sphere. They complained that more than 30 scholars lost their jobs due to this purely bureaucratic criterion, and reminded the authorities that the 1975 Helsinki Accords prohibited discrimination on the basis of political beliefs.[27]

Paradoxically, even the avant-garde has fallen victim to Finlandization. Forced to earn a living to survive, Indjić recanted and left the "Belgrade Eight." Other avant-garde theorists fell silent or retreated into safe havens of non-controversial themes, waiting for a change in the political climate. Yet, the avant-garde may be "waiting for Godot," since one of the first actions of the post-Tito "collective leadership" was to renew Tito's warning to all dissenters in general and independent Marxist thinkers in particular. To this effect, the party rammed legislation through the Serbian Parliament amending the Law on Higher Education once more in June 1980, which confronted the remaining "Belgrade Seven" with an ultimatum to find new employment, retire, or lose their salaries.[28]   By January 1981, all seven professors were formally dismissed from the University of Belgrade.

Some, like Marković, even began to reconsider their basic philosophical stance. By 1979, Marković rewrote the first section of his 1976 assessment of Marxist philosophy in Yugoslavia, cautioning that Marxist humanist thought might turn into "a dead end track of a shallow, sentimental, commonsense humanism."[29]   Should avant-garde theorists confirm Marković's hypothesis, they will have repudiated not only the humanist content of their philosophical critique, but also their freedom of thought and personal dignity.   In justification of his new orientation, Marković advances the conception of the critically minded intellectual, who "wisely recognizes imposed limits and moves as close to them as possible, but always moves within them in all his public activities."[30]   But this conception only begs the question: what distinguishes such a critically minded intellectual from an apologist?   And how can there be genuine socialist enlightenment and universal human emancipation via a cultural revolution—advocated by Marković, Bahro, Marcuse, and others—when socialist educators themselves evade the truth?   Such ethical antinomies of revolutionary existence—articulated by Stojanović and Supek—find an echo in Djilas' lament that:

> One cannot be a Communist and preserve an iota of one's personal integrity! . . . it is only a question of time before you are asked to prostrate yourself before the Party and castrate your conscience.[31]

3.   A Revolution Within the Revolution?

The drastic action against the "Belgrade Eight" and other avant-garde theorists, preceded by a long build-up, took place within the context of a vigorous regime suppression of all dissent in Yugoslavia, regardless of its orientation.   It was parallel somewhat to similar actions elsewhere in Eastern Europe and the Soviet Union.[32]   In Yugoslavia, there was the second trial and conviction of ex-Professor Mihajlov on charges of spreading "hostile propaganda."   This time, for publishing abroad assertions about lack of freedom of speech and thought, continuing one-party dictatorship, and a return to Stalinism in Yugoslavia.   Even more intense was the crackdown on a kaleidoscope of diverse ethnic/nationalist individuals and groups, particularly Croats, Albanians and Montenegrins, on charges ranging from ethnic separatism to alleged plotting to form a rival communist party with links to Moscow.[33]   All this followed on the heels of the purge of government and party leaders accused of Croatian separatism in 1971-72, and the increasing disorganization, confusion, and even disintegration of both the party and the federal and republic governmental machineries.

This state of affairs prompted the decisive action by the aging Marshal himself.   As succession to Tito loomed ever larger as *the* problem on the Yugoslav political horizon, the regime perceived the need to streamline and centralize governmental functions and reassert the leading ideological-political role of the party.   The goal was: national unity and socialism.   The means were: institutional pluralization and ideological re-Stalinization.   The two major threats to the stability of the Yugoslav system—national separatism and potential Soviet intervention—were to be fought with a re-centralized party and absolute unity of thought and action.   But the vexing question remains: will this policy prevent a break-up of Yugoslavia along national/ethnic lines and hold back Soviet imperialism now that Tito has left the scene?

The party finds itself in an unenviable position as it faces monumental and often contradictory tasks of acting as a unifying force for the diverse republic, regional, economic, and other interests while promoting economic and political decentralization with decision-making expected to revolve increasingly on self-managing units within organizations of associated labor, local communities, communes, and communities of interest.   This contradiction is exacerbated by political and economic realities which include party disorientation and national divisions, massive unemployment (worsened by the return of Yugoslav migrant workers from abroad), persistent inflation, speculation (especially in the import-export and labor-for-export sectors), general as well as regional underdevelopment, misuse of public funds, bureaucratic mismanagement, privileges, and personal enrichment tied to a variety of socio-economic and political factors.

The serious challenges of economic and political development faced by the party are overshadowed by an even more complex *human* challenge: how to realize the goals of the socialist revolution not only as a political and economic reorganization of society, but also as a revolution in man himself and in human relationships. This dilemma has bedevilled philosophers, theologians, and statesmen alike since time immemorial. Indeed, it is the central challenge of which the avant-garde Marxist humanist philosophers and sociologists constantly remind the party, to which many of them belong(ed). How is it possible, then, that the party found it necessary to silence its most revolutionary and creative interpreters of Marxist-Leninist teachings? What has contributed to the present Kafkaesque situation in Yugoslavia in which Marxist *slogans* are everywhere, but creative Marxist *thinking* is banned from self-managing universities in a socialist country?

The major formal charge against the avant-garde Marxist philosophers, apart from corrupting and misleading the youth (Socrates *redivivus*?), is that they challenged the leading role of the party and, by implication, the class nature of contemporary socialist development, and thus opened the door to "bourgeois" ideas and counterrevolution.[34] According to Kardelj, the New Left in Yugoslavia is characterized by its lack of faith in the working class, denial of the party's leading role and of all institutions as bureaucratic and manipulative, elitism, and monopoly in deciding on the theory and goals of the socialist movement.[35]

In their critique of liberalism since Djilas, Dragan Marković and Savo Kržavac berate the illusions of the ultra-left as right-wing revisionism favoring nationalism, Trotskyism, and anarchism. But they reserve special ire for Vojin Milić as an "anti-Marxist"; for Stojanović's characterization of the LCY as a party of the Stalinist type; and for Nebojša Popov's claim that Stalinism is a general trait of socialism. Nor do the ideas of other avant-garde theorists fare any better in the Marković-Kržavac dossier on the New Left, which concludes with lengthy citations from Kardelj's *Directions of Development of the Political System of Socialist Self-Management* on extreme left-wing radicalism.[36]

Significantly, party ideologues have accused avant-garde theorists for their Copernican revolution in Marxism. Thus, Živojin D. Denić argues that Yugoslav philosophers developed a theoretical orientation based on man as a "private property-owner," who interacts with society as an individual unit.[37] He takes special displeasure with Petrović's notion of permanent human alienation; Korać's emphasis on the individual, rather than society; Marković's metaphysics and subjective idealism; and Vojan Rus' "eternal individual." Denić concludes that Yugoslav philosophers merely repeat the speculative thought of German philosophers exposed by Marx, the "scientist."[38]

A more balanced assessment of Marxist humanist thought is that by Miloje Petrović, who considers the philosophical critique of Stalinism as a measure of the contradictions inherent in contemporary socialism. He admits that the Yugoslav philosophical critique has contributed a good deal toward the destruction of Stalinism. However, Petrović finds both major currents of avant-garde critique based on the early Marx and Engels-Lenin, respectively, wanting. In his view, both critiques end up as sectarian in the philosophical and political sense.[39]

But how are these charges to be reconciled with the avant-garde's insistence expressed as early as the first issue of *Praxis* that a critical stance is the hallmark of all genuine philosophy and that no one should have a monopoly in the sphere of social critique?[40] And what about the Marxist humanists' thesis regarding the need for a unifying force in society? Even Milan Kangrga's disputed and banned article on the rise of a new Yugoslav middle class admitted that:

Only a communist movement in our country (in our case the League of Communists of Yugoslavia) which leans first of all on the working class and the Marxist (left) intelligentsia can be the carrier, guarantor, and executor of the socialist revolution, the principle of self-management, and thus also of the solution to the questions of nationalities and classes . . . .[41]

The original sin of avant-garde Yugoslav Marxist philosophers seems to be, rather, that they embarked on a reexamination of Marxist-Leninist teachings independently of party tutelage. This, in itself, could not have irked the party since its leading ideologues like Kardelj admit that the dialectic is "untutored."[42] However, the avant-garde has, in addition, been transforming Marxism-Leninism from a set of eternal and unchanging truths—or ideology—into a critical philosophy in the classic sense. In the avant-garde's vision, Marxism emerged as a method of critique of all existing social conditions which limit human freedom and development whether in capitalism, state capitalism (Stalinism), or socialism (communism).

The avant-garde thus became society's critical conscience, pointing continuously to the discrepancies between the reality of socialist practice and the futurist project of a classless, free community of equal and free men immanent in Marxist theory. The avant-garde's chief contribution has been their insistence on a *humanist* revolution within the *socialist* revolution. The aim of the humanist revolution, which they interpret as the heart of the socialist revolution, is the realization not only of political and economic development, but a profound change in the very consciousness of man and a radical humanization of social relationships at whose center is the free, creative, and self-actualizing human individual. Thus, Danilo Pejović notes that:

> A revolution in human relations and a turnabout in man himself are . . . the goals of socialism, not [merely] the build-up of the productive forces.[43]

Avant-garde theorists thus reached the conclusion that the ultimate goal of history is not simply socialism or communism, but humanism or a truly *human* society in which the liberated individual is socialized and society individualized:

> Socialism is . . . not Marx's ultimate aim but an approximation. His ultimate aim is *human* society; society in which dehumanization ceases, human labor is truly emancipated, and man has all the conditions necessary to his development and self-affirmation.[44]

Surprisingly, these are also precisely the goals which the party has repeatedly claimed as its own in charting the country's future. Such ideals were reflected in the resolutions adopted at the Tenth and Eleventh Party Congresses.

The tragic confrontation between the avant-garde and the party hinges on the central issue of who is to be the authoritative interpreter of Marxist-Leninist scripture. The avant-garde's transformation of Marxist-Leninist doctrine into a method of critique, a process, resulted in an *open-ended* Marxism critical of all absolute statements and final truths. As Gajo Petrović remarks, the most important of Marx's theses is that there are no unchallengeable theses, since man is a being of *praxis*, a free, creative being whose future is open.[45] The party, on the other hand, needs a *closed* Marxism of definitive, authoritative statements as the basis for its socio-political programs. The avant-garde's conception of the Promethean function of Marxist philosophy as a radical critique of all existing social conditions which limit the all-round development of the human individual clashes with the party's need for a specific action program to deal with complex problems in everyday life. It is the classic tension between the man of thought and the man of action. Ralph Pervan concludes that the *Praxis* Marxists were punished as convenient scapegoats for challenging not only the party leadership's prerogative of final authority, but also its claim that "the problems faced were only of a secondary nature and did not reflect on the efficacy of the system as a whole."[46]

4.   Class Struggle or Human Struggle?

By suppressing its most creative interpreters of Marxism-Leninism, the party seems to have achieved a Pyrrhic victory. It may have bartered away the soul of Marxism in the hope of preserving the body politic—a socialist version of Mission Impossible? The Faustian dynamic of its action is enhanced by the fact that both the avant-garde Marxist humanists and the party are, in reality, victims of the generic paradoxes inherent in the dogmatic, totalitarian, anti-humanist components of their common *Weltanschauung*. Thus, the party accuses its avant-garde theorists of attempting to monopolize the interpretation of Marxism-Leninism and erect a "new" or "critical dogmatism."[47] Yet, it is the avant-garde, not the party, which has been banned from public discourse.

Conspicuously, the avant-garde and the party set up their confrontation by continuing to see the world through Marx's distorted glasses through which all human and societal problems have a common root cause: the alienation in the sphere of economics and politics, as well as the class nature and origin of conflict. There is an intriguing parallel between Marx and Freud. Wherever Freud looked, he saw sex and the Œdipus complex.   And everywhere Marx looked, he saw exploitation, alienation, and conflict.   Indeed, Friedrich A.   Hayek calls the twentieth century an "age of superstition," drawing its inspiration from Marx and Freud.[48]   The accusations between the avant-garde and the party display a strange symmetry, too.   The party accuses the avant-garde of being the "ideological-theoretical 'elite' of the right" and the precursor of bourgeois class society.[49]   The avant-garde, in turn, presses an equally obtuse charge that the party has joined the nascent middle class, bureaucracies, and technocracies to form new centers of alienated economic and political power, and that self-management is impossible unless the party "withers away."[50]   And, following the utopian tradition, both the avant-garde and the party call for the abolition of power, instead of its institutionalization, dispersion, and limitation.

Hence, the party and the avant-garde are, in an important sense, equally responsible for reopening the central question of the unity of theory and practice in socialism.   Nowhere is the socialist dilemma more apparent than in the quixotic confrontation of self-management and direct participatory democracy with institutionalization and bureaucratization.   The dilemmas engendered by this confrontation, popular among the New Left both East and West, are not only abstract, but guarantee a largely artificial, insoluble, and constant tension between socialist ideals (theory) and their implementation (practice).   Veljko Rus is a rare avant-garde theorist aware of the fact that:

> . . . radical criticism of everything which exists was dogmatic in
> the sense that it had never attempted a "revision" of fundamental
> values in the name of practice but rather merely emphasized the
> fact that social practice is far removed from proclaimed ideals.[51]

Utopia's dilemma is compounded by another factor. And that is that both the party and the avant-garde wield master symbols such as bureaucracy, class, revolution, and self-management on the highly abstracted level of revolutionary rhetoric which is in sharp contrast to the country's largely evolutionary and reformist practice.   This phenomenon prompted eminent social democrats like Bernstein to remark that socialists would make much more headway if they could only find the courage to emancipate themselves from an outworn phraseology and would concentrate instead on democratic practice.[52]   Contrary to his detractors from all shades of the philosophical-political spectrum, Bernstein's emphasis on social practice never entailed the abandonment of either socialist ideals or democratic principles.   Indeed, his chief contribution was the inimitable welding together of the two sets of ideals in the fire of everyday social practice.   It is another issue whether socialist ideals or practices are adequate to a resolution of the major dilemmas confronting mankind in the latter part of the twentieth century.

Significantly, individual Marxist thinkers in Yugoslavia have come to question key master symbols like the universally derogatory analyses of bureaucracy. Bureaucracy has served as a whipping boy, if not a *bête noire*, for both party and avant-garde Marxist humanist theoreticians. It is, hence, refreshing and highly original for Dobrica Ćosić to point out that:

> There are obvious reasons for no longer blaming all the evils of socialism on the existence of bureaucracy as such, nor can that bureaucracy be simply explained and deduced in a doctrinaire or ideological way from the political nature of power to be shown as tyranny over the people in order to pocket the profits.[53]

The party's suppression of its intellectual avant-garde brings into serious question also the major postulate of socialism regarding the simultaneous liberation of the individual and society. It is becoming increasingly clear to some among the avant-garde that economic democracy presupposes political democracy. Also, that abstract (formal or negative) freedom is a prerequisite for realized (positive) freedom. In Pejović's view, human and civil rights are not merely "bourgeois phrases" which conceal the "exploitation of the proletariat." Rather, they are fundamental preconditions for a truly democratic socialist society.[54] According to Pešić-Golubović, former Director of the Institute for Sociological Research at Belgrade University and the female member of the ousted "Belgrade Eight:"

> ... the question of civil liberties is still topical in socialist societies today, and when this question is posed it is not because it ends the struggle for human emancipation, but because this struggle *cannot even begin* without it.[55]

The world is still waiting for the historical *novum*. One does not have to be either a socialist or communist to favor the realization of such socialist ideals as self-fulfillment and the all-round development of each individual within a context of humanized social relationships. Yet, the Marxist promise of fulfilled human beings, equality, liberty, and fraternity, as well as realized economic, political, and social freedoms remains thus far largely an unrealized goal and challenge. The party's treatment of its own avant-garde is the clearest indication that socialism is incompatible with freedom. It demonstrates that socialism, even in its liberalized Yugoslav variant, has not only not surpassed the so-called formal freedoms of "bourgeois," capitalist, class societies, but has not yet even attained to them. Perhaps, to reformulate Marx, socialism and communism are inherently primitive. Hayek notes that the Rousseauan nostalgia for a primitive community based on visible "social justice," which is gratifying to people's natural emotions, leads necessarily to totalitarianism and a closed society. In his critique of the "master thinkers," André Glucksmann reproaches Marx for "the cult of the total and final Revolution, of the State that terrorizes for the good of the collectivity, and of Social Science that permits the masses to be guided in spite of themselves."[56]

The central problem of freedom, the Achilles' heel of socialism and communism, is summed up in the poignant question addressed to the Faculty of Philosophy by the "Belgrade Eight," following their suspension:

> As Marxist philosophers and social scientists, we have *critically* and *publicly* discussed serious problems of the contemporary world, including our own society. What kind of Marxist movement and socialism is it when freedom of speech and criticism is denied even to Marxists themselves, and when at any moment such acts may be persecuted as criminal acts?![57]

The formation of an International Committee of Concern for Academic Freedom in Yugoslavia and the numerous letters of protest to Yugoslav authorities from scholars, writers, intellectuals, scientists, and concerned laymen from all over the world underscore the fundamental nature and scope of the human challenge of free thought and freedom of scientific inquiry. Nevertheless, the Yugoslav regime stepped up its efforts to silence once and for all its own Marxist intelligentsia dedicated to national unity and the further democratization, liberalization, and humanization of its self-managing socialist system. Only Prometheus himself could have felt a greater pain as he spoke about his fate:

> You see me a wretched God in chains, the enemy of Zeus, hated of all the Gods that enter Zeus's palace hall, because of my excessive love for Man.[58]

5. Humanism, Freedom, and Tolerance

As we concluded in Chapter IX, avant-garde Yugoslav Marxist humanist thought is likely to go down in history as an attempt to revive the Promethean function of Marxist philosophy as a radical critique and critical conscience of a highly institutionalized world. Prometheus is the classic symbol of man's rebellion against the gods and, by extension, against the uncontrolled forces of both nature (*physis*) and civilization (*nomos*). As Marx remarked in the Preface to his doctoral dissertation: "Prometheus is the foremost saint and martyr in the philosopher's calendar."[59] Yet, in the third part of Aeschylus' trilogy, lost to posterity, there is a reconciliation between Zeus and Prometheus, who come to terms by maturing in time.

Similarly, the avant-garde's radical reconstruction of the Marxist-Leninist intellectual heritage is both a rebellion and a reconciliation. It is a rebellion against all those inhuman and unnatural conditions which dehumanize man and render his existence in Hobbes' immortal words "solitary, poor, nasty, brutish, and short." Or, as Marx once exclaimed: "Wretched dogs! They want to treat you like men!"[60] It is a reconciliation as well, since the avant-garde's new philosophical orientation with its humanist paradigm appears as a vehicle for promoting dialogue and understanding within their own society as well as possibly bridging ideological gaps between civilizations.

The silencing of avant-garde Marxist humanists, these "last Mohicans" of creative Marxist thought in the communist world,[61] represents a distinct loss to both East and West, communists and democrats, philosophers and statesmen, theologians, scientists, and laymen. This is not because their vision or findings were faultless. They never made such a claim. Rather, it is because their genuine concern, moral stance, and affirmation of human dignity, ethical values, dialogue, and openness contributed to a genuine renaissance of both Marxist and humanist thought. Even their "abstract humanism" and heady utopianism grew out of their concern for humanness and a better future for the species commonly known as *homo sapiens.* Their crime and the crown of their achievement could also be summed up in Prometheus' utterance: "I dared."[62] They dared to affirm the openness and the value of the human individual. How could anyone ask for more; or less?

Crucially, the avant-garde's emphasis on the need to integrate means and ends and to question all unchallengeable truths and final solutions is in the best of the humanist tradition. Indeed, they were dealing with both aspects of the human dilemma which the late Jacob Bronowski summarized this way:

> One is the belief that the end justifies the means. That push-button philosophy, the deliberate deafness to suffering, has become the monster in the war machine. The other is the betrayal of the human spirit; the assertion of dogma that closes the mind and turns a nation, a civilization, into a regiment of ghosts—obedient ghosts or tortured ghosts.[63]

Avant-garde Marxist humanists confronted our joint enemy, whether East or West, North or South: the lack of tolerance and openness and the tendency to absolutize one's position and turn it into ideology and dogma. But the avant-garde's tragic role in this classical Greek drama may be eclipsed by that of the party itself which appears as the ultimate victim, spellbound by Stalin's ghost. How could the League of Communists revert to Stalinism when it had declared boldly as early as 1958 that:

> Marxism is not a doctrine established forever or a system of dogmas. Marxism is a theory of the social process which develops through successive historic phases. Marxism, therefore, implies a creative application of the theory and its further development, primarily by drawing general conclusions from the practice of socialist development and through attainments of scientific thinking of mankind.[64]

This leads to the conclusion that both the party and its avant-garde stand before an epochal task: to confront their common enemy in the dogmatic, totalitarian, and anti-humanist *a priori* notions constituting Marxism's generic paradoxes. It is these *a priori* notions, along with the dialectic, which make the fatal relapse into Stalinism in theory and practice almost unavoidable. Even avant-garde theorists themselves labor in the shadow of Stalinism. And, were one to conjecture, if the avant-garde ever came to power, they would most likely traverse the same practical, if not theoretical, terrain as the party. In Ljubo Sirc's view, the paradox of the New Left theorists centers on the fact that "given a chance they would try yet again to abolish reality."[65]

On the brighter side, it seems that at times both the avant-garde Marxist philosophers and the party forget that while philosophies, as Camus noted, may define a way of thinking, the point is—to live. The human dilemma is reflected in the fact that we all too often lose sight of the fundamental humanist creed, articulated so well by Danko Grlić that:

> Man does not exist for the sake of an idea, social system, and order, but rather all these derive their value only and exclusively from truly serving the human being.[66]

Perhaps the fact of simply being *human* constitutes today the most radical and revolutionary stance in a world of reified institutions, doomsday weapons, and ideological dogmas, adding their alienations to those of both man and nature.

6.   Phoenix: The Avant-Garde and Popular Culture

It is possible that the only future for the avant-garde Yugoslav Marxist humanists may, indeed, be their past. Yet, their ideas show promise of surviving in party programs as well as in high and popular culture, although their relationship is anything but simple and uncontroversial.

In order to understand this relationship, one needs to recall first of all that there is no such thing in Yugoslavia as a single "popular culture," or "high culture," for that matter. There is, rather, a bewildering variety or mosaic of popular and high cultures and sub-cultures in a land of six constituent republics, five South Slav nationalities (along with numerous minorities), four official languages, three major religions, and two alphabets, all trying to get along in one state. Yugoslavia can for these and other reasons be called, not altogether inappropriately, a land of one thousand popular (sub-)cultures.

This rich variety of popular cultures in Yugoslavia has been exposed to three major influences: (1) the communist party; (2) the intellectual community, notably the avant-garde; and (3) Western liberal tradition and ideas. Each of these three powerful agents of change has had a significant impact on the original popular culture(s). In sum, the party has attempted to *socialize* popular culture, the avant-garde to *humanize* it, and Western influence to *modernize* and *liberalize* it in the Weberian sense, while the folks back home are just trying to enjoy it.

The party sees its role relative to culture in a similar light as its role toward society as a whole: that of the leading ideological-political force whose task is to harness popular science, education, and culture in the service of building the classless self-managing socialist society.[67] Popular culture, in other words, has to contribute to the formation of the new socialist man living in a de-alienated community of freely associated producers. Predictably enough, popular culture has not always responded well to this sort of ideological tutelage. The continued party injunctions to popular media, education, and the arts bear out this ubiquitous and multi-faceted tension.[68]

But what about the relationship of the avant-garde to popular culture? Avant-garde Marxist humanist ideas became popular among youth and intellectuals during the 1960s, but their relationship to the wider audience and popular culture remains problematic. The esoteric and complex nature of many avant-garde ideas shielded for a time its proponents from party ideologues and their wrath. At the same time, the often impenetrable, if not metaphysical, contours of their ideas slowed and at times blocked their absorption into popular culture. Paradoxically, it was the third agent, Yugoslav popular contact with Western, primarily European, ideas, technology, culture, social, political, economic, and legal institutions and practices, especially since the opening of the country's frontiers to freer movement in the 1960s, which has influenced the avant-garde as well as helped spread their ideas into the wider popular culture.[69]

There is no mistaking of the essential transformation of Yugoslav society and popular culture in the direction of a more open, modern, industrialized, commercialized, and sceptical society. This obtains in spite of the ideological, political, economic, legal, and cultural streamlining taking place in Yugoslavia since the Croatian crisis in 1971. Nihilism, corruption, egotism, Western "decadence" in the style of dress, work, entertainment, family life, and social habits, and the incipient embourgeoisement and increasing commercialization of society and popular culture alike are decried equally by the party leadership and the avant-garde. If anything, more so by the latter! Yet, the Westernization of indigenous popular cultures and the growth of a more standardized *mass consumption culture* as a second skin over them have been promoted, inadvertently perhaps, by both the party and the avant-garde.

The party insists on industrialization, urbanization, science, technology, productivity, and mass production, and an astonishing flexibility of economic and other means employed, which can be termed "un-socialist." One need only refer to Yugoslavia's *market socialism.* And, to sharpen the dissonance between means and ends, the avant-garde in their attempt to find new theoretical guidelines for socialist practice has emphasized the development of the whole man, including the satisfaction of material needs within a societal framework boasting equality in abundance.

If one of the major characteristics of popular culture is its subversive nature and challenge to the *status quo* and the Establishment,[70] then avant-garde Marxist humanist thought may likely become incorporated into and even transform popular culture. Avant-garde thinking, especially in the form of its critique of Stalinist bureaucracy and state socialism, and in its espousal of direct workers' control and self-management, has already spread beyond the country's borders to other nations in Eastern Europe, the USSR, and the developing Third World. Within Yugoslavia itself, avant-garde thought became the prevailing orientation in culture, the social sciences and humanities, among youth and intellectuals, and has also significantly influenced the party and the larger society.

The chief contribution of avant-garde Marxist humanist thought to a growing socialist humanist popular culture has been its exploration of the phenomenon of man via the esoteric concept of alienation. It is true that popular culture in Yugoslavia is saturated with party slogans about intensification of the "class struggle," establishment of a self-governing society, elimination of special privileges, injustice, poverty, inequality and other pejoratives commonly associated with capitalism and class society; slogans which bear little relationship to reality. But there are also nascent ideas about the liberation, humanization, and full development and realization of each individual within a society of humanized relationships.   Thus, it appears that the avant-garde's single major impact on popular culture, both at home and abroad, may be their rekindling of the inquiring, sceptical, and critical spirit.   This critical spirit corrodes all established final truths and ideological dogmas.   And it enhances the central precondition for the growth and self-realization of each individual human being: the freedom to be you and me.

The concept of culture, particularly that of popular and avant-garde culture, needs to be explored further and differentiated in general and elaborated with greater care within the context of East European nations and the Soviet Union in particular.[71] When comparing socialist cultures, we cannot overlook the fact that Marxism—understood both as theory and practice—is not merely an official ideology, but moreover, a dynamic ideational force which has increasingly permeated the different culture contexts within socialist systems. At the same time, it is the intelligentsia in Russia as well as in Eastern Europe which has traditionally assumed the role of the most articulate spokesman, critic, and co-creator of both high and popular culture.

The many-faceted and dynamic contemporary cultural revival in the socialist systems of Eastern Europe and the Soviet Union presents us with unique opportunities in exploring socialist cultures. This cultural revival reflects an a-political mood born of alienation from the overpoliticized nature of the official culture of socialist realism. It is also a rebellion against the dogmatic and repressive features of bureaucratized Stalinism. The new cultural mood seeks a revival of more liberal, open-ended, Western, non-dogmatic, democratic, and humanist values, both material and spiritual, which promise to enhance individual human lives in the here and now. All this is blended into a sort of existentialist socialist humanism.

The prevailing popular cultural orientation is not, however, one of a "textbook" humanism characterized by scientific precision and dogmatic certainty. It is, rather, a humanism of trial and error in everyday practice in search of man. It is also significant that man in this equation is spelled with a small "m," meaning each individual human being, rather than abstract entities such as Society, State, and Mankind. The full significance of this Copernican revolution in socialist societies, for which the Yugoslav avant-garde has provided the fullest theoretical framework, has yet to be appreciated, East and West. The contemporary cultural revival in Eastern Europe and the Soviet Union is embedded within a deeper transvaluation of values encompassing both Marxist theory and socialist practice. It is dominated by a humanism of trial and error, a quest for openness, and stress on the creative as well as the unabashedly hedonistic aspects in the individual's everyday life.

Poetry, drama, theatre, music, literature, mass consumption, and the like are thus increasingly fulfilling the function of escape mechanisms from the drudgery, drabness, and politicization of everyday life in socialist systems. And this in spite, or even because of, the ideological demands of socialist realism. Culture, in its broadest conceptualization, presents opportunities for a Dionysian celebration of lighter moments of human existence, joy, and laughter. These, too, are in great demand in socialist societies. Finally, forbidden fruits of "decadent" Western culture figure prominently in the popular quest for material enjoyment and spiritual abandon in a socialist version of *la dolce vita.*

This is not to minimize the continuing import of culture in the socialist states as vehicles for regimentation, socialization, and mobilization. Nor is it to deny its Promethean function as a radical critique of all existing social processes and institutions. Or its unique feature as an axiological, linguistic, and historic link between the past, present, and the future. It is merely to point out the most general yet quintessential aspect of culture across time and space as an echo of man's deepest longings, hopes, fears, doubts, struggles, and aspirations. Understood in this context, culture may well emerge as that special medium containing the message that to be immersed in culture in its broadest sense is to be fully human.

Chapter XI · Tito's Legacy and Human Rights

> If socialism fails to contribute to reducing the scope and depth of human alienation, if it fails to represent a gradual "return of man to himself," if it does not bring about such a social system which will allow an increasingly fuller human development and the development of human needs, if it does not liberate the human imagination from centuries of oppression responsible for but a partial utilization of the entire human potential thus far, and if, furthermore, it fails to be a truly open society (not in the sense of open borders, but openness for new ideas), which would encourage human initiative and inventiveness, without any prejudice or fear of novelty, and without fearing freedom—for all of which culture should and can serve best—then socialism will have to be conquered henceforth only by force of arms.
>
> Zagorka Pešić-Golubović, *Čovek i njegov svet* (banned in 1973)

1. Tito's Legacy: Dictator or Philosopher-King?

Tito's passing from the socio-political scene has moved the question of Yugoslavia's future to the center stage of world public attention riveted by the Soviet invasion of Afghanistan in December 1979. What will happen to Yugoslavia now that its founder and champion is no longer at the helm? Will the federation simply fall apart under the pressures of economic crises and national/ethnic separatism? What are the prospects for and consequences of a Soviet invasion of Yugoslavia? And what are the chances for further democratization, liberalization, and respect for basic human rights in post-Tito Yugoslavia? These questions call clearly for an assessment of Tito's legacy.

In 1979, the Yugoslav experiment in self-managing socialism lost its major architect and ideologue, Edvard Kardelj, and, in 1980, its uncontested leader and *deus-ex-machina*, Marshal Josip Broz-Tito. Yugoslavia thus stepped into the post-Tito era. Some believe that the post-Tito era began long before the Marshal's death on May 4. The old man's (Tito's nickname among his closest associates) grip on the country appeared to wane during his final decade in favor of the new Constitution, a re-centralized party, and "collective leadership" in the party and state Presidencies. Following the amputation of his leg, compounded by several other ailments—each by itself sufficient to overcome a much younger man—Tito was incapacitated in January 1980. Soon thereafter, pictures and interviews stopped, leading to the conjecture that Tito may have died long before the official obituary which preceded his 88th birthday and the customary reception of the annual Youth Day relay trophy by mere three weeks.

Indeed, Tito's passing away was as mysterious as his rise to power: from a peasant Croatian boy, a locksmith apprentice, volunteer in the Austro-Hungarian Army, prisoner in Russia and witness of the October Revolution, clandestine Comintern agent sent by Stalin to reorganize the pre-war Yugoslav Communist Party, leader of the communist-dominated National Liberation Front (Partisans) during World War II, bitter foe of all non-communist and anti-communist movements during and after Yugoslavia's civil war, to founder of SFRY, challenger of Stalin, and co-creator of the non-aligned movement. Josip Broz—alias Comrade Walter, Tito, and a dozen other pseudonyms[1]—the rebel who became an uncrowned king,[2] passed into history. But his legend, woven into the rich tapestry of Illyrian folklore in the tradition of Prince Marko, the South Slav rebel and nemesis of the infidel Ottoman invaders in centuries past, remains.

Tito's funeral rivaled that of the world's greatest statesmen. It drew some 100 official foreign delegations and such leaders as Soviet President Leonid Brezhnev, Chinese Premier Hua Guofeng, the British Prime Minister Margaret Thatcher, and the West German Chancellor Helmut Schmidt. Among heads of state of the non-aligned nations were Presidents Sekou Toure of Guinea, Kenneth Kaunda of Zambia, and Julius Nyerere of Tanzania, along with India's Prime Minister Indira Gandhi. From the Arab world came Jordan's King Hussein, Libya's Moammar Kaddafi, and PLO's Yasser Arafat. They were all paying homage to a myth: the myth of the invincible, if not immortal, warrior, hero, father of the people, founder of an independent nation-state, builder of socialism, fighter for freedom, equality, justice, and brotherhood. Tito was eulogized not only by his party colleagues, but by the world community of nations as well. Prime Minister Thatcher called Tito "a great statesman," French President Valery Giscard d'Estaing praised Tito's role as "an international leader who, having preserved the liberty and independence of his country, gave the world the authentic voice of nonalignment," whereas U.N. Secretary-General Kurt Waldheim designated Tito "a true hero . . . the last of the great figures of our times."[3]

Scholars followed the diplomats in their flamboyant appraisal of Tito's personal achievements and legacy. Bogdan Denitch reported that Tito's innovations with respect to the party, governmental institutions, the economy, succession, and non-alignment resulted in "the most open and permissive regime ruled by a Communist party, one in which religious toleration is the norm, and the decentralization of political and economic power has gone further not only than in any other Communist regime, but probably further than in many of the West European polities."[4] Denitch's encomium was seconded by John C. Campbell writing in *Foreign Affairs* about Tito as the "genial father of his country, in time respected by all; world statesman, the last of the giants, genuinely and universally mourned."[5] Campbell's list of Tito's major achievements included the preservation of national independence; unification of the country, separate road to socialism (Titoism); socialist self-management; market socialism; and non-alignment. Campbell concluded that "none, colleague or critic, would question the magnitude of his achievement."[6]

Had Hitler succeeded in his plans of world conquest even partially, and in particular had he developed sufficient cunning to rephrase his national socialism in more universal and, hence, congenial terms (dropping the adjective "national" from socialism), undoubtedly he would have been hailed by many as the world's greatest statesman. Such is the dialectical logic of a Nietzschean *Realpolitik* beyond good and evil. By the same token, had Khrushchev not found it advantageous to his career to expose Stalin's crimes (and the Gulag system of terror, which claimed an estimated 60 million lives in the USSR alone) before a closed session of highest party functionaries at the 20th CPSU Congress in 1956—and had there been no "leaks" of these revelations to the outside world—undoubtedly Stalin would have been regarded by many as a demi-god and savior of humanity. Such are the fruits of ignorance, compounded by censorship and self-censorship. As Solzhenitsyn put it, silence was confidently shaping Russian destiny.

Meanwhile, on April 25, 1980, Momčilo Selić, an unemployed architect and writer, co-editor of the *samizdat* journal *The Clock* (banned in 1979), was sentenced to 7 years imprisonment for "hostile propaganda" for a 6-page essay entitled "Contents," distributed among his friends in the Yugoslav capital. In this stream-of-consciousness essay, Selić reminisces about the darker side of the myth of Tito's legacy. Thus, he notes laconically that Tito as a Comintern agent unified the pre-war CPY using Leninist-Stalinist methods, purging many; that he is responsible for retribution in Serbia during the war, the fratricidal civil war in Montenegro, and heavy losses of manpower in the attack on Kupres and the 4th and 5th Offensives; that Tito's personal safety cost thousands of lives; that in Montenegro communists killed their opponents as early as August 1941, which drove the population to the Chetniks; and that in June 1968 Tito was ready to "unleash the army against the students."[7]

Out of Selić's rambling prose and the more detailed (auto-) biographical volumes by Milovan Djilas such as *Wartime* and his biography of Tito there emerges a portrait of Tito, the CPY, the Partisans and their actions both during and after World War II which contradicts the official Yugoslav historiography as well as the uncritical views of some Western scholars and diplomats. From these and other sources it is possible to sketch the first outlines of a truly objective assessment of Tito and his legacy as a case study in contradictions, marked by traits of a dictator as well as a Philosopher-King.

World War II leader of the Partisan guerrilla movement against foreign occupation and the executioner of General Dragoljub "Draža" Mihailović (who headed the first anti-Nazi resistance in Europe); liberator of his country and the butcher of Bleiburg and Kočevje; father of socialist Yugoslavia and its Gulag; architect, with Kardelj and Djilas, of workers' self-management, market socialism, and totalitarian democracy; Periclean statesman and a communist in Stalin's mold; champion of national independence and the bane of all internal dissent, including nationalism; exponent of inter-party democracy and intra-party monolithism in the communist world; challenger of Soviet hegemony and "Western imperialism"; founder of the non-aligned movement and Russia's Trojan Horse; brilliant politico-military strategist and a coward; proletarian who enjoyed royal splendor; critic of the Stalin-Mao personality cults and a legend in his own time; Philosopher-King and dictator—Tito was a phenomenon stranger than science fiction and as paradoxical as the experiment which bears his name.

2. The Phenomenon Called Tito

As in ancient mythologies and folk epics, Tito's origins and identity remain shrouded in mystery. Even Djilas, one of Tito's closest associates during World War II, knows only that Tito is the same man whom Stalin sent to Yugoslavia in 1937, following the purge of CPY leaders in the USSR. Official Yugoslav historiography has built up the image of Tito as an infallible leader, patriot, warrior, humanist, democrat, and father of the country. Tito's personality cult was only reinforced by his defiance of Stalin in 1948, his prestige as a leader of the non-aligned nations, and crisis management at home, particularly the ouster of the secret police chief and rival, Aleksander Ranković, in 1966. Indeed, Tito's popularity reached such a high point during the "golden age" of liberal reforms, 1966-71, that he might have been elected to his leading role, while the party would have lost a genuine election.

Tito's charisma among party members was based on his leadership qualities during and after the war of "national liberation," enhanced by the messianic nature of the Marxist-Leninist ideology. As Robert C. Tucker notes, times of distress call for a charismatic leader, "one in whom, by virtue of unusual personal qualities, the promise or hope of salvation—deliverance from distress—appears to be embodied."[8] Djilas writes that Tito's cult grew out of his followers' need for personal identity and autonomy, particularly during periods of crisis. Thus, World War II and the civil war set the stage for the phenomenon called Tito. Djilas concludes that an "ideological movement and an insurgent people felt the need for an infallible leader and benign protector."[9]

Tito's cult of personality was built on the need for leadership in times of distress, bolstered by the charisma of a party claiming the exclusive historical mandate to liberate the nation from a foreign oppressor and lead it toward a classless, communist future of equality and brotherhood. The eschatology of a movement and a party were thus fused with the personal eschatology of the infallible leader. Svetozar Stojanović remarks that Stalin's unlimited authority rested on the power of charisma of the Bolshevik party and its *apparat*.[10] But, the Tito, Stalin, Mao, Hitler, and similar cults of the leader were not totally manufactured nor dependent upon organizational structures alone. They were rooted in the popular psyche of man, whom Freud called "a horde animal, an individual creature in a horde led by a chief."[11] In the Yugoslav context in particular, Tito's cult of the hero and deliverer found fertile soil in the Illyrian folklore of the native son as the champion of the common folk against both internal and external enemies.

The problem with Tito's cult and the related notions of party infallibility and the liberation of the country by the Partisans alone is that they constitute an elaborate mythology substituting for a complex reality. More important, the mythology continues to serve as a justification or rationalization for Tito's Gulag archipelago and the suppression of basic human rights. Thus, people are still prosecuted in contemporary Yugoslavia for alleged transgressions during World War II and the civil war, while Yugoslav émigrés are blackmailed, kidnapped, or assassinated. As Djilas observes, communists continue to wage a civil war against society.[12] And the roots of this civil war stretch back to World War II and before.

With regard to Tito, Djilas sketches the portrait of a man of considerable organizational and leadership abilities. But, Djilas' Tito is far from an infallible, fearless leader or superman. Djilas records Tito's failures as a commander such as indecision, lack of professional military skills, contradictory orders, and excessive concern for his personal safety. Tito's retention of troops for the defense of his headquarters and his refusal to leave a cave at Drvar under enemy fire characterize a man of caution, if not cowardice. At any rate, Tito emerges very much a human being, with his share of strengths and weaknesses, and a military commander whose defeats in the First Offensive in the Fall of 1941 reportedly led to his offering to resign.[13] But, Tito's stature as an outstanding statesman and military leader are not diminished by Djilas' realistic portrayal. One need only recall that Pericles, another famous statesman and general, was censured for serious mistakes and even fined by the Athenian Assembly, only to be reelected general once more in 429 B.C. during the Peloponnesian War. Djilas admits that Tito, in spite of all his failings, possessed the rare gift of understanding the true nature of the war: the struggle for a new social order within the war against foreign occupation, secured by transforming guerrilla bands into a regular army.

Even more controversial is the larger picture of Yugoslavia during World War II. According to official Yugoslav historiography, only the communist-led Partisans fought for national liberation, while everyone else collaborated in one way or another with the enemy. In fact, as a Commission of Inquiry reported to the U.S. State Department in 1946, it was Colonel Mihailović, a Royalist officer, who declined to surrender during the German occupation of the country in April 1941, and fled instead to the mountains to organize his Chetniks, the first anti-Nazi resistance movement in Europe.[14] Tito and his Partisans did not fight the occupier until after Hitler's invasion of the USSR on June 22, 1941.

Even today, the communist regime in Yugoslavia accuses Mihailović's Chetniks of collaborating with the enemy, a baseless charge. It is true that some Chetnik guerrilla formations, especially those under Pećanac, and the Ljotić (assassinated in Munich by the Yugoslav secret police in 1974) militia, collaborated with the Germans or otherwise sought various forms of accommodation. But these formations were not under Mihailović's command. On the contrary, Mihailović fought both the Nazis and the communists, the Italians and the Croatian Ustashi. The tragedy of Mihailović consisted in the fact that he lacked understanding of domestic, let alone international politics. A 19th century royal military officer, who pledged allegiance to "God, King and Country," in a century of increasing

cynicism toward such ideals and a situation in which God seemed to be incommun-
icado, the King fled the country, and the country itself disintegrated under foreign
occupation and internal civil war between Croats and Serbs, Ustashi and Chetniks,
communists versus anti-communists, brother against brother, Mihailović offered to
his countrymen the archaic vision of a Greater Serbian Kingdom, appealing to few
among disillusioned Serbs and Montenegrins, and disingenious to other Yugoslav
nationalities. Nominated Minister of War and advanced to the rank of General by
the Royal Yugoslav government-in-exile, Mihailović, "the mountain czar of the
Serbian people,"[15] was executed on July 17, 1946. In 1948, President Truman
awarded Mihailović posthumously the Legion of Merit, the highest U.S. decoration
to a foreigner, for his contributions to the Allied cause during World War II.

During World War II, British and American military missions were sent to both
Tito's and Mihailović's headquarters. Tito persuaded the Allies that his Partisans
fought the Germans more effectively. The Partisans claimed credit for operations
against Germans and Italians conducted by Mihailović and other forces. According
to an American eyewitness, Tito's headquarters produced even fake photographs
showing fraternization between Chetniks and Germans.[16] From September 1943
on, BBC broadcasts to Yugoslavia credited all resistance activity to Tito and the
Partisans, without mentioning Mihailović or the Chetniks, or the fact that the
Germans offered a reward of 100,000 gold Reichsmarks for the capture, dead or
alive, of either Mihailović or Tito. Duncan Wilson recounts that at the summit
meeting in Tehran, December 1943, Churchill, Roosevelt, and Stalin "agreed to
give Tito all possible help."[17]

In the meantime, General Mihailović directed the construction of airstrips at
Pranjani and elsewhere for the evacuation and repatriation of over 500 Allied
airmen—majority American, but also British, French, and Russians shot down in
the S-E European theatre. American transport planes would first drop supplies,
weapons, and ammunition to the Partisans, then pick up American airmen rescued
by Mihailović's Chetniks. In September 1944, the Partisans attacked the Pranjani
airfield with the aid of those American supplies, forcing the withdrawal of
Mihailović's forces and the American rescue mission.[18] Thus, Americans were
already reaping the first bitter fruits of détente. Unswerving, Mihailović built
more airstrips and refused the generous offer by the last American officer
attached to his headquarters to be evacuated to Allied territory. Condemned by
some and worshipped by others, General Mihailović fought and died a patriot.

It is a truism that Mihailović's forces, short on supplies, fighting on multiple
fronts, engaged at various times in accommodation or *de facto* truce with the
Germans. What is taboo in Yugoslavia, however, is the fact corroborated
independently by German documents and Djilas' memoirs, that the Partisans were
involved in accommodations with the Nazis as well. A German memorandum of
March 13, 1943 of a meeting between Lt. General Benignus Dippold, commander of
the German 717th Infantry Division, and three top leaders of the Partisan
movement—Djilas, Dr. Vladimir Velebit, and General Koča Popović—showed that
the two sides agreed to an exchange of prisoners, considered the Chetniks as the
main enemy, and promised joint action against the Allies should they land in
Yugoslavia. It was Hitler who forbade further negotiations with Tito's Partisans.[19]

As to the intensity of the civil war—a war within a war—and World War II in
Yugoslavia, it might suffice to note that few prisoners were taken or kept.
Partisan heroism in battle is counterbalanced by their execution of an estimated
80,000 German POWs and the pogrom against the German and Hungarian minorities
in Yugoslavia after the war.[20] Djilas admits to killing an unarmed German POW
without the slightest apprehension then or now, yet elsewhere praises German
heroism.[21] It will probably never be known which of the principal combatants in
Yugoslavia killed more people during the course of the Second World War, 1941-45.
Was it the Nazi SS commanders, who took Hitler's "Nacht und Nebel" punitive
measures against the Slav population literally by taking entire villages and shooting
one and all, following the infernal ratio: 50 villagers for each German wounded,
100 for each German soldier killed in that area? Was it the Croatian Ustashi, who
vented their centuries-long pent-up anger against all oppressors, domestic and

foreign, by setting the torch to entire Serbian villages? In Dr. Franjo Tudjman's estimate, some 60,000 people of various nationalities, including Croats, Serbs, Jews, and Gypsies, perished in the prisons of the Independent State of Croatia.[22] Was it the Serbian Chetniks, who retaliated in kind for the Ustashi terror and swept through the Croatian villages, in addition to fighting the Nazis, Italians, and the communists? Or, was it the communist-led and dominated Partisans, who killed indiscriminately all unwilling to fight under their command aginst the Ustashi, Chetniks, Nazis, Italians, and whomever else the party leadership considered undesirable? Andreas Graf Razumofsky cites Kardelj's letter of August 2, 1941 ordering political commissars to stir up hatred between Croatian and Serbian villages in order to incite conflict, attacks on fascist soldiers, and German reprisals.[23] The distraught villagers would then most likely take to the hills and join the Partisans, whose all-Yugoslav ideological orientation appealed to all nationalities. Djilas admits that Pijade and Pekić, top party functionaries, set fire to the village of Žabljak in order to deny it to the Chetniks as a stronghold.[24] After the war, the communists shot the entire Hungarian minority population of Žabljak.[25]

The fanaticism of revolution and the ruthlessness of civil war were thus juxtaposed to the hysteria of a World War. The result: some two million people, including 300,000 Partisans, perished in the Yugoslav holocaust during and after World War II. Each combatant blames the other(s) for the most eggregrious crimes, not without good reason. Only the victims—and God knows there were many—are silent. The inhumanity and futility of all ultimate revolutions, civil and world wars find an echo in the banned *samizdat* play by Matija Bećković and Dušan Radović—a wry satire of the Ché Guevara mystique of Revolution:

> Do you hear? No! Listen!... The dead complain...Those below ... I don't hear a thing ... But you can hear it ... Yes, they shout and protest! Again?... What do they want? They are dissatisfied ... What are they dissatisfied with? Their death? No, our life ... They offer countless observations ... They say that this isn't it ... They inquire: why did they perish?[26]

History books do not record dialogues with the dead. And they seldom record dialogues among the living, which fail to conform to conventional norms. Yet, the situation in Yugoslavia during the war was anything but conventional. How is one to explain such phenomena as that which occurred on September 14, 1941, when a German punitive tank detachment sent to raze a Serbian village to the ground for Partisan activity in the area, reneged on its task, since a hundred villagers on horseback with white flags offered their lives in exchange for the village? The unarmed horsemen promised that if the Germans kept out of their village, the villagers themselves would keep the Partisans away.[27] Those "reactionary" peasants: typical of peasants anywhere, they merely wanted to be left alone. And we are left to ponder Lenin's afterthought that:

> History generally, and the history of revolutions in particular, is always richer in content, more varied, more many-sided, more lively and "subtle" than even the best parties and the most class-conscious vanguards of the most advanced classes imagine.[28]

There is little doubt that history will survive and prosper. The prospect for man, on the other hand, remains an open question. Should man survive, even revolutions might have a future.

3.   Tito's Gulag Archipelago, 1945-1956

The war ended, but the hatred of the victors over the vanquished did not. Russian troops aided Tito's Partisans to liberate Belgrade. Even card-carrying

Yugoslav communists, including Djilas, had difficulty justifying the widespread looting and raping by the Red Army. Again, not all Russian officers and men behaved like the common criminals, whom Stalin let out of jails to bolster the sagging morale of his forces, just as Hitler threw German youth and old men into the juggernaut toward the end. Russian attrocities on Yugoslav soil are well known; those of the Partisans are not.

Nicholas Bethell and Nikolai Tolstoy drew the world's attention to the epochal tragedy of forced repatriation by the Allies of some two million anti-Soviet Russians, Cossacks, and others, whom Solzhenitsyn found languishing in Stalin's camps after World War II.[29] Tito's Gulag archipelago opened with the forced repatriation of some 250,000 anti-communist fighters and civilians by the British Military Command in May-June, 1945. Djilas, who is aware of only 20,000-40,000 victims, admits that it was foolish for the British to return all those peasants, along with Ustashi, Chetniks, Croatian and Slovenian home guards, and others, just as it was wrong for the Partisans to shoot them all.[30]

Based on eyewitness accounts, Bor. M. Karapandzich details the monumental tragedy of anti-communist forces who surrendered to the British in Austria, only to be disarmed and handed over for execution by the Partisans. Serbian volunteers, Slovenian home-guardsmen, Serbian and Montenegrin Chetniks, and the entire Croatian army of some 200,000, plus civilians, were turned over to Tito's executioners.[31] Some Croats who surrendered at Bleiburg, Austria, were executed on the spot, others were transported to places in Slovenia and killed, yet others were decimated on forced marches through Yugoslavia. The lucky survivors of the death march, like Captain Joseph Hećimović, were used and abused in various prisons and forced labor camps. Hećimović witnessed the disappearance of German and Croatian POWs in the Fall of 1945, but survived miraculously till his amnesty in 1955.[32] Among the survivors of the communist inferno unknown to the general public and even to many party members, Tito earned the accolade of the butcher of Bleiburg and Kočevje.

But the communist genocide in Yugoslavia—relatively minor in comparison to USSR, China, or Cambodia—was only the opening salvo of a new civil war and the ground-breaking for the establishment of Tito's Gulag system of terror. Half-crazed from suffering, lust for revenge, and greed, the Partisans opened their campaign to punish all "class enemies," settling personal and ideological scores at once. All those who did not join the Partisans were automatically suspect. People of all nationalities, beliefs, political or non-political orientations, were taken away at night, interned, questioned, expropriated, abused, trucked away at night and shot. The lucky ones, like R. Oraški, were sentenced to 15 years of imprisonment. Oraški testifies that all villagers of Žabljak were shot, as were German POWs as late as March 1950.[33] The Gulag archipelago was metastasizing in Yugoslav society.

Following the Marxist-Leninist blueprint of eliminating all real or potential enemies and alternative sources of authority, Tito moved against his major military-political rival, General Mihailović, who was trapped, sentenced to death by a kangaroo court, and executed. Next came the religious communities: the Croatian and Slovenian Catholic churches and the Serbian and Montenegrin Orthodox churches. All religious denominations were decimated both during and after the war, including at Bleiburg and Kočevje. The communist hatred for all "class enemies" was so intense that Svetozar Vukmanović-Tempo refused to intervene on behalf of his own brother Luka, a Montenegrin Orthodox priest and scholar, murdered along with Joanikije, the Metropolitan of Montenegro, and other clergy, by the Partisans.[34]

In 1946, Tito staged a show trial against Aloysius Stepinac, the popular Croatian Catholic Archbishop of Zagreb (designated Cardinal in 1952 by Pope Pius XII), whose moral and spiritual attributes were an alternative source of authority even in the Axis-dominated Independent State of Croatia. Archbishop Stepinac was accused on standard trumped-up charges of collaborating with the enemy, sentenced to 16 years of imprisonment, later converted to house arrest due to his failing health (died in 1960). Buried in the Zagreb Cathedral, the tomb of this man of courage became a national shrine for Croatian Catholics, who regard Stepinac as a martyr-saint, a great spiritual leader, and a patriot.[35] But the back of the religious community, whose lands were expropriated and leaders imprisoned or silenced, was broken. The resulting accommodation between church and state in Yugoslavia, lauded by Stella Alexander[36], was a necessity at best and a tragedy at worst.

Stepinac's successor, Archbishop Franjo Kuharić, remarked during a May 23, 1979 interview by Stockholm Radio-TV that Yugoslavia boasts an all-powerful and omniscient state ideology which limits religious freedom, controls the small religious press, and denies permits for building churches in new settlements.[37] Kuharić's statement is corroborated by J. Nikolić, a Serbian Orthodox clergyman, who complains about arson and destruction of churches, abuse and psychological and moral pressure on adults and children for their religious orientation, dismissal from jobs, interference with rebuilding fallen temples and the like—all of which are contrary to the official party program banning discrimination against religious activity.[38]

As to the new social order, Desimir Tochitch writes that the elections of November 11, 1945 were a farce, a "political manifestation" and not at all the expression of popular will.[39] Leaders of the pre-war political parties were summoned to appear before the police. Most of them fled, disappeared, or were imprisoned. What is surprising is that Tito's reign of terror did not extinguish all dissent and organized political opposition at once. At the height of Stalinism in Yugoslavia, 1945-50, when some 20 big political trials were staged to neutralize pre-war political parties and intimidate others, clandestine student organizations sprang up like the League of Democratic Youth of Yugoslavia.[40] All such groups were suppressed.

Then came the Tito-Stalin duel for control of Yugoslavia in 1948, outlined in Chapter III. While the West hailed Tito as a champion of freedom and national independence, he was setting up the concentration camp on the Naked Island (*Goli Otok*) for his former comrades-in-arms, who remained faithful to Stalin. The pro-Soviet leaders in the CPY were executed. Thousands of party members were sent to the Yugoslav Dachau on the Naked Island to die like Sisyphus in the stone quarry, eternally rolling stones from one end of the island to the other. Djilas conjectures that some 15,000 party members went through the brutal "re-education" course on the Island.[41] Those who survived Hell's Island as psychological or physical cripples fell silent. Radoslav Kostić-Katunac, Yugoslavia's Solzhenitsyn, recounts in his stories of Tito's Gulag that survivors of the Naked Island did not blame communism, but rather Tito's revisionism—his alleged betrayal of the communist ideals in favor of bourgeois liberalism.[42]

To show Stalin that he was a better communist, Tito ordered forced collectivization of agriculture in 1949, which resulted in expropriations, hiding of crops, peasant revolts, imprisonment of Yugoslav "kulaks," and a serious economic crisis. Mass famine was averted only by stepped-up U.S. food shipments under UNRRA auspices. According to Milan Radovich, in the prison camp Zabela where he served, there were some 12,000 prisoners in 1951-52: 75 percent peasants, and 5 percent students.[43] Radovich points out that the massive opposition by the peasantry forced Tito to abandon his collectivization blueprint by 1952, just as the thousands of "frontiersmen"—people voting with their feet, fleeing Yugoslavia, shot or imprisoned when captured in the 1950s—eventually led to the open borders policy in the 1960s.

As to the surviving "Stalinists" on the Naked Island and in other prisons and camps, most seem to have been amnestied by 1956, like Vitomil Župan, who was arrested in August 1948 and sentenced in February 1949 to fifteen years of forced labor. Due to his courageous defense in court, considered as "improper conduct," his sentence was extended to eighteen years. Župan, a gifted writer who won a number of decorations while fighting as a Slovenian Partisan, was found guilty of hostile propaganda, anti-state agitation, espionage, immorality, murder, attempted murder and attempted rape. No evidence was produced by the court; no witnesses admitted—a procedure which was to become standard for the new higher, socialist "class justice." Following his release, Župan published award-winning plays and novels. But his 2,000-page autobiographical tetralogy—*Creation, Minuet for a Guitar, Levitan,* and *Destruction*—among other works, remains unpublished. *Levitan,* already set in type, was banned in 1972.[44] Like Solzhenitsyn, Djilas concludes that Tito's Gulag was built on and owed its existence to secrecy and the official management of information—the greatest evil of all communist regimes. Yet, Solzhenitsyn reminds us that there would have been no Stalinism, terror, or Gulag archipelago without obedient accomplices willing to carry out Stalin's (or Tito's) orders.[45]

In marked contrast to Tito's Gulag were the early attempts by the regime to democratize, liberalize, and humanize the system in quest of an independent path to socialism. In human terms, it meant that if you were a landless peasant or unemployed worker, you could finally give up your right to starve, since the state guaranteed employment and a minimum subsistence. If you were poor, now probably for the first time in your life you could afford a vacation or treatment in one of the famous health spas in which the country abounds. If you were a child with a precarious constitution, whose parents were too poor to send you to summer camp, now it would be paid for by public funds. The new religion of the state seemed to be: work, education, and physical culture. "Voluntary" shock brigades of young and old were organized to rebuild the country. By working as a Stakhanovite you might prove that you were "progressive," rather than "reactionary." Volunteering meant jumping on the socialist bandwagon, if not into the new class of party and government functionaries, with first crack at scarce consumer goods and apartments. Sports clubs sprang up everywhere. Health and physical fitness became integral parts of all school curricula. Many adults learned to read and write and acquired new skills on the job or in evening courses. A free eight-grade education became mandatory for all children. Thus, the first decade after the war saw a phenomenal reconstruction of the country as well as investment in human capital. Truly, Tito was Yugoslavia's Pericles, and not only Yugoslavia's Stalin.

4.   Human Rights in Yugoslavia, 1956-1980

Pericles maintained in his famous Funeral Oration, preserved by Thucydides, that the warriors who fell defending the polis died for a noble cause since Athens was not only a city, but a school for Hellas—and, by implication, the entire civilized world. In Pericles' immortal words:

> We need no Homer to sing our praises, nor any poet whose verses shall give fleeting delight, while his notion of the facts suffers at the hands of truth; nay, we have forced every sea and land to be pathways for our daring, and have everywhere established reminders of what our enmity or our friendship means, and they will abide forever. It was for such a city, then, that these dead warriors of ours so nobly gave their lives in battle; they deemed it their right not to be robbed of her, and every man who survives them should gladly toil in her behalf.[46]

Above all, as Lowell Edmunds relates, Pericles put forward the notion of rational freedom and of "conscious choice of the city's ends, based on knowledge of the alternatives."[47] The greatness of the city was thus based on rational human will or intelligence (*techne*), rather than pure chance (*tyche*). Pericles, like Rousseau, Marx, and Tito, genuinely believed that the most rational choice embodied in the general will could be internalized by the enlightened citizen. The signal Athenian contribution to the world, according to Cecil M. Bowra, was respect for the individual based on the discovery that "the first task of government is to treat men as ends in themselves."[48]

In contrast to Pericles, who was elected general annually between 443-429

B.C., and who founded Athenian democracy on free speech and freedom of choice (excepting slaves), Tito—following Plato, Rousseau, Marx, Engels, Lenin, and Stalin—was determined to realize the general will by restricting basic human rights and freedoms, particularly freedom of speech, press, thought, religion, and association. However, unlike his intellectual mentors and other communist party states, Tito did not persist in prior censorship. The result is paradoxical: the most open and "liberal" state in the communist world, Yugoslavia apparently has more political prisoners and prosecutions for "verbal crimes" than the most Stalinist of the communist party states.

Rusko Matulić's representative list of political arrests in Yugoslavia between 1956-76 and banned publications, films, and plays between 1959-76 are baffling when one recalls that Yugoslavia ratified such documents as the U.N. Charter of Universal Human Rights, the International Covenants of Civil and Political, and Economic, Social and Cultural Rights, and the Helsinki Final Act. No less damning for the regime are the *samizdat* dossier on "Repression in Yugoslavia" which focuses on the period between 1974-1976 and the "Memorandum on Human Rights in Yugoslavia" by the Democracy International Committee to Aid Democratic Dissidents in Yugoslavia, summarizing human rights violations between 1975-80, which was inserted into the *Congressional Record* on September 5, 1980, by Congressman John M. Ashbrook of Ohio.[49]

As indicated in Chapter X, the U.S. Commission on Security and Cooperation in Europe ("Helsinki Commission") omitted Yugoslavia from its 1977 Report to Congress on the implementation of the Helsinki Accords by the Soviet Union and East European nations. The same is true of its 1980 Report.[50] Human rights activists, East and West, fear that the 1980-82 Madrid Conference to review progress toward human rights, free flow of people and ideas, may end up as a replay of the futile Belgrade Conference in 1977-78.

Patricia M. Derian, Assistant Secretary for Human Rights and Humanitarian Affairs at the U.S. State Department, echoed in her September 16, 1980 Statement before the U.S. House of Representatives, Subcommittee on International Organizations of the Committee on Foreign Affairs, the Department's 1979 *Report* to Congress on human rights practices in Yugoslavia, which states that Yugoslavs "enjoy broad freedom of movement and access to foreign publications and radio broadcasts."[51] This is true insofar as it concerns those citizens, publications, and broadcasts which are *not* critical of the regime or its ideology. In contrast, a new law on the abuse of press freedom promulgated in 1973 aims at preventive censorship and is considered unconstitutional by some of Yugoslavia's leading *Marxist* theorists. The avant-garde claims that in the first ten months of 1976 alone, this press law resulted in 100 bans affecting some 35 publications, including such foreign papers as the *Neue Kronen Zeitung* of March 12 and the *International Herald Tribune* of March 1.[52] Emigré sources claim 114 cases of bans on publications in 1976, and 93 cases in 1977. Among foreign publications in summer 1977, were: *Paris Match, Allgemeine Frankfurter Zeitung,* and *Süddeutsche Zeitung.* In October 1977, *Paris Match* 21, Il *Picolo* 25 (Trieste), and *Südost Tagespost* (Austria) of October 25 were proscribed, as were the London *Daily Telegraph* of October 4 and the *International Herald Tribune* of October 5, which carried reports concerning the disappearance of Tito's estranged wife, Jovanka.[53]

During 1977-78, some 85 Serbian writers, public figures, university professors, and Orthodox clergy had to surrender their passports to the Secretariat of the Interior (SUP) and thus could not travel abroad.[54] As to foreign broadcasts, Mihajlov points out that Radio Free Europe has not broadcast to Yugoslavia for a quarter century, and other stations such as the Voice of America avoid all reference to Yugoslavia's internal conditions. This Western Finlandization, combined with internal censorship—whether official or self-censorship—leads Mihajlov to conclude that:

> Yugoslavia is the only communist country in the world whose citizens cannot find out or hear about the conditions in their own country, even from the West.[55]

Amnesty International Report for 1977 notes numerous allegations of harassment, interrogation, and imprisonment of Yugoslav migrant workers returing home such as the cases of Mr. Govan and Father Cvitković, who were sentenced in 1976 to 3 and 6 years of imprisonment, respectively, for importing publications "hostile" to Yugoslavia.[56] By 1977, AI had adopted about 100 Yugoslav prisoners of conscience.

Yugoslavia's human rights record remains largely unpublicized. Thus, in Spring 1975, a letter was smuggled out of the Psychiatric Hospital of the Belgrade Central Prison appealing to public opinion to "take urgent measures" to obtain the release of 100 normal people interned there who have committed no crime.[57] In 1976, Radovan Rajić, a lawyer, was prosecuted for his intention to publish a novel, *Fire and Ashes*, for alleged "false representation of conditions" in the country; Nikola Ristić's *Serbia at War, 1912-1914* and *Serbia's Struggle to Achieve National Aspirations* were banned; Radovan Blagojević, a Belgrade lawyer, was committed to an insane asylum for his letter to Tito requesting that the government honor the Yugoslav Constitution and freedom of thought; nine citizens in Novi Sad were sentenced from 4-15 years for "creating an illegal organization"; and Milan Petrajkić from Zaječar was sentenced to 13 years for "attempting to create an illegal organization."[58]

Even more questionable is the State Department's assertion that Yugoslavia is "not a significant offender with respect to violations of the integrity of the person." Yet, in May 1977, Amnesty International designated Dušan Brkić as its Prisoner of the Month. Brkić, who served a term in the 1950s, was imprisoned again in 1975 as a Cominformist, and freed only by the November 1979 amnesty. Twice, in August 1977 and July 1980, AI chose Dr. Nikola Novaković, former head of the Croatian Peasant Party, in poor health, sentenced to 12 years for association with the Party in exile, as its Prisoner of Conscience. On August 27, 1977, Franja Rupić was sentenced to 3 years for possession of "hostile" pro-Western publications dated 1975.[59] In early 1977, Dobrica Cosić, a World War II Partisan veteran-commissar, member of Parliament after the war, author of a World War I epic, was elected to the prestigious Serbian Academy of Arts and Sciences in Belgrade, but his Acceptance Speech on "Literature and History" was not published in the *Annals* of the Academy or any other Yugoslav publication. An *Anthology of Postwar Short Stories in Bosnia-Hercegovina* was banned because of Djuro Damjanović's short story, "Golimjesto" ("The Naked Place"), critical of life in a Bosnian village.[60]

Amnesty International Report for 1978-79 records that even private conversations are considered "hostile propaganda" and carry heavy prison terms. AI adoptee Dr. Veselin Masić, a gynæcologist from Brčko, was sentenced to 6 years in 1978 for alleged false depiction of social and political conditions in Yugoslavia. Other AI adoptees, like the lawyer Nenad Vasić and the high school teacher Mirko Kovačević, were sentenced in 1977 to 10 and 8 years, repectively, for "hostile propaganda."[61]

The Yugoslav performance in the area of human rights has, if anything, deteriorated since the Belgrade Conference. The State Department *Report* holds that human rights are becoming "increasingly a legitimate subject for discussion" in Yugoslavia. Yet, President Tito's address to the Eleventh Party Congress in June 1978 would indicate otherwise:

> Even the question of human rights, which are a part of overall progress, is being used as a weapon in bloc confrontation and intervention in the internal affairs of other independent countries.[62]

And Tito went on to renew his call for increased vigilance and a "continual ideological struggle against alien theoretical and ideological conceptions."[63] By December 1978, Tito declared that the "opposition" would no longer be tolerated. The Second Plenary Session of the CC of LCY on December 19, 1978 issued the guidelines for the intensification of the "class struggle." Vladimir Bakarić attacked the internal opposition of nationalists, liberals, and bureaucrats, who are attempting to create a new common platform based on the Helsinki documents and the fight for freedom.

The first to be attacked were Mihajlo Mihajlov, who is visiting the United States since 1978, and Djilas, deprived of his passport since 1970, as alleged organizers of a united front of dissent across republic boundaries, particularly Serbia-Croatia. Thus, Djilas was called in by the police in April 1979 and given a "final warning" to cease and desist from his activities and contacts. In August 1979, Yugoslav authorities issued a warrant for Mihajlov's arrest upon his return. Other dissidents, including Dragoljub Ignjatović, had their homes searched or were detained briefly by the police.[64] Djilas and Mihajlov thus continue to serve as the prime scapegoats for the regime. However, the human rights ferment in contemporary Yugoslavia is much broader in scope.

While the regime concentrates on bridling one group of dissidents, another group pops up somewhere else. In fact, the regime has intensified its campaign against all dissent—from Cominformists, former Chetniks, Croatian and Albanian nationalists, the clergy, students, independent Marxist thinkers, and liberals, to émigrés, foreign scholars, journalists, and diplomats.[65] Thus, the Yugoslav secret police (OZNA/UDBA/SDB) went to the trouble of kidnapping Mileta Perović, head of the Yugoslav pro-Stalinist forces, from Zurich. Perović was sentenced in 1978 to 20 years for establishing an illegal CPY.

Representative of regime action against former Chetniks is the re-imprisonment of three old men in 1979: Milojko Marić, imprisoned from 1946-58, was sentenced to 20 years for alleged war crimes; Djuro Djurović, who served 17 years, got another 20; and Slavko Vranješević, who served 20 years, received another 9, but mercifully passed away before completing his second term. In early 1980, Vojislav Rajčić "Požarevac," who served 8 years of a 20-year term handed down in 1946, was sentenced to death in Zaječar for killing 49 people during World War II as a Chetnik. Former guest workers in Germany like Milorad Joksimović and D. Aleksić were imprisoned in Doboj for Chetnik ties and "enemy propaganda." In April 1980, Žarko Aleksić, a lawyer, was sentenced to 7 years for praising the Chetnik movement and deprecating the LCY and self-management since October 1973.

The regime campaign against Croatian nationalists is reminiscent of 1971-72: In October 1979, Stjepan Brezovečki and Slavko Jelušić were sentenced in Zagreb to 10 and 6 months, respectively, for singing, while drunk, songs which lampooned the state leadership. In December 1979, five Croats—Dragoja Ljubomir (whose extradition from Germany is sought by the regime), Janko Kovačević, Vlado Pocrnja, Ante Jurić, Josip Žutić, and Ivan Lozić—were sentenced in Sarajevo from 5-15 years. In early 1980, Miroslav Večenaj and Željko Zec received 5-year sentences in Split for membership in a "terrorist Ustashi organization Croatian Liberation Movement" in Germany. Ivan Zelember also garnered a "fiver" in Osijek for "enemy propaganda" for bringing banned publications from Germany. Nediljka Šarić was meted out 6 years for membership since 1978 in the émigré organization "Croatian Revolutionary Brotherhood" in FRG. Writer Zlatko Tomičić, who edited the Croatian literary magazine *Književni list* in the 1960s, apprehended in Zagreb on January 24, 1980, was released temporarily from prison in March due to poor health (previously sentenced to 5 years in 1972, but amnestied due to heart ailment and an international campaign on his behalf). In April, Pavao Despot, Professor of Croatian, sentenced to 4 months in 1974 for "inciting national hatred," was apprehended in Zadar for "enemy propaganda." Professor Davor Aras, temporarily released from prison, underwent successful surgery at Zurich University Medical Clinic. In May, Dragutin Trumbetaš, famous Croatian painter apprehended by the police upon his return from Germany, had his apartment searched, émigré publications seized, temporarily released from investigative imprisonment on June 17, sentenced to 1 ½ years in Zagreb on October 2. In June, a new "terrorist" group—Andrija Mart, Franjo Bilandžić, Stjepan Janković, Ivo Jurić, Djuro Krznar Branko Hodak, and Vladimir Uzelac—were sentenced in Zagreb from 5-15 years (apprehended toward the end of 1979). In 1981, three prominent Croatian dissidents—the writer Vlado Gotovac (imprisoned, 1972-76), Dr. Tudjman (sentenced to 15 years in 1971, reduced to 2, released after one year thanks to international campaign), and Dr. Marko Veselica (imprisoned, 1972-78)—were sentenced to 2, 3, and 11 years of imprisonment, respectively.

Manifestations of Albanian nationalism have been prosecuted with equal vigor: In March 1980, a group of 50 Albanian nationalists in Priština were accused of distributing leaflets advocating union of the Autonomous Province of Kosovo with Albania. On June 10, another group of 8 Albanians—Sefcet Jasair, Ramadan Plana, Avdi Kelmendi, Avdulj Ljahu, Isa Demaj, Sulejman Djucala, Skender Jasari, and Hisen Grvala—were sentenced in Priština from 3-8 years for "enemy propaganda and for forming a coalition for enemy activities." On July 7, 1980, three Albanians—Professor Gani Sula, lawyer Muharan Shaliani, and student Ms. Hatixhte Maliqui—were sentenced in Skopje from 3-6 years for "anti-state activities." And the regime employed the army for the first time since World War II to quash the massive Albanian demonstrations in Kosovo during Spring 1981.

The religious communities in Yugoslavia have not escaped official censure, either. The regime is worried particularly about the Islamic renaissance among the Moslems of Bosnia-Hercegovina, Kosovo, and Macedonia. But the greatest pressure is applied to Croatian and Slovenian Catholics. Thus, in November 1978, France Rode, Professor of Theology, delivered a lecture on "True Christianity in Our Midst (in Slovenia), Today and Tomorrow," at the traditional theology seminar for students and youth at the Catholic Faculty of Theology in Ljubljana, in which he concluded that Christians were the proletarians of socialism and that the Church was locked out of social life. Rode's essay was left out of the anthology, *Do Not Extinguish the Spirit*, which contained the other lectures. In October 1979, Valenta Halić, a Catholic priest in Čadljavici, was sentenced to 5 months for his letter published in the October 20, 1977, issue of *Glas Koncila*. In November 1979, an official campaign was launched against two other Catholic periodicals, *Družina* (Ljubljana) and *Naša luč* (Celovec). By November 29, 1979, Rode and another young Slovenian Catholic theologian at Ljubljana University, France Križnik, were being investigated for critical remarks at the student symposium at which Križnik defended Ljubljana Bishop Rožman, killed by the communists in 1945, and Professor Ehrlich, Dean of the Ljubljana Theology Faculty, also killed by Slovenian Partisans in 1942. In February 1980, Marinko Jurišin, a young Croatian Catholic priest from the Split Archdiocese, fled to Germany, after questioning by the secret police. In April, Professor Vojmilo Rabadan, member of the Croatian Writers Association, was charged in Varaždin with "inciting national, racial or religious hatred" in his contribution to *Marulić*, a Catholic literary review. In May, Franciscan novices Franjo Vidović and Ivan Turndić were sentenced to 6 and 5 ½ years, respectively, for "enemy propaganda." By October 16, 1980, *Večernje novosti* reported that Professor Ivan Lalić, President of the Executive Commission of the Croatian Parliament, stated to the Republic Committee for Information in Croatia that the Catholic periodical *Glas Koncila* was without doubt an opposition political organ and the focal point of all inimical forces.

Students have also been drawn into the political maelstrom. Five law students in the liberal Marxist tradition of the *Praxis* group—Ante Rakić, Mirko Rajčić, Marko Juranović, Vjekoslav Rojnica, and Fabijan Dumančić—were tried in October 1978 in the Zagreb district court and sentenced from 1-5 years for "hostile propaganda," for compiling a dossier of human rights violations, including denial of nationality rights, in Yugoslavia. In May 1979, Vladimir Marković, a self-professed Marxist interested in the Christian-Marxist dialogue, was tried under Article 118 of the Criminal Code for "spreading false information," and confined to a hospital for the criminally insane in Belgrade. His "crime": Marković protested the denial of a pension to Father Sava Banković (an Orthodox priest/monk, arrested for the second time in 1975, who served long prison terms) and published an article about the Yugoslav leftist opposition in a West German journal. Marković appealed to the New York-based Research Center for Religion and Human Rights in Closed Societies to publicize his case as well as that of Josip Veznarović and other prisoners. In November 1979, Jakoslav Rojnica was sentenced to 3 years in Zagreb and sent to the Naked Island, as was Dobroslav Paraga in December 1981. In April 1980, a group of Croatian students in Sarajevo received 5-15-year sentences for allegedly planning to dynamite a road outside town. During 1980, a number of student and youth periodicals such as *Izbor* (Pula), *Bereklin* (Split), *Omladinska iskra* (Split), *Polet* (Zagreb), as well as an April issue of *Student* (Belgrade), were banned.

Independent Marxist thinkers were also served notice that the era of experimentation has ended—as explored in Chapter X. On January 10, 1980, the authorities called in Mihailo Marković, Zagorka Pešić-Golubović, and Ćosić and told them that lectures in private homes (since 1978) would no longer be tolerated. On June 26, 1980, the "Belgrade Seven" appealed to the Constitutional Court of Serbia, through their lawyer Srdja Popović, requesting that the Court declare unconstitutional the 1980 revisions in the University law, which would terminate their salaries within 6 months. The University law was revised once more in June 1980 to bring its letter in harmony with Convention No. 111 of the International Labor Organization, which proscribes discrimination in employment and the selection of professions. Previous appeals by these independent thinkers remain ineffective. A new international edition of *Praxis* appeared in April 1981 in—Oxford. While Ćosić's pro-Serbian Acceptance Speech was not published in Yugoslavia, Vladimir Dedijer, elected to the Serbian Academy of Arts and Sciences in 1979, was not allowed even to read his speech about "Revolution and Heroic Suicides."

The liberals continue to be *persona non grata* in Yugoslavia. On February 7, 1979, Jovan Barović, Yugoslavia's leading civil rights lawyer, who fought for due process and guarantees of fair and impartial trial, died in a mysterious car accident without witnesses. It recalls another "accident" during a ceremonial hunt staged by Tito for foreign diplomats in 1976, which resulted in the death of Pierre Sebilleau, the French ambassador to Yugoslavia, who successfully negotiated Mirko Vidović's release from his 5-year ordeal in Tito's Gulag (1971-76). In August 1979, 16 persons, including Bogdan Stefanović, were sentenced in Šapac from 1½-6 years for organizing a "Realistic Unification of Europe—Yugoslav European Movement." On October 15, 1979, Ignjatović was sentenced to 30 days. Djilas fined 10,000 dinars (equal to his monthly pension of $530), and Selić reprimanded for publishing the literary journal, *The Clock*, without prior registration, while legal proceedings were instituted *in absentia* against the fourth contributor, Mihajlov, for previous "criminal acts." As mentioned above, Selić was apprehended again in February 1980 and sentenced on April 25 to 7 years for his *samizdat* essay, "Contents." On June 19, Josip Cesarec was sentenced in Osijek to 4 years for stating that "a day will come when the political system in Yugoslavia will collapse." On October 21, 1980, lawyer Nikola Barović, the son of the late Jovan Barović, was physically accosted in front of his Belgrade office and suffered injuries.

Following Tito's death, appeals for the liberalization and democratization of Yugoslavia's socio-political system have grown in scope and intensity. Thus, on June 11, 1980, some 50 Slovenian cultural workers, including Niko Grafenauer, Tino Hribar, Andreja Inkret, Svetlana Makarovič, Boris Novak, and Dimitrije Rupel, petitioned M. Ribičič, President of the Socialist Alliance of Slovenia, for the establishment of a new liberal non-ideological journal. In summer 1980, 36 prominent Belgrade intellectuals, including Matija Bećković, Srdja Popović, and Ljubomir Tadić, petitioned the SFRY Presidency to grant an unconditional amnesty for all political prisoners. Laslo Sekelj, one of the signers, is already under investigation for his "moral-political suitability" as a lecturer at the University of Novi Sad. In the Fall of 1980, Ćosić and Tadić were gathering signatures throughout Yugoslavia, petitioning the authorities to allow the establishment of a new independent left-wing literary journal, *Forum (Javnost)*. By November 1980, on the eve of the Madrid conference, some 100 Yugoslav intellectuals—lawyers, writers, professors, and university students—petitioned the post-Tito collective leadership to repeal the law against "hostile propaganda."

A violent secret war continues to rage between the Yugoslav secret police and Yugoslav, particularly Croatian, émigré organizations abroad. The world is perturbed by the rise of terrorism on an international scale. Hence, President Carter assured the post-Tito collective leadership during his June 1980 visit to Belgrade that terrorism against Yugoslav diplomats and missions abroad would not be tolerated. And rightly so, since terrorism is a direct threat to civilization in general and democracy in particular. This fact is reflected in the 1980 State Department *Report* on human rights practices in Yugoslavia. However, the Report contains only a passing reference to the kidnapping of émigrés by the Yugoslav secret police,[66] and fails to mention the extensive blackmail and assassination of émigrés as well as the infiltration of their organizations by Yugoslav police agents, even though most émigrés oppose terrorism.

In 1979, the German magazine *Neue Bildpost* started a petition demanding the release of Vjenceslav Čižek (*Aktion Freiheit für Vjenceslav Čižek*), kidnapped from Italy by UDBA. Čižek, a Croatian nationalist adopted by AI in 1978 as a Prisoner of Conscience, was sentenced in August 1978 to 15 years for "counter-revolutionary" activities and for entering Yugoslavia "illegally." The 1978-79 AI Annual Report notes that Čižek sought political asylum in West Germany in 1971, joined the émigré Croatian Republic Party, and contributed articles and cartoons to Croatian émigré journals, critical of the Yugoslav political system, calling for the establishment of an independent Croatian state. During a trip to Milan in November 1977, Čižek vanished, only to appear again at his trial in Sarajevo in August 1978.

Speaking in the U.S. House of Representatives on October 1, 1976, Congressman Philip M. Crane of Illinois drew attention to Tito's campaign of terror in the West, concluding that:

> In the area of terrorism, of the brutal elimination of critics of the regime, and of total governmental power, the Tito government is, in no major respect, different from other Communist governments.

He then entered into the *Congressional Record* the names of several Serbian émigrés killed by UDBA between 1969-76 from a list prepared by Dr. Urosh L. Seffer, President of the Serbian National Committee, and Dragiša Kasikovich, associate editor of the anti-communist weekly, *Liberty*, published by the Serbian National Defense Council of America. On June 19, 1977, Kasikovich and his 9-year-old stepdaughter-to-be were found shot-to-death in his Chicago office, a few days after Kasikovich presented a document on political murders of dissident Yugoslavs to the U.S. State Department. Dr. Seffer charged the Yugoslav secret police for the slayings.[67] Nor was this the only incident of Tito's terrorism on American soil. On January 16, 1978, Dr. Mihailo Naumović, another editor of *Liberty*, died in a mysterious car accident, falling from a bridge into the Chicago river.[68] Karapandžić's list of Tito's victims abroad includes Borislav Vasiljević, member of the "Ravna Gora" Serbian Chetnik organization in the U.S., who was found shot on February 1, 1979 in Gary, Indiana; and Križan Brkić, a prominent Croatian émigré, shot on November 22, 1978 in Glendale, California.[69]

Apart from immorality, cowardice, and inordinate human waste, Titoist terrorism abroad is likely to be counterproductive by alienating world public opinion as well as Yugoslav guest workers abroad. After all, Tito and his colleagues are creating martyrs in the same way that Czarist Russia did before the October Revolution. The martyrdom of such men as the Croatian patriot Bruno Bušić, shot in Paris on October 16, 1978, and Dušan Sedlar, leading Serbian émigré, shot in Düsseldorf on April 16, 1980, bodes ill for the post-Tito regime. Consider the caliber of just these two men: Bušić (38), a gifted writer and orator, who fled from Zagreb on a forged passport in 1975, after serving 2 ½ years for his writings, elected Secretary-General for press and propaganda of the Croatian National Congress—which seeks self-rule for Croatia—in 1977, has already become the symbol of Croat national resistance. And Sedlar (72): President of Serbian National Defense in Germany; editor of the *White Eagle (Beli Orao)* since 1979; Secretary-General of the Association of European Refugees ("European Union"), and consultant on refugees to the United Nations in Bonn, killed on the eve of preparing a Congress which was to elect a Serbian émigré government.[70] In October 1980, shots were fired at the Paris home of Kosta Hristić, a French citizen, journalist, former contributor to *Le Monde* and presently on the editorial board of *La Point*, and translator of Djilas' works into French.

Yugoslav citizens abroad, including those with dual citizenship, have been targeted by Yugoslav security services for blackmail and recruitment to spy on their fellow countrymen. Thus, in summer 1980, the Swedish public was surprised and dismayed to find out that Josip Bubas, Yugoslav Consul-General in Malmö, tried to blackmail Tonci Percan, a Croatian radio reporter for Radio Malmöhus, into spying. According to Martin Marinković, a Serbian colleague of Percan, dual citizenship forces many Yugoslav radio reporters abroad to practice self-censorship for fear of official reprisals upon their return. Even U.S.-Yugoslav citizens are not exempt from such blackmail. On August 28, 1980, Mirko Blažo Markotić, an American of Croatian origin, visiting Yugoslavia, was sentenced in Mostar to 11 years for belonging to an "Ustashi organization" in Chicago between 1970-80.

Finally, foreign journalists, scholars, and diplomats critical of Tito's Yugoslavia have encountered some strange welcomes. In early 1975, the Yugoslav government lodged a formal protest with the Italian government concerning the publication in 1974 of a well-documented biography of Cardinal Stepinac by Aleksa Benigar. On July 31, 1975, Laszlo Toth, a naturalized U.S. citizen and laboratory manager for Great Western Sugar Company of Loveland, Colorado, was arrested for taking pictures of a Yugoslav sugar refinery, while visiting Yugoslavia, and sentenced in a secret trial to 7 years for espionage. Due to repeated intervention by Laurence Silberman, U.S. ambassador to Yugoslavia, Toth was released on July 23, 1976. The Yugoslav regime then started a campaign against Silberman, which led the East European Section of the U.S. State Department to request the Secretary of State that the ambassador be reprimanded for "undiplomatic conduct" in pressing Yugoslav authorities for Toth's release. The Secretary of State judiciously turned down the request, but ambassador Silberman resigned his post by January 1977.

In June 1976, Reverend Ljubo Krasic, a Croatian Franciscan priest, sociologist, and project director of the Center for Migration Studies at Staten Island, permanent U.S. resident since 1974, attending his father's funeral in Čitluk, Hercegovina, was detained by Yugoslav authorities who seized his passport. On August 16, 1977, Edo Pivčević, Yugoslav-born lecturer in philosophy at Bristol University, on holiday in Yugoslavia, was expelled for refusing to spy on Yugoslav émigrés in Britain. On July 31, 1977, Ilios Yannakakis, Professor of Social History, University of Lille; Jean-Edem Hallier, writer and publisher; François de Negroni, sociologist; and Bruno Bachelet, journalist—were arrested during the Belgrade Conference and deported. Yugoslav authorities also barred entry to some 100 German refugees, who carried to the Belgrade Conference a list of 3,400 Germans seeking to leave the USSR, Rumania, and East Germany. On October 18, 1977, Richard Schwertfeger, correspondent for Radio Bern, attending the Belgrade Conference, was deported, while Yugoslav authorities later apologized for the "mix-up." On May 16, 1978, Jakov Bakić, a Canadian citizen, who emigrated from Yugoslavia in 1943, was apprehended in Titograd and accused of killing Partisans during World War II. At the same time, Dr. Vladimir Pavlov, another Canadian citizen, lecturer at the Plymouth Polytechnic Institute in the United Kingdom, was apprehended in Pula while on vacation with his family, sentenced to 10 days and fined 500 dinars for openly criticizing state organs. On May 17, 1978, the Swedish daily *Sydsvenska* reported that Bora Žurovac, the Yugoslav Consul in Malmö, organized émigré Yugoslav school children to spy on their parents and that a Yugoslav secret police agent had attempted to infiltrate the Swedish police. The Yugoslav Consul was asked to quit his post by the end of May.

In early 1980, several West European newsmen were taken to police head-quarters in Belgrade for taking pictures of the "May 25" Museum housing Tito's decorations and gifts, and for interviewing citizens concerning Tito's illness. They were informed that they had to obtain prior authorization for both activities. On February 20, 1980, Peter Miroschnikoff, correspondent for the ARD German TV network, was deported for the second time and barred from Yugoslavia till the end of 1980 for seeking an interview with Dr. Tudjman; his previous interview-with the General was confiscated and he was deported on January 20. In May 1980, Michel

Barthélémy, special correspondent for Radio-France International, was apprehended at Zagreb airport, deported, and barred for 2 years from visiting Yugoslavia, for interviewing Tudjman, Gotovac, and other dissidents. In August 1980, Amy Young-Anawaty, Executive Director of the New York-based International Human Rights Law Group, and Charles Kolb, a Washington lawyer, who attended the conference of the World Association for International Law in Belgrade and visited prominent Yugoslav dissidents, were shadowed by the Yugoslav secret police who also searched their hotel room. In September 1980, a group of French citizens traveling through Europe, collecting signatures for a petition requesting that future Olympic Games be held only in Greece, was frustrated in their efforts in Yugoslavia by the "people's police."

Undaunted by the fact of numerous human rights violations in Yugoslavia stands the State Department's Aesopian logic that: "Freedom of thought is honored in principle, but public expression of dissident views is strongly discouraged."[71] As if anyone ever forbade praise of the government! In contrast, the 1980 Comparative Survey of Freedom in the World by Freedom House puts Yugoslavia in the "not free" category.[72] This, too, is not fully convincing. If Poland merits a "partly free" rating, then such a characterization would appear appropriate for Yugoslavia as well. One cannot overlook the fact that dissent, which is ordinarily repressed in other communist party states, is all out in the open in Yugoslavia's semi-open society. Hence, even if Yugoslavia should harbor the maximum estimated 6,000-8,000 political prisoners (officially only 500), it remains the most "liberal" country in the communist world.

Chief liberalizing and humanizing agents in Yugoslavia are the Western cultural heritage, the pragmatism of its rulers, and the lack of crusading zeal or obtuse ideological training among the party rank and file. Doder believes that repression in Yugoslavia is due often to Balkan traditions and the pettyness of local chieftains and officialdom, rather than to the central leadership.[73] Djilas, on the other hand, points out that life and society in Yugoslavia are more pluralistic than the official ideology, a fact which the leadership is willing to acknowledge only in a roundabout way—such as Kardelj's notion of the "pluralism of self-management interests." The chief weakness of the Yugoslav system in general and self-management in particular, according to Djilas, is the lack of real political and ideological pluralism.[74]

5. Homo Duplex, Socialist Style

Yugoslavia's human rights record mirrors a curious dialectic:

(1) Yugoslavia has open borders, but is closed to new ideas; and

(2) In the absence of prior censorship, controversial ideas abound —a state of affairs which the regime has sought to remedy by passing a new press law in 1973 tightening freedom of expression.

The result, summed up by Leszek Kolakowski, is that: " . . . there are many more political prisoners in Yugoslavia than in Poland or Hungary, yet in those countries the police control of cultural matters is more severe."[75]

The key to understanding the Yugoslav socio-political and cultural scene is "self-censorship," the attempt to implant a new Superego of enlightened socialist consciousness in the human psyche. In this enterprise, the regime has borrowed heavily not only from the classics of utopian thought like Plato, Rousseau, Marx, Engels, and Lenin, but from Freud as well. According to the Marxist-Leninist blueprint, enriched by psychoanalysis, the human being is to be molded into a new selfless individual, conscious of the general will, by peer group pressure and the sublimation of libidinal/instinctual drives into socially useful forms of expression. Societal pressure for conformism is not a novel phenomenon. Freud remarked that "the psychology of groups is the oldest human psychology."[76] Nor is this phenomenon restricted in time or place. Yet, communist systems have gone furthest in their attempts to create a new "collective individual."

In Yugoslavia specifically, the regime has sought to exploit three existing cultural trends favorable to conformism: (1) The Illyrian Dinaric patriarchal culture with its traditional social and personal ideal of *zadruga*—a form of extended family agricultural unit; (2) The Partisan tradition, grafted onto the Dinaric culture of heroism and violence, personified in Tito himself; and (3) The revolution of rising expectations—the quest for modernization and material well-being raised to the level of a new secular faith.[77] The regime also found a natural ally in another archaic cultural value among the South Slavs: an apolitical orientation resting on the belief that the rulers are inherently power-hungry, greedy, and corrupt, and since there is very little the average man can do about it, it is best to submit to authority, or ignore it, if possible, and, above all, to mind one's own business. The problem with such an apolitical orientation in a communist system is that it clashes with the authorities' project of building the new socialist man, which makes each individual's life the regime's business. The peculiar solution of this contradiction in communist party states is the emergence of a new *homo duplex*, socialist style, a man who is afraid to voice his real opinions in public life, which subverts his private life by politicizing all life.

Avant-garde Marxist humanist thinkers have been among the most incisive critics of the new *homo duplex*, and the socio-economic, political, and cultural values, which feed this socialist Frankenstein. Ćosić expresses the avant-garde consensus about the fundamental social malaise characterizing contemporary Yugoslav reality:

> There is little in our society which binds and inspires us to intellectual steadfastness and to the dignity of mind and con-science. Truth sinks ever deeper into illegality. Courage has passed over into the territory of the absurd and to the tragedy of quixotism. Self-sacrifice for one's beliefs is a discarded tradition. Morality has been completely subordinated to the political calculus and to material self-interest. The great human virtues, in our country, now reside on library shelves. Under the rule of nihilists, even those who create become nihilists out of selfishness and despair.[78]

The avant-garde agrees on the major source of the social malaise and *homo duplex:* the restriction of freedom via censorship and self-censorship. Thus, Esad Ćimić's critique of conformism focuses on the mechanism of self-censorship which prompts people to encourage everyone to speak their minds freely, on the one hand, yet cautions them at the same time about possible implications and abuse of freedom, on the other.[79] Yet, Milan Mirić notes that it is precisely this bogeyman of the possible "abuse of freedom," which constitutes the foundation of the reservation for thought and action in Yugoslav society.[80] The fear from the possible abuse of freedom and attendant social sanctions—from criticism to imprisonment—has led to the Finlandization of some and the rebellion of others, while confirming the majority in their apathy.

Gojko Borić in the West and Predrag Matvejević in the East wonder about the causes for the absence of controversial themes in contemporary Yugoslav litera-ture and critical analyses of current affairs. Borić contends that Yugoslav intellectuals have retreated into the safe havens of non-controversial, highly subjective, personal themes, waiting for better times, satisfying their curiosity about the real world by travelling abroad, whereas the general public is interested mainly "in gaudily illustrated journals that imitate the Western gutter press."[81] Hardly a promising situation for socialist enlightenment. Matvejević considers the absence of a genuinely critical culture as the major threat to both artistic/intel-lectual creativity and socialism. While Borić deplores the lack of a *samizdat* tradition in Yugoslavia, Matvejević traces the history of the suppression of critical works—books, journals, articles, and plays—noting the absence of genuine polemics in Yugoslav society. The greatest need in contemporary Yugoslav socialism, concludes Matvejević, is for broadening the range of critical free speech.[82]

Yet, what needs explaining in Yugoslav reality today is not conformism or Finlandization—commonplace occurrences in all societies regardless of time and place—but rather the persistence and scope of critical thought which refuses to die. The persistent demands for basic freedoms and human rights in Yugoslavia mirror another basic contradiction observed by Doder: that between a Western-oriented liberal life style and a dogmatic Eastern political system, that is, communism. Doder argues that: "Psychologically, the West has become Yugoslavia's new frontier: men driven by ambition or by desperation trek northward into a life of personal sacrifices and uncertainty."[83]

Even more curious is the phenomenon that in a society in which leading civil rights lawyers are disbarred or killed, poets imprisoned, and critics silenced—where, in Vidović's view, clerics flee from religious truth, leftists from their own truth, and conservatives retreat into the past[84]—that such a society could give rise to world-class literature of Nobel quality and epic grandeur. A kind of literature that compares favorably with Homer's *Iliad* and *Odyssey*, Shakespeare's *Hamlet*, and Alfred Lord Tennyson's *Idylls of the King*. That such literature should arise from the depths of human suffering in the desolate reaches of the system of prisons and camps in Yugoslavia's timeless Gulag archipelago is further testimony to the indomitability of the human spirit. But that such camp literature could express the quintessential alienation of man in the twentieth century as well as his most sublime hopes and aspirations is but inadequately understood.

The poets of Tito's Gulag follow in Solzhenitsyn's footsteps. The most pervasive theme of Yugoslav camp literature is the one articulated in Solzhenitsyn's works: the struggle for meaning and for touchstones of judgment in the quest for genuine liberation and inner freedom. According to Vidović, no one else is left in contemporary communist societies but visionaries, these last Mohicans in search of truth. Vidović is appalled by the scale of the tragedy of contemporary man in socialism: in the dark Middle Ages, only the contagious and the lepers were sequestered from society and quarantined, whereas in the modern era even poets suffer the same fate.[85]

Another basic theme in camp literature is liberation from the split personality of *homo duplex* characterizing our era in general and socialist societies in particular, where people believe one thing, say another, and do a third. Vladislav Musa writes that he felt free for the first time in his life following his return from Austria, when he began to speak his mind. It was in that moment that Musa felt he had regained his own self.[86] An aspect of freedom incomprehensible to many in the West is Musa's contention—echoing Solzhenitsyn—that he felt freer within than outside the prison walls. For one thing, in prison he could talk freely to fellow political prisoners, without fear of the consequences.

On a deeper level, Kostić-Katunac discovers that genuine freedom is the freedom from fear, and concludes that, hence, there cannot be any freedom outside the prison in a socialist system. Katunac's odyssey reflects the full scope of the fateful crossroads for mankind, groping toward the twenty-first century. He wonders whether mankind has the spiritual strength and moral courage to withstand the combined onslaught of a totalitarian regime with its brutalizing ideology and the moral/ethical relativism of rampant materialism, which are attempting to choke the human spirit and annihilate all sense of justice, truth, love, and compassion. Like Moses, Katunac worries about his people, whom he once knew as "raw, but proud; uneducated, yet noble; shy, but righteous," and who now appear to him as crippled beings, shackled by fear and lust for material goods, adrift without a moral or spiritual anchor.[87]

The tragedy of the poets of Gulag is that they are prophets without honor in their own country. They are the embodiment of the permanent tragedy of the civil war which communists everywhere wage against society. And, as Katunac and Oraški testify, political prisoners in Yugoslavia are permanent social outcasts. They cannot return to society, and often are rejected by their own family, relatives, and friends as well.[88] It is also problematic whether they can be understood in the West. For they remind people, East and West, of the depths to which human beings and societies may plunge and of the extraordinary effort required to break the chains of the Gulag archipelago, forged by *homo duplex* in "freedom." The challenge of Yugoslavia's epic camp literature is its attempt to come to grips with the nature of man, civilization, and culture in late twentieth century. It asks but one central question:

> . . . is there a God? Man, His image and likeness, is crucified in the greater part of the contemporary world: black, dirty, and unworthy of *Him, God-Man.* Is humanity stumbling today, only to find itself tomorrow in front of narrow prison cells, with a bloody head and its feet in excrement?[89]

The spectacular spiritual renaissance among poets of Yugoslavia's Gulag is epitomized by Mihajlov's writings. In his *Underground Notes,* reminiscent of Dostoevsky, this dean of Yugoslav dissenters explores man's spiritual quest as a reflection of the quintessential dimension of freedom. Mihajlov concludes that the struggle in totalitarian countries today is religious, rather than political, in essence, since it is a struggle for the liberation of the human soul or the individual self.[90]

Imbedded within the larger eschatological framework of human destiny is the question of the future of socialism in general and the Yugoslav experiment in particular.

Chapter XII · Post-Tito Yugoslavia: A Socialist Camelot?

The twentieth century spread great misconceptions and grave misunderstandings among people and nations on our soil as well. Aligned with those who think differently, literature, too—with its humanistic spirit and truths—is called upon to transcend existing misconceptions and misunderstandings. However, freedom, knowledge, and conscience are indispensable for such a task . . ..In the quest for the meaning of our existence, it is really indispensable that we discern man in history, human destiny in national destiny, the individual in the collective, that behind national and societal ideologies which move people in great events we recognize also the wholly personal motives in the "making of history," and that behind all the flags, guns, and rhetoric of patriotism we perceive the human face, hear his heartbeat, and divine his soul.

Dobrica Ćosić, *"Književnost i istorija danas"* (Acceptance Speech to the Serbian Academy of Arts and Sciences, 1977)

1.   Scenarios for Post-Tito Yugoslavia

The general consensus in the post-war era holds that nationalism and potential Soviet intervention constitute the two major threats to the Yugoslav experiment. The realization is growing also that this dual internal/external threat to the country's unity and independence is but a symptom of a much more fundamental malaise. And that is the question of freedom—the Achilles' heel of socialist/communist systems. Michael M. Milenkovitch and Dusko Doder agree that the central dilemma facing the country and the party in Yugoslavia is how much freedom may be allowed.[1]

The major failing of Tito's leadership has been the inability to develop a new political culture conducive to full democratization, liberalization, and humanization of Yugoslavia's socio-economic and political system. A new political culture which respects basic human rights and freedoms—such as freedom of speech, thought, press, religion, association, private enterprise, and the inviolability of the person—would have to encompass a pluralism of ideas and value orientations, and not merely the façade of institutional pluralization. Such pluralism of values and ideas is incompatible with the ruling ideology which claims a monopoly on truth.

Milovan Djilas and Leszek Kolakowski advance the thesis that the Marxist-Leninist ideology in contemporary communist systems is both dead and very much alive: dead at the level of faith, but indispensable as a justification or legitimation of the party's monopoly of power.[2]   Hence, the post-Tito "collective leadership" is unlikely to part with the ideology—its sole source of legitimacy. Yet, in Yugoslavia's secularized society open to Western influence and receptive to democratic life styles and ideals, a moribund Marxist-Leninist ideology might prove insufficient to legitimate the continuing party monopoly on the outcome of decision-making in a system boasting direct democracy and self-management/self-government.

This raises the question of the limits of tolerance in Yugoslav political culture. If post-Tito Yugoslavia does indeed have the potential for a full democratization, liberalization, and humanization, it would have to crystallize in a new social consensus combining such disparate individual and group claims for a share in decision-making and the levers of political power as the various currents within the party itself, the demands for greater autonomy by the various nationalities/ethnic groups, the independent New Left intelligentsia around *Praxis*, the technical and managerial elites in the economy, organized labor, the religious communities, and all other individuals and groups willing to abide by fair democratic rules of the game. How do the various social actors in Yugoslavia perceive their roles and what kind of socio-economic, political, and cultural framework would they prefer given an unconstrained free choice?

2. Titoism Without Tito: Periclean or Stalinist?

It is a fine historical irony that Tito starred in the conflicting roles of Pericles and Stalin in post-war Yugoslavia. Tito as the Periclean statesman preserved Yugoslavia's national independence and led the country half-way to democracy. During its "golden age," 1966-71, the Yugoslav experiment in socialist self-management witnessed a genuine pluralization of ideas and institutions reflected in socio-economic and political decentralization leading to a *de facto* Illyrian league of six republic and two provincial communist parties, a confederate government, and the renunciation of all monopoly, including that of the LCY at the Ninth Party Congress. By 1971, Yugoslavia was well on its way to fulfilling the promise of democracy in socialism. By 1974, however, Tito—the communist in Stalin's mold—had repudiated not only the Sixth Congress which put forth the notion of a *League* of Communists, but the essence of the liberal reforms of the 1960s as well, leaving behind only the empty shell of institutional pluralism dominated by a recentralized party based on the Marxist-Leninist-Stalinist tenet of democratic centralism.

Tito thus left behind a dual legacy: Periclean and Stalinist. The question arises: can the post-Tito collective leadership match Tito's virtuoso performance at home and abroad? What sort of a party did Tito bequeath to his successors? Is it like the centralized, elitist, monolithic, Stalinist party of 1937 or 1945? Or, is it a mass party of bureaucrats, managers, professionals, organization men, and ambitious individuals climbing the ladder of success in a modernizing society claiming to be socialist? Tito attempted to build several safeguards into the party: (1) Ideological re-Stalinization and emphasis on Marxist indoctrination at all levels; (2) Re-intertwining the party and government from the BOALs to the federation; (3) "Collective leadership" at all levels, culminating in the party and state Presidencies; and (4) Resurrecting the wartime triumvirate of party-army-state. Do these safeguards guarantee the survival of Titoism without Tito? And would such a system be liberal or dogmatic, Periclean or Stalinist?

Western observers of the Yugoslav socio-political scene disagree about the respective strengths of the Periclean and Stalinist elements, and, hence, about the prospects for the further liberalization of the system in the post-Tito era. Some, like R. V. Burks and A. Ross Johnson, regard the pluralization of Yugoslav society as nearly irreversible.[3] Others, like Doder and Mihajlo Mihajlov, believe that post-Tito Yugoslavia is at the point where it will have to make a definite choice: continuing its liberal reforms toward full democracy or backsliding into totalitarianism[4]—the classic choice between a Periclean and a Stalinist future. Yet, Robert A. Dahl points out that mixed regimes like Yugoslavia's are likely to oscillate between liberalization and repression.[5] The key to understanding this peculiar dynamic in the Yugoslav context is the nature and composition of the party as well as of social forces outside the party.

First of all, one must note that the Yugoslav party is Tito's creature. With Tito's departure, the party has lost its most authoritative interpreter, source of legitimacy, and *deus-ex-machina*. In Robin Remington's view, the passage of this "Godfather of Yugoslav communism" may lead to an organizational crisis within the party.[6] More fundamental, the party faces a major identity crisis. Left with organization men, deprived of such ideological heirs to Tito as the late Kardelj and the disgraced World War II Partisan leaders Djilas and Ranković, the party confronts a multiple crisis of leadership, purpose, and orientation, compounded by ideological uncertainty. This multidimensional crisis has accumulated during Tito's lifetime and jelled into conflicting currents within the party itself. In fact, the party is at war with itself in a house divided between liberals and dogmatists, nationalists and centralists, exponents of market versus planning, innovators and bureaucrats, younger communists and the "Club of 1941," democrats and Stalinists. These internal divisions surfaced with explosive force during the 1971 Croatian Spring and the 1972 purge of party liberals in Serbia and other republics. But the full scope of these divisions became clear only in the official critique of liberalism since Djilas, published in 1978. In the second tome on the "Political Crisis in the League of Communists of Serbia and the New Revolutionary Course," Dragan Marković and Savo Kržavac criticize the phenomenal transformation of the League of Communists into a social democratic party, which prompted Tito to remind his colleagues that: "We are a revolutionary party, not a social-democratic party."[7]

It is quite clear by now that the numerically small group of Cominformists or pro-Soviet dogmatic communists are not a significant threat to the party, barring Soviet intervention. Johnson contends that the deposed chief of the secret police, Ranković, represents a greater challenge, since his followers, excluded from the party, remain a significant political underground with considerable influence in the veteran's organization.[8] The liberal contingent of thousands of communists expelled from the party and/or imprisoned since 1971-72 constitutes another major threat to the post-Tito leadership as well as the single most important exponent of liberalization and democratization of the party from within. Liberal communists like Marko Nikezić and Latinka Perović, former President and Secretary of the CC of LCS, respectively; former Croatian party chiefs Mika Tripalo, the late Pero Pirker, and Savka Dabčević-Kučar; and the former Macedonian party spokesman Krsta Crvenkovski represent the kind of national leaders who could assume Tito's Periclean role in further democratizing the party and the country. The platform of liberal communists is summed up by Nikezić—echoing avant-garde theorists: "The transformation of society, under party leadership, presupposes the transformation of the party as well."[9]

The present post-Tito collective leadership at the level of the party and state Presidencies prefers Tito's Stalinist mantle, with its legitimation of continuing party monopoly in social life. But even the post-Tito leadership is not unaware of the need for social consensus. Remington points out that the military has been accorded a greater role as an "interest group" in Yugoslav politics. No less than 21 high-ranking officers were nominated in 1974 to top party bodies. On May 17, 1974, General Franjo Herljević was appointed head of UDBA, returning control of the secret police to the military.[10] At the Eleventh Party Congress in 1978, 23 high-ranking army officers were elected to the 166-member LCY Central Committee. The party-army-state triumvirate was rejuvenated by the appointment of a number of generals to civilian government posts: General Herljević, as Minister of Internal Affairs; General Vuko Goce-Gučetić, Federal State Attorney (Public Prosecutor): General Ivan Dolničar, Secretary-General of the SFRY Presidency; Colonel Veljko Miladinović, Editor-in-Chief of *Komunist*; General Petar Matić, Chairman of the Commission for Nationwide Defense, CC Presidium, and member of the National Defense Council (NDC), SFRY Presidency; General Džemil Šarac, NDC and Deputy Minister of National Defense; and General Milan Daljevič, Executive Secretary, CC Presidium, and NDC. In addition, Generals Nikola Ljubičić (Minister of Defense) and Herljević are also ex-officio members of the

Federal Council for the Protection of the Constitutional Order, headed by Dr. Bakarić. And in June 1979, General Ivan Miškovic became the new President of the Council for Civil Defense.[11]

As to the interlocking directorate between the SFRY Presidency and the LCY Presidium, top state and party bodies, it too metamorphosed into a triumvirate on February 6, 1980, when seven ex-officio members were added to the SFRY Presidency: Dragoslav Marković, President of the Federal Assembly: Veselin Djuranović, Prime Minister; Dušan Dragosavac, Secretary of the CC Presidium; General Ljubičić, Minister of Defense; General Herljević, Minister of Internal Affairs; and Josip Vrhovec, Foreign Minister. Dr. Bakarić, Petar Stambolić, Stevan Doronjski, Fadil Hoxha, Veselin Djuranović, Dušan Dragosavac and General Ljubičić are members of both the SFRY Presidency and the LCY Presidium.[12]

Yet, the party-army-state triumvirate in Yugoslavia and other communist systems does not portend greater liberalization, pluralization or "interest group" politics, since the decision-making elites in the army (the officer corps) and the government (high state functionaries) are all party members. In the Yugoslav context, a strong case can be built for the thesis that such a party-army-state triumvirate which co-opts the military into civilian executive roles not only bolsters the party's grip on the country, but insures that the conservative, dogmatic, ideologically stable wing of the party holds sway. Predictably, Tito drew on the military for reliable organization men—those unwilling to "rock the boat" after his departure.

Tito's death brought into operation the cumbrous mechanism of succession by the "collective leadership." On May 4, 1980, Lazar Koliševski (formerly Vice-President) became President of the SFRY Presidency, vacated by Tito, according to Article 328, Paragraph 6 of the Constitution. On May 15, Cvijetin Mijatović (member of the SFRY Presidency from Bosnia-Hercegovina) rotated into Koliševski's position, since the latter's Vice-Presidential mandate expired on that day, while Sergej Krajger (Slovenia) was elected Vice-President. In the Central Committee Presidium, the top party body, a similar game of musical chairs took place: Stevan Doronjski (Vojvodina) was elected to fill the LCY Presidency, vacated by Tito, but was succeeded in the one-year rotating post by Lazar Mojsov (Macedonia) on October 20, 1980.[13] However, the real test of the Yugoslav socio-political system is not the success or failure of succession—important as that may be—but the future orientation of the party toward internal and external dissent and the universal challenge of free speech and thought expressed by Boško Šiljegović, a retired Partisan colonel-general and former member of the CC of LCY:

> Criticism neither is nor can be destructive of the creative process. On the contrary. If viewpoints and principles, even those which were once already checked in practice . . . , are not reconsidered and checked again and again, the result will be stagnation and dogmatism. Criticism and dogma cannot coexist . . . . We shall gradually have to get used to the fact that progressive, democratic, socialist ideas are not anybody's monopoly.[14]

Threatened by dissent inside and outside its ranks and hypnotized by fear of potential Soviet intervention, the post-Tito leadership has retreated into dogma, reviving the old true and tested mythology of internal and external enemies and the need for intensifying the "class struggle." In his report on the current political situation and the tasks of communists, prepared for the 11th Session of the CC of LCC on June 5, 1980, Milutin Baltić called for a resolute struggle against the "class enemy," who is allegedly building a new united front of dissent focusing on democracy understood as a multi-party system rather than class-based democracy. Baltić promised that such "quasi-democratic, anti-socialist, and reactionary politics" will be resisted by all means.[15] Once again, Marx's tortured vision burst upon an unsuspecting world in which:

> The government hears only *its own voice,* it knows that it hears
> only its own voice, yet it harbours the illusion that it hears the
> voice of the people, and it demands that the people, too, should
> themselves harbour this illusion. For its part, therefore, the people
> sinks partly into political superstition, partly into political dis-
> belief, or, completely turning away from political life, becomes a
> *rabble of private individuals.*[16]

Tito's heirs appear to be following in Marx's footsteps, haunted by Stalin's ghost. In the past, as Ralph Pervan writes, the party has been all too prone to obscure problems with rhetoric, shift responsibility, and find scapegoats.[17] Yet, ideological re-Stalinization is a poor substitute for real solutions to concrete problems. The epochal question facing the party today is whether it can adapt to a democratic challenge. Teresa Rakowska-Harmstone doubts it, since "the ruling elite controls the process of decision making and will not acquiesce in its own demise."[18] On the other hand, Richard Löwenthal's research indicates that the communist ship of state is bound to navigate between the Scylla of growing pluralism of interests vital for effective party rule in complex societies and the Charybdis of the institutionalization of those interests which threatens party legitimacy.[19] What are the implications of such a dialectic in the particular framework of post-Tito Yugoslavia?

3. The Nationalist Alternative: Illyrian League of Socialist Republics?

Marshall McLuhan and Quentin Fiore sketched a puzzling scenario of the re-tribalization of humanity and its quest for a global village in an environment of electric information.[20] The modern counterculture impulse to "tune in, turn on, and cop out" mirrors a basic malaise in advanced industrial civilization: the loss of personal identity and meaning. Viktor Frankl, founder of Logotherapy (Third Viennese School of Psychotherapy), conjectures that the human being is able to cope with physical deprivation and can bear physical and psychological hardship, but it cannot survive without some ideal or value—religious or secular—which gives life meaning.[21]

The phenomenon of national/ethnic separatism appears within this context as a more archaic, group, or tribal expression of the universal quest for personal identity and anchoring of the self within the swift currents of enormous scientific-technological, social, economic, political, and cultural changes in a world swept by *Future Shock.* National/ethnic consciousness is thus a collective counterculture ethos dominating Toffler's third wave of post-industrial *practopia,* cresting upon the spent waves of agricultural and industrial civilization.[22] Gail Stokes considers nationalism a successful modern ideology, since it satisfies simultaneously "the ancient human need for community and the modern need for personal autonomy."[23]

Of the three major internal agents of change in communist systems, identified by Rakowska-Harmstone as revisionism, modernization, and nationalism[24], it is nationalism—symbolized by language and religion—which has traditionally been the repository of collective identity in the Balkans. That language plays a distinct role in personal identity was affirmed dramatically in 1967 when a "Declaration on the Designation for and the Position of the Croatian Language," signed by distinguished Croatian writers, intellectuals, and cultural institutions, petitioned authorities to elevate Croatian as a separate official language of Yugoslavia, along with Serbian, Slovenian, and Macedonian.[25] It is also a truism that nationalism and religion have always been associated together in the minds of Croat and Slovenian Catholics, Serb, Montenegrin and Macedonian Orthodox, and Moslem communities of Kosovo, Bosnia-Hercegovina, and Macedonia.[26] In the course of centuries of wars and foreign conquests, language, religion, and ethnic consciousness served as the last refuge from physical extermination and psychological terror. As a result, ethnicity in the Balkans (and elsewhere) is rooted deep in the collective uncon-scious mind explored by such luminaries as Freud and Jung.

The elemental force of nationalism as a collective consciousness became clear during the Croatian Spring of 1971 when the League of Communists of Croatia attempted to harness national sentiment to socialist ends—only to find socialism itself submerged in the tidal wave of nationalism. Finally, nationalism was confirmed when communists themselves joined the Croatian mass movement. Why, then, did Tito veto the nationalist renaissance, oust the Croatian party leaders, and order the resumption of Marxist education? He did so because national/ethnic consciousness is the most potent alternative source of authority and legitimacy in contemporary Yugoslavia and, hence, a potential rival to the party and its monopoly of power. Does this mean that nationalism/ethnicity is a force for the further democratization, liberalization, and humanization of socio-political systems? That would presuppose:

(1) A developed political culture of a pluralism of ideas and values based on the principle of tolerance; and
(2) Respect for basic human rights and freedoms attached to each *individual*, regardless of sex, religion, race, color, ethnic or national origin.

In Yugoslavia, both sets of values essential for the genuine democratization, liberalization, and humanization of societal institutions and practices are still in their infancy.

It is a tribute to the political farsightedness of Tito and his party that they proclaimed the unity, equality, and brotherhood of all nations and nationalities in Yugoslavia as a basic ideal of the revolution and the struggle for national liberation from both domestic prejudice and foreign oppression. Probably more peasant youths joined the Partisans and fought and died for this ideal during World War II than all the other planks in the party program put together. Yet, Tito and the party failed to promote a new political culture advocating genuine pluralism and tolerance. The dilemma facing the Yugoslavs as a multi-national state is that a more humane future depends on the successful conjoining of the values of pluralism and individual freedom.

In the meantime, the spectre of *group rights* is haunting the South Slavs— these ancient tribes in Toffler's *practopia.* Such rights, attached to tribes, nations, classes, or churches, leave the question of *individual rights* in limbo. In the past, as Cynthia W. Frey and George Klein point out, nationalism has served all kinds of other *isms*—from fascism to communism.[27] It has yet to find its true home in the Periclean concept of rational freedom and *human* rights. The inflamed passions and violence attending ethnic separatist movements worldwide—from Yugoslavia's majorities and minorities, to Protestants versus Catholics in Northern Ireland, Basques versus Castilians in Spain, Bretons and Corsicans versus French in France, French versus English-speaking Canadians in Quebec, Walloons versus Flemish in Belgium, Welsh and Scots versus English in the United Kingdom, Russians versus Ukrainians in the USSR, Czechs versus Slovaks in Czechoslovakia, Palestinians versus Jews in the Middle East—confirm the hypothesis that the concept of group rights is a prescription for non-negotiable and insoluble conflict, terrorism, tribal warfare, and disaster.

Tito boasted in 1969 that the national question had been solved in Yugoslavia.[28] The Croatian Spring in 1971 showed otherwise. In fact, Tito and his heirs chose to suppress nationalism and thus confine the genie of national/ethnic separatism. Frey sees a parallel between the Soviet invasion of Czechoslovakia in 1968 and Tito's handling of Croatian nationalism in 1971. While Brezhnev invoked the doctrine of "limited sovereignty" in the socialist commonwealth, Tito rested his case on the concept of "socialist internationalism."[29] In Yugoslavia at least, all nations and ethnic groups have been treated *equally,* protestations to the contrary notwithstanding. Serbian nationalist writers have been censored as severely as their Croatian counterparts. Moslems have been forewarned just like the Catholic and Orthodox churches. And the Albanians were reminded that Kosovo belongs to Yugoslavia, not Albania.

On the other hand, the post-Tito collective leadership may have overstepped the bounds when it decided to abolish *Matica Hrvatska*, the leading Croatian cultural organization founded in 1842, which played the role of a major power broker in aggregating diverse interests during the Croatian Spring. Mirko Vidović speaks for Croat intellectuals everywhere who were shocked that this national institution, a symbol of Croatian nationhood, a bastion of independence and resistance to foreign assimilation via Turkification, Germanization, Magyarization, and Italianization for more than a century, has been extinguished.[30] On April 10, 1980, *Matica Hrvatska* was disbanded and its inventory and archives transferred to the Yugoslav Academy. The question remains: could genuine peace, equality, and brotherhood be achieved in the absence of freedom?

Marx and Engels provided South Slavs with very little inspiration and sparse practical guidance, mostly negative, on the question of national self-determination. Even Marxist theorists in Yugoslavia turn purple from embarrassment and anger when they recall the Marx-Engels summary judgment over the South Slavs as a plebeian, "reactionary" people, who richly deserve foreign domination by more "progressive" nations. Marx and Engels wrote in 1848-49 that the South Slavs:

> . . . never had any history of their own, they have no future, no capacity for survival, and will never be able to attain any kind of independence . . . [since they] lack the primary historical, geographical, political and industrial conditions . . .. The South Slavs, who have trailed behind the Germans and Hungarians for a thousand years, only rose up to establish their national independence in 1848 in order to suppress the German-Magyar revolution at the same time. They represent the *counter-revolution.*[31]

Yugoslavia's "ethnic key"—featured prominently in the 1974 Constitution—concerning appointments to federal executive posts based on proportional representation, in reality bypasses the problem of national/ethnic discrimination. There are no strictly legal solutions to the dilemma of nationalism/ethnicity in Yugoslavia or elsewhere, since it is not a legal problem, but an existential one. The United Nations' Universal Declaration of Human Rights (1945) states clearly in Article 21, Point 3 that:

> The will of the people shall be the basis of the authority of government; this will shall be expressed in periodic and genuine elections which shall be by universal and equal suffrage and shall be held by secret vote or by equivalent free voting procedures.

Why is it, then, that democratic elections and even plebiscites such as the 1980 Quebec Vote do not necessarily satisfy the advocates of national/ethnic separatism? The reason appears simple enough: nationalism/ethnicity is a badge of collective identity and personal security—a psychological, that is, emotional construct. Walker Connor argues that:

> . . . ethnic strife is too often superficially discerned as principally predicated upon language, religion, customs, economic inequity, or some other tangible element. But what is fundamentally involved in such a conflict is that divergence of basic identity which manifests itself in the "us-them" syndrome.[32]

Hence, the question of national self-determination, including secession, is not amenable to purely empirical, or exclusively rational, solutions via a "calculus of legitimacy" proposed by some. Moreover, Lee C. Buchheit's standards for determining the legitimacy of secessionist claims strike one as highly subjective since the claimant must:

> (1) Demonstrate that it is in fact a "self" . . . capable of independent existence or willing to annex itself to an existing viable

entity; and

(2) Show that acquiescence in its demands would be likely to
result in a greater degree of world harmony . . ..[33]

Even constitutional laws and international conventions do not offer realistic
solutions, when their theoretical precepts of national self-determination, while
universally affirmed in theory, are just as consistently denied in actual state
practice. It is as if the world had inscribed in its set of invisible laws Abraham
Lincoln's dictum that "a house divided against itself cannot stand," and decided to
stick it out no matter what the price: dissension, oppression, or civil war. But, is
there no better way?

The dilemma of national self-determination, ethnicity, and separatism reflects
the much more fundamental challenge of individual freedom. This accounts for the
fact that problems of nationalism cannot be resolved within the narrow conceptual
framework of nationalism per se. Solutions may be found only within the larger
universe of *individual* freedoms and *human* rights. In sum, the realization of basic
human rights and freedoms on the individual level is a necessary precondition and
the only credible foundation for achieving collective or group rights as well,
whether national, ethnic, or class, and *not* vice versa. There are indications that
some Yugoslav intellectuals may be approaching such a conceptual breakthrough.
Thus, Vlado Gotovac, a leading Croatian writer (imprisoned 1972-76, 1981--),
concluded in a 1977 interview for Swedish television that the achievement of
freedom and justice as general *all-European* ideals would also represent the
attainment of *Croatian* ideals.[34]

It is a paradox that the pursuit of group rights as exclusive ends guarantees to
divide society into warring factions, jeopardizing the realization of both individual
and group rights. Nathan Glazer cautions that the pursuit of group rights by
government action in particular leads to the formal division of the nation into
"racial and ethnic categories with differential rights" and a growing resentment of
the favored by the disfavored groups.[35] The potential anarchy of competing
irreconcilable claims in a zero-sum-game calls for the authority of a *deus-ex-
machina,* a dictator or Philosopher-King, and the attendant centralization of
power. The conclusion follows that totalitarianism may be the final outcome of
the quest for unlimited group rights, while those rights themselves recede into the
future.

The consensus, East and West, seems to be that only a confederate structure
of genuinely autonomous units in a Yugoslav (con-)federation based on extensive
home rule could provide a realistic blueprint for the affirmation of Yugoslavia's
multiple nationalities and promote economic prosperity, national harmony, and
peace. An *Illyrian League* of autonomous socialist republics, drawing on the rich
cultural heritage of rebellion, independence, national unity, and social purpose
among the South Slavs, might represent that *tertium quid* between national/ethnic
separatism and communist monolithism, which has eluded social engineers and
critics alike. But whether such a League would be democratic or totalitarian would
depend to a large extent on whether basic human rights and freedoms were defined
in individual or group/class terms. The South Slavs thus find themselves at a
historic juncture where their choice will be symbolic for mankind: Periclean
democracy or Stalinist dictatorship. *Tertium non datur.*

What marks contemporary Yugoslavia as mankind's giant experimental station
is the fact that its East-West conflict is overshadowed by a North-South conflict as
well. This lends credence to the notion that Yugoslavia is a microcosm of the
world's most intractable problems. All points of the compass meet in Yugoslavia:
the watersheds of different worlds run right through this country of amazing
natural beauty and diversity. The industrial, developed North of Slovenia and
Croatia faces uneasily the developing regions of Bosnia-Hercegovina, Kosovo,
Montenegro, and Macedonia to the South (see Figure 5).

The ethnic divisions in Yugoslavia are exacerbated by economic dilemmas and
religious affiliation, which coincide with the spacial distribution of various
nationalities (see Table X). The national/ethnic orientation of the churches is

TABLE 10. Nationalities in Yugoslavia, 1971 Census

	SFRY	Bosnia & Hercegovina	Montenegro	Croatia	Macedonia	Slovenia	Serbia Total	Kosovo	Vojvodina

Number of Inhabitants (in thousands)

	SFRY	Bosnia & Hercegovina	Montenegro	Croatia	Macedonia	Slovenia	Total	Kosovo	Vojvodina
TOTAL	20,523	3,746	530	4,426	1,647	1,727	8,447	1,244	1,953
Serbs	8,143	1,393	40	627	46	20	6,017	228	1,089
Croats	4,527	772	9	3,514	4	43	185	8	139
Moslems	1,730	1,483	70	19	1	3	154	26	3
Slovenes	1,678	4	3	32	1	1,624	16	*	5
Albanians	1,310	4	36	4	280	1	985	916	3
Macedonians	1,195	2	1	6	1,142	1	43	1	17
Montenegrins	509	13	356	10	3	2	125	32	36
Hungarians	477	1	*	36	*	10	430	*	424
"Yugoslavs"	273	44	11	84	3	7	124	1	47
Turks	128	1	*	*	109	*	18	12	*
Others	486	19	3	75	56	13	320	18	184
Unknown	67	10	3	19	2	3	30	2	6

Percentage Composition

	SFRY	Bosnia & Hercegovina	Montenegro	Croatia	Macedonia	Slovenia	Total	Kosovo	Vojvodina
TOTAL	100.0	100.0	100.0	100.0	100.0	100.0	100.0	100.0	100.0
Serbs	39.7	37.2	7.5	14.2	2.8	1.2	71.2	18.3	55.8
Croats	22.1	20.6	1.7	79.4	0.2	2.4	2.2	0.6	7.1
Moslems	8.4	39.6	13.2	0.4	0.1	0.2	1.8	2.1	0.2
Slovenes	8.2	0.1	0.2	0.7	0.1	94.0	0.2	*	0.3
Albanians	6.4	0.1	6.8	0.1	17.0	0.1	11.7	73.6	0.2
Macedonians	5.8	0.1	0.2	0.2	69.3	0.1	0.5	0.1	0.9
Montenegrins	2.5	0.3	67.2	0.2	0.2	0.1	1.5	2.6	1.8
Hungarians	2.3	*	*	0.8	*	0.6	5.1	*	21.7
"Yugoslavs"	1.3	1.2	2.1	1.9	0.2	0.4	1.5	0.1	2.4
Turks	0.6	*	*	*	6.6	*	0.2	1.0	*
Others	2.4	0.5	0.6	1.7	3.4	0.7	3.8	1.4	9.4
Unknown	0.3	0.3	0.5	0.4	0.1	0.2	0.3	0.2	0.3

Statistički godišnjak Jugoslavije, 1981, p. 410.   * Under 1,000 or 0.1 percent.

perceived as a threat by the regime and infringement of the separation between church and state. As to society, the demands, charges, and counter-charges of the contending factions in the tribal war of "dinar nationalism"[36] are framed in terms of traditional ethnic group rights. Thus, the Croatian students demonstrating at Zagreb University in 1971 sought *Croatian*, not human rights, accused Belgrade and the Serbs of exploitation, and chided the developing regions for the inordinate waste of resources drawn from federal development funds with their heavy Croatian and Slovenian contributions.

Undoubtedly, the Croatian charges were not without foundation. But their articulation in ethnic group terms only obscured the factual essence of real problems by emotional rhetoric, inhibiting genuine dialogue and consensus formation and, hence, in effect, precluding rational solutions. For their part, Kosovo Albanians and others sought justification in the conspiracy theory of the rich republics exploiting the developing regions, keeping their inhabitants in abject poverty. Again, these people did not complain about the violation of human rights, but merely of Albanian, Bosnian, Montenegrin, or Macedonian rights. The Serbs were caught in the middle, their attempts to mediate automatically suspect to all non-Serbs.

In a world conceived as a zero-sum-game between competing tribes, nations, or classes, whatever one group achieves can only be at the expense of other groups. How can there be meaningful dialogue in such a world about complex issues of development, which encompass not only palpable variables of economic policy, finances, science, technology, organization, and management, but also such ethereal human concerns as social, psychological, and cultural values and attitudinal/behavioral prerequisites crucial for successful modernization strategies?

Ellen Turkish Comisso notes that the party abandoned central planning in the 1960s, since communists themselves could no longer agree on economic priorities or development goals.[37] Paul Shoup observed even before the Croatian Spring that Yugoslav communists were "succumbing to the sterile pattern of national conflict which so weakened the interwar regime."[38] David Andelman concludes that at present the Yugoslavs appear to lack a real program for the future. In his view, their energies are spent on "political manipulations within the apparat of the Central Committee of the party organizations of each of the republics."[39] In Gary Bertsch's analysis, the post-Tito leadership confronts what may be mutually exclusive goals: if it respects national interests, it may be unable to govern; and if it fails to take those interests into account, its task may prove even more difficult.[40]

The Yugoslavs are by no means alone in such straits. Hélène Carrère d'Encausse traces the demographic revolution in the USSR, the displacement of *Homo Sovieticus* by *Homo Islamicus*, and the rising tide of nationalism and ethnic consciousness (*mirasism*) among its national minorities. D'Encausse regards these minorities as the most stubborn problem for the Soviet leadership. And she wonders whether the Soviet state has the capability to surmount its "nationality impasse."[41] According to Rakowska-Harmstone, communist party leaderships in Eastern Europe face three major social demands: (1) national sovereignty; (2) political democratization and pluralism; and (3) improvement in living standards. Yet, the party's leading role epitomized by monopoly of power and communications, democratic centralism, and the lack of mechanisms for conflict resolution frustrates the effective pursuit of problem-solving strategies to meet those demands.[42]

The question of who can win a zero-sum-game—nationalism or communism—should probably be superseded by one inquiring about the potential losers: individuals, nationalities, and society as a whole. And, were it possible to expand Lincoln's vision, it might read: can a people long endure, half free and half slave, in a world in which children are condemned to deprivation and despair, human sentiment turns to rage, and the spirit of man becomes hostage to the winds of war?

4. The Praxis Alternative: Self-Management Without the Party?

Andrew C. Janos observes that while other communist party states have tended to settle into the normalcy of managerial middle age, the Yugoslav experiment remains genuinely millenarian and chiliastic.[43] The quest for the classless utopia—a socialist Camelot—is represented most effectively by avant-garde Marxist humanist theorists gathered around *Praxis*. These modern knights of the Round Table engineered a Copernican revolution in Marxism with their paramount focus on the individual. Yet, the avant-garde's conception of man as a being of *praxis* is plagued by the contradictory demands of *praxis* as process—freedom—and *praxis* as end goal—communism—which requires a *positive* choice. This dialectic pervades avant-garde thought as the most spectacular and convincing expression of the basic dualism characterizing the Marxist *Weltanschauung*: the ubiquitous tension between its humanist, democratic, and liberal elements and its anti-humanist, dogmatic, and totalitarian components. This contradiction is present also in the avant-garde's conception of self-management and its relationship to the party.

The avant-garde's conception of self-management and direct democracy rests on Marx's myth of the artificial unity of civil and political society, and of the individual and the collective, which requires the abolition of bureaucracy, the state, intermediary organizations, and politics. Paradoxically, Marx's quest for perfect social harmony, unity, and the abolition of power in theory leads to its direct opposite—distopia, totalitarianism, and dictatorship—in everyday practice. Kolakowski draws attention to the "Rousseauist" and "neoplatonic" sources of Marx's vision and concludes that:

> The dream of perfect unity may come true only in the form of a caricature which denies its original intention: as an artificial unity imposed by coercion from above, in that the political body prevents real conflicts and real segmentation of the civil society from expressing themselves.[44]

The Yugoslavs did Marx one better. They *camouflaged* reality via the self-management rhetoric which continues to pay lip service to the dream of unity. In Chapter X, we conjectured that if the avant-garde ever came to power, it would most likely traverse the same practical, if not theoretical, terrain as the party. The avant-garde, no less than the party or nationalist spokesmen, thus confronts the epochal choice between a Periclean or Stalinist, democratic or totalitarian, future. This is evident particularly in the classic Marxist conception of bourgeois versus socialist human rights held by seven members of the original "Belgrade Eight," who continue public action. Their conception of the preeminence of material/economic/social over legal/political/civil rights envelops them in an enchanted Hegelian circle, a socialist Camelot, haunted by Stalin's ghost.[45]

The avant-garde's conception of self-management is anchored in their concept of man as a being of *praxis*, on the one hand, and of egalitarian material/economic/social rights, on the other. But, as we saw above, *praxis* is bound up with the imperative of a *positive* choice, whereas egalitarianism in the economic sphere leads directly to authoritarianism in the political sphere. In either case, the self-managers cannot be trusted to arrive unaided at the correct, "socialist," choice. Guidance or tutelage thus appears to be implicit in the theory of *praxis*. The avant-garde is first to acknowledge the need for socialist enlightenment. But, how can the avant-garde then reproach the party for attempting to operationalize their credo and realize *praxis* by guiding the self-managers to the classless, communist future, where power and politics would be abolished once and for all? Even Svetozar Stojanović can come up only with the notion that the party ought to become "the initiator" of the socialist movement, democratizing itself and society in the process. The question of the use and abuse of *power* is thus left unanswered. Marković admits that:

> . . . Marx did not solve the problem: how will the *whole* prole-
> tariat form its common will, make the step from a "class in itself"
> toward a "class for itself," win power and run society "organized as
> the ruling class."[46]

Crucially, Marković's formulation of the central problem of power—in the
utopian tradition—precludes a solution. From Madison to Tocqueville, Friedman,
and Hayek, the dilemma of power is seen not in how to *win* it, but how to
institutionalize, disperse, and *limit* it. Friedman expresses the general Western
consensus that "the greatest threat to human freedom is the concentration of
power, whether in the hands of government or anyone else."[47] Hence the need for
institutions for conflict resolution, checks and balances, and the separation of
powers between executive, legislative and judicial, which avant-garde theorists
have been discovering surreptitiously and, as it were, by a back door. The avant-
garde's advocacy of such institutionalization of power is in direct conflict with the
larger universe of their Marxist heritage which calls for the abolition of power.

Even more complex and elusive to avant-garde theorists is the dilemma that
egalitarianism in the economic sphere leads to the centralization of power,
bureaucracy, and authoritarianism in the political sphere, as pointed out by Kardelj
and Županov in the East, and Friedman and Hayek in the West. Hayek considers
"social justice" as the Trojan Horse of totalitarianism, since the quest for absolute
equality of outcomes demands that a central authority control "every circumstance
which could affect any person's well-being."[48] And such pervasive control of all
aspects of private and public life can only be exercised by a government with
totalitarian powers.

The avant-garde also remains totally oblivious of the Western liberal precept
that economic freedom is an essential prerequisite for political freedom. Not in
the sense advocated by avant-garde theorists—that the individual has a *right* to
free education, health care, cultural goods, leisure, and the like—since nothing is
"free," but must be produced by individuals. Rather, in the sense expressed by
Friedman that:

> By enabling people to cooperate with one another without coercion
> or central direction, it reduces the area over which political power
> is exercised.[49]

Hence, concludes Friedman, economic freedom inherent in the free market results
in the dispersion of power, offsetting the concentration of political power. The
market, however, is anathema to the avant-garde who consider it the natural ally
of bureaucracy. It is only unclear how in the absence of real economic
independence or political/civil rights the self-managers can possibly actualize
themselves as beings of *praxis.*

Is it true, then, as Albert Camus wrote that: "Every revolutionary ends up as
an oppressor or heretic?" Is it possible as Bernard-Henri Lévy charges that:

> In fact, the "revolutionary" intellectual is a pitiful figure—the salt
> of the earth, he thinks; in reality an executioner. The perennial
> "guides" speak a shameful and abject language, and they always, in
> the end, justify massacre and repression.[50]

What would prevent the avant-garde from becoming an oppressor, if not an
executioner, should it ever come to power? Does Marxist humanist thought
exclude Stalinism? Is the avant-garde democratic or totalitarian, Periclean or
Stalinist, Menshevik or Bolshevik? We have seen that Marxist humanist thought
remains hostage to anti-humanist, dogmatic, and totalitarian aspects of Marx's
Weltanschauung. Hence, it is Bolshevik. Yet, curiously, it contains also important
Menshevik or social democratic elements.

It is common knowledge that Plekhanov joined the Mensheviks after the
Second Congress of the Russian Social Democratic Workers' Party in 1903, after

initially siding with Lenin. The major issues which divided the Mensheviks from the Bolsheviks—the nature of the party, the revolution, the transition period, and ethics (Bolshevik terror)—appeared to have little theoretical significance at the time. Yet these political and organizational issues, which have divided socialist/ communist ranks ever since, were only the outward manifestations of much deeper theoretical/philosophical/ethical dilemmas. Thus, Plekhanov's revisionist views censuring Lenin's elitist conception of a highly centralized and clandestine party of professional revolutionaries, and his critique of Bolshevik terror, especially upon return to Russia in 1917, can be fully understood only in light of the later developments of Leninism and Stalinism, and the critique of the latter phenomena by avant-garde Yugoslav theorists. With regard to both the party and terror, the Yugoslav avant-garde is clearly Menshevik, not Bolshevik. One need only recall Stojanović's critique of the Leninist party in his *History and Party Consciousness*.

But, the avant-garde's greatest contribution to the liberalization, democratization, and humanization of Yugoslavia's socio-political system has been its insistence upon freedom of inquiry and communications, critical thought, and an open society. Ljubomir Tadić summed up the avant-garde consensus regarding free speech:

> The principal difference between socialism and every form of authoritarian thought is best expressed in the difference between the status of the *citizen* and that of the *subject*. For only the citizen is a being with the "gift" of free speech. The mentality of the subject, in contrast, is distinguished by *silence* and respect toward higher authority.[51]

That socialism is incompatible with freedom since it needs subjects rather than citizens is not yet clear to the avant-garde, even though the party has sought to silence them. New Left theorists, East and West, refuse to acknowledge Levy's conclusion that Stalinism is inherent in socialism and, hence, that there is: "No socialism without camps, *no classless society without its terrorist truth*."[52]

There remains also the perplexing question of just how open-minded or receptive to new ideas are avant-garde theorists themselves. The consensus among the avant-garde seems to be that genuine liberation of the individual or society is impossible without socialist enlightenment. And socialist enlightenment, in turn, requires an open society, critical thought, availability of information, creativity, and new ideas. Djuro Šušnjić remarks that: "In a society in which there is a monopoly of ideas, there is no possibility of thinking in terms of alternatives."[53] The party appears comfortable enough with its monopoly of ideas. But, what about the avant-garde theorists? What kind of enlightenment and guidelines for individual and social liberation can be expected from educators who seem receptive only to those ideas which bolster their preconceptions? Why do avant-garde theorists read only Marx, but not Mises, Marcuse but not Hayek, Galbraith but not Friedman? Is it because of the dynamic mentioned by Rudolf Bahro where:

> Every thinking communist who meets with two other thinking communists to exchange ideas must consider himself as already expelled by party rules.[54]

Or, is it because avant-garde theorists persuade themselves that they are in possession of the Truth as latter-day representatives of Plato's Philosopher-King? Karl R. Popper, for one, has voiced serious doubts about the credentials as well as the desirability of such a creature:

> What a monument of human smallness is this idea of the philosopher king. What a contrast between it and the simplicity and humaneness of Socrates, who warned the statesman against the danger of being dazzled by his own power, excellence, and wisdom, and who tried to teach him what matters most—that we are all

frail human beings. What a decline from this world of irony and reason and truthfulness down to Plato's kingdom of the sage whose magical powers raise him high above ordinary men; although not quite high enough to forgo the use of lies, or to neglect the sorry trade of every shaman—the selling of spells, of breeding spells, in exchange for power over his fellow-men.[55]

What distinguishes the Philosopher-King from a dictator? Does the former's claim to the legitimacy of Absolute Knowledge differ from the latter's claim to the legitimacy of power? And, where does that leave freedom and individual self-realization?

Notwithstanding its failings, avant-garde thought should not be underestimated. Milton Yinger comments that the most important lesson taught by countercultures is what they tell us about the human condition.[56] Those who would understand the full axiological-epistemological-ontological and existential ramifications of avant-garde Yugoslav Marxist humanist thought may well consult, apart from the Marxist classics, also Shakespeare's *Hamlet* and Tennyson's *Idylls of the King.* For, while Promethean, the avant-garde's conception of man as a being of *praxis,* a free, creative, and self-actualizing being, is in the final analysis deeply tragic. In the end, the revolutionary Prometheus metamorphoses into Sisyphus and the latter into Hamlet, an imperfect being who knows that he must die.

Transposed onto the larger canvas of society and the world, it becomes obvious that the *Praxis* theorists' quest for a socialism which would liberate rather than enslave society and men contains essentially all the dramatic elements of Tennyson's great epic heralding the fall of the West. Hence, the intellectual terrain of *Praxis* may be likened to a socialist Camelot—that legendary land- and time-scape in which King Arthur's pristine vision of a kingdom of ends was debauched repeatedly by friend and foe alike. The lions engraved on Sir Lancelot's shield were symbolic not only of the heat of battle and the glory of victory in just wars, but also, and more important, of the warring passions within man himself.

In the *Idylls of the King,* just like in *Praxis* thought, the spectacular tensions and conflicts which characterize the human condition, individually and collectively, remain largely unresolved. It is this fact perhaps, more than any other, which lends avant-garde Yugoslav Marxist humanist thought the earmarks of an epic as well as philosophy in the classic sense. The avant-garde is seeking desparately for a way out of the Sherwood Forest of closed or circular Marxist-Leninist reasoning. Yet, the Marxist classics provide no guides for finding the pathway leading out of this enchanted universe. *Verschollen* in Camelot! And through the enchanted forest echo the words of Sir Percivale:

> 'Thereafter, the dark warning of our
>   King,
> That most of us would follow wandering
>   fires,
> Came like a driving gloom across my
>   mind.
> Then every evil word I had spoken once,
> And every evil thought I had thought of
>   old,
> And every evil deed I ever did,
> Awoke and cried, "This Quest is not for
>   thee."
> And lifting up mine eyes, I found myself
> Alone, and in a land of sands and thorns,
> And I was thirsty even unto death;
> And I, too, cried, "This Quest is not for
>   thee."[57]

Man's quest for self-understanding may be likened to the quest for the Holy

Grail by the Knights of the Round Table. Few of those illustrious noblemen returned from their journey. And those who did were something of a disappointment. It turned out that most of them had but faint glimpses and even fainter recollections of the Holy Grail. Are we, then, but sojourners in a land called Camelot? And how much do we really know? Tennyson said that: "Poetry is like shot-silk with many glancing colours. Every reader must find his own interpretation according to his ability, and according to his sympathy with the poet." In Shakespeare's view, all the world is a stage and men but actors on it. If that is true, where do the actors' lines come from? And, is the world but poetry?

5. Democratic Socialism: Plebiscitary Dictatorship?

Of all the alternative scenarios for post-Tito Yugoslavia, the one that is universally overlooked, or perhaps taken for granted, is the possible emergence of a genuinely democratic, pluralist order: *democratic* socialism, rather than *socialist* democracy. The reticence of even Western observers to consider the alternative of a democratic future for Yugoslavia is an oddity, yet understandable in the face of the crisis of democratic theory and practice in the Western world. Daniel Bell notes that: "The decline of liberal democracy—especially in Europe—and a shift to the political extremes may well be the most unsettling fact of the last quarter of the century."[58] How, then, can one reasonably raise the question of the possibility of democratic evolution of a *communist* state?

Again, the Yugoslav experiment contains all the essential ingredients of a great epic of democratization, liberalization, and humanization of socio-political systems, or *political development*. And the outcome is uncertain. Yugoslavia is at a threshold where it can choose between three alternatives: (1) genuine pluralistic democracy based on the rule of law and the principle of tolerance; (2) totalitarian democracy; and (3) plebiscitary dictatorship. The post-Tito collective leadership has clearly opted for the second alternative, continuing Tito's heritage. That leaves only two alternatives open: genuine democracy or plebiscitary dictatorship. If egalitarianism or "social justice" is the Trojan Horse of totalitarianism—as Hayek and others intimate—then the Yugoslav experiment might skip the democratic stage and catapult itself from totalitarian democracy into plebiscitary dictatorship. Could plebiscitary dictatorship be the outcome of a fateful East-West convergence of a third kind?

But what is "plebiscitary dictatorship?" Plebiscitary dictatorship is the rule of men, rather than laws. Furthermore, it is the rule of men based on power unconstrained by political, legal, moral, or religious principles. That such a totalitarian order based on *popular* choice might emerge in Yugoslavia and elsewhere is inadequately understood. Hayek, Friedman, William Simon, and Bell agree that the quest for equality of outcomes leads to the centralization of power, bureaucracy, and totalitarianism. In Bell's view: " . . . equality can be achieved only by administrative determination, by the enhancement of bureaucratic power in society," whereas Simon recalls that egalitarianism and despotism have been linked throughout history.[59] As summed up by Friedman:

> . . . there is a fundamental conflict between the *ideal* of "fair shares" or of its precursor, "to each according to his needs," and the *ideal* of personal liberty. This conflict has plagued every attempt to make equality of outcome the overriding principle of social organization. The end result has invariably been a state of terror.[60]

The most comprehensive re-statement of the classic conflict between equality and liberty has flowed from the pen of Friedrich A. Hayek in his three-volume *Law, Legislation and Liberty*. In this *tour de force*, Hayek outlines the theoretical basis for the metamorphosis of socio-political systems from democracy into new totalitarian forms. At the heart of this transformation is the concept of social justice which requires progressively more regulation of all aspects of individual and public life and the concomitant concentration of power. Hayek sees the fundamental flaw of contemporary democratic systems in the absence of any (legal, constitutional, popular) limits on power. Whereas Charles Lindblom considers the autonomy of the private corporation as the major barrier to fuller democracy, Hayek believes that it is the selfishness of organized *groups* which threatens the market order—the guarantor of liberty and pluralist democracy.[61]

A body of thought has arisen in the West concerning the desirable features of a rejuvenated, fuller, genuine democracy which would meet the needs of individuals and societies in late twentieth century. The common denominator of such theories seems to be pluralization and decentralization of institutions and practices. Thus, Arend Lijphart's model of *consociational democracy* is based on: (1) a grand coalition of political leaders reflecting societal pluralism; (2) mutual veto or "concurrent majority" rule; (3) proportionality as the standard of political representation, appointments, and allocation of public funds; and (4) high degree of autonomy for each segment of society.[62] Toffler argues in his *Third Wave* for a *practopia* based on minority power, semi-direct democracy, and decision division.[63] And, James A. Ogilvy's *Many Dimensional Man* highlights the new desiderata of paraconsciousness, paratechnology, and parapolitical pluralism.[64] Nevertheless, all these imaginative theoretical frameworks leave the question of social conflict in limbo.

Yet, it is precisely social conflict based on unlimited demands on the body politic by organized groups with effective political power which constitutes the greatest threat today not only to liberty and democracy, but the attainment of genuine equality as well. Hayek surmises that:

> So long as it is legitimate for government to use force to effect a redistribution of material benefits—and this is the heart of socialism—there can be no curb on the rapacious instincts of all groups who want more for themselves.[65]

Hence, continues Hayek, we should not really blame politicians for their corrupt pork-barrel politics advantageous to special interests, since we as a society have created the very framework of expectations, justification for, and legitimation of their activities. Hayek reminds us that a government which has unlimited power to grant the wishes of any and all constituencies, "can stay in office only by satisfying a sufficiently large number of pressure groups to assure itself of the support of a majority."[66] His conclusion follows that the only way to limit the powers of organized interests is to limit the powers of government. What we need, adds Friedman, is no less than an *economic* Bill of Rights to limit government power in the economic and social spheres.[67] Yet, for such a new Bill of Rights to be effective in a democracy, it would have to be based on a socio-cultural-psychological change in people's expectations of and demands on government. As Bell cautions, it is the chiliasm of modern man, self-infinitization, hubris, the refusal to accept limits, which are at the root of our contemporary crisis.[68]

The Yugoslav experiment is a quintessential expression of modern hubris and chiliasm haunting mankind in the latter part of the twentieth century. Central to this dynamic is the Yugoslav system of workers' self-management. It is a great curiosity that while many (nearly half of all) Yugoslav guest workers sojourned in Germany, Yugoslav self-managers model themselves on British labor in their disregard for productivity and the competitive status of their enterprise at home and abroad. Hence, it is *not* surprising that Yugoslavia today suffers from low productivity and high unemployment, excessive taxes, slow real economic growth (discounting borrowing) and high inflation, unrealistic consumption, low savings and investment—stagflation. Winston Churchill identified the basic cause of what among Western economists came to be known as the "British disease" in the reckless pursuit of egalitarianism in theory and policy:

> I am sure that this policy of equalizing misery and organizing

> scarcity instead of allowing diligence, self-interest and ingenuity
> to produce abundance has only to be prolonged to kill this British
> island stone dead.[69]

In spite of its North Sea oil deposits, Britain registered two million unemployed and an inflation rate of 22 percent in 1980. A Marxist analysis might
contend that organized labor constitutes the new capitalist class in Great Britain
based on incessant strikes, inflationary wage increases (anything in excess of
productivity growth), and beggar-thy-neighbor policies of exploiting society, particularly those on fixed incomes. In fact, organized labor might be an anachronism
in developed economies in which 85-90 percent of the national product is paid out
to employes in the form of wages and salaries. Peter F. Drucker writes that
employes own a good part of American industry through pension fund investments
and, hence, that employes are the only "capitalist" left. Since most of the
economic pie goes to labor in Western "employe societies," and since no "more"
may be obtained for labor, the unions feel genuinely threatened and thus obliged to
re-invent worker militancy, class solidarity, sacrifice and struggle in the form of
strikes or "organized civil war" against society. In Drucker's analysis:

> All one labor union can do is increase the share of its members at
> the expense of other employes. The unions thus become represen-
> tatives of a special interest that holds up the rest of society
> through the threat of power, rather than the representatives of a
> "class," let alone the representatives of an "oppressed majority."[70]

In the Yugoslav context, it is individual self-managed enterprises with market
power which fulfill the function of unions in the West. The justification for the
inflationary wage demands of the Illyrian firm rests on Marx's labor theory of value
and the notion that profits are "obscene," and, in any case, belong to labor. In
Chapter VI we noted that any theory of value that fails to incorporate all factor
inputs—land, labor, capital, management/entrepreneurship—does not reflect the
fundamentals of economic organization, but leads to faulty accounting principles,
excessive distribution, lack of capital formation and thus resources for investment,
technological innovation, creation of new jobs, greater production, and incomes. In
fact, the very notion of "profit" is seen increasingly among some youth and
intellectuals, East and West, as synonymous with "capitalism" which in turn means
"petty-bourgeois" egoism, exploitation, and alienation. Yet, this is a highly
irrational notion. For, as economists, East and West, point out, there can be no
investment, growth, jobs, and hence equality, without profits. Drucker even claims
that profit is an "accounting illusion," since it means nothing more than earning
today the costs of staying in business tomorrow. This is so because managers
everywhere have to earn "the costs of risk, of change, of innovation, and of
tomorrow's jobs for today's young people and the new entrants into the work
force."[71] The major problem facing the world economy is, indeed, falling
productivity and the drop in capital formation.

The Illyrian firm is notoriously inefficient in capital formation and innovation.
Western economists like Ljubo Sirc note the difficulty of allocating authority and
responsibility in the self-managed firm based on social ownership. In the absence
of private ownership of capital, the market does not function, either, as a rational
allocator of society's scarce resources. Hence, Sirc recommends that self-
managers be linked in some manner to their capital.[72] John H. Moore concludes
that faster economic growth in Yugoslavia presupposes such measures as liberalizing the laws governing ownership of land, size of private firms, rights of
enterprise founders to capital, and rights of enterprise members to the capital of
the enterprise.[73] In sum, economic efficiency in Illyria requires individual
responsibility, and the latter in turn presupposes private property. As Lord Acton
remarked in his *History of Freedom:* "A people averse to the institution of private
property is without the first element of freedom."

The dilemma of how to connect responsibility and ownership is central to the future of economies and societies, East and West. Contrary to some expectations, it has not been solved in the West, either. This in spite of the fact—affirmed by Drucker—that big business in the United States has become socialized (employe ownership via pension funds) without being nationalized. Drucker maintains that while employes own big business, they do not realize it, hence there is ownership without power, knowledge without responsibility, and function without status. As a result, both management and labor are enveloped in a crisis of authority and legitimacy. There is a need to institutionalize the employe's knowledge, responsibility, and economic stake in the enterprise, while enhancing effective management and preserving societal flexibility and individual mobility. Although critical of worker participation and co-determination, Drucker proposes greater labor responsibility in decision-making at all levels within the enterprise:

> . . . the employe on all levels from the lowest to the highest needs to be given genuine responsibility for the affairs of the plant community, including responsibility for designing and administering benefit programs. He must be held responsible for setting the goals for his own work and for managing himself by objectives and self-control. He must be held responsible for the constant improvement of the entire operation—what the Japanese call "continuous learning." He must share responsibly in thinking through and setting the enterprise's goals and objectives, and in making the enterprise's decisions.[74]

Drucker's postulates for greater employe responsibility and participation in decision-making are true to a page from Yugoslav self-management manuals. The problem is that in real life labor and management, East and West, pull in opposite directions. While organized labor in the West and self-managers in the East appear to be set to kill the goose which lays the golden egg, managements are frozen in equally antiquated conceptions of their role resting on bureaucratic organization, hierarchy, preservation of the status quo instead of innovation, and a Faustian disregard of the ecological imperative of husbanding human and natural resources. Robert H. Hayes and William J. Abernathy hypothesize that the decline in U. S. productivity and technological superiority is due, in part, to U. S. executives' concentration on short-term profits rather than investment, research, and development of new technologies.[75] In spite of declining productivity in the United States or Yugoslavia, labor militancy shows no sign of slackening.

Since big labor is as powerful politically, financially, and organizationally as big business or big government, Robert Nozick wonders why workers do not set up their own businesses or factories which would solve alleged exploitation by the "capitalists" once and for all.[76] In fact, worker-owned and operated factories have been set up in the United States and elsewhere, in spite of great difficulties. On March 1, 1978, Congressmen Peter H. Kostmayer, Stanley N. Lundine and Mathew F. McHugh introduced H. R. 12094, the *Voluntary Job Preservation and Community Stabilization Act,* to assist employe or employe-community organizations to purchase a shutdown factory or plant and thus maintain jobs. Preliminary findings show that worker-owned and managed enterprises succeed where conventional ones fail. Thus, William Foot Whyte, Director of Cornell University's New Systems of Work and Participation Program, reports that employment was maintained or expanded in four case studies: Saratoga Knitting Mill, Mohawk Valley Community Corporation (formerly the Library Bureau), Jamestown Metal Products, and Vermont Asbestos Group.[77] As to the productivity of the new worker-owned enterprises, the National Center for Economic Alternatives shows increases of 25 percent at South Bend Lathe in Indiana, 32 percent at a Kaiser steel pipe mill, and a 17 percent return on equity at Mohawk Valley Community Corporation.[78]

Worker-owned and managed enterprises are fascinating laboratories of "people's capitalism," exploring solutions to labor-management, productivity, and profitability dilemmas, East and West. Extrapolating to the theoretical level, such enterprises appear to combine the best features of capitalist ingenuity, entrepreneurship, and productivity with the socialist ideals of equality, humanizing the workplace, and more humane social relationships.

Worker-owned and managed enterprises may be also an important institutional safeguard against the erosion of genuine pluralism, constitutionalism, and democracy based on the rule of law, adumbrated by the principle of tolerance. In Yugoslavia, as in the West, the unlimited pursuit of private interest by competing factions in non-negotiable terms of *group rights* endangers not only economic and social progress, but *individual* freedom, *human* rights, and democracy itself. The unlimited power of such contending groups demanding special privileges enforced by the authority of government can only lead to the centralization of power, the erosion of social consensus, and the weakening of the respect for societal institutions and the rule of law. The resulting anarchy of competing claims dividing society into warring factions may endanger the delicate fabric of social harmony and the peaceful resolution of conflict. If such conflict led to a breakdown of authority and civil war, compounded by runaway inflation, depression, and widespread unemployment—as in Germany in the 1920s—the historic preconditions for the rise of a dictator or Philosopher-King would be realized once more.

6. Operation Polarka: Prelude to World War Three?

The Yugoslav experiment remains a real cliffhanger, not only with respect to the evolution of a genuine democratic order, but also with regard to possible Soviet intervention. Indeed, the evolution of such a democratic order could lead to a prompt Soviet intervention in Yugoslavia, as in Hungary in 1956 and Czechoslovakia in 1968. Western observers agree that the USSR never gave up its original goal of bringing Tito's maverick state back into the Warsaw Pact fold and of extending Soviet reach to the Mediterranean—a goal which Russia has pursued even in tsarist times. Duncan Wilson writes that Soviet strategic interests would be better served by returning Yugoslavia to the socialist camp as an obedient satellite.[79] The return of Yugoslavia to the Soviet orbit would be also a Russian gain ideologically, since it would mean an end to a rival Marxist "church" and its pernicious influence among Soviet allies in Eastern Europe and Eurocommunists in Western Europe.

The Titoist mutation and the significance of its "independent road to socialism" to the communist world were explored in previous chapters. The Soviet strategic interest in Yugoslavia, the Adriatic coast, and the Mediterranean are outlined by Aurel Braun, who concludes that the USSR's powerful new blue water navy and air force need permanent bases in Yugoslavia as part of an overall rapid deployment and multi-force strategy in the South European theatre aimed at neutralizing NATO's southern flank. In Braun's assessment:

> . . . Soviet naval aircraft flying from Yugoslavia could cover all the eastern half of the Mediterranean, provide mid-term guidance instructions to Soviet cruise missiles which would make them truly effective at over-the-horizon ranges, and directly threaten both surface and undersea shipping through their own armaments.[80]

In view of Yugoslavia's geo-political and strategic significance, it is not surprising that the Soviet Union has drawn up contingency plans for armed intervention in Yugoslavia, dubbed Operation *Polarka*, revealed in 1974 by Jan Sejna, a defecting Czechoslovak general. Operation *Polarka* calls for a two-pronged invasion of Yugoslavia by Warsaw Pact forces (USSR, Czechoslovakia, Hungary, and Bulgaria) via Austrian territory toward Ljubljana and the Adriatic combined with airborne landings in Belgrade, Zagreb, and other key cities, with terrorist acts by pro-Soviet Cominformist agents and perhaps even Croat separatists.[81]

However, Western observers believe that a direct Soviet military intervention in Yugoslavia is unlikely in the absence of considerable internal turmoil and/or Western, that is U. S., waiver of interest in Yugoslavia. Andrew Borowiec, David Andelman, and Carl Gustav Ströhm agree that the greatest threat to Yugoslavia's independence and territorial integrity is slow internal disintegration and Soviet infiltration resulting in a "peaceful" victory for the USSR.[82] According to Gavriel D. Ra'anan, the most likely scenarios for Soviet intervention in Yugoslavia are:

(1) Soviet *covert* or surrogate assistance to groups seeking national autonomy or independence;

(2) Soviet support of a strongly "centralist" Serb-Montenegrin regime (essentially military, in all probability);

(3) Moscow assistance to a group in a Yugoslav succession crisis caused by factional, rather than primarily ethnic strife; and

(4) A pro-Moscow faction in Belgrade as a result of concessions by Tito to USSR after 1974.[83]

Ra'anan argues convincingly that the extensive Belgrade-Moscow rapprochement which Tito engineered in the 1970s, appeasing Moscow, might in fact foreclose the options of his successors. But the Belgrade-Moscow rapprochement of the 1970s is only the expression of a much broader and pervasive dynamic underlying the love-hate relationship between Yugoslavia and the USSR, reaching back to World War II and before. Thus, Aleksa Djilas, son of Milovan Djilas, cautions that Tito never broke completely with the Soviet Union, hence in Yugoslav schools and the army, the USSR is defined as a "socialist" state, anti-imperialism (the essence of non-alignment) is applied mostly to the U. S. and Western Europe, rather than to the USSR, Soviet ships and submarines are overhauled in Yugoslav ports, and Soviet military transport aircraft land at Yugoslav airports en route to Africa, while the USSR is the major supplier of arms to Yugoslavia and Yugoslav officers are sent for training courses to the USSR.[84]

Indeed, if the extensive Soviet-Yugoslav rapprochement—initiated in 1967—continues, there may no longer be the need for outright Soviet military intervention in post-Tito Yugoslavia. Soviet-Yugoslav rapprochement advanced with giant steps during the 1967 and 1973 Middle East crises. Even Wilson admits that on both occasions Tito "allowed overflight and refuelling of Soviet aircraft," while Johnson notes the renewed political and military cooperation between Yugoslavia and the USSR on behalf of the Arab cause in the 1973 Middle East war.[85] The extent of Soviet-Yugoslav politico-military cooperation that has developed during the 1970s is not quite clear. Ra'anan records that Yugoslavia and the USSR signed a Joint Protocol in 1973 which provided Soviet Mi-8 helicopters, Yak-40 airplanes, aviation fuel, roller bearings, and the like to the Yugoslavs.[86] Perhaps as a quid pro quo, the USSR used the Adriatic port of Rijeka for sealifting heavy equipment, including T-54 tanks, to the Middle East. Ra'anan estimates that some 60,000 tons of material per week were shipped via land link from Hungary to Rijeka, destined for Egypt and Syria. He shows also that the Soviet navy quietly increased its utilization of Yugoslav ports, especially after 1975 when Yugoslavia changed its ports rights regulations and a floating drydock was installed in the port of Tivat for Soviet submarine and submarine tender repairs, thus enhancing Soviet capacity to support its Mediterranean fleet. Borowiec confirms that the USSR at present enjoys a refueling and repair facility in Tivat (Kotor Bay), and Braun mentions the rumor that Soviet submarines may be using the Bay of Martinščica.[87] Laurence Silberman, former U. S. ambassador to Belgrade, points out that the Yugoslavs permitted Soviet military overflights at the height of the Angolan civil war in 1976.[88] Indications are that the Soviets continue to use Yugoslav air and sea space in their tracking missions of the U. S. Sixth Fleet in the Mediterranean.

It is an open secret that Yugoslavia is associated with both the Common Market and Comecon, and is expanding its trade relations with China. Yugoslav trade statistics reflect this dual orientation. In 1978, Yugoslavia's trade with China amounted to $200 million, U. S. $1.3 billion, USSR $2.76 billion, and EEC $5.1 billion.[89] In September 1980, a new Yugoslav-Soviet long-term Agreement on Economic and Scientific-Technological Cooperation, 1981-90, was signed by the post-Tito leadership, which envisages transactions in both directions between 1981-85 on the order of $26-30 billion.[90] This would be the largest single commercial transaction agreement yet between the two countries. It would represent not only closer economic cooperation between "two socialist countries," according to the *Komunist* editorial, but also the linkage of scientific institutions and common scientific and technical projects. Such comprehensive economic, scientific, and technological cooperation between Yugoslavia and the USSR would appear to reflect similar levels of cooperation between the military and security services of the two socialist states.

The question remains, however, whether the post-Tito collective leadership can buy the nation's security, independence, and territorial integrity from the motherland of socialism. Can Tito's virtuoso performance as Pericles and Stalin at home and abroad be duplicated by the post-Tito collective leadership? What about Tito's policies of non-alignment and active peaceful coexistence? Would the continuation of Tito's policies toward the Third World appease the Soviet behemoth? Is it true that Titoism in its Periclean dimension represents a Trojan Horse in the communist world, and in its Stalinist function a Trojan Horse in the Western world?

It is quite clear by now that Tito's insistence on "independent roads to socialism," equality, democratization, and dialogue in the communist movement, and condemnation of power blocs, imperialism and hegemony, including Soviet intervention in Afghanistan, has been a constant source of embarrassment to the USSR and a source of inspiration for independent-minded communists in Eastern Europe and elsewhere. Hence, Tito's foreign policy contained a liberal, democratic, Periclean element universally acclaimed. Tito even became the head of the nonaligned movement, admired by many leaders of the Third World. Yet, Tito remained a communist and, hence, Stalinist. Could that mean that the world, particularly the developing nations, have been sold a false bill of goods? Evidence for Tito's Stalinist impact in the realm of foreign policy has accumulated. The clearest indication of this impact was the de facto Sovietization of the nonaligned movement in 1979, when Cuba—a Soviet proxy in Africa and Latin America—ascended to the chairmanship of the nonaligned movement at the 6th Conference of Nonaligned in Havana. The Soviet allies called the Conference and Tito was outmaneuvered—to his own surprise and chagrin. Yet, Tito had contributed more to the Soviet hijacking of the nonaligned movement than any other single statesman. How can this dialectic be explained?

Borowiec contends that Tito promoted not only non-alignment, but Yugoslavia's brand of socialism as well.[91] On the international plane, Titoism became identified with active peaceful coexistence, opposition to power blocs, and national independence. Moreover, Titoism tried to sell itself in the nonaligned movement as a system of popular, participatory, direct socialist democracy of workers' self-management and a champion against Western "imperialism, colonialism, racism, and apartheid," and only occasionally a critic of Soviet "hegemony." Third World nations have proven uncommonly receptive to such ideological incantations proceeding from a small, friendly, developing, "socialist," "nonaligned" nation as Yugoslavia. In fact, the nonaligned movement has welded together all the essential Marxist notions regarding monopoly capitalism and exploitation by multinational corporations into scenarios which call for a "holy war" against the Western world—the alleged bastion of imperialism, colonialism, racism, zionism, and apartheid. One need only compare Tito's writings like his Address to the Eleventh Party Congress in 1978 with the Manifestos issued by nonaligned nations at Havana in 1979, and the World Trade Union Conference on Development and UNESCO at Belgrade in 1980. The latter were the more significant since Tito no longer took part in them, yet his ideas held sway.

At the Eleventh Party Congress, Tito summed up the new correlation of forces in the world and Yugoslavia's foreign policy based on the Marxist-Leninist notion that capitalism is in crisis, that socialism has become a world process, and that it behooves all "forces of freedom, independence, peace and progress" to wage a resolute struggle against "imperialism, colonialism, neocolonialism, racism and all other forms of oppression" in order to establish a new world order. As to Yugoslavia, Tito claimed that:

> We are in the front ranks of the struggle of socialist forces in the world. To the best of our ability we are providing all-round assistance to all democratic, progressive and liberation aspirations of peoples and countries.[92]

Tito affirmed Yugoslavia's dedication to national liberation movements and the establishment of a new international economic order at the Havana Conference of the Nonaligned on September 4, 1979. The theme of his speech was the need for "decolonization" in the fields of technology, information, and culture in general. In Tito's view, present international economic relations were based on inequality and discrimination against developing countries, on the one hand, and resistance of leading industrial powers to any substantive changes in those relations, on the other. Hence, the nonaligned movement had acquired a historic responsibility, since it expressed "the essential interests of all mankind."[93] Upon his return from Havana, Tito could boast that the policy of non-alignment—with its anti-colonial and anti-imperialist character—supported liberation movements and that Cuba and Yugoslavia "agreed on the necessity for closer cooperation between our two countries at the bilateral level and in the realization of the policy of non-alignment."[94]

Walter Laqueur observes that the nonaligned movement became effectively mobilized for the aims of Soviet policy reflected in the Final Declaration of the Havana Conference, and the fact that Cuba, a "Soviet vassal," now appears to head the movement, whereas "some twenty Soviet proxies dictate policy to the majority."[95] Laqueur notes that not all nonaligned nations are happy about the radical change in the character of the movement. Thus, U Nu of Burma, one of the founders of the movement, no longer considers it nonaligned. The unanswered question remains: did Tito help "deliver" the nonaligned movement to the USSR thanks to his "socialist" rhetoric? Djilas thinks that:

> Emphasis on the anti-imperialist motif had prepared the ground for the Soviets, and they promptly focused on those situations offering them the widest range of opportunities.[96]

Undaunted by Tito's possible contribution to the Sovietization of the non-aligned movement and Stalinization of developing nations, the International Monetary Fund and the World Bank held their 34th Annual Meeting in Belgrade in October 1979. In his address to the meeting, Tito sounded his favorite theme of inequality, oppression, and preservation of privileges, colonialism, and racism in the world, calling for the establishment of a new international economic order based on effective mechanisms for a "much greater transfer of resources to developing countries."[97] True to its Marxist heritage, the post-Tito leadership reaffirmed Yugoslavia's support of national liberation movements in the joint Declaration of the CC of LCY and the SFRY Presidency issued upon Tito's death, proclaiming him "citizen of the world," while restating to the World Trade Union Conference on Development in Belgrade, April 22-25, 1980, Tito's battle cry against exploitation, domination, imperialism, colonialism, neo-colonialism, hegemony, racism and apartheid, protectionism, regional isolation, and the monopolies of multinational companies.[98]

A comparison of the Welcoming Speech to the participants in the World Trade Union Conference on Development by Veselin Djuranović, President of Yugoslavia's via's Federal Executive Council, and the final Conference Declaration shows complete identity of views in form as well as substance. This is the more surprising since the Conference was attended by 184 delegates from 108 trade union organizations from 74 countries representing all points of the compass. The basic thesis of the Declaration is that the present international economic order is unjust and unbalanced, since it is based on domination and exploitation reflecting the "logic of capitalism," resting on an "intensified exploitation of the working class, and threats to its social attainments and rights." In a classic Marxist analysis, monopoly capitalism—represented by the multinational corporation—is blamed for exploitation of workers both at home and abroad and, hence, for the perpetuation of inequality, domination, waste of human and natural resources, widening the gap in development, preservation of privileges and dependency in international economic relations subordinated to the "logic of profit." Therefore, the Conference participants consider:

> ... the struggle for the establishment of the new international economic order to be an eminent political goal and a constituent part of the peoples' struggle for their full national, economic and political liberation—against imperialism, colonialism, and all other forms of expansionism, racial discrimination, apartheid and external domination.[99]

The goal of this struggle is a "permanent and automatic transfer of funds from the industrially developed to the developing countries" on the order of 0.7 percent of the GNP of developed countries, without strings attached. The analysis of the plight of developing nations and the proposed remedies are typically Marxist. Curiously, the document fails to mention the OPEC cartel's role in driving the developing nations to the wall by escalating oil prices. Except for a single sentence, the Declaration ignores the responsibility of developing nations for their own plight such as indigenous socio-economic, political, and cultural frameworks inimical to modernization, socio-cultural change, and economic-political development. It ignores also the developing countries' limits in absorptive capacity for the transfer of technology and capital as well as the developing nations' responsibility for their own development, particularly by limiting exploding population growth, expanding technical-scientific cadres, encouraging private initiative and enterprise, raising productivity, capital formation and investment, and developing socio-economic and political institutions favorable to modernization and economic growth. Tito's classic answer to problems of development in the Marxist tradition—eagerly adopted by developing nations—is distribution rather than production. Such analyses and remedies are not only scientifically wrong and morally suspect, but grievously misleading as well. Even if the entire present wealth of the industrialized world were distributed among the developing nations, it would not secure affluence to the latter. A Chinese proverb put it graphically: "Give man a fish, and he will have a meal. Teach man to fish, and he will provide for himself for the rest of his life."

Complementing the quest for a "new international economic order" is an equally quixotic quest for a "new international information order." Again, Tito played a key role in misleading the developing nations. In his address to the Second Conference of the Nonaligned News Agencies Pool in Belgrade, November 22-24, 1979, Tito voiced his concern about equal relations in the world, calling for a "decolonization of information."[100] Tito's prescription for government control over the news media was carried by Third World representatives to the October 1980 meeting of UNESCO in Belgrade. Encouraged by the USSR and its East European allies, Third World delegates demanded that UNESCO become involved in the regulation of international news gathering, broadcasting satellites, codes of conduct for journalists, and even the content of their dispatches. If the Third World plan were carried out, the press throughout the world would be subordinated to the whims of governments. Despite Western opposition to this Orwellian scheme, Third World members voted a 1981 UNESCO budget funding a number of programs which observers see as an attempt to realize their plan piecemeal. Ominously, Western delegates failed to eliminate the notion that UNESCO should set press standards.

Thus, among UNESCO programs paid for mainly by the West, are studies to define the makeup of a new world information order, fundamental principles for the mass media, responsibility and the protection of journalists, as well as communication programs helping the PLO and other "liberation" organizations to improve their propaganda capabilities, and shifting the control of programs for training and equipping Third World communications agencies from Western donors to UNESCO.

The threat to free institutions and human rights of one of Tito's last Stalinist initiatives among the nonaligned was summed up by Akhtar Mohammed Paktiawal, the Afghan delegate to the Conference, who denounced the Soviet invasion as well as his government—and, hence, had to seek political asylum in the West—noting that he could not vote for the new information order when his people needed to tell their sufferings to the world, but were prevented from doing so. And Paktiawal warned the delegates to the 21st UNESCO Conference that: "We have this problem today. You will have it tomorrow."[101]

But why should Operation *Polarka* be a prelude to World War Three? The theory is gaining currency that due to Yugoslavia's standing among nonaligned nations and Western interest in Yugoslavia's independence—which goes back to the wartime "gentlemen's agreement" between the West and the USSR concerning respective spheres of influence in Eastern Europe—the Soviet Union is unlikely to invade Yugoslavia *except* as part of a larger operation. Hence, a Soviet invasion of Yugoslavia could very well presage a full-scale assault on Western Europe and, thus, the beginning of World War III.

7.   Human Rights and Détente: Toward a New U. S. Foreign Policy

The Western world welcomed Yugoslavia's nominal independence from the Soviet Union, following the Tito-Stalin split in 1948, hoping that the forces of nationalism would establish a beachhead in the Soviet empire, thus initiating its ultimate dissolution, or, at least, checking its advance toward world domination. To preserve Yugoslavia's independence, the United States poured some $2 billion worth of economic and military aid into the country, in effect underwriting the Titoist experiment in "independent roads to socialism." The preservation of Yugoslavia's national independence, unity, and territorial integrity thus became the cardinal orientation points of U. S. foreign policy toward this communist maverick. Such policy orientation demanded that Yugoslavia be treated as an ally, rather than a neutral or an adversary. In everyday diplomacy, this meant that Tito's domestic and foreign policies should be lauded and encouraged, rather than carefully scrutinized and assessed critically.

The result of the unrealistic approach of U. S. foreign policy decision-makers toward Yugoslavia has been a growing asymmetry in the relations between the two countries. Critics of U. S. foreign policy point to the dual aspect of U. S.-Yugoslav relations as allies when it comes to preserving Yugoslavia's independence from the Soviet Union, and adversaries with regard to the larger universe of Western, including U. S., interests in preserving free institutions, democracy, and pluralism in the world. Silberman argues that the United States shares with Yugoslavia a limited sphere in which interests coincide, yet the two nations have fundamentally divergent goals and values in other areas equally important to the U. S. national interest. Hence, a realistic U. S. foreign policy toward Yugoslavia would qualify its present unconditional support of Yugoslav independence in the face of Soviet pressure with a demand that Yugoslav leaders honor America's bilateral and multilateral concerns.[102]

The need for a more balanced U. S. foreign policy approach toward Yugoslavia should be clear from Tito's championing of orthodox Marxist-Leninist-Stalinist causes among the developing nations of the Third World at a variety of forums, particularly the United Nations. Yugoslavia's continuing ideological, and at times material, support to so-called national liberation movements in Africa, Asia, and Latin America would counsel caution in regarding this nation as other than communist and, hence, opposed to democracy and basic human rights and freedoms.

Thus, in 1977, Yugoslavia appears to have begun its own foreign aid program to Marxist movements, when it transferred a number of U. S.-supplied M-47 tanks to Ethiopia without U. S. consent.[103] While U. S. military assistance to Yugoslavia ended in 1961, the United States continues to sell military hardware to Yugoslavia. During the 1970s, the Yugoslavs requested from the United States TOW Precision-Guided Anti-Tank munitions, sophisticated communications and radar equipment, F-16s, and the like, but withdrew their request due to unfavorable publicity in the West. In 1978, President Carter requested from Congress authorization to increase arms sales to Yugoslavia up to $15 million. In 1979, U. S. military equipment sales to Yugoslavia were an estimated $356,000.   What is curious is the rise of a Yugoslav armaments industry featuring such sophisticated military electronics equipment as the ADL-M2 lightweight laser rangefinder which measures range as well as azimuth and elevation angles to targets; the TLMD-2 laser rangefinder designed especially for Soviet T-type battle tanks, including the T-34, T-54, T-55 and T-62; hand-held laser rangefinders; PRC 638 FM manpack transceiver for VHF-FM communications for military and paramilitary operations; and LID laser irradiation detectors—exhibited at the 1979 Military Electronics Defense Exposition in Wiesbaden, Germany, by Iskra, Yugoslavia's leading electronics company which is expanding its military technology equipment export markets with emphasis on Third World nonaligned nations.[104] The surrealistic nature of Yugoslav foreign aid was reflected in 1980 by a $40 million loan to Castro's Cuba, while a consortium of Western banks extended some $500 million in loans to Belgrade.[105]

Emigré publications hint at Yugoslavia's possible links with international terrorism.   In one instance, a Lebanese merchant ship with contraband—Soviet-made SAM rockets from Palestinian sources—hid from the Italian Coast Guard in Yugoslav territorial waters. In another instance, the Italian police investigating "Red Brigade" terrorism accused Zoran Grbelj, a Yugoslav citizen, of complicity in the assassination of Francesca Coca, Italy's top public prosecutor. Grbelj declined to return to Italy or furnish any statement against the Brigade.[106] Tito's unofficial campaign of secret police terrorism among Yugoslav émigrés abroad has earned him additional admirers and imitators like the Lybian dictator Kaddafi who in a July 21, 1980 interview in the West German *Der Spiegel* justified the assassination of Lybian émigrés abroad by reference to Tito. Kaddafi reasoned that: "Tito sent to the Federal Republic his hirelings to liquidate his Croatian opponents. And yet Tito's prestige in Germany has not suffered in the least. Why should only Tito be free to do it, and not me . . . ?"

The official U. S. foreign policy response to Yugoslav violations of human rights at home and U. S. interests abroad can be summed up by the proverbial adage: "See no evil, hear no evil, speak no evil." In plain English: by ignoring those violations. The U. S. foreign policy establishment retreated in effect into self-Finlandization. In compliance with such a policy of deliberate self-deception, data and events which fail to conform to the prevailing one-dimensional perspective of Yugoslavia as a friendly country are filtered out of consciousness and covered up. Bor. M. Karapandzich ponders the rationale for the U. S. State Department action concerning the Legion of Merit medal and citation which President Truman awarded to General Mihailović posthumously in 1948, only to have it placed under "Classified" and forwarded to the U. S. Congress for "safekeeping."[107] The State Department rationale was spelled out clearly in opposition to a proposed monument to the World War II guerrilla leader executed by Tito: "A live Marshal [Tito] is more important than a dead hero [Mihailović]." Frank J. Lausche, former Senator and Governor of Ohio, deplores the destruction by the State Department of its copy of the 1946 Report of the Commission of Inquiry of the Committee for a Fair Trial for Draja Mihailovich and concludes that: "The cause of history is certainly not served by the destruction of such important documentations."[108]

U. S. foreign policy decision-makers have apparently attempted to get rid of not only the unsavory wartime and immediate post-war period in Yugoslav history, but also of less auspicious later developments. A case in point is the Yugoslav transfer of U. S.-supplied tanks to Marxist Ethiopia in 1977. During hearings on

U. S. policy toward Eastern Europe on September 7, 1978, William H. Luers, Deputy Assistant Secretary of State for European Affairs, revealed that the Yugoslav transfer was a *classified* document. Although the transfer of the M-47 tanks violated the U. S.-Yugoslav agreement, the United States would not seek to retaliate "in any significant way" due to the "U.S. interest in maintaining good relations with Yugoslavia . . . ."[109] Daniel P. Moynihan, U.S. ambassador to the United Nations in the mid-1970s, was continually baffled by State Department reluctance to confront Yugoslav representatives in the Decolonization Committee with the fact that their country's support of the Puerto Rican Liberation Movement (accorded "nonaligned" status in August 1975 at Lima) was equivalent to American support for a Croatian Liberation Movement in the U.N. Even Helmut Sonnenfeldt had to admit with respect to U.S. policy toward Yugoslavia that:

> . . . we would like them to be less obnoxious, and we should allow
> them to get away with very little. We should especially disabuse
> them of any notion that our interest in their relative independence
> is greater than their own and, therefore, they have a free ride.[110]

Tito and his collective leadership have, indeed, enjoyed a free ride, particularly with respect to human rights violations in Yugoslavia, as outlined in Chapter XI. Reflecting on the Western euphoria concerning Tito's achievements and legacy, Senator Jesse Helms of North Carolina wondered:

> How can we, a Government proclaiming human rights, pretend that
> we do not know the appalling price of this so-called achievement,
> which we naively ascribe to Tito's credit?[111]

All indications are that the U.S. foreign policy establishment has developed by now a vested interest in maintaining the status quo in U.S.-Yugoslav relations and, hence, continuing to ignore human rights violations in Yugoslavia. Such a stance was confirmed at the State Department Daily Press Briefing on July 29, 1980, at which a Department spokesman answered in the negative when asked whether the United States intended to support the movement for the amnesty of political prisoners in Yugoslavia launched by the petition of 36 intellectuals and whether the United States intended to approach the Yugoslav government concerning the incarceration of Momcilo Selić.

Wooing the post-Tito leadership, the United States has already expressed its willingness to cooperate with Yugoslav authorities in tracking down Nazi collaborators accused of mass murders. Yet, State Department reports on human rights practices in Yugoslavia have yet to acknowledge Yugoslav secret police terror in the West, including America. This has led Yugoslav émigrés to question whether the Western democracies realize the extent of the erosion of their own independence and democratic order as a result of Yugoslav secret police terrorism on their soil. An *Iskra* (Munich) editorial of May 1, 1980, asks the taboo question: "is it possible to build better relations between two regimes over the corpses of citizens of either nation?" And where does that leave President Carter's pledge to promote human rights throughout the world as an integral aspect of American foreign policy?

The unrealistic nature of U.S. foreign policy toward Yugoslavia is but a symptom of a much more fundamental malaise: the inability to comprehend that nationalism and communism are compatible, but that democracy and communism are not. Hence, the consensus among such thinkers, East and West, as Djilas, Solzhenitsyn, Kuznetsov, Podhoretz, Laqueur, and Nitze is that the United States confronts the greatest danger to its survival as a free nation due to its failure to realize the nature of the Soviet threat. The Western failure of vision is anchored in its perception of détente as peace instead of a continuation of war by other means, to rephrase von Clausewitz.

Djilas and Solzhenitsyn note that Soviet imperialism is on the march, yet the West refuses to read the evidence. Both critics are appalled at Western unpreparedness and unwillingness to stand up to the Russians. On the contrary, observes Djilas, the West, at present, is "actively supporting the Soviet system with vast shipments of grain, technology, and credit."[112] Solzhenitsyn concurs in Djilas' assessment, adding that, hence, détente is definitely in the Soviet interest, since it allows the USSR to continue its subjugation of dissent at home, while obtaining all necessary technology abroad.[113] The greatest surprise which awaited Edward Kuznetsov upon his arrival in the West was the lack of concern about the Soviet military buildup.[114] Could it be that Western governments have sold a false bill of goods to their own people?

In a candid essay on "The Present Danger," Norman Podhoretz outlines the major sinews of a remarkable Finlandization which threatens America and its allies. Podhoretz writes that the seizure of American hostages in Tehran and the subsequent Soviet invasion of Afghanistan clearly indicate that the era of "cold war" has not been superseded by "détente," nor has the East-West conflict yielded to a North-South conflict. Rather, the basic fact characterizing our era is the relentless expansion of Soviet power whose aim is the Finlandization of Western Europe, Japan and, ultimately, the United States. Podhoretz cautions that détente stands for U.S. strategic retreat and the forceful absorption of countries in the "South" by Cuban and East German troops and Soviet advisers into the "East." The basic problem, concludes Podhoretz, is the West's incomprehension of the nature of the Soviet Union as a revolutionary communist state.[115]

To critics of détente like Laqueur, it has been clear all along that détente and cold war are "two sides of the same coin."[116] Thus, Soviet leaders see nothing contradictory between their insistence on arms limitation talks with the West, trade, aid, credits and technology transfer, on the one hand, and the intensification of the ideological-political struggle against the West by espionage, terrorism, subversion, and even local wars of "national liberation," on the other. In fact, argues Laqueur, Brezhnev and his colleagues regard détente as a means of creating "better conditions for the expansion of Soviet influence."[117] According to Paul H. Nitze, the major Soviet strategic objectives for the 1980s are:

(1) Political separation of NATO Europe from the U.S.;

(2) Increase in Soviet influence and control over the Persian Gulf;

(3) Encirclement and neutralization of China;

(4) Stimulating trouble for the U. S. in the Western hemisphere, especially the Caribbean;

(5) Dealing successfully with the contingency of direct Soviet military confrontation with Western military forces;

(6) Building an image of the Soviet regime as "a responsible, legitimate, peace-loving participant in the international community"; and possibly

(7) Covert operations, including the training, organization, and support of terrorist activities "to break down the confidence of groups not under their control."[118]

Seasoned observers of the world scene like Richard Nixon and Brian Crozier argue that World War III began even before World War II ended. What is novel about World War III is that it is waged at all levels: military, social, economic, political, cultural. Nixon claims in *The Real War* (1980) that the Russians have perfected a new "warfare by remote control" via international terrorism, and that Soviet actions in Africa and Afghanistan are aimed at depriving the West of essential oil and raw materials. Crozier agrees with Nixon that the target area of Soviet imperialism is the non-communist world, and that World War III is "a different kind of war" focusing on subversion, disinformation, terrorism, psychological warfare, and diplomatic negotiations.[119] As Nitze quipps: "The Kremlin leaders do not want war; they want the world."[120]

This prosaic Soviet strategy appears to be working. Antony C. Sutton documents in his 3-volume study the phenomenal contribution of Western trade and technology transfer to Soviet economic development between 1917-65. Sutton's major thesis is that the West has bailed out repeatedly Soviet economic planners from the failures of their centrally planned economy which remains in crisis, necessitating continous assistance, provided generously by the West. Thus, by 1967, the West had built about two-thirds of the Soviet merchant fleet.[121] The appetite of the USSR and its East European allies for Western equipment and technology has, if anything, increased during the 1970s, judging by more than $50 billion in credits extended by the West. Drucker, who considers the Soviet bloc "grossly overborrowed today and probably the worst credit risk around," is sceptical about the ability of the Soviet bloc or China to pay for much except food and energy.[122] Even more disconcerting is the fact noted by the London *Times* that OECD trade with the East based on government-subsidized low-interest loans smacks more of aid than trade.[123]

It is a truism that most technology has military applications. Yet, the pressure of Western businessmen on their respective governments to open the floodgates to unlimited exports of most goods to communist nations is increasing. It is as if Lenin's prophetic words that the capitalists would vie with each other to sell the rope to the communists with which the latter could hang them, remain unknown. Lenin wrote in 1921 that:

> . . . the so-called cultural strata of Western Europe and America are not capable of understanding the contemporary state of affairs nor the actual alignment of forces; we must regard these strata as deaf mutes and act with respect to them accordingly . . . . The capitalists of the entire world, and their governments, in the rush of conquering Soviet markets, will close their eyes to the realities, and will thus become blind deaf mutes. They will open credits which will serve as a support for the Communist Party in their countries and will provide us with essential materials and technology thus restoring our military industries, essential for our future victorious attacks on our suppliers. Speaking otherwise, they will be working to prepare their own suicides.[124]

While Western businessmen will sell even high-technology laser mirrors to the Soviet Union, if they can get away with it, the United States government was willing to lend in 1976 a super magnet to Russia which is "ideal for powering laser weaponry and death-ray type weapons," in the opinion of Dr. John B. Dicks, President of the University of Tennessee's Space Institute, and which the U. S. will probably never get back.[125] According to Jack Vorona, a science and technology specialist with the Defense Intelligence Agency, the USSR is apparently using sophisticated machines bought from the United States to improve the accuracy of its SS-18 heavy missile, the largest and most deadly nuclear missile. Moreover, Senator James R. Sauser of Tennessee discovered that U.S. documents, including military manuals on the operation of the Lance surface-to-surface missile system deployed here and in Europe, are routinely sent to the Soviet Union, Cuba, Iran and other nations.[126] Little wonder that the United States could not win in Vietnam.

Silberman complains that for years the United States has sold civilian technology of strategic significance to Yugoslavia with the proviso that it not be resold to Eastern Europe.[127] In fact, American corporations have invested an estimated $2 billion in joint ventures with Yugoslav firms, encouraged since 1972 by investment guarantees by the U. S. Overseas Private Investment Corporation. The largest American venture in Yugoslavia is the $750 million petrochemical complex built by Dow Chemical on the Adriatic. The most controversial, however, is the U. S. Export-Import Bank-financed nuclear power plant at Krsko, Yugoslavia's first, built by Westinghouse Corporation in a joint venture with the republics of Slovenia and Croatia. This in spite of the fact—mentioned by Ra'anan—that by 1975 over 200 Yugoslav firms and organizations had ties with Soviet trade organizations, while U. S. Secretary of Commerce, Elliot Richardson, obtained evidence in 1976 concerning Yugoslav re-export to the USSR of sophisticated American technology (computers, -components, and -systems).[128] And, with the new long-term commercial agreement signed in 1980, Soviet-Yugoslav cooperation in economic, scientific, and technical areas, and joint projects is scheduled to expand further.

George Meany, the late President of the AFL-CIO, summed up the Soviet view of détente during the 1974 Senate Foreign Relations Committee hearings on the subject as based on U. S. weakness, intensification of ideological warfare, undermining of NATO, ultimate Soviet military superiority over the West, Western recognition of Soviet ownership of Eastern Europe, and withdrawal of American forces from Europe, concluding that:

> The decision to provide the Soviet Union with Western technology
> is a decision to bail out the Russian leaders. It is a decision to save
> them the hard choice between production for war and production
> for people.[129]

Yet, technology transfer to the communist world is not the greatest failure of Western Chamberlainian diplomacy in an age dominated, in Solzhenitsyn's conviction, by the "spirit of Munich." The major failure of U. S. and allied foreign policy is the reluctance to live up to our own ideals of freedom and human rights by restricting the flow of information to people living in communist party states. If the United States is really serious about President Carter's pledge to promote human rights throughout the world, and if the Helsinki Final Act's dedication to the free flow of people and ideas is to be meaningful at all, then the first order of business for Western powers, especially the United States and Great Britain, would be to acknowledge their role in turning over some two million Russian, Cossack, Ukrainian, Croatian, Serbian, Slovenian, Montenegrin, and other POWs to the USSR and Yugoslavia for execution or internment. The Third Reich was justly condemned at the Nuremberg Trials for the holocaust in which six million Jews perished. But the greater holocaust of the estimated 60 million lives in the USSR, 100 million in China, 2-3 million in Cambodia, and the millions in other communist party states remains to be investigated before an international tribunal. As Solzhenitsyn advocates, it is the crimes against humanity, more than their perpetrators, which need to be put on trial so that the truth about such social cancer may come to light and serve as a warning to future generations.[130] Santayana admonished posterity that those who fail to learn from history are condemned to repeat it.

Mihajlov, Laqueur, and Sakharov postulate that human rights and world security are intimately linked. According to Mihajlov:

> . . . the abdication regarding strict defense of human rights would
> mean an *end to détente,* reinforcement of totalitarianism, and the
> first step toward European war, which would mean world war.[131]

Mihajlov believes that only growing pluralism, democracy, and the opening of societies in the communist world can assure détente. He is seconded by Laqueur, who considers the emergence of an informed public opinion behind the Iron Curtain as a growing factor of political influence in Soviet decision-making our "best, perhaps the only, hope of peaceful coexistence."[132] Yet, Sakharov notes that Soviet and East European leaderships have intensified the repression of basic civil and political rights in their societies following Helsinki.[133] Thus, throughout the Soviet bloc members of the Helsinki Watch groups have been persecuted and imprisoned. Apparently, Soviet block leaders believe that peace is divisible, that they can obtain needed technology, trade, and credits from the West, coupled with

Western acquiescence in the post-war division of Europe and arms limitation agreements without international inspection, while they continue to violate human rights at home and promote subversion abroad.

Laqueur, Solzhenitsyn, and Mihajlov argue that it is high time for the West, at least, to tell the truth without fearing the likes and dislikes of the Soviet and other communist leaderships. Laqueur suggests the desirability of a new departure in the field of broadcasting to disseminate factual information on the state of the world as an important instrument of U. S. foreign policy.[134] Solzhenitsyn considers the airwaves as a means of "establishing direct contact with the subjugated peoples and of furthering the growth of their self-awareness and emancipation."[135] And Mihajlov emphasizes the linkage between freedom of speech and information, on the one hand, and pluralism in the sphere of thought and ideas, on the other. To Mihajlov:

> A single newspaper, independent of the monopolistic party in Communist lands, would mean much more for peace and security in Europe than all the possible international and interbloc agreements on disarmament or trade credits.[136]

However, a free flow of information and ideas is incompatible with the present self-censorship of Western government media such as the Voice of America. While the Soviet leaders' blueprint of détente calls for the intensification of the ideological struggle against Western democracies, particularly the United States, the Voice of America guidelines to program directors forbid practically all criticism of communist regimes. VOA "Restraints" counsel the avoidance of emotionalism, vituperation, vindictiveness, stridency, belligerency, arrogance, pomposity, pretentiousness, condescension, sweeping generalizations, propagandistic argumentation, gratuitous value judgments, unsupported criticism of communist regimes, inflammatory programming, incitement to revolt, tactical advice, rumors, unsubstantiated information, gossip, slander or spiteful references, while "attacks on the stations by the Soviet and East European media should not be commented upon without prior consultation with the director." In other words, the VOA appears effectively Finlandized. Hence, it is not surprising that Mihajlov and others can no longer distinguish between VOA and Yugoslav broadcasts. And the more basic question arises: could Western foreign policies become hostage to what Jean-François Revel calls *The Totalitarian Temptation?*

With respect to Yugoslavia, U. S. foreign policy decision-makers entertain the notion that only a communist party dictatorship can hold the country together. On the contrary, argues Mihajlov, it is only the democratization of the country, pluralism, and an open society which can insure genuine unity and thus the survival of an independent Yugoslavia.[137] Mihajlov considers a de-Titoization process to be inevitable in Yugoslavia after Tito's death due to the new leadership's need to distance itself from Tito's aura and establish its own legitimacy. And he cautions the West that the failure to support pro-Western democratic opposition in left- or right-wing dictatorships causes such opposition to become anti-Western and anti-democratic, as in the case of Iran.[138] The conclusion follows that it is in the West's interest to support democratic forces throughout the world. Mihajlov proposes that a U. S. foreign policy designed to safeguard both American and Yugoslav interests would, therefore, have to include the following elements:

(1) Broadening of human rights in Yugoslavia, encouraging greater diversity in public debate and freedom of speech in general;

(2) Improvement of the economic situation by increasing economic freedom and fostering private initiative;

(3) A shift in Yugoslavia's foreign policy from "non-alignment" to genuine neutrality, guaranteed by the West;

(4)   Dealings with the Yugoslav communist leadership on an equal basis, without compromising American principles;

(5)   Economic and military aid to be mutually administered;

(6)   Establishment of contacts with democratic dissidents in Yugoslavia by inviting them to official functions at American embassies and consulates;

(7)   Encouragement and facilitation of non-party views inside Yugoslavia to be aired in the West;

(8)   Removal of restrictions at VOA on subjects considered sensitive regarding Yugoslavia;

(9)   Establishment of Yugoslav section broadcasts by Radio Free Europe;

(10) Responding to Yugoslav media reporting on America from an exclusively Marxist viewpoint, and demanding balanced reporting on the United States;

(11) Insistence that not only technocrats, but social scientists and others, who influence public policy, visit the United States as exchange students on U. S.-paid grants; and

(12) Restricting Yugoslav diplomats to their diplomatic duties, denying them access to émigré organizations which they are trying to intimidate and imbue with Marxist-Leninist ideas.[139]

The epochal challenge confronting the United States and other Western democracies in late twentieth century is not whether human rights and détente are compatible or not, but whether they should remain true to their own ideals of representative government, pluralism, democracy, and basic human rights and freedoms. The basic human challenge is—us. And the kind of world that we fashion shall hopefully strive to increase human freedom and diversity, rather than restrict it in the face of the irrational fear of the possible "abuse of freedom." In this quest for a more humane future, East and West, we might recall Dobrica Čosić's humanist plea that:

> In the history of the world and of this country, *the greatest abuse of freedom has always been committed by men of power and political ambition*. And in modern times, freedom can be abused much more frequently, and with graver consequences for socialism, by men of power than by scientists, artists, and philosophers. It must be stated again: *the most fatal social act is to deprive a person of his freedom*. The wise and those who would like to see that values might last in history, find it most difficult to take the risk of depriving an individual or a nation of its freedom. For in principle and essence, creativity is man's highest expression and function made possible by freedom. And a social order whose existence may be threatened by science, art, and philosophy lacks human rationale for existing at all.[140]

Looking to the future, one might ask how would a 21st century historian assess the human predicament of war and peace in the latter part of the twentieth century? If mankind does not blow up the world with atomic warfare—and Edward Teller assures us that that is impossible, given the *present* state of knowledge[141]—such a historian might write that nuclear Armageddon was averted due to the basic sensibility of the human psyche, a sensibility bolstered by self-interest, rather than love of one's fellow men. The Third World War saw only limited nuclear engagements which persuaded all participants that—if continued—the victor would preside over a nuclear cemetery in which the living would envy the dead.[142] Self-interest and the instinct for survival proved stronger even than ideological predispositions. Geo-political considerations also played a crucial part. It was obvious to the three major powers—foreshadowed in the Orwellian scenario—that whoever controlled the Eurasian land mass controlled the world. Hence, the Free World—primarily the United States, Canada, Western Europe, Japan, Australia, New Zealand—had to ally itself once more with a totalitarian power (as in World War II)—this time with China—in order to subdue the Soviet Union's drive for world domination. What came as a surprise was the overwhelming numerical superiority and fanaticism of Chinese communist forces, which, if unchecked, would have laid waste not only Russia, but Europe as well. Hence, the Western allies had to switch sides toward the end of the war and oppose the Chinese war machine continuing the quest for world domination where the Russians had left off. Thus, World War III ended without real victors or vanquished. Yet, the casualties exceeded those of all previous wars put together. The only major gain to mankind from the war was the new international convention banning nuclear, along with chemical and biological, warfare.

The basic human dilemmas remained: war and peace, hunger and affluence, intolerance and forgiveness, hate and love, bondage and freedom, dictatorship and democracy. In the realm of knowledge and the sciences, Alfred North Whitehead's admonition to natural scientists to "seek simplicity and distrust it" and to social scientists to "seek complexity and order it" acquired new meaning by the end of the century. So did Kant's categorical imperative in the realm of ethics. The most surprising development of all was the emerging vision of unity among all the arts and sciences, faith and knowledge. An unknown 21st century poet expressed it poignantly in rounding out Tennyson's Arthuriad with the following stanzas sketching the Return of the King:

> 'And one enchanted evening
> The Knights of the Round Table shall
>   return
> Carrying the Holy Grail
> Led by King Arthur with his
>   Excalibur
> Retrieved from that misty pond in
>   Camelot.
>
> They shall present to us the
>   Holy Grail
> To light our way until a
>   better day
> When the arms of yesteryear
> Symbolized by the Excalibur
> Become plowshares and pruning hooks
> While the spectre of warring men
> Yields to the peace of a
>   Kingdom of Ends.

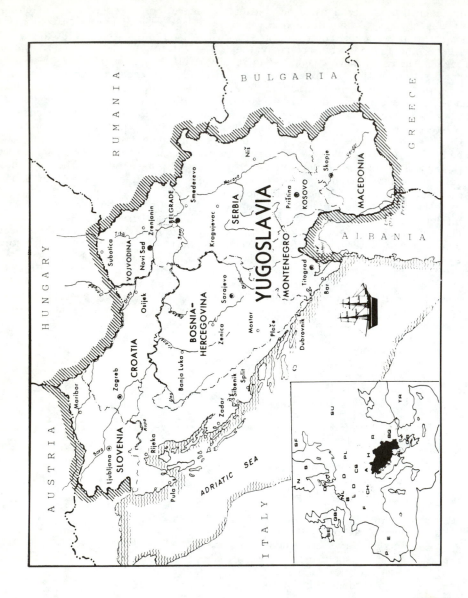

Abbreviations
in the References

A. *YUGOSLAV JOURNALS*

I. *Journals in Serbo-Croatian:*

Ekonomist: Ekonomist (Zagreb)
EP: Ekonomska politika (Belgrade)
EM: Encyclopædia moderna (Zagreb)
Filosofija: Filosofija (Belgrade)
Gledišta: Gledišta (Belgrade)
HR: Hrvatska Revija (Munich)
Komunist: Komunist (Belgrade)
NAR: Naša reč (Harrow, UK)
NH: Nova Hrvatska (London)
NIN: NIN or Nedeljne Informativne Novine (Belgrade)
NT: Naše teme (Zagreb)
Politika: Politika (Belgrade)
Praxis (Y): *Praxis* (Zagreb: Yugoslav edition)
Socijalizam: Socijalizam (Belgrade)
Sociologija: Sociologija (Belgrade)
VUS: VUS or Vjesnik u Srijedu (Zagreb)

II. *Journals in Translation:*

EA: Ekonomska Analiza (Belgrade)
Praxis (I): *Praxis* (Zagreb: International edition)
Review: Review of the Study Centre for Jugoslav Affairs (London)
STP: Socialist Thought and Practice (Belgrade)
YFV: Yugoslav Facts and Views (New York)
YL: Yugoslav Life (Belgrade)
YS: Yugoslav Survey (Belgrade)
YTU: Yugoslav Trade Unions (Belgrade)

B. *WESTERN JOURNALS*

AER: American Economic Review
APSR: American Political Science Review
AS: American Scholar
ASR: American Sociological Review
AUFSR: American Universities Field Staff Reports
AAAPSS: Annals of the American Academy of Political and Social Science
BAS: Bulletin of the Atomic Scientists
CSM: Christian Science Monitor
CPS: Comparative Political Studies
CH: Current History
Dialogue: Dialogue (Vienna: International edition)
EE: East Europe
EEQ: East European Quarterly
Encounter: Encounter (London)
FA: Foreign Affairs

FP: Foreign Policy
GAO: Government and Opposition (London)
IOC: Index on Censorship (London)
IR: Industrial Relations
Inquiry: Inquiry (Oslo)
IPQ: International Philosophical Quarterly
JBSP: Journal of the British Society for Phenomenology (Manchester)
JEL: Journal of Economic Literature
JIA: Journal of International Affairs
LAT: The Los Angeles Times
MA: Modern Age
NL: The New Leader
NR: The New Republic
NYRB: The New York Review of Books
NYT: The New York Times
PR: Partisan Review
PPR: Philosophy and Phenomenological Research
PPA: Philosophy and Public Affairs
PT: Political Theory
PC: Problems of Communism
PQ: The Political Quarterly (London)
RT: The Round Table (London)
SLR: Slavic Review
SR: Social Research
SOS: Soviet Studies (Glasgow)
SS: Soviet Survey (since 1961: *Survey*)
SCC: Studies in Comparative Communism
SST: Studies in Soviet Thought (Dordrecht)
Survey: Survey (London)
WAP: The Washington Post
WP: World Politics
WT: The World Today (London)

C. WESTERN ASSOCIATIONS

AAASS: American Association for the Advancement of Slavic Studies
APSA: American Political Science Association

References

CHAPTER I: WHAT IS MARXIST HUMANISM?

1. See "Humanist Manifesto II," in *The Humanist,* XXXIII, 5, September/October, 1973, pp. 4-9; also, *Socialist Humanism,* ed. Erich Fromm, Garden City, N. Y.: Doubleday, 1966; and *Tolerance and Revolution,* eds. Paul Kurtz & Svetozar Stojanović, Belgrade: Philosophical Society of Serbia, 1970.
2. See Svetozar Stojanović, "Contemporary Yugoslavian Philosophy," *Ethics,* LXXVI, 4, July 1966, pp. 297-301; Howard L. Parsons, *Humanistic Philosophy in Contemporary Poland and Yugoslavia,* New York: American Institute for Marxist Studies, 1966; Albert W. Levi, "Humanism and the Marxist Tradition: The Young Marx, Lukacs, the Yugoslavian School," in his *Humanism and Politics,* Bloomington: Indiana University Press, 1969.
3. Robert C. Tucker, "The Deradicalization of Marxist Movements," *APSR,* LXI, 2, June 1967, pp. 343-358.
4. "A l'occasion des critiques les plus récentes adréssées à 'Praxis'," *Praxis* (I), IV, 3-4, 1968, pp. 507-516.
5. "Za slobodu akademske diskusije" ("For Freedom of Academic Discussion"), *Praxis* (Y), IX, 3-4, May-August, 1972, p. 613.
6. *Ibid.,* p. 612; see also the editorial board's introduction to the edition's theme, "Marxism and Social Consciousness," *ibid.,* pp. 307-311, in which it reported that some of the student critics at the 1972 Korčula Summer School were detained as alleged "Trotskyites" and that their trial was in preparation. *NH,* November-December, 1972, p. 15, reported that Dr. Mihajlo Djurić of the University of Belgrade's School of Law and a member of *Praxis'* editorial board, was already in prison.
7. "The Extreme Left—Actually the Right," *STP,* 14, 3, March 1974, pp. 87-88.
8. Vladimir Slijepčević, "Nije spor oko marksističke kritike: Rasprava o 'Praxisu' na Filozofskom fakultetu u Zagrebu" ("No Contention About Marxist Criticism: Debate on *Praxis* at the Faculty of Philosophy in Zagreb"), *Komunist,* December 31, 1973, p. 28, and "Politikanstvo opozicije: Filozofski fakultet u Beogradu" ("Opposition's Politicking: The Faculty of Philosophy in Belgrade"), *ibid.,* p. 3.
9. Josip-Broz Tito, "Borba za dalji razvoj socijalističkog samoupravljanja u našoj zemlji i uloga Saveza komunista Jugoslavije" ("The Struggle for the Further Development of Socialist Self-Management in Our Country and the Role of the League of Communists of Yugoslavia"), Address to the Tenth Party Congress, May 27, 1974, *Komunist,* May 28, 1974, pp. 5-24; for Resolutions adopted at the Congress, see insert to *Komunist,* June 3, 1974, especially p. 55.
10. On student and faculty support for the "Belgrade Eight," see Slijepčević, "Politikanstvo opozicije," *op. cit.*; "Sprega protivrečnih snaga" ("The Teaming of Conflicting Forces"), *Komunist,* February 18, 1974, p. 3; and Joe Alex Morris, Jr., "Yugoslavian Regime Challenged by Liberal 'Belgrade 8'," *LAT,* June 19, 1974, I-A, p. 3.
11. Mihailo Marković, "Struktura moći u jugoslavenskom društvu i dilema revolucionarne inteligencije" ("The Power Structure in Yugoslav Society and the Dilemma of the Revolutionary Intelligentsia"), *Praxis* (Y), VIII, 6, November-December, 1971, pp. 812-813.
12. "Dokumenti o zabrani 'Praxisa'" ("Documents Concerning the Ban on

Praxis"), *Praxis* (Y), VIII, 5, September-October, 1971, p. 790.

13. Gajo Petrović, *Marx in the Mid-Twentieth Century,* Garden City, N. Y.: Doubleday, 1967, pp. 9-30, 154-169.

14. See Fred Warner Neal & Winston M. Fisk, "Yugoslavia: Towards a Market Socialism?," *PC,* XV, 6, November-December, 1966, pp. 28-37.

15. Petrović, *Marx in the Mid-Twentieth Century, op. cit.,* pp. 67-89; Mihailo Marković, "Basic Characteristics of Marxist Humanism," *Praxis* (I), V, 3-4, 1969, pp. 606-615 and *From Affluence to Praxis,* Ann Arbor: University of Michigan Press, 1974.

16. Based on Marx's Third Thesis on Feuerbach.

17. Petrović, *Marxism in the Mid-Twentieth Century, op. cit.,* pp. 31-66; Mihailo Marković, "Marx and Critical Scientific Thought," *Praxis* (I), IV, 3-4, 1968, pp. 391-403 and "Critical Social Theory in Marx," *Praxis* (I), VI, 3-4, 1970, pp. 283-297; Stojanović, "Contemporary Yugoslavian Philosophy," *op. cit.,* and *Between Ideals and Reality,* New York: Oxford University Press, 1973.

18. Miladin Zivotić, "The End of the Ideals or of Ideology," *Praxis* (I), V, 3-4, 1969, pp. 409-429; Predrag Vranicki, "Socialism and the Problem of Alienation," in *Socialist Humanism, op. cit.,* pp. 299-313; *Humanizam i socijalizam (Humanism and Socialism),* I and II, eds. Branko Bošnjak & Rudi Supek, Zagreb: Naprijed, 1963, especially Ljubomir Tadić, "The Proletariat and Bureaucracy," I, pp. 35-65; *Marks i savremenost (Marx and the Contemporary Age),* I-II, eds. Mihailo Marković, et. al., Belgrade: Institut Društvenih Nauka, 1964, especially Vojan Rus, "Problems of the Avant-Garde in the Contemporary Development of Socialism," II, pp. 7-15, and Boris Ziherl, "Socialist Policies and the De-Alienation of Man," II, pp. 547-553; and Rudi Supek, *Sociologija i socijalizam (Sociology and Socialism),* Zagreb: Znanje, 1966, pp. 23-43.

19. Mihailo Marković, "Marxist Humanism and Ethics," *Inquiry,* No. 6, 1963, p. 23.

20. Danko Grlić, "On Abstract and Real Humanism," in *Humanizam i soci- jalizam,* I, *op. cit.,* p. 138. See also Veljko Vlahović, "Theoretical Movements in the Contemporary Phase of Our Development and Further Tasks for the LCY," in *Osmi Kongres SKJ (Eighth Congress of the LCY),* Belgrade: Kultura, 1964, p. 178.

21. Marković, "Marxist Humanism and Ethics," *op. cit.,* p. 34.

22. Mihailo Marković, "Economism or the Humanization of Economics," *Praxis* (I), V, 3-4, 1969, pp. 451-475. Indeed, Predrag Vranicki claims that alienation is the central problem not of capitalism, but of socialism: see his "Socialism and the Problem of Alienation," *op. cit.,* p. 304.

23. See Rudi Supek, "Workers' Self-Management and the Humanization of Work and Consumption," in *Humanizam i socijalizam,* II, *op. cit.,* pp. 139-170; Ziherl, "Socialist Policies and the De-Alienation of Man," *op.cit.*

24. *STP,* No. 33, January-March, 1969, p. 90, emphasis added.

25. Tito, Address to the Tenth Party Congress, *op. cit.,* p.5; emphasis added.

26. Karl Marx, "On the Jewish Question," in *Karl Marx,* ed. T. B. Bottomore, New York: McGraw-Hill, 1964, p. 31; Friedrich Engels, "Socialism: Utopian and Scientific, " in *Marx & Engels,* ed. Lewis S. Feuer, Garden City, N. Y.: Doubleday, 1959, p. 106.

27. Petrović, *Marx in the Mid-Twentieth Century, op. cit.,* pp. 90-114; Marković, "Economism or the Humanization of Economics," *op. cit.*

28. Petrović, *Marx in the Mid-Twentieth Century, op. cit.,* pp. 67-89, 115-134; Marković, "Basic Characteristics of Marxist Humanism," *op. cit.,* pp. 610, 614; Vladimir Filipović, "A Contibution to the Idea of Humanity," in *Humanizam i socijalizam,* I, *op. cit.,* pp. 174-191.

29. Stojanović, "Contemporary Yugoslavian Philosophy," *op. cit.,* p. 299; Marković, "Critical Social Theory in Marx," *op. cit.,* p. 286.

30. Vranicki, "Socialism and the Problem of Alienation," *op. cit.,* p. 308.

31. See also Veljko Korać, "In Search of Human Society," in *Socialist*

Humanism, op. cit., pp. 1-15; Vojin Milić, "The Concept of Alienation and Contemporary Sociology," in *Humanizam i socijalizam,* I, *op. cit.,* pp. 89-138.

32. Petrović, *Marx in the Mid-Twentieth Century, op. cit.,* p.32.
33. *Ibid.,* p. 153.
34. Marković, "Marx and Critical Scientific Thought," *op. cit.,* p. 402.
35. Marković, "Economism or the Humanization of Economics," *op. cit.,* p. 466.
36. Veljko Rus, "Self-Management Egalitarianism and Social Differentiation," *Praxis* (I), VI, 1-2, 1970, p. 254.
37. Vojislav Stanovčić, "Konfliktne situacije u našem društvu" ("Situations of Conflict in Our Society"), *Socijalizam,* XIII, 1, January 1970, pp. 36-58.
38. Vranicki, "Socialism and the Problem of Alienation," *op. cit.;* Marković, "Economism or the Humanization of Economics," *op. cit.*
39. Mihailo Marković, "Humanism and Dialectic," in *Socialist Humanism, op. cit.,* p. 96.
40. Marković, "Struktura moći u jugoslavenskom društvu . . . ," *op. cit.,* p. 815.
41. Milan Kangrga, "Phänomenologie des ideologisch-politischen Auftretens der jugoslawischen Mittelklasse," *Praxis* (I), VII, 3-4, 1971, pp. 453-454. See also Zagorka Golubović, "Why is Functionalism More Desirable in Present-Day Yugoslavia than Marxism?," *Praxis* (I), IX, 4, 1973, pp. 357-368.
42. Ivan Kuvačić, "Middle Class Ideology," *Praxis* (I), IX, 4, 1973, pp. 351-352.
43. Kangrga, "Phänomenologie . . . ," *op. cit.,* pp. 457-458.
44. Stojanović in *Praxis* (I), VIII, 3-4, 1972, p. 383, quoted (disapprovingly) by Fuad Muhić, "Exponents of Destruction of the Proletarian Party—Who Are the Non-Party Marxists?," *STP,* 14, 1, January 1974, p. 77.
45. Ivan Kuvačić, "Scientific and Technical Progress and Humanism," *Praxis* (I), V, 1-2, 1969, pp. 181-184; Abdulah Šarčević, "Philosophy and a Human, Truly Productive World," in *Humanizam i socijalizam,* I, *op. cit.,* pp. 145-173.
46. Svetozar Stojanović, "The Dialectics of Alienation and the Utopia of Dealienation," *Praxis* (I), V, 3-4, 1969, p. 397.
47. Petrović, *Marx in the Mid-Twentieth Century, op. cit.,* pp. 160-163. Vranicki contends (in his "Observations on the Problem of Humanism," in *Humanizam i socijalizam,* I, *op. cit.,* p. 295) that the conception of communism as an eschatological end goal is quite "foreign" to Marxism.
48. Petrović, *Marx in the Mid-Twentieth Century, op. cit.,* p. 67.
49. Korać, "In Search of Human Society," *op. cit.,* p. 8.
50. Filipović, "A Contribution to the Idea of Humanity," *op. cit.,* p. 189.
51. Gajo Petrović, "Marx's Concept of Man," in *Humanizam i socijalizam,* I, *op. cit.,* p. 40.
52. Stojanović, "The Dialectics of Alienation and the Utopia of Dealienation," *op. cit.,* p. 390.
53. Marković, "Critical Social Theory in Marx," *op. cit.,* p. 296.
54. Marković, "Struktura moći u jugoslavenskom društvu . . .," *op. cit.,* p. 816.
55. *Ibid.,* p. 818.
56. Stanovčić, "Konfliktne situacije u našem društvu," *op. cit.,* p. 57.
57. Petrović, *Marx in the Mid-Twentieth Century, op. cit.,* pp. 34, 162.
58. *Ibid.,* p. 32.
59. University Committee of the LCY, Belgrade, "Sa opozicijom nema pogodbe" ("No Compromise With the Opposition"), *Komunist,* March 22, 1973, p. 10. Specifically named were the following members of the University of Belgrade's Faculty of Philosophy, Departments of Philosophy and Sociology: Mihailo Marković, Svetozar Stojanović, Miladin Životić, Ljubomir Tadić, Zagorka Pešić-Golubović, Dragoljub Mićunović, Trivo Indjić, and Nebojša Popov. The Committee blamed their influence for student demonstrations and "left-wing extremism," exemplified by

Vladimir Mijanović (convicted) and student "Trotskyites," and warned party members that there could be no "ideological coexistence."

60. *Praxis'* last international issue was No. 1-2, 1974, on "Dogmatism and Charisma" (how appropriate!); it was forced to shut down by February 1975, following the January 1975 dismissal of the eight Marxist scholars named above from the University of Belgrade—see Chapter X. Reference to *Praxis'* statement is in "Šta izjavljuje 'Praksis'" ("What is *Praxis'* Statement"), *Komunist,* May 7, 1973, p. 4, see also "Politički neodgovorni istupi 'Praksisa'" ("Politically Irresponsible Acts of *Praxis*"), joint statement by the City and University Committees of the League of Communists of Croatia, Zagreb, May 7, 1973, condemning *Praxis'* support (in issue No. 1-2, 1973) of the Belgrade and other academicians as "negative and unacceptable political action," *Komunist,* May 14, 1973, p. 4.

61. Staniša Novaković, letter to the editor regarding "Javno o Filozofiji" ("Publicly About *Filosofija*"), *Komunist,* April 26, 1973, p. 2; separate letter to the editor by Jovan Arandjelović on the same page. For *Komunist's* reply to *Filosofija,* see "Kako tome dati ime?" ("How Shall We Name That?"), on the same page; for *Komunist's* attack on *Praxis* for the latter's continued support of the Belgrade academicians (in No. 3-4, 1973), see "Jedna politikantska taktika" ("A Politicking Tactic"), *Komunist,* July 30, 1973, p. 4.

62. "The Extreme Left—Actually the Right," *op. cit.,* pp. 93, 101-102; compare with the Serbo-Croatian version, "'Nova levica' ili platforma antikomunizma" ("The 'New Left' or the Platform of Anti-Communism"), *Komunist,* March 11, 1974, pp. 20-21.

63. "The Extreme Left—Actually the Right," *op. cit.,* p. 86; Muhić, "Exponents of Destruction of the Proletarian Party . . .," *op. cit.,* p. 83; Milija Komatina, "Desničarenje u levičarskom ruhu" ("Right-Wingism in Left-Wing Clothes"), *Komunist,* March 4, 1974, p. 5; "Praksisov' prilog kampanji protiv Jugoslavije" ("*Praxis'* Contribution to the Campaign Against Yugoslavia"), *Komunist,* April 15, 1974, p. 3.

64. "The Extreme Left—Actually the Right," *op. cit.,* p. 94.

CHAPTER II: EAST-WEST DIALOGUE AND MARXIST HUMANISM

1. Mark Schorer, "The Necessity of Myth," in *Myth and Mythmaking,* ed. Henry A. Murray, Boston: Beacon, 1968, p. 355.
2. Mircea Eliade, *Myth and Reality,* New York: Harper & Row, 1963, p. 19.
3. Joseph Campbell, "The Historical Development of Mythology," in *Myth and Mythmaking, op. cit.,* p. 20.
4. Clyde Kluckhohn, "Recurrent Themes in Myths and Mythmaking," in *Myth and Mythmaking, op. cit.,* p. 58.
5. Mircea Eliade, "The Yearning for Paradise in Primitive Tradition," in *Myth and Mythmaking, op. cit.,* p. 62.
6. James G. Hart, "Mythic World as World," *IPQ,* XV, 1, March 1975, pp. 58-60.
7. Peter L. Berger & Thomas Luckmann, *The Social Construction of Reality,* Garden City, N. Y.: Doubleday, 1967, p. 102.
8. Ernest Becker, *The Birth and Death of Meaning,* New York: Free Press of Glencoe, 1962, p. 18.
9. *Ibid.,* p. 19.
10. *Ibid.,* pp. 39, 47.
11. In the sense indicated by Harold D. Lasswell in his *World Politics and Personal Insecurity,* New York: Free Press, 1965, p. 35: "Personalities display prodigious skill in justifying private goals in terms of master symbols; insofar as this process is unconscious, it is rationalization; insofar as it is conscious, it is justification."
12. *Ibid.,* pp. 30-31.

13. *Ibid.*, p. 31. For Lasswell's definition of political man as an individual who displaces private affects upon public objects and rationalizes them in terms of the public interest: p - d - r = P, see his *Psychopathology and Politics*, New York: Viking, 1962, p. 124.

14. Norbert Wiener, *The Human Use of Human Beings*, Garden City, N. Y.: Doubleday, 1956, pp. 7-12.

15. Peter L. Berger, *Pyramids of Sacrifice*, New York: Basic Books, 1974, p. 231.

16. Lewis S. Feuer, *Ideology and the Ideologists*, New York: Harper & Row, 1975, p. 1.

17. Berger & Luckmann, *The Social Construction of Reality, op. cit.*, p. 104.

18. Feuer, *Ideology and the Ideologists, op. cit.*, p. 188.

19. *Ibid.*, p. 191.

20. Quoted by Frederick L. Schuman, *Russia Since 1917*, New York: Knopf, 1957, p. 482.

21. Charles E. Osgood, *An Alternative to War or Surrender*, Urbana: University of Illinois Press, 1962, p. 88.

22. Anatol Rapoport, *Strategy and Conscience*, New York: Harper & Row, 1964, p. 176.

23. Fred Warner Neal, "Co-Existence: Practical Problems and Politics," *Co-Existence*, 3, 1, January 1966, pp. 8, 18.

24. Gustav A. Wetter, "Freedom of Thought and Ideological Coexistence," in *Philosophy in the Soviet Union*, ed. Ervin Laszlo, Dordrecht: Reidel, 1967, p. 172.

25. Andrei D. Sakharov, *Progress, Coexistence, and Intellectual Freedom*, New York: Norton, 1968, p. 27.

26. *Ibid.*, pp. 83-85.

27. Sakharov, "Peace, Progress and Human Rights," *IOC*, 5, 2, Summer 1976, p. 5.

28. *Ibid.*, p. 3; Sakharov, *My Country and the World*, New York; Vintage, 1975, pp. 63-64, 99-109.

29. Sakharov, *My Country and the World, op. cit.*, pp. 100-102.

30. *Ibid.*, pp. 102-103 and "Peace, Progress and Human Rights," *op. cit.*, p. 9.

31. Aleksandr I. Solzhenitsyn, "Letter of 12 November 1969," protesting his expulsion from the Soviet Writers' Union, in *Solzhenitsyn*, enl. ed., ed. Leopold Labedz, Bloomington: Indiana University Press, 1973, pp. 219-220.

32. Solzhenitsyn, "America: You Must Think About the World," in *Solzhenitsyn: The Voice of Freedom*, Washington, D. C.: AFL-CIO Publication No. 152, 1975, pp. 19-20.

33. Solzhenitsyn, "Communism: A Legacy of Terror," in *Solzhenitsyn: The Voice of Freedom, op. cit.*, p. 39.

34. Solzhenitsyn, *Letter to the Soviet Leaders*, New York: Harper & Row, 1975, pp. 3, 15, 19, 50, 55-66, 77.

35. Roy A. Medvedev, *On Socialist Democracy*, New York: Knopf, 1975, p. 282.

36. *Ibid.*, pp. xv-xx, 30-47.

37. *Ibid.*, p. 104.

38. *Ibid.*, p. 324.

39. Karl Marx & Friedrich Engels, *The German Ideology*, New York: International Publishers, 1969, pp. 39-41; *The Communist Manifesto*, in *Marx & Engels*, ed. Lewis S. Feuer, Garden City, N. Y.: Doubleday, 1959, pp. 20-29.

40. Robert Adolfs, "Church and Communism," in *The Christian Marxist Dialogue*, ed. Paul Oestreicher, London: Macmillan, 1969, pp. 29-54.

41. Santiago Alvarez, "Towards an Alliance of Communists and Catholics (New Features of the Spanish Scene)," in *The Christian Marxist Dialogue, op. cit.*, pp. 68-93.

42. Milan Machovec, *et. al.*, "Tasks for the Dialogue," in *The Christian*

Marxist Dialogue, op. cit., pp. 115-130.

43. Roger Garaudy, *From Anathema to Dialogue,* New York: Vintage, 1966, pp. 31-38, 120-124.

44. Vincenzo Miano, "Through Dialogue to Alliance," *Dialogue,* I, 1, Spring 1968, pp. 55-57.

45. Johannes B. Metz, "Christianity and Social Action—Three Hypotheses for Discussion," in *The Christian Marxist Dialogue, op. cit.,* p. 195.

46. Cardinal Franz König, "Man Moulded by Society," *Dialogue,* I, 1, Spring 1968, p. 7.

47. Franz Boeckle, "More than Individual Morals," *Dialogue,* I, 1, Spring 1968, p. 25.

48. Johannes Baptist Metz, "Through Religion to Revolution," *Dialogue,* I, 1, Spring 1968, p. 43.

49. Giulio Girardi, "Through Revolution to Peace," *Dialogue,* I, 1, Spring 1968, p. 49.

50. A. .O. Dyson, "God and Man in the Marxist Christian Dialogue," in *The Christian Marxist Dialogue, op. cit.,* pp. 282-283.

51. Vassily P. Tugarinov, "More than Class Morals," *Dialogue,* I, 1, Spring 1968, p. 19.

52. Lucio Lombardo-Radice, "Marxism Embracing Pluralism," *Dialogue,* I, 1, Spring 1968, pp. 26-30.

53. Robert Kalivoda, "Christian Origins of Marxism," *Dialogue,* I, 1, Spring 1968, p. 39.

54. Milan Machovec, quoted by Günther Nenning, "Minutes of Marienbad," *Dialogue,* I, 1, Spring 1968, p. 66.

55. Lombardo-Radice, *op. cit.,* p. 27; Kalivoda, *op. cit.,* p. 37; Alan Ecclestone, "Priest and Communist," in *The Christian Marxist Dialogue, op. cit.,* pp. 59-60; Ylena Marculescu, "Dogmatism and Integrity," in *ibid.,* p. 206; Konrad Farner, "A Marxist View of Dialogue," in *ibid.,* p. 216; Milan Prucha, "Marxism as a Philosophy of Human Existence," in *ibid.,* p. 266; Garaudy, *op. cit.,* pp. 72-76.

56. J. Čvekl, quoted by Nenning, "Minutes of Marienbad," *op. cit.,* p.70.

57. Garaudy, *From Anathema to Dialogue, op. cit.,* p. 86.

58. J. Claude Evans, "Beyond Dogmatism in Europe's Marxist-Christian Dialogue," *Christian Century,* XCI, 3, January 23, 1974, p. 70.

59. Garaudy, *From Anathema to Dialogue, op. cit.,* p. 86.

60. Garaudy was expelled from the Partie Communiste Française in the Spring of 1970. For the circumstances surrounding his expulsion as well as a brief account of the thought of this most unusual French Marxist philosopher, see Maurice Cranston, "The Thought of Roger Garaudy," *PC,* XIX, 5, September-October, 1970, pp. 11-18.

61. Quoted by Schuman, *Russia Since 1917, op. cit.,* p. 265.

62. Since Lenin's classic statement in his "Theses on the Question of the Immediate Conclusion of a Separate and Annexationist Peace" of 1918, much has happened to undermine even his thesis of a common proletarian or Marxist strategy if we read the post-World War II history of the communist movement carefully. Suffice it to draw attention to the differences in their respective conceptions of proletarian internationalism and Marxist strategy of the USSR, China, and Yugoslavia.

63. Adam B. Ulam, *Expansion and Coexistence: Soviet Foreign Policy, 1917-1973,* 2nd ed., New York: Praeger, 1975. The conflict between Russian national interest and the demands of world revolution constitutes the underlying theme of this encyclopaedic study of Soviet foreign policy.

64. George W. Hoffman & Fred W. Neal, *Yugoslavia and the New Communism,* New York: Twentieth Century Fund, 1962, p. 4.

65. See Dan N. Jacob's "Introduction" to *The New Communisms,* ed. D. N. Jacob, New York: Harper & Row, 1969, pp. 1-17.

66. Adopted, with slight modifications, from Zbigniew K. Brzezinski's *The Soviet Bloc,* Cambridge: Harvard University Press, 1967.

67. The most exhaustive treatment of this paradox in the Yugoslav case is that by Hoffman & Neal, *Yugoslavia and the New Communism, op. cit.*, especially pp. 155-173.

68. Carl J. Friedrich & Zbigniew K. Brzezinski, *Totalitarian Dictatorship and Autocracy,* Cambridge: Harvard University Press, 1965, pp. 21-22.

69. Joseph M. Bochenski, "The Great Split," *SST,* VIII, 1, March 1968, pp. 1-15.

70. *Ibid.,* pp. 10-11.

71. Wolfgang Leonhard, *Three Faces of Marxism,* New York: Holt, Rinehart & Winston, 1974, p. 360.

72. Richard T. De George, *The New Marxism,* New York: Pegasus, 1968, p. 51.

73. De George distinguishes among three groups of Marxists: scientific dogmatists, critical humanists, and negative critics, in his "Communism and the New Marxists," in *Marxism and Religion in Eastern Europe,* eds. R. T. De George & James P. Scanlan, Dordrect: Reidel, 1976, pp. 3-12.

74. Maurice Cranston, "Neocommunism and the Students' Revolts," *SCC,* I, 1-2, July-October, 1968, p. 45.

75. Edmund Demaitre, "In Search of Humanism," *PC,* XIV, 5, September-October, 1965, pp. 18-30, arrives at the same conclusion.

76. See Sidney Hook, *Marx and the Marxists,* New York: Nostrand, 1955, pp. 65-75; Karl Kautsky's evolutionary and democratic socialism also contains an essential humanist element, although his determinism detracts from it.

77. Daniel Bell, "In Search of Marxist Humanism: The Debate on Alienation," *SS,* No. 32, April-June, 1960, p. 29.

78. Quoted by Leonhard, *Three Faces of Marxism, op. cit.,* pp. 283-284.

79. See Serge Frankel & Daniel Martin, "The Budapest School," *Telos,* No. 17, Fall 1973, pp. 122-133, and Ervin Laszlo, "Trends in East-European Philosophy: A Case Study on Hungary," *SST,* VII, 2, June 1967, pp. 130-141.

80. András Hegedüs & Mária Márkus, "Modernization and the Alternatives of Social Progress," *Telos,* No. 17, Fall 1973, p. 156.

81. See "Hungarian Party Document," *Telos,* No. 17, Fall 1973, pp. 134-145.

82. Adam Schaff, "Marxism and the Philosophy of Man," in *Socialist Humanism,* ed. Erich Fromm, Garden City, N.Y.: Doubleday, 1966, p. 141.

83. Bronislaw Baczko, "Marx and the Idea of the Universality of Man," in *Socialist Humanism, op.* cit., p. 192.

84. Howard L. Parsons, *Humanistic Philosophy in Contemporary Poland and Yugoslavia,* New York: American Institute for Marxist Studies, 1966, pp. 3-4. Marx defined "praxis" in his First Thesis on Feuerbach as "sensuous human activity:" See Marx & Engels, *The German Ideology, op. cit.,* p. 197.

85. Quoted by Demaitre, "In Search of Humanism," op. cit., p. 22.

86. Leszek Kolakowski, *Toward a Marxist Humanism,* New York: Grove, 1969, especially in his famous essay "The Priest and the Jester," pp. 9-37. Expelled from the Polish CP in 1966 for his left-wing views and in 1968 from his Philosophy chair at the University of Warsaw because of his support of student rebels, had to leave the country. Kolakowski's little-known sixty-five theses on "What Socialism is Not" can be compared to Martin Luther's ninety-five theses; see *The Christian Marxist Dialogue,* op. cit., pp. 165-169.

87. Kolakowski, *Toward a Marxist Humanism,* op. cit., p. 119.

88. Adam Schaff, *Marxism and the Human Individual,* New York: McGraw-Hill, 1970, p. 247.

89. For a minimal understanding of these events, see Ludvik Vaculik, "Two Thousand Words," *SCC,* I, 1-2, July-October, 1968, pp. 237-243 and the Soviet reply by I. Alexandrov, "Attack on the Socialist Foundations of Czechoslovakia," in *ibid.,* pp. 243-247 "Action Program of the Czechoslovak Party," in *ibid.,* pp. 178-181; for the Soviet ultimatum and the Czech response, see *EE,* 17, 8, August 1968, pp. 34-35 & 36-37; and H.

Gordon Skilling, *Czechoslovakia's Interrupted Revolution*, Princeton: Princeton University Press, 1976.

90. Compare Svitak's lecture at Charles University, published by *Student* (Prague) on April 10, 1968, excerpted in *EE*, 17, 6, June 1968, pp. 25-26: "Czechoslovakia: Revolution or Revolt," with his earlier article on "The Sources of Socialist Humanism," in *Socialist Humanism, op. cit.,* pp. 16-28.

91. Svitak, *"The Sources of Socialist Humanism," op. cit.,* p. 21.

92. Demaitre, *"In Search of Humanism," op. cit.,* p. 25.

93. *Ibid.,* p. 23 Schaff, *Marxism and the Human Individual, op. cit.,* pp. 128, 137-138, 196-197.

94. Schaff, *Marxism and the Human Individual, op. cit.,* p. 254; compare with his statement on p. 189: " . . . through its abolition of alienation communism creates the conditions for true freedom for men."

95. Leonhard, *Three Faces of Marxism, op. cit.,* p. 370.

96. Roger Garaudy, *The Alternative Future*, New York: Simon & Schuster, 1974, p. 78. Garaudy's open-ended, liberal, and democratic vision of the Christian-Marxist dialogue contrasts with the dogmatic official view in the East: see Janusz Kuczyński, "The Marxist-Christian Dialogue," *Dialectics and Humanism* (Warsaw), I, 2, Spring 1974, pp. 117-132.

97. Pavel Kovaly, "Is it Possible to Humanize Marxism?," *SST*, 11, 4, December 1971, p. 289.

CHAPTER III: TITOISM: ALTERNATIVE TO STALINISM?

1. Fred Warner Neal, "Yugoslav Communist Theory," *American Slavic and East European Review*, XIX, 1, February 1960, p. 42 and in F. W. Neal & George W. Hoffman, *Yugoslavia and the New Communism*, New York: Twentieth Century Fund, 1962, p. 151.

2. M. George Zaninovich, *The Development of Socialist Yugoslavia*, Baltimore: Johns Hopkins University Press, 1968, pp. 67-97.

3. Wolfgang Leonhard, *Three Faces of Marxism*, New York: Holt, Rinehart & Winston, 1974, p. 360.

4. These exchanges were actually between Tito, with Kardelj participating, on the one side, and Stalin, joined by Molotov, on the other; see *Yugoslavia and the New Communism, op. cit.,* p. 129.

5. Letters from CC of CPSU to CC of CPY of March 27, May 4, and May 22, 1948, in *The Soviet-Yugoslav Controversy, 1948-1958*, eds. Robert Bass & Elisabeth Marbury, New York: East Europe Institute, 1959, pp. 6, 33, 38-39; see also *Yugoslavia and the Soviet Union, 1939-1973*, ed. Stephen Clissold, New York: Oxford University Press, 1975.

6. Letter from the CC of CPY to the CC of CPSU of May 17, 1948, in *The Soviet-Yugoslav Controversy, op. cit.,* p. 36.

7. Official Yugoslav statistics on this are available; I am drawing on the account by Tito's semi-official biographer, Vladimir Dedijer, *Tito Speaks*, London: Weidenfeld & Nicolson, 1953, p. 271: "Reports were received by our authorities that Red Army officers and men had committed 1,219 rapes on Yugoslav territory, 329 attempted rapes, 11 rapes with murder, 248 rapes and attempts at murder and 1,204 robberies with violence." These official statistics underestimate the true extent of Red Army vandalism, because: (1) Most victims were afraid to report them for fear of reprisals; and (2) Even Yugoslav communist officials often would or could not admit this kind of "unsocialist" behavior on the part of Red Army troops to themselves and others.

8. *Tito Speaks, op. cit.,* pp. 264-265.

9. On Stalinism in Yugoslavia, see F. W. Neal, *Titoism in Action*, Berkeley: University of California Press, 1958, pp. 3-6, and *Yugoslavia and the New Communism, op. cit.,* pp. 67-102.

10. According to Bass & Marbury in *The Soviet-Yugoslav Controversy, op. cit.,* p. 2, the Yugoslavs requested a "partial withdrawal" of Soviet advisers.

11. Letter from CC of CPY to CC of CPSU of April 13, 1948, in *The Soviet-Yugoslav Controversy, op. cit.,* p. 15.

12. A. Ross Johnson, *The Transformation of Communist Ideology,* Cambridge, Mass.: MIT Press, 1972, p. 241.

13. *White Book on Aggressive Activities by the Governments of the USSR, Poland, Czechoslovakia, Hungary, Rumania, Bulgaria and Albania Towards Yugoslavia,* Belgrade: Ministry of Foreign Affairs, 1951; it lists no less than 46 breaches of treaties, agreements, conventions, and protocols by the governments of Cominform countries (p. 447).

14. For the rationale behind American support to Tito, see John C. Campbell, *Tito's Separate Road,* New York: Harper & Row, 1967, pp. 10-29.

15. For a condensed account of the East European equivalent of the notorious Soviet *Yezhovshchina,* see Zbigniew K. Brzezinski, *The Soviet Bloc,* Cambridge, Mass.: Harvard University Press, 1967, pp. 91-97.

16. See Alvin Z. Rubinstein, *Yugoslavia and the Nonaligned World,* Princeton: Princeton University Press, 1970; and *Tito on Non-Alignment,* ed. Ranko Petković, Belgrade: Federal Committee for Information, 1976. The principles of the 1955 Belgrade Declaration were reaffirmed by Soviet party chief Leonid I. Brezhnev on several occasions, including Tito's last trip to Moscow in 1979.

17. Neal, *Yugoslavia and the New Communism, op. cit.,* p. 151.

18. *Yugoslavia's Way,* trans. Stoyan Pribichevich, New York: All Nations Press, 1958 (translation of *Sedmi Kongres* [*Seventh Congress*], Belgrade: Kultura, 1958), pp. 28-29; earlier, Tito went even further in his indictment of Stalinism, if we are to believe Dedijer quoting Tito in *Tito Speaks, op. cit.,* p. 263: "Never in history has the individual been so subjugated to the State machine as in the Soviet Union today. Nowhere are men so inhumanly treated as they are in the Soviet Union after thirty-four years of Soviet rule, when the world expected the Soviet Union to become a model country for all, not only materially but also as the embodiment of a free socialist people. Instead, it has betrayed socialism."

19. Josip-Broz Tito, "Fifty Years of Revolutionary Struggle by the Communists of Yugoslavia," Opening Address to the Ninth Party Congress, March 11, 1969, *STP,* No. 33, January-March, 1969, p. 17.

20. *Yugoslavia's Way, op. cit.,* p. 104.

21. *Ibid.,* p. 136.

22. *The Constitution of the Socialist Federal Republic of Yugoslavia,* Belgrade: Federal Secretariat for Information, 1963, p. 20.

23. *Osmi Kongres SKJ (Eighth Congress of the LCY),* Belgrade: Kultura, 1964, p. 27; and Resolution on "Socialist Development in Yugoslavia on the Basis of Self-Management and the Tasks of the League of Communists" adopted at the Ninth Party Congress, *STP,* No. 33, January-March, 1969, pp. 48-53.

24. Tito, "The Struggle for the Further Development of Socialist Self-Management in Our Country and the Role of the League of Communists of Yugoslavia," Address to the Tenth Party Congress, *STP,* XIV, 6-7, June-July, 1974, pp. 21-29; and Tito, "The LCY in the Struggle for the Further Development of Socialist, Self-Managing and Nonaligned Yugoslavia," Report to the Eleventh Party Congress, *STP,* XVIII, 6, June 1978, pp. 28-41.

25. *Osmi Kongres SKJ, op. cit.,* p. 161; Resolution adopted at the Ninth Party Congress, *op. cit.,* p. 54; Tito's Address to the Tenth Party Congress, *op. cit.,* pp. 34-37; Tito's Report to the Eleventh Party Congress, *op. cit.,* pp. 48-52, 63.

26. *Osmi Kongres SKJ, op. cit.,* p. 177; Tito's Addresses to the Ninth & Tenth Party Congresses, *op. cit.,* pp. 33 & 34, respectively; Tito's Report to the

Eleventh Party Congress, *op. cit.,* pp. 43-48, 63.

27. *Yugoslavia's Way, op. cit.,* p. 30. For the Soviet critique of the 1958 Yugoslav Draft Program, see *Kommunist* (Moscow), April 19, 1958, and *Pravda* (Moscow) editorial of May 9, 1958; for communist Chinese criticism of the Program, see editorial in *Jenmin Jihpao* (Peiping) of May 5, 1958; instructive are also Nikita S. Krushchev's speech in Sofia and Tito's speech at Labin; all in *The Soviet-Yugoslav Controversy, op. cit.,* pp. 141-190.

28. *Yugoslavia's Way, op. cit.,* p. 176.

29. *Ibid.,* p. 135.

30. "Constitutional System of the Socialist Federal Republic of Yugoslavia," *YS,* XV, 3, August 1974, p. 4. See also *Ustav Socijalističke Federativne Republike Jugoslavije (The Constitution of the Socialist Federal Republic of Yugoslavia),* Belgrade: Sekretarijat Saveznog izvršnog veća za informacije, 1974.

31. *Ibid.,* p. 93.

32. Milovan Djilas, *The New Class,* New York: Praeger, 1963 and *The Unperfect Society,* New York: Harcourt, Brace & World, 1969; for the ethical roots of Djilas' discontent, see his *Anatomy of a Moral,* New York: Praeger, 1959.

33. *Yugoslavia's Way, op. cit.,* p. 235.

34. Tito, quoted by Paul Lendvai, *Eagles in Cobwebs,* Garden City, N. Y.: Doubleday, 1969, p. 127.

35. Tito, Address to the Ninth Party Congress, *op. cit.,* p. 29; and Edvard Kardelj, "The Class Position of the League of Communists Today," *STP,* No. 37, December 1969, pp. 12-13. The Yugoslav view of the strengthening of the party's role in the process of its withering away is reminiscent of Stalin's dictum that the authority of the state must be increased before it could be abolished!

36. "Resolution on the Ideological-Political Foundations for the Further Development of the League of Communists of Yugoslavia," *STP,* No. 33, January-March, 1969, p. 90; emphasis added.

37. Tito, Address to the Tenth Party Congress, *op. cit.,* p. 56.

38. Edvard Kardelj, *Socijalistička demokratija u jugoslovenskoj praksi (Socialist Democracy in Yugoslav Practice),* Belgrade: Kultura, 1957, p. 5.

39. *Yugoslavia's Way, op. cit.,* p. 71.

40. *Ibid,* pp. 71-77. See also Zvonko Štaubringer, "Humanistic Vision of a New World," *STP,* No. 39, April-June, 1970, pp. 100-102; Čazim Sadiković, "Etatizam i odnosi medju socijalističkim zemljama" ("Etatism and Relations Between Socialist Countries"), *Socijalizam,* XIII, 9, September 1970, p. 1086; and Zlatko Čepo, "Proleterski internacionalizam danas" ("Proletarian Internationalism Today"), *VUS,* No. 1251, May 1, 1976, pp. 21-24.

41. "Etatism and Relations Between Socialist Countries," *op. cit.,* p. 1086.

42. Branko Pribičević, "For an Open Dialogue in the Communist Movement," *STP,* No. 30, April-June, 1968, p.61.

43. Resolution on the "Socialist Development in Yugoslavia on the Basis of Self-Management and the Tasks of the LCY," adopted at the Ninth Party Congress, *op. cit.,* p. 44.

44. Pribičević, "For an Open Dialogue in the Communist Movement," *op. cit.,* pp. 69-74.

45. Rubinstein, *Yugoslavia and the Nonaligned World, op. cit.,* p. xii.

46. Milovan Baletić, "Triumf u Lusaki" ("Triumph in Lusaka"), *VUS,* No. 960, September 23, 1970, pp. 14-17; "Fifth Conference of Non-Aligned Countries," *YFV,* No. 105, September 1976, pp. 18-19; "Recognition to Tito," *YL,* XXIV, 9-10, September-October, 1979, p. 1.

47. Charles P. McVicker, *Titoism,* New York: St. Martin's, 1957, p. 296.

48. Albert W. Levi, *Humanism and Politics,* Bloomington: Indiana University Press, 1969, p. 445; Ghița Ionesco, "Djilas, Tito and Yugoslav Socialism," *PQ,* 41, 3, July-September, 1970, p. 308.

49. Neal, *Yugoslavia and the New Communism, op. cit.*, p. 172.
50. Tito, Report to the Fifth Party Congress, Belgrade, July 1948, in *The Essential Tito*, ed. Henry M. Christman, New York: St. Martin's, 1970, p. 72; emphasis added.
51. *Yugoslavia's Way, op. cit.*, p. 233.
52. *Osmi Kongres SKJ, op. cit.*, p. 183.
53. Resolution on the "Socialist Development in Yugoslavia on the Basis of Self-Management and the Tasks of the LCY," *op. cit.*, pp. 44-45.
54. Tito, Address to the Tenth Party Congress, *op. cit.*, p. 74.
55. Tito, "On Workers' Management in Economic Enterprises," in *The Essential Tito, op. cit.*, p. 91.
56. Kardelj, *Socijalistička demokratija u jugoslovenskoj praksi, op. cit.*, p. 35.
57. On the Socialist Alliance of the Working People of Yugoslavia, see the 1958 Draft Program; also, *Šesti kongres Socijalističkog Saveza radnog naroda Jugoslavije (Sixth Congress of the Socialist Alliance of the Working People of Yugoslavia)*, Belgrade: Kultura, 1966; and "Constitutional System of the Socialist Federal Republic of Yugoslavia," *op. cit.*, p. 52. The Socialist Alliance has been one of the party's major transmission belts.
58. Kardelj, "Ustavni osnovi socijalističkih društveno-ekonomskih odnosa i društvenog samoupravljanja" ("The Constitutional Bases of Socialist Socio-Economic Relations and Social Self-Government"), in Kardelj, et al., *O Ustavnom sistemu Socijalističke Federativne Republike Jugoslavije (On the Constitutional System of the Socialist Federal Republic of Yugoslavia)*, Belgrade: Komunist, 1963, p. 16.
59. See Winston M. Fisk & Alvin Z. Rubinstein, "Yugoslavia's Constitutional Court," *EE*, XV, 7, July 1966, pp. 24-28; Fisk, "A Communist *Rechtsstaat?*—The Case of Yugoslav Constitutionalism," *GAO*, 5, 1, Winter 1969-70, pp. 41-53, and "The Constitutionalism Movement in Yugoslavia: A Preliminary Survey," *SLR*, 30, 2, June 1971, pp. 277-297.
60. Tito, quoted by Staubringer, "Humanistic Vision of a New World," *op. cit.*, p. 109; see also Tito's Address to the Sixth Congress of the Socialist Alliance, in *Šesti kongres Socijalističkog Saveza radnog naroda Jugoslavije, op. cit.*, pp. 8-10, and his Address to the Tenth Party Congress, *op. cit.*, p. 47.
61. On the "Four Ds," see Lendvai, *Eagles in Cobwebs, op. cit.*, pp. 140-172, and Dennison I. Rusinow, "Crisis in Croatia," II, *AUFSR*, SE Europe Series, XIX, 5, September 1972, pp. 1-17.
62. Quoted by Sharon Zukin, *Beyond Marx and Tito*, New York: Cambridge University Press, 1975, p. 147.
63. Lendvai, *Eagles in Cobwebs, op. cit.*, p. 54.
64. Claire Sterling, "Tito's New Balancing Act," *The Atlantic*, 231, 6, June 1973, p. 44.
65. Paul Sweezy, cited by Bogdan D. Denitch, *The Legitimation of a Revolution*, New Haven: Yale University Press, 1976, p. 10.
66. "Constitutional System of the Socialist Federal Republic of Yugoslavia," *op. cit.*, p. 52.
67. Fred Singleton, "Yugoslavia: Democratic Centralism and Market Socialism," *WT*, 29, 4, April 1973, p. 168.
68. "Constitutional System," *op. cit.*, p. 56.
69. Jacob Walkin, "Yugoslavia After the 10th Party Congress," *Survey*, 98, 1, Winter 1976, pp. 72-73; Denitch, *The Legitimation of a Revolution, op. cit.*, p. 186; D. I. Rusinow, "Laissez-Faire Socialism in Yugoslavia: Experiences and Compromises in Efforts to Liberalize a Command Economy," *AUFSR*, SE Europe Series, XIV, 2, September 1967, p. 15.
70. Walkin, "Yugoslavia After the 10th Party Congress," *op. cit.*, pp. 55-56.
71. Edvard Kardelj, "Democracy in Socialism and Not Against Socialism," *STP*, XIV, 5, May 1974, pp. 5-12.
72. Tito, "Borba za dalji razvoj socijalističkog samoupravljanja u našoj zemlji

i uloga Saveza komunista Jugoslavije" ("The Struggle for the Further Development of Socialist Self-Management in Our Country and the Role of the League of Communists of Yugoslavia"), Address to the Tenth Party Congress, *Komunist,* No. 897, May 28, 1974, p. 5; emphasis added.

73. Zukin, *Beyond Marx and Tito, op. cit.,* pp. 164-191.
74. *Ibid.,* p. 247.
75. Dusko Doder, "Slovenia Mixes Red Rule, West's Ways," *LAT,* October 22, 1976, I-A, p. 6.
76. See Rusinow, "Laissez-Faire Socialism in Yugoslavia," *op. cit.,* pp. 1-19; Deborah D. Milenkovitch, "Which Direction for Yugoslavia's Economy?," in *Comparative Communism,* eds. Gary K. Bertsch & Thomas W. Ganschow, San Francisco: Freeman, 1976, pp. 352-360; and George W. Hoffman, "Migration and Social Change," *PC,* XXII, 6, November-December, 1973, pp. 16-31.
77. See K. F. Cviić, "Yugoslavia After Tito," *WT,* 32, 4, April 1976, p. 127, for the 1955 per capita income at $375; the 1975 per capita income of $1,000 referred to by Kiro Gligorov, President of the SFRY Assembly, in an interview "Produktivnost—jedino moguća osnova stabilizacije" ("Productivity—The Only Possible Basis for Stabilization"), *EP,* No. 1245, February 9, 1976, p. 19; the minimal monthly expenditures for a family of four at 3,800 (new) dinars indicated in "Strah nazvan uravnilovkom" ("Fear Called *Uravnilovka*"), *NIN,* No. 1313, March 7, 1976, p. 15; a Personal Income Table for March 1975 shows that 79.3 percent of all employed had monthly incomes no higher than 3,500 dinars (official exchange rate, November 1976: 1 U. S. dollar = 18.5 dinars), "Koliko nam je socijalna politika socijalistička" ("How Socialist Is Our Social Welfare Policy?"), *VUS,* No. 1241, February 21, 1976, p. 21.
78. "Fiziognomija jednog štrajka" ("The Physiognomy of a Strike"), *Pogledi* (Split), No. 3, 1970, pp. 22-28; an unusually candid analysis of the dynamics of a strike for the Yugoslav press which, in general, carries such superficial reports as "Zašto nisu radili?" ("Why Did They Not Work?"), *VUS,* No. 1246, March 27, 1976, pp. 10-11.
79. Tito, Address to the Tenth Party Congress, *op. cit.,* p. 26.
80. "Fear Called *Uravnilovka*," *op. cit.,* p. 14. The *socialist* principle of "From each according to his ability, to each according to his *work*" differs from the principle "From each according to his ability, to each according to his *needs,*" to be operationalized in *communism.*
81. Zukin, *Beyond Marx and Tito, op. cit.,* p. 62.
82. Vojo Srzentić, "Opasnosti uravnilovke" ("Dangers of the *Uravnilovka*"), *NIN,* No. 1316, March 28, 1976, p. 8.
83. *Ibid.,* p. 6.
84. Županov, cited in "Fear Called *Uravnilovka*," *op. cit.,* p. 15.
85. Tito, "Building the Ethics of the Socialist Order of Self-Management," *STP,* XVI, 2, February 1976, p. 5; Tito urged the elimination of three categories of "misdemeanor" in the economy: (1) Those who engage in corrupt behavior for the benefit of their collective; (2) Those guilty of petty and major thefts; and (3) "Big-time operators" who join forces with "various people in our foreign trade," *ibid.,* p. 19.
86. Matija Bećković, "O Jugoslovenima" ("On Yugoslavs"), in *Dr. Janez Paćuka o medjuvremenu (Dr. Janez Pacuka on the Meantime),* Novi Sad: Matica Srpska, 1969, pp. 81-84, quoted in Zukin, *Beyond Marx and Tito, op. cit.,* p. 113.
87. A Yugoslav respondent, quoted by Zukin, in *ibid.,* p. 109.
88. Bećković, quoted by Zukin, in *ibid.,* pp. 113-114.
89. *Ibid.,* pp. 206, 257-260.
90. Kardelj, "Towards a New Type of Socialist Democracy," *STP,* XVI, 4, April 1976, pp. 6-7.
91. Milton & Rose Friedman, *Free to Choose,* New York: Harcourt Brace Jovanovich, 1980, p. 24.

92. Lendvai, *Eagles in Cobwebs, op. cit.,* pp. 118-119; see also D. Plamenić, "The Belgrade Student Insurrection," *The New Left Review,* No. 54, 1969, pp. 61-78.

93. D. I. Rusinow, "Anatomy of a Student Revolt," I, *AUFSR,* SE Europe Series, XV, 4, August 1968, p. 8. For the most comprehensive study on student unrest, see Ralph Pervan, *Tito and the Students,* Nedlands: University of Western Australia Press, 1978.

94. D. I. Rusinow, "Anatomy of a Student Revolt," II, *AUFSR,* SE Europe Series, XV, 5, November 1968, pp. 2-3.

95. Zukin, *Beyond Marx and Tito, op. cit.,* p. 65.

96. D. I. Rusinow, "Crisis in Croatia," I, *AUFSR,* SE Europe Series, XIX, 4, June 1972, p. 10; see also Gary K. Bertsch, "The Revival of Nationalisms," *PC,* XXII, 6, November-December, 1973, pp. 1-15; Barbara Jancar, "Yugoslavia: The Case for a Loyal Opposition under Communism," in *Comparative Communism, op. cit.,* pp. 205-220; George Schöpflin, "The Ideology of Croatian Nationalism," *Survey,* 19, 1, Winter 1973, pp. 122-146; and Paul Shoup, *Communism and the Yugoslav National Question,* New York: Columbia University Press, 1968.

97. Singleton, "Yugoslavia," *op. cit.,* pp. 161-162.

98. Čepo, "Proleterski internacionalizam danas," *op. cit.,* p. 22; emphasis added.

99. Rusinow, "Crisis in Croatia," II, *op. cit.,* pp. 2, 6.

100. Lendvai, *Eagles in Cobwebs, op. cit.,* p. 139.

101. George Klein, "The Role of Ethnic Politics in the Czechoslovak Crisis of 1968 and the Yugoslav Crisis of 1971," *SCC,* VIII, 4, Winter 1975, p. 360.

102. D. I. Rusinow, "The Price of Pluralism," *AUFSR,* SE Europe Series, XVIII, 1, July 1971, p. 10.

103. Kladjanin, quoted in Rusinow, "Crisis in Croatia," I, *op. cit.,* p. 13.

104. Planinc, quoted in *ibid.,* p. 12.

105. Anonymous, quoted in Lendvai, *Eagles in Cobwebs, op. cit.,* p. 119.

106. D. I. Rusinow, "Yugoslavia's Return to Leninism: Notes on the Tenth Congress of the Yugoslav League of Communists," *AUFSR,* SE Europe Series, XXI, 1, June 1974, pp. 1-13.

107. Prvoslav Ralić, "Dogma komandovanja partije" ("The Dogma of Party Command"), *Komunist,* No. 981, January 5, 1976, p. 22.

108. Lendvai, *Eagles in Cobwebs, op. cit.,* pp. 132-133.

109. Rusinow, "Yugoslavia's Return to Leninism," *op. cit.,* pp. 4-5; see also D. I. Rusinow, *The Yugoslav Experiment, 1948-1974,* Berkeley: University of California Press, 1977.

110. Title of Chapter 8 in Dusko Doder's perceptive *The Yugoslavs,* New York: Random House, 1978, p. 116.

111. Tito, Report to the Eleventh Party Congress, *op. cit.,* p. 59.

112. Edvard Kardelj, *Pravci razvoja političkog sistema socijalističkog samoupravljanja (Directions of Development of the Political System of Socialist Self-Management),* 2nd. enl. ed., Belgrade: Komunist, 1978, p. 107. This last major work by Kardelj has emerged as his *magnum opus,* the theoretical basis for deliberations at the Eleventh Party Congress, and a summary of the Yugoslav experiment (Titoism).

113. Some Marxist humanist theorists imply that the *Leninist* party is Stalinist: see Svetozar Stojanović, *Geschichte und Parteibewusstsein,* Munich: Carl Hanser, 1978, p. 39. However, the notion of communists as the vanguard of the proletariat, capable of seeing further than the masses, was articulated already in 1848 by Marx and Engels in the *Communist Manifesto.*

114. Lewis S. Feuer, *Ideology and the Ideologists,* New York: Harper & Row, 1975, p. 197.

115. Leonhard, *Three Faces of Marxism, op. cit.,* p. 351.

CHAPTER IV: YUGOSLAV MARXISM DISCOVERS MAN

1.   Albert W. Levi, *Humanism and Politics,* Bloomington: Indiana University Press, 1969, p. 397.
2.   Arnold Künzli, "Marxists on the Beach," *Dialogue,* I, 1, Spring 1968, p. 79.
3.   A. J. P. Taylor, "The Independent Habit," *NYRB,* XVI, 2, February 11, 1971, p. 27.
4.   M. George Zaninovich, *The Development of Socialist Yugoslavia,* Baltimore: Johns Hopkins University Press, 1968, p. 140.
5.   Levi, *Humanism and Politics, op. cit.,* p. 443; Howard L. Parsons, *Humcnistic Philosophy in Contemporary Poland and Yugoslavia,* New York: American Institute for Marxist Studies, 1966, p. 8.
6.   For Yugoslav periodicization, see Svetozar Stojanović, "Contemporary Yugoslavian Philosophy," *Ethics,* LXXVI, 4, July 1966, p. 297; and Mihailo Marković, "Marxist Philosophy in Yugoslavia: The *Praxis* Group," in *Marxism and Religion in Eastern Europe,* eds. Richard T. De George & James P. Scanlan, Dordrecht: Reidel, 1976, pp. 63-89. Yugoslav neo-Marxist or Marxist humanist theorists (who do not necessarily belong to the *Praxis* group) are "avant-garde" in at least four related senses: (1) *Historically*—since they are contemporary interpreters of Marxist-Leninist teachings; (2) *Culturally*—since they transformed the social sciences arᴊ numanities, and contributed to a unique socialist humanist culture; (3) *Philosophically*—and most important—since they elaborated the most radical, comprehensive, and far-reaching reconstruction of Marxist-Leninist theory, and the most incisive Marxist critique of socialist practice in the communist world; and (4) *Politically*—since their critique of Stalinism, monolithism, and one-party dictatorship led to the most severe *Marxist* theoretical challenge to communist one-party rule thus far. This, very briefly, is the rationale for calling them avant-garde.
7.   *Humanizam i socijalizam,* 2 vols., eds. Branko Bošnjak & Rudi Supek, Zagreb: Naprijed, 1963.
8.   According to Gajo Petrović's Presidential Address at the Annual Meeting of the Yugoslav Philosophical Association in Zagreb, on December 27, 1966, the Dubrovnik symposium marked the entrance of Yugoslav philosophy on the world scene.   See Petrović, "La philosophie Yougoslave d'aujourd'hui," *Praxis* (I), III, 2, 1967, p. 320.
9.   These colloquia on contemporary problems of Marxism were scheduled to be held at five-year intervals beginning with the first double Scientific Meeting in 1963-64, honoring the 145th anniversary of Karl Marx's birth and the 80th anniversary of his death.   See Preface by the editorial board and introduction by Milka Minić to *Marks i savremenost (Marx and the Contemporary Age),* I-II, eds. Mihailo Marković, *et al.,* Belgrade: Institut za izučavanje radničkog pokreta i Institut društvenih nauka, 1964, pp. xvii and 3, respectively.   The subsequent Third, Fourth, and Fifth Meetings were held in 1967, 1970, and 1971, honoring the centenaries of the publication of the first volume of Marx's *Capital,* of Lenin's birth, and of the Paris Commune, respectively.   The proceedings have been published since 1970 by the "Institut za medjunarodni radnički pokret" in Belgrade, edited by Predrag Vranicki, *et al.* Marković and other avant-garde theorists are conspicuous for their absence since they were apparently no longer invited to these colloquia after 1963-64.
10.   See Rudi Supek, "Dix ans de l'Ecole D'Eté de Korčula (1963-1973)," *Praxis* (I), X, 1-2, 1974, pp.   3-15; and Marković, "Marxist Philosophy in Yugoslavia," *op. cit.*
11.   *Praxis* became the focal point for the new Marxist humanist dialogue in Yugoslavia and the avant-garde reconstruction of the Marxist-Leninist *Weltanschauung.*   See Petrović, "La philosophie Yougoslave d'aujourd'hui," *op. cit.,* p. 320; Zaninovich, *The Development of Socialist Yugoslavia, op. cit.,* pp. 140-141; and Marković, "Marxist Philosophy in Yugoslavia," *op.*

cit.

12. For the Yugoslav avant-garde's view on the need for dialogue, see Zdravko Kučinar, "Nécéssité et possibilité du dialogue," *Praxis* (I), III, 4, 1967, pp. 463-468.

13. Gajo Petrović's *Marx in the Mid-Twentieth Century,* Garden City, N.Y.: Doubleday, 1967, remains the most readable summary of avant-garde Marxist humanist philosophy in contemporary Yugoslavia translated into English.

14. See the review article by Jure Juras, "Simpozij 'O socijalističkom humanizmu' u Srpskoj akademiji" ("Symposium 'On Socialist Humanism' in the Serbian Academy"), *EM,* No. 3-4, March-June, 1967, pp. 168-176.

15. *Socialist Humanism,* ed. Erich Fromm, Garden City, N.Y.: Doubleday, 1966.

16. Toma Stamenković, "Meeting of Czechoslovak and Yugoslav Philosophers," *Praxis* (I), V, 3-4, 1969, pp. 620-623.

17. *Revolutionäre Praxis,* ed. Gajo Petrović, Freiburg im Breisgau: Rombach, 1969; Predrag Vranicki, *Mensch und Geschichte,* Frankfurt a. M.: Suhrkampf, 1969; Miladin Životić, *Čovek i vrednosti,* Belgrade: Prosveta, 1969.

18. Marković, "Marxist Philosophy in Yugoslavia," *op. cit.,* pp. 76-79. Among *Praxis* pocketbook editions in this period were No. 1: Branko Bošnjak & Mijo Škvorc, *Marksist i kršćanin (Marxist and Christian),* 1969; No. 2-3: *Dijalektika oslobodjenja (Dialectics of Liberation),* ed. David Cooper, 1969; No. 4-5: Ivan Kuvačić, *Obilje i nasilje (Affluence and Tyranny),* 1970; No. 6: Milan Kangrga, *Razmišljanja o etici (Thoughts on Ethics),* 1970; No. 7-8: Milan Damjanović, *Estetika i razočaranje (Aesthetics and Disillusionment),* 1971; No. 9: Danko Grlić, *Contra dogmaticos,* 1971; No. 10-11: Gajo Petrović, *Čemu Praxis (Why Praxis?),* 1972.

19. See Avdo Humo, *Svetozar Marković—filozof i revolucionar (Svetozar Marković: Philosopher and Revolutionary),* Belgrade: Institut za politicke studije, 1975; also, Predrag Matvejević, *Te Vjetrenjače (Those Windmills),* Zagreb: Cesarec, 1977, pp. 133-137.

20. Petrović, "La philosophie Yougoslave d'aujourd'hui," *op. cit.,* pp. 316-319; emphasis added.

21. Petrović, *Marx in the Mid-Twentieth Century, op. cit.,* p. 22.

22. Mihailo Marković, "Humanism and Dialectic," in *Socialist Humanism, op. cit.,* p. 84.

23. *Ibid.,* p. 86 on the dialectic; Mihailo Marković, "Marxist Humanism and Ethics," *Inquiry,* No. 6, 1963, p. 24 on Marx's philosophy.

24. Predrag Vranicki, "O dijalektici" ("On the Dialectic"), in *Marks i savremenost,* I, *op. cit.,* p. 141.

25. Mihailo Marković, "Marx and Critical Scientific Thought," *Praxis* (I), IV, 3-4, 1968, p. 397.

26. *Mala politička enciklopedija,* Belgrade: Savremena Administracija, 1966, p. 1179.

27. Predrag Vranicki, *Historija Marksizma (History of Marxism),* Zagreb: Naprijed, 1961, pp. 596-598.

28. See Andrija Krešić, *Političko društvo i politička mitologija (Political Society and Political Mythology),* Belgrade: Vuk Karadžić, 1968; and *Mala politička enciklopedija, op. cit.,* p. 569.

29. *Humanizam i socijalizam,* I, *op. cit.,* p. 7.

30. Predrag Vranicki, *Marksizam i socijalizam,* Zagreb: Znanje, 1979, pp. 104, 126; Svetozar Stojanović, *Geschichte und Parteibewusstsein,* Munich: Carl Hanser, 1978, pp. 106, 64.

31. Rudi Supek, *Sociologija i socijalizam (Sociology and Socialism),* Zagreb: Znanje, 1966, pp. 26-34; Supek draws on Garaudy's critique of Stalinism in *Cahiers du communisme,* No. 7-8, 1962.

32. Milan Kangrga, "Problem otudjenja u Marxovu djelu" ("The Problem of Alienation in Marx's Work"), in *Humanizam i socijalizam,* I, *op. cit.,* p. 102.

33. Marković, "Marxist Humanism and Ethics," *op. cit.*, p. 19.
34. The first point is my synthesis of the views expressed by Stojanović in "Contemporary Yugoslavian Philosophy," *op. cit.*, p. 298, and Marković in "Marx and Critical Scientific Thought," *op. cit.*, p. 395; points (2) and (3) are taken from Marković.
35. Mihailo Marković, "Marksova dijalektika i humanizam danas" ("Marx's Dialectic and Humanism Today"), in *Marks i savremenost*, I, *op. cit.*, p. 47.
36. Danilo Pejović, "On the Power and Impotence of Philosophy," in *Socialist Humanism, op. cit.*, p. 206.
37. Petrović, *Marx in the Mid-Twentieth Century, op. cit.*, pp. 14, 34.
38. Stojanović, "Contemporary Yugoslavian Philosophy," *op. cit.*, p. 298.
39. Milan Kangrga, "Program SKJ—Oslobadjanje stvaralačkih snaga socijalizma" ("The LCY Program—Liberation of the Creative Forces of Socialism"), in *Humanizam i socijalizam*, II, *op. cit.*, p. 17; emphasis added.
40. Mihailo Marković, "Marksistički humanizam i problem vrednosti" ("Marxist Humanism and the Problem of Values"), in *Humanizam i socijalizam*, I, *op. cit.*, pp. 105-106.
41. Stojanović, "Contemporary Yugoslavian Philosophy," *op. cit.*, p. 298.
42. Petrović, *Marx in the Mid-Twentieth Century, op. cit.*, p. 29.
43. *Ibid.*, pp. 42-43.
44. Karl Marx, "On the Jewish Question," in *Karl Marx*, ed. T. B. Bottomore, New York: McGraw-Hill, 1964, p. 31.
45. Veljko Korać, "Paradoxes of Power and Humanity," *Praxis* (I), VI, 1-2, 1970, p. 9.
46. Pejović, "On the Power and Impotence of Philosophy," *op. cit.*, p. 208.
47. Danko Grlić, "O apstraktnom i realnom humanizmu" ("On Abstract and Real Humanism"), in *Humanizam i socijalizam*, I, *op. cit.*, pp. 133-144.
48. Miladin Životić, "The End of the Ideals or of Ideology?," *Praxis* (I), V, 3-4, 1969, p. 420.
49. Predrag Vranicki, "Socialism and the Problem of Alienation," in *Socialist Humanism, op. cit.*, pp. 309-313.
50. Mihailo Marković, "Economism or the Humanization of Economics," *Praxis* (I), V, 3-4, 1969, p. 471.
51. Marx, quoted in Engels' letter to C. Schmidt, August 5, 1890, in *Karl Marx & Friedrich Engels, Selected Correspondence, 1843-1895*, Moscow: Foreign Languages Publishing House, 1953, p. 496.
52. Karl Marx and Friedrich Engels, *The German Ideology*, New York: International Publishers, 1969, p. 26; the second sentence is quoted by Marković in "Marx and Critical Scientific Thought," *op. cit.*, p. 400.
53. Petrović, *Marx in the Mid-Twentieth Century, op. cit.*, pp. 162-163.
54. *Ibid.*, p. 160.
55. *Ibid.*, p. 162; emphasis added.
56. Veljko Korać, "In Search of Human Society," in *Socialist Humanism, op. cit.*, p. 14.
57. Petrović, *Marx in the Mid-Twentieth Century, op. cit.*, p. 118.
58. See Svetozar Stojanović, "Marksistička koncepcija slobode" ("The Marxist Conception of Freedom") and discussion in *Marks i savremenost*, I, *op. cit.*, pp. 102-107 and 107-113.
59. Svetozar Stojanović, *Between Ideals and Reality*, New York: Oxford University Press, 1973, p. 98.
60. Rudi Supek, "Od državnog totalitarizma do individualnog totaliteta" ("From State Totalitarianism to Individual Totality"), in *Marks i savremenost*, IV, eds. Predrag Vranicki, *et al.*, Belgrade: Institut za izučavanje radničkog pokreta i Institut društvenih nauka, 1967, p. 307; Petrović, *Marx in the Mid-Twentieth Century, op. cit.*, p. 129.
61. Mihailo Marković, *The Contemporary Marx*, Nottingham: Spokesman Books, 1974, p. 75.
62. Gary C. Shaw, "Socialist Individualism," paper presented at the *AAASS*

Annual Meeting, St. Louis, Missouri, October 6-9, 1976, p. 3; David B. Meyers, "Marx's Concept of Truth: A Kantian Interpretation," *Canadian Journal of Philosophy,* VII, 2, June 1977, pp. 318-319.

63. Karl Marx, First Thesis on Feuerbach, in Marx & Engels, *The German Ideology, op. cit.,* p. 197.

64. Marković, *The Contemporary Marx, op. cit.,* p. 124.

65. Zagorka Pešić-Golubović, *Problemi savremene teorije ličnosti (Problems of the Contemporary Theory of Personality),* Belgrade: Kultura, 1966, p. 347.

66. Zagorka Pešić-Golubović, *Čovek i njegov svet (Man and His World),* Belgrade: Prosveta, 1973, pp. 39, 213. Her book went on trial in 1973, with the judge ordering critical passages removed; to her protest that those passages were published already in 1971, the judge retorted that this was 1973, not 1971!

67. Gajo Petrović, *Mogućnost čovjeka (The Possibility of Man),* Zagreb: Studentski centar sveučilišta, 1969, p. 70.

68. Vojan Rus, *Dijalektika čoveka i sveta (The Dialectic of Man and World),* Belgrade: Institut za medjunarodni radnički pokret, 1969, p. 546.

69. Richard T. De George, *The New Marxism,* New York: Pegasus, 1968, p. 58; see also Antón Donoso, "The Notion of Man in Kolakowski, Kosik and Marković," paper presented at the *AAASS Annual Meeting,* St. Louis, Missouri, October 6-9, 1976.

70. Marković, *The Contemporary Marx, op. cit.,* p. 85; Stojanović, *Between Ideals and Reality, op. cit.,* p. 27.

71. Mihailo Marković, *From Affluence to Praxis,* Ann Arbor: University of Michigan Press, 1974, p. 75.

72. Mihailo Marković, *Preispitivanja (Reassessments),* Belgrade: Srpska književna zadruga, 1972, p. 67. This book was banned in 1972, although the objectionable essays (written between 1967-71) had appeared previously in *Praxis et al.*

73. Miladin Životić, "Socijalistički humanizam i jugoslovenska filosofija" ("Socialist Humanism and Yugoslav Philosophy"), *Filosofija,* No. 1-2, 1968, p. 116.

74. Ljubomir Tadić, *Poredak i sloboda (Order and Freedom),* Belgrade: Kultura, 1967, p. 73.

75. Radojica Bojanović, "Despotic Socialism and the Authoritarian Personality," *Praxis* (I), IX, 3-4, 1973, p. 73.

76. Stojanović, *Between Ideals and Reality, op. cit.,* p. 205.

77. Marković, *From Affluence to Praxis, op. cit.,* p. 144.

78. Marković, *The Contemporary Marx, op. cit.,* p. 201.

79. Tadić, *Poredak i sloboda, op. cit.,* p. 100; see also James J. O'Rourke, *The Problem of Freedom in Marxist Thought,* Dordrecht: Reidel, 1974.

80. Marković, *Preispitivanja, op. cit.,* p. 70.

81. On Djilas and Mihajlov, see my unpublished Master's Thesis on "The Third Revolution," Claremont Graduate School, 1966; on Solzhenitsyn, see my "The Essential Solzhenitsyn: The Political Nexus or the Russian Connection," *Thought,* LV, 217, June 1980, pp. 137-152.

82. V. I. Lenin, "The Tasks of the Youth Leagues" (Address to the Third All-Russian Congress of the Young Communist League of the Soviet Union, October 2, 1920), in *The Lenin Anthology,* ed. Robert C. Tucker, N.Y.: Norton, 1975, p. 668; Marx & Engels, "The Communist Manifesto," and Engels, "On Morality" (From *Anti-Dühring*), in *The Marx-Engels Reader,* ed. Robert C. Tucker, N.Y.: Norton, 1972, pp. 351 & 667, respectively; and Marx & Engels, *The German Ideology, op. cit.*

83. Anonymous author, quoted in Thomas Molnar, *The Decline of the Intellectual,* Cleveland: World, 1961, pp. 114-115.

84. Kangrga, *Razmišljanja o etici, op. cit.,* p. 89.

85. *Ibid.,* p. 38. For the full quotation of Marx's remark in a letter to Arnold Ruge, September 1843, see *The Marx-Engels Reader, op. cit.,* p. 8; one of

the avant-garde's favorite quotations.

86. Supek, "Od državnog totalitarizma do individualnog totaliteta," *op. cit.*, p. 311; for a non-Yugoslav exploration of the ethical potential of Marx's thought, see Eugene Kamenka, *The Ethical Foundations of Marxism*, 2nd ed., Boston: Routledge, 1972.

87. Stojanović, *Geschichte und Parteibewusstsein*, *op. cit.*, p. 143.

88. Marković, "Marxist Humanism and Ethics," *op. cit.*, p. 23.

89. Stojanović, *Between Ideals and Reality*, *op. cit.*, p. 181.

90. Marx, quoted in *ibid.*, p. 179.

91. Svetozar Stojanović, "Stalinist 'Partiinost' and Communist Dignity," *Praxis* (I), X, 1-2, 1974, p. 137; greatly expanded in his *Geschichte und Parteibewusstsein*, *op. cit.*, pp. 99-157.

92. Marković, *The Contemporary Marx*, *op. cit.*, p. 154.

93. Stojanović, *Between Ideals and Reality*, *op. cit.*, p. 199.

94. Stojanović, *Geschichte und Parteibewusstsein*, *op. cit.*, pp. 156-157.

95. Richard T. De George, "The Foundations of Marxist-Leninist Ethics," in *Philosophy in the Soviet Union*, ed. Ervin Laszlo, Dordrecht: Reidel, 1967, p. 59.

96. Rus, *Dijalektika čoveka i sveta*, *op. cit.*, pp. 561-562.

97. Seweryn Żurawicki, "Stvaralački marksizam ili ljevičarski 'radikalizam'?" ("Creative Marxism or Left-Wing 'Radicalism'?"), *Praxis* (Y), VIII, 1, 1971, p. 156. Translated from *Studia Filozoficzne* (Warsaw), No. 6, 1970, pp. 103-117.

98. Danilo Pejović, *Sistem i egzistencija (System and Existence)*, Zagreb: Zora, 1970, p. 115.

99. Gajo Petrović, *Mišljenje revolucije (Thought of the Revolution)*, Zagreb: Naprijed, 1978, p. 171.

100. Miladin Životić, "Značaj fundamentalno-ontološkog stanovišta" ("The Significance of the Fundamental-Ontological Standpoint"), *Delo* (Belgrade), XXIII, 12, December 1977, pp. 110-126; special issue on "The Paths of Heidegger's Fundamental Ontology."

101. Gajo Petrović, "Izreka Heideggera" ("Heidegger's Saying"), *Praxis* (Y), VI, 5-6, 1969, p. 798.

102. Petrović, *Marx in the Mid-Twentieth Century*, *op. cit.*, p. 186.

103. Kangrga, *Razmišljanja o etici*, *op. cit.*, p. 179.

104. Marković, *The Contemporary Marx*, *op. cit.*, p. 30.

105. Vladimir Filipović, *Novija filozofija Zapada i odabrani tekstovi (Modern Western Philosophy and Selected Texts)*, Zagreb: Matica Hrvatska, 1968, pp. 155-156.

106. Kasim Prohić, "Edmund Husserl--Mislilac Krize" ("Edmund Husserl--Thinker of the Crisis"), *Praxis* (Y), IV, 5-6, 1967, pp. 744-745.

107. Paul Piccone, "Phenomenological Marxism," *Telos*, No. 9, Fall 1971, pp. 3-31; William McBride, "Marxism and Phenomenology," *JBSP*, 6,1, January 1975, pp. 13-22; Efraim Shmueli, "Can Phenomenology Accommodate Marxism?," *Telos*, No. 17, Fall 1973, pp. 169-180. For Soviet views on existentialism and phenomenology, see Thomas Nemeth, "Husserl and Soviet Marxism," *SST*, 15, 3, September 1975, pp. 183-196; R. T. De George, "Heidegger and the Marxists," *SST*, V, 4, December 1965, pp. 289-298; Thomas J. Blakeley, "Sartre's *Critique de la raison dialectique* and the Opacity of Marxism-Leninism," *SST*, VIII, 2-3, June-September, 1968, pp. 122-135; Nicolà Abbagnano & Nikolaus Lobkowicz, "Existentialismus," in *Ideologie und Philosophie*, I, ed. N. Lobkowicz, New York: Herder & Herder, 1973, pp. 232-248.

108. Marković, *The Contemporary Marx*, *op. cit.*, p. 191.

109. Trivo Indjić, "The Tyranny of Culture and the Resistance of the Existing State of Affairs," *Praxis* (I), IX, 3-4, 1973, p. 87.

110. Marković, *From Affluence to Praxis*, *op. cit.*, p. 195.

111. Marković, *The Contemporary Marx*, *op. cit.*, p. 188.

112. Svetozar Stojanović, "The June Student Movement and Social Revolution

in Yugoslavia," *Praxis* (I), VI, 3-4, 1970, p. 395.

113. Marx, quoted in Stojanović, *Between Ideals and Reality, op. cit.,* p. 202.

114. Marković, *The Contemporary Marx, op. cit.,* p. 190.

115. Ljubomir Tadić, "Herbert Marcuse: Zwischen Wissenschaft und Utopie," *Praxis* (I), VIII, 1-2, 1972, pp. 141-168.

116. Pejović, *Sistem i egzistencija, op. cit.,* p. 152.

117. Vojin Milić, "Method of Critical Theory," *Praxis* (I), VII, 3-4, 1971, p. 655.

118. Abdulah Šarčević, "Theodor W. Adorno (1903-1969): Die Unwahrheit der modernen Gesellschaft zwischen Revolution und Kritik," *Praxis* (I), VI, 1-2, 1970, p. 211.

119. Gajo Petrović,"The Development and the Essence of Marx's Thought," *Praxis* (I), IV, 3-4, 1968, p. 344.

120. *Ibid.,* p. 345.

121. Stojanović, *Between Ideals and Reality, op. cit.,* p. 173.

122. V. I. Lenin, *What Is to Be Done?,* in *The Lenin Anthology, op. cit.,* p. 19; Marković, *From Affluence to Praxis, op. cit.,* p. 139.

123. Marx, quoted in Petrović, *Mogućnost čovjeka, op. cit.,* pp. 104-105; for the full quotation from Marx's Postscript to the Second German edition of *Capital,* much quoted by the avant-garde, see *The Marx-Engels Reader, op. cit.,* p. 198.

124. Rus, *Dijalektika čoveka i sveta, op. cit.,* p. 36.

125. Stojanović, *Between Ideals and Reality, op. cit.,* p.5; Pejović, *Sistem i egzistencija, op. cit.,* p. 211.

126. Golubović, *Čovek i njegov svet, op. cit.,* p. 590.

127. Svetozar Stojanović, "Marxism and Socialism Now," *NYRB,* XVI, 12, July 1, 1971, p. 16.

128. Karl Marx, Letter to Arnold Ruge, September 1843, in *The Marx-Engels Reader, op. cit.,* p. 8; quoted by Marković, *The Contemporary Marx, op. cit.,* p. 18, and other avant-garde theorists.

129. Gerson S. Sher, *Praxis,* Bloomington: Indiana University Press, 1977, pp. 48-49, 196-197, 254-255, 268; for a critique, see my "*Praxis:* A Socialist Camelot?," *EEQ,* forthcoming.

130. Ludvik Vrtačič, *Der jugoslawische Marxismus,* Freiburg im Breisgau: Walter-Verlag, 1975, p. 132.

131. Tadić, *Poredak i sloboda, op. cit.,* p. 8; on the avant-garde's affinity to Antonio Gramsci's Marxism, see Mihailo Marković, "Gramsci on the Unity of Philosophy and Politics," *Praxis* (I), III, 3, 1967, pp. 333-339.

132. Dobrica Ćosić, "A Critique of Ideological A Priori and Doctrinaire Attitudes," *Praxis* (I), IX, 3-4, 1973, p. 71.

133. Hannah Arendt, *The Origins of Totalitarianism,* New York: Harcourt, Brace & World, 1966, pp. 470-471.

134. Ljubomir Tadić, "L'Intelligentsia dans le socialisme," *Praxis* (I), V, 3-4, 1969, p. 407.

135. Ljubomir Tadić, "Bureaucracy--Reified Organization," in *Praxis,* eds. Mihailo Marković & Gajo Petrović, Dordrecht: Reidel, 1979, p. 295; Krešić, *Političko društvo i politička mitologija, op. cit.,* pp. 165-170.

136. Molnar, *The Decline of the Intellectual, op. cit.,* p. 96.

137. *Ibid.,* p. 345.

138. Juras, "Simpozij 'O socijalističkom humanizmu' u Srpskoj akademiji," *op. cit.,* p. 172.

CHAPTER V: THE CONCEPT OF ALIENATION

1. Bertram D. Wolfe, *Marxism,* New York: Dial, 1965, p. 380.

2. On the social science, humanist, and phenomenological implications of Heisenberg's principle of indeterminacy in quantum physics, see the late Jacob Bronowski's engaging essay on "The Principle of Tolerance," *The Atlantic,* December 1973, pp. 60-66; also, Paul Kurtz, "In Defense of

Tolerance," in *Tolerance and Revolution*, eds. P. Kurtz & Svetozar Stojanović, Belgrade: Philosophical Society of Serbia, 1970, pp. 53-60.

3. Svetozar Stojanović, "Revolutionary Teleology and Ethics," in *Tolerance and Revolution, op. cit.*, p. 29.
4. Paul Piccone, "Phenomenological Marxism," *Telos*, 9, Fall 1971, p. 15.
5. *Ibid.*; quotations from Paul Piccone, "Dialectic and Materialism in Lukacs," *Telos*, 11, Spring 1972, p. 133.
6. Paul Piccone, "Reading the *Crisis*," *Telos*, 8, Summer 1971, p. 128.
7. Troun Overend, "Alienation: A Conceptual Analysis," *PPR*, XXXV, 3, March 1975, p. 302. See also George Armstrong Kelly, "A Note on Alienation," and Bertell Ollman's comment in *PT*, I, 1, February 1973, pp. 46-50 and 51-53, respectively; on alienation as a "concept of political theology," see Lewis S. Feuer, "What Is Alienation? The Career of a Concept," in his *Marx and the Intellectuals*, Garden City, N. Y.: Doubleday, 1969, pp. 70-99; for the avant-garde's critique of Western analyses of the concept, see Zagorka Pešić-Golubović, "Kritičko razmatranje interpretacija i upotrebe pojma alijenacije u sociološkim istraživanjima" ("Critical Review of Interpretations and Use of the Concept of Alienation in Sociological Research"), *Sociološki pregled* (Belgrade), VIII, 2-3, 1974, pp. 257-277.
8. Gajo Petrović, "Marxovo shvaćanje čovjeka" ("Marx's Conception of Man"), in *Humanizam i socijalizam (Humanism and Socialism)*, 2 vols., eds. Branko Bošnjak & Rudi Supek, Zagreb: Naprijed, 1963, I, p. 40.
9. Mihailo Marković, "Basic Characteristics of Marxist Humanism," *Praxis* (I), V, 3-4, 1969, p. 614.
10. Gajo Petrović, *Marx in the Mid-Twentieth Century*, Garden City, N. Y.: Doubleday, 1967, p. 81.
11. Vojin Milić, "Ideja otudjenja i savremena sociologija" ("The Concept of Alienation and Contemporary Sociology"), in *Humanizam i socijalizam*, II, *op. cit.*, p. 122.
12. Rudi Supek, *Sociologija i socijalizam (Sociology and Socialism)*, Zagreb: Znanje, 1966, p. 34.
13. Svetozar Stojanović, "The Dialectics of Alienation and the Utopia of Dealienation," *Praxis* (I), V, 3-4, 1969, p. 389; also in his *Between Ideals and Reality*, New York: Oxford University Press, 1973, p. 20; Mihailo Marković, "Marxist Humanism and Ethics," *Inquiry*, 6, 1963, p. 24.
14. Predrag Vranicki, "Socialism and the Problem of Alienation," in *Socialist Humanism*, ed. Erich Fromm, Garden City, N. Y.: Doubleday, 1966, p. 304.
15. Petrović, *Marx in the Mid-Twentieth Century, op. cit.*, p. 146; Stojanović, *Between Ideals and Reality, op. cit.*, pp. 19-20. Quotation from Petrović.
16. Stojanović, *Between Ideals and Reality, op. cit.*, pp. 27-28.
17. Jovan Djordjević, *Novi Ustavni sistem (The New Constitutional System)*, Belgrade: Savremena Administracija, 1964, pp. 110-111.
18. Milan Kangrga, "Problem otudjenja u Marxovu djelu" ("The Problem of Alienation in Marx's Work"), in *Humanizam i socijalizam*, I, *op. cit.*, p. 99.
19. Petrović, *Marx in the Mid-Twentieth Century, op. cit.*, p. 147.
20. Veljko Korać, "In Search of Human Society," in *Socialist Humanism, op. cit.*, p. 8, quotes Marx on the idea of freedom in the *Communist Manifesto*, one of the avant-garde's favorite references. For the full quotation, see *The Marx-Engels Reader*, ed. Robert C. Tucker, New York: Norton, 1972, p. 353.
21. Mihailo Marković, "Marksistički humanizam i problem vrednosti" ("Marxist Humanism and the Problem of Values"), in *Humanizam i socijalizam*, I, *op. cit.*, p. 126, on man and nature; and "Marxism versus Technocracy," *Dialogue*, I, 1, Spring 1968, p. 36, on unfettered human development.
22. Marx, "Third Manuscript," in *Karl Marx*, ed. T. B. Bottomore, New York: McGraw-Hill, 1964, p. 155.

23. Thomas Hobbes, *Leviathan,* New York: Collier, 1962, p. 100.
24. Jean-Jacques Rousseau, "On the Moral Effects of the Arts and Sciences," in his *The Social Contract and Discourses,* New York: Dutton, 1950, pp. 150, 157, 161.
25. Jean-Jacques Rousseau, "On the Origin and Foundation of the Inequality of Mankind," in *ibid,* pp. 251-252.
26. *Ibid.,* p. 267.
27. Rousseau, *The Social Contract, op. cit.,* p. 94.
28. Marx, "First Manuscript," in *Karl Marx, op. cit.,* p. 125.
29. Marx, "On the Jewish Question," in *ibid.,* p. 37.
30. Rousseau, "On the Origin and Foundation of the Inequality of Mankind," *op. cit.,* p. 271.
31. Ernest Becker, *Beyond Alienation,* New York: Braziller, 1967, p. 99.
32. Rousseau, *The Social Contract, op. cit.,* p. 3.
33. Andrija Krešić, "Filozofski izvori Marksova humanizma: Fragmenti o Hegelu, Fojerbahu i Marksu" ("Philosophical Sources of Marx's Humanism: Fragments on Hegel, Feuerbach and Marx"), in *Humanizam i socijalizam,* I, *op. cit.,* p. 14.
34. Petrović, *Marx in the Mid-Twentieth Century, op. cit.,* p. 136.
35. Marx, "Contribution to the Critique of Hegel's Philosophy of Right," in *Karl Marx, op. cit.,* p. 44, formulated it as follows: "The immediate *task of philosophy,* which is in the service of history, is to unmask human self-alienation in its *secular form* now that it has been unmasked in its *sacred form.* Thus the criticism of heaven is transformed into the criticism of earth, the *criticism of religion* into the *criticism of law,* and the *criticism of theology* into the *criticism of politics.*"
36. Andrija Krešić, "The Proletariat and Socialism in the Works of Marx and in the World Today," *Praxis* (I), V, 3-4, 1969, p. 373.
37. Vanja Sutlić, "Macht und Menschlichkeit," *Praxis* (I), VI, 1-2, 1970, pp. 18-19.
38. Mihailo Marković, "Critical Social Theory in Marx," *Praxis* (I), VI, 3-4, 1970, p. 286; see also his *From Affluence to Praxis,* Ann Arbor: University of Michigan Press, 1974, pp. 51-52; "Basic Characteristics of Marxist Humanism," *op. cit.,* p. 613; and "Hegelian and Marxist Dialectic," in his *The Contemporary Marx,* Nottingham: Spokesman Books, 1974, pp. 17-41.
39. See Supek's elaboration in his *Sociologija i socijalizam, op. cit.,* p. 194.
40. Mihailo Marković, "Economism or the Humanization of Economics," *Praxis* (I), V, 3-4, 1969, p. 460; also in his *From Affluence to Praxis, op. cit.,* pp. 122-123.
41. G. W. F. Hegel, *The Phenomenology of Mind,* New York: Harper & Row, 1967, p. 229.
42. *Ibid.,* p. 239.
43. Alexandre Kojève, *Introduction to the Reading of Hegel,* New York: Basic Books, 1969, pp. 3-30.
44. Marx, "Critique of Hegel's Dialectic and General Philosophy," in *Karl Marx, op. cit.,* p. 202.
45. *Mala politička enciklopedija,* Belgrade: Savremena Administracija, 1966, p. 806; Milić, "Ideja otudjenja i savremena sociologija," *op. cit.,* p. 97; the categorization of the forms of alienation is based, in part, on Djordjević, *Novi Ustavni sistem, op. cit.,* pp. 108-109.
46. Petrović, *Marx in the Mid-Twentieth Century, op. cit.,* p. 84; paraphrased.
47. Marx, "First Manuscript," *op. cit.,* p. 127.
48. Petrović, "Marxovo shvaćanje čovjeka," *op. cit.,* p. 49.
49. Marx, "First Manuscript," *op. cit.,* p. 133. This passage in Marx's "Alienated Labor" is referred to quite often by the Yugoslavs; besides Petrović, see also Kangrga, "Problem otudjenja u Marxovu djelu," *op. cit.,* pp. 80-81.
50. Marx, "First Manuscript," *op. cit.,* p. 127.

51. Krešić, "The Proletariat and Socialism in the Works of Marx and in the World Today," *op. cit.*, p. 381.

52. Predrag Vranicki, "Socijalizam i alijenacija" ("Socialism and Alienation"), in *Marks i savremenost (Marx and the Contemporary Age)*, II, ed. Mihailo Marković, *et al.*, Belgrade: Institut Društvenih Nauka, 1964, p. 481.

53. Danilo Pejović, "Industrijsko društvo i humanističko obrazovanje" ("Industrial Society and Humanistic Education"), in *Humanizam i socijalizam*, II, *op. cit.*, pp. 183-184.

54. Milić, "Ideja otudjenja i savremena sociologija," *op. cit.*, p. 100.

55. Rudi Supek, "Radničko samoupravljanje i humanizacija rada i potrošnje" ("Workers' Self-Management and the Humanization of Work and Consumption"), in *Humanizam i socijalizam*, II, *op. cit.*, pp. 139-170.

56. Marx, "Second Manuscript," in *Karl Marx, op. cit.*, p. 138.

57. Vranicki, "Socijalizam i alijenacija," *op. cit.*, p. 480.

58. Supek, *Sociologija i socijalizam, op. cit.*, p. 194.

59. Vranicki, "Socijalizam i alijenacija," *op. cit.*, p. 482; and his "Socialism and the Problem of Alienation," in *Socialist Humanism, op. cit.*, p. 304.

60. Supek, "Radnicko samoupravljanje i humanizacija rada i potrosnje," *op. cit.*, p. 154.

61. Supek, *Sociologija i socijalizam, op. cit.*, p. 74.

62. Danko Grlić, "O apstraktnom i realnom humanizmu" ("On Abstract and Real Humanism"), in *Humanizam i socijalizam*, I, *op. cit.*, p. 135.

63. Petrović, *Marx in the Mid-Twentieth Century, op. cit.*, p. 87.

64. Stojanović, *Between Ideals and Reality, op. cit.*, p. 12; Marković, "Gleichheit und Freiheit," *Praxis* (I), IX, 2-3, 1973, p. 152.

65. Gajo Petrović, *Čemu Praxis (Why Praxis?)*, Zagreb: *Praxis* Pocketbook Edition No. 10-11, 1972, p. 175.

66. Figure of speech in Aleksandr I. Solzhenitsyn, *The First Circle*, New York: Bantam, 1969, p. 114.

67. Marković, *From Affluence to Praxis, op. cit.*, pp. 131-132; emphasis added to "collective capitalists and collective exploiters."

68. Stojanović, *Between Ideals and Reality, op. cit.*, p. 125.

69. Marković, *From Affluence to Praxis, op. cit.*, p. 237.

70. *Ibid.*, p. 131.

71. Krešić, "The Proletariat and Socialism in the Works of Marx and in the World Today," *op. cit.*, p. 373.

72. Nicholas Lobkowicz, *Theory and Practice*, Notre Dame: University of Notre Dame Press, 1967, p. 311.

73. Petrović, *Marx in the Mid-Twentieth Century, op. cit.*, p. 153; Milić, "Ideja otudjenja i savremena sociologija," *op. cit.*, p. 102.

74. Marx, "Third Manuscript," in *Karl Marx, op. cit.*, pp. 153-154.

75. Marković, *From Affluence to Praxis, op. cit.*, p. 139.

76. Božidar Jakšić, "Yugoslav Society Between Revolution and Stabilization," *Praxis* (I), VII, 3-4, 1971, p. 446.

77. Stojanović, *Between Ideals and Reality, op. cit.*, p. 121.

78. Zagorka Pešić-Golubović, "Why is Functionalism More Desirable in Present-day Yugoslavia Than Marxism?," *Praxis* (I), IX, 4, 1973, pp. 364-365.

79. Marković, *From Affluence to Praxis, op. cit.*, pp. 140-141, 144.

80. Stojanović, *Between Ideals and Reality, op. cit.*, p. 131.

81. Robert C. Tucker, *Philosophy and Myth in Karl Marx*, London: Cambridge University Press, 1969, p. 215.

82. Stojanović, *Between Ideals and Reality, op. cit.*, p. 34.

83. Grlić, "O apstraktnom i realnom humanizmu," *op. cit.*, p. 140; Abdulah Šarčević, "Filozofija i humani, iskonsko proizvodni svijet" ("Philosophy and a Human, Truly Productive World"), in *Humanizam i socijalizam*, I, *op. cit.*, pp. 150, 157.

84. Jure Kaštelan, "Pjesnik i svijet stroja" ("The Poet and the World of Machines"), in *Humanizam i socijalizam*, I, *op. cit.*, p. 245.

85. Gajo Petrović, "The Development and the Essence of Marx's Thought,"

Praxis (I), IV, 3-4, 1968, p. 345.

86. Petrović, *Čemu Praxis, op. cit.*, pp. 173-174.
87. Milić, "Ideja otudjenja i savremena sociologija," *op. cit.*, p. 138.
88. Marković, *From Affluence to Praxis, op. cit.*, p. 233; see also his "Descriptive and Normative Conceptions of Human Nature," in his *Contemporary Marx, op. cit.*, pp. 81-91.
89. Stojanović, *Between Ideals and Reality, op. cit.*, p. 21, emphasis added.
90. For the concept of creativity *as* alienation and humanism, see Milovan Djilas, "On Alienation," *Encounter*, XXXVI, 5, May 1971, pp. 8-15; and critique by Mihajlo Mihajlov, "Djilas versus Marx: The Theory of Alienation," *Survey*, 18, 2, Spring 1972, pp. 1-13.
91. *The Socialist Idea*, eds. Leszek Kolakowski & Stuart Hampshire, New York: Basic Books, 1974, p. 34; see also Kolakowski, "Marxist Roots of Stalinism," in *Stalinism*, ed. Robert C. Tucker, New York: Norton, 1977, pp. 283-298.
92. Karl R. Popper, *The Open Society and Its Enemies*, 5th rev. ed., 2 vols., Princeton: Princeton University Press, 1966, I, pp. 169-201; II, pp. 27-80; Friedrich A. Hayek, *Law, Legislation and Liberty*, 3 vols., Chicago: University of Chicago Press, 1973-79, I, p. 32; II, p. 147.
93. André Glucksmann, *The Master Thinkers*, New York: Harper & Row, 1980, pp. 155-175, 265-287; on the theoretical affinities between Hegel, Marx and Freud, and their followers, see my "The Myth of Id: A Touch of Modernity," *Political Psychology*, IV, 3, Fall 1982, forthcoming.
94. Mihailo Marković, "Stalinism and Marxism," in *Stalinism, op. cit.*, p. 312.
95. Dragoljub Mićunović, "Bureaucracy and Public Communication," in *Praxis*, eds. Mihailo Marković & Gajo Petrović, Dordrecht: Reidel, 1979, p. 305; Andrija Krešić, "Political Dictatorship: The Conflict of Politics and Society," in *ibid,*. p. 131.
96. Aleksandr I. Solzhenitsyn, *The Gulag Archipelago*, 3 vols., New York: Harper & Row, 1974-78, I, p. 168.
97. Thomas J. Blakeley, *Soviet Scholasticism*, Dordrecht: Reidel, 1961, p. 83; and "Marxist-Leninist Scientific Atheism," in *Philosophy in the Soviet Union*, ed. Ervin Laszlo, Dordrecht: Reidel, 1967, pp. 61-78.
98. Eric Voegelin, *The New Science of Politics*, Chicago: University of Chicago Press, 1952, p. 124.
99. Joseph M. Bochenski, *Soviet Russian Dialectical Materialism*, Dordrecht: Reidel, 1963, p. 119.
100. Vojan Rus, *Dijalektika čoveka i sveta (The Dialectic of Man and World)*, Belgrade: Institut za medjunarodni radnički pokret, 1969, p. 48.
101. Marković, *From Affluence to Praxis, op. cit.*, p. 218; Svetozar Stojanović, "Marxism and Socialism Now," *NYRB*, XVI, 12, July 1, 1971, p. 18.
102. Rudi Supek, *Humanistička inteligencija i politika (The Humanist Intelligentsia and Politics)*, Zagreb: Studentski centar sveučilišta, 1971, p. 38.
103. Gajo Petrović, "The Philosophical and Sociological Relevance of Marx's Concept of Alienation," in *Marx and the Western World*, ed. Nicholas Lobkowicz, Notre Dame: University of Notre Dame Press, 1967, p. 151.
104. Marx W. Wartofsky, "Comment," in *ibid.*, p. 159.
105. Rus, *Dijalektika čoveka i sveta, op. cit.*, p. 28.
106. Martin Heidegger, *Being and Time*, New York: Harper, 1962, p. 298.
107. Petrović, *Marx in the Mid-Twentieth Century, op. cit.*, p. 188.
108. Milan Kangrga, *Razmišljanja o etici (Thoughts on Ethics)*, Zagreb: *Praxis* Pocketbook Edition No. 6, 1970, p. 177.
109. Branko Bošnjak & Mijo Škvorc, *Marksist i kršćanin (The Marxist and the Christian)*, Zagreb: *Praxis* Pocketbook Edition No. 1, 1969, pp. 16-17.
110. *Ibid.*, p. 24.
111. Dobrica Cesarić, quoted by Škvorc, in *ibid.*, p. 27.
112. Bošnjak, as related by J. Claude Evans, "Beyond Dogmatism in Europe's Marxist-Christian Dialogue," *Christian Century*, XVI, 3, January 23, 1974, pp. 71-72.

113. Roger Garaudy, *The Alternative Future,* New York: Simon & Schuster, 1974, p. 83.

114. T. S. Eliot, *The Waste Land and Other Poems,* New York: Harcourt, Brace & World, 1962, pp. 29-30; for Heidegger's assessment of Hölderlin's poetry, see Martin Heidegger, "Hölderlin and the Essence of Poetry," in his *Existence and Being,* Chicago: Regnery, 1949, pp. 270-291.

115. Hannah Arendt, *The Human Condition,* Garden City, N.Y.: Doubleday, 1959, p. 222.

116. Jack Jones, "Does God Exist?," *The Human Context,* VII, 3, Autumn 1975, p. 465, and "Art Between Magic and Revolution," *The Psychoanalytic Review,* 63, 3, Fall 1976, p. 446.

117. Marković, *From Affluence to Praxis, op. cit.,* p. 191.

118. Mark Reader & Donald J. Wolf, "On Being Human," *PT,* I, 2, May 1973, p. 191.

119. Bronowski, "The Principle of Tolerance," *op. cit.,* p. 66; see also my "The Principle of Tolerance in Kant's *Critique of Pure Reason,*" in *Proceedings of the Fifth International Kant Congress,* 2 vols., ed. Gerhard Funke, Bonn: Bouvier, 1981, II, pp. 803-811.

120. Arendt, *The Human Condition, op. cit.,* p. 216.

121. Karl Menninger, *Whatever Became of Sin?,* New York: Hawthorn, 1973, p. 188.

122. Lobkowicz, *Theory and Practice, op. cit.,* p. 421.

123. Carl von Linné, quoted by Škvorc, in *Marksist i kršćanin, op. cit.,* p.69.

124. Lionel Trilling, *The Middle of the Journey,* quoted in Daniel Patrick Moynihan, *Coping,* New York: Vintage, 1975, p. 414.

125. Milan Mirić, *Rezervati (Reservations),* Zagreb: Studentski centar sveučilišta, 1970, p. 38.

126. See Os Guinness, *The Dust of Death,* Downers Grove, Ill.: InterVarsity Press, 1973.

CHAPTER VI: MARKET SOCIALISM: WHAT PRICE EQUALITY?

1. Paul A. Samuelson, *Economics,* 9th ed., New York: McGraw-Hill, 1973, p. 865.

2. Paul A. Samuelson, *The Samuelson Sampler,* Glen Ridge, N. J.: Thomas Horton, 1973, p. 221.

3. David McLellan, "Marx and the Missing Link: On the Importance of the 'Grundrisse'," *Encounter,* XXXIV, 5, November 1970, pp. 35-45.

4. A view corroborated by Svetozar Pejovich in his "The Relevance of Marx and the Irrelevance of Marxian Revivals," *MA,* 21,1, Winter 1977, pp. 30-38.

5. Deborah D. Milenkovitch, *Plan and Market in Yugoslav Economic Thought,* New Haven: Yale University Press, 1971, p. 54.

6. Dennison I. Rusinow, "Laissez-Faire Socialism in Yugoslavia: Experiences and Compromises in Efforts to Liberalize a Command Economy," *AUFSR,* SE Europe Series, XIV, 2, September 1967, pp. 8-9.

7. *Ibid.,* p.18.

8. Karl Marx, *Capital,* 3 vols., New York: International Publishers, 1967: I, p.80 and III, p.820; Marx, *Grundrisse,* New York: Random House, 1973, pp. 704-706, 831-833.

9. John E. Elliott, "Marx and Contemporary Models of Socialist Economy," *History of Political Economy,* 8, 2, Summer 1976, p. 177.

10. Joel Dirlam & James Plummer, *An Introduction to the Yugoslav Economy,* Columbus, Ohio: Merrill, 1973, p. 61.

11. Deborah D. Milenkovitch, "Which Direction for Yugoslavia's Economy?," in *Comparative Communism,* eds. Gary K. Bertsch & Thomas A. Ganschow, San Francisco: Freeman, 1976, p. 352.

12. American Embassy, Belgrade, "Yugoslavia," *Foreign Economic Trends and*

Their Implications for the U. S. Series, August 1976, p. 4.

13. Rikard Lang, "Društveno-ekonomski ciljevi u koncepciji dugoročnog razvoja" ("Socio-Economic Goals in the Concept of Long-Range Development"), *Ekonomist,* No. 1, 1975, p. 23; special issue covering the Symposium on "The Concept of Yugoslavia's Long-Range Development till 1985," held in Dubrovnik, February 20-21, 1975.

14. Nikola Čobeljić, "Koncepcija razvoja i proizvodna orijentacija Jugoslavije" ("The Concept of Development and Yugoslavia's Production Orientation"), *Ekonomist,* No. 1, 1975, pp. 39-40.

15. "Constitutional System of the Socialist Federal Republic of Yugoslavia," *YS,* XV, 3, August 1974, p. 2.

16. Ludwig von Mises, *Human Action,* Rev. ed., New Haven: Yale University Press, 1963, p. 710.

17. OECD, *Yugoslavia,* Paris: OECD Economic Surveys, 1976, p. 27.

18. Joel Dirlam, "Problems of Market Power and Public Policy in Yugoslavia," in *Comparative Economic Systems,* 3rd ed., ed. Morris Bornstein, Homewood, Ill.: Irwin, 1974, p. 206.

19. Dirlam & Plummer, *An Introduction to the Yugoslav Economy, op. cit.,* p. 90.

20. Dirlam, "Problems of Market Power and Public Policy in Yugoslavia," *op. cit.,* p. 209.

21. Dirlam & Plummer, *An Introduction to the Yugoslav Economy, op. cit.,* p. 209; see also S. Popov & M. Jovičić, *Uticaj ličnih dohodaka na kretanje cena (The Effect of Personal Incomes on Price Movements),* Belgrade: Institut ekonomskih nauka, 1971.

22. M. Aćimović, "Raspodela: Grupno-svojinska ponašanja" ("Distribution: Group-Property Behavior"), *Komunist,* XXXVIII, 1199, February 29, 1980, p. 3.

23. M. Predragović, "Rasponi osobnih dohodaka: Privatizacija dohotka" ("Personal Income Differentials: Privatization of Income"), *Komunist,* XXXVII, 1188, December 7, 1979, pp. 3-4.

24. Egon Neuberger & Estelle James, "The Yugoslav Self-Managed Enterprise: A Systemic Approach," in *Plan and Market,* ed. Morris Bornstein, New Haven: Yale University Press, 1973, p. 263.

25. See *The Economics of Property Rights,* eds. Eirik G. Furubotn & Svetozar Pejovich, Cambridge, Mass.: Ballinger, 1974, esp. Pejovich, "Towards a General Theory of Property Rights," pp. 341-353 and Warren G. Nutter, "Markets Without Property: A Grand Illusion," pp. 217-224.

26. Dirlam & Plummer, *An Introduction to the Yugoslav Economy, op. cit.,* p. 73.

27. George F. Klein, "Social Deviance in Yugoslavia," in *Social Deviance in Eastern Europe,* ed. Ivan Völgyes, Boulder, Colo.: Westview, 1978, p. 173.

28. Branko Horvat, in interview with Dragan Jovanović, "Prava cena stanovanja" ("The True Price of Housing"), *NIN,* XXVIII, 1449, October 15, 1978, p. 16.

29. Gavrilo Mihaljević, quoted in *ibid.,* pp. 16-17.

30. Paul Lendvai, *Eagles in Cobwebs,* Garden City, N. Y.: Doubleday, 1969, pp. 116-117.

31. T. Wilson & G. R. Denton, *Economic Reform in Yugoslavia,* London: Chatham House, July 1968, p. 239.

32. "Privatne fabrike u Sloveniji" ("Private Factories in Slovenia"), *NIN,* XXVI, 1322, May 9, 1976, pp. 11-12.

33. Martin Schrenk, *et al, Yugoslavia,* Baltimore: Johns Hopkins University Press, 1979, p. 274.

34. Aleksandr Tijanić, "U malom je veliko" ("Small is Big"), *NIN,* XXIX, 1468, February 25, 1979, p. 16.

35. For obstacles to private business, see *ibid.,* pp. 16-17; Ljiljana Zorkić, "Priča o makazama" ("Tale of the Scissors"), *NIN,* XXIX, 1466, February 11, 1979, p. 10; and Schrenk, *Yugoslavia, op. cit.,* pp. 265-266.

36. Robert Nisbet, *Twilight of Authority*, New York: Oxford University Press, 1975, pp. 251-252.

37. George Macesich, *Yugoslavia*, Charlottesville: University Press of Virginia, 1964, p. 203.

38. Branko Horvat, "An Institutional Model of a Self-Managed Socialist Economy," in *Self-Governing Socialism*, 2 vols., eds. Branko Horvat, Mihailo Marković & Rudi Supek, White Plains, N.Y.: International Arts & Sciences Press, 1975: II, p. 314; see also Horvat's *An Essay on Yugoslav Society*, White Plains, N.Y.: International Arts & Sciences Press, 1969; for a review of Horvat's thought, see Benjamin Ward, "Marxism-Horvatism: A Yugoslav Theory of Socialism," *AER*, LVII, 3, June 1967, pp. 509-523.

39. Dirlam & Plummer, *An Introduction to the Yugoslav Economy, op. cit.*, p. 240.

40. Lendvai, *Eagles in Cobwebs, op. cit.*, pp. 135-136.

41. Marx, *Capital*, I, *op. cit.*, p. 186.

42. Benjamin N. Ward, "The Illyrian Firm," in *Self-Governing Socialism*, II, *op. cit.*, p. 247.

43. *Ibid.*, pp. 248, 257; for critiques, see Horvat, "On the Theory of the Labor-Managed Firm," in *Self-Governing Socialism*, II, *op. cit.*, pp. 229-240; and Jaroslav Vanek, *The Economics of Workers' Management*, London: Allen & Unwin, 1972.

44. Benjamin N. Ward, *The Socialist Economy*, New York: Random House, 1967, p. 212; Svetozar Pejovich, "The Firm, Monetary Policy, and Property Rights in a Planned Economy," in *Self-Governing Socialism*, II, *op. cit.*, pp. 265-266; E. Furubotn, "Bank Credit and the Labor-Managed Firm: The Yugoslav Case," in *The Economics of Property Rights, op. cit.*, p. 276.

45. Furubotn, "Bank Credit and the Labor-Managed Firm," *op. cit.*, pp. 267-271; Pejovich, "The Firm, Monetary Policy, and Property Rights in a Planned Economy," *op. cit.*, pp. 268-271.

46. Mitja Kamušić, "Economic Efficiency and Workers' Self-Management," in *Self-Governing Socialism*, II, *op. cit.*, p. 223.

47. Edvard Kardelj, "The Organizing of Associated Labour Along Self-Management Lines," *STP*, 13, 1, January 1975, p. 17.

48. Laura D'Andrea Tyson, "Liquidity Crises in the Yugoslav Economy: An Alternative to Bankruptcy?," *SOS*, XXIX, 2, April 1977, p. 295.

49. "Monetarni doprinos inflaciji" ("The Monetary Contribution to Inflation"), *EP*, XXIX, 1408, March 26, 1979, pp. 19-20; "Restrikcijom do stabilizacije" ("Stabilization via Restrictions"), *EP*, XXIX, 1410, April 9, 1979, pp. 18-19.

50. "Motivi za udruživanje akumulacije" ("Motives for Pooling Accumulation"), *EP*, XXVII, 1351, February 20, 1978, pp. 21-22.

51. OECD, *Yugoslavia*, Paris: OECD Economic Surveys, June 1979, p. 46 vs. Ljubo Sirc, *The Yugoslav Economy Under Self-Management*, London: Macmillan, 1979, pp. 242, 248.

52. Svetozar Vukmanović-Tempo, quoted by Dennison I. Rusinow, "Notes From a Yugoslav Party Congress," *AUFSR*, Europe, No. 41, 1978, p. 17.

53. Sirc, *The Yugoslav Economy . . ., op. cit.*, p. 244.

54. Milenkovitch, *Plan and Market in Yugoslav Economic Thought, op. cit.*, p. 214.

55. Horvat, "An Institutional Model of a Self-Managed Socialist Economy," *op. cit.*, p. 323.

56. Neuberger & James, "The Yugoslav Self-Managed Enterprise," *op. cit.*, p. 264.

57. Ward, *The Socialist Economy, op. cit.*, pp. 215-217; Milenkovitch, *Plan and Market in Yugoslav Economic Thought, op. cit.*, pp. 272-273.

58. Dirlam & Plummer, *An Introduction to the Yugoslav Economy, op. cit.*, p. 241; Ichak Adizes, *Industrial Democracy*, New York: Free Press, 1971, p. 209.

59. Sirc, *The Yugoslav Economy . . ., op. cit.*, p. 252.

60. Gudrun Lemân, "Economic Units in Yugoslav Enterprises," in *Self-Governing Socialism*, II, *op. cit.*, p. 200.

61. Sharon Zukin, *Beyond Marx and Tito,* New York: Cambridge University Press, 1975, p. 112.

62. Ivan Kuvačić, *Sukobi (Conflicts),* Zagreb: Razlog, 1972, pp. 35-38.

63. Mihailo Marković, "Gleichheit und Freiheit," *Praxis* (I), IX, 2-3, 1973, p. 147; Milan Mirić, *Rezervati (Reservations),* Zagreb: Studentski centar sveučilišta, 1970, p. 54.

64. Mihailo Marković, *The Contemporary Marx,* Nottingham: Spokesman Books, 1974, p. 136.

65. Miroslav Radovanović, "Savremeno jugoslovensko društvo u sukobu sa samim sobom" ("Contemporary Yugoslav Society in Conflict With Itself"), *Sociologija,* XIII, 3, 1971, p. 413; special issue devoted to the Symposium on "Social Conflicts and Yugoslavia's Socialist Development."

66. Srdjan Vrcan, "Social Equality and Inequality in the Bourgeois World and in Socialism: Challenge and Alternative," *Praxis* (I), X, 1-2, 1974, pp. 116-117; paper presented at the 1973 Korčula Summer School.

67. Srdjan Vrcan, "Some Comments on Social Inequality," *Praxis* (I), IX, 2-3, 1973, pp. 227-230.

68. Miladin Životić, "Is Equality a Moral Value of Our Society," *Praxis* (I), II, 4, 1966, p. 403.

69. Albert Meister, *Où va l'autogestion yougoslave?,* Paris: Anthropos, 1970, pp. 315-316.

70. "Opasnosti uravnilovke: Čovek u proseku" ("Dangers of the *Uravnilovka:* Man on the Average"), *NIN,* XXVI, 1316, March 28, 1976, p. 6.

71. "Strah nazvan uravnilovka: Jednakost sa više lica" ("Fear Called *Uravnilovka:* Equality With Several Faces"), *NIN,* XXVI, 1313, March 7, 1976, p. 14.

72. Vrcan, "Some Comments on Social Inequality," *op. cit.*, pp. 223-224.

73. Josip Županov, "Egalitarizam i industrijalizam" ("Egalitarianism and Industrialism"), *Sociologija,* XII, 1, 1970, p. 9; the paper aroused the greatest interest at the Fourth Meeting of the Yugoslav Association for Sociology in Split, February 12-14, 1970.

74. Mises, *Human Action, op. cit.*, p. 840.

75. Robert Nozick, *Anarchy, State, and Utopia,* New York: Basic Books, 1974, pp. 213-231; Friedrich von Hayek, *The Constitution of Liberty,* Chicago: University of Chicago Press, 1960, pp. 85-102; Županov, "Egalitarizam i industrijalizam," *op. cit.*, p. 14.

76. Hayek, *The Constitution of Liberty, op. cit.*, p. 100; see also his *Law, Legislation and Liberty,* 3 vols., Chicago: University of Chicago Press, 1973-79, II, pp. 83-85.

77. Županov, "Egalitarizam i industrijalizam," *op. cit.*, p. 27.

78. Adizes, *Industrial Democracy, op. cit.*, pp. 209-211.

79. On Yugoslavia's need for professional cadres, see Čobeljić, "Koncepcija razvoja i proizvodna orijentacija Jugoslavije," *op. cit.*, p. 39; on anti-professionalism as a basic cultural norm, see Županov, "Egalitarizam i industrijalizam," *op. cit.*, pp. 35-36.

80. Božidar Jakšić, "Culture and Development of the Contemporary Yugoslav Society," *Praxis* (I), VIII, 3-4, 1971, p. 664.

81. Robert McNamara, quoted by Županov, "Egalitarizam i industrijalizam," *op. cit.*, p. 35.

82. *Ibid.*, pp. 38-43.

83. Edvard Kardelj, *Pravci razvoja političkog sistema socijalističkog samoupravljanja (Directions of Development of the Political System of Socialist Self-Management),* 2nd enl. ed., Belgrade: Komunist, 1978, pp. 88-91.

84. "Constitutional System . . .," *op. cit.*, p. 9.

85. Radovanović, "Savremeno jugoslovensko društvo u sukobu sa samim sobom," *op. cit.*, p. 408.

86. Aleksander Bajt, "Social Ownership—Collective and Individual," in *Self-*

Governing Socialism, II, *op. cit.,* p. 160.

87. Mihailo Marković, *From Affluence to Praxis,* Ann Arbor: University of Michigan Press, 1974, p. 237; Rudi Supek, "Some Contradictions and Insufficiencies of Yugoslav Self-Managing Socialism," *Praxis* (I), VII, 3-4, 1971, p. 389.

88. Radomir Lukić, "Društveno raslojavanje kao uzrok društvenih sukoba u Jugoslaviji" ("Social Segmentation as a Cause of Social Conflicts in Yugoslavia"), *Sociologija,* XIII, 3, 1971, p. 343.

89. *Ibid.,* pp. 348-349.

90. Branko Horvat, "The Labor-Managed Enterprise," in *Self-Governing Socialism,* II, *op. cit.,* p. 172.

91. Branko Horvat, "The Pricing of Factors of Production," in *Self-Governing Socialism, II, op. cit.,* pp. 294-306; for Western critiques of Marx's labor theory of value, see Samuelson, *Economics, op. cit.,* pp. 839-866; Mark Blaug, *Economic Theory in Retrospect,* Rev. ed., Homewood, Ill.: Irwin, 1968, pp. 227-297; Eugen von Böhm-Bawerk, *Karl Marx and the Close of His System,* New York: Kelley, 1949, pp. 64-101; Mises, *Human Action, op. cit.,* pp. 812-820.

92. Blaug, *Economic Theory in Retrospect, op. cit.,* p. 237; on the transformation problem, see also Paul A. Samuelson, "Understanding the Marxian Notion of Exploitation: A Summary of the So-Called Transformation Problem Between Marxian Values and Competitive Prices," *JEL,* IX, 2, June 1971, pp. 399-431, and the exchange between Samuelson, William J. Baumol & Michio Morishima in "Colloquium: On Marx, the Transformation Problem," *JEL,* XII, 1, March 1974, pp. 51-77.

93. Milenkovitch, "Which Direction for Yugoslavia's Economy?," *op. cit.,* pp. 356-360; *Plan and Market in Yugoslav Economic Thought, op. cit.,* pp. 258-265.

94. Hannah Arendt, *The Human Condition,* Garden City, N. Y.: Doubleday, 1959, p. 233.

95. Mirić, *Rezervati, op. cit.,* p. 54; Svetozar Stojanović, *Between Ideals and Reality,* New York: Oxford University Press, 1973, p. 114; Neca Jovanov, *Radnički štrajkovi u SFRJ, 1958-1969 (Workers' Strikes in the SFRY, 1958-1969),* Belgrade: Zapis, 1979; Jovanov is considered Yugoslavia's leading authority on the causes and nature of worker unrest.

96. Dirlam & Plummer, *An Introduction to the Yugoslav Economy, op. cit.,* p. 57.

97. Nebojša Popov, "Streiks in der gegenwärtigen jugoslawischen Gesellschaft," *Praxis* (I), VI, 3-4, 1970, p. 411.

98. Blaug, *Economic Theory in Retrospect, op. cit.,* pp. 245-246.

99. Nozick, *Anarchy, State, and Utopia, op. cit.,* p. 253.

100. Edvard Kardelj, "Towards a New Type of Socialist Democracy," *STP,* XVI, 4, April 1976, p. 19.

101. Nozick, *Anarchy, State, and Utopia, op. cit.,* p. 199; for John Rawls' theory of distributive justice, see his *A Theory of Justice,* Cambridge, Mass.: Harvard University Press, 1971.

102. Ivan Kuvačić, "Additional Thoughts on Synchrony and Diachrony," *Praxis* (I), VII, 3-4, 1971, p. 429.

103. Marx, *Capital, I, op. cit.,* p. 352.

104. Heinz Kontetzki, *Agrarpolitischer Wandel und Modernisierung in Jugoslawien,* Nürnberg: Nürnberger Forschungsberichte, 1976, pp. 493-520.

105. Derek T. Healey, "Development Policy: New Thinking About an Interpretation," *JEL,* X, 3, September 1972, p. 794.

106 Stipe Šuvar, *Sociološki presjek jugoslavenskog društva (Sociological Cross Section of Yugoslav Society),* Zagreb: Školska knjiga, 1970, p. 57; the classic Yugoslav study on peasant-workers is by Cvetko Kostić, *Seljaci industrijski radnici (Peasants-Industrial Workers),* Belgrade, 1955; see also Andrei Simić, *The Peasant Urbanites,* New York: Seminar Press, 1973.

107. *Ibid.;* Horst Günther, *Die Verstädterung in Jugoslawien,* Wiesbaden: Har-

rassowitz i. Komm., 1966, pp. 141-142.

108. Šuvar, *Sociološki presjek jugoslavenskog društva, op. cit.,* pp. 68-85; Joel M. Halpern, "Yugoslavia: Modernization in an Ethnically Diverse State," in *Contemporary Yugoslavia,* ed. Wayne S. Vucinich, Berkeley: University of California Press, 1969, pp. 323-327; George W. Hoffman, "Migration and Social Change," *PC,* XXII, 6, November-December, 1973, pp. 17-18.

109. Kiro Gligorov, "SKJ i razvojna politika Jugoslavije" ("The LCY and Yugoslavia's Development Policy"), paper presented at conference on "The LCY and the Socialist Revolution," Bled, February 7-9, 1980, quoted in "Mnogo raskoraka izmedju zacrtanih i realizovanih ciljeva" ("Great Divergences Between Projected and Realized Goals"), *Komunist,* XXXVIII, 1201, March 14, 1980, p. 7.

110. Klein, "Social Deviance in Yugoslavia," *op. cit.,* p. 175.

111. Branko Krstin, "Na putu stabilizacije: Rezerve u brazdi" ("On the Road to Stabilization: Reserves in the Furrow"), *Komunist,* XXXVIII, 1201, March 14, 1980, pp. 12-13; Rastko Jovetić, "Duže brazde" ("Longer Furrows"), *Komunist,* XXXVIII, 1202, March 21, 1980, p. 17.

112. B. Krstin, "Korak do 'zelenog plana'" ("A Step Toward the 'Green Plan'"), *Komunist,* XXXVIII, 1202, March 21, 1980, p. 5.

113. Günther, *Die Verstädterung in Jugoslawien, op. cit.,* p. 208; for a portrait of Transitional Man, see my "Modell der Modernisation und Einstellungsänderung für jugoslawische Arbeitnehmer im Herkunftsland und in der BRD: Soziokulturelle Herkunft jugoslawischer Arbeitnehmer," Nürnberg: Sozialwissenschaftliches Forschungszentrum der Universität Erlangen-Nürnberg, 1972, pp. 31-35; also, Vera St. Erlich, *Family in Transition,* Princeton: Princeton University Press, 1966.

114. Zagorka Pešić-Golubović, "Socialist Ideas and Reality," *Praxis* (I), VII, 3-4, 1971, pp. 419-420.

115. Rudi Supek, "Robno-novčani odnosi i socijalistička ideologija" ("Commodity-Money Relations and Socialist Ideology"), *Praxis* (Y), V, 1-2, April 1968, p. 176.

116. Stojanović, *Between Ideals and Reality, op. cit.,* p. 132.

117. Josip Županov, "Neke dileme u vezi s robno-novčanim odnosima" ("Some Dilemmas Concerning Commodity-Money Relations"), *Praxis* (Y), V, 1-2, April 1968, p. 166.

118. Supek, "Robno-novčani odnosi i socijalistička ideologija," *op. cit.,* p. 177.

119. Marković, *From Affluence to Praxis, op. cit.,* p. 139.

120. Gajo Petrović, "The Philosophical and Sociological Relevance of Marx's Concept of Alienation," in *Marx and the Western World,* ed. Nicholas Lobkowicz, Notre Dame: University of Notre Dame Press, 1967, p. 152.

121. Marković, *The Contemporary Marx, op. cit.,* p. 130.

122. Mihailo Marković, "Marxism versus Technocracy," *Dialogue,* I, 1, Spring 1968, pp. 31-36.

123. Ivan Kuvačić, "Scientific and Technical Progress and Humanism," *Praxis* (J), V, 1-2, 1969, p. 182.

124. Živojin D. Denić, "Sociologija nastanka, egzistencije i funkcija robnog privredjivanja" ("Sociology of the Origin, Existence, and Functions of Commodity Production"), *Praxis* (Y), IX, 1-2, April 1972, p. 207; Vojan Rus, *Dijalektika čoveka i sveta (The Dialectic of Man and World),* Belgrade: Institut za medjunarodni radnički pokret, 1969, p. 547.

125. Josip Županov, "The Yugoslav Enterprise," in *Comparative Economic Systems, op. cit.,* pp. 187-188; see also J. Obradović, "Participation and Work Attitudes in Yugoslavia," *IR,* 9, 2, February 1970, pp. 161-169.

126. Nozick, *Anarchy, State, and Utopia, op. cit.,* p. 262.

127. Kardelj, *Pravci razvoja . . ., op. cit.,* p. 91.

128. On "human servitude," see *Karl Marx,* ed. T. B. Bottomore, New York: McGraw-Hill, 1964, pp. 132-133; on the inversion of relations between persons and things, see Marx, *Capital, op. cit.:* I, p. 73 and III, p. 830;

also, *Grundrisse, op. cit.,* p. 157.

129. Pešić-Golubović, "Socialist Ideas and Reality," *op. cit.,* p. 408.

130. Slaven Letica, "Samoupravno društvo i teorija tržišta radne snage" ("The Self-Managing Society and the Theory of the Market for Labor Power"), *Gledišta* (Belgrade), XVI, 3, March 1975, pp. 270-271.

131. *Ibid.,* p. 271.

132. Josip-Broz Tito, "Building the Ethics of the Socialist Order of Self-Management, " *STP,* XVI, 2, February 1976, p. 19.

133. Radovanović, "Savremeno jugoslovensko društvo u sukobu sa samim so-bom," *op. cit.,* pp. 409-410.

134. Vladimir Milanović, quoted in "Zašto smo nejednaki" ("Why Are We Unequal?"), *NIN,* XXVI, 1320, April 25, 1976, p. 8.

135. Marković, *The Contemporary Marx, op. cit.,* p. 137.

136. Supek, "Robno-novčani odnosi i socijalistička ideologija," *op. cit.,* p. 176.

137. Stojanović, *Between Ideals and Reality, op. cit.,* p. 213.

138. *Ibid.,* p. 203.

139. *Ibid.,* pp. 201-202; for the full quotation from Marx, see *Karl Marx, op. cit.,* pp. 153-154.

140. Stojanović, *Between Ideals and Reality, op. cit.,* p. 214.

141. Lukić, "Društveno raslojavanje kao uzrok društvenih sukoba u Jugoslaviji," *op. cit.,* p. 342.

142. Stojanović, *Between Ideals and Reality, op. cit.,* pp. 215-216.

143. Ljubomir Tadić, "Private Property and Political Economy Suppress Human Freedom," *Praxis* (I), IX, 1, 1973, p. 23; Proceedings of the First Philosophical Winter Meeting, Tara, Serbia, February 8-10, 1971, first published in *Filosofija,* No. 1, 1971.

144. Marković, *From Affluence to Praxis, op. cit.,* p. 144.

145. Županov, "Neke dileme u vezi s robno-novčanim odnosima," *op. cit.,* pp. 165-166.

146. Marx, *Grundrisse, op. cit.,* p. 163.

147. Paul C. Roberts & Matthew A. Stephenson, *Marx's Theory of Exchange, Alienation and Crisis,* Stanford: Hoover Institution Press, 1973, p. 80.

148. Petrović, "The Philosophical and Sociological Relevance of Marx's Concept of Alienation," *op. cit.,* p. 146.

149. Marx, *Grundrisse, op. cit.,* p. 693.

150. Marx, "Critique of the Gotha Program," in *The Marx-Engels Reader,* ed. Robert C. Tucker, New York: Norton, 1972, p. 388; versus *Capital,* III, *op. cit.,* p. 820.

151. Arendt, *The Human Condition, op. cit.,* p. 91.

152. Marković, *From Affluence to Praxis, op. cit.,* p. 91.

153. Milton & Rose Friedman, *Free to Choose,* New York: Harcourt Brace Jovanovich, 1980, p. 23.

154. John Kenneth Galbraith, *The New Industrial State,* 2nd ed., Boston: Mifflin, 1972 and *Economics and the Public Purpose,* New York: New American Library, 1975; Robert L. Heilbroner, *An Inquiry Into the Human Prospect,* New York: Norton, 1974 and "The American Plan," *NYT Magazine,* January 25, 1976, pp. 9, 35-40; Willis W. Harman, "Humanistic Capitalism: Another Alternative," *Journal of Humanistic Psychology,* 14, 1, Winter 1974, pp. 5-32; Howard R. Bowen, "Toward a Humanist Economics," *Nebraska Journal of Economics and Business,* 11, 4, Autumn 1972, pp. 9-24; Kenneth E. Boulding, *Beyond Economics,* Ann Arbor: University of Michigan Press, 1968; for a critique of New Left economics, see Assar Lindbeck, *The Political Economy of the New Left—An Outsider's View,* 2nd ed., New York: Harper & Row, 1977.

155. Friedman, *Free to Choose, op. cit.,* p. 214.

156. Horvat, "An Institutional Model of a Self-Managed Socialist Economy," *op. cit.,* p. 313; the Neo-Austrian School is likely to disagree, as would the Chicago School of Economics; for the latter's viewpoint, see Milton Friedman (Nobel Prize in Economics, 1976), *Capitalism & Freedom,*

Chicago: University of Chicago Press, 1963, *An Economist's Protest,* 2nd ed., Glen Ridge, N. J.: Thomas Horton, 1975, and, with Rose, *Free to Choose, op. cit.*

157. "Quarterly Economic Review of Yugoslavia, 1st Quarter 1980," London: Economist Intelligence Unit, 1980, p. 5; "Prvi propisi o racioniranju hrane i robe" ("First Regulations on Food and Commodities Rationing"), *NH,* XXII, 13, June 29, 1980, p. 5.

158. Friedman, *Free to Choose, op. cit.,* p. 234; William E. Simon, *A Time for Truth,* New York: Reader's Digest, 1978, p. 219.

159. Dušan Bilandžić, interview in *Start* (Zagreb), December 12, 1979, quoted by Slobodan Stanković, "Yugoslav Party Theorist Defends Market Economy," *Radio Free Europe Research,* December 19, 1979, p. 2.

160. Sirc, *The Yugoslav Economy . . ., op. cit.,* p. 243.

161. *Ibid.,* p. 245.

162. Kiro Gligorov, "Jasan kurs omogućava brži napredak" ("A Clear Course Facilitates Faster Progress"), *Komunist,* XXXVIII, 1188, December 7, 1979, p. 7.

163. Blaug, *Economic Theory in Retrospect, op. cit.,* p. 273.

164. Friedrich A. Hayek, *The Road to Serfdom,* Chicago: University of Chicago Press, 1962, p. 210.

165. For a Manhattan-type project to achieve a scientific-technological breakthrough in solar power, see my "Project: SOLARMOBILE," in *Proceedings of the 1978 Annual Meeting, American Section of the International Solar Energy Society,* 2 vols., Killeen, Texas: AS-ISES, 1978, II, pp. 649-654.

CHAPTER VII: SELF-MANAGEMENT AND THE PARTY

1. Maurice Duverger, *Les partis politiques,* Paris: Colin, 1964, p. 83; Eric Voegelin, *The New Science of Politics,* Chicago: University of Chicago Press, 1966, pp. 162-189.

2. Michel Crozier, Samuel P. Huntington & Joji Watanuki, *The Crisis of Democracy,* New York: New York University Press, 1975, p. 159.

3. John H. Kautsky, "Comparative Communism versus Comparative Politics," *SCC,* VI, 1-2, Spring-Summer, 1973, p. 170.

4. William A. Welsh, "Elites and Leadership in Communist Systems: Some New Perspectives," *SCC,* IX, 1-2, Spring-Summer, 1976, p. 171.

5. Joseph LaPalombara, "Monoliths or Plural Systems: Through Conceptual Lenses Darkly," *SCC,* VIII, 3, Autumn 1975, p. 325.

6. Jacob Walkin, "Yugoslavia After the 10th Party Congress," *Survey,* 98, 1, Winter 1976, pp. 55-56; Dennison I. Rusinow, *The Yugoslav Experiment, 1948-1974,* Berkeley: University of California Press, 1977, p. 346.

7. M. George Zaninovich, *The Development of Socialist Yugoslavia,* Baltimore: Johns Hopkins University Press, 1968, p. 38.

8. Bogdan D. Denitch, *The Legitimation of a Revolution,* New Haven: Yale University Press, 1976, pp. 186, 154.

9. Fred B. Singleton, *Twentieth-Century Yugoslavia,* New York: Columbia University Press, 1976, p. 312.

10. Fred W. Neal & George W. Hoffman, *Yugoslavia and the New Communism,* New York: Twentieth Century Fund, 1962, p. 504.

11. Stephen Miller, "The Poverty of Socialist Thought," *Commentary,* 62, 2, August 1976, p. 36.

12. David Levy, "Not For Marx," *MA,* 21, 1, Winter 1977, p. 29.

13. Jacob L. Talmon, *The Origins of Totalitarian Democracy,* New York: Praeger, 1960, p. 252.

14. Milovan Djilas, *The Unperfect Society,* New York: Harcourt, Brace & World, 1969, pp. 4-5.

15. Leszek Kolakowski, "The Myth of Human Self-Identity: Unity of Civil and Political Society in Socialist Thought," in *The Socialist Idea,* eds. L.

Kolakowski & Stuart Hampshire, New York: Basic Books, 1974, p. 35.

16. Mihajlo Mihajlov, "Yugoslavia—The Approaching Storm," *Dissent,* Summer 1974, p. 372.

17. Patrick O'Brien, "On the Adequacy of the Concept of Totalitarianism," *SCC,* I·I, 1, January 1970, p. 58.

18. Jean-Jacques Rousseau, *The Social Contract and Discourses,* New York: Dutton, 1950, pp. 37-42. For Plato's contributions to the theory of a closed society, see Karl R. Popper, *The Open Society and Its Enemies,* 5th rev. ed., 2 vols., Princeton: Princeton University Press, 1966, I: "The Spell of Plato."

19. Rousseau, *The Social Contract and Discourses, op. cit.,* pp. 23, 24, 94.

20. *Ibid.,* p. 37.

21. *Ibid.,* p. 17.

22. *Ibid.,* p. 18.

23. Talmon, *The Origins of Totalitarian Democracy, op. cit.,* p. 48.

24. Edvard Kardelj, "Kritika partijskog sistema i problemi razvoja socijalis-tičke demokracije" ("Critique of the Party System and Problems of Development of Socialist Democracy"), in *Političke stranke kao faktor savremenog političkog sistema (Political Parties as a Factor in the Contemporary Political System),* ed. Stjepan Pulišelić, Zagreb: Naprijed, 1971, p. 357; also, Kardelj, "Towards a New Type of Socialist Democracy," *STP,* XVI, 4, April 1976, pp. 24-25.

25. Najdan Pašić, "Selfmanagement as an Integral Political System," in *Yugoslav Workers' Selfmanagement,* ed. M. J. Broekmeyer, Dordrecht: Reidel, 1970, pp. 27, 39.

26. Andrija Krešić, "The Production-Relations Basis of Self-Management," in *Self-governing Socialism,* 2 vols., eds. Branko Horvat, Mihailo Marković & Rudi Supek, White Plains, N. Y.: International Arts & Sciences Press, 1975, I, p. 452.

27. Dragomir Drašković, "Socijalna dinamika i konflikti u razvoju samoupravl-janja" ("Social Dynamics and Conflicts in the Development of Self-Management"), in *Teorija i praksa samoupravljanja u Jugoslaviji (Theory and Practice of Self-Management in Yugoslavia),* eds. Jovan Djordjević, *et al.,* Belgrade: Radnička štampa, 1972, p. 985.

28. Andrija Krešić, *Političko društvo i politička mitologija (Political Society and Political Mythology),* Belgrade: Vuk Karadžić, 1968, p. 122.

29. Rudi Supek, "Historicitet, sistem i sukobi" ("Historicism, the System, and Conflicts"), *Sociologija,* XIII, 3, 1971, p. 328; Special Issue: Symposium on Social Conflicts and Socialist Development of Yugoslavia.

30. Neil McInnes, *The Western Marxists,* New York: Library Press, 1972, p. 39.

31. Jovan Mirić, *Interesne grupe i politička moć (Interest Groups and Political Power),* Zagreb: Narodno sveučilište grada Zagreba, Centar za aktualni politički studij, 1973, p. 110.

32. Jean-Jacques Rousseau, "A Discourse on Political Economy," in his *The Social Contract and Discourses, op. cit.,* p. 306.

33. Ghiţa Ionesco, "Djilas, Tito and Yugoslav Socialism," *PQ,* 41, 3, July-September, 1970, p. 305.

34. Djilas, *The Unperfect Society, op. cit.,* p. 227.

35. Edvard Kardelj, "Ekspoze Pretsednika Komisije za Ustavna Pitanja Ed-varda Kardelja" ("Exposé of the President of the Commission for Consti-tutional Questions"), in *Ustav Socijalističke Federativne Republike Jugo-slavije (The Constitution of the SFRY),* Belgrade: Izdanje Službenog Lista SFRJ, 1965, p. 13; Mijalko Todorović, "Self-Management—Historical Aspiration of the Working Class," *STP,* 40, July-September, 1970, pp. 3-27.

36. Miroslav Pečujlić, *Budućnost koja je počela (The Future Which Has Begun),* Belgrade: Institut za političke studije Fakulteta političkih nauka, 1969, p. 52.

37. Mihailo Marković, *From Affluence to Praxis*, Ann Arbor: University of Michigan Press, 1974, p. 227; Marković, *The Contemporary Marx*, Nottingham: Spokesman Books, 1974, p. 207.

38. Svetozar Stojanović, *Between Ideals and Reality*, New York: Oxford University Press, 1973, p. 58.

39. Dragutin Leković, "O osnovnim vidovima dijalektike konstituisanja beskla-snog komunističkog društva" ("On Basic Aspects of the Dialectical Forma-tion of the Classless Communist Society"), in *Marks i savremenost (Marx and the Contemporary Age)*, II, eds. Mihailo Marković, *et al.*, Belgrade: Institut Društvenih Nauka, 1964, p. 262; Predrag Vranicki, "Teorijsko zasnivanje ideje o samoupravljanju" ("Theoretical Foundations of the Concept of Self-Management"), *Socijalizam*, XIII, 6, June 1970, p. 743.

40. Karl Marx, "Third Manuscript," in *Karl Marx*, ed. T. B. Bottomore, New York: McGraw-Hill, 1964, p. 152.

41. Rudi Supek, "The Statist and Self-Managing Models of Socialism," in *Opinion-Making Elites in Yugoslavia*, eds. Allen H. Barton, Bogdan D. Denitch & Charles Kadushin, New York: Praeger, 1973, pp. 306-307.

42. Mihailo Marković, "Self-government and Planning," in *Self-governing Socialism*, I, *op. cit.*, p. 481.

43. Marković, *From Affluence to Praxis, op. cit.*, p. 227.

44. Jovan Djordjević, *Socijalizam i demokratija (Socialism and Democracy)*, Belgrade: Savremena Administracija, 1962, pp. 94-97; Vranicki, "Teorij-sko zasnivanje ideje . . .," *op. cit.*, p. 729. For the Yugoslav definition of "politics," see *Mala politička enciklopedija (Small Political Encyclopædia)*, Belgrade: Savremena Administracija, 1966, pp. 891-896; note the "dialec-tical" Yugoslav conception of the simultaneous withering away of (class-) and expansion of (socialist, self-managing-) politics, *ibid.*, p. 896.

45. Rudi Supek, "Humanizam i naturalizam" ("Humanism and Naturalism"), in *Humanizam i socijalizam (Humanism and Socialism)*, 2 vols., eds. Branko Bošnjak & Rudi Supek, Zagreb: Naprijed, 1963, I, p. 61.

46. Vranicki, "Teorijsko zasnivanje ideje . . .," *op. cit.*, pp. 729-731.

47. Krešić, "The Production-Relations Basis of Self-management," *op. cit.*, p. 446.

48. Zagorka Pešić-Golubović, "Socialist Ideas and Reality," *Praxis* (I), VII, 3-4, 1971, p. 417.

49. Ljubomir Tadić, *Poredak i sloboda (Order and Freedom)*, Belgrade: Kultu-ra, 1967, p. 8.

50. Mihailo Marković, "Economism or the Humanization of Economics," *Praxis* (I), V, 3-4, 1969, p. 453.

51. *Ibid.*, p. 469.

52. Rudi Supek, *Participacija, radnička kontrola i samoupravljanje (Participa-tion, Workers' Control, and Self-Management)*, Zagreb: Naprijed, 1974, p. 141.

53. Leon Trotsky, *The Revolution Betrayed*, 5th ed., New York: Pathfinder, 1972, p. 105.

54. Jovan Djordjević, *Ogled o birokratiji i birokratizmu (Essay on Bureaucracy and Bureaucratism)*, Belgrade: Kultura, 1962, pp. 113-116. Yugoslav textbooks and treatises in sociology, political science, and related disci-plines customarily devote space to an analysis of the phenomena of bureaucracy and bureaucratization; for a summary of these issues, see *Mala politička enciklopedija, op. cit.*, pp. 100-103, and related concepts of technocracy, managerialism, and economism, pp. 1229-1230, 658-659, and 272-273, respectively.

55. *Yugoslavia's Way*, trans. Stojan Pribichevich, New York: All Nations, 1958, pp. 48-49, 145-148; Predrag Vranicki, *Historija Marksizma (History of Marxism)*, Zagreb: Naprijed, 1961, pp. 585-588; see also Proceedings of the Ninth, Tenth, and Eleventh Party Congresses.

56. Radomir D. Lukić, *Teorija države i prava (Theory of the State and Law)*, Belgrade: Savremena Administracija, 1964, pp. 317, 319-320; Marković,

"Economism or the Humanization of Economics," *op. cit.*, p. 466.

57. Josip-Broz Tito, "On Workers' Management in Economic Enterprises," in *The Essential Tito*, ed. Henry M. Christman, New York: St. Martin's, 1970, p. 84; emphasis added.
58. Vranicki, "Teorijsko zasnivanje ideje . . .," *op. cit.*, pp. 738, 742.
59. Vladimir I. Lenin, *State and Revolution*, New York: International Publishers, 1932, p. 25.
60. The classic statement is in Friedrich Engels' *Socialism: Utopian and Scientific:* "The [proletarian] state is not 'abolished.' *It dies out.*" in *Marx & Engels*, ed. Lewis S. Feuer, New York: Doubleday, 1959, p. 106. For the Yugoslav conception of the state and its withering away, see summaries in *Mala politička enciklopedija, op. cit.*, pp. 241-247 and 767-779; for related concepts of de-etatization, unity of power, and the withering away of power, pp. 146-147, 442-443, and 1313-1314, respectively. A good introduction to Yugoslav concepts of the state and law is Ivo Lapenna's *State and Law*, New Haven: Yale University Press, 1964.
61. Richard Adamiak, "The 'Withering Away' of the State: A Reconsideration," *Journal of Politics*, 32, 1, February 1970, pp. 3-18.
62. Miladin Životić, "The End of the Ideals or of Ideology?," *Praxis* (I), V, 3-4, 1969, p. 420.
63. Boris Ziherl, "Socijalistička politika i dezalijenacija čoveka" ("Socialist Politics and the De-Alienation of Man"), in *Marks i savremenost*, II, *op. cit.*, p. 552.
64. Todorović, "Self-Management . . . ," *op. cit.*, p. 16.
65. Andrija Krešić, "The Proletariat and Socialism in the Works of Marx and in the World Today," *Praxis* (I), V, 3-4, 1969, pp. 380-381.
66. Marx, "On the Jewish Question," in *Karl Marx, op. cit.*, p. 11.
67. Karl Marx & Friedrich Engels, *The German Ideology*, New York: International Publishers, 1969, p. 78.
68. Marković, *The Contemporary Marx, op. cit.*, p. 167.
69. Karl Marx, *A Contribution to the Critique of Political Economy*, excerpted in *Marx & Engels, op. cit.*, p. 43.
70. Djordjević, *Socijalizam i demokratija, op. cit.*, p. 94.
71. Jovan Djordjević, *Novi Ustavni sistem (The New Constitutional System)*, Belgrade: Savremena Administracija, 1964, p. 73; Krešić, "The Proletariat and Socialism . . . ," *op. cit.*, p. 381.
72. Vranicki, *Historija Marksizma, op. cit.*, p. 573.
73. Vranicki, discussing Pero Damjanović's "Marks o društvenom samoupravljanju" ("Marx on Social Self-Government"), in *Marks i savremenost*, I, *op. cit.*, p. 375.
74. Vranicki, "Teorijsko zasnivanje ideje . . .," *op. cit.*, p. 725.
75. Marx's conception of freedom as man's rational exchange with nature in volume III of his *Capital* is cited often by Yugoslav Marxists; see Vuko Pavićević, "Neki moralni aspekti Jugoslovenskog puta u socijalizam" ("Some Moral Aspects of the Yugoslav Road to Socialism"), in *Humanizam i socijalizam*, II, *op. cit.*, p. 23.
76. Vranicki, "Teorijsko zasnivanje ideje . . .," *op. cit.*, p. 743.
77. Djordjević, *Socijalizam i demokratija, op. cit.*, p. 101.
78. Vranicki, "Teorijsko zasnivanje ideje . . .," *op. cit.*, p. 743.
79. Rudi Supek, *Sociologija i socijalizam (Sociology and Socialism)*, Zagreb: Znanje, 1966, pp. 83-84, 194.
80. "Constitutional System of the Socialist Federal Republic of Yugoslavia," *YS*, XV, 3, August 1974, p. 4.
81. Mihajlo Velimirović, "The Organization of Associated Labour," *STP*, XVII, 1, January 1977, p. 87.
82. Vladimir Bakarić, "From Associated Labour to the Association of Free Producers," *STP*, 17, 10, October 1974, p. 12.
83. Slaven Letica, "Samoupravno društvo i teorija tržišta radne snage" ("Self-Managing Society and the Theory of the Market for Labor Power"),

Gledišta, XVI, 3, March 1975, pp. 270, 274-275.

84. Edvard Kardelj, "The Organizing of Associated Labour Along Self-Management Lines," *STP*, 13, 1, January 1975, pp. 11, 23. In 1976, some 1,500 BOALs ran a cumulative deficit of ca. 18 billion dinars: See "Samoupravljanje i gubici" ("Self-Management and Losses"), *EP*, XXVI, 1297, February 7, 1977, p. 8.

85. Velimirović, "The Organization of Associated Labour," *op. cit.*, p. 77.

86. Kardelj, "Towards a New Type of Socialist Democracy," *op. cit.*, p. 18.

87. Edvard Kardelj, "Protivrečnosti društvene svojine u savremenoj socijalističkoj praksi" ("Contradictions of Social Property in Contemporary Socialist Practice"), in *Teorija i praksa samoupravljanja u Jugoslaviji, op. cit.*, pp. 48-49.

88. *The Constitution of the Socialist Federal Republic of Yugoslavia*, Belgrade: Federal Secretariat for Information, 1963, pp. 7-9.

89. *Mala politička enciklopedija, op. cit.*, pp. 234-236.

90. Čeda Djurdjević, discussing Damjanović's "Marks o društvenom samoupravljanju," *op. cit.*, p. 375.

91. Vranicki, "Teorijsko zasnivanje ideje . . .," *op. cit.*, pp. 724-725.

92. *Ibid.*, p. 742.

93. Tito, "On Workers' Management in Economic Enterprises," *op. cit.*, p. 82.

94. *Radničko samoupravljanje (Workers' Self-Management)*, ed. Živan Tanić, Belgrade: Institut Društvenih Nauka, 1963, pp. 50-51, 119.

95. Jiri Kolaja, *Workers' Councils*, New York: Praeger, 1966, p. 77.

96. Rudi Supek, "Radničko samoupravljanje i humanizacija rada i potrošnje" ("Workers' Self-Management and the Humanization of Work and Consumption"), in *Humanizam i socijalizam*, II, *op. cit.*, p. 151.

97. David Tornquist, *Look East, Look West*, New York: Macmillan, 1966, p. 194.

98. Denitch, *The Legitimation of a Revolution, op. cit.*, p. 154.

99. Singleton, *Twentieth-Century Yugoslavia, op. cit.*, p. 285.

100. Djilas, *The Unperfect Society, op. cit.*, p. 223; Nenad D. Popović, *Yugoslavia*, Syracuse: Syracuse University Press, 1968, p. 205.

101. *Ibid.*, p. 227.

102. Edvard Kardelj, "The Class Position of the League of Communists Today," *STP*, 37, December 1969, pp. 6-7.

103. Pešić-Golubović, "Socialist Ideas and Reality," *op. cit.*, p. 408.

104. Stipe Šuvar, "Neformalne grupe kao centri moći u samoupravnom društvu" ("Informal Groups as Power Centers in Self-Governing Society"), in *Teorija i praksa samoupravljanja u Jugoslaviji, op. cit.*, p. 626.

105. Josip-Broz Tito, "Sixty Years of Revolutionary Struggle of the League of Communists of Yugoslavia," *STP*, XIX, 6, June 1979, p. 29.

106. Pečujlić, *Budućnost koja je počela, op. cit.*, p. 66.

107. Supek, *Participacija, radnička kontrola i samoupravljanje, op. cit.*, p. 127.

108. Marković, *From Affluence to Praxis, op. cit.*, pp. 235-236.

109. Rudi Supek, "Problems and Perspectives of Workers' Self-Management in Yugoslavia," in *Yugoslav Workers' Self-Management, op. cit.*, p. 231.

110. Kardelj, "Protivrečnosti društvene svojine . . .," *op. cit.*, p. 62; Branko Horvat, "An Institutional Model of a Self-managed Socialist Economy," in *Self-governing Socialism*, II, *op. cit.*, p. 323.

111. Stephen M. Sachs, "Implications of Recent Developments in Yugoslav Self-Management," paper presented at the *Second International Conference on Self-Management*, Ithaca, New York, June 1975, p. 9.

112. Paul Lendvai, *Eagles in Cobwebs*, Garden City, N. Y.: Doubleday, 1969, p. 137.

113. Gerry Hunnius, "Workers' Self-Management in Yugoslavia," in *Workers' Control*, eds. G. Hunnius, G. David Garson & John Case, New York: Random House, 1973, p. 283.

114. Ichak Adizes, *Industrial Democracy*, New York: Free Press, 1971, pp. 209-212.

115. Veljko Rus, "Self-Management Egalitarianism and Social Differentiation," *Praxis* (I), VI, 1-2, 1970, pp. 254-257.

116. *Ibid.*, pp. 258-261.

117. Egon Neuberger & Estelle James, "The Yugoslav Self-Managed Enterprise: A Systemic Approach," in *Plan and Market*, ed. Morris Bornstein, New Haven: Yale University Press, 1973, p. 277; Sharon Zukin, *Beyond Marx and Tito*, New York: Cambridge University Press, 1975, p. 190.

118. Benjamin N. Ward, *The Socialist Economy*, New York: Random House, 1967, p. 254.

119. Jakov Blažević, *Aktualnosti revolucije (Current Questions of the Revolution)*, Zagreb: Narodno sveučilište grada Zagreba, Centar za aktualni politički studij, 1973, p. 101.

120. Sidney Verba & Goldie Shabad, "Workers' Councils and Political Stratification: The Yugoslav Experience," paper presented at the *APSA Annual Meeting*, San Francisco, September 2-5, 1975, p. 67.

121. Sachs, "Implications of Recent Developments . . . ," *op. cit.*, p. 7.

122. Joel Dirlam & James Plummer, *An Introduction to the Yugoslav Economy*, Columbus, Ohio: Merrill, 1973, p. 246.

123. Aleksander Bajt, "Management in Yugoslavia," in *Comparative Economic Systems*, 3rd ed., ed. Morris Bornstein, Homewood, Ill.: Irwin, 1974, p. 196.

124. S. Bolčić, quoted by Branko Horvat, "The Labor-Managed Enterprise," in *Self-governing Socialism*, II, *op. cit.*, p. 168. Radoslav Ratković calls this phenomenon where everyone decides about everything "coventioneering" ("zborovanje") rather than self-management: see "Opasnosti tehnokratizma" ("Dangers of Technocracy"), *NIN*, No. 1370, April 10, 1977, pp. 12-13.

125. Mirić, *Interesne grupe i politička moć*, *op. cit.*, p. 161.

126. Adizes, *Industrial Democracy*, *op. cit.*, pp. 223-224.

127. Sachs, "Implications of Recent Developments . . . ," *op. cit.*, p. 18.

128. Zukin, *Beyond Marx and Tito*, *op. cit.*, p. 97; on the inversion of functions between workers' self-management and trade unions, see Paul Blumberg, *Industrial Democracy*, New York: Schocken, 1969, p. 206.

129. David A. Dyker, "Yugoslavia: Unity Out of Diversity?," in *Political Culture and Political Change in Communist States*, eds. Archie Brown & Jack Gray, New York: Holmes & Meier, 1977, p. 86.

130. Marius J. Broekmeyer, "Self-Management in Yugoslavia," *AAAPSS*, 431, May 1977, p. 139; Veljko Rus, "Limited Effects of Workers' Participation and Political Counter-Power," in *Work and Power*, eds. Tom R. Burns, Lars Erik Karlsson & V. Rus, Beverly Hills: Sage, 1979, p. 237.

131. Rus, "Limited Effects of Workers' Participation . . .," *op. cit.*, p. 240; Tom Baumgartner, Tom R. Burns & Dusko Sekulić, "Self-Management, Market, and Political Institutions in Conflict: Yugoslav Development Patterns and Dialectics," in *Work and Power*, *op. cit.*, pp. 117-118.

132. Ellen Turkish Comisso, *Workers' Control Under Plan and Market*, New Haven: Yale University Press, 1979, pp. 2, 216, 218, 222-223.

133. Zukin, *Beyond Marx and Tito*, *op. cit.*, pp. 191-192.

134. Josip Obradović, "Participation and Work Attitudes in Yugoslavia," *IR*, 9, 2, February 1970, p. 165.

135. Veljko Rus, "Influence Structure in Yugoslav Enterprise," *IR*, 9, 2, February 1970, p. 160.

136. Rus, "Self-Management Egalitarianism . . . ," *op. cit.*, pp. 264-265.

137. Zoran Polić, "Smisao i problemi ostvarivanja novih odnosa u upravi" ("The Meaning and Problems of Creating New Relations in Administration"), in *Zbirka zakona i drugih propisa o upravi (Collection of Laws and Other Regulations on Administration)*, ed. Nikola Balog, Belgrade: Savezni Zavod za Javnu Upravu, 1966, p. 5.

138. Svetozar Stojanović, "From Post-Revolutionary Dictatorship to Socialist Democracy: Yugoslav Socialism at the Crossroads," *Praxis* (I), IX, 4,

1973, p. 320.

139. Mirić, *Interesne grupe i politička moć, op. cit.*, p. 128.

140. "Local Communities—Development and Results," *YS*, XIII, 3, August 1972, p. 11.

141. Zdravko Tomac, "Komuna u ustavnoj reformi" ("The Commune in the Constitutional Reform"), in *Ustavna reforma komune (The Constitutional Reform of the Commune)*, eds. D. Božić, *et al.*, Zagreb: Centar za aktualni politički studij, 1971, p. 88.

142. Leon Gershković, "Samoupravljanje u društveno-političkim zajednicama" ("Self-Government in Socio-Political Communities"), in *Teorija i praksa samoupravljanja u Jugoslaviji, op. cit.*, p. 578; Bogdan Pilić, "Jugoslovenska socijalistička samoupravna komuna" ("The Yugoslav Socialist Self-Governing Commune"), in *Marks i savremenost*, VII, eds. Dragutin Leković, *et al.*, Belgrade: Institut za medjunarodni radnički pokret, 1974, p. 292.

143. "Local Communities . . . ," *op. cit.*, p. 1.

144. "Constitutional System . . .," *op. cit.*, p. 6.

145. Tomac, "Komuna u ustavnoj reformi," *op. cit.*, p. 92.

146. Gersković, "Samoupravljanje u društveno-političkim zajednicama," *op. cit.*, p. 586.

147. Zukin, *Beyond Marx and Tito, op. cit.*, p. 157.

148. Quoted in *ibid.*, p. 180.

149. *Ibid.*, p. 183.

150. Edvard Kardelj, *Socijalistička demokratija u jugoslovenskoj praksi (Socialist Democracy in Yugoslav Practice)*, Belgrade: Kultura, 1957, p. 7. For Marx's conflicting views on the Paris Commune, see Bertram D. Wolfe, *Marxism*, New York: Dial, 1965, pp. 126-147.

151. Vranicki, "Teorijsko zasnivanje ideje . . .," *op. cit.*, p. 739.

152. Kardelj, *Socijalistička demokratija . . .* , *op. cit.*, p. 40.

153. *The Constitution of the Socialist Federal Republic of Yugoslavia, op. cit.*, p. 50; for elaborations on the Yugoslav concept of the commune, see Jovan Djordjević & Najdan Pašić, "The Communal Self-Government System in Yugoslavia," *International Social Science Journal* (UNESCO), XIII, 3, 1961, pp. 389-407; and Edvard Kardelj, *Samoupravljanje u komuni (Self-Government in the Commune)*, Belgrade: Stalna Konferencija Gradova Jugoslavije, 1961.

154. "Constitutional System . . .," *op. cit.*, p. 79.

155. Jack C. Fisher, *Yugoslavia—A Multinational State*, San Francisco: - Chandler, 1966, p. 147.

156. Kardelj, *Socijalistička demokratija . . .* , *op. cit.*, p. 40.

157. "Constitutional System . . .," *op. cit.*, pp. 43-48.

158. Šuvar, "Neformalne grupe kao centri moći . . . ," *op. cit.*, p. 639; Hunnius, "Workers' Self-Management in Yugoslavia," *op. cit.*, p. 312.

159. Josip-Broz Tito, "The LCY in the Struggle for the Further Development of Socialist, Self-Managing and Nonaligned Yugoslavia," *STP*, XVIII, 6, June 1978, p. 77.

160. Svetozar Stojanović, "The June Student Movement and Social Revolution in Yugoslavia," *Praxis* (I), VI, 3-4, 1970, p. 398.

161. Milentije Popović, "Samoupravljanje kao osnova društveno-ekonomskog sistema" ("Self-Management as the Basis of the Socio-Economic System"), in *Teorija i praksa samoupravljanja u Jugoslaviji, op. cit.*, p. 231.

162. Damjanović, "Marks o društvenom samoupravljanju," *op. cit.*, p. 364.

163. Radivoje Marinković, "Uticaj komune na proces integracije u privredi" ("The Influence of the Commune on the Process of Integration in the Economy"), in *Marks i savremenost*, II, *op. cit.*, pp. 325-326; Tomac, "Komuna u ustavnoj reformi," *op. cit.*, pp. 35-38.

164. Rus, "Self-Management Egalitarianism . . . ," *op. cit.*, p. 267.

165. Blažević, *Aktualnosti revolucije, op. cit.*, p. 111.

166. Edvard Kardelj, "Development of the System of Communities of Interest,"

STP, 18, 11, November 1974, pp. 3-4; on the 20th Assembly of the Standing Conference of Towns in Herceg-Novi, October 4, 1974, see Miroslav Koraksić, "Interesne zajednice su izraz i potvrda jedinstva samoupravnog sistema" ("Communities of Interest are the Expression and Affirmation of the Unity of the Self-Governing System"), *Komunist,* XXXII, 917, October 14, 1974, p. 7.

167.   *Ibid.,* p. 13.

168.   Pečujlić, *Budućnost koja je počela, op. cit.,* p. 104; Vojan Rus, "Demokratizacija: Naše osnovno raskršće" ("Democratization: Our Basic Crossroads"), in *Marks i savremenost,* VII, *op. cit.,* p. 298.

169.   Časlav Strahinjić, "Self-Management Agreements and Social Compacts," *STP,* XVI, 6, June 1976, pp. 43-44.

170.   Svetozar Stojanović, "Socijalistička demokratija i SKJ" ("Socialist Democracy and the LCY"), in *Marks i savremenost,* II, *op. cit.,* p. 27.

171.   Mihailo Marković, *Preispitivanja (Reassessments),* Belgrade: Srpska književna zadruga, 1972, pp. 58-60.

172.   Tomac, "Komuna u ustavnoj reformi," *op. cit.,* p. 55.

173.   Milan Matić, "Samoupravljanje i skupštinski sistem" ("Self-Government and the Assembly System"), in *Teorija i praksa samoupravljanja u Jugoslaviji, op. cit.,* p. 655.

174.   Djordji Caca, "Karakter delegatskog mandata" ("The Nature of the Delegate's Mandate"), *Komunist,* XXXII, 925, December 9, 1974, p. 15.

175.   Angel Čemerski, "The Delegates' System--Strengthening of the Role of the Working Class," *STP,* XVI, 3, March 1976, p. 22.

176.   Edvard Kardelj, *Pravci razvoja političkog sistema socijalističkog samoupravljanja (Directions of Development of the Political System of Socialist Self-Management),* 2nd enl. ed., Belgrade: Komunist, 1978, p. 174.

177.   Tito, Report to the Eleventh Party Congress, *op. cit.,* pp. 72, 76.

178.   Dragan Jovanović, "Lenji delegati" ("Lazy Delegates"), *NIN,* XXVIII, 1451, October 29, 1978, pp. 12-13.

179.   Gavriel D. Ra'anan, *Yugoslavia After Tito,* Boulder, Colo.:   Westview, 1977, p. 43.

180.   Mirić, *Interesne grupe i politička moć, op. cit.,* p. 169.

181.   *Ibid.,* pp. 164-166.

182.   Rus, "Demokratizacija," *op. cit.,* pp. 304-307.

183.   Svetozar Stojanović, *Geschichte und Parteibewusstsein,* Munich: Carl Hanser, 1978, pp. 81, 84-85.

184.   "Neophodnost razvijenije ideologije" ("The Necessity of a More Developed Ideology"), *Socijalizam,* XIII, 2, February 1970, pp. 151-152.

185.   Josip-Broz Tito, "Introductory Address" at the Ninth Party Congress, *STP,* 33, January-March, 1969, p. 33.

186.   Kardelj, "The Class Position of the League . . . ," *op. cit.,* p. 13; emphasis added.

187.   Antun Žvan, "Ecstasy and Hangover of a Revolution," *Praxis* (I), VII, 3-4, 1971, p. 484.

188.   Mihailo Marković, "The Possibilities and Difficulties of Overcoming Liberalism and the Present Form of Socialist Society," *Praxis* (I), IX, 3-4, 1973, p. 36.

189.   Marković, *From Affluence to Praxis, op. cit.,* p. 241.

190.   Supek, "Problems and Perspectives of Workers' Selfmanagement in Yugoslavia," *op. cit.,* p. 217.

191.   Milan Mirić, *Rezervati (Reservations),* Zagreb: Studentski centar sveučilišta, 1970, p. 27.

192.   Krešić, *Političko društvo i politička mitologija, op. cit.,* pp. 165-170.

193.   Dragoljub Mićunović, "Bureaucracy and Public Communication," in *Praxis,* eds. Mihailo Marković & Gajo Petrović, Dordrecht: Reidel, 1979, pp. 309-310.

194.   Zagorka Pešić-Golubović, *Čovek i njegov svet (Man and His World),* Belgrade: Prosveta, 1973, pp. 213-214; Ljubomir Tadić, "Authority and

Authoritarian Thinking: On the Sense and Senselessness of Subordination," in *Marxist Humanism and Praxis,* ed. Gerson S. Sher, Buffalo, N. Y.: Prometheus, 1978, p. 89.

195. Mihailo Marković, "Reason and Historical Praxis," in *Marxist Humanism and Praxis, op. cit.,* pp. 27-31; Predrag Vranicki, *Marksizam i socijalizam (Marxism and Socialism),* Zagreb: Liber, 1979, p. 179.

196. Marković, *From Affluence to Praxis, op. cit.,* p. 241.

197. Tadić, *Poredak i sloboda, op. cit.,* p. 191.

198. Danilo Pejović, *Sistem i egzistencija (System and Existence),* Zagreb: Zora, 1970, p. 209; Marković, *Preispitivanja, op. cit.,* p. 68.

199. Stevan Vračar in *Gledišta,* VII, 8-9, August-September, 1967, pp. 1053-1066, quoted by Wolfgang Leonhard, *Three Faces of Marxism,* New York: Holt, Rinehart & Winston, 1974, p. 312. Djilas' call for a multi-party system was echoed in the 1960s even by some party leaders like Krste Crvenkovski, head of the Macedonian LC, who envisaged a pluralistic party and a loyal opposition: see Lendvai, *Eagles in Cobwebs, op. cit.,* p. 124.

200. Radomir Lukić, *Političke stranke (Political Parties),* 2nd ed., Belgrade: Naučna knjiga, 1975, pp. 243-244.

201. Marko Nikezić, former Minister for Foreign Affairs and 1971-72 President of the Serbian LC, ousted from state functions in 1972 and from the party in 1974, cited by William Zimmerman, "The Tito Succession and the Evolution of Yugoslav Politics," *SCC,* IX, 1-2, Spring/Summer, 1976, p. 73.

202. Ivan Kuvačić, *Sukobi (Conflicts),* Zagreb: Razlog, 1972, pp. 15-16; Svetozar Stojanović, "Stalinist 'Partiinost' and Communist Dignity," *Praxis* (I), X, 1-2, 1974, pp. 129-138.

203. *Ibid.,* p. 137; Rudi Supek, *Humanistička inteligencija i politika (The Humanist Intelligentsia and Politics),* Zagreb: Studentski centar sveučilišta, 1971, p. 120.

204. Stojanović, *Between Ideals and Reality, op. cit.,* pp. 182-183.

205. *Ibid.,* p. 186.

206. Mihailo Djurić, "Homo Politicus," in *Praxis, op. cit.,* p. 117.

207. Svetozar Stojanović, "Revolutionary Teleology and Ethics," in *Tolerance and Revolution,* eds. Paul Kurtz & S. Stojanović, Belgrade: Philosophical Society of Serbia, 1970, p. 43.

208. Gajo Petrović, *Marx in the Mid-Twentieth Century,* Garden City, N. Y.: Doubleday, 1967, p. 156.

209. Tadić, *Poredak i sloboda, op. cit.,* p. 226.

210. Stjepan Pulišelić, "Političke stranke" ("Political Parties"), lead essay in *Političke stranke kao faktor suvremenog političkog sistema, op. cit.,* p. 34.

211. Stojanović, "From Post-Revolutionary Dictatorship to Socialist Democracy," *op. cit.,* p. 324.

212. Lendvai, *Eagles in Cobwebs, op. cit.,* p. 56.

213. Tito, quoted in *ibid.,* p. 127.

214. Aleksandr I. Solzhenitsyn, "Letter of 12 November 1969 to the Soviet Writers' Union," protesting his expulsion, in *Solzhenitsyn,* enl. ed., ed. Leopold Labedz, Bloomington: Indiana University Press, 1973, p. 220.

215. Marković, *The Contemporary Marx, op. cit.,* p. 154.

216. Srdjan Vrcan, "Social Equality and Inequality in the Bourgeois World and in Socialism: Challenge and Alternative," *Praxis* (I), X, 1-2, 1974, p. 128.

217. Marković, *From Affluence to Praxis, op. cit.,* p. 237.

218. Stojanović, *Between Ideals and Reality, op. cit.,* p. 125.

219. Božidar Jakšić, "Yugoslav Society Between Revolution and Stabilization," *Praxis* (I), VII, 3-4, 1971, p. 448.

220. Zagorka Pešić-Golubović, "Why is Functionalism More Desirable in Present-Day Yugoslavia Than Marxism?," *Praxis* (I), IX, 4, 1973, p. 363; Mihailo Marković, "Gleichheit und Freiheit," *Praxis* (I), IX, 2-3, 1973, p. 147.

221. Srdjan Vrcan, "Some Comments on Social Inequality," *Praxis* (I), IX, 2-3, 1973, pp. 239-241; for Kuvačić's views, see his "Additional Thoughts on Synchrony and Diachrony," *Praxis* (I), VII, 3-4, 1971, pp. 423-430.

222. Radomir Lukić, "Društveno raslojavanje kao uzrok društvenih sukoba u Jugoslaviji" ("Social Differentiation as the Cause of Social Conflicts in Yugoslavia"), *Sociologija,* XIII, 3, 1971, pp. 356-358.

223. Kuvačić, *Sukobi, op. cit.,* p. 138.

224. Pečujlić, *Budućnost koja je počela, op. cit.,* p. 66.

225. Supek, *Humanistička inteligencija i politika, op. cit.,* p. 78.

226. Milan Kangrga, "Phänomenologie des ideologisch-politischen Auftretens der jugoslawischen Mittelklasse," *Praxis* (I), VII, 3-4, 1971, pp. 457-459. This essay in particular led to a confrontation between the regime and *Praxis* theorists.

227. Marković, *The Contemporary Marx, op. cit.,* p. 196.

228. Mijo Biličić, "Srednja klasa u samoupravljanju" ("The Middle Class in Self-Management"), *NT,* No. 9, September 1975, p. 1339.

229. Kardelj, "Protivrečnosti društvene svojine . . . ," *op. cit.,* p. 22 on self-management vs. monopoly; p. 64 on workers as exploiters.

230. *Ibid.,* pp. 25, 48-49.

231. Mirić, *Rezervati, op. cit.,* p. 61.

232. Pešić-Golubović, "Socialist Ideas and Reality," *op. cit.,* p. 417.

233. Marković, *From Affluence to Praxis, op. cit.,* p. 234.

234. Jakšić, "Yugoslav Society Between Revolution and Stabilization," *op. cit.,* pp. 443-444.

235. Supek, "The Statist and Self-Managing Models of Socialism," *op. cit.,* p. 298.

236. Marković, *From Affluence to Praxis, op. cit.,* p. 235.

237. Mihailo Marković, "Struktura moći u jugoslovenskom društvu i dilema revolucionarne inteligencije" ("The Power Structure in Yugoslav Society and the Dilemma of the Revolutionary Intelligentsia"), *Praxis* (Y), VIII, 6, November-December, 1971, p. 812; Blažević, *Aktualnosti revolucije, op. cit.,* p. 101.

238. Sidney Verba, Norman H. Nie & Jae-On Kim, *Participation and Political Equality,* New York: Cambridge University Press, 1978, pp. 225-231.

239. Baumgartner, Burns & Sekulić, "Self-Management, Market, and Political Institutions in Conflict," *op. cit.,* p. 115.

240. Ralph Pervan, *Tito and the Students,* Nedlands: University of Western Australia Press, 1978, pp. 149-150.

241. Žvan, "Ecstasy and Hangover of a Revolution," *op. cit.,* p. 481.

242. Marković, *From Affluence to Praxis, op. cit.,* p. 182.

243. Marković, "Struktura moći u jugoslovenskom društvu . . . ," *op. cit.,* p. 816.

244. Gršković, "Samoupravljanje u društveno-političkim zajednicama," *op. cit.,* p. 575.

245. Marković, *The Contemporary Marx, op. cit.,* p. 197.

246. Mihailo V. Popović, "Heterogenost društvenih sistema i sadašnja kriza jugoslovenskog društva" ("The Heterogeneity of Social Systems and the Contemporary Crisis of Yugoslav Society"), *Sociologija,* XIII, 3, 1971, pp. 422-423.

247. Vladimir Arzenšek, "Socijalna struktura i karakter konflikata" ("The Social Structure and the Nature of Conflicts"), *Sociologija,* XVII, 2, 1975, p. 257.

248. Vladimir Arzenšek, "'Konfliktni model' i struktura jugoslovenskog društva" ("The 'Conflict Model' and the Structure of Yugoslav Society"), *Sociologija,* XIII, 3, 1971, p. 369.

249. Zdravko Mlinar, "Društvene vrednosti, razvoj i konflikti" ("Societal Values, Development, and Conflicts"), *Sociologija,* XIII, 3, 1971, pp. 393-395.

250. Kardelj, "Protivrečnosti društvene svojine . . . ," *op. cit.,* p. 68.

251. Jakšić, "Yugoslav Society Between Revolution and Stabilization," *op. cit.,* p. 446.

252. Nebojša Popov, "Les formes et le caractere des conflits sociaux," *Praxis*

(I), VII, 3-4, 1971, p. 364.

253. Stojanović, "From Post-Revolutionary Dictatorship to Socialist Democracy, "*op. cit.*, p. 328.
254. Rus, "Self-Management Egalitarianism . . . ," *op. cit.*, p. 258.
255. Popović, "Heterogenost društvenih sistema . . . ," *op. cit.*, p. 424; Supek, "The Statist and Self-Managing Models of Socialism," *op. cit.*, p. 314.
256. Stojanović, "Socijalistička demokratija i SKJ," *op. cit.*, p. 30; Vojislav Stanovčić, "Konfliktne situacije u našem društvu" ("Situations of Conflict in Our Society"), *Socijalizam*, XIII, 1, January 1970, pp. 36-58; Rus, "Self-Management Egalitarianism . . . ," *op. cit.*, pp. 258-261.
257. Mirić, *Interesne grupe i politička moć*, *op. cit.*, p. 170.
258. Stipe Šuvar, *Samoupravljanje i alternative (Self-Management and Alternatives)*, 2nd enl. ed., Zagreb: Centar za aktualni politički studij Narodnog sveučilišta grada, 1976, pp. 448-449.
259. Kardelj, *Pravci razvoja . . .*, *op. cit.*, pp. 65-66.
260. Stanovčić, "Konfliktne situacije u našem društvu," *op. cit.*, p. 41; David Easton, *A Systems Analysis of Political Life*, New York: Wiley, 1965.
261. Mirić, *Interesne grupe i politička moć*, *op. cit.*, p. 170.
262. Stanovčić, "Konfliktne situacije u našem društvu," *op. cit.*, pp. 43-44, 57.
263. Marković, *From Affluence to Praxis*, *op. cit.*, pp. 166-167.
264. Mihailo Marković, "Is it Possible to Abolish Political Mediation?," *Praxis* (I), IX, 3-4, 1973, p. 53.
265. Marković, "Struktura moći u jugoslovenskom društvu . . . ," *op. cit.*, p. 818.
266. Stojanović, *Between Ideals and Reality*, *op. cit.*, p. 91.
267. Stojanović, *Geschichte und Parteibewusstsein*, *op. cit.*, p. 90; vs. Kardelj, *Pravci razvoja . . .*, *op. cit.*, p. 66.
268. Vladimir I. Lenin, *Collected Works*, Vol. 32, Moscow: Progress, 1970, pp. 85-86; for Stalin's conception of the party boasting "iron discipline," see his *Foundations of Leninism* (1924).
269. Robert Nozick, *Anarchy, State, and Utopia*, New York: Basic Books, 1974, p. 330.
270. Winston M. Fisk, "A Communist *Rechtsstaat?*—The Case of Yugoslav Constitutionalism," *GAO*, 5, 1, Winter 1969-70, pp. 41-53 and "The Constitutionalism Movement in Yugoslavia: A Preliminary Survey," *SLR*, 30, 2, June 1971, pp. 277-297. For the Yugoslav view of constitutionalism and legality, see Najdan Pašić, "Društveno-političke pretpostavke Ustavnosti i zakonitosti" ("The Socio-Political Assumptions of Constitutionalism and Legality"), in *Marks i savremenost*, II, *op. cit.*, pp. 38-48; and Ivan Maksimović, "Constitutional Socialism in Yugoslavia," *AAAPSS*, 358, March 1965, pp. 159-169.
271. Zimmerman, "The Tito Succession and the Evolution of Yugoslav Politics," *op. cit.*, pp. 75-76; Singleton, *Twentieth-Century Yugoslavia*, *op. cit.*, pp. 307-312; George Klein, "The Role of Ethnic Politics in the Czechoslovak Crisis of 1968 and the Yugoslav Crisis of 1971," *SCC*, VIII, 4, Winter 1975, pp. 363-366.
272. Gary K. Bertsch, "Yugoslavia: The Eleventh Congress, the Constitution and the Succession," *GAO*, 14, 1, Winter 1979, p. 105; Robin Alison Remington, "Yugoslavia," in *Communism in Eastern Europe*, eds. Teresa Rakowska-Harmstone & Andrew György, Bloomington: Indiana University Press, 1979, p. 224.
273. Hunnius, "Workers' Self-Management in Yugoslavia," *op. cit.*, p. 272; Robert Sharlet, "Introduction: Comparative Political Development in Eastern Europe," in *The Politics of Modernization in Eastern Europe*, ed. Charles Gati, New York: Praeger, 1974, p. 48; on the interlock between the party and other elites in Yugoslavia, see also Howard M. Wachtel, *Workers' Management and Workers' Wages in Yugoslavia*, Ithaca, N.Y.: Cornell University Press, 1973, pp. 77-81.
274. Šuvar, *Samoupravljanje i alternative*, *op. cit.*, p. 134.
275. Lenard J. Cohen, "Yugoslavia: The Political Role of the Administrative

Elite," in *The Politics of Modernization in Eastern Europe, op. cit.,* p. 186.

276. Lendvai, *Eagles in Cobwebs, op. cit.,* p. 164.

277. *Ibid.,* p. 96.

278. Stojanović, *Geschichte und Parteibewusstsein, op. cit.,* p. 82.

279. This does not solve all problems. The institutional imperative is a framework for conflict resolution, not a conflict-less framework. See Irving Kristol, *et al., America's Continuing Revolution,* Garden City, N.Y.: Doubleday, 1976; for a humorous view, see Robert N. Kharasch, *The Institutional Imperative,* New York: Charterhouse, 1976.

280. O'Brien, "On the Adequacy of the Concept of Totalitarianism," *op. cit.,* p. 59.

281. LaPalombara, "Monoliths or Plural Systems," *op. cit.,* p. 325.

282. Talmon, *The Origins of Totalitarian Democracy, op. cit.,* p. 253.

283. Bernard-Henri Lévy, *Barbarism With a Human Face,* N. Y.: Harper & Row, 1979, pp. 148-149.

CHAPTER VIII: IS MARXISM THE ONLY HUMANISM?

1. Albert W. Levi, *Humanism and Politics,* Bloomington: Indiana University Press, 1969, p. 20.

2. Howard L. Parsons, *Humanism and Marx's Thought,* Springfield, Ill.: Charles C. Thomas, 1971, p. 182.

3. George E. Novack, "Basic Differences Between Existentialism and Marxism," in *Existentialism versus Marxism,* ed. G. E. Novack, New York: Dell, 1966, pp. 317-340.

4. John Hoffman, *Marxism and the Theory of Praxis,* New York: International Publishers, 1976, pp. 199-232.

5. Henryk Skolimowski, "Are There No Consequences of Open Marxism?," *SCC,* IV, 1, January 1971, p. 49.

6. Richard T. De George, *Patterns of Soviet Thought,* Ann Arbor: University of Michigan Press, 1966, pp. 61-62.

7. Paul C. Roberts & Matthew A. Stephenson, *Marx's Theory of Exchange, Alienation and Crisis,* Stanford: Hoover Institution Press, 1973, p. 86.

8. George L. Kline, "Was Marx an Ethical Humanist?," *SST,* 9, 2, June 1969, p. 96.

9. Predrag Vranicki, "Socialism and the Problem of Alienation," in *Socialist Humanism,* ed. Erich Fromm, Garden City, N. Y.: Doubleday, 1966, p. 308.

10. Walter Odajnyk, *Marxism and Existentialism,* Garden City, N. Y.: Doubleday, 1965, pp. xxi-xxii.

11. Raymond Aron, *Marxism and the Existentialists,* New York: Harper & Row, 1969, p. 176.

12. Thomas J. Blakeley, "Sartre's *Critique de la raison dialectique* and the Opacity of Marxism-Leninism," *SST,* VIII, 2-3, June-September, 1968, p. 129.

13. Odajnyk, *Marxism and Existentialism, op. cit.,* p. 171.

14. Nicola Abbagnano & Nicholas Lobkowicz, "Existentialismus," in *Ideologie und Philosophie,* 3 vols., ed. N. Lobkowicz, New York: Herder & Herder, 1973, I, p. 245.

15. Jovan Djordjević, *Socijalizam i demokratija (Socialism and Democracy),* Belgrade: Savremena Administracija, 1962, p. 101.

16. Mijalko Todorović, "Self-Management—Historical Aspiration of the Working Class," *STP,* 40, July-September, 1970, p. 14.

17. R. N. Carew-Hunt, *The Theory and Practice of Communism,* Baltimore, Md.: Penguin, 1963, pp. 171-210.

18. See Tito's view in Zvonko Štaubringer, "Humanistic Vision of a New World," *STP,* 39, April-June, 1970, p. 106; the Yugoslavs base their conception of a possible peaceful transition to socialism and communism

on Marx's address to the Hague Conference of the Amsterdam section of the International in 1872 in which he conceded this possibility in the case of the United States and Great Britain.

19. Gajo Petrović, *Marx in the Mid-Twentieth Century*, Garden City, N. Y.: Doubleday, 1967, p. 156.

20. "Resolution on the Ideological-Political Foundations for the Further Development of the League of Communists of Yugoslavia," *STP*, 33, January-March, 1969, pp. 89-120.

21. Rudi Supek, "Discours d'ouverture" ("Opening Address" to the 1969 Korčula Symposium on Power and Humanity), *Praxis* (I), VI, 1-2, 1970, pp. 3-7.

22. Ćazim Sadiković, "Etatizam i odnosi medju socijalističkim zemljama" ("Etatism and Relations Between Socialist Countries"), *Socijalizam*, XIII, 9, September 1970, pp. 1081-1090.

23. Petrović indicates in his *Marx in the Mid-Twentieth Century, op. cit.,* pp. 17-18, that the relationships between existentialism, pragmatism, symbolic logic, and Marxism remain unexplored. It is possible that the Yugoslavs would decline the designation of their thought as Marxism-Existentialism suggested here.

24. Fromm in *Socialist Humanism, op. cit.,* pp. vii-xiii.

25. Levi, *Humanism and Politics, op. cit.,* p. 445; Howard L. Parsons, *Humanistic Philosophy in Contemporary Poland and Yugoslavia*, New York: American Institute for Marxist Studies, 1966, p. 10; Ghiţa Ionesco, "Djilas, Tito and Yugoslav Socialism," *PQ*, 41, 3, July-September, 1970, p. 308.

26. Ludvik Vrtačić, *Der jugoslawische Marxismus*, Freiburg im Breisgau: Walter-Verlag, 1975, p. 132.

27. Gerson S. Sher, *Praxis*, Bloomington: Indiana University Press, 1977, p. 247.

28. H. J. Blackham, *Humanism*, Baltimore, Md.: Penguin, 1968, p. 128.

29. Jacques Maritain, *True Humanism*, New York: Scribner's, 1938, p. 80.

30. Petrović, *Marx in the Mid-Twentieth Century, op. cit.,* p. 37; Mihailo Marković, "Basic Characteristics of Marxist Humanism," *Praxis* (I), V, 3-4, 1969, p. 610.

31. J. P. Van Praag, "Humanistički pogled na svijet" ("A Humanist View of the World"), *EM*, 3-4, March-June, 1967, p. 114.

32. "Humanist Manifesto II," *The Humanist*, XXXIII, 5, September/October, 1973, p. 8.

33. Van Praag, "Humanistički pogled na svijet," *op. cit.,* pp. 114-115.

34. Blackham, *Humanism, op. cit.,* p. 80.

35. *Ibid.,* p. 204.

36. Gerald Wendt, "Humanistički doprinos" ("A Humanist Contribution"), *EM*, 3-4, March-June, 1967, pp. 117-119.

37. "Humanist Manifesto II: Qualifying and Dissenting Statements," *The Humanist*, XXXIII, 6, November/December, 1973, pp. 9-10.

38. *Ibid.,* p. 7.

39. Maritain, *True Humanism, op. cit.,* p. 84.

40. Van Praag, in *Tolerance and Revolution*, eds. Paul Kurtz & Svetozar Stojanović, Belgrade: Philosophical Society of Serbia, 1970, p. 154.

41. Paul Kurtz, "In Defence of Tolerance," in *ibid.,* p. 53.

42. Os Guinness, *The Dust of Death*, Downers Grove, Ill.: InterVarsity Press, 1973, p. 18.

43. *Ibid.,* p. 38.

44. Kurtz, "In Defence of Tolerance," *op. cit.,* p. 57.

45. Jacob Bronowski, "The Principle of Tolerance," *The Atlantic*, 232, 6, December 1973, p. 60.

46. William James, *The Meaning of Truth*, Ann Arbor: University of Michigan Press, 1970, pp. 89-90.

47. Some students of Marxism contend that Marx accepted none of the components of dialectical materialism, and that he never used the

expression. Yet, Marx's entire life and work were characterized by efforts to develop a dialectical *and* historical materialism. As Marx wrote in the Preface to the Second Edition of *Capital* in 1873: "My dialectic method is not only different from the Hegelian, but its direct opposite . . . . With me . . . the ideal is nothing else than the material world reflected by the human mind and translated into forms of thought." Gustav A. Wetter stated in *Marxism, Communism and Western Society*, 8 vols., ed. C. D. Kernig, New York: Herder & Herder, 1972-73, II, that: "For the most part dialectical materialism is today understood as a philosophy initially conceived by Marx, systematically worked out by Engels and elaborated in somewhat greater detail by Lenin." And, the late Herbert Marcuse concluded in the same volume that: "In its fundamental structure Marxian materialism is at once historical and dialectical, as Marxian dialectics is at once materialistic and historical."

48. Max Weber, "The Meaning of 'Ethical Neutrality' in Sociology and Economics," in his *On the Methodology of the Social Sciences*, eds. Edward A. Shils & Henry A. Finch, Illinois: Free Press of Glencoe, 1949, p. 14.

49. See my "Human Science and Ethics: A Prolegomenon," *Epistemologia* (Genova), II, 1, January-June, 1979, pp. 155-178; also in Castilian translation: *Logos* (México), VI, 17, May-August, 1978, pp. 83-101.

50. Gordon Leff, *The Tyranny of Concepts*, London: Merlin, 1969, p. 17.

51. Paul A. Samuelson, *Economics*, 9th ed., New York: McGraw-Hill, 1973, p. 862.

52. Mark Blaug, *Economic Theory in Retrospect*, Rev. ed., Homewood, Ill.: Irwin, 1968, p. 237.

53. Predrag Vranicki, "Moral i historija" ("Morals and History"), *Praxis* (Y), VIII, 6, 1971, p. 919.

54. Mihailo Marković, *The Contemporary Marx*, Nottingham: Spokesman Books, 1974, p. 124.

55. Jacob L. Talmon, *The Origins of Totalitarian Democracy*, New York: Praeger, 1960, p. 254.

56. David A. Crocker, "Marković's Concept of *Praxis* as Norm," *Inquiry*, 20, 1, Spring 1977, pp. 31-32.

57. Veljko Korać, "In Search of Human Society," in *Socialist Humanism, op. cit.*, p. 6.

58. Rudi Supek, *Sociologija i socijalizam (Sociology and Socialism)*, Zagreb: Znanje, 1966, pp. 63-88.

59. Mihailo Marković, "Economism or the Humanization of Economics," *Praxis* (I), V, 3-4, 1969, p. 473; Ivan Kuvačić, "Scientific and Technical Progress and Humanism," *Praxis* (I), V, 1-2, 1969, pp. 183-184; Svetozar Stojanović, "Marxism and Socialism Now," *NYRB*, XVI, 12, July 1, 1971, p. 20; Mihailo V. Popović, "Heterogenost društvenih sistema i sadašnja kriza jugoslavenskog društva" ("The Heterogeneity of Social Systems and the Contemporary Crisis of Yugoslav Society"), *Sociologija*, XIII, 3, 1971, p. 423; Rudi Supek, "Some Contradictions and Insufficiencies of Yugoslav Self-Managing Socialism," *Praxis* (I), VII, 3-4, 1971, pp. 386-388; Miroslav Radovanović, "Savremeno jugoslovensko društvo u sukobu sa samim sobom" ("Contemporary Yugoslav Society in Conflict with Itself"), *Sociologija*, XIII, 3, 1971, pp. 408-409; Mijo Biličić, "Srednja klasa u samoupravljanju" ("The Middle Class in Self-Management"), *NT*, No. 9, September 1975, p. 1335; Zoran Vidojević, "The Role of the League of Communists in the Process of Society's Material Life," *STP*, XVII, 1, January 1977, p. 63.

60. Mihailo Marković, *From Affluence to Praxis*, Ann Arbor: University of Michigan Press, 1974, p.132; Svetozar Stojanović, *Between Ideals and Reality*, New York: Oxford University Press, 1973, p.130.

61. Supek, "Some Contradictions and Insufficiencies of Yugoslav Self-Managing Socialism," *op. cit.*, pp. 386-387.

62. Ivan Kuvačić, *Sukobi (Conflicts)*, Zagreb: Razlog, 1972, p. 74.

63. Edvard Kardelj, "Protivrečnosti društvene svojine u savremenoj socijalis-tičkoj praksi" ("Contradictions of Social Ownership in Contemporary Socialist Practice"), in *Teorija i praksa samoupravljanja u Jugoslaviji (Theory and Practice of Self-Management in Yugoslavia)*, eds. Jovan Djordjević, *et al.*, Belgrade: Radnička štampa, 1972, p. 44.

64. Jovan Mirić, *Interesne grupe i politicka moć (Interest Groups and Political Power)*, Zagreb: Narodno sveučilište grada Zagreba, Centar za aktualni politički studij, 1973, p. 161.

65. Branko Horvat, "Fundamentals of a Theory of Distribution in Self-Governing Socialism," *EA*, X, 1-2, 1976, p. 40.

66. Mihailo V. Popović, "Heterogenost društvenih sistema i sadašnja kriza jugoslovenskog društva, "*op. cit.*, p. 422; Stojanović, *Between Ideals and Reality, op. cit.*, p. 124; "Zaostajanje prakse ili teorije" ("The Lag in Practice or Theory"), *EP*, XXVI, 1315, June 13, 1977, p. 22.

67. Radovanović, "Savremeno jugoslovensko društvo u sukobu sa samim so-bom," *op.cit.*, p. 413.

68. Oliver Wendell Holmes, Jr., quoted by Friedrich A. Hayek, *The Constitution of Liberty*, Chicago: University of Chicago Press, 1960, p. 85.

69. Marković, *From Affluence to Praxis, op. cit.*, p. 223; Stojanović, *Between Ideals and Reality, op. cit.*, p. 27.

70. Marković, *From Affluence to Praxis, op. cit.*, pp. 218-219; on the phenomenon of projection of evil onto other people, see Rade Bojanović, "Lucifer and the Lord," *Praxis* (I), VI, 3-4, 1970, pp. 369-380.

71. Mihailo Marković, *Preispitivanja (Reassessments)*, Belgrade: Srpska knji-ževna zadruga, 1972, pp. 152-154.

72. Svetozar Stojanović, "Contemporary Yugoslavian Philosophy," *Ethics*, - LXXVI, 4, July 1966, p. 298.

73. Biličić, "Srednja klasa u samoupravljanju," *op. cit.*, p. 1327.

74. Kardelj, "Protivrečnosti društvene svojine . . . ," *op. cit.*, p. 62.

75. Prvoslav Ralić, "Mogućnost i granice etike samoupravnosti" ("Possibilities and Limits of a Self-Management Ethics"), in *Teorija i praksa samoupravljanja u Jugoslaviji, op. cit.*, p. 1099.

76. Friedrich A. Hayek, *The Road to Serfdom*, Chicago: University of Chicago Press, 1962, p. 211.

77. Stipe Šuvar, "Osnovni oblici i alternative u razvoju socijalizma" ("Basic Forms and Alternatives in the Development of Socialism"), in *Marksizam i samoupravljanje (Marxism and Self-Management)*, 2 vols., ed. Predrag Radenović, Belgrade: Zavod za udžbenike i nastavna sredstva, 1977, I, p. 666.

78. Danko Grlić, "The Determinism of Economy and the Freedom of the Individual," *Praxis* (I), IX, 1, 1973, p. 33.

79. Kardelj, "Protivrečnosti društvene svojine . . . ," *op. cit.*, pp. 48-49; Ivan Maksimović, "Ekonomski problemi društvene svojine u socijalizmu" ("Economic Problems of Social Ownership in Socialism"), in *Marks i savremen-ost (Marx and the Contemporary Age)*, VII, eds. Dragutin Leković, *et al.*, Belgrade: Institut za medjunarodni radnički pokret, 1974, p. 388.

80. Blaug, *Economic Theory in Retrospect, op. cit.*, p. 292.

81. "Uzroci neefikasnosti" ("The Causes of Inefficiency"), *EP*, XXV, 1273, August 23, 1976, p. 19.

82. D. R. Denman, "Capitalism and Property," in *The Case for Capitalism*, eds. Michael Ivens & Reginald Dunstan, London: Michael Joseph, 1967, p. 17.

83. Warren G. Nutter, "Markets Without Property: A Grand Illusion," in *The Economics of Property Rights*, eds. Eirik G. Furubotn & Svetozar Pejo-vich, Cambridge, Mass.: Ballinger, 1974, p. 223.

84. Josip Županov, "Neke dileme u vezi s robno-novčanim odnosima" ("Some Dilemmas Concerning Commodity-Money Relations"), *Praxis* (Y), V, 1-2, April 1968, pp. 166-167; Deborah D. Milenkovitch, *Plan and Market in Yugoslav Economic Thought*, New Haven: Yale University Press, 1971, p.

252.

85.　Ibid., p. 266.

86.　Edvard Kardelj, "Democracy in Socialism and Not Against Socialism," *STP*, 14, 5, May 1974, p. 24.

87.　Mika Tripalo, former Executive Secretary of the LCC: " . . . we have to put an end to parasitism. Those who are able to earn cannot be punished all the time . . . ," quoted by Paul Lendvai, *Eagles in Cobwebs*, Garden City, N. Y.: Doubleday, 1969, p. 140; Stojanović, *Between Ideals and Reality, op. cit.*, p. 132.

88.　"Ekonomska sadržina društvene svojine" ("The Economic Content of Social Ownership"), *EP*, XXV, 1266, July 5, 1976, p. 21; see also "Ekonomisti o udruženom radu" ("Economists on Associated Labor"), *EP*, XXV, 1264, June 21, 1976, pp. 18-19. The two articles summarize the June 14-15, 1976, meeting of some 250 Yugoslav economists discussing the Draft Law on Associated Labor which came under heavy fire for lack of economic substance.

89.　Radovanović, "Savremeno jugoslovensko društvo . . . ," *op. cit.*, p. 410; Kuvačić, *Sukobi, op. cit.*, pp. 35-37.

90.　Vukašin Pavlović, "Socijalne nejednakosti u samoupravnom društvu i sindikalna akcija" ("Social Inequalities in Self-Managing Society and Trade Union Action"), *NT*, XXI, 1, January 1977, p. 78.

91.　Aleksander Bajt, "Social Ownership—Collective and Individual," in *Self-Governing Socialism*, 2 vols., eds. Branko Horvat, Mihailo Marković & Rudi Supek, White Plains, N. Y.: International Arts & Sciences Press, 1975, II, p. 159.

92.　Veljko Rus, "Self-Management Egalitarianism and Social Differentiation," *Praxis* (I), VI, 1-2, 1970, p. 254.

93.　Marković, "Economism or the Humanization of Economics," *op. cit.*, p. 475.

94.　Robert C. Tucker's incisive socio-psychological analysis of capital as the personification of the alienated part of the human being in his *Philosophy and Myth in Karl Marx*, London: Cambridge University Press, 1969, pp. 203-217, points out the mythical-religious qualities in Marx's concepts of labor and capital. Among avant-garde theorists, Supek holds the unconventional view that capital accumulation is due today more to the increasing rationalization of production than to the exploitation of labor, and argues that students of 20th century capitalism should overcome the sloganeering and vulgar political conceptions which are the residues of an earlier era, in his "Karl Marx i neki problemi kapitalizma XX vijeka" ("Karl Marx and Some Problems of 20th Century Capitalism"), in *Marks i savremenost (Marx and the Contemporary Age)*, I-II, eds. Mihailo Marković, *et al.*, Belgrade: Institut društvenih nauka, 1964, I, pp. 258-264, and discussion with reply, pp. 264-278.

95.　Marx, "Contribution to the Critique of Hegel's Philosophy of Right," in *Karl Marx*, ed. T. B. Bottomore, New York: McGraw-Hill, 1964, p. 56.

96.　Gustav Wetter, "Überwindung der Klassenspaltung durch Beseitigung des Privateigentums?," *Praxis* (I), II, 1-2, 1966, p. 170.

97.　Stojanović, *Between Ideals and Reality, op. cit.*, p. 208.

98.　Karl Marx & Friedrich Engels, "The Communist Manifesto," & Engels, "On Morality (From *Anti-Dühring)"*, in *The Marx-Engels Reader*, ed. Robert C. Tucker, New York: Norton, 1972, pp. 351 & 667, respectively; V. I. Lenin, "The Tasks of the Youth Leagues" (Address to the Third All-Russian Congress of the Young Communist League of the Soviet Union, October 2, 1920), in *The Lenin Anthology*, ed. Robert C. Tucker, New York: Norton, 1975, p. 668.

99.　Herbert Marcuse, "Repressive Tolerance," in Robert P. Wolff, *et al.*, *A Critique of Pure Tolerance*, Boston: Beacon, 1969, pp. 81-123.

100.　Maurice Merleau-Ponty, *Humanism and Terror*, Boston: Beacon, 1969, p. 107.

101. Gajo Petrović, *Mišljenje revolucije (Thought of the Revolution)*, Zagreb: Naprijed, 1978, pp. 138, 216.
102. Svetozar Stojanović, *Geschichte und Parteibewusstsein*, Munich: Carl Hanser, 1978, pp. 118, 124.
103. Ljubomir Tadić, "The Marxist and Stalinist Critiques of Right," in *Marxist Humanism and Praxis*, ed. Gerson S. Sher, Buffalo, N. Y.: Prometheus, 1978, p. 170.
104. Leo Tolstoy, quoted by Guinness, *The Dust of Death, op. cit.*, p. 174.
105. Arif Tanović, discussing Miladin Životić's "Humanistička problematika u marksizmu i savremenoj zapadnoevropskoj filozofiji" ("The Humanist Dilemma in Marxism and Contemporary West European Philosophy"), in *Marks i savremenost, op. cit.*, I, pp. 163-64; Danko Grlić, "O apstraktnom i realnom humanizmu" ("On Abstract and Real Humanism"), in *Humanizam i socijalizam (Humanism and Socialism)*, 2 vols., eds. Branko Bošnjak & Rudi Supek, Zagreb: Naprijed, 1963, I, p. 138; Veljko Vlahović, "Idejna kretanja na sadašnjem stepenu našeg razvoja i dalji zadaci Saveza Komunista Jugoslavije" ("Theoretical Movements in the Contemporary Phase of Our Development and Further Tasks for the League of Communists of Yugoslavia"), in *Osmi kongress SKJ (Eighth Congress of the LCY)*, Belgrade: Kultura, 1964, p. 178; Mihailo Marković, "Marxist Humanism and Ethics," *Inquiry*, 6, 1963, p. 23; Petrović, *Marx in the Mid-Twentieth Century, op. cit.*, p. 156; Djordjević, *Socijalizam i demokratija, op. cit.*, p. 67.
106. Stojanović, *Between Ideals and Reality, op. cit.*, p. 180.
107. Vlahović, "Idejna kretanja na sadašnjem stepenu našeg razvoja . . . ," *op. cit.*, p. 178.
108. Miladin Životić, "The End of the Ideals or of Ideology?," *Praxis* (I), V, 3-4, 1969, p. 423.
109. Sharon Zukin, Review of Marković, *From Affluence to Praxis* and Stojanović, *Between Ideals and Reality*, in *Telos*, No. 21, Fall 1974, pp. 209, 212-213.
110. Hoffman, *Marxism and the Theory of Praxis, op. cit.*, p. 211.
111. Marković, *The Contemporary Marx, op. cit.*, pp. 154-155.
112. Mihailo Marković, "Is It Possible to Abolish Political Mediation?," *Praxis* (I), IX, 3-4, 1973, p. 53.
113. Stojanović, *Between Ideals and Reality, op. cit.*, p. 184.
114. Rudi Supek, *Humanistička inteligencija i politika*, Zagreb: Studentski centar sveučilišta, 1971, p. 119.
115. Svetozar Stojanović, "Stalinist 'Partiinost' and Communist Dignity," *Praxis* (I), X, 1-2, 1974, p. 138.
116. Albert Camus, *The Rebel*, New York: Vintage, 1956, p. 292.
117. Marković, *The Contemporary Marx, op. cit.*, p. 216.
118. Jack Gray, "Conclusions," in *Political Culture and Political Change in Communist States*, eds. Archie Brown & J. Gray, New York: Holmes & Meier, 1977, p. 272.
119. Kardelj, "Protivrečnosti društvene svojine . . . ," *op. cit.*, pp. 35, 67.
120. Mirić, *Interesne grupe i politička moć, op. cit.*, p. 111.
121. Damir Grubiša, "O nekim proturječnostima u konstituiranju udruženog rada" ("On Some Contradictions in the Establishment of Associated Labor"), *NT*, XXI, 1, January 1977, p. 71.
122. Edvard Kardelj, *Pravci razvoja političkog sistema socijalističkog samoupravljanja (Directions of Development of the Political System of Socialist Self-Management)*, 2nd enl. ed., Belgrade: Komunist, 1978, p. 66.
123. Veljko Rus, "Influence Structure in Yugoslav Enterprise," *IR*, 9, 2, February 1970, p. 160; Vladimir Arzenšek, "Socijalna struktura i karakter konflikata" ("The Social Structure and the Nature of Conflicts"), *Sociologija*, XVII, 2, 1975, p. 257; Mirić, *Interesne grupe i politička moć, op. cit.*, pp. 111-112, 128-139, 138-139, 166, 169-170.
124. Popović, "Heterogenost društvenih sistema . . . ," *op. cit.*, p. 424.

125. Rudi Supek, "The Statist and Self-Managing Models of Socialism," in *Opinion-Making Elites in Yugoslavia,* eds. Allen H. Barton, Bogdan D. Denitch & Charles Kadushin, New York: Praeger, 1973, p. 314.

126. Svetozar Stojanović, "From Post-Revolutionary Dictatorship to Socialist Democracy: Yugoslav Socialism at the Crossroads," *Praxis* (I), IX, 4, 1973, p. 329.

127. Marković, "Basic Characteristics of Marxist Humanism," *op. cit.,* p. 608.

128. Životić, "The End of the Ideals or of Ideology?," *op. cit.,* p. 417.

129. Rus, "Self-Management Egalitarianism . . . ," *op. cit.,* p. 264.

130. Marković, *From Affluence to Praxis, op. cit.,* p. 79.

131. Milton & Rose Friedman, *Free to Choose,* New York: Harcourt Brace Jovanovich, 1980, p. 309.

132. Marković, "Is It Possible to Abolish Political Mediation?," *op. cit.,* p. 53.

133. Stojanović, "From Post-Revolutionary Dictatorship to Socialist Democracy," *op. cit.,* p. 320.

134. Kostas Axelos, *Alienation, Praxis and Techné in the Thought of Karl Marx,* Austin: University of Texas Press, 1976, p. 305.

135. Max Weber, *The Theory of Social and Economic Organization,* New York: Free Press, 1966, p. 248.

136. Friedman, *Free to Choose, op. cit.,* p. 3.

137. Marković, "Basic Characteristics of Marxist Humanism," *op. cit.,* p. 609.

138. Petrović, *Marx in the Mid-Twentieth Century, op. cit.,* p. 65; and "Marx kao filozof" ("Marx as a Philosopher"), in *Marks i savremenost, op. cit.,* I, pp. 78-79.

139. Staniša Novaković, "Metaphysics and Marxist Philosophy," in *Dialogues on the Philosophy of Marxism,* eds. John Somerville & Howard L. Parsons, Westport, Conn.: Greenwood Press, 1974, pp. 154-177.

140. Mihailo Marković, "Critical Social Theory in Marx," *Praxis* (I), VI, 3-4, 1970, pp. 288-296.

141. For a concise analysis of the dialectic, see Carew-Hunt, *The Theory and Practice of Communism, op. cit.,* pp. 42-54.

142. Stojanović, "Stalinist 'Partiinost' and Communist Dignity," *op. cit.,* p. 135.

143. Stojanović, *Geschichte und Parteibewusstsein, op. cit.,* p. 110.

144. Nicholas Lobkowicz, "Theorie und Praxis," in *Ideologie und Philosophie, op. cit.,* III, p. 204.

145. Guinness, *The Dust of Death, op. cit.,* p. 101.

146. Aleksandr I. Solzhenitsyn, *The First Circle,* New York: Bantam, 1969, pp. 126-127.

147. Stojanović, *Geschichte und Parteibewusstsein, op. cit.,* pp. 107-108.

148. Marković, "Marxist Humanism and Ethics," *op. cit.,* p. 20.

149. Engels, quoted by Nike Martinović, in Jure Juras, "Simpozij 'O socijalističkom humanizmu' u Srpskoj akademiji" ("Symposium 'On Socialist Humanism' in the Serbian Academy"), *EM,* 3-4, March-June, 1967, p. 169.

150. Friedrich Engels, Letter to Joseph Bloch, September 21-22, 1890, in *The Marx-Engels Reader, op. cit.,* p. 640.

151. Živko Surčulija, "Uslovljenost podela i kontroverzi u marksizmu i oko njega" ("The Rationale for Divisions and Controversies in Marxism"), in *Marksizam i samoupravljanje, op. cit.,* I, p. 133.

152. James J. O'Rourke, *The Problem of Freedom in Marxist Thought,* Dordrecht: Reidel, 1974, p. 35.

153. Max Weber, "'Objectivity' in Social Science and Social Policy," in his *On the Methodology of the Social Sciences, op. cit.,* p. 71.

154. Stojanović, *Geschichte und Parteibewusstsein, op. cit.,* p. 27.

155. Grlić, "The Determinism of Economy . . . ," *op. cit.,* p. 33.

156. Petrović, *Marx in the Mid-Twentieth Century, op. cit.,* p. 105.

157. Miladin Životić, "Socijalistički humanizam i jugoslovenska filosofija" ("Socialist Humanism and Yugoslav Philosophy"), *Filosofija,* No. 1-2, 1968, pp. 112, 116.

158. Axelos, *Alienation, Praxis and Techné . . . , op. cit.,* p. 325.

159. Hannah Arendt, *The Human Condition*, Garden City, N. Y.: Doubleday, 1959, pp. 62-63.
160. Merleau-Ponty, *Humanism and Terror, op. cit.*, p. 103.
161. Marx, "First and Second Manuscripts," in *Karl Marx, op. cit.*, pp. 90, 108, & 144, respectively.
162. De George, *Patterns of Soviet Thought, op. cit.*, p. 75.
163. Roberts & Stephenson, *Marx's Theory of Exchange. . . , op. cit.*, p. 93.
164. Tito, quoted by Staubringer, "Humanistic Vision . . . ," *op. cit.*, p. 104.
165. Kardelj, "Democracy in Socialism . . . ," *op. cit.*, p. 16; Josip-Broz Tito, "The Struggle for the Further Development of Socialist Self-Management in Our Country and the Role of the League of Communists of Yugoslavia," Address to the Tenth Party Congress, May 27, 1974, *STP*, 14, 6-7, June-July, 1974, pp. 45, 48-49.
166. Andrija Krešić, *Političko društvo i politička mitologija (Political Society and Political Mythology)*, Belgrade: Vuk Karadžić, 1968, pp. 160-168.
167. Ljubomir Tadić, *Poredak i sloboda (Order and Freedom)*, Belgrade: Kultura, 1967, p. 226.
168. Danilo Pejović, *Sistem i egzistencija (System and Existence)*, Zagreb: Zora, 1970, p. 210.
169. Milan Mirić, *Rezervati (Reservations)*, Zagreb: Studentski centar sveučilišta, 1970, p. 68.
170. Kuvačić, "Scientific and Technical Progress and Humanism," *op. cit.*, p. 182; Supek, "Karl Marx i neki problemi kapitalizma XX vijeka," *op. cit.*, pp. 261-262.
171. Marković, *The Contemporary Marx, op. cit.*, pp. 201-202.
172. Zagorka Pešić-Golubović, "Self-Fulfilment, Equality and Freedom," *Praxis* (I), IX, 2-3, 1973, p. 160.
173. Stojanović, "From Post-Revolutionary Dictatorship to Socialist Democracy," *op. cit.*, p. 324.
174. Tadić, *Poredak i sloboda, op. cit.*, p. 153.
175. Marković, *From Affluence to Praxis, op. cit.*, p. 241.
176. Karl Marx & Friedrich Engels, "Manifesto of the Communist Party," in *Marx & Engels*, ed. Lewis S. Feuer, Garden City, N. Y.: Doubleday, 1959, p. 20.
177. Danko Grlić, *Contra dogmaticos*, Zagreb: *Praxis* Pocketbook Edition No. 9, 1971, p. 124.
178. Stojanović, *Geschichte und Parteibewusstsein, op. cit.*, pp. 55-56.
179. Stojanović, "Stalinist 'Partiinost' and Communist Dignity," *op. cit.*, p. 132.
180. Svetozar Stojanović, "Društvena kritika u socijalizmu" ("Social Criticism in Socialism"), in *Etičko-humanistički problemi socijalizma (Ethical-Humanistic Problems of Socialism)*, eds. Ljubinka Krešić & S. Stojanović, Belgrade: Rad, 1964, p. 276; Radovanović, "Savremeno jugoslovensko društvo . . . ," *op. cit.*, p. 401.
181. Hoffman, *Marxism and the Theory of Praxis, op. cit.*, p. 215.
182. Budislav Soškić, "Položaj i uloga Saveza komunista u sistemu socijalističkog samoupravljanja" ("The Position and Role of the League of Communists in the System of Socialist Self-Management"), in *Teorija i praksa samoupravljanja u Jugoslaviji, op. cit.*, p. 446.
183. Roger Garaudy, *The Alternative Future*, New York: Simon & Schuster, 1974, p. 78.
184. Predrag Vranicki, "Marginalije uz problem humanizma" ("Observations on the Problem of Humanism"), in *Humanizam i socijalizam, op. cit.*, I, p. 295; Jovan Djordjević, *Novi Ustavni sistem (The New Constitutional System)*, Belgrade: Savremena Administracija, 1964, p. 110; Marković, "Critical Social Theory in Marx," *op. cit.*, p. 295.
185. Marković, "Critical Social Theory in Marx," *op. cit.*, p. 296.
186. Danko Grlić, *Zašto? (Why?)*, Zagreb: Studentski centar sveučilišta, 1968, p. 8.
187. Danilo Pejović, "On the Power and Impotence of Philosophy," in *Socialist*

Humanism, op. cit., p. 202.

188. Životić, "Humanistička problematika u marksizmu . . . ," *op. cit.,* p. 158.
189. Petrović, "Marx kao filozof," *op. cit.,* p. 77; Zdravko Kučinar, "Nécéssité et possibilité du dialogue," *Praxis* (I), III, 4, 1967, pp. 466-467.
190. Marx, "Third Manuscript," in *Karl Marx, op. cit.,* p. 167.
191. Tito, Address to the Tenth Party Congress, *op. cit.,* p. 39.
192. Marković, *From Affluence to Praxis, op. cit.,* p. 199.
193. Jovan Djordjević, "Rad, (dez)alijenacija i država, država i (dez)alijenacija političke moći" ("Labor, (De-)Alienation and the State, State and the (De-)Alienation of Political Power"), in *Marksizam i samoupravljanje, op. cit.,* I, p. 518.
194. Vojan Rus, *Dijalektika čoveka i sveta (The Dialectics of Man and World),* Belgrade: Institut za medjunarodni radnički pokret, 1969, p. 569.
195. Gajo Petrović, *Mogućnost čovjeka (The Possibility of Man),* Zagreb: Studentski centar sveučilišta, 1969, p. 60.
196. Grlić, *Zašto?, op. cit.,* p. 8.
197. Stephen Miller, "The Poverty of Socialist Thought," *Commentary,* 62, 2, August 1976, p. 36.
198. Mihailo Djurić, "Homo Politicus," in *Praxis,* eds. Mihailo Marković & Gajo Petrović, Dordrecht: Reidel, 1979, p. 112.
199. Staniša Novaković, "Two Concepts of Science and Humanism," *Praxis* (I), V, 1-2, 1969, p. 195.
200. Dobrica Cosić, "A Critique of Ideological A Priori and Doctrinaire Attitudes," *Praxis* (I), IX, 1, 1973, p. 71.
201. Gajo Petrović, *Čemu Praxis? (Why Praxis?),* Zagreb: *Praxis* Pocketbook Edition No. 10-11, 1972, p. 14.
202. Surčulija, "Uslovljenost podela i kontroverzi . . . ," *op. cit.,* p. 148.
203. Stojanović, *Between Ideals and Reality, op. cit.,* p. 15.
204. Guinness, *The Dust of Death, op. cit.,* pp. 13-14.
205. *Ibid.,* p. 273.
206. A. Robert Caponigri & Richard T. De George, "Humanismus," in *Ideologie und Philosophie, op. cit.,* II, pp. 42-43.
207. Thomas J. Blakeley, "Marxist-Leninist Scientific Atheism," in *Philosophy in the Soviet Union,* ed. Ervin Laszlo, Dordrecht: Reidel, 1967, pp. 77-78.
208. Bertram D. Wolfe, *Marxism,* New York: Dial, 1965, pp. 378-379; Karl R. Popper, *The Open Society and Its Enemies,* 2 vols., Princeton: Princeton University Press, 1966, II, p. 280.
209. Bernard-Henri Lévy, *Barbarism With a Human Face,* New York: Harper & Row, 1979, pp. 19-25.
210. Friedrich A. Hayek, *Law, Legislation and Liberty,* 3 vols., Chicago: University of Chicago Press, 1973-79, III, p. 80.
211. Lewis S. Feuer, *Ideology and the Ideologists,* New York: Harper & Row, 1975, pp. 192-193.
212. Tucker, *Philosophy and Myth in Karl Marx, op. cit.,* pp. 233-235; Leff, *The Tyranny of Concepts, op. cit.,* pp. 1-16; John A. Hutchison, *Living Options in World Philosophy,* Honolulu: University Press of Hawaii, 1977, pp. 131-133; Wolfe, *Marxism, op. cit.,* pp. 356-381; Popper, *The Open Society and Its Enemies, op. cit.,* I., pp. 169-201 & II, pp. 259-280.
213. David Levy, "Not For Marx," *MA,* 21, 1, Winter 1977, p. 28.
214. Hutchison, *Living Options in World Philosophy, op. cit.,* p. 133.
215. Ludwig von Mises, *Human Action,* Rev. ed., New Haven: Yale University Press, 1963, p. 693.
216. Mirić, *Rezervati, op. cit.,* p. 109; capitalization of God and Nothingness added.
217. Axelos, *Alienation, Praxis and Techné . . . , op. cit.,* p. 292.
218. Leff, *The Tyranny of Concepts, op. cit.,* p. 16.
219. Levi, *Humanism and Politics, op. cit.,* p. 445.
220. Pavel Kovaly, "Is It Possible to Humanize Marxism?," *SST,* 11, 4, December 1971, p. 292.

221. Richard T. De George, "Communism and the New Marxists," in *Marxism and Religion in Eastern Europe*, eds. R. T. De George & James P. Scanlan, Dordrecht: Reidel, 1976, p. 8.

222. Hoffman, *Marxism and the Theory of Praxis, op. cit.*, p. 225.

223. Wolfgang Leonhard, *Three Faces of Marxism*, New York: Holt, 1974, p. 370.

224. *Ibid.*, p. 365.

225. Antón Donoso, "The Notion of Man in Kolakowski, Kosik and Marković," paper presented at the *AAASS Annual Meeting*, St. Louis, Missouri, October 6-9, 1976, p. 11.

226. Kovaly, "Is It Possible to Humanize Marxism?," *op. cit.*, p. 289.

227. Kline, "Was Marx an Ethical Humanist?," *op. cit.*, p. 96.

CHAPTER IX: TOWARD A NEW HUMANISM

1. Robert C. Tucker, "The Deradicalization of Marxist Movements," *APSR*, LXI, 2, June 1967, pp. 343-358.

2. Lewis S. Feuer, "Alienation: The Marxism of Contemporary Student Movements," in *Marxist Ideology in the Contemporary World*, ed. Milorad M. Drachkovitch, New York: Praeger, 1966, p. 58.

3. Quoted by Daniel & Gabriel Cohn-Bendit, *Obsolete Communism*, New York: McGraw-Hill, 1968, pp. 253-254; note the original German title: *Linksradikalismus—Gewaltkur gegen die Alterskrankheit des Kommunismus*, Hamburg: Rowohlt, 1968.

4. Karl Reyman & Herman Singer, "The Origins and Significance of Eastern European Revisionism," and William E. Griffith, "The Decline and Fall of Revisionism in Eastern Europe," in *Revisionism*, ed. Leopold Labedz, New York: Praeger, 1962, pp. 215-222 and 223-238, respectively; quotation from Reyman & Singer, p. 222.

5. Charles Gati, "From Cold War Origins to Détente: Introduction to the International Politics of Eastern Europe," in *The International Politics of Eastern Europe*, ed. C. Gati, New York: Praeger, 1976, pp. 10-11.

6. Mihajlo Mihajlov, "Yugoslavia—The Approaching Storm," *Dissent*, Summer 1974, p. 372.

7. Marius J. Broekmeyer, "Self-Management in Yugoslavia," *AAAPSS*, 431, May 1977, p. 139.

8. Svetozar Stojanović, "From Post-Revolutionary Dictatorship to Socialist Democracy: Yugoslav Socialism at the Crossroads," *Praxis* (I), IX, 4, 1973, p. 321.

9. Bogdan D. Denitch, *The Legitimation of a Revolution*, New Haven: Yale University Press, 1976, p. 186; M. George Zaninovich, *The Development of Socialist Yugoslavia*, Baltimore: Johns Hopkins University Press, 1968, p. 38; Dennison I. Rusinow, *The Yugoslav Experiment, 1948-1974*, Berkeley: University of California Press, 1977, p. 346; Jacob Walkin, "Yugoslavia After the 10th Party Congress," *Survey*, 98, 1, Winter 1976, pp. 55-56.

10. Duncan Wilson, *Tito's Yugoslavia*, New York: Cambridge University Press, 1979, pp. 243, 249.

11. Fred B. Singleton, *Twentieth-Century Yugoslavia*, New York: Columbia University Press, 1976, p. 312; Paul Lendvai, *Eagles in Cobwebs*, Garden City, N.Y.: Doubleday, 1969, p. 120; Lenard J. Cohen, "Political Participation, Competition, and Dissent in Yugoslavia: A Report of Research on Electoral Behavior," in *Political Development in Eastern Europe*, eds. Jan F. Triska & Paul M. Cocks, New York: Praeger, 1977, pp. 207-208.

12. Edvard Kardelj, "The Political System of Socialist Self-Management," *STP*, XVII, 7-8, July-August, 1977, p. 14.

13. Veljko Rus, "Self-Management Egalitarianism and Social Differentiation," *Praxis* (I), VI, 1-2, 1970, pp. 264-265.

14. See Tucker, "The Deradicalization . . . ," *op. cit.*, pp. 349-352.
15. Eduard Bernstein, *Evolutionary Socialism*, New York: Schocken, 1965, p. 197.
16. Josip-Broz Tito, "The Struggle for the Further Development of Socialist Self-Management in Our Country and the Role of the League of Communists of Yugoslavia," Address to the Tenth Party Congress, May 27, 1974, *STP*, 14, 6-7, June-July, 1974, pp. 34, 36-37, 45; Edvard Kardelj, "Democracy in Socialism and Not Against Socialism," *STP*, 14, 5, May 1974, p. 16.
17. Vladimir V. Kusin, "An Overview of East European Reformism," *SOS*, XXVIII, 3, July 1976, p. 361.
18. Jean-François Revel, *The Totalitarian Temptation*, Garden City, N.Y.: Doubleday, 1977, pp. 299-300, 28, 128.
19. *Ibid.*, p. 311.
20. Peter C. Ludz, "Eastern Europe and Eurocommunism as Indicators of Soviet Change," in *Innovation in Communist Systems*, eds. Andrew György & James A. Kuhlman, Boulder, Colo.: Westview, 1978, pp. 185-193.
21. Svetozar Stojanović, *Geschichte und Parteibewusstsein*, Munich: Carl Hanser, 1978, pp. 92-93.
22. Edvard Kardelj, *Pravci razvoja političkog sistema socijalističkog samoupravljanja (Directions of Development of the Political System of Socialist Self-Management)*, 2nd enl. ed., Belgrade: Komunist, 1978, pp. 47-53.
23. Leszek Kolakowski, *Main Currents of Marxism*, 3 vols., Oxford: Oxford University Press, 1978, III, p. 474.
24. H. Malcolm Macdonald, "Marxism and Revisionism: The Case of Yugoslavia," *Il Politico* (Pavia), XXIX, 1, 1964, p. 90.
25. Mihailo Marković, "Critical Social Theory in Marx," *Praxis* (I), VI, 3-4, 1970, p. 286.
26. Arnold Künzli, "Marxists on the Beach," *Dialogue*, I, 1, Spring 1968, p. 79.
27. Bernstein, *Evolutionary Socialism, op. cit.*, p. 202.
28. Rudi Supek, *Participacija, radnička kontrola i samoupravljanje (Participation, Workers' Control, and Self-Management)*, Zagreb: Naprijed, 1974, p. 115.
29. Svetozar Stojanović, *Between Ideals and Reality*, New York: Oxford University Press, 1973, p. 105.
30. Mihailo Marković, *From Affluence to Praxis*, Ann Arbor: University of Michigan Press, 1974, p. 184.
31. Marx, Letter to W. Bracke, May 5, 1875, in Karl Marx & Friedrich Engels, *Selected Correspondence*, Moscow: Foreign Languages Publishing House, 1953, p. 360.
32. Kardelj, "The Political System . . . ," *op. cit.*, p. 13.
33. Marx, "Circular Letter to Bebel, Liebknecht, Bracke, and Others," in *The Marx-Engels Reader*, ed. Robert C. Tucker, New York: Norton, 1972, p. 405.
34. B. Vojvodić & J. Djurčić, "Jednoglasnost ne mora uvek da znači i ravnopravnost," *Borba*, XLIX, 85, March 29, 1971 (review of the inconclusive findings of the Symposium on the National Question and Federalism, Novi Sad, March 1971), p. 6; "Postojeći pravni i politički sistem sputava razvoj društva," *Politika*, LXVIII, 20648, March 30, 1971 (editorial on the speech of the President of the Constitutional Commission for Drafting the Amendments, Milentije Popović, to the Council of Nationalities of the Federal Assembly, March 1971), pp. 5-6.
35. Radoslav Ratković, "Opasnosti tehnokratizma" ("Dangers of Technocracy"), *NIN*, No. 1370, April 10, 1977, pp. 12-13; "Zaostajanje prakse ili teorije" ("The Lag in Practice or Theory"), *EP*, XXVI, 1315, June 13, 1977, pp. 22-23; "Ekonomska sadržina društvene svojine" ("The Economic Content of Social Ownership"), *EP*, XXV, 1266, July 5, 1976, pp. 20-21.
36. Ralph K. White, "'Socialism' and 'Capitalism': An International Misunderstanding," *FA*, 44, 2, January 1966, p. 218.
37. Milton & Rose Friedman, *Free to Choose*, New York: Harcourt Brace

Jovanovich, 1980, p. 97; Friedrich A. Hayek, *Law, Legislation and Liberty*, 3 vols., Chicago: University of Chicago Press, 1973-79, II, p. 87.

38. See Matthew Mestrovic, "The Paunchy Revolution: Tito's Twilight," *Commonweal*, 83, 11, December 17, 1965, pp. 336-339; Ernest Dumbar, "Karl Marx in a Mercedes," *Look*, XXXIII, 4, February 18, 1969, pp. 23-29.

39. Daniel Bell, *The Coming of Post-Industrial Society*, New York: Basic Books, 1973, p. 467.

40. John Kenneth Galbraith, *The New Industrial State*, 2nd ed., Boston: Mifflin, 1972, pp. 59-71.

41. *Ibid.*, p. 393; John K. Galbraith, *Economics & the Public Purpose*, New York: New American Library, 1975, p. 307.

42. Milton Friedman, *An Economist's Protest*, 2nd ed., Glen Ridge, N.J.: Hornton, 1975, p. 293.

43. Bell, *The Coming of Post-Industrial Society, op. cit.*, pp. 433, 481-482, 453.

44. Alexis de Tocqueville, *Democracy in America*, New York: New American Library, 1956, pp. 298-317.

45. Josip Županov, "Egalitarizam i industrijalizam" ("Egalitarianism and Industrialism"), *Sociologija*, XII, 1, 1970, pp. 42-43.

46. Miroslav Pečujlić, *Budućnost koja je počela (The Future Which Has Begun)*, Belgrade: Institut za političke studije Fakulteta političkih nauka, 1969, p. 26.

47. Karl Marx, *Grundrisse*, New York: Random House, 1973, pp. 704-705.

48. Rudi Supek, "Robno-novčani odnosi i socijalistička ideologija" ("Commodity-Money Relations and Socialist Ideology"), *Praxis* (Y), V, 1-2, April 1968, p. 176.

49. Mihailo Marković, *The Contemporary Marx*, Nottingham: Spokesman - Books, 1974, p. 213.

50. *Ibid.*, p. 149.

51. Danilo Pejović, *Sistem i egzistencija (System and Existence)*, Zagreb: Zora, 1970, p. 207.

52. Rudi Supek, *Humanistička inteligencija i politika (The Humanist Intelligentsia and Politics)*, Zagreb: Studentski centar sveučilišta, 1971, pp. 60-61.

53. Rudi Supek, *Ova jedina zemlja (Only One Earth)*, 2nd enl. ed., Zagreb: Liber, 1978, pp. 234-249.

54. Rudolf Bahro, *The Alternative in Eastern Europe*, London: NLB, 1978, p. 262.

55. Ivan Kuvačić, "Die Analyse der bürgerlichen Gesellschaft von Marx und die Konvergenz-Theorie," *Praxis* (I), X, 1-2, 1974, p. 92.

56. Nenad Kecmanović, "Marksistička kritika i valorizacija teorije konvergencije" ("Marxist Critique and Assessment of the Theory of Convergence"), in *Marksizam i samoupravljanje (Marxism and Self-Management)*, 2 vols., ed. Predrag Radenović, Belgrade: Zavod za udžbenike i nastavna sredstva, 1977, I, pp. 497-499.

57. Editorial Board of *Praxis*, "Uvod" ("Introduction" to the 1971 Korčula Summer School on "Marxism and Social Consciousness"), *Praxis* (Y), IX, 3-4, May-August, 1972, p. 311.

58. Djuro Šušnjić, "The Idea of Manipulation and Manipulation of Ideas," *Praxis* (I), VI, 1-2, 1970, p. 155.

59. Popović, quoted in "Postojeći pravni i politički sistem . . . ," *op. cit*, pp. 5-6; see also Milentije Popović, "Jačanje samoupravljanja" ("Strengthening Self-Management"), *Komunist*, XXIX, 732, April 1, 1971, p. 3; and in "Ustavne promene—otklanjanje sukoba izmedju etatizma i samoupravljanja" ("Constitutional Changes—Eliminating the Conflict Between Etatism and Self-Management"), *Borba*, XLIX, 86, March 30, 1971, pp. 5-7.

60. David A. Andelman, "Yugoslavia: The Delicate Balance," *FA*, 58, 4, Spring 1980, p. 843.

61. Roger E. Kanet, "Political Groupings and Their Role in the Process of

Change in Eastern Europe," in *Innovation in Communist Systems, op. cit.,* p. 52.

62. Dan N. Jacobs, "Overview and Projection," in *The New Communisms,* ed. D. N. Jacobs, New York: Harper & Row, 1969, p. 300.

63. Alvin Z. Rubinstein, *Yugoslavia and the Nonaligned World,* Princeton: Princeton University Press, 1970, p. 196.

64. Andrzej Korbonski, "External Influences on Eastern Europe," in *The International Politics of Eastern Europe, op. cit.,* p. 259; Christopher Cviić, "Jugoslavia, Russia and the West: Possible Political Developments After Tito Leaves the Scene," *RT,* No. 265, January 1977, p. 28.

65. Kevin Devlin, "The Challenge of Eurocommunism," *PC,* XXVI, 1, January-February, 1977, p. 15.

66. William Zimmerman, "The Tito Legacy and Yugoslavia's Future," *PC,* XXVI, 3, May-June, 1977, p. 47.

67. Laurence Silberman, "Yugoslavia's 'Old' Communism: Europe's Fiddler on the Roof," *FP,* No. 26, Spring 1977, p. 3.

68. Fred Warner Neal, "Yugoslav Foreign Policy: International Balancing on a High Wire," *AUFSR,* Europe, No. 24, 1978, p. 11.

69 Andrew György, "Communism in Eastern Europe," in *The New Communisms, op. cit.,* p. 161.

70. Milosav Janićijević, "Jugoslovenski studenti o marksizmu" ("Yugoslav Students on Marxism"), in *Marks i savremenost (Marx and the Contemporary Age),* eds. Mihailo Marković, *et al.,* Belgrade: Institut društvenih nauka, 1964, I, p. 201.

71. See Gajo Petrović, "Praxis: Deux ans de plus," *Praxis* (I), V, 1-2, 1969, pp. 335-344.

72. "A l'occasion des critiques les plus récentes adréssées à 'Praxis'," *Praxis* (I), IV, 3-4, 1968, pp. 509-515.

73. *Ibid.,* p. 516.

74. Zdravko Kučinar, "Nécéssité et possibilité du dialogue," *Praxis* (I), III, 4, 1967, pp. 463-464.

75. Bell, *The Coming of Post-Industrial Society, op. cit.,* p. 386.

76. Richard Kostelanetz, "Introduction," to *Beyond Left & Right,* ed. R. Kostelanetz, New York: Morrow, 1968, p. xix.

77. Herman Kahn, William Brown & Leon Martel, *The Next 200 Years,* New York: Morrow, 1976, p. 164.

78. B. F. Skinner, *Beyond Freedom and Dignity,* New York: Bantam, 1972; for a critique, see Francis A. Schaeffer, *Back to Freedom and Dignity,* Downers Grove, Ill.: Inter-Varsity Press, 1972.

79. June Goodfield, *Playing God,* New York: Random House, 1977, p. 152.

80. Kahn, *et al., The Next 200 Years, op. cit.,* p. 225.

81. Erich Fromm, *The Revolution of Hope,* New York: Harper & Row, 1968; Herbert J. Muller, *The Children of Frankenstein,* Bloomington: Indiana University Press, 1970; Herbert Marcuse, *One-Dimensional Man,* Boston: Beacon, 1968, and *An Essay on Liberation,* Boston: Beacon, 1969.

82. Norbert Wiener, *The Human Use of Human Beings,* Garden City, N.Y.: Doubleday, 1956; Ernest Becker, *Beyond Alienation,* New York: Braziller, 1967; Andrei D. Sakharov, *Progress, Coexistence, and Intellectual Freedom,* New York: Norton, 1968; Nikolai M. Amosoff, *Notes From the Future,* New York: Schuster, 1970.

83. Ivan Kuvačić, "Scientific and Technical Progress and Humanism," *Praxis* (I), V, 1-2, 1969, pp. 181-184.

84. Mihailo Marković, "Marx and Critical Scientific Thought," *Praxis* (I), IV, 3-4, 1968, p. 392.

85. Danilo Pejović, "On the Power and Impotence of Philosophy," in *Socialist Humanism,* ed. Erich Fromm, Garden City, N.Y.: Doubleday, 1966, p. 208.

86. Živojin D. Denić, "Sociologija nastanka, egzistencije i funkcija robnog privredjivanja" ("Sociology of the Creation, Existence and Functioning of Commodity Production"), *Praxis* (Y), IX, 1-2, April 1972, p. 207.

87. Dragomir Drašković, "Socijalna dinamika i konflikti u razvoju samoupravljanja" ("Social Dynamics and Conflicts in the Development of Self-Management"), in *Teorija i praksa samoupravljanja u Jugoslaviji (The Theory and Practice of Self-Management in Yugoslavia)*, ed. Jovan Djordjević, *et al.*, Belgrade: Radnička štampa, 1972, p. 985.

88. Marković, *From Affluence to Praxis, op. cit.*, pp. 71-72.

89. Mihailo Marković, "Marxism versus Technocracy," *Dialogue*, I, 1, Spring 1968, p. 31.

90. *Ibid.*, p. 35.

91. Rudi Supek, "Der technokratische Szientismus und der sozialistische Humanismus," *Praxis* (I), III, 2, 1967, p. 163.

92. *Ibid.*, p. 161.

93. Becker, *Beyond Alienation, op. cit.*, p. 97.

94. Gajo Petrović, *Marx in the Mid-Twentieth Century*, Garden City, N.Y.: Doubleday, 1967, p. 119.

95. Roland Huntford, *The New Totalitarians*, New York: Stein, 1972, pp. 344-348.

96. Roger Garaudy, *The Alternative Future*, New York: Simon & Schuster, 1974, p. 102.

97. Becker, *Beyond Alienation, op. cit.*, p. 88.

98. James A. Ogilvy, *Many Dimensional Man*, New York: Oxford University Press, 1977, p. 285.

99. Alvin Toffler, *The Third Wave*, New York: Morrow, 1980, p. 375.

100. *Ibid.*, p. 454.

101. Albert Camus, *The Rebel*, New York: Vintage, 1956, p. 11.

102. Milan Mirić, *Rezervati (Reservations)*, Zagreb: Studentski centar sveučilišta, 1970, p. 39.

103. Roger Garaudy, *From Anathema to Dialogue*, New York: Vintage, 1966, p. 31.

104. Peter L. Berger, *Pyramids of Sacrifice*, New York: Basic Books, 1974, p. 231.

105. Stojanović, *Geschichte und Parteibewusstsein, op. cit.*, p. 51.

106. Arthur Koestler, *The Ghost in the Machine*, London: Hutchinson, 1967, p. 339.

107. Arthur Koestler, *Darkness at Noon*, New York: New American Library, 1961, p. 215.

108. Bell, *The Coming of Post-Industrial Society, op. cit.*, pp. 475-488.

109. Daniel Bell, *The Cultural Contradictions of Capitalism*, New York: Basic Books, 1976, pp. 155, 168.

110. Esad Cimić, *Čovjek na raskršću (Man at the Crossroads)*, Sarajevo: Svjetlost, 1975, p. 108. Banned in December 1975.

111. Bernard-Henri Lévy, *Barbarism With a Human Face*, New York: Harper & Row, 1979, pp. 135-142.

112. Francis A. Schaeffer, *How Should We Then Live?* Old Tappan, N.J.: Revell, 1976, p. 55.

113. *Ibid.*, p. 224.

114. Kahn, *et al., The Next 200 Years, op. cit.*, p. 226; emphasis added.

115. Schaeffer, *How Should We Then Live?, op. cit.*, p. 245.

116. Tocqueville, *Democracy in America, op. cit.*, p. 34.

117. *Ibid.*, p. 35.

118. Nikolai M. Amosoff, paraphrased and quoted by George St. George, "1991," *Look*, July 14, 1970, p. 61.

119. Leo Strauss, *On Tyranny*, Ithaca: Cornell University Press, 1968, p. 224.

120. Karl R. Popper & John C. Eccles, *The Self and Its Brain*, New York: Springer International, 1977, p. 144.

121. Immanuel Kant, *Critique of Pure Reason*, London: Macmillan, 1929, p. 472.

122. See my "The Principle of Tolerance in Kant's *Critique of Pure Reason*," in *Proceedings of the Fifth International Kant Congress*, 2 vols., ed. Gerhard

Funke, Bonn: Bouvier, 1981, II, pp. 803-811, on which this section draws heavily.

123. Popper & Eccles, *The Self and Its Brain, op. cit.*, p. 472.
124. *Ibid.*, p. 362.
125. Nicholas Rescher, "Noumenal Causality," in *Proceedings of the Third International Kant Congress*, ed. Lewis White Beck, Dordrecht: Reidel, 1972, p. 470; Kant, *Critique of Pure Reason, op. cit.*, p. 631.
126. Max Weber, "The Meaning of 'Ethical Neutrality' in Sociology and Economics," in his *On the Methodology of the Social Sciences*, eds. E. A. Shils & H. A. Finch, Illinois: Free Press of Glencoe, 1949, p. 7.
127. Popper & Eccles, *The Self and Its Brain, op. cit.*, p. 557.

CHAPTER X: PROMETHEUS BOUND

1. Friedrich Engels, Letter to Herson Trier, December 18, 1889, quoted by Ljubomir Tadić, "Proletarijat i birokratija" ("The Proletariat and Bureaucracy"), in *Humanizam i socijalizam (Humanism and Socialism)*, 2 vols., eds. Branko Bošnjak & Rudi Supek, Zagreb: Naprijed, 1963, II, p. 61.
2. Branko Bošnjak, "Tko suprotstavlja radnike i filozofe?" ("Who Opposes Workers to Philosophers?"), *Praxis* (Y), X, 3-4, 1973, p. 546.
3. Dragan Bartolović, "On Freedom and 'Freedoms'," *STP*, XVII, 3, March 1977, p. 77.
4. On Živojin Radović, see *IOC*, 6, 4, July-August, 1977, Index, p. 74; on Viktor Blažić, Franc Miklavčić & Edward Kocbek, see *Amnesty International Index* EUR/04/77, June 22, 1977, pp. 3-7 and *Newsletter*, February 1977; also, *IOC*, 6, 1, January-February, 1977, Index, p. 66 and A.S., "Letter from Slovenia," *IOC*, 6, 5, September-October, 1977, pp. 49-52.
5. Vitomir Djilas, quoted in "Question and Answer," *IOC*, 6, 4, July-August, 1977, p. 78.
6. *Ibid.*; also, *IOC*, 6, 5, September-October, 1977, Index, p. 72; according to *IOC*, 6, 4, July-August, 1977, p. 74, Djilas was asked to testify against Radović and, after refusing, was arrested shortly thereafter.
7. See *IOC*, 6, 5, September-October, 1977, Index, p. 72.
8. U.S. Commission on Security and Cooperation in Europe, *Report to the U. S. Congress on Implementation of the Final Act of the Conference on Security and Cooperation in Europe: Findings and Recommendations Two Years After Helsinki*, Washington, D. C., August 1, 1977.
9. Andrei D. Sakharov, "Peace, Progress and Human Rights," 1975 Nobel Lecture, *IOC*, 5, 2, Summer 1976, pp. 3-9; Aleksandr I. Solzhenitsyn, "America: You Must Think About the World" and "Communism: A Legacy of Terror," in *Solzhenitsyn: The Voice of Freedom*, Washington, D. C.: AFL-CIO Publication No. 152, 1975, pp. 3-25 & 27-48; Walter Laqueur, "The Issue of Human Rights," *Commentary*, 63, 5, May 1977, pp. 29-35; Daniel P. Moynihan, "The Politics of Human Rights," *Commentary*, 64, 2, August 1977, pp. 19-26. For the conclusion of the Belgrade Conference, see "Weak Belgrade Statement Finally Wins Acceptance," *LAT*, March 9, 1978, I, pp. 1, 15.
10. Jean-François Revel, *The Totalitarian Temptation*, Garden City, N.Y.: Doubleday, 1977, pp. 74-75.
11. "Carter Welcomes Tito as 'True Friend' of U.S.," *LAT*, March 8, 1978, I, p. 5 for a critique, see Senator Daniel P. Moynihan's comments in the *Congressional Record*, March 10, 1978.
12. "Yugoslavia [sic.] Author, 217 More Dissidents Pardoned," *LAT*, November 25, 1977, I, p. 5.
13. U.S. Department of State, *Report on Human Rights Practices in Countries Receiving U.S. Aid*, submitted to the Senate Committee on Foreign Relations and the House Committee on Foreign Affairs, February 8, 1979, Washington, D.C.: GPO, 1979, pp. 510-515.

14. "8 Dissident Yugoslav Professors Dropped From Posts by Serbia," *NYT*, January 29, 1975, p. 2; "Dean in Yugoslavia Reported to Resign," *NYT*, January 26, 1975, p. 2. For background, see Noam Chomsky & Robert S. Cohen, "The Repression at Belgrade University," *NYRB*, XXI, 1, February 7, 1974, pp. 32-33; Gerson S. Sher, "'The Belgrade Eight': Tito Muzzles the Loyal Opposition," *The Nation*, 220, 10, March 15, 1975, pp. 294-297; and Robert S. Cohen's informal "Yugoslav Notes," V-VII, Boston: February 1975, June 1976 & June 1977, mimeo.

15. Lazo M. Kostić, *Sve su to laži i obmane (All Those Lies and Deceptions)*, Munich: Samizdat, 1975, p. 296.

16. Cohen, "Yugoslav Notes V," *op. cit.*; also, "Yugoslav Notes VI," excerpted in "East Wind Over Yugoslavia: The Case of the *Praxis* Philosophers and the Trial of Srdja Popović," *IOC*, 5, 4, Winter 1976, pp. 55-65.

17. Statement by the "Belgrade Eight" of November 21, 1974, at the Faculty of Philosophy meeting at Belgrade University, delivered by Mihailo Marković, member of the Serbian Academy of Sciences, excerpted in "Yugoslav Notes V," *op. cit.*, pp. 17-22.

18. LCY, quoted in *ibid.*, p. 3.

19. See the release by the Yugoslav Information Center, New York, "Concerning the Case of the Eight Belgrade Philosophers," *YFV*, February 1975; Special Issue.

20. "East Wind Over Yugoslavia," *op. cit.*; for a petition by 30 Yugoslav intellectuals on behalf of Popović, see pp. 64-65. Popović must have been quite a thorn in the side of Yugoslav authorities because of his extensive record of defending political prisoners, *inter alia*: In 1972, defended Ivan Ivanović whose book, *The Red King*, was banned; 1973: defended Božidar Jakšić, University of Sarajevo, a member of the *Praxis* group who was sentenced to six months, but set free on probation; Kosta Čavoški, Faculty of Law, Belgrade, supporter of the *Praxis* group, sentenced to six months, but sentence suspended; Vladimir Mijanović, a student, sentenced for second time for one year; 1974: acted on behalf of Miodrag Stojanović & Zoran Djindjić, students at Belgrade Philosophy Faculty, accused of "hostile propaganda" for expressing sympathies for the "Belgrade Eight" at a student meeting in Ljubljana, received ten months imprisonment; Jovan Vukelić, a student, Philosophy Faculty, for public support of the "Eight" at a student meeting, ten months imprisonment.

21. On *Filosofija*, see "East Wind Over Yugoslavia," *op. cit.*, p. 64; on *Praxis*, see "Yugoslavia Closes Magazine Critical of Regime," *NYT*, February 22, 1975, p. 2.

22. Rudi Supek, Presidential Letter to Members of the Yugoslav Sociological Association, February 20, 1976, excerpted in "East Wind Over Yugoslavia," *op. cit.*, pp. 61-62; see also "Yugoslavia Presses Drive on Academic Dissidents," *NYT*, February 16, 1975, p. 12.

23. Appeal to the Presidium of the Socialist Republic of Serbia by the "Belgrade Eight," October 20, 1975, excerpted in "East Wind Over Yugoslavia," *op. cit.*, p. 59.

24. See *IOC*, 2, 1, Spring 1973, Index, p. xvi.

25. Predrag Matvejević, *Te Vjetrenjače (Those Windmills)*, Zagreb: Cesarec, 1977, pp. 89-94.

26. Open Letter of October 1, 1976, by Tadić, Stojanović, Životić, Golubović, Popov, Mićunović & Marković, to the Presidencies of Serbia and Yugoslavia, translated in Cohen, "Yugoslav Notes VII," *op. cit.*, pp. 1-3, and commentary, pp. 3-5.

27. "Opozicioni Marksisti protiv karakteristike" ("Opposition Marxists Against Characterization"), *NAR*, XXXI, 295, May 1978, pp. 3-4.

28. "'Praksisovci' opet na udaru" ("*Praxists* Under Attack Again"), *NH*, XXII, 14, July 13, 1980, p. 6.

29. Mihailo Marković, "Praxis: Critical Social Philosophy in Yugoslavia," in *Praxis*, eds. M. Marković & Gajo Petrović, Dordrecht: Reidel, 1979, p. xii;

compare with his "Marxist Philosophy in Yugoslavia: The *Praxis* Group," in *Marxism and Religion in Eastern Europe*, eds. R. T. De George & J. P. Scanlan, Dordrecht: Reidel, 1976, pp. 63-66.

30. Marković, "Praxis," *op. cit.*, p. xiii.
31. Djilas, quoted by George Urban, "A Conversation With Milovan Djilas," *Encounter*, LIII, 6, December 1979, p. 34. Banned in Yugoslavia.
32. Malcolm W. Browne, "Two Hungarian Dissidents in Pact With Government" and "Dissident in Hungary Protests Delay on Promised Exit Visa," *NYT*, January 29 & February 8, 1975, p. 3 & p. 8; "Soviet Writer Gets Suspended Sentence After He Apologizes," *NYT*, February 22, 1975, p. 2; Solzhenitsyn was expelled from the Soviet Union in February 1974.
33. "Yugoslav Critic is on Trial Again," *NYT*, February 26, 1975, p. 4; "Yugoslavs Sentence 15 as Croatian Secessionists," *NYT*, February 18, 1975, p. 6; Eric Bourne, "Yugoslav 'Albanci' Turn Assertive," *CSM*, February 6, 1975, p. 3B; Malcolm W. Browne, "In the Twilight, Tito is Creating a Rigid Legacy," *NYT*, February 16, 1975, p. E3.
34. See Fuad Muhić, "Exponents of Destruction of the Proletarian Party—Who Are the Non-Party Marxists?," *STP*, 14, 1, January 1974, pp. 75-92.
35. Edvard Kardelj, quoted in "Liberalizam od Djilasa do danas" ("Liberalism From Djilas Till Today"), *NIN*, 1395, October 2, 1977, p. 62; see also V. Milanović, "Neoanarhistička kritika savremenog jugoslovenskog društva" ("The Neo-Anarchist Critique of Contemporary Yugoslav Society"), in *Marksizam i samoupravljanje (Marxism and Self-Management)*, ed. Predrag Radenović, Belgrade: Zavod za udžbenike i nastavna sredstva, 1977, II, pp. 644-657.
36. Dragan Marković & Savo Kržavac, *Liberalizam od Djilasa do danas (Liberalism Since Djilas)*, 2 vols., Belgrade: Sloboda, 1978, I, pp. 299-345.
37. Živojin D. Denić, *Marks i jugoslovenska 'Sveta Porodica' (Marx and the Yugoslav "Holy Family")*, Priština: Jedinstvo, 1977, p. 105.
38. *Ibid.*, p. 420.
39. Miloje Petrović, *Kontroverzije u savremenom marksizmu (Controversies in Contemporary Marxism)*, Belgrade: Komunist, 1977, p. 81.
40. Gajo Petrović, *Čemu Praxis? (Why Praxis?)*, Zagreb: *Praxis* Pocketbook Edition No. 10-11, 1972, pp. 15-16.
41. Milan Kangrga, "Fenomenologija ideološko-političkog nastupanja jugoslavenske srednje klase" ("Phenomenology of the Ideological-Political Appearance of the Yugoslav Middle Class"), *Praxis* (Y), VIII, 3-4, May-August, 1971, pp. 445-446.
42. Edvard Kardelj, "The Class Position of the League of Communists Today," *STP*, 37, December 1969, pp. 3-14.
43. Danilo Pejović, "On the Power and Impotence of Philosophy," in *Socialist Humanism*, ed. Erich Fromm, Garden City, N. Y.: Doubleday, 1966, p. 208.
44. Veljko Korać, "In Search of Human Society," in *ibid.*, p. 8.
45. Gajo Petrović, "Philosophie und Sozialismus—Wiederaufnahme einer Diskussion," *Praxis* (I), X, 1-2, 1974, p. 64.
46. Ralph Pervan, *Tito and the Students*, Nedlands: University of Western Australia Press, 1978, pp. 59, 180.
47. Miloje Petrović, "Kritika svega postojećeg ili 'novi' dogmatizam" ("Critique of Everything Existing or the 'New' Dogmatism"), *Komunist*, November 18, 1974, p. 24.
48. Friedrich A. Hayek, *Law, Legislation and Liberty*, 3 vols., Chicago: University of Chicago Press, 1973-79, III, pp. 175-176.
49 "The Extreme Left—Actually the Right," *STP*, 14, 3, March 1974, pp. 101-102.
50. Zagorka Pešić-Golubović, "Why is Functionalism More Desirable in Present-Day Yugoslavia Than Marxism?" and Svetozar Stojanović, "From Post-Revolutionary Dictatorship to Socialist Democracy: Yugoslav Socialism at the Crossroads," both in *Praxis* (I), IX, 4, 1973, pp. 357-368 & 311-

334; also, Mihailo Marković, *From Affluence to Praxis*, Ann Arbor: University of Michigan Press, 1974, p. 241.

51. Veljko Rus, "Self-Management Egalitarianism and Social Differentiation," *Praxis* (I), VI, 1-2, 1970, pp. 264-265.

52. Eduard Bernstein, *Evolutionary Socialism*, New York: Schocken, 1965, p. 197.

53. Dobrica Ćosić, "A Critique of Ideological A Priori and Doctrinaire Attitudes," *Praxis* (I), IX, 1, 1973, pp. 71-72.

54. Pejović, *Sistem i egzistencija, op. cit.*, p. 210.

55. Zagorka Pešić-Golubović, "Self-Fulfillment, Equality and Freedom," *Praxis* (I), IX, 2-3, 1973, p. 159.

56. Hayek, *Law, Legislation and Liberty, op. cit.*, II, p. 147; Glucksmann, quoted by Max Gallo, "An Interview With André Glucksmann," *Telos*, No. 33, Fall 1977, p. 97.

57. Statement to the Faculty of Philosophy, University of Belgrade, by the "Belgrade Eight," following their suspension, excerpted in Cohen, "Yugoslav Notes V," *op. cit.*, pp. 5-6.

58. Aeschylus, *Prometheus Bound*, in *Greek Tragedies*, eds. David Grene & Richard Lattimore, Chicago: University of Chicago Press, 1963, I, p. 69.

59. Karl Marx, *Early Texts*, ed. David McLellan, London: Blackwell, 1971, p. 14.

60. Thomas Hobbes, *Leviathan*, New York: Collier, 1962, p. 100; Marx, quoting a Frenchman, in his "Contribution to the Critique of Hegel's Philosophy of Right," in *Karl Marx*, ed. T. B. Bottomore, New York: McGraw-Hill, 1964, p. 52.

61. Mihajlo Mihajlov, "Yugoslavia—The Approaching Storm," *Dissent*, Summer 1974, p. 371, in which he observed that activities for which the Pulitzer Prize is awarded in the United States are regarded as political crimes in Yugoslavia.

62. Aeschylus, *Prometheus Bound, op. cit.*, p. 73.

63. Jacob Bronowski, "The Principle of Tolerance," *The Atlantic*, December 1973, p. 66.

64. *Sedmi Kongres (Seventh Congress)*, Belgrade: Kultura, 1958, trans. Stoyan Pribichevich, *Yugoslavia's Way*, New York: All Nations, 1958, p. 233.

65. Ljubo Sirc, "The 'New Left' in Yugoslavia," *Review*, II, 3, 1977, p. 228.

66. Danko Grlić, "O apstraktnom i realnom humanizmu" ("On Abstract and Real Humanism"), in *Humanizam i socijalizam, op. cit.*, I, p. 138.

67. "Resolution on the Tasks of the League of Communists of Yugoslavia in the Field of Culture," *STP*, 14, 6-7, June-July, 1974, pp. 265-273.

68. On the party's campaign urging the intensification of the "class struggle" throughout society, see *Komunist* since September 1975; even the country's leading popular magazine of humor, "Jež" ("The Hedgehog"), has not escaped scathing criticism by the party for its lack of *partiinost*, classness, and proletarian socialist consciousness.

69. On national-international linkages, see William Zimmerman, "National-International Linkages in Yugoslavia: The Political Consequences of Openness," in *Political Development in Eastern Europe*, eds. Jan F. Triska & Paul M. Cocks, New York: Praeger, 1977, pp. 334-364.

70. Marshall Fishwick, "Popular Culture and the New Journalism," *Journal of Popular Culture*, IX, 1, Summer 1975, p. 101.

71. See my "Comparing Socialist Cultures: A Meta-Framework," *SCC*, XI, 1-2, Spring/Summer, 1978, pp. 75-95.

CHAPTER XI: TITO'S LEGACY AND HUMAN RIGHTS

1. Tito had 21 pseudonyms before 1945, according to his official biographer, Pero Damjanović, in *NIN*, June 1, 1975, cited in *NAR*, XXX, 289, November 1977, p. 18.

2. Dusko Doder, *The Yugoslavs*, New York: Random House, 1978, p. 116.

3. Thatcher, d'Estaing & Waldheim, quoted in "World Leaders Grieve for Tito, a 'Towering Figure'," *LAT*, May 5, 1980, I, pp. 1, 26.

4. Bogdan Denitch, "The Tito Legacy," *Commonweal*, CVII, 5, March 14, 1980, p. 143.

5. John C. Campbell, "Tito: The Achievement and the Legacy," *FA*, 58, 5, Summer 1980, p. 1046.

6. *Ibid.*, p. 1055.

7. Momčilo Selić, "Sadržaj" ("Contents"), *NAR*, XXXIII, 316, June-July, 1980, p. 16. English trans. in *Freedom Appeals*, 5, May-June, 1980, pp. 15-19.

8. Robert C. Tucker, "The Theory of Charismatic Leadership," in *Philosophers and Kings*, ed. Dankwart A. Rustow, New York: Braziller, 1970, p. 80.

9. Milovan Djilas, *Wartime*, New York: Harcourt Brace Jovanovich, 1977, p. 362. Djilas' works are banned in Yugoslavia. Imprisoned: 1957-61, 1963-67.

10. Svetozar Stojanović, *Geschichte und Parteibewusstsein*, Munich: Carl Hanser, 1978, p. 39.

11. Sigmund Freud, *Group Psychology and the Analysis of the Ego*, New York: Bantam, 1965, p. 68.

12. Djilas, quoted by George Urban, "A Conversation With Milovan Djilas," *Encounter*, LIII, 6, December 1979, p. 30. Banned in Yugoslavia.

13. Milovan Djilas, *Tito*, New York: H. B. Jovanovich, 1980, excerpted in *NH*, XXII, 17, September 7, 1980, p. 15; and Djilas, *Wartime, op. cit.*, pp. 222, 349.

14. Report of the Commission of Inquiry of the Committee for a Fair Trial for Draja Mihailovich, in *Patriot or Traitor*, ed. David Martin, Stanford: Hoover Institution Press, 1978, p. 481.

15. According to Mihailović's defense attorney, Dragić Jaksimović, before the Belgrade court, July 12, 1946, in *ibid.*, p. 167.

16. *Ibid.*, p. 483.

17. Duncan Wilson, *Tito's Yugoslavia*, New York: Cambridge University Press, 1979, p. 29.

18. *Patriot or Traitor, op. cit.*, p. 488.

19. *Ibid.*, pp. 43-53; Djilas, *Wartime, op. cit.*, pp. 230-231, 242-245; Walter R. Roberts, *Tito, Mihailović and the Allies, 1941-1945*, New Brunswick, N.J.: Rutgers University Press, 1973, p. 110.

20. "80,000 ubijenih Nijemaca u Jugoslaviji" ("80,000 Germans Killed in Yugoslavia"), *HR*, XXV, 2, June 1975, p. 257; *NAR*, XXXII, 309, November 1979, p. 18, Djilas, *Wartime, op. cit.*, pp. 415-450.

21. Djilas, *Wartime, op. cit.*, pp. 283,446; the night following the death of the German POW, Christ appeared to Djilas—an atheist—in a dream (pp. 284-285).

22. Swedish TV interview with Dr. Franjo Tudjman, excerpted in *HR*, XXVIII, 1, January 1978, p. 134.

23. Edvard Kardelj, Letter of August 2, 1941, cited by Andreas Graf Razumofsky, *Ein Kampf um Belgrad*, excerpted in *NH*, XXII, 16, August 10, 1980, p. 9.

24. Djilas, *Wartime, op. cit.*, p. 178.

25. Mirko Vidović, *Sakrivena strana mjeseca (The Hidden Side of the Moon)*, 2nd ed., Munich: Hrvatska Revija, 1978, p. 281. Imprisoned: 1971-76.

26. Matija Bećković & Dušan Radović, *Će, tragedija koja traje (Ché, The Permanent Tragedy)*, Belgrade: Samizdat, 1970, p. 48.

27. R. Oraški, *Panonija (Panonia)*, Mainz: Samizdat, 1976, pp. 15-27. Imprisoned: 1945-60.

28. Vladimir I. Lenin, *"Left-Wing" Communism, An Infantile Disorder*, New York: International Publishers, 1940, p. 76.

29. Nicholas Bethell, *The Last Secret*, London: André Deutsch, 1974; Nikolai Tolstoy, *The Secret Betrayal*, New York: Scribner, 1978; Aleksandr I. Solzhenitsyn, *The Gulag Archipelago*, 3 vols., New York: Harper & Row,

1974-78.

30. Urban's interview with Djilas, *op. cit.,* pp. 40-41; Djilas, *Wartime, op. cit.,* pp. 446-447.

31. Bor. M. Karapandzich, *Jugoslovensko krvavo proleće 1945—Titovi Katini i Gulazi,* Cleveland/Munich: Iskra, 1976 (condensed English edition: *The Bloodiest Yugoslav Spring 1945—Tito's Katyns and Gulags,* New York: Carlton, 1980); *Bleiburška tragedija (The Bleiburg Tragedy),* Munich/Barcelona: Hrvatska Revija, 1976; "The End of the Croatian Army at Bleiburg, Austria in May 1945 According to English Military Documents," eds. Jerome Jareb & Ivo Omrčanin, *Journal of Croatian Studies,* XVIII-XIX, 1977-1978, pp. 115-180.

32. Joseph Hećimović, *In Tito's Death Marches and Extermination Camps,* New York: Carlton, 1962, p. 85.

33. Oraški, *Panonija, op. cit.,* pp. 123, 201-204.

34. Svetozar Vukmanović-Tempo, *Revolucija koja teče (The Permanent Revolution),* 2 vols., Belgrade: Komunist, 1971, cited in Karapandzich, *Jugoslovensko krvavo proleće 1945, op. cit.,* p. 159.

35. Aleksa Benigar, *Alojzije Stepinac Hrvatski Kardinal (Aloysius Stepinac, Croatian Cardinal),* Rome: Ziral, 1974.

36. Stella Alexander, *Church and State in Yugoslavia Since 1945,* New York: Cambridge University Press, 1979, pp. 292-293.

37. Archbishop Franjo Kuharić, quoted by *NAR,* XXXII, 307, August-September, 1979, p. 17.

38. J. Nikolić in *Pravoslavlje* (Belgrade), December 1, 1979, quoted by *NAR,* XXXIII, 313, March 1980, p. 22.

39. Desimir Tochitch, *Totalitarisme et Droits de l'homme,* Paris: Samizdat, 1948, p. 63.

40. "Savez demokratske omladine Jugoslavije," *NAR,* XXX, 286, June-July, 1977, p. 49.

41. Djilas, *Tito,* excerpted as "Red Monarch Without the Mask," in *NH,* XXII, 16, August 10, 1980, p. 16. On the Naked Island, see "Dokumenti o Golom Otoku, jednom od jugoslavenskih logora" ("Documents on the Naked Island, One of the Yugoslav Camps"), *HR,* XXVI, 1, March 1976, pp. 152-155.

42. Radoslav Kostić-Katunac, *Pogledaj, Gospode, na drugu stranu!—Jugoslovenski Gulag (Look, Lord, To The Other Side—Yugoslavia's Gulag),* New York: Naša Reč, 1978, pp. 76-77. Imprisoned: 1963-69.

43. Milan Radovich, Letter of February 13, 1979 to author.

44. Eva Lapuh, "Chronicler of a Critical Time," *IOC,* 9, 2, April 1980, pp. 42-45.

45. Djilas, *Tito,* excerpted in *NH, op. cit.,* p. 16; Solzhenitsyn, *The Gulag Archipelago, op. cit.,* I, p. 174.

46. Pericles, in *Plutarch's Cimon and Pericles,* with the Funeral Oration of Pericles (Thucydides, II, 35-46), ed. Bernadotte Perrin, New York: Scribner's Sons, 1910, p. 169.

47. Lowel Edmunds, *Chance and Intelligence in Thucydides,* Cambridge, Mass.: Harvard University Press, 1975, pp. 44-45.

48. Cecil M. Bowra, *Periclean Athens,* New York: Dial, 1971, p. 285.

49. Rusko Matulić, "Repression of Dissent in Yugoslavia," *Review,* II, 3, 1977, pp. 216-225; "Repression in Yugoslavia," London: Committee in Defence of Soviet Political Prisoners, 1977, pp. 1-24, "White House Looks Other Way on Yugoslavian Human Rights Violations," *The Congressional Record,* September 5, 1980, pp. E4239-4240.

50. U.S. Commission on Security and Cooperation in Europe, *Report to the U.S. Congress on Implementation of the Final Act of the Conference on Security and Cooperation in Europe: Five Years After Helsinki,* Washington, D. C., August 1, 1980.

51. U.S. Department of State, *Report on Human Rights Practices in Countries Receiving U.S. Aid,* submitted to the Senate Committee on Foreign Relations and the House Committee on Foreign Affairs, February 8, 1979,

Washington, D.C.: GPO, 1979, p. 510.

52. "Opozicioni marksisti za slobodu štampe" ("Opposition Marxists for Freedom of the Press"), *NAR,* XXXII, 306, June-July, 1979, pp. 7-9.
53. *NAR,* November 1977, February 1978, May 1978, pp. 17, 19, 15; *IOC,* 7, 1, January-February, 1978, Index, p. 72.
54. *Iskra* (Munich), XXX, 682, September 15, 1979, p. 5.
55. "Mihajlo Mihajlov Before Helsinki Commission," *The Congressional Record,* August 1, 1978, p. E4242.
56. *Amnesty International Report 1977,* London: AI, 1977, p. 288.
57. "Repression in Yugoslavia," *op. cit.,* p. 24.
58. *Iskra,* XXX, 682, September 15, 1979, p. 5.
59. *NAR,* August-September, 1977, November 1977, February 1978, pp. 13, 19, 18-19.
60. *Review,* II, 3, 1977, p. 213.
61. *Amnesty International Annual Report, 1978-79,* London: AI, 1979, pp. 149-150.
62. Josip-Broz Tito, "The LCY in the Struggle for the Further Development of Socialist, Self-Managing and Nonaligned Yugoslavia," *STP,* XVIII, 6, June 1978, p. 11.
63. *Ibid.,* p. 63.
64. "Tito Opens Drive Against Dissent; Djilas Warned," *WAP,* April 9, 1979.
65. Major sources for the following representative (not exhaustive) account of recent human rights violations in Yugoslavia: *Bulletin of the Democracy International Committee to Aid Democratic Dissidents in Yugoslavia, Naša reč, Nova Hrvatska, Iskra, Croatia Press, Review of the Study Centre for Yugoslav Affairs, Hrvatska Revija, Jugosloven* (Sweden).
66. U.S. Department of State, *Country Reports on Human Rights Practices for 1979,* Washington, D.C.: GPO, 1980, p. 700.
67. "Serbian Editor in Chicago Slain; Anti-Reds Blame Yugoslav Secret Police," *The Plain Dealer* (Cleveland), June 20, 1977, p. 4-B.
68. *NAR,* April 1978, p. 13.
69. Karapandzich, *The Bloodiest Yugoslav Spring 1945, op. cit.,* p. 160.
70. On Bruno Bušić, see *ibid.,* pp. 159-160, *NH,* 2, 1980, p. 8; and *Cleveland Press,* October 18, 1978, A-18; on Dušan Sedlar, *NAR,* May 1980, p. 10; *NH,* 9, 1980, pp. 5-6; *Iskra,* May 1, 1980, p. 1; and *Jugosloven,* March-April, 1980, p. 30.
71. State Department, *Report on Human Rights Practices . . ., op. cit.,* p. 513.
72. Raymond D. Gastil, "The Comparative Survey of Freedom—X," *Freedom at Issue,* No. 54, January-February 1980, p. 5.
73. Doder, *The Yugoslavs, op. cit.,* p. 159.
74. Milovan Djilas, March 1978 interview with Radio Free Europe/Radio Liberty, summarized in *NAR,* XXXI, 299, November 1978, pp. 3-4.
75. Leszek Kolakowski, *Main Currents of Marxism,* 3 vols., Oxford: Oxford University Press, 1978, III, p. 476.
76. Freud, *Group Psychology . . ., op. cit.,* p. 70.
77. First two points summarized in David A. Dyker, "Yugoslavia: Unity Out of Diversity?" in *Political Culture and Political Change in Communist States,* eds. Archie Brown & Jack Gray, New York: Holmes & Meier, 1977, pp. 70-71, 88-89.
78. Dobrica Ćosić, "Culture and Revolution," in *Praxis,* eds. Mihailo Marković & Gajo Petrović, Dordrecht: Reidel, 1979, pp. 224-225.
79. Esad Cimić, *Čovjek na raskršću (Man at the Crossroads),* Sarajevo: Svjetlost, 1975, p. 100.
80. Milan Mirić, *Pisma iz rezervata (Letters from the Reservation),* Belgrade: Samizdat, 1976, p. 88.
81. Gojko Borić, "Why is There No *Samizdat* in Yugoslavia?" in *Kontinent,* II, ed. Vladimir Maximov, Garden City, N. Y.: Anchor, 1977, pp. 49-51.
82. Predrag Matvejević, *Te Vjetrenjače (Those Windmills),* Zagreb: Cesarec,

1977, pp. 10-11.

83. Doder, *The Yugoslavs, op. cit.,* p. 80.
84. Mirko Vidović, Letter of April 13, 1971 to Vinko Nikolić, in his *Sakrivena strana mjeseca, op. cit.,* p. 363.
85. *Ibid.,* p. 61.
86. Vladislav Musa, *U Titovim pandžama (In Tito's Claws),* Munich: Samizdat, 1973, p. 42. Imprisoned: 1967-70.
87. Kostić-Katunac, *Pogledaj, Gospode . . ., op. cit.,* p. 57.
88. Radoslav Kostić-Katunac, "The Umbilical Cord—A Story," in *Human Rights in Yugoslavia,* eds. O. Gruenwald & Karen Rosenblum-Cale, forthcoming; Oraški, *Panonija, op. cit.,* pp. 95-97, 115.
89. Kostić-Katunac, *Pogledaj, Gospode . . ., op. cit.,* p. 160.
90. Mihajlo Mihajlov, *Underground Notes,* Kansas City: Andrews & McMeel, 1976, pp. 176-177. Mihajlov's works are banned in Yugoslavia. Imprisoned: 1965, 1966-70, 1975-77.

CHAPTER XII: POST-TITO YUGOSLAVIA: A SOCIALIST CAMELOT?

1. Michael M. Milenkovitch, "Yugoslav Marxism: Retrospect and Prospect," *Review,* II, 3, 1977, p. 288; Dusko Doder, *The Yugoslavs,* New York: Random House, 1978, p. 241.
2. George Urban, "A Conversation With Milovan Djilas," *Encounter,* LIII, 6, December 1979, p. 19; Leszek Kolakowski, *Main Currents of Marxism,* 3 vols., Oxford: Oxford University Press, 1978, III, p. 473.
3. R. V. Burks, "Problems Facing the Yugoslav Communist Movement: A Comment," in *Innovation in Communist Systems,* eds. Andrew György & James A. Kuhlman, Boulder, Colo.: Westview, 1978, pp. 99-100; A. Ross Johnson, *Yugoslavia: In the Twilight of Tito,* Bevery Hills: Sage, 1974, p. 55.
4. Doder, *The Yugoslavs, op. cit.,* p. 242; Mihajlo Mihajlov, "The Dissident Movement in Yugoslavia," *Washington Quarterly,* 2, 4, Autumn 1979, p. 73.
5. *Regimes and Oppositions,* ed. Robert A. Dahl, New Haven: Yale University Press, 1973, p. 18.
6. Robin Alison Remington, "Yugoslavia," in *Communism in Eastern Europe,* eds. Teresa Rakowska-Harmstone & Andrew György, Bloomington: Indiana University Press, 1979, p. 235.
7. Tito, quoted by Dragan Marković & Savo Kržavac, *Liberalizam od Djilasa do danas (Liberalism Since Djilas),* 2 vols., Belgrade: Sloboda, 1978, II, p. 87.
8. Johnson, *Yugoslavia, op. cit.,* pp. 28-29.
9. Marko Nikezić, quoted disparagingly by Marković & Kržavac, *Liberalizam . . ., op. cit.,* II, p. 147.
10. Robin A. Remington, "The Military as an Interest Group in Yugoslav Politics," in *Civil-Military Relations in Communist Systems,* eds. Dale R. Herspring & Ivan Völgyes, Boulder, Colo.: Westview, 1978, p. 194.
11. Slobodan Stanković, "Yugoslav Paper Denies Army's Political Role," Munich: Radio Free Europe Research Report, November 13, 1979, pp. 3-4.
12. Slobodan Stanković, "Yugoslavia's 'Collective State Leadership' Enlarged," Munich: RFE Research Report, February 29, 1980, pp. 2-3.
13. *Komunist,* Special Issue, May 5, 1980, pp. 2-3; *Komunist,* XXXVIII, 1210, May 16, 1980, p. 7; *LAT,* June 13, 1980, I, p. 2; *NYT,* October 21, 1980, p. A6.
14. Boško Šiljegović, in an interview with *Expres nedeljna revija* (Sarajevo) on January 26, 1969, quoted by Dennison Rusinow, *The Yugoslav Experiment, 1948-1974,* Berkeley: University of California Press, 1977, pp. 379-380 (footnote ¨47).

15. Milutin Baltić, "Report on the Political Situation and the Tasks of Communists," 11th Session of the CC of LCC, June 5, 1980, excerpted in *Vjesnik,* June 6, 1980, p. 4.
16. Marx, "Die Verhandlungen des 6. Rheinischen Landtags," in Karl Marx & Friedrich Engels, *Collected Works,* New York: International Publishers, 1975, I, pp. 167-168.
17. Ralph Pervan, *Tito and the Students,* Nedlands: University of Western Australia Press, 1978, pp. 171, 180.
18. *Perspectives for Change in Communist Societies,* ed. Teresa Rakowska-Harmstone, Boulder, Colo.: Westview, 1979, p. 24.
19. Richard Löwenthal, "The Ruling Party in a Mature Society," in *Social Consequences of Modernization in Communist Societies,* ed. Mark G. Field, Baltimore: Johns Hopkins University Press, 1976, p. 109.
20. Marshall McLuhan & Quentin Fiore, *War and Peace in the Global Village,* New York: Bantam, 1968, pp. 5, 36-37.
21. Viktor E. Frankl, *Man's Search for Meaning,* New York: Washington Square Press, 1967, p. 179.
22. Alvin Toffler, *The Third Wave,* New York: Morrow, 1980, pp. 20, 375,435.
23. Gail Stokes, "The Undeveloped Theory of Nationalism," *WP,* XXXI, 1, October 1978, p. 157.
24. Rakowska-Harmstone, in *Perspectives for Change . . ., op. cit.,* pp. 7-8.
25. See George Schöpflin, "The Ideology of Croatian Nationalism," *Survey,* XIX, 1, Winter 1973, p. 135.
26. See Michael B. Petrovich, "Yugoslavia: Religion and the Tensions of a Multi-National State," *EEQ,* VI, 1, March 1972, pp. 118-135.
27. Cynthia W. Frey, "Yugoslav Nationalisms and the Doctrine of Limited Sovereignty," I-II, *EEQ,* X, 4, Winter 1976, pp. 427-57 & XI, 1, Spring 1977, pp. 79-108; George Klein, "The Role of Ethnic Politics in the Czechoslovak Crisis of 1968 and the Yugoslav Crisis of 1971," *SCC,* VIII, 4, Winter 1975, p. 356.
28. Tito, in *Borba,* September 22, 1969, cited by Remington, "Yugoslavia," *op. cit.,* p. 223.
29. Frey, "Yugoslav Nationalisms . . .," *op. cit.,* I, p. 428.
30. Mirko Vidović, "Matica hrvatska—hrvatsko narodno ognjište nasilno ugušeno" (Matica Hrvatska—Croatian National Hearth Extinguished by Force"), *NH,* XXII, 10, May 18, 1980, pp. 4-5.
31. Marx & Engels, in *Neue Rheinische Zeitung* (1848-49), quoted by Mihailo Marković, "Stalinism and Marxism," in *Stalinism,* ed. Robert C. Tucker, New York: Norton, 1977, p. 316.
32. Walter Connor, "Nation-Building or Nation-Destroying?" *WP,* XXIV, 3, April 1972, p. 341.
33. Lee C. Buchheit, *Secession,* New Haven: Yale Universtiy Press, 1978, p. 228.
34. Vlado Gotovac, November 1977 interview with Swedish TV; Serbo-Croatian text in *HR,* XXVIII, 1, January 1978, p. 144.
35. Nathan Glazer, *Affirmative Discrimination,* New York: Basic Books, 1975, p. 220.
36. Coined by Johnson, *Yugoslavia, op. cit.,* p. 8.
37. Ellen Turkish Comisso, *Workers' Control Under Plan and Market,* New Haven: Yale University Press, 1979, p. 212.
38. Paul Shoup, *Communism and the Yugoslav National Question,* New York: Columbia University Press, 1968, p. 261.
39. David Andelman, "Yugoslavia: Into the Post-Tito Era," *The Atlantic,* 245, 3, March 1980, p. 24.
40. Gary K. Bertsch, "Yugoslavia: The Eleventh Congress, the Constitution and the Succession," *GAO,* 14, 1, Winter 1979, p. 109.
41. Hélène Carrère d'Encausse, *Decline of an Empire,* New York: Newsweek Books, 1979, pp. 47-90, 248, 265-274.
42. Teresa Rakowska-Harmstone, "Nationalism and Integration in Eastern

Europe: The Dynamics of Change," in *Communism in Eastern Europe, op. cit.,* p. 315.

43. *Authoritarian Politics in Communist Europe,* ed. Andrew C. Janos, University of California, Berkeley: Institute of International Studies, 1976, p. 22.

44. *The Socialist Idea,* eds. Leszek Kolakowski & Stuart Hampshire, New York: Basic Books, 1974, p. 34.

45. Mihailo Marković, Ljubomir Tadić, Dragoljub Mićunović, Svetozar Stojanović, Zagorka Golubović, Miladin Životić & Nebojša Popov, "Smisao borbe za ljudska prava" ("The Meaning of the Struggle for Human Rights"), *NAR,* XXXI, pp. 296-299, June-November, 1978, pp. 11-12, 9-10, 4-6 & 4-5; English version in *Marxist Humanism and Human Rights,* ed. O. Gruenwald (in preparation).

46. Marković, "Stalinism and Marxism," *op. cit.,* p. 312.

47. Milton & Rose Friedman, *Free to Choose,* New York: Harcourt Brace Jovanovich, 1980, p. 309.

48. Friedrich A. Hayek, *Law, Legislation and Liberty,* 3 vols., Chicago: University of Chicago Press, 1973-79, II, p. 85.

49. Friedman, *Free to Choose, op. cit.,* pp. 2-3.

50. Bernard-Henri Lévy, *Barbarism With a Human Face,* New York: Harper & Row, 1979, p. 194.

51. Ljubomir Tadić, "Authority and Authoritarian Thinking: On the Sense and Senselessness of Subordination," in *Marxist Humanism and Praxis,* ed. Gerson S. Sher, Buffalo, N.Y.: Prometheus, 1978, p. 90.

52. Lévy, *Barbarism With a Human Face, op. cit.,* p. 158.

53. Djuro Šušnjić, "Ideas and Life," in *Praxis,* eds. Mihailo Marković & Gajo Petrović, Dordrecht: Reidel, 1979, p. 204.

54. Rudolf Bahro, *The Alternative in Eastern Europe,* London: NLB, 1978, p. 345.

55. Karl R. Popper, *The Open Society and Its Enemies,* 5th rev. ed., 2 vols, Princeton: Princeton University Press, 1966, I, p. 156.

56. J. Milton Yinger, "Countercultures and Social Change," *ASR,* 42, 6, December 1977, pp. 850-851.

57. Alfred Lord Tennyson, *Idylls of the King,* in *The Poems of Tennyson,* ed. Christopher Ricks, New York: Norton, 1972, p. 1673.

58. Daniel Bell, *The Cultural Contradictions of Capitalism,* New York: Basic Books, 1976, p. 248.

59. *Ibid.,* p. 264; William E. Simon, *A Time for Truth,* New York: Reader's Digest, 1978, p. 198.

60. Friedman, *Free to Choose, op. cit.,* p. 135.

61. Charles E. Lindblom, *Politics and Markets,* New York: Basic Books, 1977, p. 356; Hayek, *Law, Legislation and Liberty, op. cit.,* III, p. 89.

62. Arend Lijphart, *Democracy in Plural Societies,* New Haven: Yale University Press, 1977, p. 25.

63. Toffler, *The Third Wave, op. cit.,* pp. 435-450.

64. James A. Ogilvy, *Many Dimensional Man,* New York: Oxford University Press, 1977, pp. 8, 285, 311.

65. Hayek, *Law, Legislation and Liberty, op. cit.,* III, p. 150.

66. *Ibid.,* pp. 15-16.

67. Friedman, *Free to Choose, op. cit.,* p. 299.

68. Bell, *The Cultural Contradictions of Capitalism, op. cit.,* pp. 49-50.

69. Winston Churchill, quoted by Simon, *A Time for Truth, op. cit.,* p. 38.

70. Peter F. Drucker, *Managing in Turbulent Times,* New York: Harper & Row, 1980, p. 199.

71. *Ibid.,* pp. 28-29, 36-37.

72. Ljubo Sirc, *The Yugoslav Economy Under Self-Management,* London: Macmillan, 1979, p. 246.

73. John H. Moore, *Growth With Self-Management,* Stanford: Hoover Institution Press, 1980, p. 164.

74. Drucker, *Managing in Turbulent Times, op. cit.*, pp. 192-193.

75. Robert H. Hayes & William J. Abernathy, "Managing Our Way to Economic Decline," *Harvard Business Review*, 58, 4, July-August, 1980, pp. 67-68,77.

76. Robert Nozick, *Anarchy, State, and Utopia*, New York: Basic Books, 1974, p. 253.

77. William Foot Whyte, "In Support of the Voluntary Job Preservation and Community Stabilization Act," *The Congressional Record*, 124, 94, June 19, 1978, p. E3326.

78. "Worker Role in Management Can Boost Productivity, Fight Inflation, Study Says," *LAT*, March 10, 1980, IV, p. 5.

79. Duncan Wilson, *Tito's Yugoslavia*, New York: Cambridge University Press, 1979, p. 256.

80. Aurel Braun, "Soviet Naval Policy in the Mediterranean: Yugoslavia and the Sonnenfeldt Doctrine," *Orbis*, 22, 1, Spring 1978, p. 123.

81. Andrew Borowiec, *Yugoslavia After Tito*, New York: Praeger, 1977, pp. 52-53.

82. Borowiec, *Yugoslavia After Tito, op. cit.*, p. 107; David A. Andelman, "Yugoslavia: The Delicate Balance," *FA*, 58, 4, Spring 1980, p. 851; Carl Gustav Ströhm, *Ohne Tito: Kann Jugoslawien überleben?* Köhln: Styria, 1976, p. 300.

83. Gavriel D. Ra'anan, *Yugoslavia After Tito*, Boulder, Colo.: Westview, 1977, pp. 123-127.

84. Aleksa Djilas, "Tito and the Independence of Yugoslavia," *Review*, II, 4, 1980, p. 399.

85. Duncan Wilson, "Yugoslavia and Soviet Policy," in *The Soviet Threat*, eds. Grayson Kirk & Nils H. Wessell, New York: Academy of Political Science, 1978, p. 86.

86. Ra'anan, *Yugoslavia After Tito, op. cit.*, p. 49.

87. Borowiec, *Yugoslavia After Tito, op. cit.*, p. 48; Braun, "Soviet Naval Policy . . .," *op. cit.*, p. 116.

88. Laurence Silberman, "Yugoslavia's 'Old' Communism: Europe's Fiddler on the Roof," *FP*, No. 26, Spring 1977, p. 15.

89. Andelman, "Yugoslavia: The Delicate Balance," *op. cit.*, p. 845.

90. "Jugoslovenski-sovjetski ekonomski odnosi: Još stabilnija saradnja" ("Yugoslav-Soviet Economic Relations: Even Stabler Cooperation"), *Komunist*, XXXVIII, 1229, September 26, 1980, p. 10.

91. Borowiec, *Yugoslavia After Tito, op. cit.*, p. 62.

92. Josip-Broz Tito, "The LCY in the Struggle for the Further Development of Socialist, Self-Managing and Nonaligned Yugoslavia," *STP*, XVIII, 6, June 1978, p. 27.

93. Tito, "The Historical Responsibility of the Movement of Non-Alignment," *STP*, XIX, 10, October 1979, p. 13.

94. Tito, "Strengthened Action Capability for the Non-Aligned Countries," *STP*, XIX, 11, November 1979, pp. 5-6.

95. Walter Laqueur, "Containment for the 80s," *Commentary*, 70, 4, October 1980, p. 39.

96. Milovan Djilas, "Yugoslavia and the Expansionism of the Soviet State," *FA*, 58, 4, Spring 1980, p. 863.

97. Tito, "Inequitable International Economic Relations—Sources of Crisis Situations and Conflicts," *STP*, XIX, 11, November 1979, p. 28.

98. "Tito je velike ideale i misli pretvorio u akciju milionskih narodnih masa" ("Tito Transformed Great Ideals and Thoughts Into Action by Millions of People"), *Komunist*, May 5, 1980, p. 3; Veselin Djuranović, "The World of Tomorrow Must Reflect All Major Changes Through Which Mankind is Passing," *YTU*, XXI, 126, May-June, 1980, pp.4-5.

99. "The New International Economic Order—An Expression of Active Peaceful Coexistence," *YTU*, XXI, 126, May-June, 1980, p. 38.

100. Tito, "A Major Step in the Decolonization of Information," *STP*, XX, 1,

January 1980, p. 18.
101. Akhtar Mohammad Paktiawal, quoted by Arlie Schardt & Scott Sullivan, "Inching Toward Controls," *Newsweek*, November 3, 1980, p. 95.
102. Silberman, "Yugoslavia's 'Old' Communism," *op. cit.*, p. 25.
103. U.S. Congress, House of Representatives, Committee on International Relations Hearings before the Subcommittee on Europe & the Middle East, September 7 & 12, 1978, *U.S. Policy Toward Eastern Europe*, Washington, D.C.: U.S. GPO, 1979, pp. 47-49.
104. "Yugoslavian Firm Raises Military Technology Sales to Third World," *Aviation Week & Space Technology*, 111, 16, October 15, 1979, pp. 18-19.
105. Mirko Vidović, "Stanje apsurda i pripreme za Madrid" ("Absurd Conditions and Preparations for Madrid"), *NH*, XXII, 16, August 10, 1980, p. 5.
106. "Jugoslavenska veza s medjunarodnim terorizmom" ("The Yugoslav Connection With International Terrorism"), *NH*, XXII, 9, May 4, 1980, p. 16.
107. Bor. M. Karapandzich, *Jugoslovensko krvavo proleće 1945 (The Bloody Yugoslav Spring, 1945)*, Cleveland/Munich: Iskra, 1976, pp. 312-314.
108. Frank J. Lausche, "Foreword" to *Patriot or Traitor*, ed. David Martin, Stanford: Hoover Institution Press, 1978, p. ix.
109. William H. Luers, testifying at the Subcommittee on Europe & the Middle East Hearings on September 7, 1978, *op. cit.*, pp. 47-49.
110. Helmut Sonnenfeldt, cited in *Croatia Press*, XXIX, 1-2, April-June, 1976, p. 9.
111. Jesse Helms, "Tito's Death Preceded by Many Victims," *The Congressional Record*, May 9, 1980, p. S5091.
112. Djilas, in Urban, "A Conversation With Milovan Djilas," *op. cit.*, p. 36.
113. Aleksandr I. Solzhenitsyn, "Misconceptions About Russia Are a Threat to America," *FA*, 58, 4, Spring 1980, p. 833.
114. Isaac Rehert, "Soviet Refugee Acclaimed as a Hero," *LAT*, December 14, 1980, I-A, p. 2.
115. Norman Podhoretz, "The Present Danger," *Commentary*, 69, 3, March 1980, p. 39.
116. Walter Laqueur, "The Psychology of Appeasement," *Commentary*, 66, 4, October 1978, p. 47.
117. Laqueur, "Containment for the 80s," *op. cit.*, p. 34.
118. Paul H. Nitze, "Strategy in the Decade of the 1980s," *FA*, 59, 1, Fall 1980, pp. 87-91.
119. Brian Crozier, *Strategy of Survival*, New Rochelle, N.Y.: Arlington House, 1978, p. 11.
120. Nitze, "Strategy . . .," *op. cit.*, p. 90.
121. Antony C. Sutton, *Western Technology and Soviet Economic Development, 1917-1965*, 3 vols., Stanford: Hoover Institution Press, 1965-73, III, p. 415.
122. Drucker, *Managing in Turbulent Times, op. cit.*, p. 175.
123. London *Times*, cited in Laqueur, "Containment . . .," *op. cit.*, p. 35.
124. V. I. Lenin, quoted by George Meany in his statement of October 1, 1974, U. S. Senate, Committee on Foreign Relations Hearings on United States Relations With Communist Countries, *Détente*, Washington, D.C.: U.S. GPO, 1975, p. 377.
125. Charles Maher, "Couple Guilty of Selling High-Technology Optics to Soviets," *LAT*, December 13, 1980, II, pp. 1, 12; on the super magnet, see *LAT*, January 20, 1980, I, p. 2.
126. "Western 'Help' for Soviet Arms Cited," *LAT*, November 9, 1979, I, p. 5; Ward Sinclair, "Senator Disturbed by Data Exchange," *LAT*, September 4, 1980, I-B, p. 6.
127. Silberman, "Yugoslavia's 'Old' Communism," *op. cit.*, p. 17.
128. Ra'anan, *Yugoslavia After Tito, op. cit.*, pp. 111, 96.
129. Meany, in *Détente, op. cit.*, p. 383.
130. Aleksandr I. Solzhenitsyn, *The Gulag Archipelago, 1918-1956*, 3 vols., New York: Harper & Row, 1974-78, I, p. 177; see also my "Yugoslavia's GULAG and Human Rights," *South Slav Journal* (London), IV, 2, Summer

1981, pp. 61-67.

131. Mihajlo Mihajlov, "Rights Come First," *NYT*, April 8, 1978, p. L23.
132. Laqueur, "Containment . . .," *op. cit.*, p. 35.
133. Andrei Sakharov, "World Security, Human Rights Linked," *LAT*, September 9, 1980, II, p. 5.
134. Laqueur, "Containment . . .," *op. cit.*, p. 36.
135. Aleksandr I. Solzhenitsyn, "The Courage to See," *FA*, 59, 1, Fall 1980, p. 210.
136. Mihajlov, "Rights Come First," *op. cit.*, p. L23.
137. Mihajlov, "The Dissident Movement . . .," *op. cit.*, p. 72.
138. Mihajlo Mihajlov, "Human Rights: A Means or An End?," *NL*, LXIII, 20, November 3, 1980, p. 8.
139. Mihajlo Mihajlov, "The United States and Yugoslavia," unpublished draft, 1980, pp. 2-3.
140. Dobrica Ćosić, "Kultura i revolucija" ("Culture and Revolution"), *Praxis* (Y), XI, 3-5, 1974; also in *Praxis,* eds. Marković & Petrović, *op. cit.*, pp. 223-224. Free translation.
141. Edward Teller, *The Pursuit of Simplicity,* Malibu: Pepperdine University Press, 1980, pp. 131-136.
142. John W. Hackett, et al, *The Third World War, August 1985,* New York: Macmillan, 1978, turned out to be reasonably accurate in its predictions of limited nuclear engagements, but grievously mistaken concerning the combatants' incapacity for prolonged warfare.

Selected Bibliography

A. PRIMARY SOURCES:

I. *PRAXIS*: INTERNATIONAL EDITION

"A l'occasion des critiques les plus récentes adressées à 'Praxis'." IV, 3-4, 1968, pp. 507-516.

Arandjelovac, Jovan. "The Conflict Between Philosophy and Dogmatism in Contemporary Marxism." VI, 3-4, 1970, pp. 298-312.

Bojanović, Rade. "Lucifer and the Lord." VI, 3-4, 1970, pp. 369-380.

Bojanović, Radojica. "Despotic Socialism and the Authoritarian Personality." IX, 1, 1973, pp. 73-76.

Čavoški, Kosta. "The Accomplishments of Liberalism in the Organization of Government." IX, 1, 1973, pp. 63-67.

Ćosić, Dobrica. "A Critique of Ideological A Priori and Doctrinaire Attitudes." IX, 1, 1973, pp. 69-73.

"Déclaration du Comité de Rédaction de la Revue 'Praxis'." VIII, 1-2, 1972, p. 169.

Grlić, Danko. "La patrie des philosophes, c'est la patrie de la liberté." IV, 3-4, 1968, pp. 325-329.

_____. "Marginalien zum Problem der Nation." VII, 3-4, 1971, pp. 495-510.

_____. "Revolution und Terror." VII, 1-2, 1971, pp. 49-61.

_____. "The Determinism of Economy and the Freedom of the Individual." IX, 1, 1973, pp. 32-33.

_____. "There Can Be No Critical Thought Without Permanent Scepsis." IX, 1, 1973, pp. 91-93.

Indjić, Trivo. "The Tyranny of Culture and the Resistance of the Existing State of Affairs." IX, 1, 1973, pp. 85-87.

Jakšić, Božidar. "Culture and Development of the Contemporary Yugoslav Society." VII, 3-4, 1971, pp. 657-664.

_____. "Political Freedom and Freedom-Oriented Rhetoric." IX, 1, 1973, pp. 120-123.

_____. "Yugoslav Society Between Revolution and Stabilization." VII, 3-4, 1971, pp. 439-450.

Kangrga, Milan. "Phänomenologie des ideologisch-politischen Auftretens der jugoslawischen Mittelklasse." VII, 3-4, 1971, pp. 451-474.

Korać, Veljko. "Aporiae of the Bourgeois Society and the Postulate for Human Emancipation." X, 1-2, 1974, pp. 39-44.

_____. "Paradoxes of Power and Humanity." VI, 1-2, 1970, pp. 8-13.

_____. "The Phenomenon of 'Theoretical Antihumanism'." V, 3-4, 1969, pp. 430-434.

Krešić, Andrija. "The Proletariat and Socialism in the Works of Marx and in the World Today." V, 3-4, 1969, pp. 371-386.

Kučinar, Zdravko. "Nécéssité et possibilité du dialogue." III, 4, 1967, pp. 463-468.

_____. "Some Observations Concerning Liberalism and Marxism." IX, 1, 1973, pp. 115-120.

Kuvačić, Ivan. "Additional Thoughts on Synchrony and Diachrony." VII, 3-4, 1971, pp. 423-437.

_____. "Contemporary Forms of Mental Violence." VI, 1-2, 1970, pp. 130-136.

_____. "Die Analyse der bürgerlichen Gesellschaft von Marx und die Konvergenz-Theorie." X, 1-2, 1974, pp. 81-92.

_____. "Middle Class Ideology." IX, 4, 1973, pp. 335-356.

_____. "Scientific and Technical Progress and Humanism." V, 1-2, 1969, pp. 181-184.

"Liberalism and Socialism." Symposium: First Philosophical Winter Meeting, Tara, Serbia, February 8-10, 1971. IX, 1, 1973, pp. 3-131.

Maksimović, Ivan. "Teleological and Genetic Bases of the Economic Problems of Contemporary Socialism." VIII, 3-4, 1972, pp. 251-267.

Marković, Mihailo. "Basic Characteristics of Marxist Humanism." V, 3-4, 1969, pp. 606-615.

_____. "Basic Issues of Self-Management." X, 1-2, 1974, pp. 93-100.

_____. "Concluding Remarks." (First Philosophical Winter Meeting, Tara, Serbia, February 8-10, 1971). IX, 1, 1973, pp. 127-131.

_____. "Critical Social Theory in Marx." VI, 3-4, 1970, pp. 283-297. Also in his *From Affluence to Praxis.*

_____. "Economism or the Humanization of Economics." V, 3-4, 1969, pp. 451-475. Also in his *From Affluence to Praxis.*

_____. "Gleichheit und Freiheit." IX, 2-3, 1973, pp. 135-152.

_____. "Gramsci on the Unity of Philosophy and Politics." III, 3, 1967, pp. 333-339.

_____. "Is It Possible to Abolish Political Mediation?" IX, 1, 1973, pp. 50-53.

_____. "Marx and Critical Scientific Thought." IV, 3-4, 1968, pp. 391-403.

_____. "The Possibilities and Difficulties of Overcoming Liberalism and the Present Form of Socialist Society." IX, 1, 1973, pp. 33-38.

Mićunović, Dragoljub. "The Possible Comparison of Liberalism and Socialism." IX, 1, 1973, pp. 93-99.

Milić, Vojin. "Method of Critical Theory." VII, 3-4, 1971, pp. 625-656.

Mirić, Milan. "Les territoires réservés pour la parole et pour l'action." V, 1-2, 1969, pp. 266-276.

Novaković, Staniša. "Two Concepts of Science and Humanism." V, 1-2, 1969, pp. 193-195.

Pešić-Golubović, Zagorka. "Liberalism as a Philosophy of Freedom." IX, 1, 1973, pp. 101-104.

_____. "Self-Fulfilment, Equality and Freedom." IX, 2-3, 1973, pp. 153-160.

_____. "Socialist Ideas and Reality." VII, 3-4, 1971, pp. 399-421.

_____. "Why is Functionalism More Desirable in Present-Day Yugoslavia Than Marxism?" IX, 4, 1973, pp. 357-368.

Petrović, Gajo. "Bürokratischer Sozialismus?" VII, 3-4, 1971, pp. 487-493.

_____. "La philosophie Yougoslave d'aujourd'hui." III, 2, 1967, pp. 313-320.

_____. "Macht, Gewalt und Humanität." VI, 1-2, 1970, pp. 45-53.

_____. "Philosophie und Sozialismus—Wiederaufnahme einer Diskussion." X, 1-2, 1974, pp. 53-68.

_____. "Praxis: Deux ans de plus." V, 1-2, 1969, pp. 335-344.

_____. "The Development and the Essence of Marx's Thought." IV, 3-4, 1968, pp. 330-345.

Popov, Nebojša. "Les formes et le caractère de conflits sociaux." VII, 3-4, 1971, pp. 353-373.

_____. "Streiks in der gegenwärtigen jugoslawischen Gesellschaft." VI, 3-4, 1970, pp. 403-433.

Rus, Veljko. "Self-Management Egalitarianism and Social Differentiation." VI, 1-2, 1970, pp. 251-267.

Šarčević, Abdulah. "Theodor W. Adorno (1903-1969): Die Unwahrheit der modernen Gesellschaft zwischen Revolution und Kritik." VI, 1-2, 1970, pp. 184-214.

Stamenković, Toma. "Meeting of Czechoslovak and Yugoslav Philosophers." V, 3-4, 1969, pp. 620-623.

Stojanović, Svetozar. "From Post-Revolutionary Dictatorship to Socialist Democracy: Yugoslav Socialism at the Crossroads." IX, 4, 1973, pp. 311-334.

_____. "Stalinist 'Partiinost' and Communist Dignity." X, 1-2, 1974, pp. 129-138.

_____. "The Dialectics of Alienation and the Utopia of Dealienation." V, 3-4, 1969, pp. 387-398. Also in his *Between Ideals and Reality.*

_____. "The June Student Movement and Social Revolution in Yugoslavia." VI, 3-4, 1970, pp. 394-402.

Supek, Rudi, "Der technokratische Szientismus und der sozialistische Humanismus." III, 2, 1967, pp. 155-175.

_____. "Discours d'ouverture." VI, 1-2, 1970, pp. 3-7.

_____. "Dix ans de l'Ecole d'Eté de Korčula (1963-1973)." X, 1-2, 1974, pp. 3-15.
_____. "Some Contradictions and Insufficiencies of Yugoslav Self-Managing Socialism." VII, 3-4, 1971, pp. 375-397.
Šušnjić, Djuro. "The Idea of Manipulation and Manipulation of Ideas." VI, 1-2, 1970, pp. 150-155.
Sutlić, Vanja. "Macht und Menschlichkeit." VI, 1-2, 1970, pp. 14-23.
Tadić, Ljubomir. "Herbert Marcuse: Zwischen Wissenschaft und Utopie." VIII, 1-2, 1972, pp. 141-168.
_____. "L'intelligentsia dans le socialisme." V, 3-4, 1969, pp. 399-408.
_____. "Macht, Eliten, Demokratie." VI, 1-2, 1970, pp. 65-79.
_____. "Private Property and Political Economy Suppress Human Freedom." IX, 1, 1973, p. 23.
Vračar, Stevan. "Le monopolisme de parti et la puissance politique des groupes." VI, 3-4, 1970, pp. 381-393.
Vrcan, Srdjan. "Social Equality and Inequality in the Bourgeois World and in Socialism: Challenge and Alternative." X, 1-2, 1974, pp. 111-128.
_____. "Some Comments on Social Inequality." IX, 2-3, 1973, pp. 217-241.
Životić, Miladin. "Is Equality a Moral Value of Our Society?" II, 4, 1966, pp. 395-404.
_____. "The End of the Ideals or of Ideology?" V, 3-4, 1969, pp. 409-429.
Žvan, Antun. "Ecstasy and Hangover of a Revolution." VII, 3-4, 1971, pp. 475-486.

II. *PRAXIS:* YUGOSLAV EDITION

Bošnjak, Branko. "Tko suprotstavlja radnike i filozofe?" ("Who Opposes Workers to Philosophers?"). X, 3-4, 1973, pp. 537-546.
Ćosić, Dobrica. "Kultura i revolucija" ("Culture and Revolution"). XI, 3-5, 1974, pp. 515-522.
Denić, Živojin D. "Sociologija nastanka, egzistencije i funkcija robnog privred-jivanja" ("Sociology of the Origin, Existence, and Functions of Commodity Production"). IX, 1-2, April 1972, pp. 199-221.
Djodan, Šime. "Socijalizam i robno-novčani odnosi" ("Socialism and Commodity-Money Relations"). V, 1-2, April 1968, pp. 154-161.
"Dokumenti o zabrani 'Praxisa'" ("Documents Concerning the Ban on *Praxis*"). VIII, 5, September-October, 1971, pp. 757-802.
Editorial Board of *Praxis.* "Uvod" ("Introduction to Marxism and Social Conscious-ness"). IX, 3-4, May-August, 1972, pp. 307-311.
Filipović, Vladimir. "Uloga filozofije u našem vremenu po Marxu i Husserlu" ("The Role of Philosophy in Our Age According to Marx and Husserl"). IV, 5-6, 1967, pp. 716-721.
Kangrga, Milan. "Fenomenologija ideološko-političkog nastupanja jugoslavenske srednje klase" ("Phenomenology of the Ideological-Political Appearance of the Yugoslav Middle Class"). VIII, 3-4, May-August, 1971, pp. 425-446.
Marković, Mihailo. "Struktura moći u jugoslovenskom drustvu i dilema revolucion-arne inteligencije" ("The Power Structure in Yugoslav Society and the Dilem-ma of the Revolutionary Intelligentsia"). VIII, 6, November-December, 1971, pp. 811-826.
Pešić-Golubović, Zagorka. "Kultura kao most izmedju utopije i realnosti" ("Culture as a Bridge Between Utopia and Reality"). IX, 1-2, January-April, 1972, pp. 247-260.
Petrović, Gajo. "Izreka Heideggera" ("Heidegger's Saying"). VI, 5-6, 1969, pp. 781-798.
_____. "Otvoreno pismo drugu Ziherlu" ("Open Letter to Comrade Ziherl"). XI, 1-2, 1974, pp. 205-211. Reply to Boris Ziherl's article in *Borba,* January 27, 1974.
Posaveć, Zvonko. "O Kraju filozofije u Djelu Martina Heideggera" ("On the End of Philosophy in the Works of Martin Heidegger"). VIII, 1, 1971, pp. 17-24.
Prohić, Kasim. "Edmund Husserl—Mislilac Krize" ("Edmund Husserl—Thinker of

the Crisis"). IV, 5-6, 1967, pp. 741-748.

Rodin, Davor. "Ekonomija i politika" ("Economics and Politics"). V, 1-2, April 1968, pp. 162-164.

Šarčević, Abdulah. "Karl Jaspers—Tragičan mislilac suvremenosti" ("Karl Jaspers—Tragic Thinker of the Contemporary Age"). VI, 3-4, 1969, pp. 374-389.

Stojanović, Svetozar. "Sadržina, smisao i smer jednog napada" ("The Content, Meaning, and Thrust of an Attack"). X, 5-6, 1973, pp. 733-744.

Supek, Rudi. "Čemu, uostalom, sada još i ovaj marksizam?" ("Why, Now, Yet Another Marxism?"). IX, 3-4, May-August, 1972, pp. 327-338.

_____. "Robno-novčani odnosi i socijalistička ideologija" ("Commodity-Money Relations and Socialist Ideology"). V, 1-2, April 1968, pp. 170-179.

Urbančič, Ivan. "Bit nihilizma kao bit metafizike" ("The Essence of Nihilism as the Essence of Metaphysics"). VIII, 1, 1971, pp. 3-16.

Vranicki, Predrag. "Moral i historija" ("Morals and History"). VIII, 6, 1971, pp. 917-925.

"Za slobodu akademske diskusije" ("For Freedom of Academic Discussion"). IX, 3-4, May-August, 1972, pp. 611-613.

Županov, Josip. "Neke dileme u vezi s robno-novčanim odnosima" ("Some Dilemmas Concerning Commodity-Money Relations"). V, 1-2, April 1968, pp. 165-169.

III. YUGOSLAV BOOKS IN TRANSLATION

"Constitutional System of the Socialist Federal Republic of Yugoslavia." *Yugoslav Survey*, XV, 3, August 1974, pp. 1-132.

Dedijer, Vladimir. *Tito Speaks: His Self-Portrait and Struggle With Stalin.* London: Weidenfeld & Nicolson, 1953.

Djilas, Milovan. *Conversations With Stalin.* New York: Harcourt, Brace and World, 1962.

_____. *The New Class: An Analysis of the Communist System.* New York: Praeger, 1963.

_____. *The Unperfect Society: Beyond the New Class.* New York: Harcourt, 1969.

_____. *Tito: The Story From Inside.* New York: Harcourt Brace Jovanovich, 1980.

_____. *Wartime.* New York: Harcourt Brace Jovanovich, 1977.

Hečimović, Joseph. *In Tito's Death Marches and Extermination Camps.* New York: Carlton, 1962.

Horvat, Branko. *An Essay on Yugoslav Society.* White Plains, N.Y.: International Arts & Sciences Press, 1969.

Karapandzich, Bor. M. *The Bloodiest Yugoslav Spring 1945—Tito's Katyns and Gulags.* New York: Carlton, 1980.

Kardelj, Edvard. *Socialism and War: A Survey of Chinese Criticism of the Policy of Coexistence.* Belgrade: Jugoslavija, 1960.

Marković, Mihailo. *From Affluence to Praxis: Philosophy and Social Criticism.* Ann Arbor: University of Michigan Press, 1974.

_____. *The Contemporary Marx: Essays on Humanist Communism.* Nottingham: Spokesman Books, 1974.

Marxist Humanism and Praxis. Ed. Gerson S. Sher. Buffalo, N.Y.: Prometheus Books, 1978.

Mihajlov, Mihajlo. *An Historic Proposal.* New York: Freedom House, 1966.

_____. *Moscow Summer.* New York: Farrar, Straus & Giroux, 1965.

_____. *Underground Notes.* Kansas City: Andrews & McMeel, 1976.

Petrović, Gajo. *Marx in the Mid-Twentieth Century: A Yugoslav Philosopher Reconsiders Karl Marx's Writings.* Garden City, N.Y.: Doubleday, 1967.

Praxis: Yugoslav Essays in the Philosophy and Methodology of the Social Sciences. Eds. Mihailo Marković & Gajo Petrović. Dordrecht: Reidel, 1979.

Self-Governing Socialism. 2 vols. Eds. Branko Horvat, Mihailo Marković & Rudi

Supek. White Plains, N.Y.: International Arts & Sciences Press, 1975.
Stojanović, Svetozar. *Between Ideals and Reality: A Critique of Socialism and Its Future*. New York: Oxford University Press, 1973.
_____. *Geschichte und Parteibewusstsein: Auf der Suche nach Demokratie im Sozialismus*. Munich: Carl Hanser, 1978.
The Constitution of the Socialist Federal Republic of Yugoslavia. Belgrade: Federal Secretariat for Information, 1963.
The Essential Tito. Ed. Henry M. Christman. New York: St. Martin's Press, 1970.
The Soviet-Yugoslav Controversy, 1948-1958: A Documentary Record. Eds. Robert Bass & Elisabeth Marbury. New York: East Europe Institute, 1959.
Tolerance and Revolution: A Marxist-Non-Marxist Humanist Dialogue. Eds. Paul Kurtz & Svetozar Stojanović. Belgrade: Philosophical Society of Serbia, 1970. Also published by Prometheus Books.
White Book on Aggressive Activities by the Governments of the USSR, Poland, Czechoslovakia, Hungary, Rumania, Bulgaria, and Albania Towards Yugoslavia. Belgrade: Ministry of Foreign Affairs, 1951.
Yugoslavia's Way: The Program of the League of Communists of Yugoslavia. Trans. Stoyan Pribichevich. New York: All Nations, 1958. Translation of *Sedmi Kongres (Seventh Congress)*. Belgrade: Kultura, 1958.

IV. YUGOSLAV BOOKS IN SERBO-CROATIAN

Baučić, Ivo. *Porijeklo i struktura radnika iz Jugoslavije u SR Njemačkoj (The Origins and Structure of Yugoslav Workers in the Federal Republic of Germany)*. Zagreb: Institute of Geography, University of Zagreb, 1970.
Bećković, Matija & Radović, Dušan. *Ce, tragedija koja traje (Ché, The Permanent Tragedy)*. Belgrade: Samizdat, 1970.
Benigar, Aleksa. *Alojzije Stepinac Hrvatski Kardinal (Aloysius Stepinac, Croatian Cardinal)*. Rome: Ziral, 1974.
Blažević, Jakov. *Aktualnosti revolucije: O novom Ustavu socijalističke samoupravne demokracije (Current Questions of the Revolution: On the New Constitution of the Socialist Self-Governing Democracy)*. Zagreb: Narodno sveučilište grada Zagreba, Centar za aktualni politički studij, 1973.
Bošnjak, Branko & Škvorc, Mijo. *Marksist i kršćanin (The Marxist and the Christian)*. Zagreb: *Praxis* Pocketbook Edition No. 1, 1969.
Ćimić, Esad. *Čovjek na raskršću: Sociološki ogledi (Man at the Crossroads: Sociological Essays)*. Sarajevo: Svjetlost, 1975.
Denić, Živojin D. *Marks i jugoslovenska "Sveta Porodica" (Marx and the Yugoslav "Holy Family")*. Priština: Jedinstvo, 1977.
Djordjević, Jovan. *Novi Ustavni sistem (The New Constitutional System)*. Belgrade: Savremena Administracija, 1964.
_____. *Socijalizam i demokratija (Socialism and Democracy)*. Belgrade: Savremena Administracija, 1962.
Etičko-humanistički problemi socijalizma (Ethical-Humanistic Problems of Socialism). Eds. Ljubinka Krešić & Svetozar Stojanović. Belgrade: Rad, 1964.
Filipović, Vladimir. *Novija filozofija Zapada i odabrani tekstovi (Modern Western Philosophy and Selected Texts)*. Filosofska Hrestomatija, Vol. VIII. Zagreb: Matica Hrvatska, 1968.
Grlić, Danko. *Contra dogmaticos*. Zagreb: *Praxis* Pocketbook Edition No. 9, 1971.
_____. *Zašto? (Why?)*. Zagreb: Studentski centar sveučilišta, 1968.
Humanizam i socijalizam (Humanism and Socialism). 2 vols. Eds. Branko Bosnjak & Rudi Supek. Zagreb: Naprijed, 1963.
Jovanov, Neca. *Radnički štrajkovi u SFRJ, 1958-1969 (Workers' Strikes in the SFRY, 1958-1969)*. Belgrade: Zapis, 1979.
Kangrga, Milan. *Razmišljanja o etici (Thoughts on Ethics)*. Zagreb: *Praxis* Pocketbook Edition No. 6, 1970.
Karapandžić, Bor. M. *Jugoslovensko krvavo proleće 1945—Titovi Katini i Gulazi (The Bloody Yugoslav Spring, 1945: Tito's Katyns and Gulags)*. Cleveland/

Munich: Iskra, 1976.

Kardelj, Edvard. *Pravci razvoja političkog sistema socijalističkog samoupravljanja (Directions of Development of the Political System of Socialist Self-Management).* 2nd enl. ed. Belgrade: Komunist, 1978.

_____, et al. *O Ustavnom sistemu Socijalističke Federativne Republike Jugoslavije (On the Constitutional System of the Socialist Federal Republic of Yugoslavia).* Belgrade: Komunist, 1963.

Kostić-Katunac, Radoslav. *Pogledaj, Gospode, na drugu stranu!—Jugoslovenski Gulag (Look, Lord, To the Other Side—Yugoslavia's Gulag).* New York: Naša Reč, 1978.

Krešić, Andrija. *Političko društvo i politička mitologija: Prilog kritici 'kulta ličnosti' (Political Society and Political Mythology: A Contribution to the Critique of the "Cult of Personality").* Belgrade: Vuk Karadžić, 1968.

Kuvačić, Ivan. *Sukobi (Conflicts).* Zagreb: Razlog, 1972.

Lukić, Radomir. *Političke stranke (Political Parties).* 2nd ed. Belgrade: Naučna knjiga, 1975.

Mala politička enciklopedija (Small Political Encyclopædia). Belgrade: Savremena Administracija, 1966.

Marković, Dragan & Kržavac, Savo. *Liberalizam od Djilasa do danas (Liberalism Since Djilas).* 2 vols. Belgrade: Sloboda, 1978.

Marković, Mihailo. *Preispitivanja (Reassessments).* Belgrade: Srpska književna zadruga, 1972.

Marks i savremenost (Marx and the Contemporary Age). Vols. I-II, IV, VII. Eds. Mihailo Marković, Predrag Vranicki, Dragutin Leković, et al. Belgrade: Institut društvenih nauka/Institut za izučavanje radničkog pokreta/Institut za medjunarodni radnički pokret, 1964-74.

Marksizam i samoupravljanje: Marksistička teorija samoupravljanja (Marxism and Self-Management: The Marxist Theory of Self-Management). 2 vols. Ed. Predrag Radenović. Belgrade: Zavod za udžbenike i nastavna sredstva, 1977.

Matvejević, Predrag. *Te Vjetrenjače (Those Windmills).* Zagreb: August Cesarec, 1977.

Mirić, Jovan. *Interesne grupe i politička moć (Interest Groups and Political Power).* Zagreb: Narodno sveučilište grada Zagreba, Centar za aktualni politički studij, 1973.

Mirić, Milan. *Pisma iz rezervata (Letters From the Reservation).* Belgrade: Samizdat, 1976.

_____. *Rezervati (Reservations).* Zagreb: Studentski centar sveučilišta, 1970.

Musa, Vladislav. *U Titovim pandžama (Svjedočanstva) (In Tito's Claws [Testimony]).* Munich: Samizdat, 1973.

Oraški, R. *Panonija: Titu u gostima (Panonia: Tito's Guest).* Mainz: Samizdat, 1976.

Osmi Kongres SKJ (Eighth Congress of the LCY). Belgrade: Kultura, 1964.

Pečujlić, Miroslav. *Budućnost koja je počela: Naučno-tehnološka revolucija i samoupravljanje (The Future Which Has Begun: The Scientific-Technological Revolution and Self-Management).* Belgrade: Institut za političke studije Fakulteta političkih nauka, 1969.

Pejović, Danilo. *Sistem i egzistencija: Um i neum u suvremenoj filozofiji (System and Existence: Reason and Unreason in Contemporary Philosophy).* Zagreb: Zora, 1970.

Pešić-Golubović, Zagorka. *Čovek i njegov svet u antropološkoj perspektivi (Man and His World in Anthropological Perspective).* Belgrade: Prosveta, 1973.

_____. *Problemi savremene teorije ličnosti (Problems of the Contemporary Theory of Personality).* Belgrade: Kultura, 1966.

Petrović, Gajo. *Čemu Praxis (Why Praxis?).* Zagreb: Praxis Pocketbook Edition No. 10-11, 1972.

_____. *Mišljenje revolucije: Od "ontologije" do "filozofije politike" (Thought of the Revolution: From "Ontology" to the "Philosophy of Politics").* Zagreb: Naprijed, 1978.

_____. *Mogućnost čovjeka (The Possibility of Man).* Zagreb: Studentski centar sveučilišta, 1969.

Petrović, Miloje. *Kontroverzije u savremenom marksizmu: O nekim filozofskim kritikama staljinizma (Controversies in Contemporary Marxism: On Some Philosophical Critiques of Stalinism)*. Belgrade: Komunist, 1977.

Političke stranke kao faktor savremenog političkog sistema (Political Parties as a Factor in the Contemporary Political System). Ed. Stjepan Pulišelić. Zagreb: Naprijed, 1971.

Rus, Vojan. *Dijalektika čoveka i sveta (The Dialectics of Man and World)*. Belgrade: Institut za medjunarodni radnički pokret, 1969.

Statistički godišnjak Jugoslavije (Statistical Yearbook of Yugoslavia). Belgrade: Savezni zavod za statistiku, 1976-81.

Supek, Rudi. *Humanistička inteligencija i politika (The Humanist Intelligentsia and Politics)*. Zagreb: Studentski centar sveučilišta, 1971.

_____. *Ova jedina zemlja. Idemo li u katastrofu ili u Treću revoluciju? (Only One Earth: Toward a Catastrophe or a Third Revolution?)*. 2nd enl. ed. Zagreb: Liber, 1978.

_____. *Participacija, radnička kontrola i samoupravljanje (Participation, Workers' Control, and Self-Management)*. Zagreb: Naprijed, 1974.

_____. *Sociologija i socijalizam (Sociology and Socialism)*. Zagreb: Znanje, 1966.

Šuvar, Stipe. *Samoupravljanje i alternative (Self-Management and Alternatives)*. 2nd enl. ed. Zagreb: Centar za aktualni politički studij Narodnog sveučilišta grada, 1976.

_____. *Sociološki presjek jugoslavenskog društva (Sociological Cross Section of Yugoslav Society)*. Zagreb: Školska knjiga, 1970.

Tadić, Ljubomir. *Poredak i sloboda: Prilozi kritici političke svesti (Order and Freedom: Contributions to a Critique of Political Consciousness)*. Belgrade: Kultura, 1967.

Teorija i praksa samoupravljanja u Jugoslaviji (Theory and Practice of Self-Management in Yugoslavia). Eds. Jovan Djordjević, et al. Belgrade: Radnička štampa, 1972.

Ustav Socijalističke Federativne Republike Jugoslavije (The Constitution of the Socialist Federal Republic of Yugoslavia). Belgrade: Sekretarijat Saveznog izvršnog veća za informacije, 1974/Izdanje Službenog Lista SFRJ, 1965.

Ustavna reforma komune (The Constitutional Reform of the Commune). Eds. D. Božić, et al. Zagreb: Centar za aktualni politički studij, 1971.

Vidović, Mirko. *Sakrivena strana mjeseca: Zapisi o Titovim tamnicama (The Hidden Side of the Moon: Notes on Tito's Prisons)*. 2nd ed. Munich: Hrvatska Revija, 1978.

Vranicki, Predrag. *Historija Marksizma (History of Marxism)*. Zagreb: Naprijed, 1961.

_____. *Marksizam i socijalizam (Marxism and Socialism)*. Zagreb: Liber, 1979.

B. SECONDARY SOURCES:

I. YUGOSLAV THEORY AND PRACTICE

Adizes, Ichak. *Industrial Democracy: Yugoslav Style. The Effect of Decentralization on Organizational Behavior*. New York: Free Press, 1971.

Alexander, Stella. *Church and State in Yugoslavia Since 1945*. New York: Cambridge University Press, 1979.

Amnesty International. *Annual Reports*. London: AI, 1965-79.

Borowiec, Andrew. *Yugoslavia After Tito*. New York: Praeger, 1977.

Campbell, John C. *Tito's Separate Road: America and Yugoslavia in World Politics*. New York: Harper & Row, 1967.

Comisso, Ellen Turkish. *Workers' Control Under Plan and Market: Implications of Yugoslav Self-Management*. New Haven: Yale University Press, 1979.

Comparative Communism: The Soviet, Chinese, and Yugoslav Models. Eds. Gary K. Bertsch & Thomas W. Ganschow. San Francisco: Freeman, 1976.

Contemporary Yugoslavia: Twenty Years of Socialist Experiment. Ed. Wayne S. Vucinich. Berkeley: University of California Press, 1969.

Denitch, Bogdan D. *The Legitimation of a Revolution: The Yugoslav Case.* New Haven: Yale University Press, 1976.

Dirlam, Joel B. & Plummer, James L. *An Introduction to the Yugoslav Economy.* Columbus, Ohio: Merrill, 1973.

Doder, Dusko. *The Yugoslavs.* New York: Random House, 1978.

Fisher, Jack C. *Yugoslavia—A Multinational State: Regional Difference and Administrative Response.* San Francisco: Chandler, 1966.

Hoffman, George W. & Neal, Fred Warner. *Yugoslavia and the New Communism.* New York: Twentieth Century Fund, 1962.

Human Rights in Yugoslavia. Eds. Oskar Gruenwald & Karen Rosenblum-Cale. New York: Irvington Publishers, forthcoming.

Johnson, A. Ross. *The Transformation of Communist Ideology: The Yugoslav Case, 1945-1953.* Cambridge, Mass.: MIT Press, 1973.

_____. *Yugoslavia: In the Twilight of Tito.* Beverly Hills: Sage, 1974.

Kolaja, Jiri. *Workers' Councils: The Yugoslav Experience.* New York: Praeger, 1966.

Kontetzki, Heinz. *Agrarpolitischer Wandel und Modernisierung in Jugoslawien: Zwischenbilanz einer sozialistischen Entwicklungsstrategie.* Nürnberg: Nürnberger Forschungsberichte, Band 7, 1976.

Lapenna, Ivo. *State and Law: Soviet and Yugoslav Theory.* New Haven: Yale University Press, 1964.

Lendvai, Paul. *Eagles in Cobwebs: Nationalism and Communism in the Balkans.* Garden City, N.Y.: Doubleday, 1969.

Meister, Albert. *Où va l'autogestion yougoslave?* Paris: Anthropos, 1970.

Milenkovitch, Deborah D. *Plan and Market in Yugoslav Economic Thought.* New Haven: Yale University Press, 1971.

Moore, John H. *Growth With Self-Management: Yugoslav Industrialization, 1952-1975.* Stanford: Hoover Institution Press, 1980.

Opinion-Making Elites in Yugoslavia. Eds. Allen H. Barton, Bogdan D. Denitch & Charles Kadushin. New York: Praeger, 1973.

OECD. *Economic Survey of Yugoslavia.* Paris: OECD Economic Surveys, 1976-81.

Parsons, Howard L. *Humanistic Philosophy in Contemporary Poland and Yugoslavia.* New York: American Institute for Marxist Studies, 1966.

Patriot or Traitor: The Case of General Mihailovich. Ed. David Martin. Stanford: Hoover Institution Press, 1978.

Pervan, Ralph. *Tito and the Students: The University and the University Student in Self-Managing Yugoslavia.* Nedlands: University of Western Australia Press, 1978.

Popović, Nenad D. *Yugoslavia: The New Class in Crisis.* Syracuse, N.Y.: Syracuse University Press, 1968.

Ra'anan, Gavriel D. *Yugoslavia After Tito: Scenarios and Implications.* Boulder, Colo.: Westview, 1977.

Roberts, Walter R. *Tito, Mihailović and the Allies, 1941-1945.* New Brunswick, N.J.: Rutgers University Press, 1973.

Rubinstein, Alvin Z. *Yugoslavia and the Nonaligned World.* Princeton: Princeton University Press, 1970.

Rusinow, Dennison I. *The Yugoslav Experiment, 1948-1974.* Berkeley: University of California Press, 1977.

Schrenk, Martin, Ardalan, Cyrus & El Tatawy, Nawal A. *Yugoslavia: Self-Management Socialism and the Challenges of Development.* Baltimore: Johns Hopkins University Press, 1979.

Sher, Gerson S. *Praxis: Marxist Criticism and Dissent in Socialist Yugoslavia.* Bloomington: Indiana University Press, 1977.

Shoup, Paul. *Communism and the Yugoslav National Question.* New York: Columbia University Press, 1968.

Singleton, Fred B. *Twentieth-Century Yugoslavia.* New York: Columbia University Press, 1976.

Sirc, Ljubo. *The Yugoslav Economy Under Self-Management.* London: Macmillan, 1979.

Ströhm, Carl Gustaf. *Ohne Tito: Kann Jugoslawien überleben?* Köln: Styria, 1976.

Sturmthal, Adolf. *Workers' Councils: A Study of Workplace Organization on Both Sides of the Iron Curtain.* Cambridge, Mass.: Harvard University Press, 1964.

Ulam, Adam B. *Titoism and the Cominform.* Westport, Conn.: Greenwood Press, 1971.

U. S. Department of State. *Country Reports on Human Rights Practices for 1979.* Washington, D.C.: U. S. GPO, 1980.

Vanek, Jaroslav. *The Economics of Workers' Management: A Yugoslav Case Study.* London: Allen & Unwin, 1972.

Vrtačić, Ludvik. *Der jugoslawische Marxismus: Die jugoslawische Philosophie und der eigene Weg zum Sozialismus.* Freiburg im Breisgau: Walter-Verlag, 1975.

Wachtel, Howard M. *Workers' Management and Workers' Wages in Yugoslavia: The Theory and Practice of Participatory Socialism.* Ithaca, N.Y.: Cornell University Press, 1973.

Wilson, Duncan. *Tito's Yugoslavia.* New York: Cambridge University Press, 1979.

Work and Power: The Liberation of Work and the Control of Political Power. Eds. Tom R. Burns, Lars Erik Karlsson & Veljko Rus. Beverly Hills: Sage, 1979.

Yugoslav Workers' Selfmanagement. Ed. Marius J. Broekmeyer. Dordrecht: Reidel, 1970.

Zalar, Charles. *Yugoslav Communism, A Critical Study.* Washington, D.C.: U. S. GPO, 1961.

Zaninovich, M. George. *The Development of Socialist Yugoslavia.* Baltimore: Johns Hopkins University Press, 1968.

Zukin, Sharon. *Beyond Marx and Tito: Theory and Practice in Yugoslav Socialism.* New York: Cambridge University Press, 1975.

II. MARX, MARXISM-LENINISM, SOCIALISM, COMMUNISM

Arendt, Hannah. *The Origins of Totalitarianism.* New York: Harcourt, Brace & World, 1966.

Aron, Raymond. *Marxism and the Existentialists.* New York: Harper & Row, 1969.

Avineri, Shlomo. *The Social and Political Thought of Karl Marx.* London: Cambridge University Press, 1971.

Axelos, Kostas. *Alienation, Praxis and Techné in the Thought of Karl Marx.* Austin: University of Texas Press, 1976.

Bahro, Rudolf. *The Alternative in Eastern Europe.* London: NLB, 1978.

Barghoorn, Frederick C. *Détente and the Democratic Movement in the USSR.* Riverside, N.J.: Free Press, 1976.

Bernstein, Eduard. *Evolutionary Socialism: A Criticism and Affirmation.* New York: Schocken, 1965.

Bethell, Nicholas. *The Last Secret: Forcible Repatriation to Russia, 1944-7.* London: Andre Deutsch, 1974.

Blaug, Mark. *Economic Theory in Retrospect.* Rev. ed. Homewood, Ill.: Irwin, 1968.

Blumberg, Paul. *Industrial Democracy: The Sociology of Participation.* New York: Schocken, 1969.

Blumenfeld, Yorick. *Seesaw: Cultural Life in Eastern Europe.* New York: Harcourt, 1968.

Böhm-Bawerk, Eugen von. *Karl Marx and the Close of His System.* New York: Kelley, 1949.

Brzezinski, Zbigniew K. *The Soviet Bloc: Unity and Conflict.* Cambridge, Mass.: Harvard University Press, 1967.

Carew-Hunt, R. N. The Theory and Practice of Communism. Baltimore: Penguin, 1963.

Civil-Military Relations in Communist Systems. Eds. Dale R. Herspring & Ivan Völgyes. Boulder, Colo.: Westview, 1978.

Cohn-Bendit, Daniel & Gabriel. Obsolete Communism: The Left-Wing Alternative. New York: McGraw-Hill, 1968.

Communism in Eastern Europe. Eds. Teresa Rakowska-Harmstone & Andrew György. Bloomington: Indiana University Press, 1979.

Comparative Communist Political Leadership. Eds. Carl Beck, et al. New York: McKay, 1973.

Comparative Economic Systems: Models and Cases. 3rd ed. Ed. Morris Bornstein. Homewood, Ill.: Irwin, 1974.

Crozier, Brian. Strategy of Survival. New Rochelle, N. Y.: Arlington House, 1978.

De George, Richard T. The New Marxism: Soviet and East European Marxism Since 1956. New York: Pegasus, 1968.

Dissent in the USSR: Politics, Ideologies, and People. Ed. Rudolf L. Tökés. Baltimore: Johns Hopkins University Press, 1975.

Engels, Friedrich. The Origin of the Family, Private Property and the State. New York: International Publishers, 1972.

Existentialism versus Marxism: Conflicting Views on Humanism. Ed. George E. Novack. New York: Dell, 1966.

Feuer, Lewis S. Marx and the Intellectuals: A Set of Post-Ideological Essays. Garden City, N.Y.: Doubleday, 1969.

Friedrich, Carl J. & Brzezinski, Zbigniew K. Totalitarian Dictatorship and Autocracy. Cambridge, Mass.: Harvard University Press, 1965.

Fromm, Erich. Marx's Concept of Man. New York: Ungar, 1961.

Garaudy, Roger. From Anathema to Dialogue: A Marxist Challenge to the Christian Churches. New York: Vintage, 1966.

_____. The Alternative Future: A Vision of Christian Marxism. New York: Simon & Schuster, 1974.

Glucksmann, André. The Master Thinkers. New York: Harper & Row, 1980.

Hayek, Friedrich A. The Constitution of Liberty. Chicago: University of Chicago Press, 1960.

Hoffman, John. Marxism and the Theory of Praxis. New York: International Publishers, 1976.

Hook, Sidney. From Hegel to Marx: Studies in the Intellectual Development of Karl Marx. Ann Arbor: University of Michigan Press, 1968.

Huntford, Roland. The New Totalitarians. New York: Stein, 1972.

Innovation in Communist Systems. Eds. Andrew György & James A. Kuhlman. Boulder, Colo.: Westview, 1978.

Kamenka, Eugene. The Ethical Foundations of Marxism. 2nd ed. Boston: Routledge, 1972.

Karl Marx: Early Writings. Ed. T. B. Bottomore. New York: McGraw-Hill, 1964.

Khrushchev, Nikita S. Crimes of the Stalin Era. New York: The New Leader, 1962.

Koestler, Arthur. Darkness at Noon. New York: New American Library, 1961.

Kolakowski, Leszek. Main Currents of Marxism: Its Origin, Growth, and Dissolution. 3 vols. Oxford: Oxford University Press, 1978.

_____. Toward a Marxist Humanism: Essays on the Left Today. New York: Grove Press, 1969.

Lenin, Vladimir I. "Left-Wing" Communism: An Infantile Disorder. New York: International Publishers, 1940.

_____. Materialism and Empirio-Criticism: Critical Comments on a Reactionary Philosophy. Moscow: Foreign Languages Publishing House, 1947.

_____. "Philosophical Notebooks." In Reader in Marxist Philosophy. Eds. Howard Selsam & Harry Martel. New York: International Publishers, 1964.

_____. State and Revolution. New York: International Publishers, 1932.

Leonhard, Wolfgang. Three Faces of Marxism: The Political Concepts of Soviet Ideology, Maoism, and Humanist Marxism. New York: Holt, 1974.

Lévy, Bernard-Henri. Barbarism With a Human Face. New York: Harper & Row, 1979.

Lindbeck, Assar. The Political Economy of the New Left--An Outsider's View. 2nd ed. New York: Harper & Row, 1977.

Löwenthal, Richard. *World Communism: The Disintegration of a Secular Faith.* New York: Oxford University Press, 1964.

Lukács, György. *History and Class Consciousness: Studies in Marxist Dialectics.* Cambridge, Mass.: MIT Press, 1971.

Luxemburg, Rosa. *The Russian Revolution and Leninism or Marxism.* Ann Arbor: University of Michigan Press, 1961.

Marcuse, Herbert. *An Essay on Liberation.* Boston: Beacon, 1969.

_____. *One-Dimensional Man: Studies in the Ideology of Advanced Industrial Society.* Boston: Beacon, 1968.

Marx, Karl. *Capital: A Critique of Political Economy.* 3 vols. New York: International Publishers, 1967.

_____. *Grundrisse: Foundations of the Critique of Political Economy.* New York: Random House, 1973.

Marx, Karl & Engels, Friedrich. *Collected Works.* New York: International Publishers, 1975.

_____. *Selected Correspondence, 1843-1895.* Moscow: Foreign Languages Publishing House, 1953.

_____. *The German Ideology.* New York: International Publishers, 1969.

Marx & Engels: Basic Writings on Politics & Philosophy. Ed. Lewis S. Feuer. Garden City, N. Y.: Doubleday, 1959.

Marxism and Religion in Eastern Europe. Eds. Richard T. De George & James P. Scanlan. Dordrecht: Reidel, 1976.

Medvedev, Roy A. *On Socialist Democracy.* New York: Knopf, 1975.

Merleau-Ponty, Maurice. *Humanism and Terror.* Boston: Beacon, 1969.

Milosz, Czeslaw. *The Captive Mind.* New York: Vintage, 1953.

Mises, Ludwig von. *Human Action: A Treatise on Economics.* Rev. ed. New Haven: Yale University Press, 1963.

Molnar, Thomas. *The Decline of the Intellectual.* Cleveland: World, 1961.

McInnes, Neil. *The Western Marxists.* New York: Library Press, 1972.

Odajnyk, Walter. *Marxism and Existentialism.* Garden City, N. Y.: Doubleday, 1965.

Opposition in Eastern Europe. Ed. Rudolf L. Tőkés. Baltimore: Johns Hopkins University Press, 1979.

O'Rourke, James J. *The Problem of Freedom in Marxist Thought.* Dordrecht: Reidel, 1974.

Parsons, Howard L. *Humanism and Marx's Thought.* Springfield, Ill.: Charles C. Thomas, 1971.

Perspectives for Change in Communist Societies. Ed. Teresa Rakowska-Harmstone. Boulder, Colo.: Westview, 1979.

Plan and Market: Economic Reform in Eastern Europe. Ed. Morris Bornstein. New Haven: Yale University Press, 1973.

Political Culture and Political Change in Communist States. Eds. Archie Brown & Jack Gray. New York: Holmes & Meier, 1977.

Political Development in Eastern Europe. Eds. Jan F. Triska & Paul M. Cocks. New York: Praeger, 1977.

Political Socialization in Eastern Europe: A Comparative Framework. Ed. Ivan Völgyes. New York: Praeger, 1975.

Polycentrism: The New Factor in International Communism. Eds. Walter Z. Laqueur & Leopold Labedz. New York: Praeger, 1962.

Popper, Karl R. *The Open Society and Its Enemies.* 5th rev. ed. 2 vols. Princeton: Princeton University Press, 1966.

Regimes and Oppositions. Ed. Robert A. Dahl. New Haven: Yale University Press, 1973.

Revel, Jean-François. *The Totalitarian Temptation.* Garden City, N. Y.: Doubleday, 1977.

Revisionism: Essays on the History of Marxist Ideas. Ed. Leopold Labedz. New York: Praeger, 1962.

Roberts, Paul Craig & Stephenson, Matthew A. *Marx's Theory of Exchange,*

    Alienation and Crisis. Stanford: Hoover Institution Press, 1973.

Sakharov, Andrei D. *Progress, Coexistence, and Intellectual Freedom.* New York: Norton, 1968.

Schaff, Adam. *Marxism and the Human Individual.* New York: McGraw-Hill, 1970.

Schumpeter, Joseph A. *Capitalism, Socialism and Democracy.* 3rd ed. New York: Harper Torchbooks, 1962.

Seton-Watson, Hugh. *The East European Revolution.* London: Methuen, 1950.

Social Consequences of Modernization in Communist Societies. Ed. Mark G. Field. Baltimore: Johns Hopkins University Press, 1976.

Social Deviance in Eastern Europe. Ed. Ivan Völgyes. Boulder, Colo.: Westview, 1978.

Socialist Humanism: An International Symposium. Ed. Erich Fromm. Garden City, N. Y.: Doubleday, 1966.

Solzhenitsyn, Aleksandr I. *The First Circle.* New York: Bantam, 1969.

_____. *The Gulag Archipelago, 1918-1956: An Experiment in Literary Investigation.* 3 vols. New York: Harper & Row, 1974-78.

Stalinism: Essays in Historical Interpretation. Ed. Robert C. Tucker. New York: Norton, 1977.

Talmon, Jacob L. *The Origins of Totalitarian Democracy.* New York: Praeger, 1960.

The Christian Marxist Dialogue: An International Symposium. Ed. Paul Oestreicher. London: Macmillan, 1969.

The Communist States in the Era of Détente, 1971-1977. Eds. Adam Bromke & Derry Novak. Oakville, Ontario: Mosaic Press, 1979.

The God That Failed. Ed. Richard Crossman. New York: Harper & Row, 1965.

The International Politics of Eastern Europe. Ed. Charles Gati. New York: Praeger, 1976.

The Lenin Anthology. Ed. Robert C. Tucker, New York: Norton, 1975.

The Marx-Engels Reader. Ed. Robert C. Tucker. New York: Norton, 1972.

The Politics of Modernization in Eastern Europe: Testing the Soviet Model. Ed. Charles Gati. New York: Praeger, 1974.

The Socialist Idea: A Reappraisal. Eds. Leszek Kolakowski & Stuart Hampshire. New York: Basic Books, 1974.

Trotsky, Leon. *The Revolution Betrayed: What is the Soviet Union and Where is It Going?* 5th ed. New York: Pathfinder, 1972.

Tucker, Robert C. *Philosophy and Myth in Karl Marx.* London: Cambridge University Press, 1969.

Ulam, Adam B. *The Unfinished Revolution: An Essay on the Sources of Marxism and Communism.* New York: Random, 1960.

U. S. Commission on Security and Cooperation in Europe. *Report to the U. S. Congress on Implementation of the Final Act of the Conference on Security and Cooperation in Europe: Findings and Recommendations Two Years After Helsinki* and *Five Years After Helsinki.* Washington, D. C.: U. S. GPO, August 1, 1977 and August 1, 1980.

U. S. Congress. House of Representatives. Committee on International Relations. *U. S. Policy Toward Eastern Europe.* Washington, D. C.: U. S. GPO, 1979.

U. S. Gongress. Senate. Committee on Foreign Relations. *Détente.* Washington, D. C.: U. S. GPO, 1975.

Ward, Benjamin N. *The Socialist Economy: A Study of Organizational Alternatives.* New York: Random House, 1967.

Wesson, Robert G. *Why Marxism? The Continuing Success of a Failed Theory.* New York: Basic Books, 1976.

Wolfe, Bertram D. *Marxism: One Hundred Years in the Life of a Doctrine.* New York: Dial, 1965.

Wolff, Robert Lee. *The Balkans in Our Time.* Cambridge, Mass.: Harvard University Press, 1956.

Wolff, Robert P., et al. *A Critique of Pure Tolerance.* Boston: Beacon, 1969.

Workers' Control: A Reader on Labor and Social Change. Eds. Gerry Hunnius, G. David Garson & John Case. New York: Random House, 1973.

III. GENERAL BOOKS

Arendt, Hannah. *The Human Condition: A Study of the Central Dilemmas Facing Modern Man.* Garden City, N. Y.: Doubleday, 1959.

Aristotle. *Politics.* New York: Oxford University Press, 1966.

Banfield, Edward C. *The Unheavenly City Revisited.* Boston: Little, Brown, 1974.

Becker, Ernest. *Beyond Alienation: A Philosophy of Education for the Crisis of Democracy.* New York: Braziller, 1967.

Bell, Daniel. *The Coming of Post-Industrial Society: A Venture in Social Forecasting.* New York: Basic Books, 1973.

_____. *The Cultural Contradictions of Capitalism.* New York: Basic Books, 1976.

Berger, Peter L. *Pyramids of Sacrifice: Political Ethics and Social Change.* New York: Basic Books, 1974.

Berger, Peter L. & Luckmann, Thomas. *The Social Construction of Reality: A Treatise in the Sociology of Knowledge.* Garden City, N. Y.: Doubleday, 1967.

Boulding, Kenneth E. *Beyond Economics: Essays on Society, Religion, and Ethics.* Ann Arbor: University of Michigan Press, 1968.

Buchanan, James M. *The Limits of Liberty: Between Anarchy and Leviathan.* Chicago: University of Chicago Press, 1975.

Buchheit, Lee C. *Secession: The Legitimacy of Self-Determination.* New Haven: Yale University Press, 1978.

Burnham, James. *Suicide of the West.* New Rochelle: Arlington House, 1970.

Camus, Albert. *The Rebel: An Essay on Man in Revolt.* New York: Vintage, 1956.

Crozier, Michel, Huntington, Samuel P. & Watanuki, Joji. *The Crisis of Democracy.* New York: New York University Press, 1975.

Dostoevsky, Fyodor. *The Grand Inquisitor.* New York: Ungar, 1956.

Drucker, Peter F. *Managing in Turbulent Times.* New York: Harper & Row, 1980.

Feuer, Lewis S. *Ideology and the Ideologists.* New York: Harper & Row, 1975.

Frankl, Viktor E. *Man's Search for Meaning: An Introduction to Logotherapy.* New York: Washington Square Press, 1967.

Freud, Sigmund. *Civilization and Its Discontents.* New York: Norton, 1962.

Friedman, Milton. *Capitalism and Freedom.* Chicago: University of Chicago Press, 1963.

_____ & Rose. *Free to Choose: A Personal Statement.* New York: Harcourt Brace Jovanovich, 1980.

Fromm, Erich. *Escape From Freedom.* New York: Avon, 1965.

Galbraith, John Kenneth. *Economics and the Public Purpose.* New York: New American Library, 1975.

_____. *The New Industrial State.* 2nd ed. Boston: Mifflin, 1972.

Glazer, Nathan. *Affirmative Discrimination: Ethnic Inequality and Public Policy.* New York: Basic Books, 1975.

Goodfield, June. *Playing God: Genetic Engineering and the Manipulation of Life.* New York: Random House, 1977.

Grazia, Sebastian de. *The Political Community (A Study of Anomie).* Chicago: University of Chicago Press, 1956.

Guinness, Os. *The Dust of Death: A Critique of the Establishment and the Counter Culture—and a Proposal for a Third Way.* Downers Grove, Ill.: InterVarsity Press, 1973.

Hackett, John W., et al. *The Third World War, August 1985.* New York: Macmillan, 1978.

Hayek, Friedrich A. *Law, Legislation and Liberty.* 3 vols. Chicago: University of Chicago Press, 1973-79.

Hegel, G. W. F. *The Phenomenology of Mind.* New York: Harper & Row, 1967.

Heilbroner, Robert L. *An Inquiry Into the Human Prospect.* New York: Norton, 1974.

Hobbes, Thomas. *Leviathan.* New York: Collier, 1962.

Hoffer, Eric. *The True Believer.* New York: New American Library, 1964.

Huxley, Aldous. *Brave New World.* New York: Bantam, 1962.

James, William. *The Meaning of Truth.* Ann Arbor: University of Michigan Press,

1970.

Kahn, Herman, Brown, William & Martel, Leon. *The Next 200 Years: A Scenario for America and the World.* New York: Morrow, 1976.

Kaplan, Abraham. *The Conduct of Inquiry: Methodology for Behavioral Science.* San Francisco: Chandler, 1964.

Kuhn, Thomas S. *The Structure of Scientific Revolutions.* 2nd ed. Chicago: University of Chicago Press, 1973.

Lasswell, Harold D. *Psychopathology and Politics.* New York: Viking, 1962.

_____. *World Politics and Personal Insecurity.* New York: Free Press, 1965.

Levi, Albert W. *Humanism and Politics: Studies in the Relationship of Power and Value in the Western Tradition.* Bloomington: Indiana University Press, 1969.

Lijphart, Arend. *Democracy in Plural Societies: A Comparative Exploration.* New Haven: Yale University Press, 1977.

Lindblom, Charles E. *Politics and Markets: The World's Political-Economic Systems.* New York: Basic Books, 1977.

Lobkowicz, Nicholas. *Theory and Practice: History of a Concept from Aristotle to Marx.* Notre Dame: University of Notre Dame Press, 1967.

Mannheim, Karl. *Ideology and Utopia: An Introduction to the Sociology of Knowledge.* New York: Harcourt, 1947.

Maritain, Jacques. *True Humanism.* New York: Scribner's, 1938.

Mills, C. Wright. *The Sociological Imagination.* New York: Grove, 1961.

Moore, Barrington, Jr. *Reflections on the Causes of Human Misery and Upon Certain Proposals to Eliminate Them.* Boston: Beacon, 1972.

More, Thomas. *Utopia.* New York: Appleton-Century-Crofts, 1949.

Myth and Mythmaking. Ed. Henry A. Murray. Boston: Beacon, 1968.

Nisbet, Robert. *Twilight of Authority.* New York: Oxford University Press, 1975.

Nozick, Robert. *Anarchy, State, and Utopia.* New York: Basic Books, 1974.

Ogilvy, James A. *Many Dimensional Man: Decentralizing Self, Society, and the Sacred.* New York: Oxford University Press, 1977.

Ortega y Gasset, José. *The Revolt of the Masses.* New York: Norton, 1960.

Orwell, George. *1984.* New York: New American Library, 1964.

Plato. *The Republic.* New York: Oxford University Press, 1965.

Political Opposition and Dissent. Ed. Barbara N. McLennan. New York: Dunellen, 1973.

Popper, Karl R. & Eccles, John C. *The Self and Its Brain.* New York: Springer International, 1977.

Rawls, John. *A Theory of Justice.* Cambridge, Mass.: Harvard Unversity Press, 1971.

Rokeach, Milton. *The Open and Closed Mind: Investigations Into the Nature of Belief Systems and Personality Systems.* New York: Basic Books, 1960.

Rostow, Walt W. *The Stages of Economic Growth: A Non-Communist Manifesto.* London: Cambridge University Press, 1965.

Roszak, Theodore. *The Making of a Counter Culture: Reflections on the Technocratic Society and Its Youthful Opposition.* Garden City, N. Y.: Doubleday, 1969.

Rousseau, Jean-Jacques. *The Social Contract and Discourses.* New York: Dutton, 1950.

Schaeffer, Francis A. *How Should We Then Live? The Rise and Decline of Western Thought and Culture.* Old Tappan, N. J.: Revell, 1976.

Simon, William E. *A Time for Truth.* New York: Reader's Digest Press, 1978.

Skinner, B. F. *Beyond Freedom and Dignity.* New York: Bantam, 1972.

Spengler, Oswald. *The Decline of the West.* Vol. I. New York: Knopf, 1926.

Strauss, Leo. *On Tyranny.* Ithaca: Cornell University Press, 1968.

Tennyson, Alfred L. *Idylls of the King.* In *The Poems of Tennyson.* Ed. Christopher Ricks. New York: Norton, 1972.

The Economics of Property Rights. Eds. Eirik G. Furubotn & Svetozar Pejovich. Cambridge, Mass.: Ballinger, 1974.

Tocqueville, Alexis de. *Democracy in America.* Ed. Richard D. Heffner. New York: New American Library, 1956.

Toffler, Alvin. *The Third Wave.* New York: Morrow, 1980.

Verba, Sidney, Nie, Norman H. & Kim, Jae-On. *Participation and Political Equality: A Seven-Nation Comparison.* New York: Cambridge University Press, 1978.

Voegelin, Eric. *The New Science of Politics.* Chicago: University of Chicago Press, 1966.

Weber, Max. *On the Methodology of the Social Sciences.* Eds. Edward A. Shils & Henry A. Finch. Ill.: Free Press of Glencoe, 1949.

Wiener, Norbert. *The Human Use of Human Beings: Cybernetics and Society.* Garden City, N. Y.: Doubleday, 1956.

Index of Subjects

Index of Names